UNCERTAINTY IN ARTIFIC

CW00544859

Machine Intelligence and Pattern Recognition

Volume 9

Series Editors

L.N. KANAL

and

A. ROSENFELD

University of Maryland
College Park, Maryland, U.S.A.

NORTH-HOLLAND
AMSTERDAM • NEW YORK • OXFORD • TOKYO

Uncertainty in Artificial Intelligence 4

Edited by

Ross D. SHACHTER
Stanford University
Stanford, California, U.S.A.

Tod S. LEVITT
Advanced Decision Systems
Mountain View, California, U.S.A.

Laveen N. KANAL
University of Maryland
College Park, Maryland, U.S.A.

John F. LEMMER
Knowledge Systems Concepts
Rome, New York, U.S.A.

1990

NORTH-HOLLAND
AMSTERDAM • NEW YORK • OXFORD • TOKYO

ELSEVIER SCIENCE PUBLISHERS B.V.
Sara Burgerhartstraat 25
P.O. Box 211, 1000 AE Amsterdam, The Netherlands

Distributors for the United States and Canada:
ELSEVIER SCIENCE PUBLISHING COMPANY, INC.
655 Avenue of the Americas
New York, N.Y. 10010, U.S.A.

ISBN: 0 444 88650 8 (hardbound)
       0 444 88737 7 (paperback)

Printed in The Netherlands

PREFACE

The papers in this volume clearly illustrate the current relationship between Uncertainty and Artificial Intelligence. They show that while much has been accomplished, much remains to be done to fully integrate Uncertainty Technology with AI.

It has been said that the research in Artificial Intelligence revolves around five basic questions asked relative to some particular domain: (1) what knowledge is required, (2) how can this knowledge be acquired, (3) how can it be represented in a system, (4) how should the knowledge be manipulated in order to provide intelligent behavior, and (5) how can the behavior be explained. The early volumes in this series concentrated on manipulation of the uncertainties associated with other knowledge in a system and often implied, at least in a general way, associated data structure.

In this volume we can observe all five of the fundamental questions of AI being addressed. Some of the papers address all five questions. Other papers address only one or several of the questions, with intelligent manipulation still being the most popular.

From the perspective of the relationship of uncertainty to the basic questions of Artificial Intelligence, this volume divides rather naturally into four sections which highlight both the strengths and weaknesses of the current state of the relationship between Uncertainty Technology and Artificial Intelligence.

The first section contains papers describing paradigms that seem to be on the same level as the Expert System Paradigm. It is in this sense that these papers address, at least implicitly, all five basic questions. In most cases the papers themselves do not take such a bold stance, but it is difficult to not understand them in this sense. All these papers seem to use the notion of causality as an organizing principle in much the same way that Expert Systems use heuristic knowledge as an organizing principle.

The second, and by far the largest section addresses specific means of representing and intelligently manipulating uncertainty information. How these representations and manipulations are to be integrated into an intelligent system is left largely to the creativity of the reader. This section naturally divides into two parts: one on manipulating uncertainties, and a second which evaluates or compares one or more representation/manipulations technologies. These papers range from ones which are specifically presented as possible solutions to well known AI problems (e.g. the problem of monotonicity) through improved computational techniques to philosophical discussions of the possible meanings of uncertainty.

The third, and regrettably the smallest of the sections (containing only two papers!) addresses the basic questions of knowledge acquisition and explanation. These questions must be addressed if intelligent systems incorporating uncertainty are ever to be widely accepted. These questions seem to provide almost virgin territory for research. It may be significant that both of the papers in this section come from the group which did some of the earliest research in Expert Systems, the group which did the original MYCIN work.

The final section reports on applications of uncertainty technology.

We hope that readers of this volume will be encouraged to work on explicit connections between Uncertainty Technology and ongoing work in mainstream AI. There has been hopeful evidence that some AI researchers are looking to the uncertainty community for help in certain problem areas such as planning. In turn, uncertainty researchers must look for inspiration from the AI community if they are to avoid working on problems whose solution will have little or no value in the larger context of Artificial Intelligence.

Ross D. Shachter
Stanford, CA

Tod S. Levitt
Mt. View CA

Laveen N. Kanal
College Park, MD

John F. Lemmer
Rome, NY

CONTENTS

Part 2: Comparisons

Section III: KNOWLEDGE ACQUISITION AND EXPLANATION

Section IV: APPLICATIONS

LIST OF CONTRIBUTORS

A.M. Agogino, *Department of Mechanical Engineering, University of California, Berkeley, CA, USA*

J.M. Agosta, *Robotics Laboratory, Stanford University, Stanford, CA, USA*

R. Aleliunas, *Centre for System Science, Simon Fraser University, Vancouver, Canada*

F. Bacchus, *Department of Computer Science, University of Waterloo, Waterloo, Ontario, Canada*

T.O. Binford, *Stanford University, Stanford, CA, USA*

P.K. Black, *Decision Science Consortium, Inc., Reston, VA, USA*

J.S. Breese, *Rockwell International Science Center, Palo Alto Laboratory, Palo Alto, CA, USA*

C. Carter, *Australian Graduate School of Management, University of New South Wales, Sydney, Australia*

M. Cecile, *Department of Computing and Information Science, University of Guelph, Guelph, Ontario, Canada*

R.M. Chavez, *Medical Computer Science Group, Stanford University, Stanford, CA, USA*

G.F. Cooper, *Medical Computer Science Group, Stanford University, Stanford, CA, USA*

B. D'Ambrosio, *Department of Computer Science, Oregon State University, OR, USA*

T. Dean, *Department of Computer Science, Brown University, RI, USA*

D. Dubois, *I.R.I.T.-L.S.I., Université Paul Sabatier, Toulouse, France*

G.J. Ettinger, *Advanced Decision Systems, Mountain View, CA, USA*

M.R. Fehling, *Rockwell International Science Center, Palo Alto Laboratory, Palo Alto, CA, USA*

A.M. Frisch, *Department of Computer Science, University of Illinois, Urbana, IL, USA*

D. Geiger, *Computer Science Department, University of California, Los Angeles, CA, USA*

P. Haddawy, *Department of Computer Science, University of Illinois, Urbana, IL, USA*

D. Heckerman, *Departments of Computer Science and Medicine, Stanford University, Stanford, CA, USA*

M. Henrion, *Department of Engineering and Public Policy, Carnegie Mellon University, Pittsburgh, PA, USA*

D. Hunter, *Northrop Research and Technology Center, Palos Verdes Peninsula, CA, USA*

P. Jain, *Andersen Consulting, Chicago, IL, USA*

H.B. Jimison, *Medical Computer Science, Stanford University, Stanford, CA, USA*

J. Kalagnanam, *Department of Engineering and Public Policy, Carnegie Mellon University, Pittsburgh, PA, USA*

K. Kanazawa, *Department of Computer Science, Brown University, RI, USA*

S.W. Kwok, *Computer Power Group, Sydney, Australia*

H.E. Kyburg, Jr., *Computer Science and Philosophy, University of Rochester, Rochester, NY, USA*

K.B. Laskey, *Decision Science Consortium, Inc., Reston, VA, USA*

T.S. Levitt, *Advanced Decision Systems, Mountain View, CA, USA*

R.P. Loui, *Department of Computer Science, Washington University, St. Louis, MO, USA*

M. McLeish, *Department of Computing and Information Science, University of Guelph, Guelph, Ontario, Canada*

E. Neufeld, *Department of Computational Science, University of Saskatchewan, Saskatoon, Canada*

P. Pascoe, *Ontario Veterinary College, Guelph, Ontario, Canada*

J. Pearl, *Computer Science Department, University of California, Los Angeles, CA, USA*

D. Poole, *Department of Computer Science, University of British Columbia, Vancouver, Canada*

H. Prade, *I.R.I.T.-L.S.I., Université Paul Sabatier, Toulouse, France*

R.D. Shachter, *Department of Engineering-Economic Systems, Stanford University, Stanford, CA, USA*

G. Shafer, *School of Business, University of Kansas, Lawrence, KS, USA*

P.P. Shenoy, *School of Business, University of Kansas, Lawrence, KS, USA*

W. Spohn, *Institut für Philosophie, Universität Regensburg, Regensburg, FRG*

S. Star, *Département d'Informatique, Université Laval, Québec, Canada*

W. Taylor, *NASA AMES, Moffett Field, CA, USA*

T. Verma, *Computer Science Department, University of California, Los Angeles, CA, USA*

W.X. Wen, *Department of Computer Science, Royal Melbourne Institute of Technology, Melbourne, Australia*

A. Yeh, *MIT Laboratory for Computer Science, Cambridge, MA, USA*

J. Yen, *Department of Computer Science, Texas A&M University, TX, USA*

Section I

CAUSAL MODELS

Uncertainty in Artificial Intelligence 4
R.D. Shachter, T.S. Levitt, L.N. Kanal, J.F. Lemmer (Editors)
© Elsevier Science Publishers B.V. (North-Holland), 1990

3

ON THE LOGIC OF CAUSAL MODELS *

Dan GEIGER and Judea PEARL
Cognitive Systems Laboratory, Computer Science Department
University of California Los Angeles, CA 90024
Net address: geiger@cs.ucla.edu
Net address: judea@cs.ucla.edu

This paper explores the role of Directed Acyclic Graphs (DAGs) as a representation of conditional independence relationships. We show that DAGs offer polynomially *sound* and *complete* inference mechanisms for inferring conditional independence relationships from a given *causal* set of such relationships. As a consequence, *d-separation*, a graphical criterion for identifying independencies in a DAG, is shown to uncover more valid independencies then any other criterion. In addition, we employ the *Armstrong* property of conditional independence to show that the dependence relationships displayed by a DAG are inherently *consistent*, i.e. for every DAG *D* there exists some probability distribution P that embodies all the conditional independencies displayed in D and none other.

1. INTRODUCTION AND SUMMARY OF RESULTS

Networks employing Directed Acyclic Graphs (DAGs) have a long and rich tradition, starting with the geneticist Wright (1921). He developed a method called *path analysis* [26] which later on, became an established representation of causal models in economics [25], sociology [1] and psychology [3]. *Influence diagrams* represent another application of DAG representation [8,19,21]. These were developed for decision analysis and contain both chance nodes and decision nodes (our definition of causal models excludes decision nodes). *Recursive models* is the name given to such networks by statisticians seeking meaningful and effective decompositions of contingency tables [11,24,10]. *Bayesian Belief Networks* (or *Causal Networks*) is the name adopted for describing networks that perform evidential reasoning [14,15]. This paper establishes a clear semantics for these networks that might explain their wide usage as models for forecasting, decision analysis and evidential reasoning.

DAGs are viewed as an economical scheme for representing conditional independence relationships. The nodes of a DAG represent variables in some domain and its topology is specified by a list of conditional independence judgements elicited from an expert in this domain. The specification list designates parents to each variable *v* by asserting that *v* is conditionally independent of all its predecessors, given its parents (in some total order of

---
*This work was partially supported by the National Science Foundation Grants #IRI-8610155, "Graphoids: A Computer Representation for Dependencies and Relevance in Automated Reasoning," and #IRI-8821444, "Probabilistic Networks for Automated Reasoning."

the variables). This input list implies many additional conditional independencies that can be read off the DAG. For example, the DAG asserts that, given its parents, v is also conditionally independent of all its non-descendants [8]. Additionally, if S is a set of nodes containing v's parents, v's children and the parents of those children, then v is independent of all other variables in the system, given those in S [14]. These assertions are examples of *valid consequences* of the input list, i.e., assertions that hold for every probability distribution that satisfies the conditional independencies specified by the input. If one ventures to perform topological transformations (e.g., arc reversal or node removal [19]) on the DAG, caution must be exercised to ensure that each transformation does not introduce extraneous, invalid independencies, and, preferably, that the number of valid independencies which become obscured by the transformation is kept at a minimum. Thus, in order to decide which transformations are admissible, one should have a simple graphical criterion for deciding which conditional independence statement is valid and which is not.

This paper deals with the following questions:

1.   What are the valid consequences of the input list ?

2.   What are the valid consequences of the input list that can be read off the DAG ?

3.   Are the two sets identical?

The answers obtained are as follows:

1.   A statement is a valid consequence of the input list if and only if it can be derived from it using the axioms of graphoids[1] [2,16]. Letting X, Y, and Z stand for three disjoint subsets of variables, and denoting by $I(X, Z, Y)$ the statement: " *the variables in X are conditionally independent of those in Y, given those in Z*", we may express these axioms as follows:

Symmetry   (1.a)
$$I(X, Z, Y) \Rightarrow I(Y, Z, X)$$

Decomposition   (1.b)
$$I(X, Z, Y \cup W) \Rightarrow I(X, Z, Y) \ \& \ I(X, Z, W)$$

Weak Union   (1.c)
$$I(X, Z, Y \cup W) \Rightarrow I(X, Z \cup W, Y)$$

Contraction   (1.d)
$$I(X, Z \cup Y, W) \ \& \ I(X, Z, Y) \Rightarrow I(X, Z, Y \cup W)$$

2.   Every statement that can be read off the DAG using the *d*-separation criterion is a valid consequence of the input list [23].

The *d*-separation condition is defined as follows [13]: For any three disjoint subsets

---

[1] In [15,16,17] axioms (1.a) through (4.b) are called the *semi-graphoid* axioms. We have changed terminology to account for the generality of these axioms.

X, Y, Z of nodes in a DAG D, Z is said to d-separate X from Y, denoted $I(X, Z, Y)_D$, if there is no path from a node in X to a node in Y along which: 1. every node that delivers an arrow is outside Z, and 2. every node with converging arrows either is in Z or has a descendant in Z (the definition is elaborated in the next section).

3. The two sets are identical, namely, a statement is valid IF AND ONLY IF it is graphically-validated under d-separation in the DAG.

The first result establishes the *decidability* of verifying whether an arbitrary statement is a valid consequence of the input set. The second result renders the d-separation criterion a *polynomially sound* inference rule, i.e., it runs in polynomial time and certifies only valid statements. The third renders the d-separation criterion a *polynomially complete* inference rule, i.e., the DAG constitutes a sound and complete inference mechanism that identifies, in polynomial time, each and every valid consequence in the system.

The results above are true only for *causal* input sets i.e., those that recursively specify the relation of each variable to its predecessors in some (chronological) order. The general problem of verifying whether a given conditional independence statement logically follows from an arbitrary set of such statements, may be undecidable. Its decidability would be resolved upon finding a complete set of axioms for conditional independence i.e., axioms that are powerful enough to derive all valid consequences of an arbitrary input list. The completeness problem is treated in [6] and completeness results for specialized subsets of probabilistic dependencies have been obtained. Result-1 can be viewed as yet another completeness result for the special case in which the input statements form a causal set. This means that applying axioms (1.a) through (1.d) on a causal input list is guaranteed to generate all valid consequences and none other. Interestingly, result-2 above holds for any statements that obey the graphoid axioms, not necessarily probabilistic conditional independencies. Thus, DAGs can serve as polynomially sound inference mechanisms for a variety of dependence relationships, e.g., partial correlations and qualitative database dependencies. In fact, the results of this paper prove that d-separation is complete for partial correlation as well as for conditional independence statements, whereas completeness for qualitative database dependencies is examined in [7].

2. SOUNDNESS AND COMPLETENESS

The definition of d-separation is best motivated by regarding DAGs as a representation of causal relationships. Designating a node for every variable and assigning a link between every cause to each of its direct consequences defines a graphical representation of a causal hierarchy. For example, the propositions "It is raining" (α), "the pavement is wet" (β) and "John slipped on the pavement" (γ) are well represented by a three node chain, from α through β to γ; it indicates that either rain or wet pavement could cause slipping, yet wet pavement is designated as the *direct cause;* rain could cause someone to slip if it wets the pavement, but not if the pavement is covered. Moreover, knowing the condition of the pavement renders "slipping" and "raining" independent, and this is represented graphically by a d-separation condition, $I(\alpha, \gamma, \beta)_D$, showing node α and β separated from each other by node γ. Assume that "broken pipe" (δ) is considered another direct cause for wet pavement, as in Figure 1. An induced dependency exists between the two events that may cause the pavement to get wet: "rain" and "broken pipe". Although they appear connected in Figure 1, these propositions are marginally independent and become dependent once we learn that the pavement is wet or that someone broke his leg. An increase in our belief in either cause would decrease our belief in the other as it would "explain away" the observation. The following definition of d-separation permits us to graphically identify such induced dependencies from the DAG (d connoted "directional").

Definition: If X, Y, and Z are three disjoint subsets of nodes in a DAG D, then Z is said to *d-separate* X from Y, denoted $I(X, Z, Y)_D$, iff there is no path[2] from a node in X to a node in Y along which every node that delivers an arrow is outside Z and every node with converging arrows either is or has a descendant in Z. A path satisfying the conditions above is said to be *active,* otherwise it is said to be *blocked* (by Z). Whenever a *statement* $I(X, Z, Y)_D$ holds in a DAG D, the predicate $I(X, Z, Y)$ is said to be *graphically-verified* (or an *independency),* otherwise it is *graphically-unverified* by D (or a *dependency).*

In Figure 2, for example, $X = \{2\}$ and $Y = \{3\}$ are d-separated by $Z = \{1\}$; the path $2 \leftarrow 1 \rightarrow 3$ is blocked by $1 \in Z$ while the path $2 \rightarrow 4 \leftarrow 3$ is blocked because 4 and all its descendents are outside Z. Thus $I(2, 1, 3)$ is graphically-verified by D. However, X and Y are not d-separated by $Z' = \{1, 5\}$ because the path $2 \rightarrow 4 \leftarrow 3$ is rendered active by virtue of 5, a descendent of 4, being in Z. Learning the value of the consequence 5, renders its causes 2 and 3 dependent, like opening a pathway along the converging arrows at 4. Consequently, $I(2, \{1,5\}, 3)$ is graphically-unverified by D.

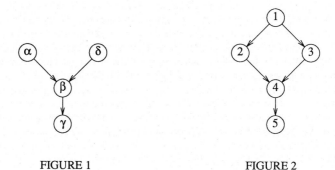

FIGURE 1   FIGURE 2

Definition: If X, Y, and Z are three disjoint subsets of variables of a distribution P, then X and Y are said to be conditionally independent given Z, denoted $I(X, Z, Y)_P$ iff

$$P(X = x, Y = y \mid Z = z) = P(X = x \mid Z = z) \cdot P(Y = y \mid Z = z)$$

for all possible values of x, y and z for which $P(z) > 0$. $I(X, Z, Y)_P$ is called a *(conditional independence)* statement. A conditional independence statement σ *logically follows* from a set Σ of such statements if σ holds in every distribution that obeys Σ. In such case we also say that σ is a *valid consequence* of Σ.

Ideally, to employ a DAG D as a graphical representation for dependencies of some distribution P we would like to require that for every three disjoint sets of variables in P (and

---

[2] By *path* we mean a sequence of edges in the underlying undirected graph, i.e ignoring the directionality of the arrows.

nodes in D) the following equivalence would hold

$$I(X,Z,Y)_D \quad \textit{iff} \quad I(X,Z,Y)_P \qquad (2)$$

This would provide a clear graphical representation of all variables that are conditionally independent. When equation (2) holds, D is said to be a *perfect map* of P. Unfortunately, this requirement is often too strong because there are many distributions that have no perfect map in DAGs. The spectrum of probabilistic dependencies is in fact so rich that it cannot be cast into any representation scheme that uses polynomial amount of storage [22]. Geiger [5] provides a graphical representation based on a collection of graphs (Multi-DAGs) that is powerful enough to perfectly represent an arbitrary distribution, however, as shown by Verma, it requires, on the average, an exponential number of DAGs. Being unable to provide perfect maps at a reasonable cost, we compromise the requirement that the graphs represent each and every dependency of P, and allow some independencies to escape representation.

Definition: A DAG D is said to be an *I-map* of P if for every three disjoint subsets X, Y and Z of variables the following holds:

$$I(X,Z,Y)_D \quad \Rightarrow \quad I(X,Z,Y)_P$$

The natural requirement for these I-maps is that the number of undisplayed independencies be minimized.

The task of finding a DAG which is a minimal I-map of a given distribution P was solved in [23,17]. The algorithm consists of the following steps: assign a total ordering d to the variables of P. For each variable i of P, identify a minimal set of predecessors S_i that renders i independent of all its other predecessors (in the ordering of the first step). Assign a direct link from every variable in S_i to i. The resulting DAG is an I-map of P, and is minimal in the sense that no edge can be deleted without destroying its I-mapness. The input list L for this construction consists of n conditional independence statements, one for each variable, all of the form $I(i, S_i, U_{(i)}-S_i)$ where $U_{(i)}$ is the set of predecessors of i and S_i is a subset of $U_{(i)}$ that renders i conditionally independent of all its other predecessors. This set of conditional independence statements is called a *causal* input list and is said to *define* the DAG D. The term "causal" input list stems from the following analogy: Suppose we order the variables chronologically, such that a cause always precedes its effect. Then, from all potential causes of an effect i, a causal input list selects a minimal subset that is sufficient to explain i, thus rendering all other preceding events superfluous. This selected subset of variables are considered the *direct causes* of i and therefore each is connected to it by a direct link.

Clearly, the constructed DAG represents more independencies than those listed in the input, namely, all those that are graphically verified by the d-separation criterion. The analysis of [23] guarantees that all graphically-verified statements are indeed valid in P i.e., the DAG is an I-map of P. However, this paper shows that the constructed DAG has an additional property; it graphically-verifies **every** conditional independence statement that logically follows from L (i.e. holds in every distribution that obeys L). Hence, we cannot hope to improve the $d-separation$ criterion to display more independencies, because all valid consequences of L (which defines D) are already captured by d-separation.

The three theorems below formalize the above discussion.

Theorem 1 (soundness) [23]: Let D be a DAG defined by a causal input list L. Then, every graphically-verified statement is a valid consequence of L.

Theorem 2 (closure) [23]: Let D be a DAG defined by a causal input list L. Then, the set of graphically-verified statements is exactly the closure of L under axioms (1.a) through (1.d).

Theorem 3 (completeness): Let D be a DAG defined by a causal input list L. Then, every valid consequence of L is graphically-verified by D (equivalently, every graphically-unverified statement in D is not a valid consequence of L).

Theorem 1 guarantees that the DAG displays only valid statements. Theorem 2 guarantees that the DAG displays all statements that are derivable from L via axioms (1). The third theorem, which is the main contribution of this paper, assures that the DAG displays all statements that logically follow from L i.e., the axioms in (1) are complete, capable of deriving all valid consequences of a causal input list. Moreover, since a statement in a DAG can be verified in polynomial time, Theorem 3 provides a complete polynomial inference mechanism for deriving all independency statements that are implied by a causal input set.

Theorem 3 is proven in the appendix by actually constructing a distribution P_σ that satisfies all conditional independencies in L and violates any statement σ graphically-unverified in D. This distribution precludes σ from being a valid consequence of L and therefore, since the construction can be repeated for every graphically-unverified statement, none of these statements is a valid consequence of L.

The first two Theorems are more general than the third in the sense that they hold for every dependence relationship that obeys axioms (1.a) through (1.d), not necessarily those based on probabilistic conditional independence (proofs can be found in [23]). Among these dependence relationships are partial correlations [16] and qualitative dependencies [4,20] which can readily be shown to obey axioms (1). Thus, for example, the transformation of arc-reversal and node removal [8] can be shown valid by purely graphical consideration, simply showing that every statement verified in the transformed graph is also graphically-verified in the original graph.

The proof of Theorem 3 assumes that L contains only statements of the form $I(i, S_i, U_{(i)}-S_i)$. Occasionly, however, we are in possession of stronger forms of independence relationships, in which case additional statements should be read of the DAG. A common example is the case of a variable that is functionally dependent on its corresponding parents in the DAG (*deterministic variable,* [19]). The existence of each such variable i could be encoded in L by a statement of *global* independence $I(i, S_i, U-S_i-i)$ asserting that conditioned on S_i, i is independent of **all** other variables, not merely of its predecessors. The independencies that are implied by the modified input list can be read from the DAG using an enhanced version of d-separation, named *D-separation*.

Definition: If X, Y, and Z are three disjoint subsets of nodes in a DAG D, then Z is said to *D-separate* X from Y, iff there is no path from a node in X to a node in Y along which 1.

every node which delivers an arrow is outside Z, 2. every node with converging arrows either is or has a descendant in Z and 3. no node is functionally determined by Z.

The new criterion certifies all independencies that are revealed by d-separation plus additional ones due to the enhancement of the input list. It has been shown that Theorem 1 through 3 hold for D-separation whenever L contains global independence statements [7].

These graphical criteria provide easy means of recognizing conditional independence in influence diagrams as well as identifying the set of parameters needed for any given computation. Shachter [18,19] has devised an algorithm for finding a set of nodes M guaranteed to contain sufficient information for computing $P(x \mid y)$, for two arbitrary sets of variables x and y. The outcome of Shachter's algorithm can now be stated declaratively; M contains every ancestor of $x \cup y$ that is not D-separated from x given y and none other. The completeness of D-separation implies that M is minimal; no node in M can be excluded on purely topological grounds (i.e., without considering the numerical values of the probabilities involved).

We conclude by showing how these theorems can be employed as an inference mechanism. Assume an expert has identified the following conditional independencies between variables denoted x_1 through x_5:

$$L = \{ I(x_2, x_1, \varnothing),\ I(x_3, x_1, x_2),\ I(x_4, \{x_2 x_3\}, x_1),\ I(x_5, x_4, \{x_1 x_2 x_3\}) \}$$

(the first statement in L is trivial). We address two questions. First, what is the set of all valid consequences of L? Second, in particular, is $I(x_3, \{x_1 x_2 x_4\}, x_5)$ a valid consequence of L? For general input lists the answer for such questions may be undecidable but, since L is a causal list, it defines a DAG that graphically verifies each and every valid consequences of L. The DAG D is the one shown in Figure 2, which constitutes a dense representation of all valid consequences of L. To answer the second question, we simply observe that $I(x_3, \{x_1 x_2 x_4\}, x_5)$ is graphically-verified in D. A graph-based algorithm for another subclass of statements, called *fixed context* statements, is given in [6]. In that paper, results analogous to Theorem 1 through 3 are proven for Markov-fields; a representation scheme based on undirected graphs [9,11].

3. EXTENSIONS AND ELABORATIONS

Theorem 3 can be restated to assert that for every Dag D and any dependency σ there exists a probability distributution P_σ that satisfies D's input set L and the dependency σ. By Theorem 2, P_σ must satisfy all graphically-verified statements as well because they are all derivable from L by the graphoid axioms. Thus, Theorems 2 and 3 guarantee the existence of a distribution P_σ that satisfies all graphically verified statements and a single arbitrary-chosen dependency. The question answered in this section is the existence of a distribution P that satisfies all independencies of D and **all** its dependencies (not merely a single dependency). We show that such a distribution exists, which legitimizes the use of DAGs as a representation scheme for probabilistic dependencies; a model builder who uses the language of DAGs to express dependencies is guarded from inconsistencies.

The construction of P is based on the Armstrong property of conditional independence.

Definition: Conditional independence is an *Armstrong relation* in a class of distributions **P**

if there exists an operation $\otimes$ that maps finite sequences of distributions in $\mathbf{P}$ into a distribution of $\mathbf{P}$, such that if σ is a conditional independence statement and if P_i $i=1..n$ are distributions in $\mathbf{P}$, then σ holds for $\otimes\{P_i \mid i=1..n\}$ iff σ holds for each P_i.

The notion of Armstrong relation is borrowed from database theory [4]. We concentrate on two families of discrete distributions **P**: *All* discrete distributions, denoted *PD* and *strictly positive* discrete distributions, denoted PD^+. Conditional independence can be shown to be an Armstrong relation in both families. The construction of the operation $\otimes$ is given below, however the proof is omitted and can be found in [6].

Theorem 4 [6]: Conditional independence is an Armstrong relation in *PD* and in PD^+.

We shall construct the operation $\otimes$ for conditional independence using a binary operation $\otimes'$ such that if $P = P_1 \otimes' P_2$ then for every conditional independency statement σ we get

$$\otimes'P_i \text{ obeys } \sigma \quad \text{iff} \quad P_1 \text{ obeys } \sigma \text{ and } P_2 \text{ obeys } \sigma. \tag{5}$$

The operation $\otimes$ is recursively defined in terms of $\otimes'$ as follows:

$$\otimes\{P_i \mid i=1..n\} = ((P_1 \otimes' P_2) \otimes' P_3) \otimes' \cdots P_n).$$

Clearly, if $\otimes'$ satisfies equation (5), then $\otimes$ satisfies the the requirement of an Armstrong relation, i.e.

$$P \text{ obeys } \sigma \quad \text{iff} \quad \forall_i P_i \text{ obeys } \sigma.$$

Therefore, it suffices to show that $\otimes'$ satisfies (5).

Let P_1 and P_2 be two distributions sharing the variables $x_1, \cdots, x_n$. Let $A_1, \cdots, A_n$ be the domains of $x_1, \cdots, x_n$ in P_1 and let an instance of these variables be $\alpha_1, \cdots, \alpha_n$. Similarly, let $B_1, \cdots, B_n$ be the domains of $x_1, \cdots, x_n$ in P_2 and $\beta_1, \cdots, \beta_n$ an instance of these variables. Let the domain of $P = P_1 \otimes' P_2$ be the product domain $A_1 B_1, \cdots, A_n B_n$ and denote an instance of the variables of P by $\alpha_1 \beta_1, \cdots, \alpha_n \beta_n$. Define $P_1 \otimes' P_2$ by the following equation:

$$P(\alpha_1\beta_1, \alpha_2\beta_2, \cdots, \alpha_n\beta_n) = P_1(\alpha_1, \alpha_2, \cdots, \alpha_n) \cdot P_2(\beta_1, \beta_2, \cdots, \beta_n).$$

The proof that P satisfies the condition of Theorem 4 uses only the definition of conditional independence and can be found in [6]. The adequacy of this construction for PD^+ is due to the fact that $\otimes$ produces a strictly positive distribution whenever the input distributions are strictly positive.

Theorem 5: For every DAG D there exists a distribution P such that for every three disjoint sets of variables X, Y and Z, the following holds;

$$I(X,Z,Y)_D \quad \text{iff} \quad I(X,Z,Y)_P$$

Proof: Let $P = \otimes\{P_\sigma \mid \sigma \text{ is a dependency in a DAG } D\}$ where P_σ is a distribution obeying all independencies of D and a dependency σ. By Theorem 3, a distribution P_σ always exists. P satisfies the requirement of Theorem 5 because it obeys only statements that hold in every P_σ and these are exactly the ones verified by D. $\square$

The construction presented in the proof of Theorem 5 leads to a rather complex distribution, where the domain of each variable is unrestricted. It still does not guarantee that a set of dependencies and independencies represented by DAGs is realizable in a more limited class of distributions such as normal or those defined on binary variables. We conjecture that these two classes of distributions are sufficiently rich to permit the consistency of DAG representation.

ACKNOWLEDGMENT

We thank Ron Fagin for pointing out the usefulness of the notion of Armstrong relation and to Ross Shachter for his insightful comments. Thomas Verma and Azaria Paz provided many useful discussions on the properties of dependency models.

REFERENCES

[1]   Blalock, H.M. 1971. *Causal Models in the Social Sciences,* London: Macmillan.

[2]   Dawid A.P. 1979. Conditional Independence in Statistical Theory, *J.R. Statist. Soc. B,* **41(1):** 1-31.

[3]   Duncan O.D. 1975. *Introduction to Structural Equation Models,* New York: Academic Press.

[4]   Fagin R. 1982. Horn Clauses and Database Dependencies, *JACM,* **29(4):** 952-985.

[5]   Geiger D. 1987. Towards the Formalization of Informational Dependencies, (M.S. thesis). UCLA Cognitive Systems Laboratory, *Technical Report R-102.*

[6]   Geiger D., Pearl J. 1988. Logical and Algorithmic Properties of Conditional Independence. In *Preliminary Papers, 2nd Intl. Workshop on AI and Statistics,* Miami, Florida, pp. (19-1)-(19-10).

[7]   Geiger D., Verma T. S., Pearl J. 1988. Recognizing Independence in Bayesian Networks. UCLA Cognitive Systems Laboratory *Technical Report (R-116).* To appear in *Networks,* 1990.

[8]   Howard R. A., Matheson J. E. 1981. Influence Diagrams, In *Principles and Applications of Decision Analysis,* Menlo Park, Ca.: Strategic Decisions Group.

[9]   Isham V. 1981. An Introduction to Spatial Point Processes and Markov Random Fields, *International Statistical Review,* **49:** 21-43.

[10]   Kiiveri H., Speed T. P., Carlin J. B. 1984. Recursive Causal Models, *Journal of Australian Math Society,* **36:** 30-52.

[11]   Lauritzen S. L. 1982. *Lectures on Contingency Tables,* 2nd Ed., University of Aalborg Press, Aalborg, Denmark.

[12]   Miller K. S. 1964. *Multidimensional Gausian distributions,* Wiley Siam series in applied math.

12

[13] Pearl J. 1985. A Constraint-Propagation Approach to Probabilistic Reasoning. In Kanal, L.N. and Lemmer, J. (eds) *Uncertainty in Artificial Intelligence*, North-Holland, Amsterdam, 357-369.

[14] Pearl J. 1986. Fusion, Propagation and Structuring in Belief Networks, *Artificial Intelligence*, **29(3)**: 241-288.

[15] Pearl J. 1988. *Probabilistic Reasoning in Intelligent Systems*, San Mateo:Morgan-Kaufmann.

[16] Pearl J., Paz A. 1987. *GRAPHOIDS: A Graph-based Logic for Reasoning about Relevance Relations*. In Du Boulay, B. et al. (eds) *Advances in Artificial Intelligence-II*, Amsterdam: North-Holland Publishing Co.

[17] Pearl J., Verma T. S. 1987. The Logic of Representing Dependencies by Directed Acyclic Graphs, *Proc. 6th Nat. Conf. on AI (AAAI-87)*, Seattle, Washington, 374-379.

[18] Shachter R. 1985. Intelligent Probabilistic Inference, In Kanal, L.N. and Lemmer, J. (eds) *Uncertainty in Artificial Intelligence*, North-Holland, Amsterdam, 371-382.

[19] Shachter R. 1988. Probabilistic Inference and Influence Diagrams, *Operations Research*, **36**: 589-604.

[20] Shafer G., Shenoy P.P., Mellouli K. 1987. Propagating Belief Functions in Qualitative Markov Trees, *International Journal of Approximate Reasoning* **1(4)**: 349-400.

[21] Smith J.Q. (1989). Influence Diagrams for Statistical Modeling. *Annals of Statistics* **17(2)**: 654-672.

[22] Verma T. S. 1987. Some Mathematical Properties of Dependency Models, UCLA Cognitive Systems Laboratory, Los Angeles, California, *Technical Report R-103*.

[23] Verma T. S., Pearl J. 1988. Causal Networks: Semantics and Expressiveness, this volume.

[24] Wermuth N., Lauritzen S. L. 1983. Graphical and Recursive Models for Contingency Tables, *Biometrika*, **70**: 537-552.

[25] Wold H. 1964. *In Econometric Model Building*, Amsterdam: North-Holland Publishing Co..

[26] Wright S. 1934. The Method of Path Coefficients, *Ann. Math. Statist.*, **5**: 161-215.

APPENDIX

Theorem 3 (completeness): Let D be a DAG defined by a causal input list L. Then, every valid consequence of L is graphically-verified by D.

Proof: Let $\sigma = I(X, Z, Y)$ be an arbitrary graphically-unverified statement in D. We construct a distribution P_σ that satisfies all conditional independencies in the input list L and violates σ. This distribution precludes σ from being a valid consequence of L and therefore, every valid consequence of L must be graphically-verified in D.

From the definition of d-separation, there must exist an active path between an element α in X and an element β in Y that is not d-separated by Z. Ensuring that P_σ violates the conditional independency $I(\alpha, Z, \beta)$, denoted σ', guarantees that σ is also violated, because any distribution that renders X and Y conditionally independent must render each of their individual variables independent as well (axiom (1.b)).

P_σ is defined in terms of a simplified DAG D_σ. This DAG is constructed by removing as many links as possible from D such that σ remains unverified in D_σ. This process clearly preserves all previously verified statements but caution is exercised not to remove links that would render σ graphically-verified in D_σ. We will conclude the proof by constructing a distribution P_σ which satisfies all graphically-verified statements of D_σ (hence also those of D) and violates σ'.

Let q be an active path (by Z) between α and β with the minimum number of head-to-head nodes (i.e. nodes with converging arrows) denoted, left to right, $h_1, h_2, ..., h_k$. Let z_i be the closest (wrt path length) descendent of h_i in Z and let p_i be the directed path from h_i to z_i (if $h_i \in Z$ then $z_i = h_i$). We define D_σ to be a subgraph of D containing only the links that form the paths p_i's and the path q. We make two claims about the topology of the resulting DAG. First, the paths p_i are all distinct. Second, for any i, h_i is the only node shared by p_i and q. The resulting DAG is depicted in Figure 3 (note that some nodes, including nodes of Z, might become isolated in D_σ).

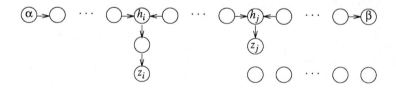

FIGURE 3

Proof of claim 1: Assume, by contradiction, that there are two paths p_i and p_j $(i < j)$ with a common node γ. Under this assumption, we find an active path between α and β that has less head-to-head nodes than q, contradicting the minimality of the latter. If γ is neither h_i nor h_j then the path $(\alpha, h_i, \gamma, h_j, \beta)$ is an active path (by Z); Each of its head-to-head nodes is or has a descendent in Z because it is either γ or a head-to-head node of q. Every other node lies either on the active path q and therefore is outside Z or lies on p_i (p_j) in which case, since it has a descendent γ, it must also be outside Z. The resulting path contradicts the minimality of q since both h_i and h_j are no longer head-to-head nodes while γ is the only newly introduced head-to-head node. If $\gamma = h_j$ then, using similar arguments, the path $(\alpha, h_i, \gamma, \beta)$ (see Figure 4), which has less head-to-head nodes then q, can readily be shown active (the case $\gamma = h_i$ is similar).

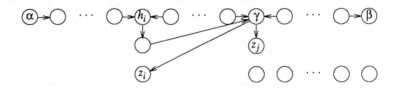

FIGURE 4

Proof of claim 2: Assume p_i and q have in common a node γ other then h_i and assume w.l.o.g that it lies between h_i and β. This node is not a head-to-head node on q because p_i is distinct from all other p_j's. The node γ cannot belong to Z because otherwise q would not have been active. Thus, the path $(\alpha, h_i, \gamma, \beta)$ must be an active path which contradicts the minimality of q (Figure 5).

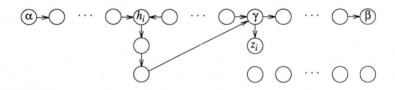

FIGURE 5

The distribution P_σ is defined as follows: Each node with no parents corresponds to an independent fair coin. Every other node corresponds to a variable that is the sum modulo 2 of the variables corresponding to its parents. Clearly, variables α and β are conditionally dependent given Z in P_σ because constraining α and Z to some specific values determines a value for β via the single trail q that connects them in D_σ. It remains to show that every graphically-verified statement in D_σ is satisfied by P_σ. Theorem 2 ensures that all graphically verified statements are derivable by the graphoid axioms from the n statements that form the causal input list L of D_σ. Since the graphoid axioms are satisfied by every distribution, it suffice to show that the statements in L hold in P_σ. But this is immediate; If i has parents in D_σ then it is independent given its parents from all its non-descendants because it is a function of its parents. Otherwise, i is a source node, thus is independent from all its non-descendants by the d-separation criteria (Theorem 1). $\square$

Uncertainty in Artificial Intelligence 4
R.D. Shachter, T.S. Levitt, L.N. Kanal, J.F. Lemmer (Editors)
© Elsevier Science Publishers B.V. (North-Holland), 1990

Process, Structure, and Modularity in Reasoning with Uncertainty

Bruce D'Ambrosio
Department of Computer Science
Oregon State University

Abstract

Computational mechanisms for uncertainty management must support interactive and incremental problem formulation, inference, hypothesis testing, and decision making. however, most current uncertainty inference systems concentrate primarily on inference, and provide no support for the larger issues. We present a computational approach to uncertainty management which provides direct support for the dynamic, incremental aspect of this task, while at the same time permitting direct representation of the structure of evidential relationships. At the same time, we show that this approach responds to the modularity concerns of Heckerman and Horvitz [Heçk87]. This paper emphasizes examples of the capabilities of this approach. Another paper [D'Am89] details the representations and algorithms involved.

1 Introduction

A review of the literature on uncertainty in AI might lead one to conclude that the problem consists solely of choosing an appropriate certainty calculus. However, a complete approach to uncertainty management requires support for interactive and incremental problem formulation, inference, hypothesis ranking, and decision making. Further, it should be based on a normative model of reasoning and decision-making under uncertainty, must provide support for defeasible decision-making about problem model formulation, and must offer ways of bounding the resources need for uncertainty management.

In this paper we present an approach which begins to address these requirements. It is based on the belief that while Bayesian inference provides one possible "gold standard" for micro-management of uncertainty, that is, describing and evaluating isolated instances of uncertainty reasoning, it ignores the macro-management aspects of reasoning with uncertainty, the problems of how an intelligent agent goes about structuring and revising situation models. In our approach, uncertainty is represented symbolically and structurally. The approach permits natural and intuitive representations of commonly occurring causal and evidential structures, permits analysis even in the face of weak, non-numeric information about beliefs, and yet conforms to a normative model of inference when full probability data is available. At the same time, the symbolic underpinnings of our approach support incremental construction, modification, and evaluation of belief networks. We believe this to be an essential aspect of uncertainty reasoning which has been ignored in most previous research. In addition, they provide a natural mechanism for modelling macro-management of uncertainty reasoning as the dynamic construction and evaluation of a set of related situation models, based on a subgoalling structure. In subsequent sections of this paper we first briefly introduce Hybrid Uncertainty Management (HUM), and then illustrate its operation by considering two examples which have appeared recently in the literature on uncertainty in AI. The reader should note that the work reported here does not include a theory of macro-management. Rather, it simply reports on an inference system (UIS) designed to provide the low level operations needed to support macro-management.

2 Related Research

Breese [Bree87] has studied the problem of model formulation, starting from a database containing both logical and probabilistic knowledge. Laskey [Lask88] has independently begun developing a mapping for probabilistic knowledge into an ATMS similar to ours. Quinlan [Quin87] has considered the problems of hard-wiring assumptions regarding model structure, and resulting limitations in expressivity. Henrion [Henr87], Pearl [Pear87], Shachter [Shac87], and others are studying performance models with the full expressivity of probability theory. More recently, Charniak and Goldman [Char89] and Levitt *et al* [Levi89] have begun exploring incremental dynamic situation model construction.

3 Hybrid Uncertainty Management

3.1 Issues and Overview

Hybrid uncertainty management is a framework for reasoning with uncertain information based on the following principles:

1. All information, including information about our uncertainty, should be represented using *explicit, local* representations. These representations should preserve the *structure* of information, as well as its "content".

2. For efficient yet robust reasoning, representations must be such that they can be incrementally constructed, evaluated, and modified, and the same uncertainty management capabilities should be available to the agent when reasoning about construction of a model, as when reasoning about the domain problem.

We are constructing[1] an Uncertainty Inference System (UIS [Henr87]) in accordance with these principles, based on the logical inference capabilities of an Assumption-Based Truth Maintenance System (ATMS) [deKl86]. An ATMS provides a complete propositional logic. That is, given a set of atomic propositions and a set of logical formulas over those propositions, it computes the set of consistent assignments of truth values to a core set of propositions, and derives the truth value of every other proposition in terms of the truth values of the core set. Derived truth values are represented as expressions, in disjunctive normal form, for the truth of every proposition in terms of the truth of core propositions. It is this DNF expression, called a *label* in ATMS parlance, which provides the core structured representation for uncertainty in HUM.

In creating HUM, we are developing mechanisms for using the representational and inferential capabilities of an ATMS for both micro- and macro-management of reasoning with uncertainty. For micro-management, we have added mechanisms which permit the interpretation of selected *assumptions* as markers for elements of *probability distributions*, and have developed mappings for the basic expressions in a probabilistic model. This required developing the following components:

---

[1] All the examples shown run in the current prototype.

1. A representation for a probability distribution - we use the ATMS *choose* operator to indicate that a set of assumptions represent a probability distribution, and annotate each assumption with the corresponding numeric probability, when available.

2. A mapping for the basic computations of probabilistic inference - we use the ATMS *justification* as the primitive component of our representation for an probabilistic relationship between variables, and the ATMS *environment propagation* mechanism to perform inference.

3. A mechanism for retrieving probabilities from ATMS labels - we have developed an algorithm which can evaluate labels on request to reduce them to a numeric representation.

For further details see [D'Am89].

Macro-management requires the ability to:

1. Represent and reason about the decisions involved in model construction.

2. Recognize when inference at the domain level indicates problems in the model formulation, and revise domain models as appropriate.

The domain models are constructed as ATMS networks, and ATMS *assumptions* are used to explicitly record defeasible model structure decisions. As we will show in an example below, this permits dynamic extension and revision, as well as incremental evaluation, of domain models. Our current implementation provides a mixed forward and backward chaining rule language in which model construction algorithms are written. Forward chaining is used to express the basic model construction algorithms, and backward chaining is invoked when information needed during model construction is unavailable. This architecture provides the same capabilities in response to model structure subgoals as are available at the domain level. We illustrate in a second example how explicit recording of structuring decisions permits revision and incremental re-evaluation of domain models.

3.2   Example One: The Three Urns

We begin with a very simple example, the three urns problem described in [Heck87]:

> Suppose you are given one of three opaque jars containing mixtures of black licorice and white peppermint jelly beans. The first jar contains one white jelly bean and one black jelly bean, the second jar contains two white jelly beans, and the third jar contains two black jelly beans. You are not allowed to look inside the jar, but you are allowed to draw beans from the jar, *with* replacement. That is, you must replace each jelly bean you draw before sampling another. Let H_i be the hypothesis that you are holding the *ith* jar. As you are told that the jars were selected at random, you believe that each H_i is equally likely before you begin to draw jelly beans.

We can represent this situation in HUM in the following fashion[2]:

---

[2]In the following psuedo-lisp examples, we simply present an expression when the value returned is not of interest. If the returned value is relevant, we precede the expression by > and show the result on the following line.

```
;;; I have one of three possible urns
(Variable Urn H1 H2 H3)
;; every draw has two possible outcomes
(Variable (Draw ?n) white black)
```

The expression (Draw ?n) above states that we are describing, not a single draw, but a class of possible draws from an urn. Actual Draws will instantiate the logical variable ?n with a number 1 ,2,.... We can express the conditional probability of drawing a white based on the urn we are holding as follows:

```
;;; probability of drawing white, for each urn:
(Relation Urn-Draw (Urn) (Draw ?n)
        (-> ((Urn H1)) (((Draw ?n) white) .5) (((Draw ?n) black) .5))
        (-> ((Urn H2)) (((Draw ?n) white) 1.0))
        (-> ((Urn H3)) (((Draw ?n) white) 0.0)))
```

Each "->" in this example corresponds to a rule, and the entire collection defines a complete conditional probability distribution. Finally, we can express our pre-existing information about jars as follows:

```
(Marginal Urn (.33 .33 .33))
```

3.2.1 Incremental Symbolic Evaluation

The above information serves to fully constrain the conditional probabilities for a class of possible situation models. Note, however, that the full joint distribution need never be explicitly represented, either in the problem statement or in the ATMS network: the label reduction algorithm can directly combine the marginals for each evidence source. At this point, the specific situation model constructed so far only contains the *Urn* variable. We can now ask HUM for the probability that we are holding H2:

```
>(Probability-of (Urn H2))
0.33
```

We can also ask for the probability of selecting a white jelly bean, by first extending the model to include a first draw, and then querying the probability of various outcomes:

```
(Instance (draw 1))
>(Probability-of ((draw 1) white))
.5
```

Any of this could easily be done in several of the various UIS's currently available, and should seem rather boring (except, perhaps, for the ability to describe a *class* of variables, (Draw ?n)). Consider, however, what happens once we actually draw a sample:

```
(Assert ((draw 1) white))
>(Probability-of (Urn H2))
0.67

(Instance (draw 2))
(Assert ((draw 2) white))

>(Probability-of (Urn H2))
0.8
```

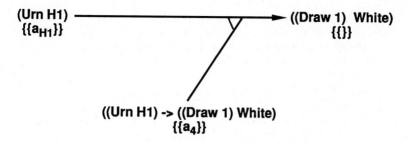

Figure 1: ATMS network for Urn Problem after Draw 1

The system *incrementally* computes the new posterior for the various Urn hypotheses, by incrementally extending the network and incrementally updating the structured representation for the probability of each urn.

A fragment of the ATMS network corresponding to this problem is shown in figure 1. Arcs in the diagram represent ATMS justifications, in this case used to express conditional probability relationships between variables. The label of each value is shown in brackets under the value. Thus, the ATMS records that hypothesis (Urn H2) is true precisely under the assumption a_{H2}, wich carries the original marginal assigned, while ((Draw 1) white) is true universally (that is, it is true in a environment which includes no assumptions). ((Draw 1) black), on the other hand, is not supported in any environment. It may not be obvious from this example how the observation of draw 1 affects the probability of holding Urn H2, since the label for Urn H2 is unchanged. Briefly, when ((Draw 1) white) is asserted, its label is saved, and used to condition subsequent queries. Since this label includes assumptions used to represent the marginal for Urns, the subsequently computed probability for any value of the Urns variable is changed. Further detail is beyond the scope of this paper, see [D'Am89].

A complete computational treatment of uncertainty must meet a variety of requirements. Some are expressivity requirements, as identified by Heckerman and Horvitz [Heck87]. Others arise from the dynamic nature of computation and interaction with the world. We have used this example to illustrate how several of these requirements are handled in HUM. We have shown how HUM handles mutual exclusivity, bidirectional inference (reasoning from causes to observables **and** observables to causes interchangeably), and one process aspect of reasoning with uncertainty, incremental construction and evaluation of models. Note also that this representation system does not suffer from the modularity problems observed by Heckerman and Horvitz when they considered the same example. The "rules" relating urns to outcomes need only be expressed once, and remain correct for any number of draws and any sequence of outcomes.

3.3   Example 2 - Thousands Dead

A major issue in uncertainty reasoning is the representation and use of correlated evidence. In this next example, taken from [Henr87], we examine reasoning about model structure and model revision. Specifically, we attempt to show that commonly occurring correlations between evidence sources are the result of *structural* relationships between such sources, and therefore are best supported by a system which permits direct expression of that structure:

Chernobyl example: The first radio news bulletin you hear on the accident at the Chernobyl nuclear power plant reports that the release of radioactive materials may have already killed several thousand people. Initially you place small credence in this, but as you start to hear similar reports from other radio and TV stations, and in the newspapers, you believe it more strongly. A couple of days later, you discover that the news reports were all based on the same wire-service report based on a single unconfirmed telephone interview from Moscow. Consequently, you greatly reduce your degree of belief again.

We see two interesting issues here. The first is expressivity. Henrion points out that "...none of the better known UISs are actually capable of distinguishing between independent and correlated sources of evidence." One view is that the problem here is not probabilistic, but rather a logical uncertainty about the possible coreference of evidence for the various reports. The second is a process issue. What changes is our beliefs about the *structure* of the evidential relationships. We are unaware of any existing UIS that is capable of accommodating this structural change. All require reconstructing the model in its entirety, which we claim is exorbitant and unrealistic.

The information we have underconstrains the possible joint evidential relationship between news reports and the number dead. One possibility, advocated by Quinlan [Quin87], is to abstain from committing, and compute a weak, interval-valued result. We believe this is unrealistic. Commitments must be made in the absence of conclusive data, based on *reasonable assumptions* about the situation being modelled. What is crucial is that a mechanism be provided through which an agent can reason about and record structural assumptions. The structured uncertainty representation provided by an ATMS provides the bookkeeping necessary for such a mechanism, as we now show.

Our initial knowledge is as follows

1. Thousands of people might have died at Chernobyl:

    (Variable 1000s-dead true false)

2. This seems unlikely a priori:

    (Marginal 1000s-dead (.01 .99)))

3. A report either has been received or it hasn't:

    (Variable (report ?n ?subject) true false)

4. Reports have sources who usually tell the truth:

    (Variable (source (report ?n ?subject)) true false)
    (Marginal (source (report ?n ?subject)) (.99 .01))

5. The relation between events, sources, and reports is as follows (in general, this can be a complete conditional distribution):

    (Relation report (1000s-dead (source (report ?n 1000s-dead)))
            (report ?n 1000s-dead)
        (-> ((1000s-dead true) ((source (report ?n 1000s-dead) false))
        ((((report ?n 1000s-dead) true) 1.0)))
        (->`((1000s-dead true) ((source (report ?n 1000s-dead) true))

```
(((((report ?n 1000s-dead) true) 1.0)))
(-> ((1000s-dead false) ((source (report ?n 1000s-dead) true))
(((((report ?n 1000s-dead) true) 1.0)))
(-> ((1000s-dead false) ((source (report ?n 1000s-dead) false))
(((((report ?n 1000s-dead) false) 1.0))))
```

6. Finally, two reports on the same subject might or might not have independent sources, but sources are usually independent:

```
(Frame (sources (report ?n ?subject) (report ?m ?subject))
       elem independent coreferent)
(Marginal (sources (report ?n ?subject) (report ?m ?subject)) (.8 .2))
```

If we now consider a report about the accident, and assert that it in fact occurred, we can compute the belief in thousands dead:

```
>(Probability-of (1000s-dead true))
.01

(Instance (report 1 1000s-dead))
(Assert ((report 1 1000s-dead) true))
>(Probability-of (1000s-dead true))
0.5
```

However, if we subsequently assert the receipt of a second report the joint distribution is underconstrained and the posterior belief in thousands-dead cannot be computed. if we assume that each report provides *independent* evidence, then we have enough information to recover the complete joint distribution. Now what happens when we change our mind about the independence of the various reports? First we show system operation, then explain what happened:

```
(Instance (report 2 1000s-dead))
(Assert ((report 2 1000s-dead) true))
** Assuming ((sources (report 1) (report 2)) independent) ***
** Monitoring ((sources (report 1) (report 2)) coreferent) ***
>(Probability-of (1000s-dead true))
0.91
(Assert ((sources (report 1) (report 2)) coreferent))
** Retracting ((sources (report 1) (report 2)) independent) ***
>(Probability (1000s-dead true))
0.5
```

When reasoning about model structure, the system has all of the reasoning capabilities available at the domain model level. When it detects an attempt to instantiate a second report about thousands dead at Chernobyl, it establishes a subgoal to determine the relationship between the two sets of antecedents. This subgoal is solved by constructing simple decision model, based on information provided above about evidence sources, which decides how to instantiate the evidence for the second report. In our example, the prior probability that sources are independent is high enough to result in the decision to instantiate the evidence for the second report as a separate, independent source of evidence. However, because the evidence for independence is not conclusive, a *monitor*, in the form of a rule

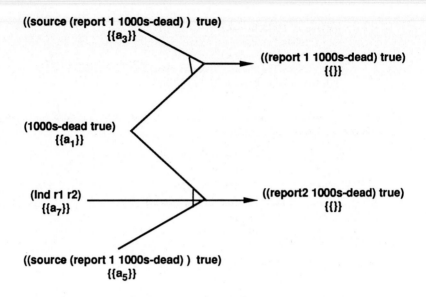

Figure 2: ATMS network for Chernobyl with Independence

which triggers on changes in the ATMS label of either the coreference or independence assertions, is installed. When evidence later arrives that the sources of evidence for the two reports are in fact identical, this triggers the monitor to re-structure the domain model in accordance with the new information. This restructuring is accomplished by invalidating the previous evidence for (report 2) and sharing the evidence source for (report 1) between the two reports. As we stated earlier, the assumption of independence is the statement of a *lack* of structural connection between the various reports. In order to make this assumption retractable, we condition the connection between the original evidence for (report 1) and (report 1) itself on the independence assumption. Thus, if the independence assumption is a_7, the above described situation is represented by the ATMS network shown in figure 2.

The purpose for explicitly recording the independence assumption is to permit later retraction. When we later discover that the evidence for the reports is not independent, we retract the independence assumption, and extend the model to reflect our updated understanding of the situation, as shown in figure 3. It is not obvious from this figure how the previous structure has been retracted, since the old arcs remain. Notice, however, that the label for the independence proposition (Ind r1 r2) has become empty.

3.4   Discussion

The above examples are intended to demonstrate desirable attributes of comprehensive computational support for inference under uncertainty. However, the above is more of a tantalizing hint than a substantive accomplishment. Several questions remain unaddressed:

1. Is there any significant complexity reduction in reformulation, as opposed to reconstruction from scratch?

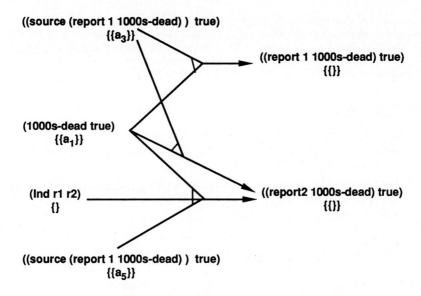

Figure 3: ATMS network for Chernobyl with co-reference

2. Is incremental refinement or reformulation always possible (this is really just a variant of the above?

3. What is a necessary and sufficient set of construction/reformulation primitives?

4. Is there a coherent theory of how construction/reformulation decisions ought to be made?

5. How might such an approach be extended to support decision making, as well as inference?

We have just begun to incorporate the machinery of decision analysis into this framework. Also, our current mechanisms for control of the reasoning process are crude and only handle a few special cases. We are in the process of examining a sample diagnostic problem in detail to identify a more complete set of control issues and techniques. The structured symbolic representation provides fertile ground for exploring the problem of explanation of results, a topic we have not yet begun to explore. A major difficulty in the current approach is that, in order for a structural component to be modifiable, it must be initially tagged as such.

4 Summary

We have argued that most research in UIS's is too narrowly focused. When viewing the larger problem solving task in which such inference is embedded, probabilistic model extension, structuring, and reformulation primitives are essential. We have presented an approach to uncertain inference which emphasizes both expressivity in the sense discussed by Heckerman and Horvitz, and process. We identify two aspects of expressivity: adequacy and economy. We have illustrated through examples that this approach is not only adequately expressive, but also economical, in that it captures *structurally* commonly occurring classes of evidential relationships. We have argued, although not demonstrated, that it is also economical in the sense that it permits efficient incremental recomputation in the presence of structural reformulation.

References

[Bree87] John S. Breese. Knowledge Representation and Inference in Intelligent Decision Systems. Phd Thesis, Department of Engineering-Economic Systems, Stanford University, Stanford, CA. March, 1987.

[Char89] Eugene Charniak and Robert Goldman. Plan Recognition in Stories and in Life. In *Proceedings of the Fifth Workshop on Uncertainty in AI*, pp 54-59, Windsor, Ontario, August, 1989.

[D'Am87a] Bruce D'Ambrosio. Truth Maintenance with Numeric Certainty Estimates. In *Proceedings Third Conference on AI Applications*, pages 244–249, Kissimmee, Florida, Computer Society of the IEEE, February, 1987.

[D'Am88] Bruce D'Ambrosio. A Hybrid Approach to Management of Uncertainty. In *International Journal of Approximate Reasoning.*, 2:29-45, February, 1988.

[D'Am89] Bruce D'Ambrosio. Symbolic Representation and Evaluation of Probabilistic Knowledge. In print.

[deKl86] Johan deKleer. An Assumption-based TMS. In *Artificial Intelligence* 28(2): 127-162, March, 1986.

[Heck87] David Heckerman and Eric Horvitz. On the Expressiveness of Rule-based Systems for Reasoning with Uncertainty. In *Proc. AAAI-87*, pp. 121-126, Seattle, WA, 1987.

[Henr87] Max Henrion. Uncertainty in Artificial Intelligence: Is probability epistemologically and heuristically adequate? In *Expert Systems and Expert Judgement*, proceedings of the NATO Advanced Research Workshop, in Porto, Portugal, August, 1986. Mumpower and Renn (Eds).

[Henr87] Max Henrion. Practical Issues in Constructing a Bayes Belief Network. In Proc. Uncertainty in AI 87, pp. 132-140, Seattle, WA, 1987.

[Lask88] Kathryn Laskey and Paul Lehner. Belief Maintenance: An Integrated Approach to Uncertainty Management. In *Proc. AAAI-88*, pp 210-214, Minneapolis, Minn, Aug. 1988, Morgan Kaufmann, publishers.

[Levi89] T. S. Levitt, J. M. Agosta, and T. O. Binford. Model-based Influence Diagrams for Machine Vision. In *Proceedings of the Fifth Workshop on Uncertainty in AI*, pp 233-244, Windsor, Ontario, August, 1989.

[Pear87] Judea Pearl. Fusion, Propagation, and Structuring in Belief Networks. In *Artificial Intelligence*, 29(3): 241-288.

[Quin87] J.R. Quinlan. Inferno: A Cautious Approach to Uncertain Inference. In *The Computer Journal*, 26(3): 255-269.

[Shac87] Ross Shachter and David Heckerman. A Backwards View of Assessment. In *AI Magazine*, 8(3):55-62, Fall, 1987.

Uncertainty in Artificial Intelligence 4
R.D. Shachter, T.S. Levitt, L.N. Kanal, J.F. Lemmer (Editors)
© Elsevier Science Publishers B.V. (North-Holland), 1990

Probabilistic Causal Reasoning

Thomas Dean*and Keiji Kanazawa
Department of Computer Science
Brown University
Box 1910, Providence, RI 02912

Abstract

Predicting the future is an important component of decision making. In most situations, however, there is not enough information to make accurate predictions. In this paper, we develop a theory of causal reasoning for predictive inference under uncertainty. We emphasize a common type of prediction that involves reasoning about *persistence*: whether or not a proposition once made true remains true at some later time. We provide a decision procedure with a polynomial-time algorithm for determining the probability of the possible consequences of a set events and initial conditions. The integration of simple probability theory with temporal projection enables us to circumvent problems that nonmonotonic temporal reasoning schemes have in dealing with persistence. The ideas in this paper have been implemented in a prototype system that refines a database of causal rules in the course of applying those rules to construct and carry out plans in a manufacturing domain.

*This work was supported in part by a National Science Foundation Presidential Young Investigator Award IRI-8957601 with matching funds from IBM, and by the Advanced Research Projects Agency of the Department of Defense and was monitored by the Air Force Office of Scientific Research under Contract No. F49620-88-C-0132. A version of this paper appears in the Proceedings of the Seventh Biennial Conference of the Canadian Society for Computational Studies of Intelligence.

1 Introduction

We are interested in the design of robust inference systems for generating and executing plans in routine manufacturing situations. We hope to build autonomous agents capable of dealing with a fairly circumscribed set of possibilities in a manner that demonstrates both strategic reasoning (the ability to anticipate and plan for possible futures) and adaptive reasoning (the ability to recognize and react to unanticipated conditions). In this paper, we develop a computational theory for temporal reasoning under uncertainty that is well suited to a wide variety of dynamic domains.

The domains that we are interested in have the following characteristics: (i) things cannot always be predicted accurately in advance, (ii) plans made in anticipation of pending events often have to be amended to suit new information, and (iii) the knowledge and ability to acquire predictive rules is severely limited by the planner's experience. Reasoning in such domains often involves making choices quickly on the basis of incomplete information. Although predictions can be inaccurate, it is often worthwhile for a planner to attempt to predict what conditions are likely to be true in the future and generate plans to deal with them.

Our theory includes (i) a polynomial-time decision procedure for probabilistic inference about temporally-dependent information, and (ii) a space and time efficient method for refining probabilistic causal rules.

2 Causal Theories

In order to explore some of the issues that arise in causal reasoning, we will consider some examples involving a robot foreman that directs activity in a factory. The robot has a plan of action that it is continually executing and revising. Among its tasks is the loading of trucks for clients. If our robot learns that a truck is more likely to leave than it previously believed, then it should consider revising its plans so that this truck will be loaded earlier. If, on the other hand, it predicts that all trucks will be loaded ahead of schedule, then it should take advantage of the opportunity to take care of other tasks which it did not previously consider possible in the available time.

In order to construct and revise its plan of action, the robot makes use of a fairly simple model of the world: a special-purpose theory about the cause-and-effect relationships that govern processes at work in the world (referred to as a *causal theory*). The robot's causal theory consists of two distinct types of rules which we will refer to as *projection rules* and *persistence rules*. We will defer discussion of persistence rules for just a bit.

As an example of a projection rule, the robot might have a rule that states that if a client calls in an order, then, with some likelihood, the client's truck will eventually arrive to pick up the order. The consequent prediction, in this case the arrival of a client's truck, is conditioned on two things: an event referred to as the *triggering event*, in this case the client calling in the order, and an enabling condition corresponding to propositions that must be true at the time the triggering event occurs. For example, the rule just mentioned might be conditioned on propositions about the type of items ordered, whether or not the caller has an account with the retailer, or the time of day. The simplest form of a projection rule is $PROJECT(P_1 \wedge P_2 \ldots \wedge P_n, E, R, \pi)$. This says that R will be true with probability π immediately following the event E given that P_1 through P_n are true at the time E occurs. Let $\langle P, t \rangle$ indicate that the proposition P is true at time t, and $\langle E, t \rangle$ indicate that an event of type E occurs at time t. Restated as a conditional probability, we might express this rule as:

$$p(\langle R, t + \epsilon \rangle | \langle P_1 \wedge P_2 \ldots \wedge P_n, t \rangle \wedge \langle E, t \rangle)) = \pi$$

In this paper, we will assume for simplicity that P_1 through P_n are independent, and that other combinations of $P_1 \ldots P_n$ and E do not affect R. In [4] we present a model of reasoning in which these restriction are removed. Projection rules are applied in a purely antecedent fashion (as in a production system) by the inference engine we will be discussing. The objective is to obtain an accurate picture of the future in order to support reasoning about plans [2] [1].

Our approach, as described up to this point, is fairly traditional and might conceivably be handled by some existing approach [13] [7]. What distinguishes our approach from that of other probabilistic reasoning approaches is that we are very much concerned with the role of time and in particular the tendency of certain propositions (often referred to as *fluents* [11]) to change with the passage of time. By adding time as a parameter to our causal rules, we have complicated both the inference task and the knowledge acquisition task. Complications notwithstanding, the capability to reason about change in an uncertain environment remains an important prerequisite to robust performance in most domains. We simply have to be careful to circumscribe a useful and yet tractable set of operations. In our case, we have allowed the computational complexity of the reasoning tasks and the availability and ease of acquisition of the data to dictate the limitations of our inference mechanism.

Our inference system needs to deal with the imprecision of most temporal information. Even if a robot is able to consult a clock in order to verify the exact time of occurrence of an observed event, most information the robot is given is imprecise (*e.g.*, a client states that a truck will pick up an order at *around* noon, or a delivery is scheduled to arrive *sometime* in the next 20 minutes). One of the most important sources of uncertainty involves predicting how long a condition lasts once it becomes true (*i.e.*, how long an observed or predicted fact is likely to *persist*). In most planning systems (*e.g.*, [14]) there is a single (often implicit) default rule of persistence [6] that corresponds more or less to the intuition that a proposition once made true will remain so until something makes it false. The problem with using this rule is that it is necessary to predict a contravening proposition in order to get rid of a lingering or persistent proposition: a feat that often proves difficult in nontrivial domains. If a commuter leaves his newspaper on a train, it is not hard to predict that the paper is not likely to be there the next time he rides on that train; however, it is quite unlikely that he will be able to predict what caused it to be removed or when the removal occurred.

When McDermott first proposed the notion of persistence as a framework for reasoning about change [12], he noted that persistence might be given a probabilistic interpretation. That is exactly what we do here. We replace the single default rule of persistence used in most planning systems with a set of (probabilistic) rules: one or more for each fluent that the system is aware of. Our robot might use a persistence rule to reason about the likelihood that a truck driver will still be waiting at various times following his arrival at the factory. The information derived from applying such a rule might be used to decide which truck to help next or how to cope when a large number of trucks are waiting simultaneously. Each persistence rule has the form $PERSIST(P, \sigma)$, where P is a fluent and σ is a function of time referred to as a *survivor* function [17]. In our implementation, we consider only two types of survivor functions: exponential decay functions and piecewise linear functions. The former are described in Section 4, and the latter, requiring a slightly more complex analysis, are described in [5]. Exponential decay functions are of the form $e^{-\lambda t}$ where λ is the constant of decay. Persistence rules referring to exponential decay functions are notated simply $PERSIST(P, \lambda)$. Such functions are used, for example, to indicate that the probability of a truck remaining at the dock decreases by 5% every 15 minutes. The persistence rule $PERSIST(P, \lambda)$ encodes a survivor function of the form:

$$p(\langle P, t \rangle) = e^{-\lambda \delta} p(\langle P, t - \delta \rangle))$$

where Δ is a positive number indicating the length of an interval of time. This is equivalent to the two conditional probabilities

$$p(\langle P, t \rangle | \langle P, t - \delta \rangle) = e^{-\lambda \delta}$$
$$p(\langle P, t \rangle | \neg \langle P, t - \delta \rangle) = 0$$

Exponential decay functions are insensitive to changes in the time of occurrence of events that cause such propositions to become true, and, hence, are easy to handle efficiently.

There are a number of issues that every computational approach to reasoning about causality must deal with. One such issue involves reasoning about dependent causes [13] (*e.g.*, the application of two probabilistic causal rules that have the same consequent effects, both of which appear to apply in a given set of circumstances but whose conditions are correlated). Another issue concerns

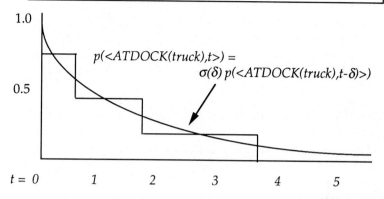

Figure 1: A causal theory illustrating the use of survivor functions

handling other forms of incompleteness and nonmonotonic inference [9] [3] (*e.g.*, the robot might have a general rule for reasoning about the patience (persistence) of truck drivers waiting to be served and a special rule for how they behave right around lunch time or late in the day). While we agree that these problems are important, we do not claim to have any startling new insights into their solution. There is one area, however, in which our theory does offer some new insights, and that concerns the form of probability functions used in causal rules and how they can be used to efficiently predict the causal consequences.

3   Probabilistic Projection

In this section, we will try to provide some intuition concerning the process of reasoning about persistence, which we will refer to as *probabilistic projection*. A planner is assumed to maintain a picture of the world changing over time as a consequence of observed and predicted events. This picture is formed by extrapolating from certain observed events (referred to as *basic facts*) on the basis of rules believed to govern objects and agents in a particular domain. These governing rules are collectively referred to as a *causal theory*.

Figure 1 depicts a simple causal theory. Predicates (*ATDOCK, CLOSE*) and constants (*TRUCK14, FACTORY1*) are in upper case, while functions (p, σ) and variables (t, *truck*) are in lower case. We refer to an instance of a (fact)

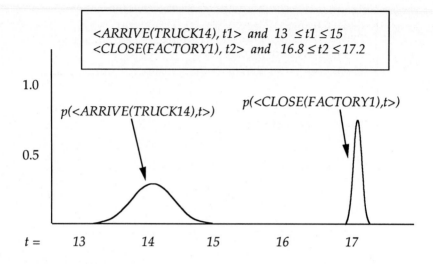

Figure 2: A set of basic facts and their probabilistic interpretation

type being true over some interval of time as a *time token*, or simply *token*. For example, *ARRIVE(TRUCK14)* denotes a general type of event whereas $\langle ARRIVE(TRUCK14), t \rangle$ denotes a particular instance of the event type becoming true. The predicate *ALWAYS* is timelessly true (*i.e.*, $\forall t \langle ALWAYS, t \rangle$).

Figure 2 shows a set of basic facts corresponding to two events assumed in our example to occur with probability 1.0 within the indicated intervals. The system assumes that there is a distribution describing the probability of each event occurring at various times, and uses some default distribution if no distribution is provided.

Evidence concerned with the occurrence of events and the persistence of propositions is combined to obtain a probability function π for a proposition Q being true at various times in the future by convolving the density function f for an appropriate triggering event with the survivor function σ associated with Q:

$$p(\langle Q, t \rangle) = \int_{-\infty}^{t} f(z)\sigma(t - z)dz \qquad (1)$$

Figure 3 illustrates a simple instance of this kind of inference. Note that the range of the resulting probability function is restricted; after the point in time labeled 17, the persistence of *ATDOCK(TRUCK14)* is said to be *clipped*, and thereafter its probability is represented by another function described below.

All probability computations are performed incrementally in our system. Each token has associated with it a vector which is referred to as its *expectation vector* that records the expected probability that the proposition corresponding to the token's type will be true at various times in the future.

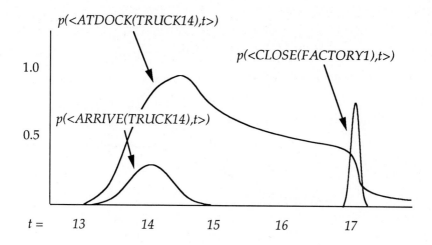

Figure 3: An example of simple probabilistic inference about persistence

The system updates the expectation vectors every time new propositions are added to the database, and also at regular intervals as time passes. In the update, a single pass sweep forward in time is made through the database. There is, according to the domain and granularity of data, a fixed *time step*, or a quantum by which we partition time. Starting at the "present time," we compute for each proposition its expected probability for the time step according to the causal theory governing that type of proposition, and record it in the expectation vector. We compute the probability for all propositions, before moving on to the next time step. The process is repeated for some finite number of time steps.

For event causation, the update is straightforward; in the simplest cases, it is just a table lookup and copying of the density function into the vector. For the convolution, it is necessary to take steps to avoid computing the convolution integral afresh at each time step. We compute the convolution as a Riemann sum, successively summing over the time axis with a mesh of fixed size (the time step). By using the exponential decay form of survivor functions, it is possible to compute the convolution at a time step by looking only at the value for the last time step, independent of the time at which the proposition of interest became true. All that is required is to multiply the last value by the constant decay rate, and add it to any contribution from the causal distribution for that time step. The process is illustrated graphically in figure 4.

There are many details concerned with indexing and applying projection rules that will not be mentioned in this paper (see, for example, [6]). The details of probabilistic projection using exponential decay functions are described in

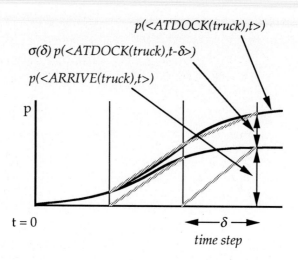

p(<ATDOCK(truck),t>)

σ(δ) p(<ATDOCK(truck),t-δ>)

p(<ARRIVE(truck),t>)

p

t = 0

←——δ——→

time step

Figure 4: Computing the convolution integral incrementally

Section 4. Our update algorithm is polynomial in the product of the number of causal rules, the size of the set of basic facts, and the size of the mesh used in approximating the integrals. For many practical situations, performance is closer to linear in the size of the set of basic facts.

The convolution equation can be easily extended to handle the case of clipping. We add to (1) a term, the function g, corresponding to the distribution of an event which clips the state of a fact being true.

$$p(\langle Q,t \rangle) = \int_{-\infty}^{t} f(z)\sigma(t-z)[1 - \int_{z}^{t} g(w)dw]dz \qquad (2)$$

The cumulative distribution of g defines the degree to which it becomes unlikely that the fact represented by π remains true in the world. We see that under certain conditions, (2) describes exactly what we desire. Unfortunately, there will be a tendency for the decay function and g to count the same effects twice. In [4] we address methods by which this problem can be attacked in a different framework.

4 The Algorithm

Probabilistic causal theories are composed of two types of rules, projection rules:

$$PROJECT(P_1 \wedge P_2 \ldots \wedge P_n, E, R, \pi)$$

and persistence rules:

$$PERSIST(Q, \lambda)$$

where P_1 through P_n, R, and Q are all fact types, and E is an event type. We assume independence of fact types so that, if we are interested in the conjunction $P_1 \wedge P_2 \ldots \wedge P_n$, we can assume that

$$p(\langle P_1 \wedge P_2 \ldots \wedge P_n, t \rangle) = \prod_{i=1}^{n} p(\langle P_i, t \rangle) \qquad (3)$$

We define a relation $\prec_C$ on fact types so that $Q \prec_C R$ just in case there exists a rule of the form $PROJECT(P_1 \wedge P_2 \ldots \wedge P_n, E, R, \pi)$ where $P_i = Q$ for some i. For any given set of causal rules, the graph $\mathcal{G}_{\prec_C}$ whose vertices correspond to fact types and whose arcs are defined by $\prec_C$ is likely to have cycles; this will be the cause of a small complication that we will have to resolve later. In this paper, we distinguish between fact types corresponding to propositions that hold over intervals and event types corresponding to instantaneous (point) events. For each occurrence (token) of a point event of type E, we will need its density function $p(\langle E, t \rangle)$. Probabilistic projection takes as input a set of initial events and their corresponding density functions. Given the restricted format for projection rules, the only additional point events are generated by the system in response to the creation of new instances of fact types. For each token of fact type P, we identify a point event of type E_P corresponding to the particular instance of that fact becoming true. In the process of probabilistic projection, we will want to compute the corresponding density function $p(\langle E_P, t \rangle)$. In addition to computing density functions, we will also want to compute the mass functions $p(\langle P, t \rangle)$ for instances of facts.

In order to describe the process of probabilistic projection, we will divide the process into two different stages: *deterministic causal projection* and *probabilistic causal refinement*. The actual algorithms are more integrated to take advantage of various pruning techniques, but this simpler, staged, process is somewhat easier to understand. Deterministic causal projection starts with a set of tokens and a set of projection rules and generates a set of new tokens T by scanning forward in time and applying the rules without regard for the indicated probabilities. This stage can be carried out using any number of simple polynomial algorithms (see [6] [10]) and will not be further detailed here. Probabilistic causal refinement is concerned with computing density and mass functions for tokens generated by deterministic causal projection. In the following, all density and mass functions are approximated by step (*i.e.*, piecewise constant) functions. We represent these functions of time using vectors (*e.g.*, $mass(T)$ denotes the mass function for the token T and $mass_i(T)$ denotes the value of the function at $t = i$). For each fact token T_P, we create a corresponding event token T_{E_P} and define a vector $mass(T_P)$. For each event token T_E, we define a vector $density(T_E)$. We define an upper bound Ω on projection and assume that each mass and density vector is of length Ω. Initially, we assume that

$$\forall T \in \mathsf{T} : 1 \leq i \leq \Omega : density_i(T) = 0 \wedge mass_i(T) = 0$$

Event tokens are supplied by the user in the form

$$\rho = \int_{est}^{lst} p(\langle E, t \rangle) dt$$

where est and lst correspond (respectively) to the earliest and latest start time for the token and ρ is the probability that the event will occur at all. We assume that the density function for such an event is defined by a Gaussian distribution over the interval from est to lst. For a token T_E corresponding to a user-supplied initial event, it is straightforward to fill in $density(T_E)$. Probabilistic causal refinement is concerned with computing $mass_i(T_P)$ and $density_i(T_{E_P})$ for all fact tokens T_P and all event tokens T_{E_P}. We partition the set of tokens T into fact tokens $\mathsf{T_F}$ and event tokens $\mathsf{T_E}$. Probabilistic causal refinement can be defined as follows:

Procedure: refine(T)
  for $i = 1$ to Ω:
      for $T \in \mathsf{T}_E$: density-update(T, i);
      for $T \in \mathsf{T}_F$: mass-update(T, i);

Of course, all of the real work is done by density-update and mass-update. Each token has associated with it a specific *derivation* that is used in computing its mass or density. For a token T_{E_R}, this derivation corresponds to a rule of the form

$$PROJECT(P_1 \wedge P_2 \ldots \wedge P_n, E, R, \pi)$$

and a set of antecedent tokens $\{T_E, T_{P_1}, T_{P_2} \ldots T_{P_n}\}$ used to instantiate the rule and generate the consequent token T_R. Given that

$$p(\langle E_R, t \rangle) = \pi * p(\langle E, t \rangle) * p(\langle P_1 \wedge P_2 \ldots \wedge P_n, t \rangle)$$

and, assuming independence (3), we have

Procedure: density-update(T_{E_R}, i)
  $density_i(T_{E_R}) \leftarrow \pi * density_i(T_E) * \prod_{j=1}^{n} mass_i(T_{P_j})$

There is one problem with this formulation: it relies on all the mass and density functions for the antecedent conditions being already computed for the instant i. In the present algorithm, refine takes no care in ordering the tokens in T. There are a number of ways of ensuring that the updates are performed in the correct order. The easiest is to partially order T according to $\prec_C$ and insist that $\mathcal{G}_{\prec_C}$ be acyclic, but this would preclude the use of most interesting causal theories. A more realistic method is to partition T with respect to an instant i into those tokens that are *open* and those that are *closed*. Deterministic causal projection defines an earliest start time (est) for each token; for event tokens a latest start time (lst) is specified. An event token is open throughout the interval est to lst and closed otherwise. For fact tokens, we modify probabilistic causal refinement so that it closes a fact token T_P as soon as $mass_i(T_P)$ drops below a fixed threshold. A fact token is open from its est until it is closed. All we require then is that for any i the set of tokens that are open define an acyclic causal dependency graph using $\prec_C$. This restriction still allows for a wide range of causal theories. To get refine to do the right thing, we would have to apply refine only to open tokens and either sort the tokens using $\prec_C$, or (as is actually done) define refine so that if, in the course of updating a consequent token, refine finds an antecedent token that hasn't yet been updated, it applies itself recursively.

The derivation of a token T_P corresponds to a persistence rule of the form $PERSIST(P, \lambda)$ where λ is the constant of decay for the fact type P, and an event token T_{E_P}. The procedure mass-update is a bit more difficult to define than density-update since it depends upon the type of decay functions used in persistence rules. In the case of exponential decay functions, the operation of density-update is reasonably straightforward.

Recall the basic combination rule for probabilistic projection:

$$p(\langle Q, t \rangle) = \int_{-\infty}^{t} f(x)\sigma(t - x)dx$$

and suppose that σ is of the form $e^{-\lambda z}$ where λ is some constant of decay, and that f can be approximated by a step function as in

$$f(x) = \begin{cases} C_1 & t_0 \leq x < t_1 \\ \ldots \\ C_n & t_{n-1} \leq x < t_n \end{cases}$$

We will take advantage of the fact that

$$\int_{t_j}^{t_k} f(x)dx = \sum_{i=j}^{k-1} \int_{t_i}^{t_{i+1}} f(x)dx$$

and

$$\sigma(t_{k+1} - x) = e^{-\lambda\delta}\sigma(t_k - x)$$

where $\delta = t_{k+1} - t_k$.

Making appropriate substitutions, we have

$$
\begin{aligned}
p(\langle Q, t_{k+1}\rangle) &= \sum_{i=j}^{k} \int_{t_i}^{t_{i+1}} f(x)\sigma(t_{k+1} - x)dx \\
&= \sum_{i=j}^{k-1} \int_{t_i}^{t_{i+1}} f(x)\sigma(t_{k+1} - x)dx + \int_{t_k}^{t_{k+1}} f(x)\sigma(t_{k+1} - x)dx \\
&= e^{-\lambda\delta} \sum_{i=j}^{k-1} \int_{t_i}^{t_{i+1}} f(x)\sigma(t_k - x)dx + \int_{t_k}^{t_{k+1}} f(x)\sigma(t_{k+1} - x)dx \\
&= e^{-\lambda\delta} p(\langle Q, t_k\rangle) + \int_{t_k}^{t_{k+1}} f(x)\sigma(t_{k+1} - x)dx
\end{aligned}
$$

It should be clear that updates depending upon such simple survivor functions can be performed quite quickly. Integration is approximated using Riemann sums with a mesh of fixed size (roughly) corresponding to δ. We define the procedure mass-update as follows:

Procedure: mass-update(T_P, i)
  $mass_i(T_P) \leftarrow e^{\lambda_P \delta} mass_{i-1}(T_P) + density_i(T_{E_P})$

The actual algorithms are complicated somewhat by the fact that the choice of mesh size may not coincide precisely with the steps in the step functions approximating survivor functions and distributions. We compensate for this by using a somewhat finer mesh in the update algorithms. The fact that we employ a fixed mesh size still causes small errors in the accuracy of the resulting mass and density functions, but these errors can be controlled. We have tried to make a reasonable tradeoff, taking into account that the finer the mesh the larger the mass and density vectors. Given that the step functions used for encoding survivor functions and distributions are only approximations, there is a point past which employing a finer mesh affords no additional information. We have found that a mesh size of half the smallest step in any step function works quite well in practice.

5 Acquiring Rules

Statistical methods have not seen particularly wide application in AI. This is largely due to problems concerning the availability of the data necessary to employ such methods. Data provided from experts has been labeled as unreliable, and the use of priors in Bayesian inference has been much maligned. An alternative to expert judgements and estimating priors, is to integrate the data acquisition process into your system: have it gather its own data. In such a scheme, all predictions made by the system are conditioned only upon what the system has directly observed. Of course, this is unrealistic in many cases (*e.g.*, diagnostic systems whose decisions could impact on the health or safety of humans). In the industrial automation applications considered in this paper, however, not only is it practical, but it appears to be crucial if we are to build systems capable of adapting to new situations.

In this section, we describe a method for continually refining a database of probabilistic causal rules in the course of routine planning and execution. Given the focus of this paper, we will concern ourselves exclusively with the acquisition (or refinement) of persistence rules. Our warehouse planner keeps track of how long trucks stay around and uses this information to construct survivor functions for various classes of trucks. The system must be told which quantities it is to track and how to distinguish different classes of trucks, but given that, the rules it acquires are demonstrably useful and statistically valid.

The survivor function for a given class of trucks is computed from a set of data points corresponding to instances of trucks observed arriving and then observed leaving without being loaded. It should be clear that, in general, a collection of data points will not define a survivor function uniquely. There are many ways in which to derive a reasonable approximation for such a function. For example, we might employ some form of curve fitting based on an expected type of function and the sample data. While such methods may yield more accurate approximations in some cases, for our application, there are simpler and more efficient methods. With both of the simple classes of functions we have considered, the exponential decay and the linear decay functions, computing, respectively, the persistence parameter (λ) and the slope is trivial. In the case of an exponential decay, we use the mean as the half-life of the function.

We can now sketch the simple algorithm utilized in our system. As noted, we need to collect data for each class of interest. The data for each class is collected in a data structure along with various intermediate quantities used by the update algorithm (*e.g.*, since the algorithm calls for the arithmetic mean of the data points it is convenient to incrementally compute the sum of the elements of the collection). The *class* data type has the following accessor functions associated with it (c is an instance of *class*):

type(c): the type of survivor function: linear or exponential
lambda(c): the rate or slope
insts(c): the number of data points in the collection
sum(c): the sum of the items in the collection

Assuming that c is an instance of *class* and p is a new data point, the acquisition algorithm can be described as follows:

```
Procedure: acquire(c, p)
   insts(c)  ←  insts(c) + 1;
   sum(c)  ←  sum(c) + p;
   lambda(c)  ←  rate(c, sum(c)/insts(c));
```

The function rate depends on the type of survivor function used:

```
Function: rate(c, μ)
   if μ = 0
      then +∞
      else if type(c) = linear
            then 0.5 / μ
            else if type(c) = exponential
                  then (ln 2) / μ
```

Although we have tested our approach extensively in simulations and have found the acquired persistence data to converge very rapidly to the correct values, we do not claim that the above methods have any wider application. The simplicity of the algorithm and its incremental nature are attractive, but the most compelling reason for using it is that the algorithm works well in practice. Probabilistic projection does not rely upon a particular method for coming up with persistence rules. As an alternative, the data might be integrated off line, using more complex (and possibly more accurate) methods.

It should be noted that our system is given the general form of the rules it is to refine. It cannot, on the basis of observing a large set of trucks, infer that trucks from one company are more impatient than those from another company, and then proceed to create two new persistence rules where before there was only one. The general problem of generating causal rules from experience is very difficult. We are currently exploring methods for distinguishing different classes of trucks based on statistical clustering techniques ([8] [15]). Using such methods, it appears to be relatively straightforward to determine that a given data set corresponds to more than one class, and even to suggest candidate survivor functions for the different classes. However, figuring out how to distinguish between the classes in order to apply the different survivor functions is considerably harder.

6   Conclusions

In this paper, we have sketched a theory of reasoning about change that extends previous theories [12] [16]. In particular, we have shown how *persistence* can be modeled in probabilistic terms. Probabilistic projection is a special case of reasoning about continuously changing quantities involving partial orders and other sorts of incomplete information, and as such it represents an intractable problem. We have tried to identify a tractable core in the inferences performed by probabilistic projection.

In [5], we describe a planning system capable of continually refining its causal rules. The system makes predictions, observes whether or not those predictions come to pass, and modifies its rules accordingly. It is capable of routine data acquisition and updates its probabilititistic rules in the course of everyday operation. Initial experiments with the prototype system have been very encouraging. We believe that the inferential and causal rule refinement capabilities designed into our system are essential for robots to perform robustly in routine manufacturing situations. We hope that our current investigations will yield a new view of strategic planning and decision making under uncertainty based on the idea of continuous probabilistic projection.

References

[1] Thomas Dean. Large-scale temporal data bases for planning in complex domains. In *Proceedings IJCAI 10*. IJCAI, 1987.

[2] Thomas Dean. An approach to reasoning about the effects of actions for automated planning systems. *Annals of Operations Research*, 12:147–167, 1988.

[3] Thomas Dean and Mark Boddy. Incremental causal reasoning. In *Proceedings AAAI-87*, pages 196–201. AAAI, 1987.

[4] Thomas Dean and Keiji Kanazawa. A model for reasoning about persistence and causation. *Computational Intelligence*, 5, 1989.

[5] Thomas Dean and Keiji Kanazawa. Persistence and probabilistic inference. *IEEE Transactions on Systems, Man, and Cybernetics*, 19(3):574–585, 1989.

[6] Thomas Dean and Drew V. McDermott. Temporal data base management. *Artificial Intelligence*, 32(1):1–55, 1987.

[7] R.O. Duda, P.E. Hart, and N.J. Nilsson. Subjective bayesian methods for rule-based inference systems. In B.W. Webber and N.J. Nilsson, editors, *Readings in Artificial Intelligence*. Tioga, Palo Alto, California, 1981.

[8] Olive Jean Dunn and Virginia A. Clark. *Applied Statistics: Analysis of Variance and Regression*. John Wiley and Sons, New York, 1974.

[9] M.L. Ginsberg. Does probability have a place in non-monotonic reasoning? In *Proceedings IJCAI 9*. IJCAI, 1985.

[10] Steve Hanks and Drew V. McDermott. Default reasoning, nonmonotonic logics, and the frame problem. In *Proceedings AAAI-86*, pages 328–333. AAAI, 1986.

[11] John McCarthy and Patrick J. Hayes. Some philosophical problems from the standpoint of artificial intelligence. *Machine Intelligence*, 4:463–502, 1969.

[12] Drew V. McDermott. A temporal logic for reasoning about processes and plans. *Cognitive Science*, 6:101–155, 1982.

[13] Judea Pearl. A constraint propagation approach to probabilistic reasoning. In John F. Lemmer and Laveen F. Kanal, editors, *Uncertainty in Artificial Intelligence 2*. North-Holland, 1988.

[14] Earl Sacerdoti. *A Structure for Plans and Behavior*. American Elsevier, New York, 1977.

[15] S. S. Shapiro and M. B. Wilk. An analysis of variance test for normality. *Biometrika*, 52:591–612, 1965.

[16] Yoav Shoham and Thomas Dean. Temporal notation and causal terminology. In *Proceedings Seventh Annual Conference of the Cognitive Science Society*. Cognitive Science Society, 1985.

[17] Ryszard Syski. *Random Processes*. Marcel Dekker, New York, 1979.

Uncertainty in Artificial Intelligence 4
R.D. Shachter, T.S. Levitt, L.N. Kanal, J.F. Lemmer (Editors)
© Elsevier Science Publishers B.V. (North-Holland), 1990   43

Generating Decision Structures and Causal Explanations For Decision Making

Spencer Star

Département d'informatique, Université Laval
Cité Universitaire, Québec, Canada G1K 7P4

ABSTRACT--This paper examines two related problems that are central to developing an autonomous decision-making agent, such as a robot. Both problems require generating structured representations from a database of unstructured declarative knowledge that includes many facts and rules that are irrelevant in the problem context. The first problem is how to generate a well-structured decision problem from such a database. The second problem is how to generate, from the same database, a well-structured explanation of why some possible world occurred.

In this paper it is shown that the problem of generating the appropriate decision structure or explanation is intractable without introducing further constraints on the knowledge in the database. The paper proposes that the problem search space can be constrained by adding knowledge to the database about causal relations between events. In order to determine the causal knowledge that would be most useful, causal theories for deterministic and indeterministic universes are proposed. A program that uses some of these causal constraints has been used to generate explanations about faulty plans. The program shows the expected increase in efficiency as the causal constraints are introduced.

1. INTRODUCTION

Decision analysis starts with a description of a problem, translates that description into a structural representation, and then uses algorithms to evaluate the structure in order to find the problem's optimal solution. The algorithms are tedious but are well-enough understood so that they can be written as a program that will do the evaluation automatically. [Shacter 1986; Pearl 1986; Lauritzen and Spiegelhalter 1987; Henrion 1986]   The key missing element of the decision analysis technology is a set of rules and procedures that specify how to translate a problem description into a structural representation [Breese 1987].   Currently, the task of creating a structural representation from a declarative description that contains many facts and rules that are irrelevant in the problem context can be described as the art of decision analysis.

The problem of generating a structural representation for a decision maker can be shown to be closely related to the problem of generating an explanation of about why some possible world occurred. These two related problems should be central concerns for anyone wanting to developing an autonomous decision-making agent, such as a robot. Both problems require generating structured representations from a database of unstructured declarative knowledge that includes many facts and rules that are irrelevant in the problem context. When the structured representation is used to find the decision acts that will maximize a decision-making agent's utility, I call it a decision structure. When the agent generates a similar structure to explain ex post why a particular set of outcomes occurred I call the structure an explanation. In this paper it is shown that at one point in time the number of possible outcomes that could be represented in a decision structure is exponentially complex in the number of events represented in the agent's database. Furthermore, when searching for the correct transition rules from one state to another over time, the number of possible rules is exponentially complex in the number of outcomes at each moment. The results show the problem to be intractable without introducing further constraints on the knowledge in the database. The paper then examines the related problem of inferring the best explanation of the causal factors that have led to the current state of the world. Inference from a known outcome to the best explanation is called abduction. The problem of abduction is shown to be of the same complexity as that of generating the appropriate decision structure. The paper proposes that the problem search space can be constrained by adding knowledge to the database about causal relations between events. In order to determine the causal knowledge that would be most useful, causal theories for deterministic and indeterministic universes are proposed. A program that uses some of these causal constraints has been used to generate explanations about faulty plans. The program shows the expected increase in efficiency as the causal constraints are introduced.

2. LEARNING A DECISION STRUCTURE

In this section I will first set out the elements of a well-structured dynamic decision problem for an autonomous decision-making agent such as a robot. By examining the difference between the structured representation of the decision problem and the unstructured database of knowledge in declarative form, we will determine what parts of the decision problem have to be learned by the agent.

The decision problem will then be recast in a possible-worlds framework and the complexity of the learning task will be described in terms of the size of the search space among the possible worlds. It will be shown that we must introduce a bias in terms of prior knowledge that constrains the search space. It is proposed that the constraints provided by encoding causal relations in the knowledge base will introduce sufficient bias to make the problem tractable.

A structured representation of the decision problem. A dynamic decision problem can be described in terms of a decision maker's search for an optimal plan. A *plan* consists of a goal, a sequence of decisions taken to achieve that goal, and the outcomes associated with those decisions. There are probabilities and utilities associated with each outcome, and the decision maker chooses decision acts that will maximize his expected utility. I will call a well-structured representation of this problem a *decision structure*. The decision problem of finding an optimal plan can be described as a dynamic maximization problem that has the following decision structure:

$$\text{Max } \Sigma_t \text{ EU}(D(t),X(t)) \text{ s.t. } X(t+1) = R(D(t), X(t))$$

where the variables and relevant features of the decision problem are defined as follows:

(i) D(t): Decision space at time t. The finite space of potential acts. A decision maker can select a specific act $\{d(t)_i\}$ from the set of k possible decision acts $D(t) = \{d(t)_1, d(t)_2,..., d(t)_k\}$.

(ii) X(t): State space at time t. The finite space of feasible outcomes of the world: $X(t) = \{x(t)_1, x(t)_2,..., x(t)_l\}$.

(iii) U(t): Utility evaluation in the state space X(t). For every decision $d(t)_i$ the decision maker assigns utility $U(d(t)_i, X(t))$ to each possible outcome in the state space at time t.

(iv) P(X(t)/d(t)$_i$): Probability assessment on X(t) conditional on decision d(t)$_i$ For every decision $d(t)_i$ the decision maker directly or indirectly assigns a joint probability measure $P(X(t)/d(t)_i)$ to each possible outcome in the state space at time t.

(v) R(D(t), X(t)): Transition rules. A set of rules that map each element of X(t) and D(t) into an element of X(t+1).

(vi) EU(t): Expected utility at time t. For each decision and all outcomes at time t the associated utilities are multiplied by the corresponding conditional probabilities. The sum over possible decisions and outcome at time t is expected utility at time t: $EU(t) = \Sigma_i U(d(t)_i, X(t)) P(X(t)/d(t)_i)$

Generating the Appropriate Decision Structure. Now that we know what the elements of a decision structure are, let us see how an intelligent agent can go about generating such a structure. The basic approach that will be used is *generate and test.* The agent uses its knowledge base and machine time to generate a set of possible decision structures and then tests these structures to find the best one given its limited resources. We will provide the decision-making agent with the following *limited resource inputs*: K, an initial database of knowledge and beliefs; M, a computing machine; and O, observations of the outside world.

The agent uses these inputs to learn things, by reasoning and observing, that enable it to generate and identify the appropriate decision structure. Learning will be defined simply as any change to the knowledge base that permits an agent to achieve greater total utility, over some time interval, than could be obtained without learning. If a particular decision is to be made only one time, a learning program should be able to make some generalization from the problem structure that would be useful (utility increasing) when considering analogous decision problems.

For expository purposes, I will describe the kinds of things that are to be learned in terms of an influence diagram that graphically represents the decision structure. An agent can learn three classes of concepts:

Learn the nodes. Nodes, which I will also call *events*, consist of decision acts (the decision to act and the act itself) and outcomes. It is assumed that the agent's knowledge base can describe a large finite number of nodes or events, only a small subset of which will be relevant to a particular problem. The determination of the appropriate context and the relevant decisions and outcomes requires searching through the space of all possible events. In order to make this problem tractable, knowledge must be introduced that indicates those events that are most likely to be relevant in the particular context. In terms of an influence diagram, let there be a set of pre-determined nodes that can be used. Choosing the appropriate subset is learning the nodes.

Learn the arcs. Define this to mean learning the topology of the minimal number of arcs that must be drawn in an influence diagram together with the transition rules. The main role of arcs in Bayes nets and influence diagrams is to indicate by their presence and absence specific independencies and conditional independencies among the nodes. Arcs in influence diagrams correspond somewhat loosely to the transition rules of the decision structure. The standard transition rule used in influence diagrams is Bayes' rule for calculating inverse probabilities. However, transition rules in a formal decision structure contain explicit references to time while arcs are ambiguous with respect to time. Arcs into a decision node show that the information flowing along the arc is available before the decision is made. Arcs between outcome nodes, however, do not clearly assume that the prior node is prior in time. They can indicate functional and definitional relationships between nodes at one point in time or they can indicate, sometimes only implicitly, transitions between time periods. This ambiguity can lead to paradoxes such as Newcombe's problem [Nozick 1969; Gardenfors and Sahlin 1988].

It should be emphasized that up to this point we have been concerned only with learning *qualitative* and *symbolic* structures--the topology of a decision structure--which is perhaps the most difficult and least understood aspect of decision analysis.

Learn the numbers. I assume that the particular decision problem to be faced is not known with certainty before it occurs, thus making it impossible to enter into the database all the appropriate probabilities and utilities. However, there will be included in the database certain reference decision problems with associated values for probabilities and utilities. One way to learn the numbers is for the agent to use analogical reasoning, comparing the symbolic structure of the problem at hand, called the target problem, with the symbolic structure of the reference problems that it knows about. The agent will then make estimates of the missing values, basing its reasoning on the strength and type of associations that are discovered. The agent may also make use of default rules such as equal probabilities among events in the basic reference class.

Note that the "equal probabilities" assumption is strongly dependent on the symbolic structure that the agent has generated. The determination of the number of homogeneous groups in the basic reference class is part of the problem of learning the nodes. Obviously the probabilities that an agent will assign to equally probable events is an inverse function of the number of possible outcomes that are considered relevant.

A possible-worlds approach. In this section I recast the decision problem in terms of a set of possible worlds to provide the basis for an analysis of problem complexity. It is assumed that sentences in standard first order predicate logic are used to describe decision acts, outcomes, transition rules, and quantitative values. The logic may be augmented if necessary to represent probability theory [Nilsson 1986].

Throughout this paper I will be discussing events and the causal relations among events. Define the union of the set of decision acts and the set of outcomes as the set of *events*. Let there be a fixed set of m possible events that the agent may have to deal with. The event set is sufficient to describe any decision problem that the decision agent will face, but not all of the events are relevant for any particular decision problem. Let $S = \{s_1, s_2, ..., s_m\}$ be the set of sentences describing the m events at time t. The time-period index is suppressed except when necessary to distinguish between different time periods. Define a sentence to be true *with respect to a possible world* only when it evaluates to true using the interpretation associated with that possible world.

Define the set of possible worlds at time t as the power set of S. Each subset of S describes a possible world $w(t)_i$ at time t and every possible combination of events is represented in some possible world. Represent the set of possible worlds at t by the binary-valued matrix $W = [w(t)_{ij}]$, where i represents the rows and j the columns. Let the jth column be the sentence corresponding the jth event, and the ith row be the ith possible world. Those events that are true in the ith possible world will be represented by ones in the appropriate columns in row i.

Generating all possible worlds and identifying the one closest to the agent's actual world is exponentially complex in the number of events. Given m possible events, the number of possible worlds at time t is $n = 2^m$. But this does not consider the dynamic problem of moving from one possible world at t to another at $t + 1$. This is the problem of learning the transition rules, or, loosely speaking, learning the arcs. The problem can be analyzed as follows.

Let $d(t)_i$ be a decision act that the agent might decide to perform. Assume that the decision to act and the performance of the act occur simultaneously. Define a *decision-world* as a possible world which is to some degree like the actual world before t and in which the agent decides to do $d(t)_i$ at t. Let $dw(t)_i^*$ be the decision world which at t is the *nearest world to the real world*. The agent has chosen to do what he believes to be the utility maximizing decision act based on his prediction of the possible worlds (and their probabilities and utilities) that were accessible from the set of decision worlds.

Due to ignorance about the real world and limited computational resources, there will not be only one possible world at $t + 1$, but many. Let the agent have generated the possible-worlds matrix $W(t + 1)$. Define the *transition relation*, $r(dw(t)_i^*, W(t + 1)_i)$, between the closest decision-world at time t and the ith subset of possible worlds $W(t + 1)_i$ that $dw(t)_i^*$ could be transformed into. Represent the possible world closest to the actual world resulting from $dw(t)_i^*$ as $w(t + 1)_i^*$.

If the universe was deterministic and the agent had perfect information and was omniscient, then it would know the transition relation $r(dw(t)_i^*, w(t + 1)_i^*)$. Limited resources and imperfect information force the agent to be satisfied with a generalization of $w(t + 1)_i^*$, represented by some subset of possible worlds. Obviously there is a tradeoff in decision making between using the most general representation of the future (all possible worlds) and using the most specific representation (only one possible world).

Choosing the proper degree of generalization means choosing how many possible outcomes will adequately describe the possible states of the world after making a decision. This is a different problem than learning the nodes. It is concerned with learning a computationally tractable transition relation: in essence, learning the transition rules.

The combinatorics of the agent's problem of learning the transition rules is exponential in the number of possible worlds. For example, suppose there is only one possible world that is accessible from $dw(t)_i^*$. There are m possible transition rules, one for each possible world at $t + 1$. If there are two possible worlds accessible from $dw(t)_i^*$, each different combination of two worlds corresponds to a different transition rule. Since there are n possible worlds, there are 2^n possible transition relations. Recall that n itself was the result of 2^m possible combinations of events. Thus if, for example, our robot operates in a microworld of four potential chance events and one decision event at time t, there are five events and $32 = 2^5$ possible worlds. Suppose that the nearest decision world $dw(t)_i^*$ has been identified. From among the 32 possible worlds in $t + 1$, there are 2^{32} different, not necessarily exclusive, transition rules. With this kind of combinatorial explosion, generate and test is clearly a computationally intractable method.

What is needed is a way of organizing the space of nodes and arcs so that only a small subset of possible worlds and transition relations need be considered. In machine learning, an effective technique for learning concepts has been to organize the search space hierarchically from the most general to the most specific concepts. Define the degree of generalization to be a function of the number of distinct possible worlds that would be included under the generalization. For n possible worlds, there are 2^n transition relations divided into n levels of generality. The result is that each level of generality has on the average 2^{n-1} transition relations, a shallow and wide hierarchy that does not help in dealing with the combinatorial explosion.

The problem of making sense of complexity is closely related to the problems of predicting events and explaining why events occur. One widely accepted view of prediction and explanation sees them as inverse functions: an event predicted with a high probability of occurring can be explained by factors yielding the prediction. An alternative view, which will be presented later, introduces causal relations. If the causal relations leading to a high-probability event are understood as well those leading to a low-probability event, the explanations have similar power. Thus, explanation is more than the identification of regularities that enable one to generalize from a sample population because it involves theoretical reasoning about causal processes that link events. Decision making is at its very foundations a based on the search for causal relations. Decisions set in motion causal processes that determine which of the possible worlds will occur.

A framework for explanation can be built very easily on the possible worlds foundation that we have developed. Consider the possible world, $w(t)_i^*$, which most closely resembles the world we are actually in. To put this in a problem context, suppose the decision agent at t-1 has made an optimal plan that predicted a different world as the most likely outcome at time t. Suppose further that the realized world was considered very unlikely and let realized utility be much lower than expected utility. Is the unexpected outcome due to a flaw in the plan or is it one of those occurrences of relatively rare outcomes that can be expected in a world of imperfect knowledge? More to the point, is there something that the agent should learn from the unexpected outcome that can be used in future decision making? In other words, why did the possible world $w(t)_i^*$ occur?

The answer to a why-question about an event in the possible world $w(t)_i^*$ requires an explanation. Inference to the best explanation has been called *abductive reasoning* to distinguish it from simple inductive generalization. Abductive reasoning can be defined with reference to a decision problem as the search for the most likely decision world $dw(t-1)_i^*$ from among the set of possible worlds *W(t-1)*, given the evidence of $w(t)_i^*$.

Decision analysis will therefore be useful to autonomous agents in contexts that use both forward predictive-based reasoning and backward explanation-based reasoning. When given a problem situation at time t, the agent should understand the causes and enabling conditions at t-1 in order to make decisions that will maximize utility at t+1. The next two sections formulate the elements of a domain independent account of causal structures that will be useful in organizing causal relations in the agent's knowledge base.

3. CAUSAL EXPLANATION IN A DETERMINISTIC UNIVERSE WITH PERFECT INFORMATION

The goal of the next two sections is to develop a theory of causal knowledge that can be used to constrain the search among possible worlds for an appropriate decision structure or explanation. These sections extend the causal analysis in [Star 1988a, 1988b] further. The theoretical structure should be useful for organizing existing causal knowledge as well as providing control knowledge about the most valuable kind of information to add to an incomplete database of causal relations. The causal theories presented here draw on the literature on explanation and causality in the philosophy of science. I have taken an eclectic approach, integrating aspects from several philosophers of science. The analysis in this section of a deterministic universe has been inspired mostly by Hume [1748/1955] and Mackie[1974].

Contiguity, priority, and constant conjunction. In artificial intelligence, there is a strong tradition of basing causal reasoning on a deterministic view of the universe. By deterministic I mean that it is assumed that every event is the result of causally sufficient conditions. This is a view of what the world is like, not a view about the knowledge we can obtain about the world. Even if the fundamental causal structure of the world is deterministic, references to probable cause will be appropriate if we are ignorant of some part of the causal complex--some "hidden factors" that, if understood, would complete the causal story.

I will, however, assume in this section that knowledge is based on perfect information: no noise, a complete causal theory, and no uncertainty. This is only adopted as a temporary convenience to allow us to proceed "as if" information is perfect. All the elements will be put in place to allow for generalizing the framework in the next section so that it can deal with difficult problems involving probable cause and uncertainty.

David Hume, the British empiricist philosopher, has been one of the most influential early writers on causality. He studied causality by considering the most obvious of situations, one billiard ball striking another. He says [1748/1955]:

> Here is a billiard ball lying on the table, and another ball moving toward it with rapidity. They strike; the ball which was formerly at rest now acquires a motion. This is as perfect an instance of the relation of cause and effect as any which we know either by sensation or reflection.

Hume found that three elements occur for all causes. The first element is *contiguity* or closeness in time and place between the cause and effect. It is often stated as "No action at a distance." Second, he found that causes have *priority* in time. No effect can occur before its cause. The third circumstance he called *constant conjunction*: Every object like the cause always produces some object like the effect. Hume concluded, "Beyond these three circumstances of contiguity, priority, and constant conjunction I can discover nothing in this cause."

What Hume meant by this last statement was that the only way we seem to "know" that one billiard ball striking another will cause the second to move is because of past experience that it has always occurred thusly. In order to prove analytically that it will occur again it would be necessary to rely on the continuing regularity over time of the nature of causal events in our universe. But this regularity is only known from observation of past regularity; certainly we cannot assume what we are trying to prove. Thus, Hume concluded, the inference from cause to effect is based on a psychological expectation based on habit or custom rather than on some "real" connection.

Accepting Hume's argument means we must reject the view that the cause of some event can be determined by some objective, logically correct proof. If there is a logical proof linking cause and effect, it only shows that no inconsistency has occurred in the form of the argument. We cannot assign any causal meaning to the terms of the proof unless we are willing to do metareasoning about causality, which will require having a causal theory that relies on heuristic judgments of causal features.

Context, causal scenarios, and the field. Hume's analysis is only a first step. It leaves unanswered numerous problems. For example, suppose we want to explain why John woke up at seven in the morning. What was the cause of this event? Few people would say that the cause of John's waking up is his going to sleep the night before. But if John typically works nights and always wakes up to an alarm, then the event to be explained is why John woke up in the morning rather than the evening and not why his sleep was interrupted at seven o'clock. Clearly, an explanation of an event must be situated in a well-defined context. As van Fraassen

[1980] has emphasized, the same event can be explained different ways if the context is different.

Suppose that a decision agent is faced with a specific decision problem that requires understanding why some undesirable event occurred and taking a decision to ensure that it does not recur. Let us focus on the elements of a causal explanation.

When most people judge that A has caused Z, they rarely mean that A is either necessary or sufficient to cause Z. Usually they mean that A together with a set of other specific conditions will be sufficient to cause Z. Define the conjunction of events sufficient to cause Z as a *causal scenario*. This brings us immediately to the problem of trying to determine which variables belong in a causal scenario. It also requires a distinction to be made within a scenario between causes and conditions.

Those events we call causes and conditions should be seen as differences that stand out against a background that helps define the problem context. Define the *field* to be the background of statements that are assumed to be true in a given context but that are omitted from the causal scenario. The single factor that distinguishes whether an event belongs in the field or in the scenario is whether or not the event should be considered as a possible cause in the given context. If it is not a possible cause but is relevant to the overall context, then it belongs in the field. If it is to be considered as a possible cause, then it belongs in the scenario. The *context* is therefore defined by the triple *{effect, scenario, field}*. Of course, if the context changes, then what was once an element of the field can become part of the scenario.

Let me introduce an example to illustrate these concepts. This example also forms the basis of a program that is mentioned later in the paper. Suppose a firm has a new cereal it plans to introduce in grocery stores. A new-product report is made that estimates the after-tax profits for eight periods after introducing the product. The report creates scenarios with optimistic and pessimistic assumptions about tax rates, discount rates, consumer spending, and store response. The report recommends introducing the cereal. After eight periods an evaluation is made and it is determined that the cereal is a flop. The president wants to know why.

Among the statements that are true and that might have entered into the report for this cereal are statements such as "cereal is usually eaten with cold milk for breakfast", "there are many competing brands", "shelf space is limited", "this cereal was made in a factory in Chicago", and that "tax rates are .4 times pretax profits". But these are statements that could be made about many of the cereals that the company has successfully introduced into the market. When the president is looking for an answer to his why-question, he wants to know why it is that this time the new product failed and other times, when cereals were introduced, they succeeded. Thus the question of failure or success is seen as a difference against a field of elements that do not enter as causal factors. More must be known before we can determine which specific factors belong in the field.

Suppose that the difference-in-a-background is that this time the cereal did not receive enough shelf space so that consumers did not notice it. We can elaborate the story by supposing that in the successful introductions the distributor supplied a special display stand that provided four feet of shelf space while this time only 10 inches was available, the width of one box. We thus see that statements such as "cereal is eaten with cold milk in the morning" or "there are many competing brands" can be set aside as belonging to the field. Given the context they are ruled out as candidates for the role of cause.

Causes and inus conditions. Among those facts that are part of the causal explanation, people usually distinguish between *proximate* or *triggering causes* and *standing conditions*. Suppose that in the cereal example the calculation of the net present value of after-tax profits from the new product depends on two other key conditions: the tax rate and the discount rate. If the tax rate had been higher, the product would not have been profitable even with the optimistic sale projections. If a lower discount rate had been used, even the realized low sales of cereal would have allowed the product to be a success.

The two conditions concerning the appropriate tax and discount rates are of a different nature than the condition requiring adequate shelf space. They should be classified as standing conditions that were true when the product failed. The tax rate is, in these circumstances, a parameter not under the control of the firm. The new-project discount rate is, in the given context, based on a policy that is independent of the particular new product. For example, the firm may require an after-tax rate of return on new projects of at least 20%. The context suggests that this is a standing condition when an executive makes a decision about launching a new product. The only variable factor is adequate shelf space. Thus the distinction between a cause and a condition also depends on the context. Since the agent is in a decision context and is searching for factors under its control that can be used to control the outcome, those events that are part of the causal scenario but not controllable are treated as conditions. In another context, say a scientific experiment, the scientist will try to control the conditions and let the "causal factor" vary. In both contexts, a single factor is nominated as the causal factor. If it does not provide the appropriate explanation, one looks at the conditions to see if in fact they varied. If so, the, *ex post*, a factor previously thought of as a condition should be treated as a cause.

We can go further in our causal analysis, following an approach first set out by Mackie [1974]. Let us continue to use the example of the introduction of a new cereal. Define the following variables: A is insufficient shelf space, B is the firm's discount rate, C is the current tax rate, and Z is the product's failed introduction. We have a scenario ABC that produces an event Z. Let the causal field F represent the statements describing the introduction of the new product and define the scenario S as the conjunction of the three factors ABC conditional on the field: $S = (ABC/F)$.

Define S to be a *minimally sufficient scenario* since the conjunct of the three elements A,B,C will always produce the effect, Z, the failed new product introduction. If a counter-factual situation is considered in which one of the conjuncts did not occur, the new cereal would have been a success. Each of these factors is, therefore, by itself an *insufficient* and *non-redundant* part of an *unnecessary* but *sufficient* scenario for Z. It will be convenient to say, using the first letters of the italicized words, that these factors are *inus* or satisfy the inus condition.

Now the statement that A caused Z means that

- A is at least inus for Z;
- A occurred;
- the other conjuncts B and C occurred; and
- all other minimally sufficient scenarios for Z not having A in them were absent on the occasion in question.

In other words, if A is a cause of Z, A is necessary for Z to occur in the context described by the scenario and the field. We do not require that A be sufficient in the context for Z to occur. Moreover, if we cannot rule out definitively the existence of every other minimally sufficient scenario, the event Z is overdetermined. In the situation of causal overdetermination due to incomplete knowledge any causal attribution must be a judgment of probable cause.

The elements of a causal theory in a deterministic universe with prefect information are now in place. A cause is related to its effect by contiguity, priority, and constant conjunction. The context of an event-to-be-explained is determined by the field and the minimally sufficient causal scenario. Irrelevant events are seen to be of two different types: those that have nothing to do with the problem and those that form part of the field. Events in the field are irrelevant in the sense that the should not be considered as conditions or possible causes. The scenario contains those events that are either standing conditions or triggering causes. The statement A causes Z has been defined in terms of inus conditions and scenarios.

The problem with this approach is that it has no room for limited knowledge, noise, statistical relations, and indeterminism. Nonetheless, it has provided us with a basic idealized model that is useful for understanding and organizing the causal relations in a domain independent way. We now turn to the more difficult problem of causal theory in an uncertain universe.

4. CAUSAL EXPLANATION IN AN UNCERTAIN UNIVERSE

In this section a theory of causal explanation will be presented that can be used in situations that involve indeterminism, partial knowledge, noisy events, and limited computing power. The theory follows closely the philosophical line of thought of Wesley Salmon [1984]. For other theories of causality that involve statistical or probabilistic notions see Reichenbach 1956; Carnap 1950; Greeno 1970; Hempel and Oppenheim 1948; Good 1983; van Fraassen 1980; and Suppes 1984]. Due to space limitations, only certain key points of the total theory will be discussed.

The inverse relationship between prediction and explanation. Perhaps the most widely accepted view of scientific explanation is that of Hempel and Oppenheim [1948]. They require an explanation to have predictive capability. They state, "...an explanation of a particular event is not fully adequate unless its explanans, if taken account of in time, could have served as a basis for predicting the event in question." They view low probability events as lacking this potential predictive force:

> Thus, we may be told that a car turned over on the road "because" one of its tires blew out while the car was traveling at high speed. Clearly, on the basis of just this information, the accident could not have been predicted, for the explanans provides no explicit general laws by means of which the prediction might be effected, nor does it state adequately the antecedent conditions which would be needed for the prediction. (p. 13)

Suppes [1984] also states a similar view, although he is not discussing explanation per se:

> ...there is a whole range of cases in which we do not have much hope of applying in an interesting scientific or commonsense way probabilistic analysis, because the causes will be surprising....Thus, although a Bayesian in such matters of individual events...I confess to being unable to make good probabilistic causal analyses of many kinds of individual events. (pp.64-65)

If we were to accept these views, an autonomous agent would be severely limited in its ability to make causal sense of low probability events. For example, if we draw one card at random from an ordinary 52-card deck, the probability of a spade or a club or a diamond is 3/4. The probability of the ace of spades is 1/52. Is it reasonable to say that the explanation of why we get a non-heart more adequate or better than the explanation of why we get the ace of spades?

The answer has been provided by Salmon [1984]:

> If determinism is false, a given set of circumstances of type C will yield an event of type E in a certain percentage of cases; and under circumstances of precisely the same type, no event of the type E will occur in a certain percentage of cases. If C defines a homogeneous reference class...then circumstances C explain the occurrence of E in those cases in which it occurs, and exactly the same circumstances C explain the nonoccurrence

of E in those cases in which it fails to occur. The pattern is a statistical pattern, and precisely the same circumstances that produce E in some cases produce non-E in others. (p. 120)

Thus although low-probability events may be difficult to predict specifically, their occurrence a small percentage of the time is highly predictable. Thus the power of explanations is independent of the ability to predict individual events. This has important implications for an autonomous decision-making agent.

To illustrate the relevance for decision making, suppose that an autonomous agent is responsible for monitoring instruments on a Mars Rover vehicle (a wheeled vehicle for exploring the surface of Mars) and for making decisions when the vehicle encounters problems. Let us assume that while rolling around on martian soil, about once every 10,000 milliseconds its wheels will slip and spin freely for about 200 milliseconds, which will show up on an instrument in terms of a high rate of spin. Although the actual time index of the two milliseconds of slip cannot be predicted, the average number of milliseconds of slip per minute of rolling is a low probability event that is highly predictable. Statisticians would speak of this in terms of sufficient statistics. The specific time sequence of spin rates cannot be predicted but the average value is a sufficient statistic to describe the state of the machine. The agent need not look further than the sufficient statistic in building its explanation. Both the high-probability event of rolling without slippage and the low-probability event of a two-millisecond spin are considered normal and are "explained" equally well.

Statistical relevance relation. Recall that Hume searched unsuccessfully for the a true causal relationship, but only found contiguity, priority, and constant conjunction. The relation of constant conjunction was illustrated by one billiard ball hitting another and always causing the second to move. There was no uncertainty in the situation. Except for artificially simple problems and mathematical problems, there is almost always some degree of uncertainty involved in a complex cause-effect relation. For an autonomous agent, it should be assumed that the cause-effect relationship is not known with certainty. It is likely that the agent will have to deal with uncertain evidence in the form of a statistical relevance (S-R) relation, which is defined as follows:

An event C is statistically relevant to the occurrence of event B in the context A if and only if

(1) $P(B/AC)$ is not equal to $P(B/A)$; or (2) $P(B/AC)$ is not equal to $P(B/A,not\text{-}C)$.

For a context A in which C occurs with a nonvanishing probability conditions (1) and (2) are equivalent.

The S-R relation makes explicit the need to refer to at least two probabilities for judging the relevance of two events: a prior probability and at least one or more posterior probabilities. But the S-R relation forms only a statistical basis for an explanation. It must be supplemented with causal factors in order to further constrain the space of possible explanations.

Causal processes. Suppose we have two events that are separated in space and time. Label event A the cause and event Z the effect. Let A be prior in time and statistically relevant to Z. Hume cited contiguity as a factor linking causal events. Yet in this case contiguity is missing. We need a *causal connection* to link together the two events in a causal relation. Salmon calls this link a *causal process.* He states:

In some cases, such as the starting of the car, there are many intermediate events, but in such cases, the successive intermediate events are connected to one another by spatiotemporally continuous causal processes. [Salmon 1984, p. 156]

The reader is referred to Salmon for further details on causal processes.

A common cause and conjunctive forks. In influence diagrams and Bayes networks a distinction is made between causal factors and evidentiary factors through their spatial orientation [Shacter and Heckerman 1987; Pearl 1986, 1987]. It is also standard practice, when two factors X and Y are caused by a single factor C, to describe X and Y as being conditionally independent given the factor C. It is said that C *screens off* X from Y. We also say that C is the *common cause* of X and Y.

Hans Reichenbach [1956, sec. 19] recognized that a natural principle of causal reasoning is to expect events that are simultaneous, spatially separate, and strongly correlated, to have a common cause, prior in time, that generates the correlation. Reichenbach introduced the notion of a *conjunctive fork* in order to try to characterize the structure of relations involving common cause. It is defined in terms of the following four necessary conditions:

(1) $P(XY/C) = P(X/C)P(Y/C)$ (2) $P(XY/\text{not-C}) = P(X/\text{not-C})P(Y/\text{not-C})$

(3) $P(X/C) > P(X/\text{not-C})$ (4) $P(Y/C) > P(Y/\text{not-C})$.

These conditions also entail

(5) $P(XY) > P(X)P(Y)$ non-independence

(6) $P(X/C) = P(X/YC)$ conditional independence

(7) $P(Y/C) = P(Y/XC)$ conditional independence.

For a discussion see [Salmon 1984, pp. 160-161; Suppes 1984]. From condition (1) we see that given a common cause, X and Y are independent of each other. The same two factors, in the absence of their common cause C (and assuming no other common cause), are independent by virtue of (2). Yet the two factors are more highly correlated than they would be under strict independence; they are thus not independent, as shown in condition (5). Therefore, the occurrence of the event C makes X and Y statistically irrelevant to each other, and the occurrence of not-C has the same effect. Note that it is not claimed that any event C that fulfills relations (1)-(4) is a common cause of X and Y. C must be connected to X and Y by a causal process.

It is possible to describe the conjunctive fork in terms of a common effect E. Simply replace C by E in all the equations. This would correspond to some symptom, say a cough, being caused by two different illnesses, say a cold X or an allergy Y. Reichenbach claimed that there is an important asymmetry in conjunctive forks. He proposed that *it is impossible to have a situation in which two events, X and Y, in the absence of a common cause C, jointly produce a common effect E*. Let us call this Reichenbach's asymmetry conjecture or just *R-asymmetry*. Salmon has made a stronger claim. He proposes [1984, pp. 166-167] that *it is impossible to have a situation in which two events, X and Y, regardless of whether or not they have a common cause C, jointly produce a common effect E*. Refer to this as Salmon's asymmetry conjecture or just *S-asymmetry*.

Equations (1)-(7) plus the conditions of R-asymmetry and S-asymmetry provide important guides to the kind of probabilistic and statistical relations that an intelligent agent should look for in the data when trying to determine causal relations. They also suggest important restrictions on how causal relations can evolve over time and often furnish insights that are not immediately apparent. Space limitations prevent me from providing illustrations here.

5. TESTING THE THEORY

A theory of the structure of causal knowledge has been presented in order to suggest the kinds of relations that should be entered into an autonomous agent's database of knowledge and beliefs. The need for additional constraints comes about because the generation of the appropriate decision structure or explanation from completely unstructured data is an intractable problem. The value of the theory is, in this context, an empirical question. Does the addition of causal relations to a database enhance the performance of a decision-making agent? Which elements of the theory are most valuable, and what can be expected in terms of increased efficiency when they are used?

I have started to test the theories with some very simple programs. Some interesting results have occurred when techniques from machine learning have been used to generate explanations. For example, a program has been developed that generates a plan to introduce a new cereal on the market if prior analysis shows that the introduction will be profitable. A structure corresponding to an influence diagram is generated and the decision is made to introduce the cereal. Several periods after the introduction, additional data are introduced to the database. The data indicate that the cereal is not profitable. The program generates an explanation of why the cereal is not profitable, doing goal regression to find the sufficient preconditions for profitability.

The program generates structures corresponding to two different influence diagrams. The first is a decision structure that terminates in a successful product introduction. The second is an explanation structure that shows the preconditions that led to the unsuccessful product introduction. By comparing the two structures, the program should be able to determine the differences and thus find the cause of the failure. The problem is that at the most detailed level, since we are dealing with numeric data, the values at almost every node are different in the two structures. The solution is to abstract from the values by generalizing until only qualitative or binary values remain. By tracing back and comparing nodes we can arrive at the conclusion that a single different ground proposition is responsible for the different outcomes. In order for this to succeed, the values that correspond to standing conditions in a causal scenario have to be protected. For example, the tax rate and the discount rate are taken as standing conditions that do not change value. If facts are identified as irrelevant, as belonging to the field, or as conditions, the number of unifications needed for the program to arrive at an answer is reduced substantially. Since the example is still quite simple, the program always finds a solution. But the number of operations needed to get to the solution drops continually as more causal knowledge is introduced into the database.

6. CONCLUSIONS AND FUTURE RESEARCH

This paper has attempted to bring together some aspects of the symbolic approaches of artificial intelligence and machine learning with the more quantitative approach of decision analysis. It is a continuation of previous work that I have done towards integrating the two approaches [Star 1987]. The problem of generating the appropriate decision structure and causal explanations relies heavily on the symbolic computing tradition of artificial intelligence. But the use of decision analysis, probabilities, and measurable utility is characteristic of quantitative methods. Perhaps one of the most important conclusions that I would like readers to reach after reading this paper is that symbolic and quantitative approaches are necessary complements to each other--both contribute to the tentative answers I have proposed about how to create a structured representation of a decision problem faced by an autonomous decision-making agent.

The theory of explanation and of the causal structure of the world has only been sketched out quite briefly. It is not meant to provide a definitive answer to the questions that philosophers ask about scientific explanation and causality; rather it draws on the philosophical literature for ideas that can be useful for solving computational problems. Thus the theory needs to be tested extensively by using it in examples and in working programs to find both its weaknesses and its strengths. Our very preliminary results are encouraging, but much additional work needs to be done.

7. ACKNOWLEDGEMENTS

I would like to thank Neeraj Bhatnagar for comments on section 2 and an anonymous referee for comments on the first draft of this paper. All remaining errors are my responsibility.

REFERENCES

Breese, J.S. (1987). *Knowledge representation and inference in intelligent decision systems*. Research report 2. April. Rockwell International Science Center, Palo Alto Laboratory, Palo Alto, CA.

Carnap, Rudolph (1950). *Logical foundations of probability*. Chicago, IL: University of Chicago Press. 2nd ed., 1962.

Gardenfors, Peter and N. Sahlin, eds. (1988). *Decision, probability, and utility*. New York, NY: Cambridge University Press.

Greeno, J.G. (1970). Evaluation of statistical hypotheses using information transmitted. *Philosophy of science* 37: 279-293.

Hempel, C.G. and P.Oppenheim (1948). Studies in the logic of explanation. *Philosophy of science*, vol 15, pp. 567-579, reprinted in J.C. Pitt (1988) *Theories of explanation*. New York, NY: Oxford University Press.

Henrion, M. (1986). Propagating uncertainty by probabilistic logic sampling in bayesian networks. In J. Lemmer, and L.N. Kanal (eds), *Uncertainty in Artificial Intelligence 2*. (Machine Intelligence and Pattern Recognition Series) New York: Elsevier. 1986.

Hume, David (1748/1955). *An inquiry concerning human understanding*. Indianapolis, IN: Bobbs-Merrill.

Lauritzen, S.L. and D.J. Spiegelhalter (1987). *Local computations with probabilities on graphical structures and their application to expert systems*. October. Department of Mathematics and Computer Science, Institute of Electronic Systems, Aalborg University, Aalborg, Denmark.

Mackie, J.L. (1974). *The cement of the universe: A study of causation*. Oxford, England: Clarendon Press.

Nilsson, N.J. (1986). Probabilistic logic. *Artificial intelligence*, 28(1): 71-87.

Nozick, R. (1969). Newcomb's problem and two principles of choice. In *Essays in honor of Carl G. Hempel*, ed. by N. Rescher, Reidel, Dordrecht, Holland, 1969:107-133.

Pearl, J. (1987). Embracing causality in formal reasoning. *Proceeding of the Sixth National Conference on Artificial Intelligence*. Seattle, WA: Morgan Kaufmann: 369-373.

Pearl, J. (1986). Fusion, propagation, and structuring in belief networks. *Artificial intelligence*, vol. 29, no. 3, September: 241-288.

Reichenbach, Hans (1956). *The direction of time*. Berkeley, CA: University of California Press.

Salmon, W.C. (1984). *Scientific explanation and the causal structure of the world*. Princeton, NJ: Princeton University Press.

Shachter, Ross D. (1986). *Evaluating influence diagrams*. Department of Engineering-Economic Systems, Stanford University, Stanford, CA 94305, January.

Shachter, Ross D. and D.E. Heckerman (1987). Thinking backward for knowledge acquisition. *AI magazine* 8(3) Fall: 55-62.

Star, S. (1988a). Learning causal explanations in an uncertain world, *Proceedings of the AAAI Spring Symposium Series: Explanation-Based Learning*, Stanford University, Stanford, CA, March: 185-189.

Star, S. (1988b). *Reasoning about causality in explanation-based learning*. Department of Computer Science, Laval University, Quebec, Canada.

Star, S. (1987). A method for doing theory-based inductive learning. In J. Lemmer, and L.N. Kanal (eds), *Uncertainty in Artificial Intelligence 3*. (Machine Intelligence and Pattern Recognition Series) New York: Elsevier. 1988.

Suppes, P. (1984). *Probabilistic metaphysics*. New York, NY: Basil Blackwell.

van Fraassen, Bas C. (1980). *The scientific image*. New York, NY: Clarendon Press.

Uncertainty in Artificial Intelligence 4
R.D. Shachter, T.S. Levitt, L.N. Kanal, J.F. Lemmer (Editors)
© Elsevier Science Publishers B.V. (North-Holland), 1990

Control of Problem Solving: Principles and Architecture

John S. BREESE and Michael R. FEHLING
Rockwell International Science Center
Palo Alto Laboratory
444 High Street
Palo Alto, CA 94301

This paper presents an approach to the design of autonomous, real-time systems operating in uncertain environments. We address issues of problem solving and reflective
control of reasoning under uncertainty in terms of two fundamental elements: 1) a set of
decision-theoretic models for selecting among alternative problem-solving methods and 2)
a general computational architecture for resource-bounded problem solving. The decision-
theoretic models provide a set of principles for choosing among alternative problem-solving
methods based on their relative costs and benefits, where benefits are characterized in
terms of the value of information provided by the output of a reasoning activity. The output may be an estimate of some uncertain quantity or a recommendation for action. The
computational architecture, called Schemer-II, provides for interleaving of and communication among various problem-solving subsystems. These subsystems provide alternative
approaches to information gathering, belief refinement, solution construction, and solution execution. In particular, the architecture provides a mechanism for interrupting
the subsystems in response to critical events. We provide a decision theoretic account for
scheduling problem-solving elements and for critical-event-driven interruption of activities
in an architecture such as Schemer-II.

1 Introduction

An autonomous system, operating in a complex and constantly changing environment, must
formulate and carry out plans to achieve desired behaviors or objectives. In such an environment the synthesis and use of plans will typically be severely constrained by limitations
on time, information, and other critical resources. We refer to problem solving under these
conditions as resource-bounded problem solving: controlling and adapting actions to meet
contextually-determined constraints.

We partition problem-solving into three fundamental activities:

1. Select a reasoning method for a particular problem.

2. Perform the reasoning activity selected in Step 1.

3. Execute the plan or recommendation generated in Step 2.

In this paper we examine several issues with respect to this general set of activities.
The computational architecture Schemer-II provides the overall framework in which problem
solving proceeds: encapsulation and invocation of alternative reasoning mechanisms, sensing
external events, inter-process communication, initiating external activities, and others. We
also address the problem of selecting among a set of alternative reasoning activities in service
of some object-level problem. This selection problem (Step 1 above) exhibits considerable uncertainty because the performance of alternative reasoning methods on the primary problem
is difficult to estimate *a priori*. The selection problem is essentially an issue of belief management: the presence of significant amounts of uncertainty in a realistic task environment
forces a system to constantly face a fundamental choice between using its current information
to carry out its primary objectives and making efforts via reasoning activities to improve its

state-of-information.[1] The third major thrust of this paper is the idea of *interrupts*. While executing either internal reasoning activities or actions in the world, sensory data may be received which invalidates the ongoing activity. Thus Steps 2 and 3 may not proceed in sequence to completion, but are interrupted as information changes.

Researchers in artificial intelligence have long been interested in the topic of problem-solving control. Some investigators have focused on developing general architectures with features that support explicit reasoning about control of problem-solving actions [3,4,6,8,11]. The primary emphasis has been on mechanisms and representations by which control knowledge might be used. With few exceptions [12], the knowledge itself has been developed heuristically with little emphasis on developing general principles of control. In this work, we will model control in terms of decision making under uncertainty as formalized in decision theory. As indicated above, control involves resource allocation under uncertainty with complex preferences and the need to reason about the cost and quality of information. Representations and tools from decision theory are a promising path for analysis of these problems from a formal basis [13].

This work has been motivated in large part by a desire to incorporate principled control procedures within autonomous real-time systems. In particular, we are extending Schemer-II, a computational architecture that allows embedding various problem-solving elements in an autonomous system designed for operation in complex, dynamic environments [7]. Although Schemer-II's design provides a robust computational framework for applying appropriately chosen techniques for control reasoning, this architecture does not by itself offer any such techniques for making the appropriate choices or defining effective interrupts. In the latter part of the paper we indicate how the analytic techniques and results derived here are being incorporated into the architecture.

2 Decision-Theoretic Selection

Our approach to selecting among alternative methods for reasoning about a particular problem is a computational version of an idea proposed by Matheson [16] and more recently Nickerson [17] and Lindley [15]. The outputs of a problem solving method are viewed as *information* in a decision-theoretic sense; that is, the outputs of a model are used to update the probability distribution about an event or potential action.

We are concerned with two classes of action: *primary* actions and *modeling* actions. Primary actions involve the system's interface to the external world, e.g. moving an item, opening a valve, or initiating communication. Modeling actions operate on the system's knowledge to produce new conclusions or recommendations. We use the term modeling to capture the set of actions regarding structuring, solving, and interpreting a model of a domain. Alternative methods may be based on different assumptions and require different amounts of data and time to run. The solutions may differ in their quality[14], perhaps expressed in terms of different attributes of a solution [12].

The formulation of the selection problem in these terms is illustrated as an influence diagram in Figure 1. Modeling actions, m, are selected from a space of modeling alternatives $\mathcal{M}$. Sequences of primary actions, d, are selected from a space of decision alternatives $\mathcal{D}$. The decisions are represented as square nodes in the figure. The overall utility is a function of the primary decision (d), some uncertain state of the world (x), and the cost of using a particular method (c). The cost can be thought of as reflecting the (possibly uncertain) time, data, and processor requirements to use a particular problem solving methodology, m.

The output of a model is s. It is available at the time the primary decision is made (indicated by the arrow from s to d in Figure 1). The output of a model is uncertain. It also is probabilistically dependent on the state of the world: the information s from using method

---

[1]Cohen [2] has referred to this tradeoff as balancing internal and external action

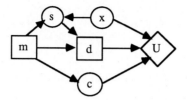

Figure 1: Selection-Problem Influence Diagram

m provides information about the uncertain state of the world. In this sense, a problem-solving methodology acts as a sensor for some unknown quantity. We express this measure of quality of output as the probability distribution, $\Pr(s|x, m, \xi)$, where ξ is the background state of information (or context) where the distribution applies.

The expected utility of the meta-level problem is

$$\mathrm{E}_{x\,s\,c}(U|d, m, \xi) = \int_c \int_s \int_x U(x, d, c) \Pr(x|s, m, \xi) \Pr(s|m, \xi) \Pr(c|m, \xi)$$

where

$$\Pr(x|s, m, \xi) = \frac{\Pr(s|x, m, \xi) \Pr(x|\xi)}{\int_x \Pr(s|x, m, \xi) \Pr(x|\xi)}$$

by application of Bayes' rule. The optimal primary decision, $d^*(m, s)$, is obtained by solving:

$$\max_{d \in \mathcal{D}} \mathrm{E}_{x\,c}(U|d, m, s, \xi)$$

The distribution over the uncertainty has been updated with the model output. The optimal model m^* is obtained by solving:

$$\max_{m \in \mathcal{M}} \mathrm{E}_{x\,s\,c}(U|d^*(m, s), m, \xi)$$

The above formulation can be extended and operationalized in several ways, as discussed below.

Resource Usage and Resource Constraints. In the previous formulation, usage of computational resources is captured in the cost, c, of using a particular method. Resources that are limited or that can be expended variably to modify the quality of a computational result can be expressed by conditioning the output, s, on the amount of resources available. In a multi-processor system, there is a tradeoff between the amount of time available for a task and the number of processors assigned to a computation. For example, the quality of an output may depend on time to the next interrupt, t_i, and the number of processors, n, involving in running method m.:

$$\Pr(s|x, m, t_i, n, \xi)$$

In this case n is a decision variable while t_i is an uncertain quantity. The form of this distribution can be used to capture the "anytime" behavior of methods whose outputs improve monotonically as additional time or processing power is applied (such as Monte Carlo methods), as opposed to those which require some threshold to provide any useful output.

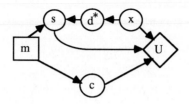

Figure 2: Control Problem Influence Diagram for Decision Recommendations

Decision Recommendations. In the previous formulation, the most natural interpretation for the output of a model is that it provides an assessment or diagnosis of some uncertain state of the world. We can modify the formulation for models and methods that provide decision recommendations. As an example, suppose we have an autonomous vehicle that needs to navigate to some objective. The system may embody several alternative means of determining a path to the destination. It could use its categorical knowledge to construct a plan while not explicitly considering uncertainty or resource usage. It could develop probability and utility models at various levels of detail, to be solved using exact or approximate methods. It could dispense with a "planning" stage altogether and use local-obstacle-avoidance and reactive-planning methods to attempt to arrive at the destination [9]. Any of these methods will produce output of the same general form: a sequence of actions to be taken, possibly conditional on observations and possibly iterated as a policy (e.g. as in a reactive algorithm).

We illustrate this model with Figure 2. Here we are assuming the existence of some "true" optimal course of action d^* dependent on the state of the world. d^* is the recommendation that would be obtained by maximizing the expectation of $U_p(x, d)$, the primary decision problem utility function ignoring the costs of reasoning. In this case d^* is an uncertain variable, reflecting the system's *a priori* uncertainty regarding the optimal action before doing the reasoning. The output of a method provides an estimate of the uncertain optimal decision. The diagram also indicates that the output of the method will be used directly as the primary decision, and the decision model can be solved using Bayes rule and maximization of expected utility in the customary way.

The burden of assessing the probability distribution $Pr(s|d^*, m, \xi)$ can be eased by expressing it in terms of deviations from the optimal value. For example, let $Pr(s = d^*|m, \xi) = p_m$—the probability method m will provide an optimal result is p_m. The dispersion about the optimum can be captured in a number of ways depending on the particular method m being considered.[2] A method is *unbiased* for real valued d^* and s when $E(s|d^*, m, \xi) = d^*$.

Cost of an Error. A key consideration in the choice among alternative problem solving methods is the extent to which a sub-optimal primary decision will reduce utility in the primary decision problem. For each world state x and alternative d we can calculate $\Delta U = U_p(x, d^*) - U_p(x, d)$. These sensitivity measures are indicative of how forgiving a domain is with respect to selection of action. Estimates of this sensitivity can be used as parameters in control strategies across domains and problems, as we would like to perform this type of reasoning without precise specification of $U(x, d, c)$.

We have developed an illustrative example using the control model described above for a specific numerical robot path planning problem [7]. The robot needs to select among a *feasible path method* (**F**), a *basic probabilistic model* (**B**), and a more complex, *information-probabilistic model* (**I**) which considers the possibility of collecting additional information

---

[2]Lindley [15] has used assumptions of normality to obtain analytic solutions in a similar problem.

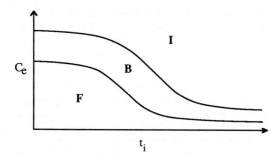

Figure 3: Optimal Reasoning Policies

as part of the primary decision problem. Each method is characterized with respect to its probability of providing an optimal solution under uncertainty. The results of the analysis are presented graphically in Figure 3. Optimal regions depend on t_i, the time to an interrupt, and the cost of an error. When t_i and C_e are low, then the non-probabilistic modeling method, F, is optimal. As these parameters increase, more complete probabilistic reasoning becomes preferred. The type of information summarized in this graph can form the basis for simple control rules, depending on contextual information. Though easy to implement and deliver, they nonetheless are developed based on defensible and clear criteria.

3   The Architecture

Schemer-II is a computational architecture for resource-bounded problem solving.[3] It has been designed to allow for the interleaving of solution-construction, solution-execution, information-gathering, and knowledge-management activities. At a coarse level of description, Schemer-II is an object-based blackboard system. Various problem-solving modules reside in a shared *knowledge space*. The invocation of these modules (or *handlers*) occurs in various ways and is further mediated by the operations of a *top level controller* which schedules various pending activities for execution, manages communication with the external world, and handles interruption and resumption of ongoing activities.

Schemer-II provides some unique and important features to support flexible, reactive control of problem solving. In particular, the architecture supports a wide variety of techniques for flexible, dynamic scheduling, the ability to employ special-purpose problem-solving modules that can modify the system's control state, and, perhaps most importantly, true pre-emptive control providing the problem-solving system the ability to react promptly and re-focus its attention in response to the occurrence of critical events. However, until recently, both scheduling and pre-emptive control were handled with strictly domain-specific techniques. In this section we use the decision-analytic framework described in Section 2 to analyze: 1) choices amongst alternative problem-solving activities and 2) generation and fielding of interrupt conditions for ongoing activities.

---

[3]See Fehling [7] for a detailed discussion of the architecture. Successful Schemer applications have been built for a number of real-time, "process management" applications such as diagnosis or control of complex manufacturing processes [3] and automated performance management of advanced avionics systems [10], among others.

3.1 Scheduling diverse problem-solving elements

The Schemer-II architecture supports encapsulation and interleaved control of multiple, independent problem-solving methods. Schemer-II's handlers, with their object-oriented modularity, meet this requirement by providing a discipline for encapsulating each problem-solving element as a distinct type of object. Each handler can encapsulate a specialized type of problem-solving skill. Handlers provide convenient data structures that support a strong distinction between the information that is strictly local to a problem-solving element and information that is to be shared with other elements.

Handlers in Schemer-II are triggered by changes in data in the system, via communication with external processes or by direct invocation. In any of these cases, a single triggering event may cause several alternative problem-solving methods to be invoked. Furthermore, at any time multiple tasks may be on the system schedule awaiting execution. The scheduling problem is selection among these alternatives based on computational costs, data requirements, and attributes of the solutions offered by each method.

In previous implementations the scheduler has used a simple pre-emptive, priority-based scheduling discipline. In this approach the carriers representing potential tasks have an initial fixed priority prescribed by the system developer as a feature of their associated handler. On each cycle of the top level controller the current priority of each task remaining on the schedule is then "aged" (viz., has its priority value modified) in some simple and application-dependent manner.

The disadvantage with this approach is that it is essentially hardwired prior to execution time—there is no general facility to adjust scheduling decisions in response to changes in environmental characteristics. As a supplement to the priority scheme currently in Schemer, we are implementing conflict-detection and -resolution routines for dynamically assigning and updating task priorities. A conflict is detected if several handlers are triggered for execution simultaneously. Once a conflict is detected, the system will look for specialized control knowledge to make a selection or allocation as exemplified by tradeoffs such as those illustrated in Figure 3. If no specialized knowledge is available or applicable, then a handler which performs decision-theoretic reasoning can examine the conflict, develop a control model such as described in Section 2 and make a recommendation regarding which task should be undertaken.

A potential problem with this approach is entailed by the computational (and other) resource requirements associated with this method of reasoning about control [18,1]. The activities of scheduling are "inner loop" in Schemer-II's overall computational activities. If the computation costs required to explicitly perform a full-blown cost/benefit analysis on each cycle are too high, they will outweigh the value of this control reasoning no matter how formally sound and general it is. Thus, it may be necessary to restrict the real-time estimations performed in scheduling on each cycle in response to limitations such as time deadlines. In extreme cases, it may even be necessary to abandon such a method entirely in favor of the default priority scheme.

3.2 Critical-event-driven Reasoning: Interrupts

One of the most important objectives in the evolution of the Schemer-II design has been to fundamentally support problem-solving processes whose control is responsive to critical changes in the problem-solving context. A problem solver dynamically formulating and executing solutions to problems in an uncertain environment must be able to react promptly to the asynchronous occurrence of such critical changes. In response to such changes, the problem-solving system may decide that its current actions are no longer the most preferable ones. In using earlier versions of Schemer in applications that must exhibit reactive, real-time performance, we found the capacity for "interrupt driven" control of problem-solving to be of paramount importance. In Schemer-II the occurrence of some critical event can initiate a response to immediately interrupt execution of the currently scheduled problem-solving tasks, suspend them gracefully, and commence tasks that are more appropriate in response to the changed information about the problem-solving context. This is readily accomplished by the use of special event-handlers that carry out these actions in response to pre-defined critical events. This aspect of Schemer-II's design is a natural evolution of the mechanisms for "opportunistic control" typical of blackboard systems such as Hearsay-II [5].

The discussion in the previous sections focused entirely on the "planning" phase of a combined control and primary decision problem. A real-time system both plans and executes actions. Suppose the system has solved both the control and primary planning problems, and is now executing the sequence of steps in the primary problem, which may involve a series of compute-intensive low-level tasks. We need to define a set of critical events that would render the current plan inappropriate or inoperable, and signal a need to replan at a higher level. A similar scenario can be applied to interruption of planning or reasoning activities: if conditions which would invalidate applicability of that planning methodology occur before reasoning has completed, it may be advantageous to interrupt that activity.

In either case, critical events are defined with respect to the modeling method used to generate a particular course of action. If the output of a reasoner is in the form of a decision recommendation, d^*, we *annotate* the recommendation with a set of assumptions on which the recommendation was based, as in (d^*, ξ^*). The use of the annotation is to continually execute the following activities:

$$EXECUTE \quad d^*$$
$$IF \quad Inconsistent(\xi^* \wedge Sensors)$$
$$THEN \quad Replan$$

Thus, the system will continually sense its knowledge base and the environment for conflicts with the set ξ^* and trigger a replanning task if a conflict occurs. The set ξ^* is a subset of the full set of assumptions which are embodied in a planning method. These assumptions can be of a number of general types, some implicit (such as reasoning axioms) and others explicit (such as defaults). One important class of assumptions relates to *mutual exclusivity*. If the system detects a condition that is not among a set of enumerated possibilities considered in generating a plan, the plan may be invalid. Other possible classes of critical assumptions relate to the validity of defaults, data, or probabilities used in a model.

The "complete" assumption set associated with a method is essentially infinite, and there are complex tradeoffs involved in identifying a "critical" subset to flag as interrupts. Providing sensitivity to critical events with an interrupt structure causes an increase in system overhead and detracts from performance on other tasks. The overhead can be crippling if the set ξ^* is large or it is time consuming to identify an inconsistency. On the other hand, ignoring information which may invalidate a plan can also be disastrous. We provide a simplified analysis of this issue below by considering the possible inclusion of each assumption into the set of interrupts independently, without consideration of cross effects with other interrupts.

Let ξ be a set of assumptions which we wish to analyze for purposes of potentially including in the set ξ^*. Let $d^*(a)$ be the optimal decision generated by the reasoning system if assumption $a \in \xi$ is true. Define $U_p(a, d)$ as the expected object-level utility given assumption a is true and decision d is selected. Thus $U_p(a, d^*(a))$ is the expected utility of the optimal decision if the system correctly assumed a was true; $U_p(\neg a, d^*(a))$ is the expected utility of a policy which was derived assuming a holds when in fact it was violated.[4] We define $C(a)$ as the cost of verifying that assumption a is true at execution time. It represents the overall degradation in object-level utility due to the overhead of checking the consistency of a. Finally, we define $P(a)$ as the probability that assumption a holds. For simplicity, we will

---

[4] We have $\max_{d \in D} U_p(a, d) \equiv U_p(a, d^*(a))$. This formulation assumes that U_p does not depend on the status of the other assumptions in ξ.

treat the probability of one assumption being violated as being independent of the status of the other assumptions being analyzed, given the structure of the model.

We can now define the following quantities:

$$EU_{in}(a) = P(a)U_p(a, d^*(a)) + P(\neg a)U_p(\neg a, d^*(\neg a)) - C(a)$$

$$EU_{out}(a) = P(a)U_p(a, d^*(a)) + P(\neg a))U_p(\neg a, d^*(a))$$

The expression for EU_{in} is the expected utility given a is included in the interrupt set. The first term on the right is the probability that the assumption was correct, and we planned using that assumption. The second term is the case where it turns out that a is violated and the violation is detected. We assume that we replan (costlessly) to account for this, achieving a utility of $U_p(\neg a, d^*(\neg a))$. The final term reflects the expected overhead cost of polling the interrupt. The equation for EU_{out} is the expected utility given a is not included in ξ^*. If assumption a is false, then the utility $U_p(\neg a, d^*(a))$ reflects the utility of acting based on an erroneous assumption.

From this we determine that we put a in the interrupt set if and only if:

$$P(\neg a)[U_p(\neg a, d^*(\neg a)) - U_p(\neg a, d^*(a))] > C(a)$$

This expression verifies our intuition. If the change in assumption would not change the decision, i.e. $d^*(\neg a) = d^*(a)$, then a is not included in ξ^*. The higher the probability of violation ,$P(\neg a)$, and the lower the overhead cost, $C(a)$, the greater propensity to include the assumption in the interrupt set. The utility difference (positive by definition of d^*) in the expression is the cost of an error with respect to the assumption.

The foregoing analysis provide some general guidelines for design interrupt sets in an architecture such as Schemer-II. Obviously approximations and independence assumptions such as those made here are necessary to make the analysis tractable. One approach is to characterize classes of assumptions and associated interrupts such that the utility and probabilistic independence conditions used above are maintained. However, this approach, in contrast to previous ad-hoc methods, makes explicit the considerations involved in developing responsive systems.

4   Conclusion

This paper has described efforts to apply decision analysis to the control of problem-solving within a computational problem-solving architecture. We have addressed control of both assessment and planning methods. The formulation makes it clear that a system's ability to make well-founded decisions about the control of its own problem-solving activities is a problem of information management, and we use concepts based on value of information to perform these allocations.

This research addresses a limitation of much previous research on problem-solving architectures. Schemer-II is a well tested and highly evolved computational approach to resource-bounded problem solving. The architecture allows encapsulating and interruption of alternative problem-solving methods so that various problem solving techniques can co-exist and be scheduled for execution as needed. One critical limitation of previous research with Schemer was that the methods for coping with uncertainty and for reasoning about control were ad hoc and application-specific. Adoption of decision-theory promises to rectify this shortcoming by providing a set of well-founded and rigorous principles for managing internal resources and other decisions under uncertainty.

5 Acknowledgements

We thank Eric Horvitz, Jackie Neider, and Sampath Srinivas for comments on an earlier draft of this paper.

References

[1] J.A. Barnett. How much is control knowledge worth? *Journal of Artificial Intelligence*, 22(1):77–89, January 1984.

[2] P.R. Cohen and D.S. Day. The centrality of autonomous agents in theories of action under uncertainty. *International Journal of Approximate Reasoning*, 2:303–326, 1988.

[3] B. D'Ambrosio, M.R. Fehling, S. Forrest, P. Raulefs, and M. Wilber. Real-time process management for materials composition in chemical manufacturing. *IEEE Expert*, pages 80–92, Summer 1987.

[4] E.H. Durfee and V.R. Lesser. Incremental planning in a blackboard-based problem solver. In *Proceedings AAAI-86 Fifth National Conference on Artificial Intelligence*, pages 53–64, Philadelphia, Pennsylvania, August 1986. American Association for Artificial Intelligence.

[5] L. Erman, F. Hayes-Roth, V.R Lesser, and D.R. Reddy. The HEARSAY-II speech understanding system: integrating knowledge to resolve uncertainty. *ACM Computing Surveys*, 12:213–253, 1980.

[6] M.R. Fehling. Soft control of cognitive processes. In *Proceedings of the 4th Annual Meeting of the Cognitive Science Society*, Ann Arbor, Michigan, August 1982.

[7] M.R. Fehling and J.S. Breese. A computational model for the decision-theoretic control of problm solving under uncertainty. Technical report, Rockwell International Science Center, April 1988. Rockwell Technical Report 837-88-5.

[8] M. Genesereth and D.E. Smith. Meta-level architecture. Technical Report HPP-81-6, Stanford University, Heuristic Programming Project, Stanford, California, 1982.

[9] M. Georgeff, A. Lansky, and M. Schoppers. Reasoning and planning in dynamic domains: An experiment with a mobile robot. Technical Report Technical Note 380, SRI International, Menlo Park, California, 1987.

[10] J. Guffey. AI takes off: Expert systems that are solving flight avionics problems. *Aviation Week and Space Technology*, February 1986.

[11] B. Hayes-Roth. A blackboard architecture for control. *Artificial Intelligence*, 26(3):251–321, 985.

[12] E.J. Horvitz. Reasoning under varying and uncertain resource constraints. In *Proceedings AAAI-88 Seventh National Conference on Artificial Intelligence*. American Association for Artificial Intelligence, August 1988. Also available as Technical Report KSL-88-35, Knowledge Systems Laboratory, Stanford University, April 1988.

[13] E.J. Horvitz, J.S. Breese, and M. Henrion. Decision theory in expert systems and artificial intelligence. *International Journal of Approximate Reasoning*, 2:247–302, 1988.

[14] V.R. Lesser, J. Pavlin, and E. Durfee. Approximate processing in real time problem solving. *AI Magazine*, 9(1):49–61, 1988.

[15] D.V. Lindley. Reconciliation of decision analyses. *Operations Research*, 20(1):289–295, 1986.

[16] J.E. Matheson. The value of analysis and computation. *IEEE Transactions on Systems Science, and Cybernetics*, 4:211–219, 1968.

[17] R. C. Nickerson and D. W. Boyd. The use and value of models in decision analysis. *Operations Research*, 20(1):139–155, 1980.

[18] J.S. Rosenschein and V. Singh. The utility of meta-level effort. Technical Report HPP-83-206, Stanford University, Heuristic Programming Project, Stanford, California, 1983.

Uncertainty in Artificial Intelligence 4
R.D. Shachter, T.S. Levitt, L.N. Kanal, J.F. Lemmer (Editors)
© Elsevier Science Publishers B.V. (North-Holland), 1990

CAUSAL NETWORKS: SEMANTICS AND EXPRESSIVENESS*

Thomas VERMA and Judea PEARL

Cognitive Systems Laboratory
Computer Science Department
University of California Los Angeles
Los Angeles, CA 90024
Internet: verma@cs.ucla.edu, pearl@cs.ucla.edu

Dependency knowledge of the form "x is independent of y once z is known" invariably obeys the four *graphoid* axioms, examples include probabilistic and database dependencies. Often, such knowledge can be represented efficiently with graphical structures such as undirected graphs and directed acyclic graphs (DAGs). In this paper we show that the graphical criterion called *d-separation* is a sound rule for reading independencies from any DAG based on a *causal input list* drawn from a graphoid. The rule may be extended to cover DAGs that represent functional dependencies as well as conditional dependencies.

1. INTRODUCTION

In several areas of research it is beneficial to reason about dependency knowledge. For example, in database design it is useful to reason about embedded-multivalued-dependence (EMVD) of attributes [2]. Similarly, in decision analysis and expert systems design it is useful to reason about probabilistic independence of variables [5,9]. These examples give two well known formalizations of the intuitive relation "knowing Z renders X and Y independent" which shall be denoted $I(X,Z,Y)$. Naturally, such a relation would have different properties for different formalizations, but it is interesting to note that most sensible definitions share the four common properties listed below:

symmetry	$I(X,Z,Y) \Leftrightarrow I(Y,Z,X)$	(1.a)
decomposition	$I(X,Z,YW) \Rightarrow I(X,Z,Y)$	(1.b)
weak union	$I(X,Z,YW) \Rightarrow I(X,ZY,W)$	(1.c)
contraction	$I(X,ZY,W) \,\&\, I(X,Z,Y) \Rightarrow I(X,Z,YW)$	(1.d)

where X, Y and Z represent three disjoint subsets of objects (e.g. variables or attributes)

* This work was partially supported by the National Science Foundation Grant #IRI-8610155. "Graphoids: A Computer Representation for Dependencies and Relevance in Automated Reasoning (Computer Information Science)."

and the notation YW is a shorthand for $Y \cup W$. These four properties, in addition to others, hold for EMVDs[1] as well as for probabilistic dependencies [1]. Three place relations which obey the four properties listed above are called *graphoids*[2]. Those relations which obey the following additional axiom:

$$\text{intersection} \quad I(X,ZY,W) \;\&\; I(X,ZW,Y) \Rightarrow I(X,Z,YW) \qquad (2)$$

are called *positive graphoids* since this axiom holds for probabilistic dependencies when the distributions are constrained to be strictly positive (non-extreme distributions).

A naive approach for representing a dependency model, i.e., particular instance of a dependency relation, would be to enumerate all triplets (X,Z,Y) for which $I(X,Z,Y)$ holds. This could require an exponential amount space since the relation I ranges over subsets of objects. In fact, any general representation scheme will require exponential space, on average, to represent a dependency model given that it is a graphoid, probabilistic dependency or EMVD [14].

The graphical representation schemes presented in this paper are appealing for three reasons. First, the graphs have an intuitive conceptual meaning. Second, the representations are efficient in terms of time and space [11]. Third, there exist various efficient algorithms that make implicit use of these representation schemes [6,7,8,9,12,13].

2. UNDIRECTED GRAPHS

The meaning of a particular undirected graph is straight forward, each node in the graph represents a variable, and a link in the graph means that the two variables are directly dependent. With this semantics, a set of nodes Z would *separate* two other sets X and Y, if and only if every path between a node in X and a node in Y passes through Z. This representation can fully represent only a small set of dependency models defined by the following properties [10]:

symmetry	$I(X,Z,Y) \Leftrightarrow I(Y,Z,X)$	(3.a)
decomposition	$I(X,Z,YW) \Rightarrow I(X,Z,Y)$	(3.b)
strong union	$I(X,Z,Y) \Rightarrow I(X,ZW,Y)$	(3.c)
intersection	$I(X,ZY,W) \;\&\; I(X,ZW,Y) \Rightarrow I(X,Z,YW)$	(3.d)
transitivity	$I(X,Z,Y) \Rightarrow I(X,Z,\gamma) \text{ or } I(Y,Z,\gamma) \; \forall \gamma \notin XYZ$	(3.e)

It is not always necessary nor feasible to have an exact representation of a dependency model; in fact, an efficient approximation called an *I-map* is often preferred to an inefficient perfect map. A representation R is an I-map of a dependency model M iff every independence statement represented by R is also a valid independence of M. Thus, R may not represent every statement of M, but the ones it does represent are correct. The rationale behind the use of I-maps is that an ignored independence will cause a redundant consultation thus only cost some time whereas use of an incorrect independence will cause

---

[1] The notation $I(X,Z,Y)$ is equivalent to the standard EMVD notation $Z \twoheadrightarrow X \mid Y$.
[2] Historically the term *semi-graphoids* was used for graphoids, and *graphoids* was used for positive graphoids.

relevant information to be ignored thereby corrupting the integrity of the system. (This rationale presupposes a specific type of use for the dependency knowledge, thus will not apply in general).

The set of undirected graphs that are I-maps of a given positive graphoid forms a complete lattice under the I-mapness relation. This means that every positive graphoid has a unique most representative I-map graph. Furthermore there is a polynomial algorithm which will find it [10]. Thus, for example, every non-extreme probability distribution P has a unique *edge-minimal* undirected graph I-map of P (i.e. no edge can be removed without destroying the I-mapness of this graph).

This is not the case for EMVD relations nor for probabilistic distributions in general. In fact, with out the intersection property there is no unique edge-minimal I-map for a given model, and, moreover, there is no effective method of constructing even one of the minimal I-maps. Hence undirected graphs are only useful as I-maps of positive graphoids.

3. DIRECTED-ACYCLIC GRAPHS (DAGS)

The dependency model represented by a particular DAG has a simple causal interpretation. Each node represents a variable and there is a directed arc from one node to another if the first is a direct cause of the second. Under this interpretation, graph-separation is not as straight forward as before since two unrelated causes of a symptom may become related once the symptom is observed [8]. In general, a set of nodes Z is defined to *d-separate* two other sets X and Y if and only if every *trail* from a node in X to a node in Y is rendered *inactive* by Z. A trail is a path which follows arcs ignoring their directionality, and is rendered inactive by a set of nodes Z in exactly two ways; either there is a *head-to-head* node on the trail which is not in Z and none of its descendents are in Z or some node on the trail is in Z but is not head-to-head. A node on the trail is head-to-head if the node before it and after it on the trail both point to it in the graph. One node is a descendent of another if there is a directed trail from the latter to the former.

There is a procedure that produces an edge-minimal I-map DAG for any graphoid. It employs an algorithm which takes a *causal input list* (or simply causal list) of a dependency model and produces a perfect map of the list's graphoid closure. A casual list of a dependency model contains two things: an ordering of the variables, and a function that assigns a *tail boundary* to each variable x. For each variable x let U_x denote the set of all variables which come before x in the given ordering. A tail boundary of a variable x, denoted B_x, is any subset of U_x that renders x independent of $U_x - B_x$. A unique DAG can be generated from each casual list by associating the tail boundary of the variable x in the list with the set of direct parents of any node x in the DAG. An equivalent specification of a casual list is an ordered list of triplets of the form $I(x, B_x, R)$, one triplet for each variable in the model, where R is $U_x - B_x$.

For a particular dependency model over n variables there are $n!$ orderings, and for each ordering there can be up to $2^{n(n-1)/2}$ different sets of tail boundaries since, in the worst case, every subset of lesser variables could be a boundary. Thus, there can be as many as $n! \, 2^{n(n-1)/2}$ casual lists for any given dependency model. But if a model posses a perfect map DAG, then one of the casual lists is guaranteed to generate that DAG by the following theorem.

Theorem 1: If M is a dependency model which can be perfectly represented by some DAG D, then there is a causal list L_θ which generates D.

Proof: Let D be a DAG which perfectly represents M. Since D is a directed acyclic graph it imposes a partial order ϕ on the variables of M. Let θ be any total ordering consistent with ϕ (i.e. $a <_\phi b \Rightarrow a <_\theta b$). For any node x in D, the set of its parents $P(x)$ constitutes a tail boundary with respect to the ordering θ, thus the pair $L_\theta = (\theta, P(x))$ is a causal list of M, and this is the very list which will generate D. QED.

Although it is possible to find a perfect map when it exists, testing for existence may be intractable. However, it is practical to find an edge-minimal I-map. The next theorem shows that any causal list of a graphoid can be used to generate an I-map of that graphoid. If the boundaries of a causal list are all subset minimal, then the graph it generates will be edge-minimal. Finding a minimal boundary is linear (in the number of variables) due to the weak union property. Hence an edge-minimal I-map of any graphoid can be found in polynomial time.

Theorem 2: If M is a graphoid, and L_θ is any causal list of M, then the DAG generated by L_θ is an I-map of M.

Proof: Induct on the number of variables in the graphoid. For graphoids of one variable it is obvious that the DAG generated is an I-map. Suppose for graphoids with fewer than k variables that the DAG is also an I-map. Let M have k variables, n be the last variable in the ordering θ, $M - n$ be the graphoid formed by removing n and all triplets involving n from M and $G - n$ be the DAG formed by removing n and all its incident links from G. Since n is the last variable in the ordering, it cannot appear in any of boundaries of L_θ, and thus $L_\theta - n$ can be defined to contain only the first $n-1$ variables and boundaries of L_θ and still be a causal list of $M - n$. In fact the DAG generated from $L_\theta - n$ is $G - n$. Since $M - n$ has $k-1$ variables, $G - n$ is an I-map of it. Let M_G be the dependency model corresponding to the DAG G, and M_{G-n} correspond to $G - n$, (i.e. M_G contains all d-separated triplets of G).

G is an I-map of M if and only if $M_G \subseteq M$. Each triplet T of M_G falls into one of four categories; either the variable n does not appear in T or it appears in the first, second or third entry of T. These will be treated separately as cases 1, 2, 3 and 4, respectively.

case-1: If n does not appear in T then T must equal (X, Z, Y) with X, Y and Z three disjoint subsets of variables, none of which contain n. Since T is in M_G it must also be in M_{G-n} for if it were not then there would be an active path in $G - n$ between a node in X and a node in Y when Z is instantiated. But if this path is active in $G - n$ then it must also be active in G since the addition of nodes and links can not deactivate a path. Since $G - n$ is an I-map of $M - n$, T must also be an element of it, but $M - n$ is a subset of M, so T is in M

case-2: If n appears in the first entry of the triplet, then $T = (Xn, Z, Y)$ with the same constraints on X, Y and Z as in case-1. Let (n, B, R) be the last triple in L_θ, B_X, B_Y, B_Z and B_0 be a partitioning of B and R_X, R_Y, R_Z and R_0 be a partitioning of R such that $X = B_X \cup R_X$, $Y = B_Y \cup R_Y$ and $Z = B_Z \cup R_Z$ as in figure 1.

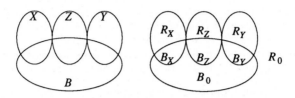

Figure 1

By the method of construction, there is an arrow from every node in B to n, but since (Xn, Z, Y) is in M_G every path from a node in Y to n must be deactivated by Z so B_Y must be empty or else there would be a direct link from Y to n (see figure 2a). The last triplet in L_θ can now be written as $(n, B_X B_0 B_Z, R_X R_Z Y R_0)$. Since $X = B_X \cup R_X$, $Y = R_Y$ and M is a graphoid it follows (from (1.b) and (1.c)) that $(n, X B_0 Z, Y) \in M$.

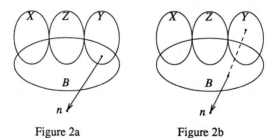

Figure 2a   Figure 2b

Since there is an arrow from every node in B_0 to n and n is separated from Y given Z in G, B_0 must also be d-separated from Y given Z in G for if it were connected there would be a path from a node in Y to a node in B_0 which was active given Z. But there is an arrow from every node in B_0 to n, thus, such a path would also connect the node in Y to n, and Y would no longer be separated from n given Z (see figure 2b). Since Y is separated from both B_0 and X given Z in the DAG G it is separated from their union, so $(XB_0, Z, Y) \in M_G$. Since n is not in this triplet, the argument of case-1 above implies that $(XB_0, Z, Y) \in M$. Since $(n, XB_0 Z, Y) \in M$ and M is a graphoid it follows (using (1.b) and (1.d)) that $T = (Xn, Z, Y) \in M$

case-3: If n appears in the second entry then $T = (X, Zn, Y)$. Now it must be the case that X and Y are separated in G given only Z for if they were not then there would be a path between some node in X and some node in Y which would be active given Z. But they are separated given Z and n, so this path would have to be deactivated by n, but n is a sink and cannot serve to deactivate any path by being instantiated. Hence there is no such path and (X, Z, Y) holds in G. This statement along with (X, Zn, Y) imply that either (Xn, Z, Y) or (X, Z, Yn) holds in G by the weak transitivity property of DAGs. Either way case-2 or case-4 would imply that the corresponding triplet must be in M, and either of these would imply that $T \in M$ by the weak union property.

case-4: If n appears in the third entry, then by symmetry the triplet T is equivalent to one with n in the first entry, and the argument of case-2 above shows that $T \in M$. QED.

This theorem constructively proves that d-separation is sound. In other words a DAG built from a causal list is an I-map since for any independence identified by d-separation there exists a derivation of that statement from the the causal input list using the graphoid axioms. The next corollary shows that for DAGs build from causal lists of graphoids, no criterion could correctly read more independencies than d-separation.

Corollary 1: If L_θ is any causal list of some dependency model M, the DAG generated from L_θ is a perfect map of the graphoid closure of L_θ. In other words, a triplet is d-separated in the DAG if and only if it can be derived from the causal input list using the graphoid axioms.

Proof: By the previous theorem, the DAG is an I-map of the closure, and it remains to show that the closure is an I-map of the DAG. Since every DAG dependency model is a graphoid, the DAG closure of L_θ contains the graphoid closure of it, thus, it suffices to show that the DAG dependency model M_G contains L_θ. If (n, B, R) is a triplet in L_θ then n is separated from R given B in the DAG, for if not then there would be a path from a node in R to n which is active given B. But since every link into n is from B the path must lead out of n into some node which was placed after n. Since every node in R was placed before n, this path cannot be directed and must contain a head-to-head node at some node which was placed after n. But this path is deactivated by B since it contains no nodes placed after n, and thus, B would separate n from R in the graph. QED.

The following corollary is needed to assert the tractability of finding an edge-minimal I-map for a graphoid.

Corollary 2: If each tail boundary in L_θ is minimal, the resulting DAG is a minimal I-map of M.

Theorem 2 and its corollaries together imply that d-separation is sound and complete for the extraction of independence information from DAGs with respect to their causal lists when those lists are drawn from graphoids. That is, a conclusion can be read from the graph using d-separation if and only if it follows from application of the graphoid axioms to the causal list. In bayesian networks [8], for example, any independence which can be read from the graph via d-separation is sound with respect to the probability distribution that it represents since the axioms of graphoids are sound for probabilistic dependence. But the axioms of graphoids are not complete for the class of probabilistic dependencies, so corollary 1 is not enough to ensure that d-separation is complete for DAGs built from the more specific probabilistic dependency models. Completeness with respect to probability has been shown in [3].

The last theorem, which is of a theoretical nature, states that it is possible to force any particular independence of a graphoid to be represented in an I-map.

Theorem 3: If M is any graphoid then the set of DAGs generated from all causal lists of M

is a perfect map of M if the criterion for separation is that d-separation must exist in one of the DAGs.

Proof: If there is a separation in one of the DAGs then the corresponding independence must hold in M since theorem 2 states that each of the DAGs is an I-map of M, thus the set is also an I-map. It remains to show that M is an I-map of the set of DAGs. Let $T = (X, Z, Y)$ be any triplet in M and $X = \{x_1, \ldots, x_n\}$. The triplets $T^* = \{(x_i, x_1 \cdots x_{i-1} Z, Y) \mid 1 \leq i \leq n\}$ must also be in M since they are implied by T using the weak union axiom of graphoids. Furthermore T is in the graphoid closure of T^* since the triplets imply T by use of the contraction axiom. Thus any causal list containing the triplets T^* would generate a DAG containing T. Such a list need only have an ordering θ such that the variables of Y and Z are less than those of X which are less than any other variables and that the variables of X are ordered such that $x_i <_\theta x_j$ if and only if $i < j$. The DAG generated by this causal list is in the set of DAGs and therefore the separation holds in the set. QED.

Since there is an effective algorithm for generating an I-map DAG for any graphoid, DAGs are a useful means for representing EMVD relations as well as probabilistic independence relations. Furthermore if the particular dependency model is stated as a causal list then it can be perfectly represented by a DAG.

4. FUNCTIONAL DEPENDENCIES

The ability to represent functional dependencies would be a powerful extension from the point of view of the designer. These dependencies may easily be represented by the introduction of *deterministic nodes* which would correspond to the deterministic variables [13]. Graphs which contain deterministic nodes represent more information than d-separation is able to extract; but a simple extension of d-separation, called D-separation, is both sound and complete with respect to the input list under both probabilistic inference and graphoid inference [4]. D-separation is very similar to d-separation, only differing in that a path is rendered *inactive* by a set of nodes Z under D-separation just in case it would be inactive under d-separation plus the case when a node on the path which is *determined* by Z.

5. CONCLUSIONS

This paper shows that d-separation is sound (i.e. correct) and briefly discusses D-separation which is also sound. They both provide a reliable and efficient method for extracting independence information from DAGs. This information may be used explicitly, for example to help guide a complex reasoning system, or implicitly as in bayesian propagation [8] or the evaluations of Influence Diagrams [12,13]. These criteria also provide a sound theoretical basis for the analysis of the properties of the corresponding graphical representations. For example, the validity of graphical manipulations such as arc reversal and node removal [5,12,13,14] can now be affirmed on solid theoretical foundations.

ACKNOWLEDGMENT

We thank Dan Geiger and Azaria Paz for many valuable discussions, and James Smith for checking the proof of Theorem 2.

REFERENCES

[1]   Dawid, A.P., Conditional Independence in Statistical Theory, *J.R. Statist. Soc. B.* (1979) **41(1):** 1-33.

[2]   Fagin, R., Multivalued Dependencies and a New Form for Relational Databases, *ACM Transactions on Database Systems* (1977) **2(3):** 262-278.

[3]   Geiger D. and Pearl J. On the Logic of Causal Models, this volume.

[4]   Geiger, D., Verma, T.S. and Pearl, J., Recognizing Independence in Influence Diagrams with Deterministic Nodes, To appear in *Networks* (1990).

[5]   Howard, R.A. and Matheson, J.E., Influence Diagrams. In Howard, R.A. and Matheson, J.E., (eds) *Principles and Applications of Decision Analysis* (Strategic Decision Group, Menlo Park, CA, 1981) **2:** 719-762.

[6]   Pearl, J., Reverend Bayes on Inference Engines: A Distributed Hierarchical Approach, *Proc. of the Natl. Conference on AI* (Pittsburgh, 1982) 133-136.

[7]   Pearl, J., A Constraint Propagation Approach to Probabilistic Reasoning. In Kanal, L.N. and Lemmer, J. (eds) *Uncertainty in Artificial Intelligence,* (North-Holland, Amsterdam, 1986) 357-369.

[8]   Pearl, J., Fusion, Propagation and Structuring in Belief Networks, *Artificial Intelligence* (1986) **29(3):** 241-288.

[9]   Pearl, J., *Probabilistic Reasoning in Intelligent Systems* (Morgan-Kaufmann, San Mateo, 1988)

[10]   Pearl, J. and Paz, A., GRAPHOIDS: A Graph-based Logic for Reasoning about Relevance Relations. In B. Du Boulay et al. (eds) *Advances in Artificial Intelligence-II* (North-Holland, Amsterdam, 1987).

[11]   Pearl, J. and Verma, T.S., The Logic of Representing Dependencies by Directed Graphs, *Proc. of the 6th Natl. Conference on AI* (Seattle, 1987) **1:** 374-379.

[12]   Shachter, R., Intelligent Probabilistic Inference. In Kanal, L.N. and Lemmer, J. (eds) *Uncertainty in Artificial Intelligence,* (North-Holland, Amsterdam, 1986) 371-382.

[13]   Shachter, R., Probabilistic Inference and Influence Diagrams, *Operations Research* (1988) **36:** 589-604.

[14]   Verma, T.S., Some Mathematical Properties of Dependency Models, *Technical Report R-102* (UCLA Cognitive Systems Laboratory, Los Angeles, 1987)

Section II

UNCERTAINTY CALCULI
AND COMPARISONS

Uncertainty in Artificial Intelligence 4
R.D. Shachter, T.S. Levitt, L.N. Kanal, J.F. Lemmer (Editors)
© Elsevier Science Publishers B.V. (North-Holland), 1990   79

STOCHASTIC SENSITIVITY ANALYSIS USING FUZZY INFLUENCE DIAGRAMS

Pramod JAIN[†] and Alice M. AGOGINO[§]

Intelligent Systems Research Group
Dept. of Mechanical Engineering, 5136 Etcheverry Hall
University of California, Berkeley, CA 94720

The practice of stochastic sensitivity analysis described in the decision analysis literature is a testimonial to the need for considering deviations from precise point estimates of uncertainty. We propose the use of Bayesian fuzzy probabilities within an influence diagram computational scheme for performing sensitivity analysis during the solution of probabilistic inference and decision problems. Unlike other parametric approaches, the proposed scheme does not require resolving the problem for the varying probability point estimates. We claim that the solution to fuzzy influence diagrams provides as much information as the classical point estimate approach plus additional information concerning stochastic sensitivity. An example based on diagnostic decision making in microcomputer assembly is used to illustrate this idea. We claim that the solution to fuzzy influence diagrams provides as much information as the classical point estimate approach plus additional interval information that is useful for stochastic sensitivity analysis.

1. INTRODUCTION AND OBJECTIVE

In discrete probability theory point estimates quantifying the likelihood of uncertain events are represented as crisp numbers. Unfortunately, even for moderately complex random processes, it can be extremely difficult to specify the probabilities of uncertain events to much precision. There is always a "fuzziness" associated with subjective assessments of uncertainty. There are Bayesians who claim that classical probability theory is equipped to handle this fuzziness (e.g., [Cheeseman:1985], [Kyburg: 1987] and [Pearl:1987]) and others who argue the opposite case and propose various schemes for higher order probabilities ([Bonissone: 1985], [Dempster: 1967], [Shafer: 1976] and [Zadeh: 1984]). However, even Bayesians show the need for considering deviations from precise estimates of point probabilities through the accepted practice of stochastic sensitivity analysis ([Howard: 1968] and [Holstein: 1973]). Howard (1968) claims that *stochastic sensitivity is a powerful tool for locating the important variables* and Holstein (1973) is of the view that it *helps in determining the level of encoding of uncertainty and risk attitude.*

We propose that fuzzy probabilities used within an influence diagram framework allow the use of linguistic probabilities when communicating with humans concerning uncertainty and provide an efficient computational scheme to perform a kind of stochastic sensitivity analysis. We do not argue that fuzzy probabilities are second-order probabilities - but that they can be convenient communication and computational tools. We insist, however, in defining Bayesian fuzzy probabilities so that they are consistent with Sage's axioms of

---

† Currently Asscociate Scientist with Andersen Consulting, Chicago.
§ Associate Professor; aagogino@tycho.berkeley.edu
This work was funded, in part, by the National Science Foundation Grant DMC-8451622.

probability theory. Within this framework, Bayesian fuzzy probabilities provide the traditional point solution, the interval probabilities, and a linear weighting distribution from the point solution to the interval endpoints.

Probability theory is one of the oldest and most widely used formalisms for representing and processing uncertain information. Discrete probabilities quantifying an individual's degree of belief of precisely defined events are encoded and Bayes' rule is used to perform probabilistic inferences given the input data. Recently probabilistic influence diagrams (also called Bayes' networks) have emerged as a tool for both graphically representing probabilistic influences and propagating uncertainties through the network ([Shachter: 1985], [Pearl: 1987], [Rege & Agogino:1988], [Heckerman & Horvitz:1987], and [Henrion & Cooley: 1987]). With the addition of decision nodes, influence diagrams also provide a representational scheme and calculus for solving complex decision problems involving uncertain variables ([Miller et al.: 1976], [Howard & Matheson: 1984], [Shachter: 1986], and [Agogino & Rege: 1987]).

In spite of the normative virtues of probability theory [Cheeseman: 1985], descriptive studies of human behavior reveal serious limitations. Cognitive scientists and knowledge engineers have documented the difficulty and biases involved in obtaining point estimates of probabilities from experts ([Kahneman et al.: 1985], [Zimmer: 1983]). Few of us can respond like Mr. Spock in the science fiction television series *Star Trek* and cite probabilities to three decimal places. The linguistic modeling approach, on the other hand, overcomes the requirement of numerical precision. Zimmer (1983,1985) reports that verbal expressions of uncertainty were more accurate than numerical values in estimating the frequency of multiple attributes in his experimental studies. These *fuzzy probabilities* are everyday linguistic expressions of likelihoods, such as *very likely, unlikely,* and *impossible.*

Fuzzy set theory was introduced by Zadeh (1965). It provides a mechanism for representing and manipulating vagueness in practical systems for computer-based decision making ([Zadeh: 1983], [Dubois & Prade: 1980]). Linguistic variables are used to represent imprecise information in a manner similar to natural language and fuzzy operators provide the inference mechanism. There have been several applications of the use of fuzzy linguistic variables in the field of process control [Kickert & Mamdani: 1978] and natural language processing [Zadeh: 1978,1981 and 1975]). Various researcher have developed techniques to map human linguistic expressions of uncertainty to point estimates of probability by means of calibration experiments and fuzzy set theory ([Zimmer: 1985], [Wallsten et al.: 1986], and [Jain & Agogino: 1988a]). The fuzzy set approach, however, is by no means devoid of numerical definitions; it may be viewed as a higher level of complexity beyond conventional point-estimate numerical methods ([Nguyen: 1979], [Tsukamoto & Hatano: 1983]). Further, opponents argue that fuzzy logic is an inadequate approximation to the more desirable calculus of probability theory.

Although there is a rich body of literature associated with probability theory and fuzzy number theory separately, there has been little work done in the area of integrating these seemingly different fields of study. Recently, Jain & Agogino (1988b) have specified the properties of a Bayesian fuzzy probability and have developed arithmetic operations that are consistent with Bayes' rule and retain closure of the required properties. The arithmetic operations developed are those necessary for Bayesian analysis: addition, multiplication, division, and expectation of joint and marginal discrete probability distributions. Application of the arithmetic operations results in a solution in which the mean of the fuzzy function is equivalent to the point estimate obtained by using conventional Bayesian probability. The resulting fuzzy function around the mean can be used for sensitivity analysis; its interpretation depending on the application.

We claim that fuzzy influence diagrams provide efficient computational techniques that contribute to both fuzzy set theory and Bayesian decision analysis. The advantages are two-fold: (1) they allow the use of fuzzy linguistic variables for representing uncertainty while maintaining the desirable properties and rigor of conventional probability theory and (2) they provide a computationally efficient method to perform sensitivity analysis in Bayesian inference and decision analysis.

2. BAYESIAN FUZZY PROBABILITIES : BASICS

In this paper, we will assume a discrete random process with precisely defined or nonfuzzy events, the likelihood of which are represented by Bayesian fuzzy probabilities. Bayesian fuzzy probabilities cannot be treated like ordinary fuzzy numbers because they are constrained by the axioms of probability theory:

- The domain of the fuzzy probability is restricted to the closed interval [0,1].
- The sum of all the fuzzy probabilities of collectively exhaustive and mutually exclusive events in a state must be equal to the nonfuzzy number 1.

2.1. Definition

A *Bayesian fuzzy probability FP* is a convex normalized fuzzy set A of [0,1] (an interval on the real line $\mathbb{R}$), such that

i) there exists a unique x_0 (also called the mean) $\in$ [0,1] satisfying $\mu_A(x_0) = 1$,

ii) μ_A is continuous on the open interval (0,1),

iii) the mean of FP satisfies the axioms of conventional probability theory,

iv) if Ω is the sample space of events then $FP (\Omega) = 1$,

v) if events E_1 and E_2 are mutually exclusive, then $FP (E_1 \cup E_2) = FP (E_1) \oplus FP (E_2)$.

In the following sections we will drop the Bayesian qualifier, thus referring to Bayesian fuzzy probability as fuzzy probability. By *FP (E)* we mean the fuzzy probability of event E and by $\oplus$ we mean the fuzzy probabilistic sum. Notice that fuzzy probability is defined only on the interval [0,1]. What we mean by this is that, the membership of any point $z \notin$ [0,1] corresponding to the fuzzy probability is 0. An example of a fuzzy probability could be a linguistic expression with a membership function as shown in Figure 1 [Jain & Agogino, 1988a].

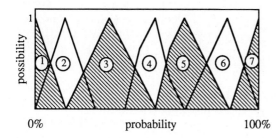

FIGURE 1. Example of fuzzy probabilities: 1. *extremely low*, 2. *quite low*, 3. *low*, 4. *even*, 5. *high*, 6. *very high*, and 7. *extremely high*

2.2. Representation of Fuzzy Probabilities

In this section we introduce the $\mathbb{P}$ representation of fuzzy probabilities. We will restrict our attention to only those fuzzy probabilities that have linear membership functions. We will therefore approximate the membership function obtained by performing arithmetic operations on fuzzy probabilities to be linear. The rationale behind this is that a linear approximation is sufficient for the purposes of sensitivity analysis and that without it the problem of manipulating them becomes extremely complex. We make a distinction between three types of fuzzy probabilities:

type-0 : zero membership at probability 0 and 1,
type-1 : nonzero membership at probability 1 and
type-2 : nonzero membership at probability 0.

The $\mathbb{P}$ representation of the three fuzzy probabilities is defined as triplets of the form, $(-(a_m)_{min}, m^*, (a_m)_{max})$ for type-0, $(\,(a_m)_{min}, m^*, [\mu_r])$ for type-1 and $([\mu_s], m^*, (a_m)_{max})$ for type-2, where a_{min}, a_{max}, μ_r and μ_s are as shown in Figure 2; m^* is the mean, m is the base variable and a_m is the spread variable of fuzzy probability M. For type-1 and type-2 fuzzy probabilities the term in the square brackets refers to the value of μ at probabilities 1 and 0, respectively. The base variable and the spread variable are related by the following formula,

$$m = m^* + a_m. \tag{1}$$

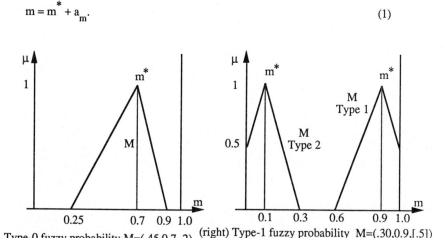

Type-0 fuzzy probability M=(.45,0.7,.2)
(right) Type-1 fuzzy probability M=(.30,0.9,[.5])
(left) Type-2 fuzzy probability M=([.5],0.1,.2)

FIGURE 2. Illustration of the three types of fuzzy probabilities

2.3. Joint and Conditional Fuzzy Probabilities

Let $X = \{x_1, ..., x_n\}$ and $Y = \{y_1, ..., y_m\}$ be two universes. If $u_i(X) = FP(X=x_i)$ and $u_j(Y) =$

$FP(Y=y_j)$ are the marginal fuzzy probabilities of events $X = x_i$ and $Y = y_j$ respectively, then let us denote the joint fuzzy probability that $X = x_i$ and $Y = y_j$ by $FP(X=x_i, Y=y_j) = v_{ij}(X,Y)$, and the conditional fuzzy probability of $X = x_i$ given $Y = y_j$ by $FP(X = x_i / Y = y_j) = w_{ij}(X/Y)$. We will drop X and Y when it is obvious which universe we are referring to. Let u_i^*, v_{ij}^* and w_{ij}^* be the means and b_i, c_{ij} and d_{ij} be the spread variables of the respective probabilities. Since $\Sigma_i\, u_i = 1$, the following condition must be satisfied by the spread variables b_i:

$$\Sigma_i\, b_i\,(X) = 0. \tag{2}$$

Similarly the conditional and joint probabilities satisfy the following relationships,

$$\Sigma_i\, w_{ij}\,(X|Y) = 1, \forall j \tag{3a}$$

$$\Sigma_i\, d_{ij}\,(X|Y) = 0, \forall j \tag{3b}$$

$$\Sigma_i\, \Sigma_j\, v_{ij}\,(X,Y) = 1 = \Sigma_j\, \Sigma_i\, v_{ij}\,(X,Y) \tag{4a}$$

$$\Sigma_i\, \Sigma_j\, c_{ij}\,(X,Y) = 0 = \Sigma_j\, \Sigma_i\, c_{ij}\,(X,Y) \tag{4b}$$

The joint and the conditional fuzzy probabilities are also related by the following formula, where $\otimes$ is the symbol for fuzzy multiplication.

$$v_{ij}\,(X,Y) = w_{ij}\,(X|Y) \otimes u_j\,(Y) = w_{ij}\,(Y|X) \otimes u_j\,(X) \tag{5}$$

2.4. Arithmetic Operations on Fuzzy Probabilities

Since we are dealing with linear membership functions it is sufficient to know the membership of two probabilities, one on either side of the mean, to construct the entire fuzzy probability. Jain & Agogino (1988b) analyze arithmetic operations involved with transformations on type-0, type-1 and type-2 fuzzy probabilities within an influence diagram computational scheme (e.g., IDES: Influence Diagram based Expert System, [Agogino & Rege: 1987]). We will not elaborate on this further except comment on the complexity of the arithmetic operations. The number of ordinary arithmetic operations to perform one fuzzy arithmetic operation is roughly three times. For instance, consider the operation of reversing an arc in an influence diagram - with point probabilities one arc reversal involves $(n-1)$ additions, n multiplications and 2 divisions; with fuzzy probabilities the same operation takes $3(n-1)$ additions, $3n$ multiplications, 6 divisions and $m \cdot log(m)$ comparisons, where n is the number of events in the goal nodes and m is the number of events in the conditioning node. Interval analysis would take roughly twice the number of operations as compared to point probabilities, but it loses information about the mean and gives a larger spread. Notice that the use of fuzzy probabilities obviates the need for evaluating the entire influence diagram at several fuzzy point probabilities (sweeping the range of a trial value of an aleatory variable) as suggested by Howard (1968). Although it may take approximately 3 times the computation, this is a local effect and can be isolated around the fuzzy variables in an influence diagram solution procedure.

3. FUZZY PROBABILISTIC INFERENCE

The solution to an inference problem using probabilistic influence diagrams involves finding conditional probability of a goal node conditioned on a given set of nodes. In a fuzzy probabilistic inference problem the above probabilities are the corresponding fuzzy probabilities. Thus it is equivalent to determining the fuzzy probability distribution FP (G (A) I B) where B is the set of conditioning nodes and G(A) is the goal-value function of the set of nodes A. One procedure for solving an inference problem consists of the following [Agogino & Ramamurthi, 1988],

- Introduce a goal-value node G(A) with conditioning arcs from nodes of set A.
- Apply transformations sequentially until the desired representation FP(G(A) I B) is obtained, that is, the final influence diagram with arcs leading from the conditioning nodes into the goal node is obtained.

3.1   Example of a Fuzzy Inference Problem: The Computer Assembly Diagnostics Problem

As an illustration of the techniques discussed so far let us consider a concrete problem [Agogino & Rege, 1987]. The problem we will examine arises in automated assembly of microcomputers.   To simplify the presentation we will assume that after complete assembly, final testing is performed on the microcomputer and a failure in it can be traced to failures in either of two components: (1) the logic board or (2) the I/O board.

Let us further assume that a sensor is available that gives rudimentary information about the operating status of the assembled microcomputer and is a function of the operating status of the logic board and the I/O board. The associated influence diagram is shown in Figure 3. This represents the Diagnostician's Inference Problem at the topological level.

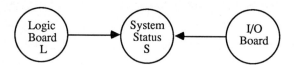

FIGURE 3. Probabilistic influence diagram

In the present structure of the influence diagram, the joint fuzzy probability can be obtained from the conditional fuzzy probability of the system status "S" and the fuzzy marginal distributions on the state of the logic board "L" and the I/0 Board "I/0" as given in the expansion below. Note that L and I/O are independent (there is no arc between them) and thus their joint probability distribution is the product of each marginal distribution.

$$FP(S, L, I/O \mid H) = FP(S \mid L, I/O, H) \otimes FP(L \mid H) \otimes FP(I/O \mid H) \qquad (6)$$

The nature of the influences is specified at the functional level. The influence diagram in Figure 3 implies that the fuzzy conditional distribution on S is known along with the fuzzy marginal distributions on L and I/O. Let us assume for illustration that the test for system status gives a <u>deterministic</u> result based on the status of the I/O and logic boards: if any of these boards (or both) is in a failure state the system status will show a failed system state. Using a subscript of "0" for a failed state and "1" for the operational state, this implies at the numerical level that the conditional distribution of the system status, S is:

$$\text{Pr}(S|L, I/O, H) = \begin{cases} 1 & \text{for } S=S_1 \text{ given } L=L_1 \text{ and } I/O=I/O_1 \\ 1 & \text{for } S=S_0 \text{ given } L=L_1 \text{ and } I/O=I/O_0 \\ 1 & \text{for } S=S_0 \text{ given } L=L_0 \text{ and } I/O=I/O_1 \\ 1 & \text{for } S=S_0 \text{ given } L=L_0 \text{ and } I/O=I/O_0 \\ 0 & \text{elsewhere} \end{cases} \qquad (7)$$

Let us further assume that the point estimate of the marginal probability of failure is 5% for the logic board and 1% for the I/O board and that the fuzzy marginal probability for failure is (.03,.05,.03) and ([.66],.01,.03), a deviation of 6% and 4% from the point estimate, respectively.

$$FP(L| H) = \begin{cases} (.03,0.95,.03) \text{ for } L= L_1 \\ (.03,0.05,.03) \text{ for } L= L_0 \end{cases} \qquad (8)$$

$$FP(I/O| H) = \begin{cases} (.03,0.99,[.66]) \text{ for } I/O=I/O_1 \\ ([.66],0.01,.03) \text{ for } I/O=I/O_0 \end{cases} \qquad (9)$$

In solving the inference problem, the fuzzy joint probability distribution associated with influence diagram in Figure 3 is first obtained. The conditional probability $FP(I/O \mid S,H)$ is then computed by initially integrating over all the states of L and then dividing by $FP(S \mid H)$ using the arithmetic operations described earlier.

$$FP(I/O \mid S,H) = \begin{cases} ([0.5],0.1681,.5076) \text{ for } I/O=I/O_0 \text{ given } S=S_0 \\ (.5076,0.8319,[.5]) \text{ for } I/O=I/O_1 \text{ given } S=S_0 \\ 1 \text{ for } I/O=I/O_1 \text{ given } S=S_1 \\ 0 \quad \text{elsewhere} \end{cases} \qquad (10)$$

The membership function of $FP(I/O_1 \mid S_0,H)$ is plotted in Figure 4. It can be clearly seen that the result is very sensitive to the fuzziness around the point estimate of the input probabilities. An advantage of such an analysis over the more common interval analysis, whose output would be a range no smaller than [0.32,1.0], is graphically illustrated in Figure 4. In our analysis information about how each of these point estimate values are weighted is also provided. In this instance, by observing the distribution of weights associated with the point estimates, one can infer that it is more likely that the probability of the event is close to 1.0 rather than close to 0.32.

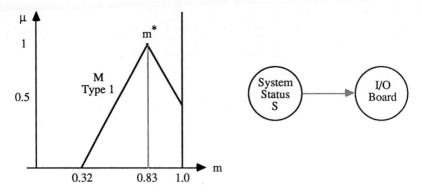

FIGURE 4. Plot of the membership function of fuzzy probability FP(I/O | S,H) and associated influence diagram.

4. SOLVING DECISION PROBLEMS

The transformations involved for solving the decision problem, within an influence diagram framework, are the same as for probabilistic inference - arc reversal and node removal. However, instead of determining the likelihood of occurrence of events, the expected value of a sequence of decisions is computed. An optimal sequence of decisions is selected that maximizes the expected value of the value function. Note that arcs to and from decision nodes cannot be reversed. This arises from informational nature of arcs to the decision node (that is, it shows exactly which variables will be known by the decision maker at the time the decision is made) and causal nature of arcs from the decision node.

4.1. Example of a Fuzzy Decision Problem

Let us continue with the computer assembly diagnostics example, but now consider the following decision problem - after having computed the likelihood of failure of the two components which component should be tested for failure first and repaired if found defective. In an automated assembly operation, this could mean deciding where the computer should be sent for "rework". If the diagnostician is wrong in his or her decision for rework, valuable time would have been wasted by the rework technician and hence in producing the final product. For purposes of illustration, let us assume that the costs of rework, which involves opening the computer and pulling out the appropriate board, testing, and repairing it, is a constant for each board. Let us define the relevant costs to be minimized as follows:

$Debug_L$	=	$150 for the logic board debugging
$Debug_{I/O}$	=	$100 for the I/O board debugging
$Repair_L$	=	$50 for the logic board repair after debugging
$Repair_{I/O}$	=	$100 for the I/O board repair after debugging

The influence diagram in Figure 5 has been modified to show the decision and value node. It has been assumed that a system failure has occurred and this information is known at the time that the rework decision is made. We will assume for the purposes of this illustration that the debugging and repair costs are known precisely. Situations when costs or risk aversion (utility function parameters) are fuzzy can be handled in a similar fashion [Gil and Jain: 1989].

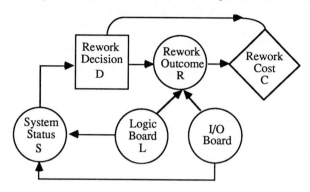

FIGURE 5. Diagnostician's decision problem.

The diagnostician has two choices given that the system status shows a failure $(S=S_0)$:
(1) D_L = Send the logic board to rework first or (2) $D_{I/O}$ = Send the I/0 board to rework first.

4.2. Diagnostician's Decision Problem Solved

Let us now work out the problem at the numerical level, using the probabilistic data given previously. If we assume that the debugging test is "perfect" and influenced only by the states of the logic board, I/O board, and rework decision as shown in Figure 5, the conditional probability distribution of the results "R" is the trivial deterministic function of the actual states of the logic and I/O boards assuming <u>any</u> initial debug decision is made:

$$Pr(R \mid L,\ I/O,\ D,\ H) = \begin{cases} 1 \text{ for } R=L_1,I/O_0, \text{ given } L=L_1 \text{ and } I/O=I/O_0 \text{ for either } D \\ 1 \text{ for } R=L_0,I/O_1, \text{ given } L=L_0 \text{ and } I/O=I/O_1 \text{ for either } D \\ 1 \text{ for } R=L_0,I/O_0, \text{ given } L=L_0 \text{ and } I/O=I/O_0 \text{ for either } D \\ 1 \text{ for } R=L_1,I/O_1, \text{ given } L=L_1 \text{ and } I/O=I/O_1 \text{ for either } D \\ 0 \quad \text{elsewhere} \end{cases}$$

The cost function (value node) depends on the rework outcome "R" and the rework decision "D".

$$C(R, D) = \$Debug\ (R, D) + \$Repair\ (R) \qquad (11)$$

Absorbing the Rework Outcome node "R", the expected value of the cost for a particular decision given the state of the *I/O* and the logic board is obtained as shown in Figure 6. Next, the fuzzy expected cost for each of the decisions is computed by doing the following transformations: reverse arc between *L* and *S*, absorb node *L*, reverse arc between *S* and *I/O* and finally absorb node *I/O*. The expected cost as a function of the remaining variables *S* and *D* is given in equation (12).

88

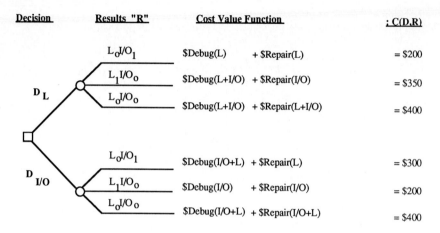

Decision	Results "R"	Cost Value Function	: C(D,R)

FIGURE 6. Conditional expected value of C(D,L,I/O) in the form of a decision tree.

$$<C(S,D)> = \begin{cases} (26, \$226, 78) & \text{for } S = S_0 \text{ and } D = D_L \\ (50, \$285, 15) & \text{for } S = S_0 \text{ and } D = D_{I/O} \end{cases} \quad (12)$$

Which rework decision minimizes the expected cost ? If one considers the range of possible outcomes in equation (12) above, it is not clear which decision - rework the logic or I/O board - is the best under the circumstances. Although the mean expected cost with D_L is lower than that of $D_{I/O}$, the largest expected cost with D_L is higher than the mean of $D_{I/O}$.

4.3. Criteria for Decision Making

The simplest criterion would be to pick the option with the lowest mean expected cost. However, this would be suboptimal if the point estimate of the input probabilities were not accurately known and were to lie in a region which yields decisions that are not optimal based on the expected cost. We would like to derive some useful information from the membership function of the expected cost that will aid in the process of decision making. The concept of *α-intersections* provides a criterion for decision making.

In simple terms we will compute the value of the largest *α-intersection* (maximum membership at the intersection of corresponding membership halves) of all the expected costs under consideration, see Figure 7. Let us call this value α^*. It has the following interpretation, with a possibility of one minus α^* or greater the decision based on the point estimate of fuzzy probabilities (same as lowest mean of the expected costs) is optimal unconditionally.

89

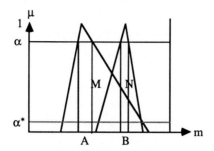

FIGURE 7. Illustration of α-intersections.

α^* can be interpreted as a sensitivity parameter. That is, if α^* is low, the decision is insensitive to input variations in the point estimate. If one decision deterministically dominates the other, then α^* will be zero. If the decision problem can be reduced to one with a single fuzzy probabilistic predecessor of the value node, α^* can also be guaranteed to be zero under first-order stochastic dominance. On the other hand, if α^* is close to one, there is an indication that the expected value of the decision is highly sensitive to the point estimate and that there is a high value for more information or precision associated with the input estimates of probability.

For the general case of multiple variables with fuzzy probabilities, it may be advantageous to consider an alternative to the *α*-intersection* approach. Prior to taking expectation, the difference between the membership functions at each expected cost, subject to constraints that require feasibility and consistency of the probabilities, could be compared. Dominance would be implied if the possibility of the difference membership function is either strictly positive or strictly negative. Other possibilities for ranking the expected cost, for different decisions, include the use of Kolodziejczyk (1986) fuzzy preference relation.

4.4. Example

Let us continue with the computer assembly diagnostics problem. The membership functions of expected costs in equation (12) are shown in Figure 7 (M represents $<C(S_0,D_L)>$ and N represents $<C(S_0,D_{I/O})>$). The two right halves of the membership functions intersect at $\alpha^* =$ 0.064. Hence the possibility that the decision made based on the point estimates is unconditionally optimal is high, around 94%. This indicates that the decision is relatively insensitive to the value of the point estimate of probability, within the range considered here.

5. CONCLUSIONS

An approach to using fuzzy probabilities at the numerical phase of the solution to an inference or decision problem using influence diagrams has been proposed. The use of fuzzy probabilities in influence diagram based expert systems was motivated by the issues that arise in knowledge engineering - reluctance of experts in initially stating precise numerical probabilities and in communicating uncertain information to the user of such a system. In addition, use of fuzzy probabilities provides an efficient computational scheme for obtaining information about the sensitivity of the solution to changes in the point estimates of the probabilities of events.

ACKNOWLEDGEMENTS

The authors wish to acknowledge the advice and discussions with Ashutosh Rege, who initiated the current research into fuzzy influence diagrams [Agogino & Rege: 1987].

REFERENCES

Agogino, A.M. and K. Ramamurthi, 1988, "Real Time Influence Diagrams for Monitoring and Controlling Mechanical Systems," in *Proceedings of the Conference on Influence Diagrams for Decision Analysis, Inference, and Prediction*, University of California, Berkeley, CA 94720 (to be published as Chapter 9, pp. 228-252 in Influence Diagrams, Belief Nets and Decision Analysis, John Wiley & Sons).

Agogino, A.M. and A. Rege, 1987, "IDES: Influence Diagram Based Expert Systems," *Mathematical Modelling*, Vol. 8, pp. 227-233.

Bonissone, P.P. and R.M. Tong, 1985, "Editorial: Reasoning with Uncertainty in Expert Systems," *International Journal of Man-Machine Studies*, Vol. 22, pp. 241-250.

Cheeseman, P., 1985, "In Defense of Probability," *Proceedings of the Ninth International Joint Conference on Artificial Intelligence*, AAAI, Vol. 2, pp. 1002-1009.

Dempster, A.P., 1967, "Upper and Lower Probabilities Induced by a Multivalued Mapping," *Annals of Math. Statistics*, Vol. 38, pp. 325-339.

Dubois, D. and Prade, H., 1980, Fuzzy Sets and Systems - Theory and Applications, Academic Press, New York.

Gil, M.A. and P. Jain, 1989, "The Effects of Perfect and Sample Information on Fuzzy Utilities in Decision-Making," *Proceedings of the Fifth Workshop on Uncertainty in Artificial Intelligence*, pp. 126-133, August 18-20.

Heckerman, D.E., and E.J. Horvitz, 1987, "On the Expressiveness of Rule-based Systems for Reasoning with Uncertainty," *Proceedings of the Sixth National AAAI Conference on Artificial Intelligence*, pp. 121-126, July 1987.

Holstein, C.S., 1973, "A Tutorial on Decision Analysis," in *Readings on The Principles and Applications of Decision Analysis,* Vol. 1, Eds. R.A. Howard and J.E. Matheson, Strategic Decisions Group, 1983, pp. 129-158.

Howard, R.A., 1968, "An Introduction to Decision Analysis," in *Readings on The Principles and Applications of Decision Analysis,* Vol. 1, Eds. R.A. Howard and J.E. Matheson, Strategic Decisions Group, 1983, pp. 21-55.

Jain, P. and Agogino, A.M., 1988a, "Calibration of Fuzzy Linguistic Variables for Expert Systems," *Proceedings of the 1988 ASME International Computers in Engineering Conference*, July, San Francisco, Vol. 1, pp. 313-318.

Jain, P. and Agogino, A.M., 1988b, "Arithmetic Operations on Bayesian Fuzzy Probabilities," Working Paper # 87-0803-3, Revision 3, Berkeley Expert Systems Technology Lab., University of California, Berkeley 94720.

Kahneman, D., P. Slovic, and A. Tversky, 1985, Judgement Under Uncertainty: Heuristics and Biases, Cambridge University Press, Cambridge, England.

Kickert, W.J.M. & Mamdani, E.H., 1979, "Analysis of Fuzzy logic Controller," *Fuzzy Sets and Systems,* Vol. 1, pp. 29-44.

Kolodziejczyk, W., 1986, "Orlovsky's concept of Decision-Making with Fuzzy Preference Relations: Further Results," *Fuzzy Sets and Systems,* Vol. 19, pp. 11-20.

Kyburg, H.E., 1987, "Higher Order Probabilities," *Proceedings of the Third AAAI Workshop on Uncertainty in Artificial Intelligence,* University of Washington, Seattle, pp. 30-38.

Nguyen, H.T., 1979, "Some Mathematical Tools for Linguistic Probabilities," *Fuzzy Sets and Systems,* Vol. 2, pp. 53-65.

Pearl, J., 1987, "Do We Need Higher Order Probabilities and If So, What Do They Mean?," *Proceedings of the Third AAAI Workshop on Uncertainty in Artificial Intelligence,* University of Washington, Seattle, pp. 47-60.

Rege, A. and A.M. Agogino, 1988, "Topological Framework for Representing and Solving Probabilistic Inference Problems in Expert Systems," *IEEE Systems, Man, and Cybernetics,* Vol. 18 (3).

Shachter, R.D., 1985, "Intelligent Probabilistic Inference," *Uncertainty in Artificial Intelligence,* L.N. Kanal and J.F. Lemmer (eds) North-Holland, Amsterdam, pp. 371-382.

Shachter, R.D., 1986, "Evaluating Influence Diagrams," *Operations Research,* Vol. 34, pp. 871-882.

Shafer, G., 1976, A Mathematical Theory of Evidence, Princeton University Press.

Tsukamoto, Y. and Hatano, Y., 1983, "Fuzzy Statement Formation by Means of Linguistic Measures," *IFAC,* France, pp. 129-134.

Wallsten, T.S., Budescu, D.V., Rapoport, A., Zwick, R. and Forsyth, B., 1986, "Measuring the Vague Meanings of Probability Terms," *Journal of Experimental Psychology: General,* Vol. 115, pp. 348-365.

Zadeh, L.A., 1965, "Fuzzy Sets," *Information and Control,* Vol. 8, pp. 338-353.

Zadeh, L.A., 1975, "The Concept of Linguistic Variable and its Application to Approximate Reasoning -I, II, III," *Information Sciences,* Vol. 8, pp. 199-249, Vol. 8, pp. 301-357, Vol. 9, pp. 43-80.

Zadeh, L.A., 1978, "PRUF - a Meaning Representation Language for Natural Languages, *Int. J. Man-Machine Studies,* Vol. 10, pp. 395-460.

Zadeh, L.A., 1981, "Test-score Semantics for Natural Languages and Meaning-representation via PRUF," *Empirical Semantics,* (ed., B.B. Reiger).

Zadeh, L.A., 1983, "The Role of Fuzzy Logic in the Management of Uncertainty in Expert Systems," *Fuzzy Sets and Systems,* Vol. 11, pp. 199-227.

Zadeh, L.A., 1984, "Fuzzy Probabilities," *Information Processing and Management,* Vol. 20, pp. 363-372.

Zimmer, A.C., 1986, "What Uncertainty Judgments Can Tell About the Underlying

Subjective Probabilities," *Uncertainty in Artificial Intelligence*, L.N. Kanal and J.F. Lemmer (eds) North-Holland, Amsterdam, pp. 249-258.

Zimmer, A.C., 1983, "Verbal vs. Numerical Processing of Subjective Probabilities," *Decision Making Under Uncertainty*, (ed., R.W. Scholz), North-Holland Press, Amsterdam.

Uncertainty in Artificial Intelligence 4
R.D. Shachter, T.S. Levitt, L.N. Kanal, J.F. Lemmer (Editors)
© Elsevier Science Publishers B.V. (North-Holland), 1990

A LINEAR APPROXIMATION METHOD
FOR PROBABILISTIC INFERENCE

Ross D. SHACHTER

Department of Engineering-Economic Systems
Terman Engineering Center
Stanford University
Stanford, CA 94305-4025
shachter@sumex-aim.stanford.edu

An approximation method is presented for probabilistic inference with
continuous random variables. These problems can arise in many practical
problems, in particular where there are "second order" probabilities. The
approximation, based on the Gaussian influence diagram, iterates over linear
approximations to the inference problem.

1.   INTRODUCTION

There have been a number of techniques developed in recent years for the efficient
analysis of probabilistic inference problems, represented as Bayes' networks or influence
diagrams (Lauritzen and Spiegelhalter [9], Pearl [12], Shachter [14]). To varying degrees
these methods exploit the conditional independence assumed and revealed in the problem
structure to analyze problems in polynomial time, essentially polynomial in the number
of variables and the size of the largest state space encountered during the evaluation.
Unfortunately, there are many problems of interest for which the variables of interest are
continuous rather than *discrete*, so the relevant state spaces become infinite and the
polynomial complexity is of little help.

In this paper, an algorithm is presented which is based on a linear approximation to the
problem structure. Each of the variables in the model is transformed, and the transformed
variables are assumed to have a Gaussian joint distribution. Through successive
iterations, this linear approximation is refined until it converges to a consistent solution.
Although this method is an approximation rather than an exact solution, it has proven
quite accurate for a variety of problems in health technology assessment. It has tended to
converge rapidly and, since each step is polynomial in the number of variables, this
provides a polynomial heuristic for probabilistic inference with continuous variable.

The algorithm presented in this paper was motivated by a technique for medical technology assessment based on second order probabilities (Eddy [5], Shachter et al [15]). The parameters of interest are the probabilities for different well-defined physical events. The probabilities are uncertain quantities and our prior knowledge about them is described by (usually "noninformative") probability distributions. The relevant medical evidence is then incorporated within a model to provide defensible, posterior distributions for these parameters.

There is an established philosophical basis for this approach, which provides a solid framework for knowledge acquisition in uncertain environments. Recent work argues persuasively that the established methodology for probabilistic reasoning applies *theoretically* to these second-order probabilities just as it does to the first-order kind (Kyburg [8], Pearl [13]). Nonetheless, the *practical* problems are considerable since the higher order probabilities are as a rule continuous distributions while the first order ones are usually discrete.

How then can these continuous probabilistic inference problems be analyzed? There are a several other approaches for dealing with this additional complexity besides the linear method.

1. **Conjugate priors:** If a model's structure allows it, prior distributions for parameters can be chosen from convenient families of conjugate distributions, so that the posterior distributions given the experimental evidence stay within those families (DeGroot [4]). This is an analytical solution to continuous inference problem and the Gaussian model is one example of this approach. Unfortunately, conjugate families are not closed in general when experimental evidence bears (indirectly) on more than one basic parameter or for different forms of experimental evidence.

2. **Discretization:** Discrete techniques can be used by partitioning the sample space. However, processing time goes up with some power of the refinement, while resolution is only grows linearly with it. A similar approach to the one in this paper could be used to iterate, determining new discretizations after each solution.

3. **Numerical integration:** This is discretization of another sort. It is impractical for more than a few dimensions.

4. **Monte Carlo integration:** This is the state-of-the-art approach to numerical integration (Geweke [7]). It can successfully solve the types of problems discussed here,

without the distributional assumptions imposed by the linear approximation method (Fung and Chang [6], Shachter and Peot [18, 19]). While it provides additional accuracy, it does so at substantially greater cost in computer time.

5. **Posterior Mode analysis:** By maximizing the posterior density, one obtains the Bayesian analog to classical maximum likelihood analysis. This can be done efficiently, especially by incorporating an approximation due to Cramèr [3], as described in Berndt et al [2] and Shachter et al [16].

Although some of these other techniques might be more appropriate for a particular problem, the linear approximation possesses a unique combination of speed and generality, providing an efficient approximation to a large class of problems.

2. NOTATION AND BASIC FRAMEWORK

The original model consists of n variables, $Y_1, \ldots, Y_n$, represented by an influence diagram, a network with an acyclic directed graph. Each variable Y_j corresponds to a node j in the diagram, thus the set $N = \{ 1, \ldots, n \}$ contains the nodes in the diagram. Y_J denotes the set of variables corresponding to the indices J. Thus, the direct predecessors of node j, denoted by C(j), represent the set of conditioning variables $Y_{C(j)}$ for Y_j. When the order of the variables is significant the sequence **s**, a vector of indices, is used to represent the vector of variables, Y_s. A sequence **s** is called *ordered* if every predecessor for any node in the sequence precedes it in the sequence.

There are three types of variables represented in the influence diagram in this paper. *Basic parameters* are quantities for which a simple prior distribution is known. They have no conditioning variables, $C(j) = \varnothing$, and they are assumed to be mutually independent a priori. *Deterministic parameters* are quantities defined in terms of other parameters. They have conditioning variables but are assumed to be deterministic functions of those conditioning variables, so that their realizations would be known with certainty if the values of their conditioning variables were known. Finally, there are *experimental evidence* variables, whose realizations have been observed. They are characterized by a conditional distribution (a priori) and an observed value (a posteriori) and are assumed to have exactly one conditioning variable, either a basic or deterministic parameter. These variables and the assumptions about them are depicted in Figure 1. (For more information, see Shachter et al [16].)

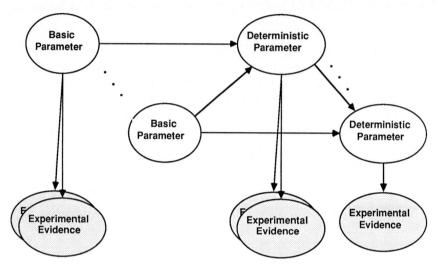

Figure 1. The model assumptions and the different types of variables

In the linear approximation method, a Gaussian variable, X_j, is associated with each parameter variable Y_j, by a deterministic function, $X_j = T_j (Y_j)$. The set of variables X_N is assumed to have a multivariate normal joint distribution characterized by its means $E X_N$ and covariance matrix

$$\Sigma = \Sigma_{NN} = \text{Var} [X_N] = E [X X^T] - E [X] E [X^T].$$

Alternatively, the Gaussian influence diagram (Shachter and Kenley [17]) represents the multivariate Gaussian distribution through its conditional regression equations

$$X_j = E X_j + B_{C(j), j}{}^T [X_{C(j)} - E X_{C(j)}] + \varepsilon_j,$$

where ε_j is a normal random variable with mean 0 and variance v_j, and B is a strictly upper triangular matrix of linear coefficients.

The resulting Gaussian model (if the original variables were integrated out) has the same structure as the original model, with basic and deterministic parameters and experimental evidence variables, except that they are assumed to have a multivariate normal distribution so that they can be manipulated using the operations of the Gaussian influence diagram. (Other similar techniques have been developed to exploit the Gaussian properties in a singly-connected network representation (Pearl [11]).

One last bit of notation denotes the the revision of probabilities over time. The superscript t as in $E^t X$ represents the prior expectation of X in the tth iteration and $E^t [X$

| D] represents its expectation after observing the experimental evidence. The superscript [t] will be omitted for readability whenever it is unambiguous to do so.

3. VARIABLE TRANSFORMATIONS

The fundamental property of the approach is that every variable in the model is transformed into a Gaussian variable, and the resulting multivariate Gaussian model will be maintained and manipulated, in order to provide indirect insight into the original variables and their dependence. Although the model could be embellished further, there are three basic transformations: *scaled*, *log-scaled* and *logistic-scaled*. These allow the representation of unbounded, semi-bounded, and bounded variables, respectively. Denoting a variable in the original model as Y, one in the transformed model as X, and the transformation function as T, the transformations are expressed in terms of *scaling parameters* a and b, where $a \neq b$:

1. **Scaled Transformation:** $Y \in (-\infty, +\infty)$
    $$X = T(Y) = (Y - a) / (b - a).$$
    $$T^{-1}(X) = a + (b - a)X$$
    $$T'(Y) = 1 / (b - a)$$

2. **Log-Scaled Transformation:** $Y \in (a, +\infty)$ if $a < b$ and $Y \in (-\infty, a)$ if $a > b$
    $$X = T(Y) = \ln(Y - a) / (b - a)$$
    $$T^{-1}(X) = a + (b - a)e^X$$
    $$T'(Y) = 1 / |Y - a|$$

3. **Logistic-Scaled Transformation:** $Y \in (a, b)$ if $a < b$ and $Y \in (b, a)$ if $a > b$
    $$X = T(Y) = \ln(Y - a) / (b - Y)$$
    $$T^{-1}(X) = b + (a - b) / (1 + e^X)$$
    $$T'(Y) = 1 / |Y - a| + 1 / |Y - b|$$

Of course, X and Y are random variables, so we must be able to transform from the *distribution* for X to the *distribution* for Y. We approximate this more complicated transformation by the function **T**, which maps the mean and variance of Y into the mean and variance for X, based on the distributional form for Y. These transformations would be exact if the X_N were truly multivariate normal.

1. **Normal Distribution:** $(Y - a) / (b - a) \sim \text{Normal}(\mu, \sigma^2))$
    with $X = (Y - a) / (b - a)$ (scaled transformation)

$$(E X, Var X) = T (E Y, Var Y) = ((E Y - a) / (b - a), Var Y / (b - a)^2)$$
$$(E Y, Var Y) = T^{-1} (E X, Var X) = (a + (b - a) E X, (b - a)^2 Var X)$$

2. **Lognormal Distribution:** $(Y - a) / (b - a) \sim$ Lognormal (μ, σ^2)

   with $X = \ln (Y - a) / (b - a)$ (log-scaled transformation)

   $(E X, Var X) = T (E Y, Var Y) = (\mu, \sigma^2)$

   where $\sigma^2 = Var X = \ln [1 + Var Y (E Y - a)^{-2}]$

   and $\mu = E X = \ln [(E Y - a) / (b - a)] - \sigma^2 / 2$.

   $(E Y, Var Y) = T^{-1} (E X, Var X)$
   $$= (a + (b - a) e^{\{ E X + Var X / 2 \}},$$
   $$(b - a)^2 (e^{Var X} - 1) e^{\{ 2 E X + Var X \}}).$$

3. **Beta Distribution:** $(Y - a) / (b - a) \sim$ Beta (α, β)

   with $X = \ln (Y - a) / (b - Y)$ (logistic-scaled transformation)

   $(E X, Var X) = T (E Y, Var Y) = (\psi (\alpha) - \psi (\beta), \psi' (\alpha) + \psi' (\beta))$

   where ψ and ψ' are the digamma and trigamma functions (Abramowitz and Stegun [1]),

   $$\psi(z) = \frac{d \ln \Gamma(z)}{dz} = \frac{\Gamma'(z)}{\Gamma(z)} \approx \sum_{i = 0}^{9} \frac{-1}{z + i} + \ln w - \frac{w^{-1}}{2} - \frac{w^{-2}}{12} + \frac{w^{-4}}{120} - \frac{w^{-6}}{252},$$

   $$\psi'(z) = \frac{d^2 \ln \Gamma(z)}{dz^2} \approx \sum_{i = 0}^{9} \frac{1}{(z + i)^2} + w^{-1} + \frac{w^{-2}}{2} + \frac{w^{-3}}{6} - \frac{w^{-5}}{30} + \frac{w^{-7}}{42} - \frac{w^{-9}}{30},$$

   and $w = z + 10$.

There is no closed-form expression for the inverse function T^{-1}. If α and β are large enough, then they can be approximated by

$$\alpha_0 \approx .5 + (1 + e^{E X}) / Var X$$

and $\beta_0 \approx .5 + (1 + e^{-E X}) / Var X$.

In general, however, α and β can be estimated using Newton's method and curve fitting using the iterative formula:

$$\begin{bmatrix} \alpha_{k+1} \\ \beta_{k+1} \end{bmatrix} = \max \left\{ \begin{bmatrix} .5\,\alpha_k \\ .5\,\beta_k \end{bmatrix}, \begin{bmatrix} \alpha_k \\ \beta_k \end{bmatrix} - \begin{bmatrix} \psi'(\alpha_k) & -\psi'(\beta_k) \\ \psi''(\alpha_k) & \psi''(\beta_k) \end{bmatrix}^{-1} \begin{bmatrix} \psi(\alpha_k) - \psi(\beta_k) - E[X] \\ \psi'(\alpha_k) + \psi'(\beta_k) - Var[X] \end{bmatrix} \right\},$$

where ψ'' is the tetragamma function (Abramowitz and Stegun [1]),

$$\psi''(z) = \frac{d^3 \ln \Gamma(z)}{dz^3} \approx \sum_{i = 0}^{9} \frac{-2}{(z + i)^3} - w^{-2} - w^{-3} - \frac{w^{-4}}{2} + \frac{w^{-6}}{6} - \frac{w^{-8}}{6}.$$

4.   EXPERIMENTAL OBSERVATIONS

The linear approximation requires that likelihood functions for experimental observations be derived in terms of the transformed, Gaussian parameter X on which the experimental evidence bears. Three kinds of experimental evidence are consider here, assuming samples from either a binomial or normal distribution. Of course, the method could be extended to other experimental designs.

1. **Normal experiment**, n exchangeable samples $\{d_j\}$ from Normal (X, σ^2) where σ^2 is known and the observed values have sample mean $m = \Sigma_j d_j / n$.
  The likelihood function for the evidence is given by
  $$D \mid X \sim \text{Normal } (X, \sigma^2 / n) \text{ with observation } d = m .$$

2. **Normal experiment**, n > 2 exchangeable samples from Normal (X, σ^2) where σ^2 is fixed but unknown and the observed values have sample mean m and sample variance $s = \Sigma_j (d_j - m)^2 / n$.
  The likelihood is t-distributed but can be approximated by
  $$D \mid X \sim \text{Normal } (X, s / (n - 3)) \text{ with observation } d = m .$$

(Note: The preceding likelihoods can also be used for exchangeable samples from a lognormal distribution by transforming each sample.)

3. **Binomial experiment**, $D \sim \text{Binomial } ((Y - a) / (b - a), n)$ with s successes observed
  with $X = \ln Y / (1 - Y)$ (logistic-scaled transformation, a = 0, b = 1)
The likelihood is binomial-distributed but can be approximated by
  $$D \mid X \sim \text{Normal } (X, v) \text{ with observation } d = v [x_2 / v_2 - x_1 / v_1]$$
  where $v = 1 / [1/v_2 - 1/v_1]$,
  $$v_1 = \psi' (\alpha) + \psi' (\beta) ,$$
  $$v_2 = \psi' (\alpha + s) + \psi' (\beta + n - s) ,$$
  $$x_1 = \psi (\alpha) - \psi (\beta) ,$$
  and $x_2 = \psi (\alpha + s) - \psi (\beta + n - s) .$

  (The estimate is most accurate if α and ß are the prior parameters for Y.
Alternatively, they can be set equal, to values such as .5 or 1, but they need not be.)

5. LINEAR APPROXIMATION ALGORITHM

1. The first step in the algorithm is to compute the linear approximations for each of the basic parameters and each of the experimental observations. These values will be used in each iteration of the algorithm. To estimate the original value for the remaining, deterministic parameters compute, in order,

$$E^0 Y_j = E^0 [f_j (Y_{C(j)})] \approx f_j (E^0 Y_{C(j)})$$

(approximating the expected value of the function by the function of the expected value) and set the conditional variance $\text{Var}^0 [Y_j \mid Y_{C(j)}] = 0$.

2. The iterative step in the algorithm proceeds until the algorithm has either converged or diverged. Define the relative difference from one iteration to the next as

$$
\begin{aligned}
r_j^t \quad &= 0 \qquad \text{if } E^t [X_j \mid D] = E^{t-1} [X_j \mid D] \\
&= | E^t [X_j \mid D] - E^{t-1} [X_j \mid D] | / \max \{ \, | E^t [X_j \mid D] |, | E^{t-1} [X_j \mid D] | \, \}
\end{aligned}
$$

otherwise .

Letting $r_{max}^t = \max_j \{ \, r_j^t \, \}$, *convergence* occurs when $r_{max}^t < \varepsilon$ and *divergence* occurs when $r_{max}^t > r_{max}^{t-1} > \dots > r_{max}^{t-m}$ for some m such as 3.

2a. The first step in each iteration is to compute the linear coefficient in the Gaussian influence diagram for the transformed variables. For each variable, in order, compute

$$B_{ij}^t = \left[\frac{\partial x_j}{\partial x_i} \right]_{x_N = E^{t-1}[X_N \mid D]} \, ,$$

taking advantage of the linearity of X_N. Now, using the approximation in 2d,

$$
\begin{aligned}
B_{ij}^t &\approx \left[\frac{\partial T_j (f_j (y_{C(j)}^{t-1}))}{\partial T_i (y_i^{t-1})} \right]_{y_N = E^{t-1}[Y_N \mid D]} \\
&\approx \frac{T_j' (f_j (E^{t-1} [Y_{C(j)} \mid D])) \dfrac{\partial f_j}{\partial y_i} (E^{t-1} [Y_{C(j)} \mid D])}{T_i' (E^{t-1} [Y_i \mid D]])} \, .
\end{aligned}
$$

2b. For basic parameters and experimental outcomes, set the mean and conditional variances for the transformed variables to their original values. For each deterministic parameter, in order,

$$
\begin{aligned}
E^t X_j &= E^t [T_j (Y_j)] = E^t [T_j (f_j (Y_{C(j)}))] \approx T_j (f_j (E^t Y_{C(j)})) \\
&\approx T_j (f_j (E^{t-1} [Y_{C(j)} \mid D])) + \sum_{i \in C(j)} B_{ij}^t (E^t [X_i] - E^{t-1} [X_i \mid D])
\end{aligned}
$$

,

and set the conditional variance to zero. (This is the first order approximation to E X, relative to the posterior from the previous iteration, in the same spirit as Maybeck [10].) Afterwards, compute the unconditional variance Σ, (assuming the variables are ordered), for $j = 1, \ldots, n$:

$$\text{let } s = (1, \ldots, j\text{-}1)$$
$$\Sigma_{sj} = \Sigma_{js}{}^T = \Sigma_{ss} B_{sj}$$
$$\Sigma_{jj} = v_j + B_{sj}{}^T \Sigma_{ss} B_{sj} .$$

2c. The evidence must now be instantiated. This can be performed in several ways, but the theoretical process is represented by the two matrix equations:

$$E [X_N | D] = E X_N + \Sigma_{ND} \Sigma_{DD}{}^{-1} (d - E D)$$
$$\text{and} \quad Var [X_N | D] = \Sigma_{NN} - \Sigma_{ND} \Sigma_{DD}{}^{-1} \Sigma_{DN} .$$

2d. Finally, compute the estimated posterior value for each basic and deterministic parameter in the model, using the inverse transform approximation,

$$(E^t [Y_j | D], Var^t [Y_j | D]) \approx T_j{}^{-1} (E^t [X_j | D], Var^t [X_j | D]) .$$

6. CONCLUSIONS

The method presented here provides a simple, efficient framework for approximating probabilistic inference over continuous distributions. The empirical evidence with the procedure has shown it to be fairly accurate and fast when there is sufficient data. (It can have convergence problems when the priors are flat and there is little experimental evidence.)

Some simple changes can improve the accuracy of the method. First, multiple (conditionally independent) experimental evidence for the same parameter can be "pooled" into a single experiment for the purposes of the approximation. Second, deterministic relationships which are analytically linear can be recognized symbolically, and the corresponding regression coefficients computed in advance. These include linear combinations of scaled variables, products of log-scaled variables, and odds-ratios of logistic-scaled variables.

Finally, there is a useful byproduct of the linear approximation algorithm: an estimate of the correlation between any two of the model parameters,

$$\text{Corr} [X_i, X_j \mid D] =$$
$$\begin{cases} 0 & \text{if Var} [X_i \mid D] = 0 \text{ or Var} [X_j \mid D] = 0 \\ \dfrac{\text{Cov} [X_i, X_j \mid D]}{(\text{Var} [X_i \mid D] \, \text{Var} [X_j \mid D])^{1/2}} & \text{otherwise} \end{cases}$$

This provides insight into the sensitivity of the posterior estimates to changes in prior distributions or additional experimental evidence.

ACKNOWLEDGEMENTS

This research was carried out during a visit to the Center for Health Policy Research And Education at Duke Univeristy, and it was supported by the John A. Hartford Foundation and the National Center for Health Services Research under Grants 1R01-HS-05531-01 and 5R01-HS-05531-02. I thank my colleagues David Eddy, Vic Hasselblad, and Robert Wolpert for their encouragement and collaboration.

REFERENCES

[1]   Abramowitz, M. and Stegun I. A., **Handbook of Mathematical Functions**, (National Bureau of Standards,Washington, 1972)

[2]   Berndt, E., Hall, B., Hall, R., and Hausman, J., Estimation and inference in nonlinear structural models, **Ann. Econ. Soc. Measure 3** (1974) 655-665.

[3]   Cramér, H., **Mathematical Methods of Statistics**, (Princeton University Press, Princton, 1946)

[4]   DeGroot, M. H., **Optimal Statistical Decisions**, (Mc-Graw Hill, New York, 1970).

[5]   Eddy, D. M. The Confidence Profile method: a Bayesian method for assessing health technologies, **Operations Research 37** (1989) 210-228.

[6]   Fung, R. and Chang, K.C., Weighing and integrating evidence for stochastic simulation in Bayesian networks, in: **Proceedings of the Fifth Workshop on Uncertainty in AI**, Windsor, Ontario (1989) 112-117.

[7]   Geweke, J., Bayesian inference in econometric models using Monte Carlo integration, **Econometrica** (to appear).

[8]   Kyburg, H. E., Higher order probabilities, in: Kanal, L. N., Levitt, T. S., Lemmer, J. F., (eds.), **Uncertainty in Artificial Intelligence 3**, (North-Holland, Amsterdam, 1989) 15-22.

[9]   Lauritzen, S. L. and Spiegelhalter, D. J., Local computations with probabilities on graphical structures and their application to expert systems, **J Royal Statist Soc.**

B 50 (1988) 157-224.

[10]   Maybeck, P. S., **Stochastic Models, Estimation, and Control** (Academic Press, New York, 1982)

[11]   Pearl, J., Distributed diagnosis in causal models with continuous variables. (Computer Science Dept, UCLA, 1985).

[12]   Pearl, J., Fusion, propagation and structuring in belief networks. **Artificial Intelligence 29** (1986) 241-288.

[13]   Pearl, J., Do we need higher-order probabilities and, if so, what do they mean? **Proceedings of the Third Workshop on Uncertainty in Artificial Intelligence,** Seattle, WA (1987) 47-60.

[14]   Shachter, R. D., Probabilistic inference and influence diagrams. **Operations Research 36** (1988) 589-604.

[15]   Shachter, R. D., Eddy, D. M., Hasselblad, V. and Wolpert, R., A heuristic Bayesian approach to knowledge acquisition: application to analysis of tissue-type plasminogen activator, in: Kanal, L. N., Levitt, T. S., Lemmer, J. F., (eds.), **Uncertainty in Artificial Intelligence 3,** (North-Holland, Amsterdam, 1989) 183-190.

[16]   Shachter, R. D., Eddy, D. M., and Hasselblad, V., An influence diagram approach to the Confidence Profile method for health technology assessment. **Proceedings, Conference on Influence Diagrams for Decision Analysis, Inference, and Prediction,** Berkeley, CA (1988) to appear in: Oliver, R. M., and Smith, J. Q., (eds.), **Influence Diagrams, Belief Nets and Decision Analysis** (Wiley, London, 1990).

[17]   Shachter, R. D., and Kenley, C. R., Gaussian influence diagrams, **Management Science 35** (1989) 527-550.

[18]   Shachter, R. D. and Peot, M. A., Simulation Approaches to General Probabilistic Inference on Belief Networks, in: **Proceedings of the Fifth Workshop on Uncertainty in AI,** Windsor, Ontario (1989) 311-318.

[19]   Shachter, R. D. and Peot, M. A., Evidential Reasoning Using Likelihood Weighting (EES Dept., Stanford University, 1989).

Uncertainty in Artificial Intelligence 4
R.D. Shachter, T.S. Levitt, L.N. Kanal, J.F. Lemmer (Editors)
© Elsevier Science Publishers B.V. (North-Holland), 1990   105

Minimum Cross Entropy Reasoning
in Recursive Causal Networks [1]

W. X. Wen [2]

Department of Computer Science
The University of Melbourne
Parkville, 3052, Victoria, Australia

A probabilistic method of reasoning under uncertainty is proposed based on
the principle of Minimum Cross Entropy (MCE) and concept of Recursive
Causal Model (RCM). The dependency and correlations among the variables
are described in a special language BNDL (Belief Networks Description
Language). Beliefs are propagated among the clauses of the BNDL programs
representing the underlying probabilistic distributions. BNDL interpreters
in both Prolog and C has been developed and the performance of the method
is compared with those of the others.

1 Introduction

In this paper we describe a scheme for reasoning over belief networks in which known
dependencies among variables can be included and multiple uncertain evidence can
be present. Our scheme is based on the principle of Minimum Cross Entropy (MCE)
(Kullback, 1968; Shore and Johnson, 1980), the concept of Recursive Causal Models
(RCM) (Kiiveri et al., 1984), and the theory of Markov fields (Kemeny et al., 1976).
In this scheme:

1. We introduce a language, the Belief Network Description Language (BNDL), in
   which known dependencies among variables can be explicitly described.

2. We use known results about RCM, Markov fields and acyclic databases to decompose the underlying probabilistic space into subspaces, each of which corresponds
   to a clause of the intermediate BNDL program. The marginal distributions of
   the subspaces exactly match with the maximum likelihood estimate of the distribution of the whole space.

3. We propagate prior information and beliefs among the subspaces according to the
   MCE principle. For reasoning with multiple uncertain evidence, the constraint
   sets created by the evidence are used iteratively, and the principle of greatest
   gradient is used to order the constraint sets.

---

[1]This research is supported by a Commonwealth Postgraduate Research Award and a Sigma Data
Research Award in Computing
[2]Current address: Department of Computer Science, Royal Melbourne Institute of Technology,
GPO Box 2476V, Melbourne, Vic. 3001, Australia

There has been much work on similar problems, this includes:

- Lemmer's *Generalized Bayesian Updating Method* (Lemmer and Barth, 1982; Lemmer, 1983). Using the Lagrange multiplier method, Lemmer derives Jeffrey's rule (Jeffrey, 1957; Diaconis and Zabell, 1982) by minimizing the cross entropy of the underlying distribution subject to one Component Marginal Distribution (CMD). This method produces an approximation of the underlying distribution when uncertain constraints on more than one CMD have to be considered simultaneously. When used with a tree of LEG's (Local Event Group), it can be quite efficient.

- Cheeseman's *Method of Maximum Entropy* (Cheeseman, 1983). Cheeseman uses the Maximum Entropy Principle (MEP) to calculate the distribution given some (not necessarily marginal) constraints by the traditional Lagrange multiplier method. The main advantage of this method is that any constraints can be handled properly while most of the other methods can only handle marginal constraints or, at most, conditional constraints. To avoid an exponential explosion of the number of states as the number of variables increases in the space, Cheeseman uses an efficient method to perform the relevant summations.

- Pearl's *Methods of Bayes Networks* (Pearl, 1986). Pearl proposes an elegant and efficient mechanism to propagate beliefs in parallel among the nodes in the networks which only needs local computation. However, it is difficult for this method to be used in multi-connected belief networks.

- Spiegelhalter's *Method of Graphical/Recursive Models in Contingency Tables* (Spiegelhalter, 1986). According to the statistical theory of graphical/recursive models in contingency tables (Darroch et al., 1980; Wermuth and Lauritzen, 1983). Spiegelhalter decomposes the underlying space into subspaces according to the above statistical theory, and guarantees that the distributions of the subspaces are the marginals of the underlying distribution. Then the beliefs for the evidence are propagated among the subspaces. Mainly Spiegelhalter discusses so called Bayes evidence, and just mentions briefly that uncertain evidence is handled by introducing some extra nodes. It is not clear how this method would deal with the case of multiple uncertain evidence (Wen, 1988c). In his method, Spiegelhalter also uses an updating rule which is quite similar to Jeffrey's rule.

In the next section, we introduce the principle of minimum cross entropy, address some special cases of MCE reasoing, and give our updating rules. Section 3 discusses the concepts of recursive causal models and recursive causal networks and presents a description language for more general belief networks. Some of the basic issues of rasoning under uncertainty in recursive causal networks are also discussed in this section. Reasoning with multiple uncertain evidence is discussed in section 4. Some other important issues for reasoning in belief networks are briefly discussed in section 5, including the issues of decomposition of belief networks, directed cycles in belief networks, and the consistency of the constraints. Finally, in section 6, we give our conclusions.

2 The Principle of Minimum Cross Entropy

Suppose that a system S of m binary random variables $x_i (i = 0, ..., m - 1)$ has a set of 2^m possible states $\{s_j | 0 \leq j < 2^m\}$ with unknown probabilities $\{P(s_j)\}$, and we know some *constraints* and a prior distribution $p^{(0)}$ that estimates p. According to the *principle of minimum cross entropy* (Kullback, 1968; Shore and Johnson, 1980), the best estimate $\hat{p}$ of p that satisfies the constraints is the one with the least cross entropy

$$CE(s_j) = CE(\hat{p}, p^{(0)}) = \sum_{j=0}^{2^m-1} \hat{P}(s_j) \, \log \frac{\hat{P}(s_j)}{P^{(0)}(s_j)}. \tag{2.1}$$

In this paper, we mainly consider marginal, conditional, and other linear equality constraint problems.

2.1 Marginal Constraints and Jeffrey's Rule

According to the values of n distinct variables, x_{i_k}, $(0 \leq i_k < m,\ k = 0, ..., n-1,\ n < m)$, in S, we partition the state space $\{s_j\}$ into 2^n exclusive and exhaustive subspaces called macro-events S_l, $l = 0, ..., 2^n - 1$ such that in each of these events the value of the vector $(x_{i_0}, ..., x_{i_{n-1}})$ is fixed.

Suppose we know the probabilities of all these events, then the MCE posterior distribution that satisfies the constraint set $\{P(S_l) \mid l = 0, ..., 2^n - 1\}$, is (Wen, 1989b)

$$\hat{P}(s_j) = P^{(0)}(s_j) \frac{P(S_l)}{P^{(0)}(S_l)} \tag{2.2}$$

for $l = 0, ..., 2^n - 1$ and $j = 0, ..., 2^m - 1$, if $s_j \in S_l$. This is equivalent to the well known Jeffrey's rule in philosophy and statistics (Jeffrey, 1957; Diaconis and Zabell, 1982) $\hat{P}(s_j) = P^{(0)}(s_j|S_l) P(S_l)$, where $s_j \in S_l$.

Suppose we only know the probabilities of some (not necessarily all) of these events, $p' = \{\nu_{l'} = P(S_{l'}) \mid 0 \leq l' < 2^n\} \subseteq \{P(S_l | l = 0, ..., 2^m - 1\}$. The MCE posterior distribution that satisfies the constraint set p' is

$$\hat{P}(s_j) = \begin{cases} P^{(0)}(s_j) \frac{\nu_{l'}}{P^{(0)}(S_{l'})}, & \exists \nu_{l'} \in p'\ (s_j \in S_{l'}) \\[2mm] P^{(0)}(s_j) \frac{1 - \sum_{\forall\ \nu_{l'} \in p'} \nu_{l'}}{1 - \sum_{\forall\ \nu_{l'} \in p'} P^{(0)}(S_{l'})}, & \forall \nu_{l'} \in p' (s_j \notin S_{l'}). \end{cases} \tag{2.3}$$

This is called "*Partial Normalized Jeffrey's (PNJ) Rule*" (Wen, 1989b). It is easy to see that incomplete information can be used by PNJ Rule.

If all these constraints are 0 or 1, the corresponding evidence is called *Bayesian evidence* (the constraint set is a Bayesian constraint set), otherwise *uncertain evidence* (an uncertain constraint set). If two or more uncertain constraint sets are simultaneously created by the evidence, the corresponding problem is called *reasoning with multiple uncertain evidence*.

2.2 Conditional Constraint Problems

Following the definitions in section 2.1, we partition each S_l further into two exclusive and exhaustive subspaces S_{l_0} and S_{l_1} according to another variable x_{i_n} in S, ($x_{i_n} \notin \{x_{i_k}\}$), such that the value of x_{i_n} is 0 and 1 in S_{l_0} and S_{l_1}, respectively.

Suppose in addition to the prior of S we also know all the conditional constraints $\{P(x_{i_n}|S_l)|l = 0, ..., 2^n - 1)\}$, then we have

$$\hat{P}(s_j) = \rho \, P^{(0)}(s_j) \left(\frac{P(\bar{x}_{i_n}|S_l) \; P^{(0)}(S_{l_1})}{P(x_{i_n}|S_l) \; P^{(0)}(S_{l_0})} \right)^{\beta}, \tag{2.4}$$

where ρ is a normalization factor to get a unit sum, and

$$\beta = \begin{cases} P(x_{i_n}|S_l), & s_j \in S_{l_0}, \\ - P(\bar{x}_{i_n}|S_l), & s_j \in S_{l_1}. \end{cases}$$

(2.4) is called conditional constraint rule (Wen, 1989b).

Similar to the case of marginal constraints, suppose we only know some (not necessarily all) of the conditional constraints $p'' = \{\mu_{l'} = P(x_{i_n}|S_{l'}) \mid 0 \leq l' < 2^n)\}$, where $p'' \subseteq \{P(x_{i_n}|S_l) \mid l = 0, ..., 2^n - 1\}$ in addition to the prior $p^{(0)}$. Then the MCE posterior distribution subject to these constraints is

$$\hat{P}(s_j) = \rho\sigma P^{(0)}(s_j) \tag{2.5}$$

where

$$\rho = \frac{1}{\sum_{\forall \mu_{l'}} \left(\alpha_{l'}^{\mu_{l'}} P^{(0)}(S_{l_1'}) + \alpha_{l'}^{1-\mu_{l'}} P^{(0)}(S_{l_0'}) \right) + 1 - \sum_{\forall \mu_{l'}} P^{(0)}(S_{l'})},$$

$$\alpha_{l'} = \frac{(1 - \mu_{l'})P^{(0)}(S_{l_1'})}{\mu_{l'} P^{(0)}(S_{l_0'})},$$

$$\sigma = \begin{cases} \alpha_{l'}^{\beta_{l'}}, & \exists \mu_{l'} \in p''(s_j \in S_{l'}), \\ 1, & \forall \mu_{l'} \in p''(s_j \notin S_{l'}), \end{cases}$$

and

$$\beta_{l'} = \begin{cases} \mu_{l'}, & \exists \mu_{l'} \in p''(s_j \in S_{l_0'}) \\ \mu_{l'} - 1, & \forall \mu_{l'} \in p''(s_j \in S_{l_1'}). \end{cases}$$

(2.5) is called *partial conditional constraint rule* (Wen, 1989b) with which incomplete information can be used in reasoning.

2.3   MCE Problems with Linear Constraints

An MCE problem with Linear Equality Constraint (LEC):

$$\begin{cases} Minimize \quad (2.1), \\ subject\ to \quad \sum_{j=0}^{2^m-1} a_{kj}\hat{P}(s_j) = b_k, \quad k = 0,...,n-1. \end{cases} \tag{2.6}$$

is equivalent to minimization of the following *Dual function* (Luenberger, 1973) with respect to the Lagrange multiplier vector $\vec{\lambda} = (\lambda_0,...,\lambda_{n-1})$ without constraints

$$D(\vec{\lambda}) = \sum_{j=0}^{2^m-1} P^{(0)}(s_j)\, e^\beta \; + \; \sum_{k=0}^{n-1} \lambda_k\, b_k,$$

The gradients of the Dual are

$$\nabla(D_k) = D'_k = -\sum_{j=0}^{2^m-1} a_{kj} P^{(0)}(s_j) e^\beta \; + \; b_k = -\sum_{j=0}^{2^m-1} a_{kj}\,\hat{P}(s_j) \; + \; b_k. \tag{2.7}$$

These gradients are very easy to obtain, which are merely the differences between the two sides of the constraint equations. This simple expression of gradients is also very important for the reasoning method proposed in section 4.

3   Recursive Causal Networks

According to Kiiveri et al (Kiiveri et al., 1984), a *Recursive Causal Model (RCM)* is characterized by an ordering of the variables $x_0,...,x_{m-1}$ and the factorization of its joint probability:

$$P(x_0,...,x_{m-1}) = P(x_0,...,x_{n-1}) \prod_{n \le j < m} P(x_j|D_j), \tag{3.1}$$

where $D_j = \{x_{j_0},...,x_{j_k}\}$, $0 \le j_0 < ... < j_k < j$. The set $S_{root} = \{x_0,...,x_{n-1}\}$ is called the root of the model.

A *Recursive Causal Network (RCNet)* is a directed acyclic graph $< V, E >$ where the nodes in V represent the variables of an RCM and the links from the nodes in D_j to the node x_j ($D_j \subset V$, $x_j \in V$) represent the dependencies (conditional probabilities $P(x_j|D_j)$) of x_j on the nodes in D_j.

For the well known example of Cooper (Spiegelhalter, 1986; Pearl, 1986):

Metastatic cancer (A) is a possible cause of a brain tumor (C) and is also an explanation for increased total serum calcium (B). In turn, either of these could explain a patient falling into a coma (D). Severe headache (E) is also possibly associated with a brain tumor.

we have the following RCM with $S_{root} = \{A\}$:

$$P(A, B, C, D, E) = P(A) \cdot P(B|A) \cdot P(C|A) \cdot P(D|B, C) \cdot P(E|C),$$

where the initial description of the distribution is:

$$
\begin{array}{llll}
P(A) & = 0.2, & & \\
P(B|A) & = 0.8, & P(B|\overline{A}) & = 0.2, \\
P(C|A) & = 0.2, & P(C|\overline{A}) & = 0.05, \\
P(D|B, C) & = 0.8, & P(D|B, \overline{C}) & = 0.8, \\
P(D|\overline{B}, C) & = 0.8, & P(D|\overline{B}, \overline{C}) & = 0.05, \\
P(E|C) & = 0.8, & P(E|\overline{C}) & = 0.6.
\end{array}
$$

The corresponding RCNet is shown in Fig. 1.

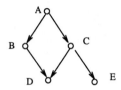

Figure 1: Cooper's Example

To describe general belief networks of which RCNet is a special case, we present a language, BNDL (Belief Network Description Language). A BNDL program consists of a set of clauses:

$$program ::= \{clause\} \tag{3.2}$$

There are three types of clauses corresponding to the three types of basic components in a recursive causal network:

$$
\begin{array}{llll}
clause & ::= & ? - query. & (3.3) \\
& | & head \rightarrow body. & (3.4) \\
& | & observation. & (3.5)
\end{array}
$$

1. **Queries** correspond to the root of the RCNet or S_{root}. In (3.3), *query* is a list of pairs each of which consists of a set of propositions corresponding to a clique in S_{root} and a list of probabilities – the joint prior of the clique, which should be known before the query.

$$
\begin{array}{lll}
query & ::= & proposition\_list : prior\{, proposition\_list : prior\} \\
proposition\_list & ::= & proposition\{, proposition\} \\
proposition & ::= & identifier \\
pr\_list & ::= & [pr\{, pr\}] \\
pr & ::= & expression.
\end{array}
$$

In most cases, the expressions are merely real numbers in [0.0, 1.0]. In the case of incomplete description, -1.0 is allowed in pr_list to represent unknown probability.

2. **Inference rule** (3.4) corresponds to a set of links from the nodes in D_j (head) to the node x_j (body) in the RCNet (the conditional probabilities $P(x_j|D_j)$ in (3.1)).

$$head \quad ::= \quad proposition\_list$$
$$body \quad ::= \quad proposition : pr\_list$$

where the list pr_list contains the conditional probabilities corresponding to $P(x_j|D_j)$ in (3.1):

3. **Observations** correspond to the leaves or terminal nodes. Here, we have

$$observation \quad ::= \quad proposition\_list.$$

where $proposition\_list$ is a set of variables to be observed.

For Cooper's example, the corresponding BNDL program is as follows

$$
\begin{aligned}
? - A \qquad\quad &: \quad [0.8000, 0.2000]. \\
A \rightarrow B \qquad &: \quad [0.2000, 0.8000]. \\
A \rightarrow C \qquad &: \quad [0.0500, 0.2000]. \\
B, C \rightarrow D \quad &: \quad [0.0500, 0.8000, 0.8000, 0.8000]. \\
C \rightarrow E \qquad &: \quad [0.6000, 0.8000].
\end{aligned}
$$

Several versions of BNDL interpreters in Prolog and C have been developed. The interpreters have two phases:

1. In the first phase, a **preprocessor** converts the BNDL source into an intermediate form which corresponds to an acyclic hypergraph (Spiegelhalter, 1986; Wen, 1989b). According to (2.2) – (2.5) or the method in section 2.3, the prior information is propagated from S_{root} around the network to give a complete description to the network. After preprocessing, each clause in the intermediate program is followed by a list of the joint probabilities of all variables in its head and body.

2. **Reasoning** under uncertainty is accomplished in the second phase of the interpreter. The constraint sets (eg. marginal, conditional, expectation, and even moment constraints) on the observed variables are ordered and propagated from clause to clause if their gradients (see (2.7)) are greater than the corresponding thresholds. If all gradients are less than the corresponding thresholds the reasoning phase stops and the result is reported.

From (3.1), generally speaking, for an intermediate BNDL program we have

$$P(S) = P(query) \prod_{i=1}^{R} P(body_i|head_i), \qquad (3.6)$$

where R is the number of rules in the intermediate program. The cross entropy of the joint probability can be expressed as (Wen, 1989b; Wise, 1986)

$$CE(S) = CE(query) + \sum_{i=1}^{R}(CE(head_i \cup body_i) - CE(head_i)) \qquad (3.7)$$

It can be shown from (3.7) (Wen, 1989b; Wise, 1986) an RCNet corresponding to an intermediate BNDL program has the following properties:

- **Parallel Intersections:** If we know all $P(head_i)$'s then the minimum $CE(S)$ is obtained by minimizing $CE(query)$ and each $CE(head_i \cup body_i)$ separately subject to $P(head_i)$ and any other constraints. This property has been used by Wise (Wise, 1986) in his algorithms.

- **Running Intersections:** If there are constraints in only one of the sets $query$ and $(head_i \cup body_i)$'s, then the minimum $CE(S)$ is obtained by minimizing the cross entropy of that particular set subject to the constraints and, step by step, minimizing the others subject to the $P(head_i)$'s obtained. This property has been used by Lemmer (Lemmer and Barth, 1982; Lemmer, 1983) and Spiegelhalter (Spiegelhalter, 1986) in their algorithms.

For Cooper's example, we have the following BNDL intermediate program:

$$
\begin{array}{llll}
A & \rightarrow & B, C & : \ [0.608, 0.032, 0.152, 0.008, 0.032, 0.008, 0.128, 0.032]. \\
B, C & \rightarrow & D & : \ [0.608, 0.032, 0.008, 0.032, 0.056, 0.224, 0.008, 0.032]. \\
C & \rightarrow & E & : \ [0.368, 0.552, 0.016, 0.064]. \\
D & & & : \ [0, 68, 0.32]. \\
E & & & : \ [0.384, 0.616].
\end{array}
$$

Thus, from (3.7) we have

$$CE(A, B, C, D, E) = CE(A, B, C) + CE(B, C, D) + CE(CE) - CE(B, C) - CE(C).$$

If the observed probabilities of D and E are 0 and 1, respectively, the reasoning procedure is as follow:

1. Use $P(D) = 0.0$ to update $\{B, C, D\}$ by (2.2), and calculate $P(B, C)$ and $P(C)$ from the result.

2. Use $P(B, C)$ and $P(C)$ obtainted in step 1 to update $\{A, B, C\}$ and $\{C, E\}$, respectively.

3. Use another constraint $P(E) = 1$ to update one of the result destributions – the distribution $\{C, E\}$ obtained in step 2 – calculate $P(C)$ from the result.

4. update $\{A, B, C\}$ by $P(C)$ obtained in step 3, and calculate $P(B, C)$ from the result. The final result $P(A) = 0.0973$ is also reported in this step.

5. Update $\{B, C, D\}$ by $P(B, C)$ obtained in step 4 to keep the consistency of the whole distribution.

4   Reasoning with Multiple Uncertain Evidence

According to (Wen, 1989b), (2.2) – (2.5) can also be used as an approximation for reasoning with multiple uncertain evidence if we use the constraint sets one at a time. It has been proved (Wen, 1989b) that

- The approximation is at each step a unit sum distribution. That is, the approximation is consistent by itself.

- The approximation improves at each step according to the MCE principle. That is, the value of cross entropy decreases at each step.

- The procedure converges to the real solution of the corresponding minimum cross entropy problem with two or more subspace constraints which are used simultaneously.

As pointed out by Brown (Brown, 1959) (see also (Diaconis and Zabell, 1982)), after one constraint set is used to update the approximation, the constraint sets used before may no longer be satisfied, and the last constraint set dominates. So, each constraint set may need be used more than once to attain convergence. The constraint sets need not be used in any particular order, but the order will have an effect on the rate of convergence. Similar to strategies in conventional nonlinear optimization (Luenberger, 1973), we have found that if we use the constraint sets in the order of greatest gradient, we can significantly speed up convergence.

Our scheme uses the following gradient-threshold method to control the termination of the reasoning iteration and the precision of the result:

1. For those constraint sets that we really don't want to be washed out by other constraint sets (Wise, 1986), give them zero thresholds or small ones.

2. For those which are not very important, specify large or even unit thresholds.

3. At each each iterative step, the inference system checks and updates the gradients of the constraint sets and uses the constraint set with the greatest gradient.

4. When the gradients of all the constraint sets are smaller than the thresholds specified beforehand, the iteration terminates.

This method is very similar to the Gauss-Southwell method (Luenberger, 1973), thus can be expected to converge linearly and with a ratio close to that of steepest descent method (see (Wen, 1988a)).

Note that, sometimes we cannot elicit a complete set of constraints for a subspace, instead, we only know a part of them. In this case, (2.3) and (2.5) still can be used to obtain a consistent MCE result.

Suppose we have a simple recursive causal model $\{A, B, C\}$ (Fig. 2) as follows:

$$P(A, B, C) = P(A) \cdot P(B|A) \cdot P(C|A)$$

and the initial description of the network is:

$$P(A) = 0.7000,$$
$$P(B|\overline{A}) = 0.2000, \quad P(B|A) = 0.4000,$$
$$P(C|\overline{A}) = 0.8000, \quad P(C|A) = 0.1000.$$

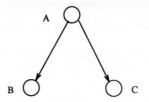

Figure 2: A simple example

We have the following BNDL source program:

$$? - A \ : [0.3000, 0.7000].$$

$$A \to B \ : [0.2, 0000.4000].$$

$$A \to C \ : [0.8000, 0.1000].$$

After preprocessing, we have the following intermediate form of the program

$$A \ \to \ B \ : \ [0.2400, 0.0600, 0.4200, 0.2800].$$

$$A \ \to \ C \ : \ [0.0600, 0.2400, 0.6300, 0.0700].$$

Suppose we know constraints (for first order marginal distributions, we only talk about constraints instead of constraint sets) $P(B) = 0.3300$ and $P(C) = 0.9500$. Because $|\nabla C| = 0.6400$ is greater than $|\nabla B| = 0.0100$, we choose P(C) to update the distribution $\{A, C\}$ first. By (2.2) we obtain a new clause

$$A \ \to \ C \ : \ [0.0043, 0.7355, 0.0457, 0.2145].$$

and $P(A) = 0.2602$. Then use it to update $\{A, B\}$ we get

$$A \ \to \ B \ : \ [0.5919, 0.1480, 0.1561, 0.1041].$$

where $P(B) = 0.2520$, and $|\nabla B| = 0.0780$. If we have specified a threshold 0.01 beforehand, then we have to use the remaining constraint P(B) to update the result again and obtain

$$A \ \to \ B \ : \ [0.5302, 0.1937, 0.1398, 0.1363],$$

which gives $P(A) = 0.2761$. Continue updating by $P(A)$, we have

$$A \ \to \ C \ : \ [0.0043, 0.7197, 0.0484, 0.2276].$$

where $P(C) = 0.9473$. $|\nabla C| = 0.0027$ is less than 0.01 which means that we may stop here. Comparing the result $P(A) = 0.2761$ here with the MCE result $P(A) = 0.2744$, we have an error is 0.0017. If we have a smaller threshold, say 0.001, then we need one more pass (by one pass we mean using the constraints or constraint sets once each), so that a more accurate result $P(A) = 0.2743$ is obtained. Both the error and $|\nabla C|$ in this case is less than 0.0001. If we use constraint $P(B)$ first, even for the threshold

0.01, two passes are needed to obtain a result of $P(A) = 0.2742$ with an error greater than 0.0001 and $|\nabla B| = 0.0005$.

For the same prior distribution, several cases of different constraints are given in Table 4.1. It is easy to see from Table 4.1 that the accuracy of our method is quite satisfactory and the greatest gradient principle for selection of constraints speeds up convergence and improves the accuracy.

Table 4.1 More Constraint Problems for Example 6.1							
Constraints					$Ps(A)$		
$P(B)$	gradient	$P(C)$	gradient	Pass	$P(B)$ first	$P(C)$ first	MCE value
0.3300	-0.0100	0.9500	0.6400	1.	0.2900	0.2761	0.2744
				2.	0.2742	0.2743	
1.0000	0.6600	0.1500	-0.1600	1.	0.8666	0.8950	0.8665
				2.	0.8666	0.8666	
0.1500	-0.1600	0.6700	0.3600	1.	0.4296	0.4188	0.4331
				2.	0.4357	0.4333	
0.2700	-0.0700	0.0500	-0.2600	1.	0.87340	0.8691	0.8711
				2.	0.8705	0.8712	
0.6500	0.3100	0.8500	0.5400	1.	0.3792	0.4154	0.3945
				2.	0.3988	0.3934	
0.9500	0.6100	0.8500	0.5400	1.	0.4435	0.4576	0.4474
				2.	0.4483	–	

In some cases, if the prior of the two paths are much different, and the constraints from both sides are quite close to 1.0, more pass may be needed to get an accurate results. For example, if we change the prior of the above example to

$$P(A) = 0.7$$
$$P(B|\overline{A}) = 0.2000, \quad P(B|A) = 0.9000,$$
$$P(C|\overline{A}) = 0.8000, \quad P(C|A) = 0.1000,$$

and the constraints are $P(B) = 0.9500$ and $P(C) = 0.8500$. We have the following results

$$P(A) = \begin{cases} 0.8947 & --MCE\ result \\ 0.9112 & --pass_1 \\ 0.8797 & --pass_2 \\ 0.8949 & --pass_3 \end{cases}$$

5 Other Important Issues

To reduce the computational amount of probabilistic reasoning, the underlying spaces are often decomposed into small subspaces. As mentioned in section 1, several authors addressed this issue, including

- Lemmer (Lemmer and Barth, 1982; Lemmer, 1983) proposes an efficient algorithm to select CMD's for underlying distributions. This may be the earliest decomposition method for belief networks. Although this method only handles the case of a tree of LEG's, it provides a good methodology to handle computational complexity in probabilistic reasoning.

- To avoid an exponential explosion of the number of states as the number of variables increases, Cheeseman (Cheeseman, 1983) gives an efficient method to perform the relevant summations in ME reasoning. The summations are grouped into some subsummations. The computational amount of the whole problem is reduced by this method significantly. It is easy to see that the basic idea behind this "grouping" is actually the same as decomposition.

- Spiegelhalter (Spiegelhalter, 1986; Lauritzen and Spiegelhalter, 1988) uses an efficient "fill-in" algorithm (Tarjan and Yannakakes, 1984), to triangulate the underlying networks. This method can often obtain good results. Computing the minimum fill-in has been proven to be NP-complete (Yannakakis, 1981). That is to say, it is very hard to obtain the optimal result by existing methods. Furthermore, as pointed by Kong (see the discussion in (Lauritzen and Spiegelhalter, 1988)), a result with a minimum fill-in is not necessarily the best result for the belief network decomposition.

- Kong and Dempster (Kong, 1986; Dempster and Kong, 1988) (see also the discussion in (Lauritzen and Spiegelhalter, 1988)) propose searching for a fill-in that minimizes the maximal clique state size to triangulate the underlying networks. Although the maximal clique state size is vital to computational cost, the solution with the minimum maximal clique state size is still not necessarily the best. The problem to find a fill-in that minimizes the maximal clique state size has also been shown to be NP-complete (Arnborg et al., 1987).

In (Wen, 1989c; Wen, 1989b), we propose a decomposition method which directly minimizes the total number of states in the decomposed space. We show that the problem of optimal decomposition of belief networks under our framework, just like all other frameworks, is NP-hard. Because of this NP-hardness, an algorithm of belief network decomposition is proposed in (Wen, 1989c) based on simulated annealing (Kirkpatrick et al., 1983).

Another advantage of our scheme is that it is easy to be generalized to handle directed cycles in the belief networks (Wen, 1989b; Wen, 1989a) based on the ME/MCE principles and the theory of Markov random fields. This can be very difficult for some other methods (Wise, 1986).

In (Wen, 1989b; Wen, 1989a), we also discuss some issues like the consistency of the constraints on the underlying networks. It has been shown that checking the global consistency in a framework (relational databases) similar to ours is NP-hard (Honeyman et al., 1980). We propose an efficient method to check the pairwise consistency between subspaces locally. The equivalence of the global consistency and the pairwise consistency is guaranteed by the acyclicity of our decomposition (Beeri et al., 1983).

6   Conclusions

In this paper, relationships among the principle of minimum cross entropy, the concept of recursive causal models, and rule-based systems are investigated. An RCNet can be decomposed into small pieces and the joint distribution of the RCNet matches with the marginal distributions of the pieces perfectly in the sense of MCE reasoning with a single constraint set or Bayesian constraint sets. The problem of multiple uncertain evidence is solved by using the constraints one at a time iteratively, and the convergence can be speeded up by careful ordering of the constraint sets. An overall scheme of MCE reasoning in recursive causal networks is proposed based on the above analysis. The dependency and correlations among the variables are described in a special language BNDL.

Our method proposed overcomes the computational difficulty in probabilistic reasoning in the case of large sparse probability space. The number of states for which the probabilities are evaluated in our method is less than $2^n \cdot k$, where n is the number of variables in the largest clause in the BNDL intermediate program and k is the number of clauses in the program. For the conventional MCE reasoning method the number of states to be evaluated is equal to 2^m, where m is the number of variables in the whole space. The efficiency of the method is quite satisfactory because of the linear convergence of the steepest gradient method. In our experiences, in most cases the method can produce quite accurate results in a few passes of updating. For Bayes evidence it always needs only one pass to produce the right result. In this case, it has Spiegelhalter's method as a special case, for which it is not clear how to handle the case of multiple uncertain evidence.

The method proposed here has been generalized to handle belief networks with directed cycles. An efficient decomposition method is also developed based on simulated annealing.

Several verions of BNDL interpreters have been developed and the scheme has been incorporated into PESS (a Probabilistic Expert System Shell) (Wen et al., 1989) and some applications have also been implemented. Based on the method proposed in this paper, a highly parallel computational model – Boltzmann-Jeffrey Machine Networks (BJMNet) – has been proposed (Wen, 1988b) and a parallel BNDL interpreter for Encore Computer – a shared memory multiprocessor system – has been developed for reasoning under uncertainty in parallel and to simulate the corresponding parallel hardware computational model (Wen, 1989d).

Acknowledgement

Thanks to E. A. Sonenberg, R. Watson, B. Marksjo, P. Cheeseman, J. Lemmer, M. Henrion, and B. Wise for valuable discussions, instructive comments, encouragement and helpfulness.

References

Arnborg, S., Corneil, D. G., and Proskurowski, A. (April 1987). Complexity of finding enbeddings in a k-tree. *SIAM J. Alg. Meth.*, 8(2):277–284.

Beeri, C., Fagin, R., Maier, D., and Yannakakis, M. (July 1983). On the desirability of acyclic database schemes. *Journal of the ACM*, 30(3):479–513.

Brown, D. (1959). A note on approximations to discrete probability distributions. *Information and Control*, 2:386–392.

Cheeseman, P. (1983). A method of computing generalized bayesian probability values for expert systems. *in Proc. IJCAI 83*, pages 198–202.

Darroch, J. N. et al. (1980). Markov fields and loglinear models for contingency tables. *Annals of Statistics*, 8:522–539.

Dempster, A. P. and Kong, A. (1988). Uncertain evidence and aritificial analysis. *Journal of Statistical Planning and Inference*, 20:355–368.

Diaconis, P. and Zabell, S. L. (1982). Updating subjective probability. *Journal of the American Statistical Association*, 77(380):822–830.

Honeyman, P., Ladner, R. E., and Yannakakis, M. (1980). Testing the universal instance assumption. *Information Processing Letters*, 10(1):14–19.

Jeffrey, R. (1957). Contributions to the theory of inductive probability. *Ph. D. thesis, Department of Philosophy, Princeton University.*

Kemeny, J. G., l. Snell, J., and Knapp, A. W. (1976). *Denumerable Markov Chains.* Springer, Heidelberg, New York,Berlin.

Kiiveri, H., Speed, T. P., and Carlin, J. B. (1984). Recursive causal models. *J. Australian Math. Soc., Ser. A*, 36:30–52.

Kirkpatrick, S., Gellat, C. D., and Vecchi, M. P. (May 1983). Optimaization by simulated annealing. *Science*, 220(4598):671–680.

Kong, A. (1986). Construction of a tree of cliques from a triangulated graph. *Technical Report S-118, Department of Statistics, Harvard University.*

Kullback, S. (1959, 1968). *Information Theory and Statistics.* Dover Publication, Inc., New York.

Lauritzen, S. L. and Spiegelhalter, D. J. (1988). Local computations with probabilities on graphical structures and their application to expert systems. *J. R. Statist. Soc. B*, 50(2).

Lemmer, J. F. (1983). Generalized bayesian updating of incompletely specified distributions. *Large Scale Systems*, 5.

Lemmer, J. F. and Barth, S. W. (1982). Efficient minimum information updating for bayesian inferencing. *in Proc. Nation. Conf. on Artificial Intelligence. AAAI, Pittsburgh.*

Luenberger, D. G. (1973). *Introduction to Linear and Nonlinear Programming.* Addison-Wesley Pub. Comp., Reading, Massachusetts.

Pearl, J. (1986). Fusion, propagation, and structuring in belief networks. *Artificial intelligence*, 29:241–288.

Shore, J. and Johnson, R. W. (Jan 1980). Axiomatic derivation of the principle of maximum entropy and the principle of minimum cross entropy. *IEEE Trans. Infor. Theory*, IT-26(1):26–37.

Spiegelhalter, D. J. (1986). Probabilistic reasoning in predictive expert systems. *in Uncertainty in artificial intelligence, (ed) L. N. Kanal and J. F. Lemmer, North-Holland, Amsterdam, New York, Oxford, Tokyo.*

Tarjan, R. E. and Yannakakes, M. (Aug. 1984). Simple linear-time algorithms to chordality of graphs, test acyclicity of hypergraphs, and selectively reduce acyclic hypergraphs. *SIAM J. Compt.*, 13(3):566–579.

Wen, W. X. (1988a). Analytical and numerical methods for minimum cross entropy problems. *Technical Report 88/26, Comput. Science., The University of Melbourne.*

Wen, W. X. (Aug. 1988b). Parallel mce reasoning and boltzmann-jeffrey machine networks. *in Proc. 3rd IEEE International Symp. on Intelligent Control, Arlington, VA, USA.*

Wen, W. X. (Aug. 1989a). Directed cycles in causal networks. *in Proc. 5th International Workshop on Uncertainty in AI, Windsor, Canada.*

Wen, W. X. (July 1988c). Probabilistic reasoning with multiple uncertain evidence. *Technical Report 88/34, Computer Science, The University of Melbourne.*

Wen, W. X. (July 1989b). Markov and gibbs fields and mce reasoning in general belief networks. *Technical Report 89/13, Computer Science, The University of Melbourne.*

Wen, W. X. (Nov. 1989d). Parallel mce reasoning in recursive causal networks. *in Proc. 1989 IEEE International Conference on Systems, Man, and Cybernetics, Boston, MA, USA.*

Wen, W. X. (Oct. 1989c). Optimal decomposition of belief networks. *Technical Report (draft), Department of Computer Science, The University of Melbourne.*

Wen, W. X., Marksjo, B., Neil, C., and Sonenberg, E. A. (Nov. 1989). An approach to probabilistic inference in belief networks. *to appear in Proc. AI-89 (Australian Joint Conference on Artifitial Intelligence), Melbourne, Australia.*

Wermuth, N. and Lauritzen, S. L. (1983). Graphical and recursive models for contingency tables. *Biometrika*, 70:537–552.

Wise, B. P. (June 1986). An experimental comparison of uncertain inference systems. *Ph.D. Thesis, Engineering and Public Policy, Carnegie-Mellon University.*

Yannakakis, M. (1981). Computing the minimum fill-in is np-complete. *SIAM J. Alg. Meth.*, 2:77–79.

Uncertainty in Artificial Intelligence 4
R.D. Shachter, T.S. Levitt, L.N. Kanal, J.F. Lemmer (Editors)
© Elsevier Science Publishers B.V. (North-Holland), 1990

PROBABILISTIC SEMANTICS AND DEFAULTS

Eric Neufeld†*, David Poole‡** and Romas Aleliunas§

†Department of Computational Science,
University of Saskatchewan,
Saskatoon, Canada, S7N 0W0

‡Department of Computer Science
University of British Columbia
Vancouver, Canada, T6G 2E1

§Centre for System Science,
Simon Fraser University,
Vancouver, Canada, V5A 1S6

There is much interest in providing probabilistic semantics for defaults but most approaches seem to suffer from one of two problems: either they require numbers, a problem defaults were intended to avoid, or they generate peculiar side effects.

Rather than provide semantics for defaults, we address the problem defaults were intended to solve: that of reasoning under uncertainty where numeric probability distributions are not available. We describe a non-numeric formalism called an inference graph based on standard probability theory, conditional independence and sentences of *favouring* where a favours $b \equiv favours(a, b) \equiv p(a|b) > p(a)$.

The formalism seems to handle the examples from the nonmonotonic literature. Most importantly, the sentences of our system can be verified by performing an appropriate experiment in the semantic domain.

1. INTRODUCTION

Though default reasoning involves reasoning under conditions of uncertainty, some argue it is not probabilistic reasoning. Reiter and Crisculo [1] distinguish the two by suggesting different interpretations for the word "most". Probabilistic reasoning gives "most" a statistical connotation, whereas default logic gives it a prototypical sense.

*Research supported by NSERC grants OGP0041937 and EQP0041938.
**Research supported by NSERC grant A6260.
* * *Supported by SFU president's fund.

On the other hand, Poole *et al* [2] claim defaults should not be thought of as having any meaning in the sense of "most" or "typical"; they are statements the user is prepared to accept as part of an explanation as to why something may be true.

What, then, does a default mean? Within the default logic camp, we know of no work which provides a semantics for defaults, in the sense that an experiment is described that can be performed in the semantic domain to verify the truth of a default. It is therefore compelling to view defaults as qualitative probabilistic statements where numeric distributions are unavailable. We survey some of these views but note most require numbers, something default reasoning intended to avoid, or have side effects.

Rather than "add semantics" to defaults, we construct a sound non-numeric probabilistic formalism called an *inference graph* based on an idea similar to Wellman's [3] qualitative influence diagrams. We explore its mathematical properties, then apply it to the standard examples.

2. WHAT'S IN A DEFAULT?

Early discussions of default inference [1, 2] considered two kinds of knowledge, a set of facts F known to be true and a set Δ of defaults. A sentence g might be *explained* by finding a set of ground instances of Δ consistent with F such that g was a logical consequence of F and D. Poole *et al* [2] argue that that if g corresponds to *observations*, then construction of appropriate sets D results in *diagnosis*. If the truth of g is not known, construction of an appropriate D might be viewed as justification for *predicting g*, or inferring g "by default".

A problem such reasoners run into is that there is often another D' such that $F \cup D'$ predicts $\neg g$; this is known as the *multiple extension problem*. (For the purpose of this paper, it is sufficient to think of an extension as the deductive closure of a maximal consistent set of defaults and facts.) This problem arises because it is assumed that sentences of default logic might be combined in arbitrary ways with sentences in F and with each other.

But as pointed out in the introduction, defaults appear to have no semantics, and many researchers seek to unify the intuitions behind default reasoning with various uncertainty calculii. Rich [4] advocates adding certainty factors to defaults to fine-tune the system and concludes "default reasoning is likelihood reasoning and treating it that way simplifies it". While some argue with her treatment, her conclusions seem to be widely held. Ginsberg [5] pursues this approach.

At the 1987 Workshop on Uncertainty in AI, Benjamin Grosof suggested defaults are interval-valued probabilities. Selection of the appropriate default in a particular setting is closely related to Kyburg's theory of selecting the correct reference class. [6, 7].

In [8], McCarthy states non-monotonic sentences can represent statements of infinitesimal probability, but does not go into detail. Pearl [9] pursues a related notion, ϵ-semantics, where defaults are viewed as constraints on sets of probability distributions.

In particular, a default $a \to b$ is interpreted as a conditional probability $p(b|a) > 1 - \epsilon$ and a default conclusion is a conclusion entailed with probability $1 - O(\epsilon)$ by our observations, where $O(\epsilon)$ tends to zero as ϵ does. We believe this interpretation has some problems. Let $e = emu$, $b = bird$, $f = fly$. If

$$p(f|b) \approx 1, p(f|e) \approx 0, p(b|e) \approx 1$$

(i.e., there are some non-bird emus) then from

$$p(f|e) = p(f|be)p(b|e) + p(f|\neg be)p(\neg b|e)$$

Pearl shows $p(f|be) \approx 0$. Then, from

$$p(f|b) = p(f|eb)P(e|b) + p(f|\neg eb)p(\neg e|b)$$

it follows $p(e|b) \approx 0$. But since a prior is always bounded by its conditionals on any evidence and the negation of that evidence, we can show $p(e) \approx 0$.

Default logics that permit contraposition of defaults also have this property: from no knowledge at all, we can prove $\neg emu$ by cases from fly and $\neg fly$ using the contrapositive forms of the defaults. This introduces the following variant of the "lottery paradox"[6].

Example 1 *(Dingo paradox)* Suppose kangaroos (k) are exceptional because they have a marsupial birth and platypusses (p) are exceptional because they lay eggs but dingos (d) have no such exceptional traits. If

$$ozzie\text{-}animal \Rightarrow e \vee k \vee p \vee d,$$

then $p(d|ozzie\text{-}animal)$ is close to one since the disjunction of the other three is close to zero. Some default reasoners and circumscription suffer the same problem. The only solutions seem to be in the form of domain dependent *constraints* [10, 11] or circumscription policies. We would argue that very little in the way of general methodology has emerged from these approaches.

Besides making subclasses vanish, Pearl's ϵ-semantics has another problem: in general, it is impossible to go out into a real problem domain and verify our default knowledge.

Bacchus[12] addresses this issue of testability and argues for thresholding, that is, that a default stands for a probability greater than some threshold $k > 1/2$. His system allows only a single defeasible inference, since $p(b|a) > k$ and $p(c|b) > k$ hardly constrain $p(c|a)$ at all.

In a similar vein, we claim it is necessary to consider the original goals of formalisms such as default reasoning, inheritance hierarchies and semantic nets and ask whether we can solve those problem without new formalisms.

3. INFERENCE GRAPHS

An inference graph is a strictly probabilistic formalism based on standard probability theory, conditional independence and influences among properties. Rather than give rules for *accepting* uncertain conclusions, the inference graph permits inferences about *shifts* in belief.

3.1. FAVOURABLE PROPOSITIONS

An interesting mathematical property of logical implication is that knowledge of the consequent increases belief in the antecedent. That is, $a \Rightarrow b$ implies that $p(a|b) \geq p(a)$. Rosenkrantz [13] calls this property *confirmation*, and we will see it has many useful computational properties. Following Chung [14], we call this the *favours* relation.

Favouring describes a *shift* in belief; it seems to be the weakest probabilistic property a default *ought* to have, whatever else a default might mean. This provides an interesting direction to explore: rather than use knowledge of the form "birds are more likely to fly than not", we consider knowledge of the form "an individual is more likely to fly once we learn that it is a bird".

Consider Nutter's example[15], where in springtime it is not true that most birds fly, since most birds are flightless nestlings. Learning that an individual is a bird still inclines us to shift belief in favour of flying.

This also admits an interesting kind of sentence. If we say "Irish Canadians have red hair", we do not mean more than half or almost all Irish Canadians have red hair, even though the stereotype is widely held.

3.2. SYNTAX

An *inference graph* contains four kinds of links, $\Rightarrow$, $\rightarrow$, $\not\Rightarrow$ and $\not\rightarrow$. Links with double arrows are called *logical links* and the others are *probabilistic links*. Each node is labelled with a name or set of names in lower case, for example, *quaker* or *pacifist*. Links are attached to a name or its negation at either endpoint.

3.3. SEMANTICS

Nodes in an inference graph denote outcomes of variables. Where a single name a appears, the variable is propositional with outcomes a and $\neg a$. Where many names appear, the variable has several mutually exclusive outcomes (not all of which need be specified), for example $\{hawk, dove\}$.

Sentences about the *favours* relation are represented by the four kinds of links in an inference graph:

$$a \rightarrow b \text{ means } 1 > p(b|a) > p(b) > 0,$$
$$a \Rightarrow b \text{ means } 1 = p(b|a) > p(b) > 0,$$
$$a \not\rightarrow b \text{ means } 1 > p(\neg b|a) > p(\neg b) > 0 \text{ and}$$
$$a \not\Rightarrow b \text{ means } 1 = p(\neg b|a) > p(\neg b) > 0.$$

Note the insistence on strict inequalities. This means that links such as $2 + 2 = 3 \Rightarrow$ *sky-is-blue* cannot appear on an inference graph. For a similar reason, we also insist that all named outcomes of variables are possible. Lastly, we assume that we are reasoning about finite populations, justifying equating certainty with probability.

The topology of the inference graph carries information about independence of variables. So long as variables are propositional, we use the same name for the variable as for the node, but distinguish the former by capitalizing. For this introductory presentation, we will assume all variables are propositional, and just touch on the need for multiattribute variables. We first need the following definitions.

Definition 1 If $p(a|b) = p(a)$, A and B are *unconditionally independent*.

Definition 2 If $p(a|bc) = p(a|b)$, $p(a|b\neg c) = p(a|b)$, $p(a|\neg bc) = p(a|\neg c)$ and $p(a|\neg b\neg c) = p(a|\neg b)$ whenever the mentioned conditional probabilities are defined, then A is *conditionally independent* of C, given B.

The inference graph encodes the knowledge that the joint probability distribution of all variables in the graph can be factored into the product of the conditional probability distributions of each node given its immediate predecessors. Thus, an inference graph may be seen as a non-numeric *influence diagram*[16]. We next explore the kinds of inferences about the *favours* relation that we can make.

4. THE FAVOURS RELATION

If $p(a|b) > p(a)$, we also write *favours(a,b)*.

4.1. SYMMETRY

Lemma 1 If *favours*(a, b), then *favours*(b, a).
Proof: Follows immediately from Bayes' Rule. □

This allows our system to be reversible; if we observe *sneeze* we can confirm *has-cold*. Alternately, if we know that someone has a cold we can predict they will sneeze. Thus we can use the same formalism for prediction and diagnosis.

4.2. NEGATION

Lemma 2 If *favours*(a, b), then *favours*$(\neg a, \neg b)$.
Proof: By definition, $p(a|b) > p(a)$. Negating both sides yields $p(\neg a|b) < p(\neg a)$. Then $p(b|\neg a) < p(b)$ by Lemma 1 and negating again yields $p(\neg b|\neg a) > p(\neg b)$. Another application of Lemma 1 yields the desired result. □

Thus, not only does *bird* increase belief in *fly*, $\neg bird$ increases belief in $\neg fly$. An interesting intermediate result is that the "contrapositive" form of a link yields a valid inference. Similarly, we can contrapose any other inference (for example, an inference based on chaining as justified by Lemma 5), but we cannot generally arbitrarily combine the contrapositive form of a link with other links. This suggests why default reasoners that permit application of the contrapositive form run into difficulties: they violate independence knowledge.

4.3. LOGICAL INFERENCES

Lemma 3 If $favours(a,c)$ and $favours(b,d)$ where c and d are outcomes of the same variable, and $a \models b$, then $favours(c,ab)$.
Proof: $p(c|ab) = p(c|a) > p(c)$, since sentences of probability hold for logically equivalent propositions. □

Some default reasoners produce separate arguments for c and d and it is argued [17] that one should choose among the arguments by appealing to "specificity", that is, we prefer the argument that depends upon the most specific knowledge.

When using the *favours* relation to make an inference about an *individual*, we simply insist on conditioning on all observations. Many default reasoning formalisms are building this idea into their inference rules by the construction of *contexts* [18, 19].

Lemma 4 If $b \models a$, but $a \not\models b$ then $favours(b,a)$.

4.4. TRANSITIVE INFERENCE

Default proofs consist of more than a single inference; part of the appeal of such reasoners is that they appear to create an argument by making inferences towards a goal. In general, if $a \to b$ and $b \to c$ are links on an inference graph, we cannot conclude $favours(c,a)$. However, if C is conditionally independent of A given B, it can be shown that $favours(c,a)$. In fact, conditional independence gives us much more than transitivity. Not only can we reverse the inference, we can perform *transduction*, inferring evidence from other evidence. We can also favour certain conjunctions.

Lemma 5 *(Probabilistic Resolution)* If there exists c such $favours(a,c)$ and $favours(b,c)$ and A is conditionally independent of B given C, then $favours(a,b)$.
Proof: Since

$$p(a|b) = p(a|cb)p(c|b) + p(a|\neg cb)p(\neg c|b)$$

and

$$p(a|\neg b) = p(a|c\neg b)p(c|\neg b) + p(a|\neg c\neg b)p(\neg c|\neg b),$$

we can simplify using the conditional independence knowledge, and subtract to obtain

$$p(a|b) - p(a|\neg b) = (p(a|c) - p(a|\neg c))(p(c|b) - p(c|\neg b)).$$

Both terms are positive by assumption, and we are done. □

The next two lemmas yield two ways of favouring conjunctions. Proofs of all remaining lemmas appear in [20] and we omit them here.

Lemma 6 *(Irrelevance)* If $favours(a,c)$ and A is conditionally independent of B given C, then $favours(a,bc)$.

Lemma 7 *(Relevance)* Suppose $favours(a,c)$ and $favours(b,c)$ and A is conditionally independent of B given C. Then $favours(ab,c)$.

4.5. OTHER INFERENCES

The following two lemmas address situations that prove to be useful in Section 5.3. The proofs are straightforward and we omit them.

Lemma 8 If $favours(\neg a, b)$, $favours(a, c)$, and $b \Rightarrow c$, then $favours(a, \neg bc)$.

Lemma 9 If r and e are the direct predecessors of g, and $r \models e$, $a \models e$, R is unconditionally independent of A, $favours(g, e)$, $favours(\neg g, r)$, then $favours(g, a)$.

5. EXAMPLES
5.1. BIRDS FLY

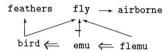

This inference graph aims to capture a lot of information. If something is a bird, we believe it is more likely that it will fly, and if it flies, it is more likely to be airborne. If something is an emu, we are less likely to believe it flies, but if it is a flemu (flying emu) we again change our belief. We are inclined to believe that birds have feathers. What inferences can we make from this graph?

Birds fly, emus don't. We can prove $favours(fly, bird)$ and $favours(\neg fly, emu)$ from the single links containing this information. More importantly, we cannot prove $favours(fly, emu)$, i.e., we do not have the multiple extension problem because we cannot chain arbitrarily. We can use Lemma 3 to conclude $favours(\neg fly, bird \wedge emu)$.

Emus don't vanish. Exactly the opposite is true: we show $favours(emu, bird)$. Note that we do not accept conclusions, just increase our belief in them.

Emus are not airborne. Naive path-based reasoners might permit a single proof of *airborne* from *emu* using the default "birds fly". We conclude an individual is less likely to be airborne given it is an emu because $favours(\neg airborne, \neg fly)$ and $favours(emu, \neg fly)$ and *Airborne* is conditionally independent of *Emu* given *Fly*.

Feathered things fly. With Lemma 5 we can show $favours(feathers, fly)$ using $c = bird$.

5.2. MODIFIED NIXON DIAMOND

The historic example of *not* wanting to draw an inference is the "Nixon Diamond" where Quakers are typically doves and Republicans are typically hawks. If Dick is both a Quaker and a Republican, we do not want to conclude he is a hawk or dove.

Suppose $hawk \equiv \neg dove$. We can represent this knowledge with arcs $quaker \rightarrow dove$, $republican \not\rightarrow dove$. We conclude that $quaker$ increases belief in $dove$ and $republican$ increases belief in $hawk$. Since the graph contains no information about the conditional probability of $dove$ given $quaker$ and $republican$, we conclude neither $hawk$ nor $dove$ if Nixon is both.

128

Suppose both *hawks* and *doves* tend to be *political*. Given this representation, either we must relax some of the strict inequalities or the graph will be inconsistent. (Equivalently, a default reasoner gives a proof by cases that *political* is true given *dove* or ¬*dove*. It is possible to prove that an object about which nothing is known is a political non-emu!)

We solve the problem in this formalism by making *hawk* and *dove* mutually exclusive but not necessarily exhaustive outcomes of some random event. Since *Political* is conditionally independent of *Quaker* given *Dove*, we can make the desired inference using Lemma 5. The price we pay for consistency and transitive inference is not being able to show that ¬*hawk* is favoured by *quaker*. This is not completely satisfying and in [21], we explore additional assumptions needed to handle this example more elegantly.

5.3. ROYAL AND AFRICAN ELEPHANTS

This appears in [22, 23]. Suppose we have links *royal* ⇒ *elephant*, *african* ⇒ *elephant*, *royal* ↛ *grey* and *elephant* → *grey*. This is supposed to capture the intuition that elephants are typically gray, but Royal elephants are not. If Clyde is both an African and a Royal elephant what do we conclude about grayness?

Lemma 9 permits the conclusion that African elephants are gray. If *royal* is true, then *elephant* is true and the conditional independence assumptions shield *gray* from the effect of *african* and we conclude *favours(¬gray,[royal african])*. This would not be true if the links from *royal* and *african* to *elephant* were probabilistic.

Intuitions clash on syntactic relabellings of this example. We claim there are no "right" answers to this question; rather, the problem is not constrained enough. Different settings need different graphs.

5.4. NAIVE DIAGNOSIS

Consider the diagnostic dual to the "birds fly" problem:

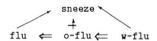

If we observe *sneeze*, a path-based reasoner might produce all three diseases as diagnoses [24]. The inference graph favours both *flu* and *w-flu*; of these, we might prefer the most probable diagnosis favoured by the observations. If we observe ¬*sneeze* only *o-flu* is favoured. A similar answer is obtained in [24], but the meaining of the undesired diagnosis is not explained.

6. CONCLUSIONS

We applied the formalism to many other problems, commonly within the province of default inference, including plan recognition and stereotyping with positive results. In general, answers agree with intuition. Where they don't, the underlying probabilistic basis has always provided the tool for understanding the structure of the particular problem.

This presentation is intended to open discussion as to whether qualitative probabilistic knowledge (including the *favours* relation, independence knowledge of all sorts, knowledge about high probabilities) is sufficient for handling the problems which nonmonotonic and other logic formalisms were invented to solve. This work has generated many interesting informal arguments, resulting in significant extensions, some of which have already appeared elsewhere. In [20], we present the theory of inference graphs containing just propositional variables from first principles and include all proofs. The use of inference graphs for plan recognition is introduced in [25]. In [21], we address the problem of multiattribute variables. In [26], Neufeld and Bacchus combine the system of accepting beliefs above certain thresholds with the *favours* relation. The resulting formalism appears to better approximate intuitions about defaults held in within the default logic community, yet remains firmly rooted in probability theory.

ACKNOWLEDGEMENTS

The work of the first author was done while a graduate student at the University of Waterloo and while a member of the School of Computer Science at the University of New Brunswick in Fredericton, New Brunswick, Canada.

Thanks to André Trudel, Bruce Spencer, Peter VanBeek, Jimmy Lee and Paul van Arragon at UW for thorough comments on an earlier draft. Fahiem Bacchus suggested Lemmas 8 and 9. Thanks to J.D. Horton at UNB for many subsequent discussions and thanks to the anonymous referees for comments.

REFERENCES

[1] Raymond Reiter and Giovanni Crisculo. On interacting defaults. In *Proceedings of the Seventh International Joint Conference on Artificial Intelligence*, pages 270–276, 1981.

[2] David L. Poole, R.G. Goebel, and R. Aleliunas. Theorist: a logical reasoning system for defaults and diagnosis. In Nick Cercone and Gordon McCalla, editors, *The Knowledge Frontier: Essays in the Representation of Knowledge*. Springer-Verlag, New York, 1987.

[3] Michael P. Wellman. Probabilistic semantics for qualitative influences. In *Proceedings of the Sixth National Conference on Artificial Intelligence*, pages 660–664, 1986.

[4] Elaine Rich. Default reasoning as likelihood reasoning. In *Proceedings of the Fourth National Conference on Artificial Intelligence*, pages 348–351, 1983.

[5] Matthew Ginsberg. Non-monotonic reasoning using Dempster's rule. In *Proceedings of the Fifth National Conference on Artificial Intelligence*, pages 126–129, August 1984.

[6] Henry E. Kyburg, Jr. *Logical Foundations of Statistical Inference*. Kluwer Academic, Dordrecht, Holland, 1971.

[7] Henry E. Kyburg, Jr. The reference class. *Philosophy of Science*, 50:374–397, 1983.

[8] J. McCarthy. Applications of circumscription to formalizing commonsense knowledge. *Artificial Intelligence*, 28:89–118, 1986.

[9] Judea Pearl. *Probabilistic Reasoning in Intelligent Systems*. Morgan Kaufmann, California, 1988.

[10] David L. Poole. A logical framework for default reasoning. *Artificial Intelligence*, 36:27–48, 1988.

[11] Denis Gagné. The multiple extension problem revisited. Technical Report CS-87-30, University of Waterloo Department of Computer Science, 1987.

[12] Fahiem Bacchus. A modest, but semantically well-founded inheritance reasoner. In *Proceedings of the Eleventh International Joint Conference on Artificial Intelligence*, pages 1104–1109, 1989.

[13] Roger D. Rosenkrantz. *Inference, Method and Decision*. Reidel, Boston, 1977.

[14] K-L. Chung. On mutually favorable events. *Annals of Mathematical Statistics*, 13:338–349, 1942.

[15] Jane Terry Nutter. Uncertainty and probability. In *Proceedings of the Tenth International Joint Conference on Artificial Intelligence*, pages 373–379, 1987.

[16] Ross D. Shachter. Probabilistic inference and influence diagrams. *Operations Research*, 36:589–604, 1988.

[17] David L. Poole. On the comparison of theories: Preferring the most specific explanation. In *Proceedings of the Ninth International Joint Conference on Artificial Intelligence*, pages 144–147, 1985.

[18] Hector Geffner. A logic for defaults. In *Proceedings of the Seventh National Conference on Artificial Intelligence*, pages 449–454, 1988.

[19] James P. Delgrande. A first order logic for prototypical properties. *Artificial Intelligence*, 33:105–130, 1987.

[20] Eric Neufeld. A probabilistic commonsense reasoner. *International Journal of Intelligent Systems*, to appear.

[21] Eric Neufeld. Ginsberg's paradox. submitted, 1989.

[22] Erik Sandewall. Nonmonotonic inference rules for multiple inheritance systems with exceptions. *Proceedings of the IEEE*, 74:1345–1353, October 1986.

[23] J.F. Horty, David S. Touretzky, and Richmond H. Thomason. A clash of intuitions: the current state of nomonotonic multiple inheritance systems. In *Proceedings of the Tenth International Joint Conference on Artificial Intelligence*, pages 476–482, 1987.

[24] Eric Neufeld and David Poole. Towards solving the multiple extension problem: combining defaults and probabilities. In L.N. Kanal, T.S. Levitt, and J.F. Lemmer, editors, *Uncertainty in Artificial Intelligence 3*, pages 35–44. North Holland, 1989.

[25] Eric Neufeld. Defaults and probabilities; extensions and coherence. In *Proceedings of the First International Conference on Principles of Knowledge Representation and Reasoning*, pages 312–323, 1989.

[26] Eric Neufeld and Fahiem Bacchus. Radically elementary default logic. in preparation, 1989.

Uncertainty in Artificial Intelligence 4
R.D. Shachter, T.S. Levitt, L.N. Kanal, J.F. Lemmer (Editors)
© Elsevier Science Publishers B.V. (North-Holland), 1990

Modal Logics of Higher-Order Probability*

Peter Haddawy and Alan M. Frisch

University of Illinois
Department of Computer Science
405 North Mathews
Urbana, Illinois 61801
U.S.A.

This paper discusses the relationship between probability and modal logic. We show that it is both natural and useful to think of probability as a modal operator. Contrary to popular belief in AI, a probability ranging between 0 and 1 represents a range between impossibility and necessity, not between simple falsity and truth. We examine two classes of probability models: flat and staged. The flat models are straightforward generalizations of models for alethic logic. We show that one of the more interesting constraints relating higher- and lower-order probabilities forces all higher-order probabilities in flat models to be either zero or one. We introduce staged models as a means of avoiding this problem. Constraints on the two types of models define various classes of probability logics. We relate some of these probability logics to alethic logic.

1 Introduction

Probability is typically treated as a metatheoretic concept; one talks in a metalanguage about the probabilities of object-language sentences. For example, this is the way Nilsson's [12] Probabilistic Logic is constructed. However, by treating probability as a logical operator in the object language, statements about probabilities may be combined freely with other statements in the object language. English, for example, permits such explicit discourse about the probability of sentences.

By introducing such a probability operator into a logical language one obtains a so-called *probability logic*. This paper deals with a probability logic that consists of first-order logic with the addition of the modal operator P, subscripted by a real number to denote the probability of a sentence. With this language one can combine ordinary logical assertions with assertions about probability—as in (1)— unambiguously represent the scopes of probability operators and quantifiers—as in (2) and (3)—and discuss the probability of a sentence that discusses probability—as in (4).

$$Plays - sax(Jane) \land P_{.8}(Miss - America(Jane)) \tag{1}$$

Jane plays the saxophone and is probably Miss America.

* This work has been partially supported by NASA under grant number NAG 1-613 and by a Cognitive Science/AI fellowship granted to the first author by the University of Illinois.

$$\forall x[Missile(x) \rightarrow P_{.8}Stopped(x)] \tag{2}$$
There is an 80% chance of stopping each missile.

$$P_{.8}(\forall x[Missile(x) \rightarrow Stopped(x)]) \tag{3}$$
There is an 80% chance of stopping all missiles.

$$P_{.2}(Cloudy \wedge P_{.3}(Rain)) \tag{4}$$
The probability is .2 that it is cloudy and that the chance of rain is 30%.

The goal of this paper is to provide a semantics for probabilistic logic that properly handles sentences with nested probability operators, such as (4). A probability operator that is applied to a sentence about probability is called a *higher-order probability* operator. A proper semantic account of higher-order probability should tell us that sentence (4) entails that the probability of rain is greater than .06.

In Section 2 we argue that probability logic should be viewed as a generalization of alethic logic in which probability one is closely related to necessity and probability zero is closely related to impossibility. From this viewpoint, it is easy to generalize the possible worlds semantics of alethic logic to a possible worlds semantics of probabilistic logic. This results in the class of *flat* probabilistic models, which are discussed in Section 3. Though these models are intuitive, they only give a proper semantic account to probability sentences that do not contain higher-order probability operators. Section 4 presents some *coherence principles* that one may wish a proper treatment of higher-order probabilities to abide by. We show that one of the more interesting constraints relating higher- and lower-order probabilities forces all higher-order probabilities in flat models to be either zero or one. This is remedied in Section 5 by introducing a class of probability models called *staged* models. Section 6 brings us full cycle by examining the relationship among a number of probability logics and alethic logics. This presentation unifies our results with previous results obtained by others, most notably Halpern [8], Gaifman [3, 4] and van Fraassen [17].

2 Probability as a Modal Operator

A common belief in AI is that probability is closely related to first-order logic, partially because probability values represent a continuum between truth and falsity.

> *In this paper we present a semantical generalization of ordinary first-order logic in which the truth values of sentences can range between 0 and 1.* — Nils Nilsson [12]

> *Formally, probability can be regarded as a generalization of predicate calculus, where instead of the truth value of a formula given the evidence (context) having only the values 0 (false) or 1 (truth), it is generalized to a real number between 0 and 1.* — Peter Cheeseman [1]

This view, however, is not quite correct. To shed light on what kind of continuum probability values represent, consider these three pairs of sentences about the next toss of a coin:

1) It is true that either the coin will land heads or that the coin will land tails.

2) It is true that the coin will land heads or it is true that the coin will land tails.

3) Necessarily either the coin will land heads or the coin will land tails.

4) Necessarily the coin will land heads or necessarily the coin will land tails.

5) With probability one either the coin will land heads or the coin will land tails.

6) With probability one the coin will land heads or with probability one the coin will land tails.

Clearly the first statement is true if and only if the second is true. The statements in the second pair, however, are not equivalent. The third statement is certainly true but the fourth would imply that the coin is either two-headed or two-tailed. The question is whether the third pair of statements more closely resembles the first or second pair. If it corresponds to the first pair then the fifth statement would have to imply the sixth statement. This is clearly not the case. It is, in fact, not the case for exactly the same reason that the third statement does not imply the fourth. Thus it is clear just from intuition that probability represents a continuum between necessity and impossibility, not between simple truth and falsity. Alethic logic, the modal logic of necessity and possibility, captures exactly this distinction. Thus it seems reasonable to expect a model theory for probability logic to be related in some way to a model theory for alethic logic.

We are not the first to suggest a modal view of probability. Nicholas Rescher [13] was perhaps the first to examine the relationship between probability and modality. He formulated a logic in which a probability of one was interpreted as necessity and showed that in a finite possibility space modal logic S5 is, "appropriately regarded, nothing more than a propositional probability logic." Several philosophers, logicians, and mathematicians have since discussed the relationship of probability to modal logics [2, 5, 3, 4, 17, 8]. The present work is closely related to that of Gaifman [3, 4] and builds on the work of van Fraassen [17] and Halpern [8].

3 Flat Probability Models

The standard way to formalize the semantics of modal logics is in terms of Kripke structures [9]. A Kripke structure is a model composed of a set of possible worlds and a binary accessibility relation between the worlds. A possible world can be considered to be a complete description of one possible reality or state of affairs. In an alethic logic, one world is accessible from a given world if it is considered possible with respect to that given world. Various alethic logics satisfying different properties may then be defined in terms of restrictions on the accessibility relations of the models. To define a semantics for probability logic we may construct our models, analogously to Kripke structures, in terms of probability distributions over possible worlds.

We simply replace the accessibility relation in a Kripke structure with a function from worlds to distributions over worlds. Alethic logic gives us a set of worlds that are accessible from a given world; probability logic adds a probability distribution over that set of worlds. So in addition to saying that a world is possible, we say how possible. We call such models *flat probability models*. A flat probability model is a four-tuple $\langle W, PD, F, D \rangle$, where W is a countable set of objects called the possible worlds, PD, the probability distribution assignment, is a function that maps each world to a probability distribution over W, D is the domain of all individuals, and F is the denotation function that maps a non-logical symbol and a world into the denotation of that symbol in that world. We write PD^w to denote the probability distribution that results from applying PD to world w.

Denotations are assigned to expressions relative to a model, a world within the model and an assignment of elements in the domain to variables. The denotation of an expression ϕ relative to a model M, a world w and an assignment g, written $[\![\phi]\!]^{M,w,g}$, is defined by the usual semantic equations with the addition of the following semantic equation for the P operator:

$$
\begin{aligned}
[\![P_\alpha \psi]\!]^{M,w,g} &= T \text{ if } PD^w(\{u : [\![\psi]\!]^{M,u,g} = T\}) = \alpha \\
&= F \text{ otherwise}
\end{aligned}
$$

A sentence is *satisfied* by a flat probability model and a world iff its semantic value in that model and world is T. A sentence is *valid* iff it is satisfied by every world in every model.

To illustrate the use of the semantic definitions, consider again two sentences from the introduction. Suppose the president can choose between two plans having the following effects:

Plan A: $\forall x[Missile(x) \rightarrow P_{.8}Stopped(x)]$

Plan B: $P_{.8}(\forall x[Missile(x) \rightarrow Stopped(x)])$

These two statements make very different assertions about the plans they are describing. In particular, if the President is a rational man he will choose plan B over plan A. The semantics should establish the proper distinction between the meaning of these formulas and show why plan B is preferable to plan A.

We assume that *Missile* is a rigid designator, i.e., that the set of missiles is the same in each possible world. This is reasonable since we are not worried about not knowing whether or not an object is a missile. Now, why should the President prefer plan B? We show that the worst case scenario for plan B is the best case for plan A. Let the expression $g[d/x]$ denote the assignment of values to variables that is identical to assignment g with the possible exception that domain element d is assigned to variable x. By the semantic definitions, sentences A and B are true at a world w iff

(A) for all $d \in D$ either $[\![Missile(x)]\!]^{M,w,g[d/x]} = F$ or $[\![P_{.8}Stopped(x)]\!]^{M,w,g[d/x]} = T$

(B) $PD^w(\{\hat{w} : \text{for all } d \in D \text{ either } [\![Missile(x)]\!]^{M,\hat{w},g[d/x]} = F$ or $[\![Stopped(x)]\!]^{M,\hat{w},g[d/x]} = T)\}) = .8$

Since the set of missiles is the same in each world, we can eliminate $Missile(x)$ from the two semantic formulas and consider only models in which the domain contains only missiles. We can then expand these two formulas out to obtain:

(A) for all $d \in D$, $PD^w(\{\hat{w} : [\![Stopped(x)]\!]^{M,\hat{w},g[d/x]} = T\}) = .8$

(B) $PD^w(\{\hat{w} : \text{for all } d \in D, [\![Stopped(x)]\!]^{M,\hat{w},g[d/x]} = T\}) = .8$

So B holds in those models that assign probability .8 to the set of worlds in which every missile is stopped. The remainder of the worlds assigned non-zero probability do not stop all of the missiles but may stop some of the missiles. So any given missile is stopped with probability at least .8. For plan A, each missile is stopped with probability exactly .8. Hence plan B is at least as good as plan A.

4 Coherence Principles

One of the main concerns of this paper is the proper treatment of sentences concerning higher-order probabilities. Depending on the interpretation we place on the probabilities, it seems reasonable to expect higher- and lower-order probabilities to be related in some way. For example, if I believe to degree .2 that next week I will believe to degree .7 that East Germany will become democratic within the next year, what does that say about my current beliefs?

We discuss three possible constraints relating higher- and lower-order probabilities. We will call them coherence principles. The principles will be reflected in constraints on the models. Two possible coherence principles that have been suggested by Brian Skyrms [15, Appendix 2] are a minimal self-knowledge principle (C1) and Miller's principle (MP), as listed below. Additionally, several researchers [10, 7] have suggested an expected value principle (Exp). Each principle below entails the previous ones. In the expressions below A denotes an event and $prob(A)$ denotes the probability of that event.

C1: if $prob(prob(A) = \alpha) = 1$ then $prob(A) = \alpha$.

Exp: $prob(A) = \int_0^1 prob(prob(A) = \alpha) \cdot \alpha \, d\alpha$

MP: $prob(A|prob(A) = \alpha) = \alpha$

Skyrms points out that the applicability of the principles is a function of the interpretation we place on the probabilities. If we interpret higher and lower order probabilities as the rational degree of belief of an agent who does not know his own mind then C1 is reasonable. An agent who violates C1 is certain that his degree of belief in A is α, although it isn't. If we wish C1 to hold under conditionalization then MP, Miller's principle, follows. This can be seen by taking C1 and conditionalizing on $pr(A) = \alpha$. The left-hand side of C1 becomes $pr(pr(A) = \alpha|pr(A) = \alpha) = 1$ which is true by definition. Thus the right-hand side follows: $pr(A|pr(A) = \alpha) = \alpha$. [1]

If we interpret higher and lower order probabilities as the degrees of belief of an agent concerning his future beliefs, then C1 and MP are justified only if an agent's belief changes are the result of learning experiences. A number of researchers have used diachronic Dutch book arguments in an attempt to show MP to be a general requirement for dynamic rationality [16, 6]. These arguments essentially attempt to show that if you accept a certain system of bets concerning your present and future beliefs and you do not adhere to MP, you are open to a Dutch book. Levi [11], however, has recently refuted these arguments.

If the outer probability represents rational degree of belief and the inner probability represents objective probability then MP is a plausible rule for assimilating knowledge about objective probability.

Finally, if the nested probability sentences represent objective probabilities of objective probabilities at later times (e.g., the inner probabilities represent the probabilities

138

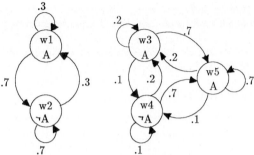

Figure 1: Uniform flat probability model.

of choosing a white ball from several different urns and the outer probability represents the probability of first choosing each of the different urns) then MP is again plausible.

We would like to formulate a logic which satisfies the strongest of the principles discussed above, i.e. Miller's principle. We express MP in the form of restrictions on the models. Weaker logics are obtainable simply by relaxing the restrictions. The problem we address, then, is how to construct the Kripke structures in such a way that all of the examples presented earlier can be modeled and such that the logic conforms to Miller's principle.

Halpern [8] has shown that the flat models in which Miller's principle holds can be characterized by a property he calls *uniformity*. A model is uniform iff $PD^w(\acute{w}) > 0$ implies $PD^w = PD^{\acute{w}}$ for any two worlds, w and $\acute{w}$. The effect of the uniformity constraint is to partition the worlds of a model into probabilistic equivalence classes. Figure 1 shows an example of a uniform model. The worlds are partitioned into two equivalence classes, $\{w_1, w_2\}$ and $\{w_3, w_4, w_5\}$. In the two worlds of the first equivalence class we have $pr(A) = .3$ while in the three worlds of the second class we have $pr(A) = .9$. Note that Nilsson's [12] Probabilistic Logic models correspond to the special case of a uniform model in which there is only one equivalence class of worlds. Furthermore, an equivalence class of worlds in a Nilsson model corresponds to a single world in a flat model.

Halpern's result stated in our terminology is:

Theorem 1 *Every instance of Miller's principle holds at every world of a flat model iff the model is uniform.*

There is, however, another effect produced by the uniformity constraint. Uniformity forces all higher-order probabilities to be either zero or one. This follows since every world to which a world assigns positive probability shares its probability distribution. For example, in world w_1 of Figure 1 we have $pr(pr(A) = .3) = 1$ and for all $\alpha \neq .3$ we have $pr(pr(A) = \alpha) = 0$. Thus by enforcing Miller's principle we have made higher-order probabilities uninteresting. For example, we can no longer use higher-order probability to represent the degrees of belief of an agent who does not know his own mind; in a uniform model, an agent is certain of all his beliefs.

Flat probability models contain too little structure to capture both Miller's principle and non-trivial higher-order probabilities. This required structure is present in the staged probability models that we consider now.

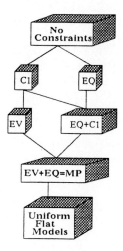

Figure 3: Lattice of probability logics.

He enforces Miller's principle by imposing the expected value constraint and a constraint on probabilities similar to our equivalence class constraint. This second constraint forces his models to assume a tree structure similar to ours. Gaifman shows that Miller's principle completely characterizes the class of his probability models that conform to the two constraints.

We have mentioned three coherence principles as well as the EQ constraint on staged probability models and the uniformity constraint on flat probability models. These five constraints admit an entire space of probability logics. Because some of the constraints entail others this space takes the shape of a lattice. Figure 3 shows the lattice of possible probability logics defined by the constraints. The stronger logics are further down in the lattice.

5.2 Semantic Definitions

The semantic value of probability sentences is defined as in flat models except that now we evaluate sentences with respect to a world and a stage. Let the semantic value of a sentence ϕ relative to a model M, a world w in M, a stage i, and an assignment g of values to variables be denoted by $[\![\phi]\!]^{M,w,i,g}$. Then $[\![\phi]\!]^{M,w,i,g}$ is defined by the usual semantic equations with the addition of the following semantic equation for the P operator:

$$\begin{aligned} [\![P_\alpha \psi]\!]^{M,w,i,g} &= T \text{ if } \vec{PD}_i^{\,w}(\{u : [\![\psi]\!]^{M,u,i+1,g} = T\}) = \alpha \\ &= F \text{ otherwise} \end{aligned}$$

A sentence is *satisfied* in a model at a world and a stage iff its semantic value in that model at that world and stage is T. A sentence is *valid* iff it is satisfied in every model at every world and stage.

Normally we evaluate sentences with respect to the stage 1. For example, in the

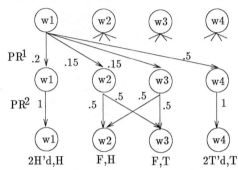

Figure 4: Probability model for coins example.

sentence $P_\alpha(P_\beta\phi \wedge P_\gamma\psi)$, the outer P is evaluated with respect to $\vec{P}D_1$ and the inner two P's with respect to $\vec{P}D_2$.

The following example illuminates the model theory and the semantic definitions. Suppose you are given a bag of coins and are told that it contains 2 double-headed coins, 3 fair coins, and 5 double-tailed coins. We would like to know what the probability is that a coin drawn at random from the bag will land heads. There are many models consistent with this description. Part of one possible probability model is shown in Figure 4. The figure shows the distribution at stage 1 and 2 for each of four worlds. World w_1 represents the event that a two-headed coin is drawn and lands heads, world w_2 that a fair coin is drawn and lands heads, etc. Notice that worlds w_2 and w_3 have the same distribution at stage 2 so, consistent with the equivalence class constraint, in each of them $\vec{P}D_2\{w_2, w_3\} = 1$. In world w_1 we have $P_{.35}H$ which we can see holds by the semantic definitions since $\vec{P}D_1^{w_1}(H) = .2 + .15 = .35$. Furthermore we can see that the expected value property holds since w_1 $P_{.2}P_1H$, $P_{.3}P_{.5}H$, and $P_{.5}P_0H$ are true and $.2(1)+.3(.5)+.5(0)=.35$. Finally we can see that Miller's principle holds in w_1 since we have that both $P_{.15}(H \wedge P_{.5})$ and $P_{.3}P_{.5}H$ are true in w_1 and $.15/.3 = .5$.

6 Relation to Modal Logic

The introduction to this paper pointed out that probability logic is the continuous case of alethic logic (not FOPC). This is easy to see for first-order probability sentences. The question is whether this still holds for higher-order probability. The development of the probability models of the previous sections was motivated by the idea that the models should generalize Kripke structures. An interesting question to ask is whether we can show the probability logics for the various models to be generalizations of any particular modal logics.

We first note that probabilistic certainty, although closely related to necessity, is not identical with necessity. In an uncountably infinite probability space we can have possible events of measure zero. [2] For example, suppose you pick a real number randomly in the interval [0 1]. For each number the probability that it will be picked is zero, yet it is possible that it will be picked. Thus if the domain is constant over possible worlds then (5) is satisfiable, but (6) is not in any serial modal logic. ($\Box$ denotes necessity.)

$$(\forall x \ P_1 \neg picked(x)) \wedge (P_1 \exists x \ picked(x)) \qquad (5)$$

$$(\forall x \ \Box \neg picked(x)) \wedge (\Box \exists x \ picked(x)) \qquad (6)$$

Necessity is a stronger notion than probability one. For a sentence to be necessary it must be true in all possible worlds. This is not the case for probability one.

This difference between probability one and necessity is one reason that we have restricted ourselves to countable models in this paper. In a countable model, sentence (5) is not satisfiable since $(P_1 \exists x \ picked(x))$ implies that at least one world in which some x is picked is assigned positive probability. Thus it cannot be the case for all x that the probability of their being picked is zero. Hence we will only be concerned with the relation between countable Kripke structures and countable probability models. First we will discuss the relationship of modal logic to probability logics characterizable by flat probability models and then we will examine the relationship to probability logics characterized by staged models.

We create the probabilistic translation of an alethic sentence by replacing all necessity operators by P_1 operators. Since any alethic sentence containing possibility operators can be represented using only necessity operators, this is sufficient to handle all alethic sentences. Thus the probabilistic translations of alethic sentences will only mention probability one. Following Halpern, we will call probability logic restricted to sentences using only probability one *certainty logic*. If ϕ is an alethic sentence then ϕ^c will denote its certainty logic equivalent. For example, the translation of $\Box \neg \Box \phi$ is $P_1 \neg P_1 \phi$.

We are interested in showing that an alethic sentence is satisfiable by a Kripke structure of a given logic iff its probabilistic translation is satisfiable by a probability model conforming to certain constraints. This requires a mapping between probability models and Kripke structures. For flat models the mapping is straightforward. Given a probability model, create the corresponding Kripke structure by replacing the function PD from worlds to probability distributions by the accessibility relation R such that $R(w, \acute{w})$ if, and only if, $PD^w(\acute{w}) > 0$.

To translate in the other direction, look at all the worlds accessible from a given world w. If the number of accessible worlds is a finite number n then make PD^w assign each world probability $1/n$. If the number of worlds is infinite then make PD^w assign probabilities according to the geometric sequence $1/2^n$. Given this mapping, one can define probabilistic versions of all the common restrictions on accessibility relations in Kripke structures. For example, reflexivity becomes $\forall w PD^w(w) > 0$. Since the probability distributions in probability models must assign positive probability to some world, probability models correspond to Kripke structures in which the accessibility relation is serial, which are precisely the Kripke structures of the modal logic D. So we have the following basic result.

Theorem 3 *An alethic sentence ϕ is satisfied by a countable Kripke structure of modal logic D iff ϕ^c is satisfied by an unconstrained probability model (flat or staged).*

Halpern [8] has studied the relation between propositional modal logic and flat probability models. Using the translation between models outlined above, he has shown how to obtain certainty logic equivalents of all the common propositional alethic logics. Furthermore, the following result follows by a slight generalization of a theorem of Halpern's relating uniform probability models to modal logic KD45, the logic characterized by structures that are serial, transitive, and Euclidean:

Theorem 4 *An alethic sentence ϕ is satisfied by a countable Kripke structure of modal logic KD45 iff ϕ^c is satisfied by a uniform flat probability model.*

Next we show that the certainty logic for our staged probability logic conforming to EQ and EV lies somewhere between modal logic KD45 and a logic whose models have a serial, transitive, and secondarily reflexive accessibility relation. We first show that if an alethic sentence is satisfied by a serial, transitive, and secondarily reflexive Kripke structure then its probabilistic translation is satisfied by a staged probability model conforming to EQ and EV. Then we show that KD45 satisfiability implies probabilistic satisfiability by a staged model conforming to EQ and EV.

Theorem 5 *For a given alethic sentence ϕ, if ϕ^c is satisfied by a staged probability model conforming to EQ and EV then ϕ is satisfied by a countable serial, transitive, and secondarily reflexive Kripke structure.*

Proof: We show that the probabilistic translation of the axioms characterizing seriality, transitivity and secondary reflexivity are valid in the probability models.
Seriality: $\neg P_1(false)$ follows directly from the axioms of probability.
Transitivity: We show that $P_1\phi \rightarrow P_1P_1\phi$ follows from the expected value property. By definition, $P_1\phi$ is true at a world w iff $\vec{PD}_1^w(\phi) = 1$. By the expected value constraint, this is true iff

$$\sum_{\acute{w}\in W} \vec{PD}_1^w(\acute{w}) \cdot \vec{PD}_2^{\acute{w}}(\phi) = 1$$

Since probabilities sum to 1, this is true iff each of the $\vec{PD}_2^{\acute{w}}(\phi) = 1$. Hence we have $P_1P_1\phi$.
Secondary Reflexivity: We show that $P_1(P_1\phi \rightarrow \phi)$ follows from Miller's principle. By MP, $pr(\phi|pr(\phi) = 1) = 1$. Let us write A for ϕ and B for $pr(\phi) = 1$. Then $pr(A \wedge B) = pr(B)$. Now,

$$
\begin{aligned}
pr(B \rightarrow A) &= pr(\neg B) + pr(A) + pr(\neg B \wedge A) \\
&= 1 - pr(A \wedge B) + pr(A) - pr(A \wedge \neg B) \\
&= 1 + pr(A) - pr(A) \\
&= 1
\end{aligned}
$$

□

Theorem 6 *If an alethic sentence ϕ is satisfied by a countable Kripke structure of modal logic KD45 then ϕ^c is satisfied by a staged probability model conforming to EQ and EV.*

Proof: It follows by a slight generalization of a result by Halpern [8][Theorem 4.1] that if an alethic sentence is satisfied by a countable Kripke structure of logic KD45 then it is satisfied by a flat probability model in which the probability distribution PD is the same for each world. We can construct a staged model conforming to EQ and EV corresponding to such a flat model by making all worlds R-accessible to one another at each stage and making each $\vec{PD}_i$ in the staged model equal to PD of the flat model. So we just create a sequence of identical flat models. Then if a sentence of probability logic is satisfied in the flat model it is satisfied in the corresponding staged model. □

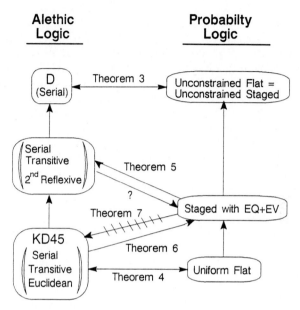

Figure 5: Relationships between probability and alethic logics.

Theorem 7 *There are alethic sentences that are falsified by a countable KD45 Kripke structure, but whose probabilistic translation is satisfied by some staged probability model conforming to EQ and EV.*

Proof: The Euclidean axiom, $\neg \Box \phi \rightarrow \Box \neg \Box \phi$, is an axiom of KD45. We present a staged probabilistic model that falsifies its probabilistic translation. Consider a model M that contains a world w such that $\vec{PD}_1^w$ assigns .5 to the set of all worlds w' for which $\vec{PD}_2^{w'}(\phi) = 1$ and assigns .5 to the set of all worlds w' for which $\vec{PD}_2^{w'}(\phi) = .4$. Then in w we have $P_{.5}P_1\phi$ and by the expected value property $P_{.7}\phi$. Thus, $\neg P_1\phi \rightarrow P_1\neg P_1\phi$ is falsified by M. $\qquad\square$

The results of this section are summarized in Figure 5.

7 Summary and Future Research

We have shown that, contrary to popular belief in AI, probability is related most closely to alethic logic, not first-order logic. A probability ranging between 0 and 1 represents a continuum between impossibility and necessity, not between simple falsity and truth.

Higher-order probabilities can be modeled by flat probability models that generalize the notion of accessibility in a Kripke structure to one of degree of accessibility. There are two coherence principles we may wish higher-order probabilities to satisfy: C1 and MP. Halpern has introduced a constraint on flat models called uniformity and has shown that it is the weakest constraint on flat models that guarantees Miller's principle holds in all models. However, uniformity also forces all higher-order probabilities to be zero or one. Staged probability models allow both Miller's principle and non-trivial higher-order probabilities. The staged models are sequences of flat models and Miller's principle holds in staged models that are hierarchies of uniform flat models.

We discussed the relation of probability logic to modal logic. Halpern has described probabilistic analogues of all the common modal logics and has shown that uniform models correspond to modal logic KD45.

We showed that the logic of staged probability models satisfying Miller's principle corresponds to an alethic logic between KD45 and a logic characterized by serial, transitive and secondarily reflexive structures. It remains open whether there is an alethic logic to which our probability logic corresponds exactly.

A number of other questions remain open to future research. The various possible constraints on probability models and combinations thereof describe a lattice of possible probability logics. Only three points in this lattice have been investigated: unconstrained models, staged models satisfying MP, and uniform flat models. The probability logics for C1, EQ, EV and EQ+C1 remain open to investigation as does the question of which alethic logics they correspond to.

The theory thus far has been developed only for unconditional probabilities. In order to represent evidence and update beliefs, conditional probabilities are required.

The results presented in this paper apply only to countable models. Many problems require uncountable probability models. A number of problems arise when we go to uncountable spaces. A formula may no longer describe a measurable set. Our mapping between probability distributions and accessibility relations no longer works. Probabilistic certainty and necessity are no longer identical.

A set of inference rules still needs to be developed for the logic. The relation of probability logic to alethic logic suggests the use of inference procedures similar to those used for modal logic. The clear correspondence of probability models to Kripke structures should help us understand how modal theorem proving methods might be applied or modified.

Acknowledgements

We thank Steve Hanks, David Selig, Peter Cheeseman, and Carl Kadie for their helpful comments on earlier drafts of this paper. We would particularly like to thank Patrick Maher for taking the time to set us straight on a number of critical issues. Discussions with Joe Halpern helped to clarify many of the issues discussed in this paper.

Notes

1. Kyburg [10] has recently dismissed the utility of higher-order probabilities by arguing that "higher-order probabilities can always be replaced by the marginal distributions of joint probability distributions." The argument claims that because Exp is an unavoidable constraint, higher- and lower-order probabilities can be combined into a joint probability space. The problem with this argument is that there are cases in which Exp need not hold and furthermore representing the higher- and lower-order probabilities in the manner Kyburg suggests requires the stronger Miller's principle, not just Exp.

2. Shimony [14] has argued that it is irrational to assign probability zero to possible events. This has the intuitive appeal that an agent would always prefer to bet on a possible event over an impossible one. If we accept Shimony's argument then we can equate probability one with necessity. One possible way of modeling this is through the use of non-standard probabilities, based on non-standard analysis [15, Appendix 4].

References

[1] P. Cheeseman. In defense of probability. In *Proceedings of the Ninth International Joint Conference on Artificial Intelligence*, pages 1002–1009, Los Angeles, California, August 1985.

[2] S. Danielsson. Modal logic based on probability theory. *Theoria*, 33(3):189–197, 1967.

[3] H. Gaifman. A theory of higher order probabilities. In *Proceedings of the Conference on Theoretical Aspects of Reasoning about Knowledge*, pages 275–292, Monterey, California, 1986.

[4] H. Gaifman. A theory of higher order probabilities. In B. Skyrms and W.L. Harper, editors, *Causation, Chance, and Credence*, pages 191–219, Kluwer Academic Publishers, 1988.

[5] P. Gärdenfors. Qualitative probability as an intensional logic. *Journal of Philosophical Logic*, 4:171–185, 1975.

[6] M. Goldstein. The prevision of a prevision. *J. American Statistical Association*, 78(384):817–819, December 1983.

[7] I.J. Good. *The Estimation of Probabilities*. MIT Press, Cambridge, MA, 1965.

[8] J. Y. Halpern. The relationship between knowledge, belief, and certainty. In *Proceedings of the Fifth Workshop on Uncertainty in AI*, pages 142–151, 1989. An expanded version appears as IBM Research Report RJ 6765, 1989.

[9] S. Kripke. Semantical considerations on modal logic. *Acta Philosophica Fennica*, 16:83–94, 1963. (Proceedings of a Colloquium on Modal and Many-Valued Logics, Helsinki, 23-26 Aug, 1962).

[10] H.E. Kyburg, Jr. Higher order probabilities. In LN Kanal, TS Levitt, and JF Lemmer, editors, *Uncertainty in Artificial Intelligence 3*, pages 15–22, North-Holland, Amsterdam, 1989.

[11] I. Levi. The demons of decision. *The Monist*, 70:193–211, 1987.

[12] N.J. Nilsson. Probabilistic logic. *Artificial Intelligence*, 28:71–87, 1986.

[13] N. Rescher. A probabilistic approach to modal logic. *Acta Philosophica Fennica*, 16:215–226, 1962.

[14] A. Shimony. Coherence and the axioms of confirmation. *Journal of Symbolic Logic*, 20:8–20, 1955.

[15] B. Skyrms. *Causal Necessity*. Yale Univ. Press, New Haven, 1980.

[16] B. van Fraassen. Belief and the will. *Journal of Philosophy*, (81):235–256, 1984.

[17] B.C. van Fraassen. A temporal framework for conditionals and chance. In W. Harper, R. Stalnaker, and G. Pearce, editors, *Ifs*, pages 323–340, D. Reidel, Dordrecht, 1980.

Uncertainty in Artificial Intelligence 4
R.D. Shachter, T.S. Levitt, L.N. Kanal, J.F. Lemmer (Editors)
© Elsevier Science Publishers B.V. (North-Holland), 1990 149

A GENERAL NON-PROBABILISTIC THEORY OF INDUCTIVE
REASONING

Wolfgang SPOHN

Institut für Philosophie
Universität Regensburg
8400 Regensburg, West Germany

1. INTRODUCTION

Probability theory, epistemically interpreted, provides an excellent, if not the best available
account of inductive reasoning. This is so because there are general and definite rules for the
change of subjective probabilities through information or experience; induction and belief
change are one and same topic, after all. The most basic of these rules is simply to conditiona-
lize with respect to the information received; and there are similar and more general rules.[1]
Hence, a fundamental reason for the epistemological success of probability theory is that there
at all exists a well-behaved concept of conditional probability.

Still, people have, and have reasons for, various concerns over probability theory. One of
these is my starting point: Intuitively, we have the notion of *plain belief*; we believe propositions[2] to be true (or to be false or neither). Probability theory, however, offers no formal
counterpart to this notion. Believing A is not the same as having probability 1 for A, because
probability 1 is incorrigible[3]; but plain belief is clearly corrigible. And believing A is not the
same as giving A a probability larger than some $1 - \varepsilon$, because believing A and believing B is
usually taken to be equivalent to believing $A \& B$.[4] Thus, it seems that the formal representation of plain belief has to take a non-probabilistic route.

Indeed, representing plain belief seems easy enough: simply represent an epistemic state
by the set of all propositions believed true in it or, since I make the common assumption that
plain belief is deductively closed, by the conjunction of all propositions believed true in it.
But this does not yet provide a theory of induction, i.e. an answer to the question how epistemic states so represented are changed through information or experience. There is a convincing partial answer: if the new information is compatible with the old epistemic state, then
the new epistemic state is simply represented by the conjunction of the new information and
the old beliefs. This answer is partial because it does not cover the quite common case where
the new information is incompatible with the old beliefs. It is, however, important to complete the answer and to cover this case, too; otherwise, we would not represent plain belief as
corrigible. The crucial problem is that there is no good completion. When epistemic states are
represented simply by the conjunction of all propositions believed true in it, the answer cannot be completed; and though there is a lot of fruitful work, no other representation of episte-

mic states has been proposed, as far as I know, which provides a complete solution to this problem.

In this paper, I want to suggest such a solution. In [4], I have more fully argued that this is the only solution, if certain plausible desiderata are to be satisfied. Here, in section 2, I will be content with formally defining and intuitively explaining my proposal. I will compare my proposal with probability theory in section 3. It will turn out that the theory I am proposing is structurally homomorphic to probability theory in important respects and that it is thus equally easily implementable, but moreover computationally simpler. Section 4 contains a very brief comparison with various kinds of logics, in particular conditional logic, with Shackle's functions of potential surprise and related theories, and with the Dempster - Shafer theory of belief functions.

2. THE THEORY

The algebraic framework has to be settled first. Let W be some non-empty set of possibilities (possible worlds, possible courses of events, or what have you). Propositions, denoted by $A,B,C,...$, are represented simply by subsets of W. Subfields of the field of all propositions will be denoted by $\mathcal{A},\mathcal{B},\mathcal{C},...$[5] Usually, W will have a structure: there will be a family $(W_i)_{i \in I}$ of variables or factors - where I is some index set and each W_i $(i \in I)$ is some non-empty set - such that $W = \Pi_{i \in I} W_i$.[6] That is, each $w \in W$ is a function defined on I with $w_i \in W_i$ for all $i \in I$ and thus represents one way how all the variables may get realized. In many physical applications, e.g., each W_i will be identical to the state space and I to the real time axis. For each $J \subseteq I$, $\mathcal{A}_J$ is to be the field $\{A \mid$ for all $w,w' \in W$, if $w_i = w'_i$ for all $i \in J$, then $w \in A$ iff $w' \in A\}$ of all propositions referring at most to the variables in J.

The central concept is now easily defined (and afterwards explained):

Definition 1: Let $\mathcal{A}$ be a field of propositions. Then κ is an $\mathcal{A}$-*measurable natural conditional function* ($\mathcal{A}$-*NCF*) iff κ is a function from W into the set N of natural numbers such that $\kappa(w) = 0$ for some $w \in W$ and $\kappa(w) = \kappa(w')$ for all atoms[7] A of $\mathcal{A}$ and all $w,w' \in A$.[8] Moreover, we define for each non-empty $A \in \mathcal{A}$: $\kappa(A) = \min\{\kappa(w) \mid w \in A\}$.[9]

The measurability condition is quite obvious; it requires that an $\mathcal{A}$-NCF does not discriminate possibilities which are not discriminated by the propositions in $\mathcal{A}$.

The crucial question, however, is how to interpret an NCF as an epistemic state. The most accurate answer is to say that an NCF κ represents a grading of disbelief: a possibility w with $\kappa(w) = 0$ is not disbelieved at all in κ; if $\kappa(w) = 1$, w is disbelieved to degree 1 in κ; etc. This means that all possibilities w with $\kappa(w) > 0$ are believed in κ not to obtain; i.e., the true possibility is believed in κ to be in $\kappa^{-1}(0) = \{w \mid \kappa(w) = 0\}$; and hence the stipulation of Definition 1 that $\kappa^{-1}(0) \neq \emptyset$. A proposition A is believed true in κ iff the true possibility is believed in κ to be in A, i.e. iff $\kappa^{-1}(0) \subseteq A$, i.e. iff $\kappa(-A) > 0$.[10] Thus, the set of propositions believed true in κ is deductively closed; and it is consistent, because $\kappa^{-1}(0) \neq \emptyset$. Note that $\kappa(A) = 0$ only means that A is not believed false in κ; this is compatible with $\kappa(-A) = 0$, i.e. with A also not being believed true in κ.

One may also talk of integer-valued degrees of firmness of belief, i.e. one may define that A is believed with firmness m in κ iff either $\kappa(A) = 0$ and $\kappa(-A) = m$ or $\kappa(A) = -m > 0$. Thus, A is believed to be true or false iff, respectively, A is believed with positive or negative firmness. This firmness-of-belief function is intuitively easier to grasp because it does not require thinking in negative terms; but it is formally less well-behaved, and the theorems would not look so simple. Therefore I prefer to stick to NCFs.

These explanations well agree with two simple consequences of Definition 1:

Theorem 1: Let κ be an $\mathcal{A}$-NCF. Then we have:

(1)   for each contingent[11] $A \in \mathcal{A}$, $\kappa(A) = 0$ or $\kappa(-A) = 0$ or both,

(2)   for all non-empty $A,B \in \mathcal{A}$, $k(A \cup B) = \min\{\kappa(A),\kappa(B)\}$.

(1) is the fundamental NCF-law for negation, saying that not both A and $-A$ can be disbelieved. (2) is the fundamental NCF-law for disjunction: It is obvious that $A \cup B$ should be believed at least as firmly as A and B. But $A \cup B$ cannot be believed more firmly than both A and B; otherwise, it might happen that both A and B are disbelieved, though $A \cup B$ is not. In order to discover a fundamental NCF-law for conjunction, we have to look at conditional NCF-values.

This brings up the crucial question how epistemic states represented by NCFs are changed through information or experience. Two plausible assumptions provide a complete answer. The first assumption is that, if the information immediately concerns only the proposition A and nothing else, then neither the grading of disbelief within A, nor that within $-A$ are changed by that information. We define:

Definition 2: Let κ be an $\mathcal{A}$-NCF and A a non-empty proposition in $\mathcal{A}$. Then, *the A-part of κ* is to be that function $\kappa(.|A)$ defined on A for which $\kappa(w|A) = \kappa(w) - \kappa(A)$ for all $w \in A$. If $B \in \mathcal{A}$ and $A \cap B \neq \emptyset$, we also define $\kappa(B|A) = \min\{\kappa(w|A) \mid w \in A \cap B)\} = \kappa(A \cap B) - \kappa(A)$.

The first assumption thus says that an information immediately concerning only A leaves the A-part as well as the $-A$-part of κ unchanged, i.e. its effect can only be that these two parts are shifted in relation to one another. Definition 2, by the way, already contains the fundamental NCF-law for conjunction:

Theorem 1 (cont.):

(3)   for all compatible $A,B \in \mathcal{A}$, $\kappa(A \cap B) = \kappa(A) + \kappa(B|A)$.

The second assumption is that information about A may come in various degrees of firmness; seeing A usually informs about A much more firmly than being told about A by some more or less reliable person. Thus, the firmness with which an information is embedded in an epistemic state cannot be fixed once and for all, but has to be conceived as a parameter of the information process itself. In view of the first assumption, this parameter completely determines belief change:

Definition 3: Let κ be an $\mathcal{A}$-NCF, A a contingent proposition in $\mathcal{A}$, and $m \in N$. Then *the A,m-conditionalization* $\kappa_{A,m}$ *of* κ is defined as that $\mathcal{A}$-NCF for which $\kappa_{A,m}(w) = \kappa(w|A)$, if $w \in A$, and $\kappa_{A,m}(w) = m + \kappa(w|\text{-}A)$, if $w \in \text{-}A$.

In the A,m-conditionalization of κ, only the A-part and the $-A$-part of κ are shifted in relation to one another, and A is believed with firmness m, as specified by the conditionalization parameter.

This account of belief change may be generalized. The information may immediately concern not only a single proposition, but a whole field $\mathcal{B}$ of propositions. The parameter characterizing the information process then consists not in a single number, but in a whole $\mathcal{B}$-NCF λ. And belief change is then defined in the following way:

Definition 4: Let κ be an $\mathcal{A}$-NCF, $\mathcal{B}$ a subfield of $\mathcal{A}$, and λ a $\mathcal{B}$-NCF. Then *the λ-conditionalization* κ_λ *of* κ is defined as that $\mathcal{A}$-NCF for which for all atoms B of $\mathcal{B}$ and all $w \in B$ $\kappa_\lambda(w) = \lambda(B) + \kappa(w|B)$.

In the λ-conditionalization of κ, $\kappa_\lambda(B) = \lambda(B)$ for all $B \in \mathcal{B}$, and only the B-parts of κ, for all atoms B of $\mathcal{B}$, are shifted in relation to each other. Definition 4 corresponds to Jeffrey's much discussed generalized probabilistic conditionalization; cf. [1], ch. 11.

It is to be expected that a workable concept of independence goes hand in hand with this account of conditionalization. This is indeed the case. The following definition is straightforward:

Definition 5: Let κ be an $\mathcal{A}$-NCF and $\mathcal{B}$ and $\mathcal{C}$ two subfields of $\mathcal{A}$. Then $\mathcal{B}$ and $\mathcal{C}$ are *independent with respect to* κ iff for all non-empty $B \in \mathcal{B}$ and $C \in \mathcal{C}$ $\kappa(B \cap C) = \kappa(B) + \kappa(C)$. Furthermore, $\mathcal{B}$ and $\mathcal{C}$ are *independent conditional on* the proposition D w.r.t. κ iff for all non-empty $B \in \mathcal{B}$ and $C \in \mathcal{C}$ $\kappa(B \cap C|D) = \kappa(B|D) + \kappa(C|D)$. If $\mathcal{D}$ is a further subfield of $\mathcal{A}$, then $\mathcal{B}$ and $\mathcal{C}$ are *independent conditional on* $\mathcal{D}$ w.r.t. κ iff $\mathcal{B}$ and $\mathcal{C}$ are independent conditional on all atoms D of $\mathcal{D}$ w.r.t. κ. Finally, these definitions are specialized to two contingent propositions B and C by taking $\mathcal{B}$ as $\{\varnothing, B, \text{-}B, W\}$ and $\mathcal{C}$ as $\{\varnothing, C, \text{-}C, W\}$.

How do all the concepts so defined behave? This may not be immediately perspicuous, but the next section will provide a surprisingly powerful answer.

3. A COMPARISON WITH PROBABILITY THEORY

The basic definitions and formulae in the previous section look very similar to those in probability theory; we only seem to have replaced the sum, multiplication, and division of probabilities by, respectively, the minimum, addition, and subtraction of NCF-values. In order to see that this is no accident, we have to move for a moment into the context of non-standard arithmetics and non-standard probability theory:

Theorem 2: Let $\mathcal{A}$ be a finite field of propositions. Then, for any non-standard $\mathcal{A}$-NCF[12] κ and for any infinitesimal z there is a non-standard probability measure P such that for all $A,B \in \mathcal{A}$ $\kappa(B|A) = n$ iff $P(B|A)$ is of the same order as z^n (i.e. $P(B|A)/z^n$ is finite, but not infinitesimal). In particular we have: whenever $P(C) = P(A) + P(B)$, then $\kappa(C) = \min\{\kappa(A), \kappa(B)\}$; whenever $P(C) = P(A)\,P(B)$, then $\kappa(C) = \kappa(A) + \kappa(B)$; $\kappa(B|A) = \kappa(A \cap B) - \kappa(A)$, as desired; and whatever is (conditionally) independent w.r.t. P, is so also w.r.t. κ.

Sketch of proof: Define P in the following way: for each atom A of $\mathcal{A}$ with $\kappa(A) = n > 0$ let $P(A) = z^n$, and distribute the rest equally among the other atoms of $\mathcal{A}$ so that the probabilities of all atoms of $\mathcal{A}$ sum up to 1. The claims of Theorem 2 are then easily checked; they in particular turn on the fact that, if x is of the same order as z^m and y of the same order as z^n, then xy is of the same order as z^{m+n} and $x + y$ is of the same order as $z^{\min(m,n)}$.

It is thus not surprising that the laws of the concepts introduced in the previous section are simply translations of the laws of the corresponding probabilistic concepts. For instance, the theorem of total probability translates into this (where $A_1,...,A_s$ partition W):

(4) $\kappa(B) = \min_{r \leq s} [\kappa(A_r) + \kappa(B|A_r)]$.

Bayes' theorem yields this (with $A_1,...,A_s$ as before):

(5) $\kappa(A_q|B) = \kappa(A_q) + \kappa(B|A_q) - \min_{r \leq s} [\kappa(A_r) + \kappa(B|A_r)]$.

Also, the probabilistic laws of independence and conditional independence hold for NCFs - e.g.:

(6) If A and C are independent w.r.t. κ, then B and C are independent w.r.t. κ iff $A \cup B$ and C are independent w.r.t. κ - provided that A and B are disjoint.

Without the proviso, (6) would not necessarily hold. And so on. Let me only mention the most important law concerning conditional independence of subfields. It says in terms of the factorization of W at the beginning of section 2, where J, K, and L are pairwise disjoint subsets of the index set I:

(7) If $\mathcal{A}_J$ is independent of $\mathcal{A}_K$ conditional on $\mathcal{A}_L$ and independent of $\mathcal{A}_L$ or independent of $\mathcal{A}_L$ conditional on $\mathcal{A}_K$ w.r.t. κ, then $\mathcal{A}_J$ is independent of $\mathcal{A}_{K \cup L}$ w.r.t. κ.[13]

These observations have a considerable import. For instance, the theory of probabilistic causation has turned out to be to a large extent a theory of conditional stochastic independence.[14] NCFs would thus allow to extend these ideas to a theory of deterministic causation.[15] In the present context, however, the crucial observation is that conditional independence is an important means for making probability measures computationally manageable. This carries over to the implementation of NCFs. In particular, the results and techniques related to such things as influence diagrams, Markov fields and trees, causal graphs, etc.[16] may be translated into NCF-theory. This is exemplified by [12] and [13]: In [12], Hunter achieves a way of parallel updating of NCFs by adapting methods of parallel probabilistic updating developed by Pearl in [11]; and in [13], Hunter shows that the results reported in [14] and [15] carry over to NCFs, i.e. that for NCFs, too, the conditional independencies implied by a given causal input list according to Definition 5, those derivable from that list by the axioms of semi-graphoids, and those implied by that list via Verma's criterion of d-separation are always the same.[17] Finally, Definition 4 suggests that the concept of a mixture may be meaningfully carried over from probability theory to the theory of NCFs and may there have fruitful applications.

Of course, there also are differences. On the one hand, NCFs are computationally simpler than probabilities; they have the advantage of formally representing the intuitively so important concept of plain belief; and it may be easier to elicit and implement the subjective judgments of experts in the coarser terms of NCFs. On the other hand, I presently do not see how NCFs would allow for a meaningful analogue to the theory of integration and expectation and thus for a useful decision theory (for which something like expected utility is essential). And most importantly, relative frequencies are so intimately tied to probabilities that I do not see how to reasonably deal with statistical data within an NCF-framework.

A final remark: I said in the introduction that plain belief in A cannot be probability 1 for A because of the incorrigibility of probability 1. This seems to be disproved by extensions of standard probability theory which allow for conditionalization by null propositions and thus render probability 1 corrigible. However, Popper measures, the best known extension of this kind, cannot account for iterated epistemic changes, as has already been observed in [16]. According to my diagnosis in [4], sect. 7, which is based on the investigation [17] into the formal structure of Popper measures, this failure can only be overcome by replacing Popper measures by, so to speak, probabilified NCFs. Thus, it seems that the probabilist cannot avoid considering NCFs as long as he takes plain belief seriously.

4. OTHER COMPARISONS

Though many have proposed non-probabilistic representations of epistemic states, I have, to my surprise, nowhere found the very structure described in section 2; aims and intuitions have presumably been different. But often, the importance of stating general and precise rules of belief change, which are tantamount to a theory of induction, has apparently not been clearly recognized; this will in any case be my standard criticism of the further comparisons pursued here.

4.1. Various Logics

The following strategy for modelling belief change has attracted many people: Suppose a language with a conditional $\rightarrow$ to be given; represent an epistemic state by a (consistent and deductively closed) set S of sentences of that language; and define the change S_A of S by information A as $S_A = \{B \mid A \rightarrow B \in S\}$.[18] Of course, this strategy crucially depends on the properties of $\rightarrow$. E.g., $\rightarrow$ must not be interpreted as material implication. Strict implication will do neither; all the conditionals in the various many-valued logics that have been proposed are unsuited, too[19]; and even the conditionals of the variants of relevance logic seem to be unhelpful.[20] However, these remarks are not meant as a criticism, because all the conditionals mentioned were not designed for the present purpose.

Indeed, no monotonic conditional will be adequate for this strategy. The best conditional for this purpose is that of conditional logic (which has always been conceived to be non-monotonic in the sense that $A \rightarrow C$ does not entail $A \& B \rightarrow C$). Most semantics of conditional logic and corresponding models of belief change basically use orderings: orderings of propositions or of certain sets of propositions, well-orderings of possible worlds, and similar or equivalent things.[21] But they don't use numbers and their arithmetical properties. As I argue in [4], this is why these semantics and the corresponding models of belief change get problems with iterated belief change and cannot provide an equally adequate concept of (conditional) independence. Moreover, epistemic changes as defined in Definition 4 seem completely inaccessible to the whole strategy. Again, this is not a criticism of conditional logic, but only of the envisaged strategy of modelling belief change.[22]

4.2. Plausibility Measures

One of the first to propose formal alternatives to the beaten tracks of probability theory was Shackle with his functions of potential surprise most extensively presented in [25]. Such a function is a function y from the set of propositions into the closed interval [0,1] such that

(8) $y(\emptyset) = 1$,

(9) either $y(A) = 0$ or $y(-A) = 0$ or both,

(10) $y(A \cup B) = \min\{y(A), y(B)\}$.

(9) and (10) are identical with (1) and (2), and (8) arbitrarily fixes the maximal degree of potential surprise to be 1. Thus, Shackle's and my functions only differ in their ranges. This is not a mere technicality, however. There is reason to accept the generalization of (2) or (10) to countable unions (without weakening min to inf), and this forces the range of these functions to be well-ordered. Moreover, I have avoided a maximal degree of disbelief, because this maximal degree could not be changed according to all rules of belief change and would thus be incorrigible. Therefore, I do not want to allow the possibility accepted by Shackle that non-empty propositions have maximal potential surprise.

The main point, however, is that Shackle didn't get a grip on conditionalization. This is clear from his proposal

(11) $y(A \cap B) = \max\{y(A), y(B|A)\}$,

where he left $y(B|A)$ undefined.[23]

Similar remarks apply to the plausibility indexing which Rescher has proposed since 1964, e.g. in [26], and to Cohen's theory of inductive probability in [27] (which is not mathematical probability, but quite similar to NCFs). The works of these authors show the wide und fruitful applicability of non-probabilistic belief representation in many areas inside and outside philosophy.

4.3. Dempster - Shafer

In [28], p.224, Shafer shows that Shackle's theory is a special case of his: the function y is a degree of doubt derived from a consonant belief function in the sense of Shafer iff it satisfies (8) - (10). Since Dempster's rule of combination governs belief change for Shafer's belief functions in general, it may be expected to complete Shackle's theory. It indeed does, but in a different way than I did in section 2:

According to [28], pp.43 + 66f., there are also conditional degrees of doubt given by the formula

(12) $y(B|A) = [y(A \cap B) - y(A)] / [1 - y(A)]$.

Apart from the denominator, this looks like my Definition 2. However, $y(.|A)$ here represents the degree of doubt which results from combining the old belief function with the belief function Bel defined by: $Bel(B) = 1$, if $A \subseteq B$, and $Bel(B) = 0$ otherwise; and this function makes A incorrigibly certain, according to Shafer's theory. Thus, one should rather know how Shafer processes evidence which makes A less than incorrigibly certain, since this is what the above Definition 3 accomplishes. Shafer does this by combining the old belief function with some belief function Bel_s defined by: $Bel_s(B) = 1$, if $B = W$, $Bel_s(B) = s$, if $A \subseteq B \neq W$, and $Bel_s(B) = 0$ otherwise $(0 < s < 1)$. (In a sense, s corresponds to the m of Definition 3.) But now the problem arises that, if the old belief function is consonant, its combination with Bel_s will in general not be consonant; this is easily checked. Thus, my conditionalizations of NCFs move within the set of all NCFs, whereas the set of all consonant belief functions in Shafer's sense is not closed with respect to Dempster's rule of combination. This entails that the NCF-theory presented here cannot be covered by the Dempster - Shafer theory of belief functions.

However, in [5] Shenoy gains a more positive perspective. He proposes a different rule of combination for NCFs which gives an account of belief change equivalent to the conditionalizations given by Definitions 3 and 4. Moreover, he defines marginalization for NCFs and shows that marginalization and combination thus explained obey the axioms presented in [29]. This means that the general scheme of local computation developed in [29] can also be applied to NCFs.[24]

NOTES

[1] Most notably Jeffrey's generalized conditionalization and the principle of maximizing relative entropy; cf. [1], ch. 11, and, e.g., [2].

[2] "Proposition" is the philosophically most common general term for the objects of belief and the one I shall use. The precise nature of these objects is philosophically very problematic, but not my present concern.

[3] Whatever has probability 1 keeps it, according to all rules of belief change within standard probability theory.

4 I am here alluding to the so-called lottery paradox, which has gained considerable importance in the writings of H.E. Kyburg, jr., I. Levi, and others. Cf., e.g., the various hints in [3].

5 In the present context W may well be assumed to be finite; so, we need not decide which kinds of fields to consider. In the infinite case, complete fields seem to me to be the most appropriate (cf. [4]), but alternative algebraic frameworks might be adapted, too.

6 Π denotes the Cartesian product.

7 A is an atom of $\mathcal{A}$ iff no proper non-empty subset of A ia a member of $\mathcal{A}$.

8 "Conditional", because these functions can be conditionalized, as we shall see; "natural", because they take natural numbers as values; in [5], Shenoy has proposed the more intuitive label "disbelief function" (which, however, cannot be translated into German). In [4], I have more generally defined "ordinal conditional functions" which take ordinal numbers as values. This generality will not be needed here (all the more as it has some awkward consequences which relate to the fact that addition of ordinal numbers is not commutative).

9 The latter function for propositions will indeed be the more important one.

10 $-A$ denotes the complement or the negation of A.

11 A is contingent iff A and $-A$ both are not empty.

12 This is to mean that κ takes non-standard natural numbers as values.

13 For a proof see [4], sect. 6. These are the properties of conditional independence which Pearl calls Contraction and Intersection, e.g. in [6], p.84.

14 As is manifested by many papers in [7], by [8], and at many other places.

15 Indeed, I originally invented them for this purpose in [9].

16 See, e.g., [10], [11], and [6], ch. 3-5. Of course, references could be easily extended.

17 Perhaps NCFs allow an easier investigation of conditional independence than probability measures, because they are mathematically simpler, because NCFs correspond only to strictly positive probabilities, and because the disturbing property of what Pearl calls weak transitivity (cf. [6], pp.128ff.), which is a special probabilistic law for binary variables, does not hold for NCFs.

18 This is the so-called Ramsey test, most thoroughly propounded by Gärdenfors, e.g. in [18], who has summarized his work in [19]. See also [20].

19 As may be easily confirmed with the help of the list in [21].

20 In order to substantiate this remark, we would have to go more deeply into [22].

21 Cf., e.g., the pioneering work [23], the overview in [24], and [19], ch. 7 together with ch. 4.

22 Another serious problem for this strategy is presented by the trivialization result in [18]. I have here avoided this problem by excluding conditional propositions as objects of belief.

23 In [25], p.205, Shackle mentions that he has considered the law (3) for NCFs instead of (11). But he says almost nothing about why he finally stuck to (11).

24 I am very grateful to Dan Hunter for having introduced my thoughts and myself to the AI community.

REFERENCES

[1]   Jeffrey, R.C., *The Logic of Decision* (University Press, Chicago, 1965, 2nd ed. 1983)

[2]   Skyrms, B., "Maximum Entropy Inference as a Special Case of Conditionalization", *Synthese* **63** (1985) 55-74.

[3]   Bogdan, R.J. (ed.), *Henry E. Kyburg, jr. & Isaac Levi* (Reidel, Dordrecht, 1982)

[4]   Spohn, W., "Ordinal Conditional Functions: A Dynamic Theory of Epistemic States", in: Harper, W.L., Skyrms, B., (eds.), *Causation in Decision, Belief Change, and Statistics* (Kluwer, Dordrecht, 1988) pp.105-134.

[5]   Shenoy, P.P., "On Spohn's Rule for Revision of Beliefs", School of Business Working Paper No. 213 (University of Kansas, Lawrence, Kansas, 1989)

[6]   Pearl, J., *Probabilistic Reasoning in Intelligent Systems: Networks of Plausible Inference* (Morgan Kaufmann, San Mateo, Ca., 1988)

[7]   Skyrms, B, Harper, W.L., (eds.), *Causation, Chance, and Credence* (Kluwer, Dordrecht, 1988)

[8]   Skyrms, B, "Probability and Causation", *Journal of Econometrics* **39** (1988) 53-68.

158

[9] Spohn, W., *Eine Theorie der Kausalität* (unpublished Habilitationsschrift, Munich, 1984)
[10] Kiiveri, H., Speed, T.P., Carlin, J.B., "Recursive Causal Models", *Journal of the Australian Mathematical Society*, Series A, **36** (1984) 30-52.
[11] Pearl, J., "Fusion, Propagation, and Structuring in Belief Networks", *Artificial Intelligence* **29** (1986) 241-288.
[12] Hunter, D., "Parallel Belief Revision", this volume.
[13] Hunter, D., "Graphoids, Semi-graphoids, and Ordinal Conditional Functions", NRTC Research Paper (Palos Verdes, Ca., 1988)
[14] Geiger, D., Pearl, J., "On the Logic of Causal Models", this volume.
[15] Verma, T., Pearl, J., "Causal Networks: Semantics and Expressiveness", this volume.
[16] Harper, W.L., "Rational Belief Change, Popper Functions and Counterfactuals", in: Harper, W.L., Hooker, C.A., (eds.), *Foundations of Probability Theory, Statistical Inference, and Statistical Theories of Science*, vol. I (Reidel, Dordrecht, 1976) pp. 73-115.
[17] Spohn, W., "The Representation of Popper Measures", *Topoi* **5** (1986) 69-74.
[18] Gärdenfors, P., "Belief Revisions and the Ramsey Test for Conditionals", *Philosophical Review* **95** (1986) 81-93.
[19] Gärdenfors, P., *Knowledge in Flux* (MIT Press, Cambridge, Mass., 1988)
[20] Rott, H., "Conditionals and Theory Change: Revisions, Expansions, and Additions", *Synthese*, in print.
[21] Rescher, N., *Many-valued Logic* (McGraw-Hill, New York, 1969)
[22] Anderson, A.R., Belnap jr., N.D., *Entailment* (University Press, Princeton, 1975)
[23] Lewis, D., *Counterfactuals* (Blackwell, Oxford, 1973)
[24] Nute, D., *Topics in Conditional Logic* (Reidel, Dordrecht, 1980)
[25] Shackle, G.L.S., *Decision, Order, and Time in Human Affairs* (University Press, Cambridge, 1969)
[26] Rescher, N., *Plausible Reasoning* (Van Gorcum, Assen, 1976)
[27] Cohen, L.J., *The Probable and the Provable* (Clarendon Press, Oxford, 1977)
[28] Shafer, G., *A Mathematical Theory of Evidence* (University Press, Princeton, 1976)
[29] Shenoy, P.P., Shafer, G., "An Axiomatic Framework for Bayesian and Belief-function Propagation", this volume.

Uncertainty in Artificial Intelligence 4
R.D. Shachter, T.S. Levitt, L.N. Kanal, J.F. Lemmer (Editors)
© Elsevier Science Publishers B.V. (North-Holland), 1990   159

EPISTEMOLOGICAL RELEVANCE AND STATISTICAL KNOWLEDGE*

Henry E. KYBURG, Jr.

Computer Science and Philosophy
University of Rochester
Rochester, NY, USA

1. BACKGROUND

For many years, at least since McCarthy and Hayes [10], writers have lamented, and attempted to compensate for, the alleged fact that we often do not have adequate statistical knowledge for governing the uncertainty of belief, for making uncertain inferences, and the like. It is hardly ever spelled out what "adequate statistical knowledge" *would* be, if we had it, and *how* adequate statistical knowledge could be used to control and regulate epistemic uncertainty.

One response to the lack of adequate statistics has been to search for non-statistical measures of uncertainty. The minimal variant has been to propose "subjective probability" as a concept to which we can turn when we lack statistics.

This proposal comes in widely differing flavors, corresponding to the dreadful ambiguity of "subjective". Sometimes this means merely "indexed by a subject". In this sense there is no conflict with statistical representations: the "subjectivity" involved just represents the fact that statistical knowledge is related to (had by) a knower. (This appears to be the sense of "subjective" employed by Cheeseman [3].)

At the other extreme, "subjective" may mean arbitrary, whimsical, subject to no objective control or constraint. Those who think we must turn in this direction are influenced by the feeling that in many cases there may be nothing better to turn to. The philosopher F. P. Ramsey, who did much to make the subjective approach to uncertainty respectable, apparently felt this way; he wrote: "...a man's expectation of drawing a white or a black ball from an urn ... may within the limits of consistency be any he likes..." [12].

Other proposals concern non-probabilistic measures of uncertainty: the certainty factors of Buchan [2], the belief functions of Shafer [14], the fuzzy membership relation of Zadeh [16].

Our purpose here is not to evaluate these alternative treatments of uncertainty, but rather to explore the question of how far you can go on the basis of statistical knowledge that you *do* have, and what considerations must be taken account of in this attempt. Relatively few people have explored the question of how far you can go using statistical knowledge. One writer who has taken this question seriously is Bacchus [1].

---

*Research underlying the results reported here has been partially supported by the Signals Warfare Center of the United States Army.

A second question, in fact the one that McCarthy and Hayes had in mind, is the question of using statistical knowledge to provide an underpinning for uncertain *inference* -- that is, inference that is based on incomplete knowledge. A basic presupposition of the non-monotonic and default industries seems to be that you cannot very often base such inferences on statistical knowledge. In part this presupposition is based on the feeling that "typicality" and "frequency" *mean* different things. Be that as it may, in formalizing non-monotonic logics many people seem to be led to considerations that (not surprisingly!) mirror considerations appropriate to the application of statistical knowledge.

Thus Etherington [4] introduces the concept of *preference* among models; Konolige [5] defines a notion of *minimal extension*; Touretzky [15] gives a metric for *inferential distance*.

These ideas will be reflected in the principles governing the relevance of statistical knowledge to be discussed below. Our analysis of the ground-rules for the use of statistical knowledge will throw light on the "cancellation principles" of non-monotonic logic as well.

2. ASSUMPTIONS

The assumptions we make here are four:

(1) We suppose that the knowledge base may have objective statistical knowledge in it. This statistical knowledge may be construed in a number of ways -- for example as statements concerning chances or statements concerning frequencies in an arbitrarily long run, or statements concerning frequencies in the actual world, or frequencies summed over possible worlds.

We do suppose that these statements are *general* -- that is, they do not directly represent the fact that we have recorded a frequency in a specific sample. We *may* have done so, and gone on to infer a general statistical statement. But we also may have gotten our statistical knowledge from a handbook, or a dependable colleague. In any event, the statistical knowledge in our knowledge base is taken to be general scientific knowledge relating properties; we will write "$\%(A, R) = p$" to represent the fact that the long-run frequency A's among R's is p.

It might seem that there are relatively few statements that can be given a probability on a direct statistical basis. But if we accept the equivalence condition -- that statements connnected in our knowledge base by a truth-functional biconditional should have the same probability -- then many more statements than might at first have been thought can have probabilities based on statistical background knowledge.[1]

The equivalence condition is very hard to get around. It follows in the standard probability calculus, for example, from the principle that any two *logically* equivalent statements be given the same probability. [Proof: $P(h\&(h\equiv g)/e) = P(g\&(h\equiv g)/e)$, by the equality of probabilities over logical equivalents. But these expand into $P(h\equiv g/e)*P(h/(h\equiv g)\&e)$ and $P(h\equiv g/e)*P(g/(h\equiv g)\&e)$, from which $P(h/(h\equiv g)\&e) = P(g/(h\equiv g)\&e)$ immediately follows.

---

[1]In fact it might be claimed that all probabilities -- all rational uncertainties -- are based on statistical knowledge. This is the underlying thrust of Kyburg [6,7].

We will weaken the assumption of exact statistical knowledge later to take account of *approximate* statistical knowledge. The long run frequency of *A*'s may be *about p*, or *at least q*.

(2) We assume that our body of knowledge -- our background knowledge -- determines equivalence classes of the statements whose uncertainty concerns us. *S* and *T* are in the same equivalence class if we know that they have the same truth values: that is, if and only if the truth functional biconditional $S \equiv T$ is part of our knowledge. Thus if we know that the next toss of this coin is the next toss of a 1979 U.S. quarter and that it lands heads if and only if it fails to land tails, and that I will choose to have chocolate ice cream if and only if it lands tails, then

> "The next toss of this coin lands heads"
> "The next toss of a 1979 U.S. quarter lands heads"
> "The next toss of this coin does not land tails"
> "I will not choose chocolate ice cream"

all fall in the same equivalence class and have the same probability.

Similarly, if we know of a certain number of *B*'s -- those we have observed for example -- that it has a relative frequency of *C*'s of 0.45, then the probability that the long run frequency of *C*'s among *B*'s is close to the sample frequency is the same as the probability that the long run frequency is close to 0.45.

The *question* to which we take statisical knowledge to be relevant is the whole equivalence class of statements. It is this assumption that makes it plausible for us to suppose that we always have statistical knowledge that bears (relevantly) on any given statement, however "unique" the subject of that statement. It is also this assumption that requires us to think about the principles of statistical relevance: if "$S \equiv T$" is in our knowlege base, then the same statistical knowledge that is potentially relevant to *S* is also potentially relevant to *T*.

(3) We assume, as usual, that our knowledge base can be expressed in a first order extensional language. (Of course this requires the inclusion of enough first order set theory to accommodate the statistics!) Of course for the manipulation of mathematical objects, such as proportions, we have no need of anything that is not built into our computer. We may still take an individual to be arbitrarily complex: for example it might be a trial of a complicated compound experiment -- say an ordered triple consisting of the selection of a room in a house, the selection of an urn in the room, and the selection of a ball from the urn.

(4) Finally, in order for statistics to be of interest, we suppose that we may know some things about an individual without knowing everything about it. Thus we might know of "the next trial" that it is a trial consisting of selecting one of a number of urns at random, and then selecting a coin at random from the urn, and then tossing the coin 10 times. And then we might be interested in whether the tenth toss landed heads on that trial, or we might know the distribution of heads in the tosses, and we might be interested in whether the urn was urn number 4, or we might be interested in knowing something about the frequency of two headed coins in the urn from which we got our sample.

In the three sections that follow, we shall be concerned with three ways in which items of statistical knowledge can interfer with each other, and three corresponding ways in which this interference can be dealt with.

3. INTERFERENCE I

The simplest and clearest case can be borrowed from non-monotonic logic.

If all we know of Tweety is that she is a bird, it is reasonable to believe -- to assign a high probabilty to -- the proposition that she can fly. If we also know that she is a penguin, then it is reasonable to believe that she cannot fly, since our knowledge about the chances of a penguin flying *interferes* with our knowledge about the chances of a bird flying and renders that statistical knowledge epistemically irrelevant as concerns Tweety.

If (as we may in our biological ignorance suppose) there is a rare kind of penguin that *can* fly, and if we know that Tweety is one of them, then this new knowledge interferes with our general knowledge about penguins, and again we may suppose it to be highly probable that Tweety *can* fly.

This relation of epistemic irrelevance has been noted by Etherington [4], Poole [11], Konolige [5], and others. It corresponds to what Reichenbach [13] had in mind when he said that we should base our posits (degrees of belief) on the "narrowest" reference class concerning which we have adequate statistics; all other reference classes are irrelevant. ("Having adequate statistics" does *not* mean having knowledge of a sample of the class in question; it means having useful *general* knowledge about that class, whatever it may be based on.)

A principle embodying this natural constraint must be stated with somewhat more generality than is at first obvious, however.

Suppose (to move to an artificial example) we know of ball #18 that it is a ball in a certain room, and that we know that 50% of the balls in that room are black. Suppose we know also that that particular ball is also one in an urn, urn A, in which 80% are black. The second piece of statistical knowledge is clearly epistemically relevant and the first is not. This intuition is based on the fact that the set of balls in the urn in the room is a subset of the set of balls in the room.

But it is more natural to be concerned with the color of a ball about which we know something more than its proper name. So suppose "#18" is the canonical designator for *the next ball to be chosen from the room.* It has been pointed out that just because 50% of the balls in the room are black doesn't mean that 50% of the balls *chosen* from the room are black. Nevertheless, under the usual conditions of such hypothetical experiments, we are entitled to infer that 50% of the choosings of balls are choosings of black balls. So we may consider the event of choosing ball #18, and the frequency with which such choosings are choosings of black balls. Fifty percent of them are, in general.

This is true, but should be irrelevant since we know that #18 came from an urn in which 80% of the balls are black. But the set of balls in that urn isn't a set of choosings at all and so not a subset of the set of objects we are now considering. The subset principle is of no direct help to us. Nor should it be of *direct* help, for it is certainly intelligible to suppose that while the frequency of black choosings corresponds to the proportion of black balls in general, it fails to do so in the set of choosings from urn *A*. If this is not the case -- if we have reason to believe that 80% of the choosings from urn *A* yield a black ball -- then either structure should be acceptable, despite the fact that one concerns choosings (events) and the other balls (objects).

It might be suggested that the whole problem can be avoided by choosing a canonical representation and using only that as a basis for generating uncertainty. We *could* stipulate that all the sentences in question have some specific canonical logical form. But, as we shall see, and as the example should already have indicated, this would be ill-advised; we need the flexibility to move to whatever form of object or event or history fragment embodies the most useful statistical information. What we can do instead is state our principle more broadly:

The Subset Principle: Suppose that "a is a B" is in our knowledge base, and that "$\%(C, B) = p$" is in our knowledge base. Suppose that we know that a' is a C' if and only if a is a C, that a' is a B', and that $\%(C', B') = p'$, where $p \neq p'$. This statistical knowledge is *epistemically irrelevant* if we know of a subset of B', B'', such that we know both a' is a B'' and $\%(C', B'') = p$.

The subset principle is one that has been frequently identified in the context of non-monotonic logic.

4. INTERFERENCE II

Here is an example that calls for a second principle: As before, suppose we have a roomful of urns, and that #18 designates a ball in the room. Suppose we know that there are 100 balls in the room, and that 50 are black. But suppose we also know that there are 10 urns, that 9 of them contain 4 black balls and one white ball, and that the tenth contains the remainder of the balls. The relative frequency of black balls in the first 9 urns is .80, and the relative frequency of black balls in the tenth urn is $14/55 = .25...$

Let us consider what statistics are relevant to the statement, "#18 is black". If we know of #18 only that it is a ball in the room, it is only the statistics about the frequency of black balls in the room that are relevant. If we know *also* something about how #18 came to be the designated ball, the other statistics may also be relevant. For example, we might know that #18 is the ball resulting from first choosing an urn at random, and then choosing a ball at random from the selected urn. If that is the case, the relevant statistics are those governing the proportion of pairs consisting of an urn, and a ball drawn from that urn, such that the second member of the pair is black. We can easily calculate the proportion of pairs having this property to be $.9 * .8 + .1 * .25... = .745$. (Note that there is no subset of the balls in the room having this frequency to which #18 is known to belong. In fact, 0.745 *cannot*, mathematically, be the relative frequency in any subset of the set of balls in the room!)

But why, under these circumstances, should we regard the general statistics concerning balls in the room to be epistemically irrelevant? The interfering set isn't a subset of its competitor. Of course, we can find a relationship: there is a possible reference class that matches the competitor, of which the correct reference set *is* a subset -- namely, the cross product of the set of urns and the set of balls. The proportion of pairs, in which the second member is a black ball, is just the original 50%. But there is a subset, the set of pairs of urns-and-balls in which the ball is paired with urn it is drawn from, that contains 74.5% pairs in which the second member is a black ball.

This construction is particularly important in the context of (so-called) Bayesian inference; the model we just looked at corresponds to a non-sampling case in which we have a prior probability of .9 combined with a conditional probability of .8, and a prior probability of .1 combined with a conditional probability of .25. We therefore call the rule the Bayesian Principle:

The Bayesian Principle: Suppose that "$<a, b>$ is a B" is in our knowledge base, and that "$\%(C, B) = p$" is in our knowledge base. Suppose that we know that a' is a C' if and only if a is a C, that a' is a B', and that $\%(C', B') = p' \neq p$. This statistical knowledge is *epistemically irrelevant* if we know of a cross product of B' with B'' and a corresponding subset C'' and a'' such that

     (1) $<a', a''>$ is known to be in $B' \times B''$,
     (2) $<a', a''>$ is in C'' if and only if a is in C,
     (3) $\%(C'', B' \times B'') = p'$,

and for some B^* known to be a subset of $B' \times B''$,

     (4) $\%(B^*, C) = p$.

To see how this works in our illustrative example, let U be the set of urns, B the set of balls, E the set of pairs corresponding to the experimental set-up, with $<x, y>$ in E just in case x is an urn and y is a ball in the urn x. Our target property is the set of pairs C in which the second member is black. The proportion is just what we calculated before: .745.

To show that a', and the statistical knowledge that the proportion of balls in B that are black is .50, is *not* epistemically relevant, we observe that $<a', u>$ is known to be a member of $B \times U$, where u is the (unknown) urn selected, that the proportion of $B \times U$ in C is 0.50, but that there is a subset of $B \times U$ -- namely E itself -- in which the proportion of members of C is the same as that in E.

The Bayesian principle is followed in constructing representations of uncertainty, particularly in cases in which uncertainties are modified by new evidence, but I have not noticed it in discussions of non-monotonic inference. It should be, of course, though it would take us too far afield to construct an example that called for it.

5. INTERFERENCE III

The final principle of epistemic irrelevance we need for dealing with statistical knowledge is in a sense the dual of our first principle, the subset principle. Suppose that you are sampling from a population C with a view to making an inference about the proportion of B's there are in C. It is a general set theoretical fact that we will not explore more deeply that almost all subsets of a given set reflect within limits the composition of the parent set. These limits depend on the number chosen to represent "almost all" and on the size of the sample, but they depend little on the proportion of B's in the parent population; the narrowness of the limits increases with sample size with surprizing speed.

Putting flesh on this observation, we might note that (using a crude approximation), whatever the proportion p_B of C's that are B's, the proportion of 10,000 member subsets of C that have a proportion of B's within .04 of the actual proportion is at least .975.

Suppose we look at 10,000 C's and find that 5000 of them are B's. Quite clearly, at a level of confidence of .975, one ought to suppose that between .46 and .54 of the C's are B's. This follows immediately from our equivalence principle. It is a set-theoretical fact -- in particular it has nothing to do with "random" selection -- that whatever p_B may be, at least 97.5% of 10,000 membered subsets of C will exhibit a proportion of B's within .04 of p_B.

It follows from the fact that we know the proportion of B's in our sample to be .50 that our particular sample of 10,000 exhibits a proportion of B's within .04 of p_B if and only if $p_B \in [.46,.54]$.

This bit of theoretical statistics may or may not be the *relevant* statistics. We might have various bits of knowledge that are relevant to this fact that fall under the first two categories. For example, it may be that we know that our sample was drawn in a special way that produces representative samples only rarely. This makes it belong to a special subclass of the 10,000-membered subclasses in which the property in question is rare rather than common. Or we may know that we are sampling from a collection of populations in which we know something about the *distribution* of the relative frequency of B's. This leads to Bayesian inference as the source of the relevant statistics.

Let us assume that neither of these are the case -- that is, that neither the subset principle nor the Bayesian principle apply. So we would like to say that the chances are at least .975 that the proportion of B's is between .46 and .54.

But there is another way in which this inference could go wrong. It is consistent with the story we have told so far that we should have observed more C's than we have mentioned. This should render the previous numbers irrelevant.

Put otherwise, note that it follows from the story we have told that we have observed a sample S' of 7500 C's, of which 2/3 have been B's. We can calculate that p_B is in $[.46,.54]$ if and only if the proportion in S' lies between $p_B +.13$ and $p_B +.21$. But the chances of a 7500 member sample of C's having this property are roughly zero.

Given the choice between "at least 0.975" and "roughly zero" we want to regard the former as relevant and the latter as irrelevant. The larger sample is the one that is epistemically relevant. A principle that captures this intuition is:

The Supersample Principle: Suppose that we know that a_n is a member of P^n and that we are interested in the chance that a_n is R_ϵ (e.g., "representative within ϵ"). Suppose that a_m is known to be a member of P^m, that a_m is a R' if and only if a_n is R_ϵ, and that $\%(R_\epsilon , P^n) = p \neq p' = \%(R', P^m)$ are all known. Then our statistical knowledge about R' -- and any equivalent statistical knowledge -- is *epistemically irrelevant* if we also know that a_m is a subset of a_n .

6. DISCUSSION

It is my belief that these three principles are all the principles we need to determine the epistemic relevance of statistical knowledge in the case in which we either have exact knowledge or none at all. It may be that other principles are needed, but I have seen no examples that intuitively require additional principles.

It might be thought that the Nixon Diamond indicates that the subset principle does not always help. (Again we see a relation between the application of statistics and non-monotonic logic.) Suppose person #18 is known to be a Quaker, and that we know that 90% of Quakers are pacifists; and also that person #18 is a Republican, and that 20% of Republicans are pacifists. It seems clear that neither the 20% nor the 90% are the relevant frequencies. If we knew the proportion of pacifists among republican quakers, we could apply the subset principle directly, but we have no reason to suppose that we know this proportion (which, so far as the story goes, may have any value from 0 to 1).

It is not entirely unreasonable that conflicting information can leave us in a state of ignorance. But sometimes we feel that we can do better. One possibility here is to turn to Shafer's rule of combination. This leads to a simple answer:

$$\frac{\%(P,Q)*\%(P,R)}{1-\%(P,Q)*\%(\sim P,R)-\%(P,R)*\%(\sim P,Q)} = 0.69$$

It is interesting that this is exactly the answer we are led to by the principles we already have. Person #18 is a pacifist if and only if the pair, consisting of him paired with himself, is among the pairs both parts of which are pacifists. This isn't as lucid a description of the goal as one might wish, but it leads to the right result.

We get to it by looking at the cross product of Q and R. Note that nobody can be both a pacifist and not a pacifist, so <#18, #18> must belong to the subset of $Q \times R$ in which the pair is uniformly pacifist or uniformly non-pacifist. Thus the subtractions in the denominator.

The proportion we get conflicts with both 0.2 and 0.9. But the Bayesian rule saves us: The proportion of pairs in $P \times Q$ in which the second member is a pacifist is just the proportion of pacifists among quakers. And the proportion of the subset at which we are looking, in which the second member is a pacifist is just 0.69. So Q is epistemically irrelevant.

Should these principles be called "principles"? It seems to me that they should, and that they are all roughly on a par, even though the subset principle is derivable from the Bayesian principle. They may be construed collectively as an articulation of our intuitive ideas about "total evidence".

The first principle directs us to use the most specific evidence at hand. The second directs us to take account of general background knowledge. The third says not to ignore available sampling data. Stated thus they seem sensible enough.

7. INEXACT KNOWLEDGE

By providing a new characterization of "difference" among statistical statements, we can easily generalize the above considerations to the general situation. Let "%(A, B) ∈ [p,q] *differ* from "%(C, D) ∈ [r, s]" just in case neither of [p, q] nor [r, s] is included in the other. Let us say that the former is stronger than the latter if [p, q] ⊂ [r, s]. Then we shall say that one item of statistical knowledge is irrelevant to another if

(a) it differs, but is rendered epistemically irrelevant by one of the three principles expounded above, or

(b) it is weaker than the other and no third item of statistical knowledge renders the first irrelevant.

Note that a consequence of thus liberalizing the notion of statistical knowledge is that we now always have statistical knowledge, even if it is only of the form, "%(A, B) ∈ [0, 1]".

In general, (b) leads us away from statistical knowledge of this form to more substantive statistical knowledge.

8. COMPUTATION

The object of providing such explicit characterizations of relevance and irrelevance is to be able to provide a feasible algorithm for computing the relevant reference class under specific epistemic conditions -- i.e., with given (plausible) knowledge base. Since (as is obvious) potential reference classes can proliferate indefinitely, we have not achieved that point yet; and providing an algorithm is not part of the present project. Nevertheless, it should be clear where we can go from here. Further details are provided in Kyburg [8] and Loui [9].

As an illustration of the mechanism we can employ, consider the following construction. Let an *inference structure* for a statement S relative to a body of knowledge be a quintuple $<a, B, C, p, q>$, where "a is a C " is known to be equivalent to S, the statement whose epistemic status interests us, "a is a B" is known, and "$\%(C, B) \in [p, q]$" represents the strongest information we have about B and C.

Consider the set I of all inference structures for S. This set is non-empty, since $<a, \{a\}, C, 0, 1>$ is a member of it, whatever else we may know. We perform pass number one: if an inference structure *differs* from an earlier inference structure [i.e., neither $[p, q]$ nor $[p', q']$ is included in the other] then delete the irrelevant inference structure, if any; otherwise delete both. The result is a set of inference structures that do not *differ* from one another. They can be partially ordered by inclusion, where we say that one inference structure $<a, B, C, p, q>$ is included in another $<a', B', C', p', q'>$ when $[p, q]$ is a subinterval of $[p', q']$.

We then perform a second pass, reflecting our concern for information, by deleting any inference structure that properly includes another inference structure in the sequence. The result is a set of inference structures -- it may well contain more than one, and, according to the details of our procedure, may potentially contain an infinite number -- that are all equally strong. This determines the epistemic probability of the statement S -- and incidentally, of every other statement in the equivalence class picked out by S.

9. CONCLUSIONS: We arrive at several conclusions.

(1) Given the equivalence condition, there will be many potential reference sets for a given statement. We therefore need a way of adjudicating our choice among these reference sets.

(2) There are three intuitive ways in which conflict between two potential reference classes can be resolved to the benefit of one of them. Only one of these ways seems to have worked its way into the literature on non-monotonic logic. All three should be taken account of.

(3) These three resolutions reflect the three principles: **the Subset Principle, the Bayesian Principle,** and **the Superset Principle.**

168

(4) The results of this analysis can be used to implement probabilistic non-monotonic acceptance as well as to determine rationally allowable distributions of uncertainty.

REFERENCES

[1]   Bacchus, Fahiem (1987): "Statistically Founded Degrees of Belief," Technical report 87-02, Alberta Center for Machine Intelligence, University of Alberta, Edmonton, Alberta, Canada.

[2]   Buchan, B.G., and Shortliffe, E. H, (eds): *Rule-Based Expert Systems*, Addison-Wesley, Reading, MA, 1984.

[3]   Cheeseman, Peter (1985): "In Defense of Probability," *IJCAI 85*, Morgan Kaufmann, Los Altos, 1002-1009.

[4]   Etherington, D. W. (1987): "A Semantics for Default Logic," *IJCAI 87*, Morgan Kaufman, Los Altos, 495-498.

[5]   Konolige, K.(1987): "On the Relation between Default Theories and Autoepistemic Logic," *IJCAI 87*, Morgan Kaufmann, Los Altos, 394-401.

[6]   Kyburg, Henry E. Jr. (1961): *Probability and the Logic of Rational Belief*, Weslyan University Press, Middletown, CT.

[7]   Kyburg, Henry E. Jr. (1974): *The Logical Foundations of Statistical Inference*, Reidel, Dordrecht.

[8]   Kyburg, Henry E. Jr. (1983): "The Reference Class," *Philosophy of Science* 50, 374-397.

[9]   Loui, Ronald P. (1986): "Computing Reference Classes," *Uncertainty in Artificial Intelligence,* Workshop, Philadelphia, 1986.

[10] McCarthy, John, and Hayes, Pat (1969): "Some Philosophical Problems from the Standpoint of Artificial Intelligence, " Melzer and Michie (eds) *Machine Intelligence* 4, Edinburgh University Press, 463-502.

[11] Poole, David L. (1985): "On the Comparison of Theories: Preferring the Most Specific Explanation," *IJCAI 85*, 144-147.

[12] Ramsey, F.D. (1931): "Truth and Probability," *The Foundations of Mathematics*, Humanities Press, New York.

[13] Reichenbach, Hans (1949): *The Theory of Probability*, University of California Press, Berkeley and Los Angeles.

[14] Shafer, Glen (1976): *A Mathematical Theory of Evidence*, Princeton University Press, Princeton.

[15] Touretzky, D., et. al. (1987): "A Clash of Intuitions: the Current State of Nonmonotonic Multiple Inheritance Systems," *IJCAI 87*, Morgan Kaufmann, Los Altos, 476-482.

[16] Zadeh, Lotfi A. (1975): "Fuzzy Logic and Approximate Reasoning," *Synthese* 30, 407-428.

Uncertainty in Artificial Intelligence 4
R.D. Shachter, T.S. Levitt, L.N. Kanal, J.F. Lemmer (Editors)
© Elsevier Science Publishers B.V. (North-Holland), 1990

AXIOMS FOR PROBABILITY AND BELIEF-FUNCTION PROPAGATION

Prakash P. SHENOY   and   Glenn SHAFER

School of Business
University of Kansas
Summerfield Hall
Lawrence, Kansas, 66045-2003, USA

In this paper, we describe an abstract framework and axioms under which exact local computation of marginals is
possible. The primitive objects of the framework are
variables and valuations. The primitive operators of
the framework are combination and marginalization.
These operate on valuations. We state three axioms for
these operators and we derive the possibility of local
computation from the axioms. Next, we describe a propagation scheme for computing marginals of a valuation
when we have a factorization of the valuation on a hypertree. Finally we show how the problem of computing
marginals of joint probability distributions and joint
belief functions fits the general framework.

1. INTRODUCTION

In this paper, we describe an abstract framework and present axioms for local computation of marginals in hypertrees. These
axioms justify the use of local computation to find marginals
for a probability distribution or belief function when the probability distribution or belief function is factored on a hypertree. The axioms are abstracted from the belief-function work
of the authors (e.g., Shenoy and Shafer [1986], Shenoy et al
[1988], Shafer et al [1987]), but they apply to probabilities as
well as to belief functions.

In the probability case, the factorization is usually a factorization of a joint probability distribution, perhaps into
marginals and conditionals. Probability factorizations sometimes arise from causal models, which relate each variable to a
relatively small number of immediate causes; see e.g., Pearl
[1986]. Probability factorizations can also arise from statistical models; see e.g., Darroch et al [1980]. Belief-function
factorizations generally arise from the decomposition of evidence into independent items, each involving only a few variables. We represent each item of evidence by a belief function
and combine these belief functions by Dempster's rule [Shafer
1976].

It is shown in Shenoy [1989b] that Spohn's [1988, 1990] theory
of epistemic beliefs also fits in the abstract framework described here. Furthermore, the axiomatic framework is extended

in Shenoy and Shafer [1988a,b] to include constraint propagation and optimization using local computation.

We first present our general axiomatic framework and then explain how it applies to probabilities and belief functions. Before we can present the axiomatic framework, we need to review some graph-theoretic concepts. We do this in section 2. We present the framework in section 3. We apply it to probabilities in section 4 and to belief functions in section 5.

2. SOME CONCEPTS FROM GRAPH THEORY

Most of the concepts reviewed here have been studied extensively in the graph theory literature (see Berge [1973], Golumbic [1980], and Maier [1983]). A number of terms we use are new, however - among them, *hypertree*, *construction sequence*, *branch*, *twig*, *bud*, and *Markov tree*. A *hypertree* is what other authors have called an acyclic (Maier [1983]) or decomposable hypergraph (Lauritzen et al [1984]). A *construction sequence* is what other authors have called a sequence with the running intersection property (Lauritzen and Spiegelhalter [1988]). A *Markov tree* is what authors in database theory have called a join tree (see Maier [1983]). We have borrowed the term *Markov tree* from probability theory, where it means a tree of variables in which separation implies probabilistic conditional independence given the separating variables. For a fuller explanation of the concepts reviewed here, see Shafer and Shenoy [1988].

As we shall see, hypertrees are closely related to Markov trees. The vertices of a Markov tree are always hyperedges of a hypertree, and the hyperedges of a hypertree can always be arranged in a Markov tree.

Hypergraphs and Hypertrees. We call a nonempty set $\mathcal{H}$ of nonempty subsets of a finite set $\mathcal{X}$ a *hypergraph* on $\mathcal{X}$. We call the elements of $\mathcal{H}$ *hyperedges*. We call the elements of $\mathcal{X}$ *vertices*.

Suppose t and b are distinct hyperedges in a hypergraph $\mathcal{H}$, $t \cap b \neq \emptyset$, and b contains every vertex of t that is contained in a hyperedge of $\mathcal{H}$ other than t; if $X \in t$ and $X \in h$, where $h \in \mathcal{H}$ and $h \neq t$, then $X \in b$. Then we call t a *twig* of $\mathcal{H}$, and we call b a *branch* for t. A twig may have more than one branch.

We call a hypergraph a *hypertree* if there is an ordering of its hyperedges, say $h_1 h_2 \ldots h_n$, such that h_k is a twig in the hypergraph $\{h_1, h_2, \ldots, h_k\}$ whenever $2 \leq k \leq n$. We call any such ordering of the hyperedges a *hypertree construction sequence* for the hypertree. We call the first hyperedge in a hypertree construction sequence the *root* of the hypertree construction sequence. Figure 2.1 illustrates hypergraphs, hypertrees, twigs and construction sequences.

If we construct a hypertree by adding hyperedges following a hypertree construction sequence, then each hyperedge we add is a twig when it is added, and it has at least one branch in the hypertree at that point. Suppose we choose such a branch, say $\beta(h)$, for each hyperedge h we add. By doing so, we define a mapping β from $\mathcal{H} - \{h_1\}$ to $\mathcal{H}$, where h_1 is the root of the hypertree construction sequence. We will call this function a *branching* for the hypertree construction sequence.

Since a twig may have more than one branch, a hypertree construction sequence may have more than one branching. In general, a hypertree will have many construction sequences. In fact, for each hyperedge of a hypertree, there is at least one construction sequence beginning with that hyperedge.

> **Figure 2.1.** Some hypergraphs on {W,X,Y,Z}. The hypergraph $\mathcal{H}_1$ is a hypertree, all of its hyperedges are twigs, and all six orderings of its hyperedges are hypertree construction sequences. The hypergraph $\mathcal{H}_2$ is a hypertree, hyperedges {W,X} and {Y,Z} are twigs, and it has only four hypertree construction sequences: {W,X}{X,Y}{Y,Z}, {X,Y}{W,X}{Y,Z}, {X,Y}{Y,Z}{W,X}, and {Y,Z}{X,Y}{W,X}. The hypergraph $\mathcal{H}_3$ is not a hypertree and it has no twigs.

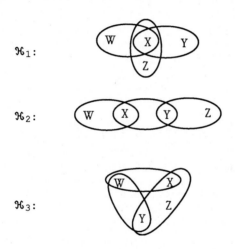

Hypertree Covers of Hypergraphs. We will justify local computation under two assumptions. The joint probability distribution function or the joint belief function with which we are working must factor into functions, each involving a small set of variables. And these sets of variables must form a hypertree.

If the sets of variables form, instead, a hypergraph that is not a hypertree, then we must enlarge it until it is a hypertree. We can talk about this enlargement in two different ways. We can say we are adding larger hyperedges, keeping the hyperedges already there. Or, alternatively, we can say we are replacing the hyperedges already there with larger hyperedges. The choice between these two ways of talking matters little, because the presence of superfluous twigs (hyperedges contained in other hyperedges) does not affect whether a hypergraph is a hypertree, and because the computational cost of the procedures we will be describing depends primarily on the size of the largest hyperedges, not on the number of the smaller hyperedges (Kong [1986],

Mellouli [1987]).

Formally, we will say that a hypergraph $\mathcal{H}*$ *covers* a hypergraph $\mathcal{H}$ if for every h in $\mathcal{H}$ there is an element h* of $\mathcal{H}*$ such that h*⊇h. We will say that $\mathcal{H}*$ is a *hypertree cover* for $\mathcal{H}$ if $\mathcal{H}*$ is a hypertree and it covers $\mathcal{H}$. Figure 2.2 shows a hypergraph that is not a hypertree and a hypertree cover for it.

Figure 2.2. *Left:* A hypergraph that is not a hypertree. *Right*: A hypertree cover for it obtained by adding hyperedges {S,L,B} and {L,E,B} and removing hyperedges {S,L} and {S,B}.

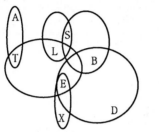 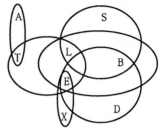

Finding a hypertree cover is never difficult. The hypertree {$\mathcal{X}$}, which consists of the single hyperedge $\mathcal{X}$, is a hypertree cover for any hypergraph on $\mathcal{X}$. Finding a hypertree cover without large hyperedges, or finding a hypertree cover whose largest hyperedge is as small as possible, may be very difficult. How to do this best is the subject of a growing literature; see e.g., Rose [1970], Bertele and Brioschi [1972], Tarjan and Yannakakis [1984], Kong [1986], Arnborg et al [1987], Mellouli [1987], and Zhang [1988].

Trees. A *graph* is a pair $(\mathcal{V}, \mathcal{E})$, where $\mathcal{V}$ is a nonempty set and $\mathcal{E}$ is a set of two-element subsets of $\mathcal{V}$. We call the elements of $\mathcal{V}$ *vertices*, and we call the elements of $\mathcal{E}$ *edges*.

Suppose $(\mathcal{V}, \mathcal{E})$ is a graph. If {v,v'} is an element of $\mathcal{E}$, then we say that v and v' are *neighbors*. We call a vertex of a graph a *leaf* if it is contained in only one edge, and we call the other vertex in that edge the *bud* for the leaf. If $v_1 v_2 \ldots v_n$ is a sequence of distinct vertices, where n>1, and $\{v_k, v_{k+1}\} \in \mathcal{E}$ for k=1,2,...,n-1, then we call $v_1 v_2 \ldots v_n$ a *path from* v_1 *to* v_n.

We call a graph a *tree* if there is an ordering of its vertices, say $v_1 v_2 \ldots v_n$ such that v_k is a leaf in the graph $(\{v_1, v_2, \ldots, v_k\}, \mathcal{E}_k)$ whenever 2≤k≤n, where $\mathcal{E}_k$ is the subset of $\mathcal{E}$ consisting of those edges that contain only vertices in $\{v_1, v_2, \ldots, v_k\}$. We call any such ordering of the vertices a *tree construction sequence* for the tree. We call the first vertex in a tree construction sequence the *root* of the tree construction sequence. Note that in a tree, for any two distinct vertices v_i and v_j, there is a unique path from v_i to v_j.

If we construct a tree following a tree construction sequence starting with the root and adding vertices, then each vertex we add is a leaf when it is added, and it has a bud in the tree at that point. Given a tree construction sequence and a vertex v that is not the root, let $\beta(v)$ denote the bud for v as it is added. This defines a mapping β from $\mathcal{V}-\{v_1\}$ to $\mathcal{V}$, where v_1 is the root. We will call this mapping the *budding* for the tree construction sequence.

The budding for a tree construction sequence is analogous to the branching for a hypertree construction sequence, but there are significant differences. Whereas there may be many branchings for a given hypertree construction sequence, there is only one budding for a given tree construction sequence. In fact, there is only one budding with a given root.

Markov Trees. We have just defined a tree as a pair $(\mathcal{V}, \mathcal{E})$, where $\mathcal{V}$ is the set of vertices, and $\mathcal{E}$ is the set of edges. In the case of a Markov tree, the vertices are themselves nonempty sets. In other words, the set $\mathcal{V}$ is a hypergraph. In fact, it turns out to be a hypertree.

Here is our full definition. We call a tree $(\mathcal{H}, \mathcal{E})$ a *Markov tree* if the following conditions are satisfied:
  (i) $\mathcal{H}$ is a hypergraph.
  (ii) If $\{h,h'\}\in\mathcal{E}$, then $h\cap h'\neq\emptyset$.
  (iii) If h and h' are distinct vertices, and X is in both h and h', then X is in every vertex on the path from h to h'.

This definition does not state that $\mathcal{H}$ is a hypertree, but it implies that it is:

> **Proposition 1.** (i) If $(\mathcal{H}, \mathcal{E})$ is a Markov tree, then $\mathcal{H}$ is a hypertree. Any leaf in $(\mathcal{H}, \mathcal{E})$ is a twig in $\mathcal{H}$. If $h_1h_2...h_n$ is a tree construction sequence for $(\mathcal{H}, \mathcal{E})$, with β as its budding, then $h_1h_2...h_n$ is also a hypertree construction sequence for $\mathcal{H}$, with β as a branching. (ii) If $\mathcal{H}$ is a hypertree, $h_1h_2...h_n$ is a hypertree construction sequence for $\mathcal{H}$, and β is a branching for $h_1h_2...h_n$, then $(\mathcal{H}, \mathcal{E})$ is a Markov tree, where $\mathcal{E} = \{(h_2,\beta(h_2)),..., (h_n,\beta(h_n))\}$; $h_1h_2...h_n$ is a tree construction sequence for $(\mathcal{H}, \mathcal{E})$, and β is its budding.

See Shafer and Shenoy [1988] for a proof of Proposition 1. The key point here is the fact that a leaf in the Markov tree is a twig in the hypertree. This means that as we delete leaves from a Markov tree (a visually transparent operation), we are deleting twigs from the hypertree.

If $(\mathcal{H}, \mathcal{E})$ is a Markov tree, then we call $(\mathcal{H}, \mathcal{E})$ a *Markov tree representative* for the hypertree $\mathcal{H}$. As per Proposition 1, every hypertree has a Markov tree representative. Most hypertrees have more than one. Figure 2.3 shows three Markov tree representations for the hypertree in Figure 2.2.

3. AN AXIOMATIC FRAMEWORK FOR LOCAL COMPUTATION

In this section, we describe a set of axioms under which exact local computation of marginals is possible.

174

Figure 2.3. If we choose {L,E,B} as the root for the hypertree in Figure 2.2, then {L,E,B} must serve as the branch for {T,L,E}, {E,B,D}, and {S,L,B}, and {T,L,E} must serve as the branch for {A,T}. This leaves only {E,X}, which can use {L,E,B}, {T,L,E}, or {E,B,D} as its branch. It follows that the hypertree has exactly three Markov tree representations, which differ only in where the leaf {E,X} is attached.

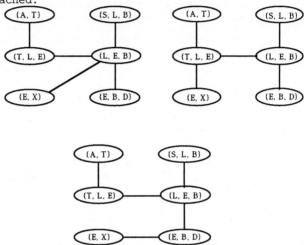

In section 3.1, we describe an axiomatic framework for local computation of marginals. The primitive objects of the framework are variables and valuations. The framework has two primitive operators, combination and marginalization. These operate on valuations. We state three axioms for these operators.

In section 3.2, we show how local computation can be used to marginalize a factorization (of a valuation) on a hypergraph to the smaller hypergraph resulting from the deletion of a twig. Once we know how to delete a twig, we can reduce a hypertree to a single hyperedge by successively deleting twigs. When we have reduced a factorization on a hypertree to a factorization on a single hyperedge, it is no longer a factorization; it is simply the marginal for the hyperedge.

In section 3.3, we shift our attention from a hypertree to the Markov tree determined by a branching for the hypertree. Using this Markov tree, we describe more graphically the process of marginalizing to a single hyperedge. Our description is based on the idea that each vertex in the tree is a processor, which can operate on valuations for the variables it represents and then send the result to a neighboring processor. In section 3.4, we generalize this idea to a scheme of simultaneous computation and message passing that produces marginals for all the vertices in the Markov tree.

3.1. The Axiomatic Framework

The primitive objects of the framework are a finite set of variables and a set of valuations. The framework has two primitive operators: combination and marginalization. These operate on valuations.

Variables and Valuations. Let $\mathcal{X}$ be a finite set. The elements of $\mathcal{X}$ are called *variables*. For each $h\subseteq\mathcal{X}$, there is a set $\mathcal{V}_h$. The elements of $\mathcal{V}_h$ are called *valuations on h*. Let $\mathcal{V}$ denote $\cup\{\mathcal{V}_h|h\subseteq\mathcal{X}\}$, the set of all valuations.

In the case of probabilities, a valuation on h will be a non-negative, real-valued function on the set of all configurations of h (a configuration of h is a vector of possible values of variables in h). In the belief-function case, a valuation is a non-negative, real-valued function on the set of all subsets of configurations of h.

Proper Valuations. For each $h\subseteq\mathcal{X}$, there is a subset $\mathcal{P}_h$ of $\mathcal{V}_h$ whose elements will be called *proper valuations on h*. Let $\mathcal{P}$ denote $\cup\{\mathcal{P}_h|h\subseteq\mathcal{X}\}$, the set of all proper valuations. The notion of proper valuations is important as it will enable us to define combinability of valuations.

In the probability case, a valuation H on h is said to be proper if the values of the function H are not zero for all configurations of h. In the belief function case, a valuation H on h is said to be proper if the values of the function H are not zero for all nonempty subsets of configurations of h.

Combination. We assume there is a mapping $\otimes:\mathcal{V}\times\mathcal{V} \rightarrow \mathcal{V}$, called *combination*, such that
    (i)   If G and H are valuations on g and h respectively, then G$\otimes$H is a valuation on g$\cup$h; and
    (ii)   If either G or H is not a proper valuation, then G$\otimes$H is not a proper valuation;
    (iii)   If G and H are both proper valuations, then G$\otimes$H may or may not be a proper valuation.
If G$\otimes$H is not a proper valuation, then we shall say that G and H are *not combinable*. If G$\otimes$H is a proper valuation, then we shall say that G and H are *combinable* and that G$\otimes$H is the *combination of G and H*.

Intuitively, combination corresponds to aggregation. If G and H represent information about variables in g and h, respectively, then G$\otimes$H represents the aggregated information for variables in g$\cup$h. In the probability case, combination corresponds to pointwise multiplication. In the belief function case, combination corresponds to Dempster's rule.

Marginalization. We assume that for each $h\subseteq\mathcal{X}$, there is a mapping $\downarrow h:\cup\{\mathcal{V}_g|g\supseteq h\} \rightarrow \mathcal{V}_h$, called *marginalization to h*, such that
    (i)   If G is a valuation on g and h$\subseteq$g, then $G^{\downarrow h}$ is a valuation on h;
    (ii)   If G is a proper valuation, then $G^{\downarrow h}$ is a proper valuation; and
    (iii)   If G is not a proper valuation, then $G^{\downarrow h}$ is not a proper valuation.

We will call $G^{\downarrow h}$ *marginal of G for h.*

Intuitively, marginalization corresponds to narrowing the focus of a valuation. If G is a valuation on g representing some information about variables in g, and $h \subseteq g$, then $G^{\downarrow h}$ represents the information for variables in h implied by G if we disregard variables in g-h. In both the probability and belief-function cases, marginalization corresponds to summation.

The Problem. We are now in a position to describe the problem. Suppose $\mathcal{H}$ is a hypergraph on $\mathcal{X}$. For each $h \in \mathcal{H}$, we have a proper valuation A_h on h. First, we need to determine if the proper valuations in the set $\{A_h | h \in \mathcal{H}\}$ are combinable. If the answer is in the affirmative, then let A denote the proper valuation $\otimes \{A_h | h \in \mathcal{H}\}$. Second, we need to find the marginal of A for each $X \in \mathcal{X}$.

If $\mathcal{X}$ is a large set of variables, then computation of $A^{\downarrow\{X\}}$ by first computing the joint valuation A on $\mathcal{X}$ and then marginalizing A to $\{X\}$ will not be possible. For example, if we have 50 variables and each variable has 2 possible values, then we will have 2^{50} possible configurations of $\mathcal{X}$. Thus in the probability case, computing A will involve finding 2^{50} values. And in the belief function case, computing A will involve finding $2^{(2^{50})}$ values. In either case, the task is infeasible. We will state axioms for combination and marginalization that make it possible to use local computation to determine if the given proper valuations are combinable and to compute $A^{\downarrow\{X\}}$ for each $X \in \mathcal{X}$ if they are.

We will assume that these two mappings satisfy three axioms.

> **Axiom A1** (*Commutativity and associativity of combination*): Suppose G, H, K are valuations on g, h, and k respectively. Then $G \otimes H = H \otimes G$, and $G \otimes (H \otimes K) = (G \otimes H) \otimes K$.
>
> **Axiom A2** (*Consonance of marginalization*): Suppose G is a valuation on g, and suppose $k \subseteq h \subseteq g$. Then $(G^{\downarrow h})^{\downarrow k} = G^{\downarrow k}$.
>
> **Axiom A3** (*Distributivity of marginalization over combination*): Suppose G and H are valuations on g and h, respectively. Then $(G \otimes H)^{\downarrow g} = G \otimes (H^{\downarrow g \cap h})$

One implication of Axiom A1 is that when we have multiple combinations of valuations, we can write it without using parenthesis. For example, $(\ldots((A_{h_1} \otimes A_{h_2}) \otimes A_{h_3}) \otimes \ldots \otimes A_{h_n})$ can be written simply as $\otimes \{A_{h_i} | i=1,\ldots,n\}$ without indicating the order in which the combinations are carried out.

Factorization. Suppose A is a valuation on a finite set of variables $\mathcal{X}$, and suppose $\mathcal{H}$ is a hypergraph on $\mathcal{X}$. If A is equal to the combination of valuations on the hyperedges of h, say $A = \otimes \{A_h | h \in \mathcal{H}\}$, where A_h is a valuation on h, then we say that A *factorizes on* $\mathcal{H}$.

If we regard marginalization as a reduction of a valuation by deleting variables, then axiom A2 can be interpreted as saying that the order in which the variables are deleted does not matter.

Axiom A3 is the crucial axiom that makes local computation possible. Axiom A3 states that computation of $(G \otimes H)^{\downarrow g}$ can be accomplished without having to compute $G \otimes H$.

3.2. Marginalizing Factorizations

In this section, we learn how to adjust a factorization on a hypergraph to account for the deletion of a twig. This can be accomplished by local computations, computations involving only the valuations on the twig and a branch for the twig. This elimination of a twig by local computation is the key to the computation of marginals from a factorization on a hypertree, for by successively deleting twigs, we can reduce the hypertree to a single hyperedge.

Suppose $\mathcal{H}$ is a hypergraph on $\mathcal{X}$, t is a twig in $\mathcal{H}$, and b is a branch for t. The twig t may contain some vertices that are not contained in any other hyperedge in $\mathcal{H}$. These are the vertices in the set t-b. Deleting t from $\mathcal{H}$ means reducing $\mathcal{H}$ to the hypergraph $\mathcal{H}-\{t\}$ on the set $\mathcal{X}' = \mathcal{X}-(t-b) = \cup(\mathcal{H}-\{t\})$.

Suppose A is a valuation on $\mathcal{X}$, suppose A factors on $\mathcal{H}$, and suppose we have stored A in a factored form. In other words, we have stored a valuation A_h for each h in $\mathcal{H}$, and we know that A $= \otimes\{A_h \mid h \in \mathcal{H}\}$. Adapting this factorization on A on $\mathcal{H}$ to the deletion of the twig t means reducing it to a factorization of $A^{\downarrow \mathcal{X}'}$ on $\mathcal{H}-\{t\}$. Can we do this? Yes. The following proposition tells us that if A factors on $\mathcal{H}$, then $A^{\downarrow \mathcal{X}'}$ factors on $\mathcal{H}-\{t\}$, and the second factorization can be obtained from the first by a local computation that involves only t and a branch.

> **Proposition 2.** Under the assumptions of the preceding paragraph,
> $$A^{\downarrow \mathcal{X}'} = (A_b \otimes A_t^{\downarrow t \cap b}) \otimes (\otimes\{A_h \mid h \in \mathcal{H}-\{t,b\}\}), \qquad (3.1)$$
> where b is any branch for t. Thus the marginal $A^{\downarrow \mathcal{X}'}$ factors on the hypergraph $\mathcal{H}-\{t\}$. The valuation on b is combined with $A_t^{\downarrow t \cap b}$, and the valuations on the other elements of $\mathcal{H}-\{t\}$ are unchanged.

Proposition 2 follows directly from axiom A3 by letting G = $\otimes\{A_h \mid h \in \mathcal{H}-\{t\}\}$ and H = A_t.

This result is especially interesting in the case of hypertrees, because in this case repeated application of (3.1) allows us to obtain A's marginal on any particular hyperedge of $\mathcal{H}$. If we want the marginal on a hyperedge h_1, we choose a construction sequence beginning with h_1, say $h_1 h_2 ... h_n$. Suppose $\mathcal{X}_k$ denotes $h_1 \cup ... \cup h_k$ and $\mathcal{H}_k$ denotes $\{h_1, h_2, ..., h_k\}$ for k=1,...,n-1. We use (3.1) to delete the twig h_n, so that we have a factorization of $A^{\downarrow \mathcal{X}_{n-1}}$ on the hypertree $\mathcal{H}_{n-1}$. Then we use (3.1) again to delete the twig h_{n-1}, so that we have a factorization of $A^{\downarrow \mathcal{X}_{n-2}}$ on the hypertree $\mathcal{H}_{n-2}$. And so on, until we have deleted all the hyperedges except h_1, so that we have a factorization of $A^{\downarrow \mathcal{H}_1}$ on the hypertree $\mathcal{H}_1$ - i.e., we have the marginal $A^{\downarrow h_1}$. At each step, the computation is local, in the sense that it involves only a twig and a branch. Note that such a step-wise computation of the marginal of A for h_1 is allowed by axiom A2.

3.3. Computing Marginals in Markov Trees

As we learned in section 2, the choice of a branching for a hypertree determines a Markov tree for the hypertree. We now look at our scheme for computing a marginal from the viewpoint of this Markov tree. This change in viewpoint does not necessarily affect the implementation of the computation, but it gives us a richer understanding. It gives us a picture in which message passing, instead of deletion, is the dominant metaphor, and in which we have great flexibility in how the message passing is controlled.

Why did we talk about deleting the hyperedge h_k as we marginalized h_k's valuation to the intersection with its branch $\beta(h_k)$? The point was simply to remove h_k from our attention. The "deletion" had no computational significance, but it helped make clear that h_k and the valuation on it were of no further use. What was of further use was the smaller hypertree that would remain were h_k deleted.

When we turn from the hypertree to the Markov tree, deletion of twigs translates into deletion of leaves. But a tree is easier to visualize than a hypertree. We can remove a leaf or a whole branch of a tree from our attention without leaning so heavily on metaphorical deletion. And a Markov tree also allows another, more useful, metaphor. We can imagine that each vertex of the tree is a processor, and we can imagine that the marginal is a message that one processor passes to another. Within this metaphor, vertices no longer relevant are kept out of our way by the rules guiding the message passing, not by deletion.

We cover a number of topics in this section. We begin by reviewing our marginalization scheme in the hypertree setting and seeing how its details translate into the Markov tree setting. We formulate precise descriptions of the operations that are carried out by each vertex and precise definitions of the messages that are passed from one vertex to another. Then we turn to questions of timing - whether a vertex uses a message as soon as it is received or waits for all its messages before it acts, how the order in which the vertices act are constrained, and whether the vertices act in serial or in parallel. We explain how the Markov tree can be expanded into an architecture for the parallel computation, with provision for storing messages as well as directing them. We explain how this architecture handles updating when inputs are changed. And finally, we explain how our computation can be directed by a simple forward-chaining production system.

Translating to the Markov Tree. We now translate our marginalization scheme from the hypertree to the Markov tree.

Recall the details in the hypertree setting. We have a valuation A on $\mathfrak{X}$, in the form of a factorization on a hypertree $\mathfrak{H}$. We want the marginal for the hyperedge h_1. We choose a hypertree construction sequence with h_1 as its root, say $h_1 h_2 \ldots h_n$, and we choose a branching β for $h_1 h_2 \ldots h_n$. On each hyperedge h_i, we have a valuation A_{h_i}. We repeatedly apply the following operation:

Operation H. Marginalize the valuation now on h_k to $\beta(h_k)$. Change the valuation now on $\beta(h_k)$ by combining it by this marginal.

We apply Operation H first for $k=n$, then for $k=n-1$, and so on, down to $k=2$. The valuation assigned to h_1 at the end of this process is the marginal on h_1.

We want now to redescribe Operation H, and the process of its repeated application, in terms of the actions of processors located at the vertices of the Markov tree $(\mathfrak{H}, \mathfrak{E})$ determined by the branching β.

The vertices of $(\mathfrak{H}, \mathfrak{E})$ are the hyperedges h_1, h_2, $\ldots$, h_n. We imagine that a processor is attached to each of the h_i. The processor attached to h_i can store a valuation defined on h_i, can compute the marginal of this valuation to h_j, where h_j is a neighboring vertex, can send the marginal to h_j as a message, can accept a valuation on h_i as a message from a neighbor, and can change the valuation it has stored by combining it by such an incoming message.

The edges of $(\mathfrak{H}, \mathfrak{E})$ are $\{h_n, \beta(h_n)\}, \{h_{n-1}, \beta(h_{n-1})\}, \ldots, \{h_3, \beta(h_3)\}$, $\{h_2, h_1\}$. When we move from h_n to $\beta(h_n)$, then from h_{n-1} to $\beta(h_{n-1})$, and so on, we are moving inwards in this Markov tree, from the outer leaves to the root h_1. The repeated application of Operation H by the processors located at the vertices follows this path.

In order to recast Operation H in terms of these processors, we need some more notation. Let Cur_h denote the valuation currently stored by the processor at vertex h of $(\mathfrak{H}, \mathfrak{E})$. In terms of the local processors and the Cur_h, Operation H becomes the following:

Operation M_1. Vertex h computes $\text{Cur}_h^{\downarrow h \cap \beta(h)}$, the marginal of Cur_h to $\beta(h)$. It sends $\text{Cur}_h^{\downarrow h \cap \beta(h)}$ as a message to vertex $\beta(h)$. Vertex $\beta(h)$ accepts the message $\text{Cur}_h^{\downarrow h \cap \beta(h)}$ and changes $\text{Cur}_{\beta(h)}$ by multiplying it by $\text{Cur}_h^{\downarrow h \cap \beta(h)}$.

At the outset, $\text{Cur}_h = A_h$ for every vertex h. Operation M_1 is executed first for $h=h_n$, then for $h=h_{n-1}$, and so on, down to $h=h_2$. At the end of this propagation process, the valuation Cur_{h_1}, the valuation stored at h_1, is the marginal of A on h_1.

An Alternative Operation. Operation M_1 prescribes actions by two processors, h and $\beta(h)$. We now give an alternative, Operation M_2, which is executed by a single processor. Since it is executed by a single processor, Operation M_2 will be easier for us to think about when we discuss alternative control regimes for the process of propagation.

Operation M_2 differs from Operation M_1 only in that it requires a processor to combine the messages it receives all at once, rather than incorporating them into the combination one by one as they arrive. Each time the Operation M_1 is executed for an h such that $\beta(h)=g$, the processor g must change the valuation it stores by combining it by the incoming message. But if processor g can store all its incoming messages, then it can delay the combination until it is its turn to marginalize. If we take this approach, then we can replace Operation M_1 with the following:

> *Operation M_{2a}.* Vertex h combines the valuation A_h with all the messages it has received, and it calls the result Cur_h. Then it computes $Cur_h^{\downarrow h \cap \beta(h)}$, the marginal of Cur_h to $h \cap \beta(h)$. It sends $Cur_h^{\downarrow h \cap \beta(h)}$ as a message to $\beta(h)$.

Operation M_{2a} involves action by only one processor, the processor h. When Operation M_{2a} is executed by h_n, there is no combination, because h_n, being a leaf in the Markov tree, has received no messages. The same is true for the other leaves in the Markov tree. But for vertices that are not leaves in the Markov tree, the operation will involve both combination and marginalization.

After Operation M_{2a} has been executed by h_n, h_{n-1}, and so on down to h_2, the root h_1 will have received a number of messages but will not yet have acted. To complete the process, h_1 must combine all its messages and its original valuation A_{h_1}, thus obtaining the marginal $A^{\downarrow h_1}$. We may call this Operation M_{2b}:

> *Operation M_{2b}.* Vertex h combines the valuation A_h with all the messages it has received, and it reports the result to the user of the system.

So Operation M_2 actually consists of two operations. Operation M_{2a} is executed successively by h_n, h_{n-1}, and so on down to h_2. Then Operation M_{2b} is executed by h_1.

Operation M_2 simplifies our thinking about control, or the flow of computation, because it allows us to think of control as moving with the computation in the Markov tree. In our marginalization scheme, control moves from one vertex to another, from the outer leaves inward towards the root. If we use Operation M_2, then a vertex is computing only when it has control.

Formulas for the Messages. We have described verbally how each vertex computes the message it sends to its branch. Now we will translate this verbal description into a formula that constitutes a recursive definition of the messages. The formula will not make much immediate contribution to our understanding, but it will serve as a useful reference in the next section, where we discuss how to extend our scheme for computing a single marginal to a scheme for computing all marginals.

Let $M^{h \to \beta(h)}$ denote the message sent by vertex h to its bud. Our description of Operation M_{2a} tells us that $M^{h \to \beta(h)} = Cur_h^{\downarrow h \cap \beta(h)}$, where $Cur_h = A_h \otimes (\otimes\{M^{g \to \beta(g)} \mid g \in \mathcal{H} \text{ and } \beta(g)=h\})$. Putting these two formulas together, we have

$$M^{h \to \beta(h)} = \left(A_h \otimes (\otimes\{M^{g \to \beta(g)} \mid g \in \mathcal{H} \text{ and } \beta(g)=h\})\right)^{\downarrow h \cap \beta(h)}. \quad (3.2)$$

If h is a leaf, then there is no $g \in \mathcal{H}$ such that $h=\beta(g)$, and so (3.2) reduces to

$$M^{h \to \beta(h)} = A_n^{\downarrow h \cap \beta(h)} . \tag{3.3}$$

Formula (3.2) constitutes a recursive definition of $M^{h \to \beta(h)}$ for all h, excepting only the root h_1 of the budding β. The special case (3.3) defines $M^{h \to \beta(h)}$ for the leaves; a further application of (3.2) defines $M^{h \to \beta(h)}$ for vertices one step in towards the root from the leaves; a third application defines $M^{h \to \beta(h)}$ for vertices two steps in towards the root from the leaves; and so on.

We can also represent Operation M_{2b} by a formula:

$$A^{\downarrow h} = A_h \otimes (\otimes \{M^{g \to \beta(g)} \mid g \in \mathcal{H} \text{ and } \beta(g) = h\}) . \tag{3.4}$$

Storing the Messages. If we want to think in terms of Operation M_2, then we must imagine that our processors have a way to store incoming messages.

Figure 3.1 depicts an architecture that provides for such storage. The figure shows a storage register at vertex g for each of g's neighbors. The registers for neighbors on the side of g away from the goal vertex are used to store incoming messages. The register for the neighbor in the direction of the goal vertex is used to store the vertex's outgoing message. The registers serve as communication links between neighbors; the outgoing register for one vertex being the incoming register for its neighbor in the direction of the goal vertex.

Figure 3.1. A typical vertex processor g, with incoming messages from vertices f and e and outgoing message to h; here $g = \beta(f) = \beta(e)$ and $h = \beta(g)$.

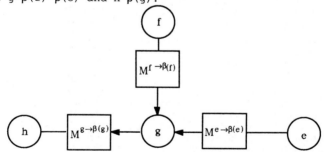

The message $M^{g \to \beta(g)}$, which vertex g stores in the register linking g to its bud, is a valuation on $g \cap \beta(g)$. It is the marginal for the bud of a valuation on g.

Flexibility of Control. Whether we use operation M_1 or M_2, it is not necessary to follow exactly the order h_n, h_{n-1}, and so on. The final result will be the same provided only that a processor never send a message until after it has received and absorbed all the messages it is supposed to receive.

This point is obvious when we look at a picture of the Markov tree. Consider, for example a Markov tree with 15 vertices, as in Figure 3.2. The vertices are numbered from 1 to 15 in this picture, indicating a construction sequence $h_1 h_2 \ldots h_{15}$. Since we want to find the marginal for vertex 1, all our messages will be sent towards vertex 1, in the directions indicated by the arrows. Our scheme calls for a message from vertex 15 to vertex 3, then a message from vertex 14 to vertex 6, and so on. But we could just as well begin with messages from 10 and 11 to 5, follow with a message from 5 to 2, then messages from 12, 13, and 14 to 6, from 6 and 15 to 3, and so on.

Figure 3.2. A tree with 15 vertices.

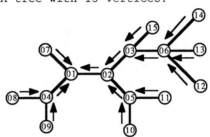

Returning to the metaphor of deletion, where each vertex is deleted when it sends its message, we can say that the only constraint on the order in which the vertices act is that each vertex must be a leaf when it acts; all the vertices that used it as a branch must have sent their messages to it and then been deleted, leaving it a leaf.

The different orders of marginalization that obey this constraint correspond, of course, to the different tree construction sequences for $(\mathcal{H}, \mathcal{C})$ that use the branching β.

So far, we have been thinking about different sequences in which the vertices might act. This is most appropriate if we are really implementing the scheme on a serial computer. But if the different vertices really did have independent processors that could operate in parallel, then some of the vertices could act simultaneously. Figure 3.3 illustrates one way this might go for the Markov tree of Figure 3.2. In step 1, all the leaf processors project to their branches. In step 2, vertices 4, 5, and 6 (which would be leaves were the original leaves deleted) project. And so on.

If the different processors take different amounts of time to perform Operation M_2 on their inputs, then the lock-step timing of Figure 3.3 may not provide the quickest way to find the marginal for h_1. It may be quicker to allow a processor to act as soon as it receives messages from its leaves, whether or not all the other processors that started along with these leaves have finished.

In general, the only constraint, in the parallel as in the serial case, is that action move inwards towards the root or goal, vertex h_1. Each vertex must receive and absorb all its messages from vertices farther away from h_1 before sending its own message on towards h_1. (In terms of Figure 3.1, each processor must wait until all its incoming registers are filled before it can compute a message to put in its outgoing register.) If we want to get the job done as quickly as possible, we will demand that each processor go to work as quickly as possible subject to this constraint. But the job will get done eventually provided only that all the processors act eventually. It will get done, for example, if each processor checks on its inputs periodically or at random times and acts if it has those inputs [Pearl 1986].

Figure 3.3. An example of the message-passing scheme for computation of the marginal of vertex 1.

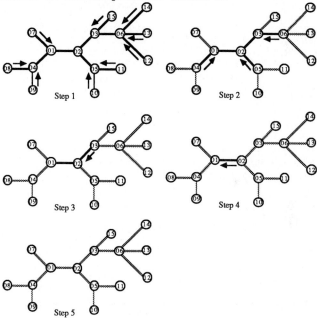

If we tell each processor who its neighbors are and which one of these neighbors lies on the path towards the goal, then no further global control or synchronization is needed. Each processor knows that it should send its outgoing message as soon as it can after receiving all its incoming messages. The leaf processors, which have no incoming messages, can act immediately. The others must wait for their turn.

Updating Messages. Suppose we have completed the computation of $A^{\downarrow h_1}$, the marginal for our goal vertex. And suppose we now find reason to change A by changing one or more of our inputs, the

A_h. If we have implemented the architecture just described, with storage registers between each of the vertices, then we may be able to update the marginal $A^{\downarrow h_1}$ without discarding all the work we have already done. If we leave some of the inputs unchanged, then some of the computations may not need to be repeated.

Unnecessary computation can be avoided without global control. We simply need a way of marking valuations, to indicate that they have received any needed updating. Suppose the processor at each vertex h can recognize the mark on any of its inputs (on A_h, our direct input, or on any message $M^{g \to \beta(g)}$ from a vertex g that has h as its bud), and can write the mark on its own output, the message $M^{h \to \beta(h)}$. When we wish to update the computation of $A^{\downarrow h_1}$, we put in the new values for those A_h we wish to change, and we mark all the A_h, both the ones we have changed, and the others, which we do not want to change. Then we run the system as before, except that a processor, instead of waiting for its incoming registers to be full before it acts, waits until all its inputs are marked. The processor can recognize when an input is marked without being changed, and in this case it simply marks its output instead of recomputing it.

Of course, updating can also be achieved with much less control. As Pearl [1986] has emphasized, hardly any control at all is needed if we are indifferent to the possibility of wasted effort. If we do not care whether a processor repeats the same computations, we can forget about marking valuations and simply allow each processor to recompute its output from its inputs periodically or at random times. Under these circumstances, any change in one of the A_g will eventually be propagated through the system to change $A^{\downarrow h_1}$.

A Simple Production System. In reality, we will never have a parallel computer organized precisely to fit our problem. Our story about passing messages between independent processors should be thought of as a metaphor, not as a guide to implementation. Implementations can take advantage, however, of the modularity the metaphor reveals.

One way to take advantage of this modularity, even on a serial computer, is to implement the computational scheme in a simple forward-chaining production system. A forward-chaining production system consists of a working memory and a rule-base, a set of rules for changing the contents of the memory. (See Brownston et al. [1985] or Davis and King [1984].)

A very simple production system is adequate for our problem. We need a working memory that initially contains A_h for each vertex h of $(\mathcal{H}, \mathcal{E})$, and a rule-base consisting of just two rules, corresponding to Operations M_{2a} and M_{2b}.

Rule 1: If A_h is in working memory and $M^{g \to \beta(g)}$ is in working memory for every g such that $\beta(g) = h$, then use (3.3) to compute $M^{h \to \beta(h)}$, and place it in working memory.

Rule 2: If A_{h_1} is in working memory and $M^{g \to \beta(g)}$ is in working memory for every g such that $\beta(g) = h_1$, then use

(3.4) to compute $A^{\downarrow h_1}$, and print the result.

Initially, there will be no $M^{g \to \beta(g)}$ at all in working memory, so Rule 1 can fire only for h such that there is no g with $\beta(g)=h$ – i.e., only for h that are leaves. But eventually Rule 1 will fire for every vertex except the root h_1. Then Rule 2 will fire, completing the computation. Altogether, there will be n firings, one for each vertex in the Markov tree.

Production systems are usually implemented so that a rule will fire only once for a given instantiation of its antecedent; this is called *refraction* [Brownston et al. 1985, pp. 62-63]. If our simple production system is implemented with refraction, there will be no unnecessary firings of rules; only the n firings that are needed will occur. Even without refraction, however, the computation will eventually be completed.

Since refraction allows a rule to fire again for a given instantiation when the inputs for that instantiation are changed, this simple production system will also handle updating efficiently, performing only those recomputations that are necessary.

3.4. Simultaneous Propagation in Markov Trees

In the preceding section, we were concerned with the computation of the marginal on a single vertex of the Markov tree. In this section, we will be concerned with how to compute the marginals on all vertices simultaneously. As we will see, this can be done efficiently with only slight changes in the architecture or rules.

Computing all Marginals. If we can compute the marginal of A on one hyperedge in $\mathcal{H}$, then we can compute the marginals on all the hyperedges in $\mathcal{H}$. We simply compute them one after the other. It is obvious, however, that this will involve much duplication of effort. How can we avoid the duplication?

The first point to notice in answering this question is that we only need one Markov tree. Though there may be many Markov tree representatives for $\mathcal{H}$, any one of them can serve for the computation of all the marginals. Once we have chosen a Markov tree representative $(\mathcal{H}, \mathcal{C})$, then no matter which element h of $\mathcal{H}$ interests us, we can choose a tree construction sequence for $(\mathcal{H}, \mathcal{C})$ that begins with h, and since this sequence is also a hypertree construction sequence for $\mathcal{H}$, we can apply the method of section 3.4 to it to compute $A^{\downarrow h}$.

The second point to notice is that the message passed from one vertex to another, say from f to g, will be the same no matter what marginal we are computing. If β is the budding that we use to compute $A^{\downarrow h}$, the marginal on h, and β' is the budding we use to compute $A^{\downarrow h'}$, and if $\beta(f) = \beta'(f) = g$, then the message $M^{f \to \beta(f)}$ that we send from f to g when computing $A^{\downarrow h}$ is the same as the message $M^{f \to \beta'(f)}$ that we send from f to g when computing $A^{\downarrow h'}$. Since the value of $M^{f \to \beta(f)}$ does not depend on the budding β, we may write $M^{f \to g}$ instead of $M^{f \to \beta(f)}$ when $\beta(f)=g$.

If we compute marginals for all the vertices, then we will eventually compute both $M^{f \to g}$ and $M^{g \to f}$ for every edge $\{f,g\}$. We will compute $M^{f \to g}$ when we compute the marginal on g or on any other vertex on the g side of the edge, and we will compute $M^{g \to f}$ when we compute the marginal on g or on any other vertex on the g side of the edge.

We can easily generalize the recursive definition of $M^{g \to \beta(g)}$ that we gave in section 3.5 to a recursive definition of $M^{g \to h}$ for all neighbors g and h. To do so, we merely restate (3.2) in a way that replaces references to the budding β by references to neighbors and the direction of the message. We obtain

$$M^{g \to h} = \left(A_g \otimes \left(\otimes \{ M^{f \to g} \mid f \in (\mathfrak{N}_g - \{h\}) \} \right) \right)^{\downarrow g \cap h},\qquad(3.5)$$

where $\mathfrak{N}_g$ is the set of all g's neighbors in $(\mathfrak{H}, \mathfrak{E})$. If g is a leaf vertex, then (3.5) reduces to $M^{g \to h} = A_g^{\downarrow g \cap h}$.

After we carry out the recursion to compute $M^{g \to h}$ for all pairs of neighbors g and h, we can compute the marginal of A on each h by

$$A^{\downarrow h} = A_h \otimes \left(\otimes \{ M^{g \to h} \mid g \in \mathfrak{N}_h \} \right).\qquad(3.6)$$

The General Architecture. A slight modification of the architecture shown in Figure 3.1 will allow us to implement the simultaneous computation of the marginals on all the hyperedges. We simply put two storage registers between every pair of neighbors f and g, as in Figure 3.4. One register stores the message from f to g; the other stores the message from g to f.

Figure 3.4. The two storage registers between f and g.

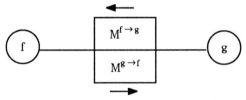

Figure 3.5 shows a more elaborate architecture for the simultaneous computation. In addition to the storage registers that communicate between vertices, this figure shows registers where the original valuations, the A_h, are put into the system and the marginals, the $A^{\downarrow h}$, are read out.

In the architecture of Figure 3.1, computation is controlled by the simple requirement that a vertex g must have messages in all its incoming registers before it can compute a message to place in its outgoing register. In the architecture of Figure 3.5, computation is controlled by the requirement that a vertex g must have messages in all its incoming registers except the one from h before it can compute a message to send to h.

This basic requirement leaves room for a variety of control regimes. Most of the comments we made about the flexibility of control for Figure 3.1 carry over to Figure 3.5.

In particular, updating can be handled efficiently if a method is provided for marking updated inputs and messages. If we change just one of the input, then efficient updating will save about half the work involved in simply reperforming the entire computation. To see that this is so, consider the effect of changing the input A_h in Figure 3.4. This will change the message $M^{g \to f}$, but not the message $M^{f \to g}$. The same will be true for every edge; one of the two messages will have to be recomputed, but not the other.

Figure 3.5. Several vertices, with storage registers for communication between themselves and with the user.

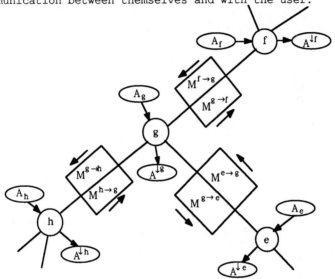

It may be enlightening to look at how the lock-step control we illustrated with Figure 3.3 might generalize to simultaneous computation of the marginals for all vertices. Consider a lock-step regime where at each step, each vertex looks and sees what messages it has the information to compute, computes these messages, and sends them. After all the vertices working are done, they look again, see what other messages they now have the information to compute, compute these messages, and send them. And so on. Figure 3.6 gives an example. At the first step, the only messages that can be computed are the messages from the leaves to their branches. At the second step, the computation moves inward. Finally, at step 3, it reaches vertex 2, which then has the information needed to compute its own marginal and messages for all its neighbors. Then the messages move back out towards the leaves, with each vertex along the way being able to compute its own marginal and messages for all its other neighbors as soon as it receives the message from its neighbor nearest vertex 2.

188

In the first phase, the inward phase, a vertex sends a message
to only one of its neighbors, the neighbor towards the center.
In the second phase, the outward phase, a vertex sends k-1 messages, where k is the number of its neighbors. Yet the number
of messages sent in the two phases is roughly the same, because
the leaf vertices participate in the first phase and not in the
second.

There are seven vertices in the longest path in the tree of
Figure 3.6. Whenever the number of vertices in the longest path
is odd, the lock-step control regime will result in computation
proceeding inwards to a central vertex and then proceeding back
outwards to the leaves. And whenever this number is even, there
will be two central vertices that send each other messages simultaneously, after which they both send messages back outwards
towards the leaves.

Figure 3.6. An example of the message-passing scheme for
simultaneous computation of all marginals.

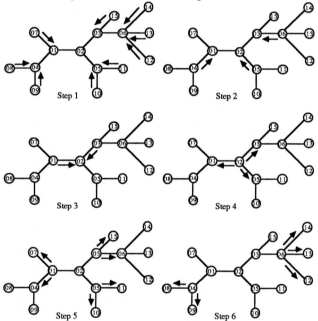

If we really do have independent processors for each vertex,
then we do not have to wait for all the computations that start
together to finish before taking advantage of the ones that are
finished to start new ones. We can allow a new computation to
start whenever a processor is free and it has the information
needed. On the other hand, we need not require that the work be
done so promptly. We can assume that processors look for work
to do only at random times. But no matter how we handle these

issues, the computation will converge to some particular vertex or pair of neighboring vertices and then move back out from that vertex or pair of vertices.

There is exactly twice as much message passing in our scheme for simultaneous computation as there was in our scheme for computing a single marginal. Here every pair of neighbors exchange messages; there only one message was sent between every pair of neighbors. Notice also that we can make the computation of any given marginal the beginning of the simultaneous computation. We can single out any hyperedge h (even a leaf), and forbid it from sending a message to any neighbor until it has received messages from all its neighbors. If we then let the system of Figure 3.6 run, it will behave just like the system of Figure 3.3 with h as the root, until h has received messages from all its neighbors. At that point, h can compute its marginal and can also send messages to all its neighbors; the second half of the message passing then proceeds, with messages moving back in the other direction.

The Corresponding Production System. Implementing simultaneous computation in a production system requires only slight changes in our two rules. The following will work:

Rule 1': If A_g is in working memory, and $M^{f \to g}$ is in working memory for every f in $\mathfrak{N}_g - \{h\}$, then use (3.5) to compute $M^{g \to h}$, and place it in working memory.

Rule 2': If A_h is in working memory, and $M^{g \to h}$ is in working memory for every g in $\mathfrak{N}_h$, then use (3.6) to compute $A^{\downarrow h}$, and print the result.

Initially, there will be no $M^{f \to g}$ at all in working memory, so Rule 1' can fire only for g and h such that $\mathfrak{N}_g - \{h\}$ is empty - i.e., only when g is a leaf and h is its bud. But eventually Rule 1' will fire in both directions for every edge {g,h}. Once Rule 1' has fired for all the neighbors g of h, in the direction of h, Rule 2' will fire for h. Altogether, there will be 3n-2 firings, two firings of Rule 1' for each of the n-1 edges, and one firing of Rule 2' for each of the n vertices.

As the count of firings indicates, our scheme for simultaneous computation finds marginals for all the vertices with roughly the same effort that would be required to find marginals for three vertices if this were done by running the scheme of section 3.5 three times.

4. PROBABILITY PROPAGATION

In this section, we explain local computation for probability distributions. More precisely, we show how the problem of computing marginals of joint probability distributions fits the general framework described in the previous section.

For probability propagation, proper valuations will correspond to potentials.

Potentials. We use the symbol $\mathbf{W}_X$ for the set of possible values of a variable X, and we call $\mathbf{W}_X$ the *frame for X*. We will be concerned with a finite set $\mathfrak{X}$ of variables, and we will assume that all the variables in $\mathcal{X}$ have finite frames. For each $h \subseteq \mathcal{X}$, we let $\mathcal{W}_h$ denote the Cartesian product of $\mathcal{W}_X$ for X in h; $\mathcal{W}_h = \times \{\mathcal{W}_X | X \in h\}$. We call $\mathcal{W}_h$ the *frame for h*. We will refer to elements of $\mathcal{W}_h$ as *configurations of h*. A *potential on h* is a real-valued function on $\mathcal{W}_h$ that has non-negative values that are not all zero. Intuitively, potentials are unnormalized probability distributions.

Projection of configurations. In order to develop a notation for the combination of potentials, we first need a notation for the projection of configurations of a set of variables to a smaller set of variables. Here projection simply means dropping extra coordinates; if (w,x,y,z) is a configuration of {W,X,Y,Z}, for example, then the projection of (w,x,y,z) to {W,X} is simply (w,x), which is a configuration of {W,X}. If g and h are sets of variables, $h \subseteq g$, and $\mathbf{x}$ is a configuration of g, then we will let $\mathbf{x}^{\downarrow h}$ denote the projection of $\mathbf{x}$ to h.

Combination. For potentials, combination is simply pointwise multiplication. If G is a potential on g, H is a potential on h, and there exists an $\mathbf{x} \in \mathcal{W}_{g \cup h}$ such that

$$G(\mathbf{x}^{\downarrow g}) H(\mathbf{x}^{\downarrow h}) > 0, \tag{4.1}$$

then their *combination*, denoted simply by GH, is the potential on $g \cup h$ given by

$$(GH)(\mathbf{x}) = G(\mathbf{x}^{\downarrow g}) H(\mathbf{x}^{\downarrow h}) \tag{4.2}$$

for all $\mathbf{x} \in \mathcal{W}_{g \cup h}$. If there exists no $\mathbf{x} \in \mathcal{W}_{g \cup h}$ such that $G(\mathbf{x}^{\downarrow g}) H(\mathbf{x}^{\downarrow h}) > 0$, then we say that G and H are *not combinable*.

Intuitively, if the bodies of evidence on which G and H are based are independent, then $G \oplus H$ is supposed to represent the result of pooling these two bodies of evidence. Note that condition (4.1) ensures that GH defined in (4.2) is a potential. If condition (4.1) does not hold, this means that the two bodies of evidence corresponding to G and H contradict each other completely and it is not possible to combine such evidence.

It is clear from the definition of combination of potentials that it is commutative and associative (axiom A1).

Marginalization. Marginalization is familiar in probability theory; it means reducing a function on one set of variables to a function on a smaller set of variables by summing over the variables omitted.

Suppose g and h are sets of variables, $h \subseteq g$, and G is a potential on g. The *marginal of G for h*, denoted by $G^{\downarrow h}$, is the potential on h defined by

$$G^{\downarrow h}(\mathbf{x}) = \begin{cases} \Sigma \{G(\mathbf{x}, \mathbf{y}) | \mathbf{y} \in \mathcal{W}_{g-h}\} & \text{if h is a proper subset of g} \\ G(\mathbf{x}) & \text{if h=g} \end{cases}$$

for all $\mathbf{x} \in \mathcal{W}_h$.

It is obvious from the above definition that marginalization operation for potentials satisfies axiom A2.

Since multiplication distributes over addition, it is easy to show that combination and marginalization for potentials satisfy axiom A3. Thus all axioms are satisfied making local computation possible.

A number of authors who have studied local computation for probability, including Kelly and Barclay [1973], Cannings, Thompson and Skolnick [1978], Pearl [1986], Shenoy and Shafer [1986], and Lauritzen and Spiegelhalter [1988], have described schemes that are variations on the the basic scheme described in section 2. Most of these authors, however, have justified their schemes by emphasizing conditional probability. We believe this emphasis is misplaced. What is essential to local computation is a factorization. It is not essential that this factorization be interpreted, at any stage, in terms of conditional probabilities. For more regarding this point, see Shafer and Shenoy [1988].

We would like to make two important observations for the case of probability propagation. First note that it is sufficient, in order for a potential A to factor on $\mathcal{H}$, that A be proportional to a product of arrays on the hyperedges. Indeed, if

$$A \propto \prod \{A_h \mid h \in \mathcal{H}\},$$

where A_h is a potential on h, then a representation of the form $A = \prod \{A_h \mid h \in \mathcal{H}\}$ can be obtained simply by incorporating the constant of proportionality into one of the A_h. In practice, we will postpone finding the constant of proportionality until we have marginalized A to a hyperedge using the scheme described in section 2.

The second observation relates to conditioning joint probability distributions. Suppose a probability distribution P represents our assessment of a given body of information, and we have been computing marginals of P from the factorization

$$P = \prod \{A_h \mid h \in \mathcal{H}\} \qquad (4.3)$$

where $\mathcal{H}$ is a hypertree on $\mathcal{X}$. Suppose we now observe the values of some of the variables in $\mathcal{X}$; say we observe $Y_1 = y_1$, $Y_2 = y_2$, and so on up to $Y_n = y_n$. We change our assessment from P to $P^{|f = \mathbf{y}}$ where $f = \{Y_1, \ldots, Y_n\}$, $\mathbf{y} = \{y_1, \ldots, y_n\}$, and $P^{|f = \mathbf{y}}$ denotes the joint probability distribution conditioned on the observations. Can we adapt (4.3) to a factorization of $P^{|f = \mathbf{y}}$? Yes, we can. More precisely, we can adapt (4.3) to a factorization of a potential proportional to $P^{|f = \mathbf{y}}$, and this, as we noted in our first observation, is good enough. The adaptation is simple. It follows from the definition of conditional probability that

$$P^{|f = \mathbf{y}} \propto B^{Y_1 = y_1} \ldots B^{Y_n = y_n} \prod \{A_h \mid h \in \mathcal{H}\}$$

where $B^{Y_i = y_i}$ is the *indicator potential for* $Y_i = y_i$ on $\{Y_i\}$ defined by

$$B^{Y_i = y_i}(x) = \begin{cases} 0 & \text{if } x \neq y_i \\ 1 & \text{if } x = y_i \end{cases}$$

for all $x \in \mathcal{W}_{Y_i}$.

We will now illustrate our propagation scheme using a simple example.

An Example. This example is adapted from Shachter and Heckerman

[1987]. Consider three variables D, B and G representing diabetes, blue toe and glucose in urine, respectively. The frame for each variable has two configurations. D=d will represent the proposition *diabetes is present* (in some patient) and D=~d will represent the proposition *diabetes is not present*. Similarly for B and G. Let P denote the joint probability distribution for {D, B, G}. We will assume that diabetes causes blue toe and glucose in urine implying that variables B and G are conditionally independent (with respect to P) given D. Thus we can factor P as follows.

$$P = P^D \ P^{B|D} \ P^{G|D}$$ (4.4)

where P^D is the potential on {D} representing the marginal of P for D, $P^{B|D}$ is the potential for {D,B} representing the conditional distribution of B given D, and $P^{G|D}$ is the potential for {D,G} representing the conditional distribution of G given D. For example, $P^{B|D}(d,b)$ represents the conditional probability of the proposition B=b given that D=d. Thus P factors on the hypertree {{D}, {D,B}, {D,G}}. Since we would like to compute the marginals for B and G, we will enlarge the hypertree to include the hyperedges {B} and {G}. It is easy to expand (4.4) so that we have a factorization of P on the enlarged hypertree - the potentials on these additional hyperedges consist of all ones. Suppose that the potentials P^D, $P^{B|D}$, and $P^{G|D}$ are as shown in Table 4.1.

Table 4.1. The potentials P^D, $P^{B|D}$, and $P^{G|D}$.

P^D		$P^{B|D}$		$P^{G|D}$	
d	.1	d,b	.014	d,g	.9
~d	.9	d,~b	.986	d,~g	.1
		~d,b	.006	~d,g	.01
		~d,~b	.994	~d,~g	.99

The enlarged hypertree and a Markov tree representation are shown in Figure 4.1.

Figure 4.1. The hypertree and a Markov tree representation.

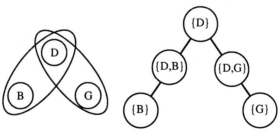

Suppose we propagate the potentials using the scheme described in section 2. The results are as shown in Figure 4.2. For each vertex h, the input potentials are shown as I^h and the output potentials are shown as O^h. All the messages are also shown. Note that the output potentials have been normalized so that they represent marginal posterior probabilities.

Figure 4.2. The initial propagation of potentials.

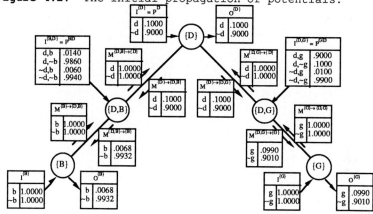

Now suppose we observe that the patient has blue toe. This is represented by the indicator potential for B=b. The other potentials are the same as before. If we propagate the potentials, the results are as shown in Figure 4.3.

Figure 4.3. The results of propagation after the presence of blue toe is observed.

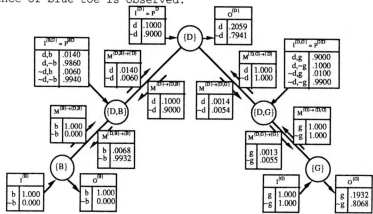

Note that the posterior probability of the presence of diabetes has increased (from .1 to .2059) and consequently the presence of glucose in urine has also increased (from .0990 to .1932).

Now suppose that after the patient is tested for glucose in urine, the results indicate that there is an absence of glucose in urine. This information is represented by the indicator potential for G=~g. The other potentials are as before. If we propagate the potentials, the results are as shown in Figure 4.4.

Figure 4.4. The results of propagation after the observation that patient does not have glucose in urine.

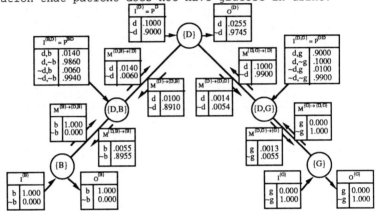

Note that the posterior probability of the presence of diabetes has decreased (from .2059 to .0255). This concludes our example.

5. BELIEF-FUNCTION PROPAGATION

In this section, we explain local computation for belief functions. More precisely, we show how the problem of computing marginals of a joint belief function fits the general framework described in section 2.

For belief-function propagation, proper valuations correspond to either probability mass assignment functions, belief functions, plausibility functions or commonality functions. For simplicity of exposition, we will describe belief-function propagation in terms of superpotentials which are unnormalized basic probability assignment functions.

Basic Probability Assignment Functions. Suppose $\mathcal{W}_h$ is the frame for a subset h of variables. A *basic probability assignment function (bpa function) for h* is a non-negative, real-valued function M on the set of all subsets of $\mathcal{W}_h$ such that
  (i) $M(\emptyset) = 0$, and
  (ii) $\Sigma\{M(\boldsymbol{a}) \mid \boldsymbol{a} \subseteq \mathcal{W}_h\} = 1$.

Intuitively, $M(\boldsymbol{a})$ represents the degree of belief assigned exactly to $\boldsymbol{a}$ (the proposition that the true configuration of h is in the set $\boldsymbol{a}$) and to nothing smaller. A bpa function is the belief function equivalent of a probability mass assignment function in probability theory. Whereas a probability mass function is restricted to assigning probability masses only to singleton configurations of variables, a bpa function is allowed to assign probability masses to sets of configurations without assigning any mass to the individual configurations contained in the sets.

Superpotentials. Suppose h is a subset of variables. A *superpotential for h* is a non-negative, real-valued function on the set of all subsets of $\mathcal{W}_h$ such that the values of nonempty subsets are not all zero. Given a superpotential H on h, we can construct a bpa function H' for h from H as follows:

$$H'(\emptyset) = 0, \text{ and } H'(\boldsymbol{a}) = H(\boldsymbol{a})/\Sigma\{H(\boldsymbol{b}) \mid \boldsymbol{b} \subseteq \mathcal{W}_h, \ \boldsymbol{b} \neq \emptyset\}.$$

Thus superpotentials can be thought of as unnormalized bpa functions. Superpotentials correspond to the notion of proper valuations in the general framework.

Projection and Extension of Subsets. Before we can define combination and marginalization for superpotentials, we need the concepts of projection and extension of subsets of configurations.

If g and h are sets of variables, $h \subseteq g$, and $\boldsymbol{g}$ is a nonempty subset of $\mathcal{W}_g$, then the *projection of $\boldsymbol{g}$ to h*, denoted by $\boldsymbol{g}^{\downarrow h}$, is the subset of $\mathcal{W}_h$ given by $\boldsymbol{g}^{\downarrow h} = \{\mathbf{x}^{\downarrow h} \mid \mathbf{x} \in \boldsymbol{g}\}$.

For example, If $\boldsymbol{a}$ is a subset of $\mathcal{W}_{\{W,X,Y,Z\}}$, then the marginal of $\boldsymbol{a}$ to $\{X,Y\}$ consists of the elements of $\mathcal{W}_{\{X,Y\}}$ which can be obtained by projecting elements of $\boldsymbol{a}$ to $\mathcal{W}_{\{X,Y\}}$.

By extension of a subset of a frame to a subset of a larger frame, we mean a cylinder set extension. If g and h are sets of variables, $h \subseteq g$, $h \neq g$, and $\boldsymbol{h}$ is a subset of $\mathcal{W}_h$, then the *extension of $\boldsymbol{h}$ to g* is $\boldsymbol{h} \times \mathcal{W}_{g-h}$. If $\boldsymbol{h}$ is a subset of $\mathcal{W}_h$, then the extension of $\boldsymbol{h}$ to h is defined to be $\boldsymbol{h}$. We will let $\boldsymbol{h}^{\uparrow g}$ denote the extension of $\boldsymbol{h}$ to g.

For example, if $\boldsymbol{a}$ is a subset of $\mathcal{W}_{\{W,X\}}$, then the vacuous extension of $\boldsymbol{a}$ to $\{W,X,Y,Z\}$ is $\boldsymbol{a} \times \mathcal{W}_{\{Y,Z\}}$.

Combination. For superpotentials, combination is called Dempster's rule [Dempster 1966]. Consider two superpotentials G and H on g and h, respectively. If

$$\Sigma\{G(\boldsymbol{a})H(\boldsymbol{b}) \mid (\boldsymbol{a}^{\uparrow(g\cup h)}) \cap (\boldsymbol{b}^{\uparrow(g\cup h)}) \neq \emptyset\} \neq 0, \qquad (5.1)$$

then their *combination*, denoted by $G \oplus H$, is the superpotential on $g \cup h$ given by

$$G \oplus H(\boldsymbol{c}) = \Sigma\{G(\boldsymbol{a})H(\boldsymbol{b}) \mid (\boldsymbol{a}^{\uparrow(g\cup h)}) \cap (\boldsymbol{b}^{\uparrow(g\cup h)}) = \boldsymbol{c}\} \qquad (5.2)$$

for all $\boldsymbol{c} \subseteq \mathcal{W}_{g\cup h}$. If $\Sigma\{G(\boldsymbol{a})H(\boldsymbol{b}) \mid (\boldsymbol{a}^{\uparrow(g\cup h)}) \cap (\boldsymbol{b}^{\uparrow(g\cup h)}) \neq \emptyset\} = 0$, then we say that G and H are *not combinable*.

Intuitively, if the bodies of evidence on which G and H are based are independent, then $G \oplus H$ is supposed to represent the result of pooling these two bodies of evidence. Note that condition (5.1) ensures that $G \oplus H$ defined in (5.2) is a superpotential. If condition (5.1) does not hold, this means that the two bodies of evidence corresponding to G and H contradict each

196

other completely and it is not possible to combine such evidence.

It is shown in Shafer [1976] that Dempster's rule of combination is commutative and associative. Thus combination for superpotentials satisfies axiom A1.

Marginalization. Like marginalization for potentials, marginalization for superpotentials corresponds to summation.

Suppose G is a superpotential for g and suppose $h \subseteq g$. Then the *marginal of G for h* is the superpotential $G^{\downarrow h}$ for h defined as follows:

$$G^{\downarrow h}(\boldsymbol{a}) = \Sigma\{G(\boldsymbol{b}) \mid \boldsymbol{b} \subseteq \mathcal{W}_g \text{ such that } \boldsymbol{b}^{\downarrow h} = \boldsymbol{a}\}$$

for all subsets $\boldsymbol{a}$ of $\mathcal{W}_h$.

It is easy to see that marginalization for superpotentials satisfies axiom A2. In Shafer and Shenoy [1988], it is shown that the above definitions of marginalization and combination for superpotentials satisfy axiom A3. Thus all axioms are satisfied making local computation possible.

Propagation of belief functions using local computation has been studied by Shafer and Logan [1987], Shenoy and Shafer [1986], Shenoy et al [1988], Kong [1986], Dempster and Kong [1986], Shafer et al [1987], Mellouli [1987], and Shafer and Shenoy [1988]. Shafer et al [1988], Shenoy [1989], Zarley [1988], Zarley et al [1988] and Hsia and Shenoy [1989, 1989b] discuss applications and implementations of these propagation schemes.

ACKNOWLEDGEMENTS

Research for this article has been partially supported by NSF grant IRI-8902444 and a Research Opportunities in Auditing grant 88-146 from the Peat Marwick Foundation. A condensed version of this paper previously appeared in the Proceedings of the Fourth Workshop on Uncertainty in Artificial Intelligence in 1988.

REFERENCES

Arnborg, S., Corneil, D. G. and Proskurowski, A. (1987), Complexity of finding embeddings in a k-tree, *SIAM Journal of Algebraic and Discrete Methods*, **8**, 277-284.

Berge, C. (1973), *Graphs and Hypergraphs*, translated from French by E. Minieka, North-Holland.

Bertele, U. and Brioschi, F. (1972), *Nonserial Dynamic Programming*, Academic Press.

Brownston, L. S., Farrell, R. G., Kant, E. and Martin, N. (1985), *Programming Expert Systems in OPS5: An Introduction to Rule-Based Programming*, Addison-Wesley.

Buchanan, B. G. and Shortliffe, E. H., eds. (1984), *Rule-based Expert Systems: The MYCIN Experiments of the Stanford Heuristic Programming Project*, Addison-Wesley.

Cannings, C., Thompson, E. A. and Skolnick, M. H. (1978), Probability functions on complex pedigrees, *Advances in Applied Probability*, **10**, 26-61.

Darroch, J. N., Lauritzen, S. L. and Speed, T. P. (1980), Markov fields and log-linear models for contingency tables, *Annals of Statistics*, **8**, 522-539.

Davis, R. and King, J. J. (1984), The origin of rule-based systems in AI, in Buchanan and Shortliffe [1984, 20-52].

Dempster, A. P. (1966), New methods for reasoning toward posterior distributions based on sample data, *Annals of Mathematical Statistics*, **37**, 355-374.

Dempster, A. P. and Kong, A. (1986), Uncertain evidence and artificial analysis, Research Report S-108, Department of Statistics, Harvard University.

Golumbic, M. C. (1980), *Algorithmic Graph Theory and Perfect Graphs*, Academic Press.

Hsia, Y. and Shenoy, P. P. (1989), An evidential language for expert systems, *Methodologies for Intelligent Systems, 4*, Ras, Z. (ed.), North-Holland, 9-16.

Hsia, Y. and Shenoy, P. P. (1989b), MacEvidence: A visual evidential language for knowledge-based systems, Working Paper No. 211, School of Business, University of Kansas.

Kelly, C. W. III and Barclay, S. (1973), A general Bayesian model for hierarchical inference, *Organizational Behavior and Human Performance*, **10**, 388-403.

Kong, A. (1986), Multivariate belief functions and graphical models, doctoral dissertation, Department of Statistics, Harvard University.

Lauritzen, S. L., Speed, T. P. and Vijayan, K. (1984), Decomposable graphs and hypergraphs, *Journal of the Australian Mathematical Society*, series A, **36**, 12-29.

Lauritzen, S. L. and Spiegelhalter, D. J. (1988), Local computations with probabilities on graphical structures and their application to expert systems (with discussion), *Journal of the Royal Statistical Society*, series B, **50**(2), 157-224.

Maier, D. (1983), *The Theory of Relational Databases*, Computer Science Press.

Mellouli, K. (1987), On the propagation of beliefs in networks using the Dempster-Shafer theory of evidence, doctoral dissertation, School of Business, University of Kansas.

Pearl, J. (1986), Fusion, propagation and structuring in belief networks, *Artificial Intelligence*, **29**, 241-288.

Rose, D. J. (1970), Triangulated graphs and the elimination process, *Journal of Mathematical Analysis and Applications*, **32**, 597-609.

Shachter, R. D. and Heckerman, D. (1987), A backwards view for assessment, *AI Magazine*, **8**(3), 55-61.

Shafer, G. (1976), *A Mathematical Theory of Evidence*, Princeton University Press.

Shafer, G. and Logan, R. (1987), Implementing Dempster's rule for hierarchical evidence, *Artificial Intelligence*, **33**, 271-298.

Shafer, G. and Shenoy, P. P. (1988), Local computation in hypertrees, Working Paper No. 201, School of Business, University of Kansas.

Shafer, G., Shenoy, P. P. and Mellouli, K. (1987), Propagating belief functions in qualitative Markov trees, *International Journal of Approximate Reasoning*, **1**(4), 349-400.

Shafer, G., Shenoy, P. P. and Srivastava, R. P. (1988), AUDITOR'S ASSISTANT: A knowledge engineering tool for audit decisions, *Auditing Symposium IX: Proceedings of the 1988 Touche Ross/University of Kansas Symposium on Auditing*

Problems, 61-84.

Shenoy, P. P. (1989), A valuation-based language for expert systems, *International Journal of Approximate Reasoning*, **3**(5), 383-411.

Shenoy, P. P. (1989b), On Spohn's rule for revision of beliefs, Working Paper No. 213, School of Business, University of Kansas.

Shenoy, P. P. and Shafer, G. (1986), Propagating belief functions using local computations, *IEEE Expert*, **1**(3), 43-52.

Shenoy, P. P. and Shafer, G. (1988a), Axioms for discrete optimization using local computation, Working Paper No. 207, School of Business, University of Kansas.

Shenoy, P. P. and Shafer, G. (1988b), Constraint propagation, Working Paper No. 208, School of Business, University of Kansas.

Shenoy, P. P., Shafer, G. and Mellouli, K. (1988), Propagation of belief functions: A distributed approach, *Uncertainty in Artificial Intelligence 2*, Lemmer, J. F. and Kanal, L. N. (eds.), North-Holland, 325-336.

Spohn, W. (1988), Ordinal conditional functions: A dynamic theory of epistemic states, in Harper, W. L. and Skyrms, B., eds., *Causation in Decision, Belief Change, and Statistics*, **II**, 105-134, D. Reidel Publishing Company.

Spohn, W. (1990), A general non-probabilistic theory of inductive reasoning, this volume.

Tarjan, R. E. and Yannakakis, M. (1984), Simple linear time algorithms to test chordality of graphs, test acyclicity of hypergraphs, and selectively reduce acyclic hypergraphs, *SIAM Journal of Computing*, **13**, 566-579.

Zarley, D. K. (1988), An evidential reasoning system, Working Paper No. 206, School of Business, University of Kansas.

Zarley, D. K., Hsia, Y. and Shafer, G. (1988), Evidential reasoning using DELIEF, *Proceedings of the Seventh National Conference on Artificial Intelligence (AAAI-88)*, **1**, 205-209, Minneapolis, MN.

Zhang, L. (1988), Studies on finding hypertree covers for hypergraphs, Working Paper No. 198, School of Business, University of Kansas.

Uncertainty in Artificial Intelligence 4
R.D. Shachter, T.S. Levitt, L.N. Kanal, J.F. Lemmer (Editors)
© Elsevier Science Publishers B.V. (North-Holland), 1990   199

A Summary of
A New Normative Theory of Probabilistic Logic

Romas Aleliunas

Simon Fraser University, Burnaby, British Columbia, Canada V5A 1S6

ABSTRACT   *By probabilistic logic I mean a normative theory of belief that explains how a body of evidence affects one's degree of belief in a possible hypothesis. A new axiomatization of such a theory is presented which avoids a finite additivity axiom, yet which retains many useful inference rules. Many of the examples of this theory—its models—do not use numerical probabilities.*

Put another way, this article gives sharper answers to the two questions—
1. What kinds of sets can used as the range of a probability function?
2. Under what conditions is the range set of a probability function isomorphic to the set of real numbers in the interval [0,1] with the usual arithmetical operations?

Any mechanical device (let's just call it a box) that makes decisions or performs actions in the real world can be analysed *as if* it were acting on the basis of—

(1) a body of statistical knowledge, and

(2) a system of utilities or preferences,

whether or not anyone can find, upon opening the box to study its mechanism, obvious embodiments of (1) or (2). Describing a box's decision-making behaviour in this way helps us see more quickly which real world situations the box can handle successfully, and which ones it cannot—mathematical statistics, and the method of performing experimental trials (on which statistics is based), are, after all, the only tools we have for making such judgements. (The difficulties with non-monotonic and default logic arise because we are in no position with these theories to make such judgements. Who knows when it is safe to say "Birds typically fly" unless this statement has a statistical interpretation?—something which is usually denied by the inventors of these theories.)

According to KEYNES, probability in its broadest sense, is the study of methods of encoding a body of statistical knowledge—item (1) above—as a set of likelihood relationships between evidence statements and hypotheses, or, more generally, between pairs of propositions. Typically this collection of statistical statements contains forumlae about conditional probabilities such as "p(A|B)=0.5".

KEYNES suggested that limiting this collection to inequality statements of the form p(A|B) ≥ p(C|D) is perhaps the weakest and least objectionable way to code statistical knowledge. This method does not require and does not introduce any specific numerical probability assignments, except in trivial cases such as p(A|B) ≥ p(A|A) which is merely a roundabout way of saying p(A|B) = 1. This idea of using only partial ordering to encode statistical knowledge was taken up again by B. O. KOOPMAN and studied in more depth in his paper of 1940. My goal here is to take pursue this idea once again from a more algebraic point of view.

The algebraic approach I take assumes that to each possible conditional probability, say p(A|B), there is assigned the formal probabilty (p,A,B), where (p,A,B) is just an uninterpreted formal mark. Thus these formal marks do not necessarily denote real numbers, for instance.

This maneuver allows us to replace inequalities between symbols of the form p(A|B) with inequalities between symbols of the form (p,A,B) which we will treat as atomic symbols. By atomic I mean that we cannot look into the internal structure of (p,A,B) to see that it is about the propositions A and B and the probability function p. Let us call the set of all possible formal marks P*. So far we have merely replaced one system for encoding statistical knowledge by a mathematically equivalent one. Our statistical knowledge is to be encoded now by the choice of partial ordering for P*.

The possible equivalence classes of P* are important. At one extreme we may have as many equivalence classes as there are elements in P*, and at the other extreme we may only have three equivalence classes. The first possibility corresponds to KEYNES's suggestion— what FINE [1973] calls a "weak comparative system of probability"—while the second one sorts likelihoods into three categories: "impossible", "certain", and "maybe". Yet another possibilty is to have equivalence classes correspond to real numbers and to deduce the inequalities between conditional probability symbols from the corresponding inequalities between real numbers.

This algebraic maneuver, therefore, gives us a uniform language for studying any sort of set of probabilities **P** that can ever be conceived. Suppose that some alien statistician chooses to assign probabilities by drawing probability values from some partially ordered set **P**. Then the set **P** must be isomorphic to one of the possible systems of equivalence classes of P*.

Obviously the interesting question is what sorts of sets **P** are sensible choices for the range of a probabilty function such as p(·|·)? Further, under what conditions, assuming they meet some weak notion of rationality, must the range of a probability function be isomorphic to the real numbers in [0,1] under the usual arithmetical operations? (This second question was studied by Richard T. COX in 1946. He attempted to show that the answer is "always".) My aim here is to provide more precise answers to these two questions. (My answer to the second question turns out to be "not always".)

Aside from streamlining the mathematical study of abstract probability, the algebraic approach promises to be both more natural from a psychological point of view, and to be more attractive computationally. Both of these points are taken up more fully in another article I am preparing.

What is Probabilistic Logic ?

Probabilistic logic is any scheme for relating a body of evidence to a potential conclusion (a hypothesis) in a rational way. We assign *degrees of belief* (which we also call *probabilities*) to the possible relationships between hypotheses and pieces of evidence. These relationships are called *conditionals*. We will use the expression "f(P|Q)" to stand for "the conditional probability of P given the evidence Q as given by the probability assignment f." We have chosen to encode the potential hypothesis, P, and the collected evidence, Q, as finite sentences of some language L. We take *probabilistic logic* to be synonymous with *theory of rational belief* , *probability* to be identical to *degree of belief*, and *probability assignment* to be the same as *belief function* . Normative theories of rational belief have had a long history (KEYNES [1921], CARNAP [1950], FINE [1973]).

Let the set of probabilities be **P**. We begin by regarding this as a set of *uninterpreted formal marks*. A theory of probabilistic logic is chiefly concerned with identifying the characteristics of a family **F** of functions from **L**x**L** to **P**. **F** is the *set of permissable belief functions* (also called the *set of possible probability assignments*) from which a rational agent is permitted to choose. Our convention is that for any f in **F**, f(P|Q) represents the probability assigned by f to the hypothesis P given the evidence Q. P and Q can be any statements in **L**—no distinction is made between hypothesis statements and evidence statements in probabilistic logic.

The set **F** of rational probability assignments clearly cannot be the set of all functions from **L**x**L** to **P**. Both **F**, and each individual element in it, must be subject to some constraints. Of course different theories of rational belief may vary in their choices for these constraints, but I believe they all share some in common. One such common constraint is: if "I believe P is certain when I see Q" then it cannot also be the case that "I believe ~P is possible when I see Q." Moreover, the correctness of these constraints—and therefore of the rules of inference they engender—cannot depend on the particular application that they are put to. Decision "theory" does not dictate the standards of correctness for inferences in probabilistic logic (TUKEY [1960]).

Does the set of probabilities **P** have any internal structure? We must, at the very least, be able to assert that some conditionals are more believable than others, or else there is no practical use for this theory. This implies that we have, at the very least, a partial ordering among conditionals. This algebraic approach does not lose us any generality because, as indicated in the introduction, we may introduce a new probability symbol into **P** for each pair of sentences drawn from the language **L** and assign whatever (partial) set of orderings between these formal symbols that we wish. In this way we can reproduce any rational partial ordering whatsoever between the conditionals as an ordering of the elements of **P**. A theory which adopts this approach is called a *weak comparative theory of probability* in FINE [1973].

A theory of rational belief is not a substitute for a decision-making procedure. Probabilistic logic does not prescribe "rules of detachment," "rules of commitment," or other decision-making rules. The only judgements a theory of probabilistic logic tells you how to make are conditional judgements—how to assign a value to a conditional probability. Conditional judgements of probability are the only judgements that can be infallible. Moreover, judgements about conditional probabilities are the natural inputs to a decision-making apparatus.

New Axioms for Probabilistic Logic

The probabilities in **P** are treated as uninterpreted formal marks in the axiomatization given below. We will exhibit some possible interpretations later.

These axioms describe the constraints that are appropriate for any rational theory of belief. The axioms fall into three groups: (1) axioms about the domain and range of each probability assignment f in **F**, (2) axioms stating consistency constraints that each individual f in **F** must obey, and (3) axioms that say something about **F** itself. Finite additivity does not appear as an axiom since it essentially forces probabilities to be numbers.

AXIOMS for PROPOSITIONAL PROBABILISTIC LOGIC

Axioms about the domain and range of each f *in* **F**.
1. The set of probabilities, **P**, is a partially ordered set. The ordering relation is " $\leq$."
2. The set of sentences, **L**, is a free boolean algebra with operations &, v, and ~, and it is equipped with the usual equivalence relation " $\approx$." The generators of the algebra are a countable set of *primitive propositions*. Every sentence in **L** is either a primitive proposition or a finite combination of them. (See BURRIS *et al.* [1981] for more details

about boolean algebra.)

3. If $P \approx X$ and $Q \approx Y$, then $f(P|Q)=f(X|Y)$.

Axioms that hold for all f *in* **F**, *and for any* P, Q, R *in* **L**.

4. If Q is absurd (*i.e.* $Q \approx R\&{\sim}R$), then $f(P|Q) = f(P|P)$.

5. $f(P\&Q|Q) = f(P|Q) \leq f(Q|Q)$.

6. For any other g in **F**, $f(P|P) = g(P|P)$.

7. There is a monotone non-increasing total function, i, from **P** into **P** such that $f({\sim}P|R) = i(f(P|R))$, provided R is not absurd.

8. There is an order-preserving total function, h, from **P**x**P** into **P** such that $f(P\&Q|R) = h(f(P|Q\&R), f(Q|R))$. Moreover, if $f(P\&Q|R) = 0^*$, then $f(P|Q\&R) = 0^*$ or $f(Q|R) = 0^*$, where we define $0^* = f({\sim}R|R)$ as a function of f and R.

9. If $f(P|R) \leq f(P|{\sim}R)$ then $f(P|R) \leq f(P|Rv{\sim}R) \leq f(P|{\sim}R)$.

Axioms about the richness of the set **F**.

Let $1 = Pv{\sim}P$. For any **distinct primitive** propositions A, B, and C in **L**, and for any arbitrary probabilities a, b, and c in **P**, there is a probability assignment f in **F** (not necessarily the same one in each case) for which—

10. $f(A|1) = a$, $f(B|A) = b$, and $f(C|A\&B) = c$.

11. $f(A|B) = f(A|{\sim}B) = a$ and $f(B|A) = f(B|{\sim}A) = b$.

12. $f(A|1) = a$ and $f(A\&B|1) = b$, whenever $b \leq a$.

Explanatory comments about these axioms can be found in the complete article. (Axiom 7 has a precondition that did not appear in some earlier versions.)

Possible Interpretations for the Set P

One can show the existence of well-defined probabilities called 0 and 1 in any set **P** that satisfies these axioms. To give a mathematical model for a **P** which satisfies these axioms we must, therefore, give a consistent interpretation to each component of the structure $(\mathbf{P}, \leq, h, i, 0, 1)$.

(Model 1)   0,1-Probabilistic Logic
$\mathbf{P}(2) = \{0, 1\}$ and $0 \cdot 0 = 0 \cdot 1 = 0$, $1 \cdot 1 = 1$, $i(0) = 1$, $i(1) = 0$, and $0 \leq 1$.

(Model 2)   Simple Real Probabilistic Logic
$\mathbf{P}(\mathbf{R}) = [0,1]$, the closed interval of real numbers from 0 to 1. Let $p \cdot q$ be the ordinary

numerical product, and let $i(p) = 1 - p$. Use the usual ordering relation.

For more examples suppose $(\mathbf{P}, \leq)$ is a totally ordered set with n elements. Then the table below (which was incorrect in earlier versions) displays the number, $N(n)$, of non-isomorphic models consistent with this constraint—

n	2	3	4	5	6	7	n
N(n)	1	1	2	4	8	16	2^{n-3}

Yet another model of these axioms is the following one mimicing English probabilities. My aim here is not to claim that this is the correct model for English probabilities, but instead to show that a good approximation to English probabilities will not be ruled out by these axioms.

(Model 3) Simplified English Probabilistic Logic
Let $\mathbf{P(E)}$ be the algebra of probabilities generated by the two formal symbols {LIKELY, UNLIKELY}, subject to the following additional constraints:
(C1)   UNLIKELY = i(LIKELY)
(C2) $0 <$ UNLIKELY $<$ LIKELY < 1.
The elements of $\mathbf{P(E)}$ are strings of symbols generated by—
(G1)   concatenating previously constructed strings in $\mathbf{P(E)}$,
(G2)   forming i(s) where s is a string in $\mathbf{P(E)}$,
(G3)   introducing the formal symbol s(p,q) for any pair of elements p and q in $\mathbf{P(E)}$ whenever $p \leq q$ and there does not yet exist a solution, r, in $\mathbf{P(E)}$ for the equation $p = q \cdot r$.
The only ordering relations are those that can be inferred from (C1), (C2), and the properties of the functions h and i. This set is not totally ordered. The symbols introduced by (G3) do not, as far as I know, have English names. But not being able to name them in English does not mean they do not exist in principle.

When Must P Be Like The Real Numbers?

Under what conditions does the familiar numerical theory of probability with the familiar arithmetical operations become the only possible theory of rational belief? Richard COX [1946, 1961] first investigated this question under the assumption that probabilities were real numbers and concluded that the algebraic operations used must then be the same as the ordinary ones. ACZEL [1966] reports stronger results under the assumption of finite additivity for probabilities. The following theorem is in the same vein, but it drops these two assumptions and even some of the axioms. I call it the Tar-Pit Theorem because it shows how easy it is to get stuck in stuff that has been lying around for a long time.

Definition

P is *archimedean ordered* if, for any p ≠ 1 and any q ≠ 0 in **P**, the repeated product p·p·...·p = p^n becomes smaller than q for some positive integer n.

The Tar-Pit Theorem

Under the conditions established by axioms 1 through to 12, the following two statements are logically equivalent:

(1) The set of probabilities **P** is totally ordered and also archimedean ordered.

(2) The algebraic structure (**P**, ≥, h, i, 0, 1) is isomorphic to a subalgebra of the system (**P(R)**, ≥, ·, i, 0, 1) given as Model 2, namely Simple Real Probabilistic Logic.

Dropping both axiom 11 and the assumption that products have no non-trivial zeroes (a part of axiom 8) does not affect the theorem.

A sketch proof of this is given in the more complete article cited below.

Note: This article partially summarises (with minor corrections) one that appears in the 1988 Proceedings of the Canadian Society for Computational Studies of Intelligence (pp.67-74). The revised version of the CSCSI article will appear in **Knowledge Representation and Defeasible Reasoning**, edited by H.E. Kyburg, R.P. Loui, and G. Carlson, and published by Kluwer Academic Publishers.

References

Janos ACZEL [1966] **Lectures on Functional Equations and Their Applications,** Academic Press, New York.

Bruce G. BUCHANAN and Edward H. SHORTLIFFE, editors [1984] **Rule-Based Expert Systems: The MYCIN Experiments of the Stanford Heuristic Programming Project,** Addison-Wesley, Reading, Massachusetts.

Stanley BURRIS and H.P. SANKAPPANAVAR [1981] **A Course in Universal Algebra,** Springer-Verlag, New York.

Rudolph CARNAP [1950] **Logical Foundations of Probability,** University of Chicago Press, Chicago.
— [1962] "The aim of inductive logic," in **Logic, Methodology, and Philosophy of Science,** eds. E. Nagel, P. Suppes, and A. Tarski, Stanford University Press, Stanford, pp.303-318.

Richard T. COX [1946] "Probability, Frequency, and Reasonable Expectation," *American*

Journal of Physics , Vol. 14, pp.1-13.
— [1961] **The Algebra of Probable Inference**, John Hopkins Press, Baltimore.

Terrence L. FINE [1973] **Theories of Probability: An Examination of Foundations**, Academic Press, New York and London.

Simon FRENCH [1984] "Fuzzy Decision Analysis: Some Criticisms" in **Studies in the Management Sciences: Fuzzy Sets and Decision Analysis**, Vol. 20, North-Holland, Amsterdam and New York.

Laszlo FUCHS [1963] **Partially Ordered Algebraic Systems**, Pergamon Press, Oxford-London-New York-Paris.

I. J. GOOD [1983] **Good Thinking, The foundations of probability and its applications**, University of Minnesota Press, Minneapolis, 1983.

David HECKERMAN [1986] "Probabilistic Interpretation for MYCIN's Certainty Factors," in **Uncertainty in Artificial Intelligence**, Laveen N. Kanal and John F. Lemmer (eds.), North-Holland, New York, 1986, pp.167-196.

John Maynard KEYNES [1921] **A Treatise on Probability**, Macmillan, London.

Bernard O. KOOPMAN [1940] "The Axioms and Algebra of Intuitive Probability," *Annals of Mathematics* , Vol. 41, No. 2, pp. 269-292, April 1940.
— [1941] "Intuitive Probabilities and Sequences," *Annals of Mathematics* , Vol. 42, No. 1, pp. 169-187, January 1941.

Henry E. KYBURG, Jr. [1987] "Bayesian and Non-Bayesian Evidential Updating," *Artificial Intelligence,* Vol. 31, No.3, March 1987, pp.271-293.

Saul KRIPKE [1980] **Naming and Necessity**, Harvard Uinversity Press, Cambridge, 1980, p.16.

D. MCDERMOTT & J. DOYLE [1980] "Non-monotonic Logic I," *Artificial Intelligence* , Vol 13, pp.27-39.

D. MCDERMOTT [1982] "Non-monotonic Logic II: non-monotonic modal theories," *Journal of the ACM* , Vol 21, No. 1, pp.33-57.

Charles G. MORGAN [1982] "There is a Probabilistic Semantics for Every Extension of Classical Sentence Logic," *Journal of Philosophical Logic* , Vol. 11, pp.431-442.

Raymond REITER [1980] "A logic for default reasoning," *Artificial Intelligence* , Vol. 13, pp.81-132.

John W. TUKEY [1960] "Conclusions vs Decisions," *Technometrics* , Vol. 2, No. 4, November, 1960.

Uncertainty in Artificial Intelligence 4
R.D. Shachter, T.S. Levitt, L.N. Kanal, J.F. Lemmer (Editors)
© Elsevier Science Publishers B.V. (North-Holland), 1990

HIERARCHICAL EVIDENCE AND BELIEF FUNCTIONS

Paul K. Black and Kathryn B. Laskey

Decision Science Consortium, Inc.
1895 Preston White Drive, Suite 300
Reston, Virginia 22094
BITNET:dsc@umdc

Dempster/Shafer (D/S) theory has been advocated as a way of
representing incompleteness of evidence in a system's knowledge
base. Methods now exist for propagating beliefs through chains
of inference. This paper discusses how rules with attached
beliefs, a common representation for knowledge in automated
reasoning systems, can be transformed into the joint belief
functions required by propagation algorithms. A rule is taken
as defining a conditional belief function on the consequent
given the antecedents. It is demonstrated by example that
different joint belief functions may be consistent with a given
set of rules. Moreover, different representations of the same
rules may yield different beliefs on the consequent hypotheses.

1. INTRODUCTION

A popular way of representing knowledge in automated reasoning systems is
by a set of rules, each asserting belief in some consequent hypothesis
conditional on belief in some set of antecedent hypotheses. Rule-based
systems are popular because they are modular (in the sense that each rule
represents a single, separable "bit" of knowledge), and because the rule
format appears to be a natural way for humans to encode knowledge. The
early idea of rule-based systems was to process knowledge entirely
symbolically, but applications soon demanded the expression of degrees of
belief or certainty associated with rules.

The developers of MYCIN (Buchanan and Shortliffe [3]) assigned "certainty
factors" to rules, which propagated in an *ad hoc* manner. Adams [1]
showed the equivalence of the MYCIN model to a probabilistic model under
certain (not too plausible) independence assumptions. Since that time,
researchers have investigated propagation mechanisms for a number of
uncertainty representations. The main focus of this paper is belief
functions, which have been advocated as a way of representing
incompleteness of evidence (i.e., the evidence may bear on the truth of a
hypothesis, but be insufficient to prove it).

A fully general model of beliefs (or probabilities) in a network of
hypotheses requires a specification of a joint belief function (or
probability distribution) over the entire space of possible combinations
of values of all the variables. Clearly, such a model would be
prohibitively difficult to assess in the absence of simplifying

assumptions. The most common simplifying assumption is to assume that
the directed graph representing the inferential model satisfies a Markov
property (Lauritzen and Spiegelhalter [10]; Shafer, Shenoy, and Mellouli
[14]). That is, a node is "screened" by its direct neighbors from all
other nodes in the graph. The Markov property means that beliefs in a
node depend on other nodes in the graph only through their effects on the
beliefs in its neighbors. This assumption not only simplifies
propagation algorithms, but also enables the assessment process to be
limited to a few hypotheses at a time.

Pearl [11] discusses a way to add probabilistic information to a
rule-based system. The simplicity and understandability of the
rule-based formalism are retained in this representation. Each rule is
associated with a strength, or degree to which the antecedents justify
the conclusion. In a probabilistic system, this strength is represented
by a conditional probability. The full joint probability distribution is
completely determined by: (i) the conditional probability distributions
over each consequent hypothesis set given each possible combination of
values of its antecedent hypothesis sets; and (ii) the marginal
probability distributions of all hypothesis sets corresponding to root
nodes.

Likewise, it seems natural to assess a belief function model by assessing
conditional belief functions on consequent hypothesis sets and marginal
belief functions on root-node hypothesis sets. Unfortunately, unlike in
the probabilistic case, this procedure is insufficient to uniquely
determine a joint belief function over the entire hypothesis space
(Dempster [6]; Shafer [12]). A full joint belief function could be
specified by direct assessment (cf., Shafer [12]), but this procedure
gives up the simplicity and transparency of the rule-based
representation.

If the belief function representation is to prove useful as a method for
representing and propagating uncertainty in automated reasoning systems,
then a simple, transparent, and reasonably general formalism for
eliciting joint belief functions must be developed. In particular,
belief functions should admit application in problems more general than
the nested partition structures studied by Shafer and Logan [13]. This
paper presents a simple example demonstrating that different joint belief
functions may be consistent with given conditional and marginal belief
functions. Several different methods for constructing a joint belief
function are described, and a rationale and associated problems are
considered for each.

2. EXAMPLE

The example concerns a company's willingness to pay expenses for a trip
to the AAAI Uncertainty Workshop this summer. Either the company will
pay $\underline{E}$xpenses (E = 1) or it will not (E = 0). Among other things, the
company's willingness to pay will depend upon whether a paper is
presented at the workshop. Let A denote $\underline{A}$cceptance or rejection of a
paper; the paper is either accepted (A = 1) or rejected (A = 0).
Graphically, the relationship between these two propositions is
represented by the directed link A $\longrightarrow$ E. These propositions actually

form part of a larger system: e.g., acceptance or rejection depends on getting the paper in before the Deadline; payment of expenses impacts attendance at the Workshop (D — A — E — W). More generally the larger system would consist of more than one branch of a tree structure. for this paper a single link of the tree is sufficient to illustrate some subtleties involved in manipulating marginal and conditional belief functions in a tree-structured network. Moreover, once propagation of beliefs across a single link is understood, further propagation is relatively straightforward. For instance, once beliefs in D have been propagated through the link D — A to result in beliefs in A, the same mechanism can then be used to propagate the resultant beliefs in A through the next link A — E to obtain marginal beliefs in E, and so on up the chain of inference.

Suppose that, in this example, an author of this paper assessed the following conditional beliefs for E given A and $\bar{A}$. (For convenience, A is denoted with A = 1, and $\bar{A}$ with A = 0; similarly for E.) "I feel that A justifies a degree of belief of *at least* .8 in E, but it may be higher. I don't want to assign any belief directly to $\bar{E}$." (It is not the purpose of this paper to discuss the various possibilities for elicitation of belief functions, it is merely assumed that an appropriate procedure is available.) This could be expressed as a conditional belief function over E given A, that assigned belief .8 directly to E, and left the rest of the belief *uncommitted* (i.e., the remaining belief of .2 does not discriminate between E and $\bar{E}$). This may be interpreted as a .8 chance that A *proves* E, and a .2 chance that A has no bearing on the truth of E. The difference between a proposition's *belief* and its *plausibility* (1 minus the belief of its complement) represents the range of permissible belief. This range is .8 to 1.0 for E given A, and 0 to .2 for $\bar{E}$ given A.

Suppose further that conditional on $\bar{A}$ the author assigned belief .5 directly to E, leaving the remaining belief of .5 uncommitted with respect to E. Assume also that the incoming beliefs (whether directly assessed or propagated) assign belief .3 directly to A and .2 directly to $\bar{A}$, leaving the remaining belief of .5 uncommitted.

Having assessed the above beliefs on A, what should be the resultant beliefs on E? Shafer, Shenoy and Mellouli [14] discuss a method analogous to Pearl's for propagating D/S beliefs in a network satisfying a Markov condition. Laskey and Lehner ([8], [9]) discuss how to use assumption-based truth maintenance to propagate beliefs when the Markov condition holds. These two propagation mechanisms are formally equivalent (except that the former cannot handle nonindependencies due to shared antecedents). Both require specification of joint beliefs. Laskey and Lehner allow direct specification of beliefs as rules with "belief tokens" as antecedents, but the joint beliefs are implicitly defined in the rule specification.

To propagate beliefs in a Markov network, the link A — E is represented by a joint belief function over the cross-product space A×E. The incoming beliefs on A implicitly define a belief function over A×E that is vacuous on E (i.e., it contains information about A, but no information about which of E or $\bar{E}$ is the case). The conditional belief functions are embedded in the cross-product space so that the marginal (embedding the belief function of E conditional on A involves vacuously extending over $\overline{A}$). Applying Dempster's Rule produces a combined belief function over A×E, which is then collapsed into a marginal belief function over E. This resultant belief function may then serve as the input to the link E ⟶ W, just as the original beliefs in A might have been propagated through the link D ⟶ A from beliefs in D.

The problem addressed here is how to obtain the joint belief function over the cross product space. In the case of a probabilistic model, the two conditional probability distributions given A and $\overline{A}$ are sufficient to represent the link A ⟶ E, and could be elicited by simply attaching numbers to rules. Unfortunately, there is no *unique* way of transforming conditional and corresponding marginal belief functions into a joint belief function so that Shafer, Shenoy and Mellouli's [14] propagation mechanism can be applied. And different ways of creating the joint beliefs result in different marginal belief functions on E. In other words, *specifying an inference "rule" (conditional belief function) from each value of A to the set E is not sufficient to uniquely determine how beliefs in A propagate to beliefs in E.*

3.   THREE WAYS OF DEFINING JOINT BELIEFS

We present three possible methods for extending the conditional belief function to the joint cross-product space: conditional embedding, consonant extension, and a third method we call dissonant extension (as the resultant joint belief function is in some sense as non-consonant as possible!). For each method the marginal belief function (on A) and the conditional belief functions (on E given A) are identical.

3.1.   Conditional Embedding

The method of conditional embedding (cf., Shafer [12]), treats each of the conditional belief functions as an *independent* source of evidence about E. The belief function conditional on A is characterized by a .8 chance that A proves E. This is represented as a .8 belief on the set {AE,$\overline{A}$E,$\overline{A}\overline{E}$} (A logically implies E), and a .2 belief on the universal set {AE,A$\overline{E}$,$\overline{A}$E,$\overline{A}\overline{E}$}. Similarly, the belief function conditional on $\overline{A}$ suggests a .5 chance that $\overline{A}$ proves E. This is represented as a .5 belief on the set {AE,A$\overline{E}$,$\overline{A}$E} ($\overline{A}$ logically implies E) and a .5 belief on the universal set.

Using Dempster's Rule, these two belief functions are combined with the incoming marginal beliefs: .3 belief on A = {AE,A$\overline{E}$}, .2 belief on $\overline{A}$ = {$\overline{A}$E,$\overline{A}\overline{E}$}, and .5 belief on the universal set. The joint belief function that results from combining these three belief functions is given in the first column of Figure 1; the marginal beliefs on E are displayed in Figure 2. Conditional embedding is the method suggested in Cohen et al. [4]. It is also the method that results from naive application of the Laskey and Lehner method (encoding the rules A ⟶ E and $\overline{A}$ ⟶ E completely separately, using different belief tokens).

Subset	Conditional Embedding			Consonant Extension			Dissonant Extension		
	m	Bel	Pl	m	Bel	Pl	m	Bel	Pl
EA	.24	.24	.8	.24	.24	.8	.24	.24	.8
$\bar{E}A$	0	0	.16	0	0	.16	0	0	.16
$E\bar{A}$	.1	.1	.7	.1	.1	.7	.1	.1	.7
$\bar{E}\bar{A}$	0	0	.35	0	0	.35	0	0	.35
$EA,\bar{E}A$	.06	.3	.8	.06	.3	.8	.06	.3	.8
*$EA,E\bar{A}$	.2	.54	1	.25	.59	1	.15	.49	1
$EA,\bar{E}\bar{A}$	0	.24	.9	0	.24	.9	0	.24	.9
$\bar{E}A,E\bar{A}$	0	.1	.76	0	.1	.76	0	.1	.76
$\bar{E}A,\bar{E}\bar{A}$	0	0	.46	0	0	.41	0	0	.51
$E\bar{A},\bar{E}\bar{A}$	.1	.2	.7	.1	.2	.7	.1	.2	.7
*$EA,\bar{E}A,E\bar{A}$	.05	.65	1	0	.65	1	.1	.65	1
$EA,\bar{E}A,\bar{E}\bar{A}$	0	.3	.9	0	.3	.9	0	.3	.9
*$EA,E\bar{A},\bar{E}\bar{A}$	.2	.84	1	.15	.84	1	.25	.84	1
$\bar{E}A,E\bar{A},\bar{E}\bar{A}$	0	.2	.76	0	.2	.76	0	.2	.76
*Ω_{ExA}	.05	1	1	.1	1	1	0	1	1

* differences

Figure 1: Joint Belief on A x E for the 3 Propagation
Mechanisms of Section 3.1.

Subset	Conditional Embedding			Consonant Extension			Third Method		
	m	Bel	Pl	m	Bel	Pl	m	Bel	Pl
E	.54	.54	1	.59	.59	1	.49	.49	1
$\bar{E}$	0	0	.46	0	0	.41	0	0	.51
Ω_E	.46	1	1	.41	1	1	.51	1	1

Figure 2: Marginal Beliefs on E for the 3 Different
Propagation Methods of Section 3.1.

3.2. Consonant Extension

A *consonant* belief function is one in which the evidence all points in a
single direction. In Shafer's terminology, the focal elements of a
consonant belief function must form a nested chain of subsets. In our
example, both conditional belief functions are consonant (because the
focal elements {E} and {E,$\bar{E}$} form a nested sequence), but the marginal
belief function over A is not (because there is no way to form a nested
sequence from {A}, {$\bar{A}$}, and {A,$\bar{A}$}). If, as in this example, we are
given consonant conditional belief functions on E given A and E given $\bar{A}$,
there is a unique way to form a consonant joint belief function with

vacuous marginals on A. (The marginal on A should be vacuous, as the conditional belief functions are meant to represent beliefs about the *link* from A to E, rather than beliefs about A itself.)

This consonant extension can be viewed as a way of representing nonindependency of the conditional belief functions. That is, in the consonant extension, these basic probabilities are assigned:

> .5 focused on {AE,$\overline{A}$E}   (A proves E *and* $\overline{A}$ proves E)
> .3 focused on {AE,$\overline{A}$E,$\overline{AE}$}   (A proves E but $\overline{A}$ is inconclusive)
> .2 focused on {AE,A$\overline{E}$,$\overline{A}$E,$\overline{AE}$} (both are inconclusive)

Thus, in conditional embedding A proves E *independently* of whether $\overline{A}$ proves E. In consonant extension, maximal nonindependency is assumed; i.e., the evidential links tend to be valid together. Figures 1 and 2 depict the joint and marginal beliefs obtained from combining this consonant extension with the incoming beliefs on A. Note that the marginal beliefs on E differ for the two methods. In particular, the range of permissible belief on E is smaller for the consonant extension.

3.3. Dissonant Extension

At one extreme of a spectrum is the nonindependency assumed by the consonant extension, where the two evidential links from A and $\overline{A}$ tend to be valid together. Conditional embedding represents a middle point, where their validity is independent. At the other extreme is the assumption that the link from A to E tends to be valid when the link from $\overline{A}$ to E is invalid, and vice versa. Making this assumption yields the following joint belief function representing the link A $\longrightarrow$ E:

> .3 focused on {AE,$\overline{A}$E}   (A proves E *and* $\overline{A}$ proves E)
> .5 focused on {AE,$\overline{A}$E,$\overline{AE}$}   (A proves E but $\overline{A}$ is inconclusive)
> .2 focused on {AE,A$\overline{E}$,$\overline{A}$E}   ($\overline{A}$ proves E but A is inconclusive)

Note that this joint belief function has *no* belief focused on the entire cross product space (although belief *is* inconclusive with respect to E for all but the first focal element). Figures 1 and 2 depict the joint and marginal beliefs after this belief function has been combined with the incoming beliefs over A. Note that the belief range widens progressively from consonant extension to conditional embedding to dissonant extension.

4. SO WHICH METHOD DO I USE?

In this simple example, we believe most people's intuition would point to the results produced by the consonant extension method. Consider the following argument: "If I have .8 belief in E when A is true and .5 belief when $\overline{A}$ is true, then I should have at least .5 belief in E no matter which is true. The difference between .8 and .5 represents the belief that A justifies *over and above* the belief when $\overline{A}$ is true." Indeed, the consonant extension propagates a *vacuous* belief function over A to a belief function focusing .5 belief on {E} and .5 belief on {E,$\overline{E}$}.

We also note that the consonant extension method gives the same results as the natural interval probability model for this example. The reader should beware, however, of interpreting belief functions as interval probabilities (cf., Black [2]; Laskey, [7]).

Conditional embedding, on the other hand, propagates vacuous beliefs on A to only .8×.5 = .40 belief focused on {E} and .60 belief focused on {E,Ē}. This "leaking out" of belief to the universal set is a consequence of the independence assumption underlying conditional embedding. The argument for using conditional embedding would go something like this: "I can prove E *no matter what* the value of A only if *both* evidential links are valid, which has probability .8×.5 = .40."

If, as we do, you find this argument less convincing than the first, it means that you think the kind of nonindependence assumed by the consonant extension model is appropriate for this problem. Unfortunately, the consonant extension method does not generalize to the case when the conditional belief functions are not consonant. (It was no accident that the only non-consonant belief function in our example was the marginal over A). Nevertheless, this method may represent a simple and compelling way of constructing joint belief functions when the input conditional belief functions are consonant. (It should be mentioned that, like probabilities, consonant belief functions may be assessed by specifying only a single number for each hypothesis. Assessing a general belief function requires specifying a number for each member of the power set of the hypothesis space.)

We grant that the restriction to consonant belief functions may not prove a problem in many applications. However, it may be the case that a more general conditional belief function is required. The chief virtue of the method of conditional embedding is that it can be applied regardless of the structure of the conditional belief functions. If the independence assumption seems untenable, the alternative is assessing a belief function over the entire cross product space, and sacrificing the simplicity of assessment based on rules.

5. "CAVEAT MODELOR"

Extending Shafer-Dempster theory to propagating beliefs in rule-based systems requires a way to represent and elicit beliefs about the *relationship* between antecedent and consequent. Specifying belief functions on qualititative rules results in conditional belief functions, which must then be transformed into joint belief functions. We have demonstrated three different ways of extending conditional and marginal belief functions to a joint belief function. Each of these methods arises from different assumptions about the joint relationship between antecedent and consequent, and produces different results when propagating beliefs. It is our view that the method of consonant extension is the most satisfying in the example of this paper, but it is limited to consonant conditional belief functions.

The differences among methods and results in our simple example may seem slight, but we feel that they point to fundamental issues that deserve further study. We suspect that many readers share our uneasiness about making the kinds of independence judgments this problem asks of us. We are not sure we really understand what it means for the evidential links A → E and A̅ → E to be "independent" or "valid together." We believe that for belief functions to be used properly in rule-based systems, knowledge engineers and experts need to have good "canonical stories" (Shafer [12]) that apply not just to single hypotheses but to the *links* between hypotheses.

In any case, all three analyses presented herein suggest that the company is likely to pay for the authors' trip to the conference. Readers are encouraged to substitute their own numbers to reach their own conclusions.

REFERENCES

[1] Adams, J.B. Probabilistic reasoning and certainty factors. In B.G. Buchanan and E.H. Shortliffe (Eds.), *Rule-based expert systems: The MYCIN experiments of the Stanford Heuristic Programming Project*, Reading, MA: Addison-Wesley Publishing Co., 1984, 263-272.

[2] Black, P.K. Is Shafer general Bayes? *Proceedings of the Third Workshop on Uncertainty in Artificial Intelligence*, Seattle, WA, 1987, pp. 2-9.

[3] Buchanan, B.G., and Shortliffe, E.H. *Rule-based expert systems: The MYCIN experiments of the Stanford Heuristic Programming Project*. Reading, PA: Addison-Wesley, 1984.

[4] Cohen, M.S., Laskey, K.B., and Ulvila, J.W. *Report on methods of estimating uncertainty: Application of alternate inference theories to ABM site localization problems* (Technical Report 87-8). Falls Church, VA: Decision Science Consortium, July 1986.

[5] Dempster, A.P. Upper and lower probabilities induced by a multivalued mapping. *Annals of Mathematical Statistics*, 1967, *38*, 325-339.

[6] Dempster, A.P. A Generalization of Bayesian Inference (with discussion). *Journal of the Royal Statistical Society,*, Series B, 1968, *30*, 205-247.

[7] Laskey, K.B. Belief in belief functions: An examination of Shafer's canonical examples. *Proceedings of the Third Workshop on Uncertainty in Artificial Intelligence*, Seattle, WA, 1987, pp. 39-46.

[8] Laskey, K.B., and Lehner, P. Belief maintenance: An integrated approach to uncertainty management. Presented at *American Association for Artificial Intelligence Conference*, 1988.

[9] Laskey, K.B., and Lehner, P.E. Assumptions, beliefs and probabilities. *Artificial Intelligence*, 41, 65-77, 1989.

[10] Lauritzen, S.L. and Spiegelhalter, D.J. Local computations with probabilities on graphical structures and their application to expert systems. *Journal of the Royal Statistical Society*, Series B, (to appear).

[11] Pearl, J. Fusion, propagation and structuring in belief networks. *Artificial Intelligence*, 1986, *29*(3), 241-288.

[12] Shafer, G. Belief functions and parametric models. *Journal of the Royal Statistical Society*, Series B, 1982, 44(3), 322-352.

[13] Shafer, G. and Logan, R. Implementing Dempster's Rule for hierarchical evidence. *Artificial Intelligence*, November 1987, *33*(3), 271-298.

[14] Shafer, G., Shenoy, P.P., and Mellouli, K. Propagating belief functions in qualitative Markov trees. *Working Paper No. 186*, Lawrence, KS: University of Kansas, School of Business, 1986.

Uncertainty in Artificial Intelligence 4
R.D. Shachter, T.S. Levitt, L.N. Kanal, J.F. Lemmer (Editors)
© Elsevier Science Publishers B.V. (North-Holland), 1990

On Probability Distributions Over Possible Worlds

Fahiem Bacchus*
Department of Computer Science
University of Waterloo
Waterloo, Ontario, Canada
N2L–3G1
fbacchus@watdragon.waterloo.edu

Abstract

In *Probabilistic Logic* Nilsson uses the device of a probability distribution over a set of possible worlds to assign probabilities to the sentences of a logical language. In his paper Nilsson concentrated on inference and associated computational issues. This paper, on the other hand, examines the probabilistic semantics in more detail, particularly for the case of first-order languages, and attempts to explain some of the features and limitations of this form of probability logic. It is pointed out that the device of assigning probabilities to logical sentences has certain expressive limitations. In particular, statistical assertions are not easily expressed by such a device. This leads to certain difficulties with attempts to give probabilistic semantics to default reasoning using probabilities assigned to logical sentences.

---

*This research was supported by a Post-Doctoral fellowship funded by the U.S. Army Signals Warfare Laboratory, while the author was a researcher at the University of Rochester.

1 Introduction

Nilsson [1] describes a method of assigning probabilities to the sentences of a logic through a probability distribution over a set of possible worlds. Each possible world in this set is a consistent assignment of truth values to the sentences of the logic, and the set consists of all unique possible worlds. A probability distribution is placed over this set. Probabilities are then assigned to the sentences by giving each sentence a probability equal to the probability of the subset of possible worlds in which it is true.

Although this approach is unproblematic when applied to propositional languages, certain difficulties arise when dealing with first-order languages. By taking a different tack these difficulties can be overcome, and indeed, it has already been demonstrated that probabilities can be coherently assigned to the sentences of any first-order language (Gaifman [2], Scott and Krauss [3]).

While the method of assigning probabilities to logical formulas is capable of representing probabilistic degrees of belief, it is incapable of effectively representing statistical assertions. It is argued that although many types of defaults have a natural statistical interpretation, this interpretation cannot be represented by probabilities over logical formulas, because of this limitation. Some authors have attempted to represent defaults by (conditional) probabilities over logical formulas (Geffner and Pearl [4], Pearl [5]), and the difficulties this causes can be demonstrated.

It is pointed out that probabilities over logical formulas fails to do the job, statistical assertions can be efficiently represented in a probability logic developed by the author [6]. This logic, however, does not use the device of assigning probabilities to first-order sentences.

2 The Propositional Case

A natural semantic model for a propositional language is simply a subset of the set of atomic symbols (Chang and Keisler [7]). This subset is the set of atomic symbols which are assigned the truth value true (t). In the propositional case Nilsson's concept of possible worlds, i.e., a set of consistent truth value assignments, has a natural correspondence with these semantic models. Each possible world is completely determined by its truth value assignments to the atomic symbols of the language, and the truth value assignments to the atomic symbols can be viewed as being the characteristic function of a semantic model (with $t = 1$, $f = 0$).

For example, in a propositional language with two atomic symbols $\{A, B\}$ there are four possible worlds with corresponding semantic models (σ is used to indicate the truth function).

1. $\{A^\sigma = \mathbf{t}, B^\sigma = \mathbf{t}\}$ or $\{A, B\}$.

2. $\{A^\sigma = \mathbf{t}, B^\sigma = \mathbf{f}\}$ or $\{A\}$.

3. $\{A^\sigma = \mathbf{f}, B^\sigma = \mathbf{t}\}$ or $\{B\}$.

4. $\{A^\sigma = \mathbf{f}, B^\sigma = \mathbf{f}\}$ or $\{\}$, i.e., the empty set.

Another way of looking at possible worlds, which will turn out to be more useful when we move to first-order languages, is to consider the *atoms*[1] of the language. When the language has a finite number of atomic symbols each possible world can be represented as a single sentence: a sentence formed by conjoining each atomic symbol or its negation, such a sentence is called an atom. Corresponding to the four worlds above we have the four atoms $A \wedge B$, $A \wedge \neg B$, $\neg A \wedge B$, and $\neg A \wedge \neg B$.

Given a probability distribution over the set of possible worlds it is possible to assign a probability to each sentence of the language. Each sentence is given a probability equal to the probability of the set of worlds in which it is true. So, for example, the sentence $A \vee B$ is true in worlds 1, 2, and 3. Hence, its probability will be equal to the probability of the set of worlds $\{1, 2, 3\}$.

Equivalently, a probability distribution can be placed directly over the sentences of the logic, more precisely over the Lindenbaum-Tarski algebra of the language. This algebra is generated by grouping the sentences into equivalence classes. Two sentences, α and β, are in the same equivalence class if and only if $\vdash_0 \alpha \leftrightarrow \beta$, where $\vdash_0$ indicates deducible from the propositional axioms.

This technique is not limited to languages with a finite number of atomic symbols. However, when the language is infinite the atoms will not be sentences of the language. If the atoms are sentences of the language, the probability distribution can be completely specified by the probabilities of the atoms (the e-classes of). Any sentence can be written as a disjunction of a unique set of atoms, and its probability will be the sum of the probabilities of these atoms. For example, if we specify the probabilities $\{A \wedge B = .5, A \wedge \neg B = .1, \neg A \wedge B = .2, \neg A \wedge \neg B = .2\}$, then the sentence $A \vee B$ will have probability 0.8 as it can be written as $(A \wedge B) \vee (A \wedge \neg B) \vee (\neg A \wedge B)$.

3 First-Order Languages

When the move is made to first-order languages certain problems arise. The first problem is that we lose the nice correspondence between possible worlds defined as complete truth value assignments to the sentences of the language

---

[1] An atom in a Boolean algebra is a minimal non-zero element (Bell and Machover, [8]).

and semantic models. The normal semantic model for a first-order language is considerably more complex than the model for a propositional language, and the truth values of the sentences in a first-order language are determined both by the model and by an interpretation (i.e., the mapping from the symbols to the semantic entities). For a given complete truth value assignment to the sentences there will be many different (in fact an infinite number) of model/interpretation pairs which will yield the same truth values. Hence, the semantic structure of a complete truth value assignment is unclear.

Another difficulty, which Nilsson is aware of, is that Nilsson's techniques depend on being able to generate consistent truth value assignments for a set of sentences. These are used as 0/1 column vectors in his V matrix. This technique is limited to languages in which the consistency of a finite set of sentences can be established. The consistency of a set of first-order sentences is not decidable, except in special cases (see Ackermann [9] for an interesting survey).

One way of avoiding these difficulties is to consider probability distributions over the Lindenbaum-Tarski (L-T) algebra of the language instead over sets of truth value assignments. It has already been demonstrated by Gaifman [2] that a probability measure can be defined over the L-T algebra of sentences of a first-order language. Every sentence in the language will have a probability equal to the probability of its equivalence class, and furthermore, the probabilities will satisfy the condition

$$\text{If } \vdash \neg(\alpha \wedge \beta) \text{ then } p[\alpha \vee \beta] = p[\alpha] + p[\beta],$$

where $\vdash$ indicates deducible from the first-order axioms. This means that the probability measure preserves the partial order of the algebra. In this partial order we have $\alpha < \beta$ if and only if $\alpha \wedge \beta = \alpha$; hence, $p[\alpha] \leq p[\alpha \wedge \beta] + p[\neg \alpha \wedge \beta] = p[\beta]$ (by the above condition). Under this partial order the conjunction and disjunction operators generate the greatest lower bound (infimum) and least upper bound (supremum).

To examine what happens to quantified sentences under such a probability measure it is sufficient to note that for L-T algebras we have that

$$(\star) \quad |\exists x \alpha| = \bigvee_{t \in T} |\alpha(x/t)|,$$

where $| \bullet |$ indicates the equivalence class of the formula, and T is the set of terms of the language. What this means is that each existentially quantified sentence is equal to the supremum of all its instantiations. This implies that the probability of any existentially quantified sentence must be greater than or equal to the probability of any of its instances. Similarly, the probability of any universally quantified sentence must be less than or equal to the probability of any of its instances.

This interpretation also makes sense in terms of Nilsson's truth value assignments. In any complete truth value assignment to the sentences of the language the existential must be true if any of its instantiations are. Hence, the set of truth assignments in which the existential is true includes the set of truth assignments in which any instantiation is true, and thus the existential must have a probability greater than or equal to the probability of any of its instances.

4 The Representation of Statistical Knowledge

Probabilities attached to logical sentences can be interpreted as degrees of belief in those sentences. Instead of either asserting a sentence or its negation, as in ordinary logic, one can attach some intermediate degree to it, a degree of belief. So, for example, one could represent a degree of belief of greater than 0.9 in the assertion "Tweety can fly" by assigning the sentence $Fly(Tweety)$ a probability > 0.9. However, it is not easy to represent statistical information, for example, the assertion "More than 90% of all birds fly."[2]

First, propositional languages do not seem to possess sufficient power to represent these kinds of statements. This particular statistical statement is an assertion which indicates some relationship between the properties of being a bird and being able to fly, but it is not an assertion about any particular bird. This indicates that some sort of variable is required. Propositional languages do not have variables, and so are inadequate for this task even when they are generalized to take on probabilities instead of just 1/0 truth values.

When we move to first-order languages we do get access to variables, variables which can range over the set of individuals. A seemingly reasonable way to represent this statement is to consider the probabilistic generalization of the universal sentence $\forall x.Bird(x) \to Fly(x)$. The universal in 1/0 first-order logic says that all birds fly, so if we attach a probability of > 0.9 perhaps we will get what we need. Unfortunately, this does not work. If there is single bird who is thought to be unable to fly, this universal will be forced to have a probability close to zero. That is, the probability of this universal must be $1 - p[\exists x Bird(x) \wedge \neg Fly(x)]$. Hence, if one believes to degree greater that 0.1 that a non-flying bird exists, then the probability of the universal must be $< .9$.

Since universal quantification or its dual existential quantification are the only ones available in a first-order language, it does not seem that moving to first-order languages allows us to represent statistical assertions. There

---

[2]It is the case that first-order logic is in some sense universally expressive. That is, set theory can be constructed in first-order logic, and thus sufficient mathematics can be built up inside the language to represent statements of this form. This is not, however, an effi̲̲.̲.̲̲ ̲ presentation, nor is there any direct reflection in the semantics of the statistical information.

is, however, one more avenue available: conditional probabilities. We have probabilities attached to sentences hence with two sentences we can form conditional probabilities. It has been suggested (Cheeseman [10]) that meta-quantified statements of the following form can be used to capture statistical statements, in particular for the statement about birds:

$$\forall x.p[Fly(x)|Bird(x)] > 0.9.$$

The reason that this is a meta-quantification is that the universal quantifier is quantifying over a formula "$p[Fly(x)|Bird(x)]$" which is not a formula of a first-order language. Once we include the "p" operator we move beyond what is expressible in a first-order language. (Hence, unconditional probability assertions like "$p[fly(x)]$" are not first-order formulas either). This statement is intended to assert that for every term, t, in the first-order language the conditional probability of the sentence $Fly(x/t)$, with the variable x substituted by the term t, given $Bird(x/t)$ is > 0.9.

However, this formulation also falls prey to any know exception. Say that there is some individual, denoted by the constant c, who is thought to be a bird, i.e., $p[Bird(c)]$ is high, and for some reason or the other is also believed to be unable to fly, i.e., $p[Fly(c)]$ is low, then clearly this statement cannot be true for the instance when x is c; hence, the meta-level universal statement cannot be true: it is not true for the instance c. It is important to note that it does not matter what other things are known about the individual c. For example, c could be known to be an ostrich, and thus there may be a good reason why c is unable to fly. However, it will still be the case that the conditional probability of $Fly(c)$ given just $Bird(c)$ will not be > 0.9. The universal statement will fail for c. That is, this problem is not resolved by conditioning on more knowledge as claimed by Cheeseman [10].

To expand on this consider the case where we have a first-order language which we use to express various assertions: each sentence of the language makes an particular assertion. In the standard subjective probability model the probabilities that are assigned to the sentences model our degree of belief in these different assertions. Shifts in our beliefs are modeled by conditionalizing on new information. If we aquire the new information that c is an ostrich, then we would represent our new distribution of subjective probabilities by conditionalizing on that information. The conditionalized distribution becomes our new prior and from here we can continue to conditionalize on further information as we receive it. However, the posterior distribution which results from conditionalizing on the fact that c is an ostrich will no longer satisfy the meta-universal constraint. In this posterior $p[ostrich(c)] = 1$ and therefore $p[fly(c)|bird(c) \wedge ostrich(c)] = p[fly(c)|bird(c)]$i. So in this posterior we cannot simultaneously believe that ostriches do not fly and that birds fly.

The problem here is that it seems unreasonable that the statistical statement "More than 90% of all birds fly" should be represented by the assertion that the conditional probability is greater than 0.9 for *all* substitutions of x: this assertion will be false for certain substitutions. The problem here is that the statistical statement implies that $p[Fly(x)|Bird(x)] > 0.9$ for a *randomly selected* x, but a universally quantified x is not the same as a x which denotes a random individual; furthermore, the simple device of assigning probabilities to sentences of a logical language does not give you access to such random designators. This point has also been raised by Schubert [11].

A logic has been constructed in which random designators exist in the language. The logic gives a very natural semantic interpretation of statistical assertions involving random designators. A powerful proof theory has also been developed. See Bacchus [6] for an exposition of this formalism. For the our purposes here, however, it is worth noting that this logic does not use a probability distribution over the sentences, instead it uses a probability distribution over the domain of discourse.

5   The Representation of Defaults

There are many different defaults which have a natural statistical justification, the famous example of "Birds fly" being one of them. A natural reason for assuming by default that a particular bird can fly is simply the fact that, in a statistical sense, most birds do fly. This is not to say that all defaults have a statistical interpretation: there are many different notions of typicality which do not have a straightforward statistical interpretation, e.g., "Dogs give live birth" (Carlson [12], Nutter [13], also see Brachman [14] for a discussion of different notions of typicality).

Since probabilities attached to the sentences of a logic do not offer any easy way of representing statistical assertions, it is not surprising that attempts to use this formalism to give an intuitive probabilistic meaning to defaults leads to certain difficulties.

Recently Geffner and Pearl [4] have proposed giving semantics to defaults through meta-quantified conditional probability statements (also Pearl [5][3]). For example, the default "Birds fly" is given meaning through the meta-quantified statement $\forall x.p[Fly(x)|Bird(x)] \approx 1$ In order to allow penguins to be non-flying birds they have the separate default rule: $\forall x.p[\neg Fly(x)|Penguin(x)] \approx 1$. They also have universal statements like $\forall x.Penguin(x) \rightarrow Bird(x)$. The probability of these universals is one; thus, as discussed above, every instantiation must also have probability one.

---

[3]Pearl uses a slightly different notion of probabilities within ϵ of one. The technical differences between this approach and that of Geffner and Pearl do not make any difference to the following discussion; the anomalies presented also appear in Pearl's system.

$$1 \approx p[Fly(t_i)|Bird(t_i)]$$
$$= \frac{p[Fly(t_i) \wedge Bird(t_i) \wedge \neg Peng(t_i)]}{p[Bird(t_i)]} + \frac{p[Fly(t_i) \wedge Bird(t_i) \wedge Peng(t_i)]}{p[Bird(t_i)]}$$
$$\leq \frac{p[Fly(t_i) \wedge Bird(t_i) \wedge \neg Peng(t_i)]}{p[Penguin(t_i)]} + \frac{p[Fly(t_i) \wedge Bird(t_i) \wedge Peng(t_i)]}{p[Penguin(t_i)]}$$
$$\leq \frac{p[\neg Penguin(t_i)]}{p[Penguin(t_i)]} + \frac{p[Fly(t_i) \wedge Penguin(t_i)]}{p[Penguin(t_i)]}$$
$$= \frac{p[\neg Penguin(t_i)]}{p[Penguin(t_i)]} + \approx 0$$

Figure 1: Conditional Probabilities close to one.

To examine the difficulties which arise from this approach consider the following example. Say that we have a logical language with the predicates $Bird$, Fly, and $Penguin$, some set of terms $\{t_i\}$ which include Skolem terms, and a probability distribution over the sentences of the language which satisfies the default rules, i.e., for all terms t_i, $p[Fly(t_i)|Bird(t_i)] \approx 1$ and $p[\neg Fly(t_i)|Penguin(t_i)] \approx 1$, and in which the universal $\forall x.Penguin(x) \rightarrow Bird(x)$, has probability one. Some simple facts which follow from the universal having probability one are that for all terms t_i, $p[Bird(t_i)] \geq p[Penguin(t_i)]$, and $p[Bird(t_i) \wedge Penguin(t_i)] = p[Penguin(t_i)]$).

Consider the derivation in figure 1.

The constraints imply that for any term t_i that

$$p[Penguin(t_i)] \leq (\approx)p[\neg Penguin(t_i)];$$

hence $p[Penguin(t_i)]$ cannot be much greater than 0.5. Since ≈ 0.5 is an upper bound on the probability of all instances of the formula $Penguin(x)$, it must also be the case that it is an upper bound on the probability of the sentence $\exists x \, Penguin(x)$, by equation $\star$.

That is, if we accept the defaults we must reject any sort of high level of belief in the *existence* of penguins.

To be fair to Geffner and Pearl their system does provide a *calculus* for reasoning with defaults. However, this result indicates that semantically their particular probabilistic interpretation of defaults causes anomalies. It does not capture the statistical notion that birds usually fly. Hence, although it provides a formal probabilistic semantics for defaults, it does not provide an intuitive, natural semantics for defaults, and in this sense does not provide any more insight into the semantics of defaults than standard logical approaches.

6 Conclusions

It has been demonstrated that although probabilities can be assigned to the sentences of any first-order language, the resulting probability logics are not powerful enough to efficiently represent statistical assertions. It has also been demonstrated that attempts to give defaults a probabilistic semantics using these types of probability logics leads to certain anomalies.

It is clear that many default inferences are based, at least in part, on statistical notions. This implies that probabilities might still be useful for giving an intuitive semantics to default rules and a justification to default inferences. For example, the default rule "Birds fly" could be represented as a statistical assertion that some large percentage of birds fly, and the default inference "Tweety flies" could be given the justification that Tweety probably does fly if to the best of our knowledge Tweety was a randomly selected bird.

This is essentially the content of work on direct inference. For example Kyburg [15] has developed a sophisticated systems in which a probability is assigned to the assertion $Fly(Tweety)$ based on underlying statistical information.

In AI, however, we need reasonable schemes of knowledge representation to duplicate these kinds of inferences. In particular, we need mechanisms for representing statistical knowledge. The probability logic developed by the author [6] addresses some of these needs, and some work has been done on duplicating direct inference style reasoning in this framework.

7 Acknowledgement

The author is thankful to Henry Kyburg for his helpful suggestions.

References

[1] Nils J. Nilsson. Probabilistic logic. *Artificial Intelligence*, 28:71–87, 1986.

[2] H. Gaifman. Concerning measures in first order calculi. *Israel Journal of Mathematics*, 2:1–18, 1964.

[3] Dana Scott and Peter Krauss. Assigning probabilities to logical formulas. In Jaakko Hintikka and Patrick Suppes, editors, *Aspects of Inductive Logic*. North-Holland, 1966.

[4] Hector Geffner and Judea Pearl. Sound defeasible inference. Technical Report CSD870058, Cognitive Systems Laboratory, U.C.L.A., Los Angeles, CA. 90024–1596, U.S.A., 1987.

[5] Judea Pearl. Probabilistic semantics for inheritance hierarchies with exceptions. Technical Report CSD870052, Cognitive Systems Laboratory, U.C.L.A., Los Angeles, CA. 90024-1596, U.S.A., 1987.

[6] Fahiem Bacchus. *Representing and Reasoning With Probabilistic Knowledge (forthcoming)*. MIT-Press, Cambridge, Massachusetts, 1990.

[7] C. C. Chang and H. J. Keisler. *Model Theory*. North-Holland, Amsterdam, 1973.

[8] John Bell and Moshé Machover. *A Course in Mathematical Logic*. Elsevier, Netherlands, 1977.

[9] W. Ackermann. *Solvable Cases of the Decision Problem*. Studies in Logic and the Foundations of Mathematics. North-Holland, Amsterdam, 1968.

[10] Peter Cheeseman. An inquiry into computer understanding. *Computational Intelligence*, 4(1), February 1988.

[11] Lenhart K. Schubert. Cheeseman: a travesty of truth. *Computational Intelligence*, 4(1), February 1988.

[12] G. Carlson. *Reference to Kinds in English*. PhD thesis, University of Massachusetts, 1977. unpublished—available from Indiana University Linguistics Club.

[13] Jane Terry Nutter. Uncertainty and probability. In *Proceedings of the 10th IJCAI*, pages 373-379, 1987.

[14] Ronald J. Brachman. I lied about the trees. *AI Magazine*, 6(3):80-93, 1985.

[15] H.E. Kyburg, Jr. *The Logical Foundations of Statistical Inference*. D. Reidel, 1974.

Uncertainty in Artificial Intelligence 4
R.D. Shachter, T.S. Levitt, L.N. Kanal, J.F. Lemmer (Editors)
© Elsevier Science Publishers B.V. (North-Holland), 1990

A Framework of Fuzzy Evidential Reasoning

John Yen

Department of Computer Science
Texas A&M University
College Station, TX 77843

With the desire to apply the Dempster-Shafer theory to complex real world problems where the evidential strength is often imprecise and vague, several attempts have been made to generalize the theory. However, the important concept in the D-S theory that the belief and plausibility functions are lower and upper probabilities is no longer preserved in these generalizations. In this paper, we describe a generalized theory of evidence where the degree of belief in a fuzzy set is obtained by minimizing the probability of the fuzzy set under the constraints imposed by a basic probability assignment. To formulate the probabilistic constraint of a fuzzy focal element, we decompose it into a set of consonant non-fuzzy focal elements. By generalizing the compatibility relation to a possibility theory, we are able to justify our generalization to Dempster's rule based on possibility distribution. Our generalization not only extends the application of the D-S theory but also illustrates a way that probability theory and fuzzy set theory can be combined to deal with different kinds of uncertain information in AI systems.

1   Introduction

The Dempster-Shafer (D-S) theory of evidence has attracted much attention in AI community in recent years for it suggests a coherent approach, which is sometimes called evidential reasoning, to aggregate evidence bearing on groups of mutually exclusive hypotheses. However, one of the major limitations in its application to plausible reasoning in expert systems is that the theory can not handle evidence bearing on vague concepts.

The knowledge base of an expert system sometimes consists of vague concepts, states that are not well defined, and qualitative descriptions of variables that do not have crisp boundaries. Therefore, an important requirement of a reasoning model for expert systems is its capabilities to manage and aggregate evidence bearing on vague concepts and inexact hypotheses. Although the D-S theory has been extended to deal with

---

† This article is partially based on the author's Ph.D. thesis at the University of California, Berkeley, which was supported by National Science Foundation Grant DCR-8513139. Part of the research described in the paper was done at USC/Information Sciences Institute and was supported by DARPA under contract No. MDA903-86-C-0178. Views and conclusions contained in this paper are those of the authors, and should not be interpreted as representing the official opinion or policy of the sponsoring agencies.

imprecise evidential strengths [1, 2, 3, 4], no previous extensions have been able to maintain the important principle that the belief and the plausibility functions are lower and upper probabilities.

In this paper, we extend the D-S theory for expressing and combining imprecise evidential strengths in a way such that degrees of belief and degrees of plausibility are still the lower and the upper probabilities constrained by the basic probability assignment. To achieve this, we first generalize the compatibility relation (i.e., multi-valued mapping) in the D-S theory to a joint possibility distribution that captures the degrees of compatibility. In order to express the way a fuzzy focal element constrains the underlying probability distribution, we decompose a fuzzy focal element into a set of consonant non-fuzzy focal elements using the resolution principle in fuzzy set theory. We also generalize Dempster's rule for combining independent sources of inexact evidential strengths. Our extension is justified by employing the noninteractive assumption in possibility theory. Finally, we discuss the similarity and the difference between consonant support functions and possibility distributions.

2   Basics of the Dempster-Shafer Theory

We briefly review the basics of the Dempster-Shafer theory in this section [5, 6]. A compatibility relation C between two spaces, S and T, characterizes possibilistic relationships between the elements of two spaces. An element s of S is compatible with an element t of T if it's possible that s is an answer to S and t is an answer to T at the same time [7], and the *granule* of s is the set of all elements in T that are compatible with s, i.e., $G(s) = \{t \mid t \in T, sCt\}$.

Given a probability distribution of space S and a compatibility relation between S and T, a basic probability assignment (bpa) of space T, denoted by $m : 2^T \rightarrow [0, 1]$, is induced:

$$m(A) = \frac{\sum_{G(s_i) = A} p(s_i)}{1 - \sum_{G(s_i) = \emptyset} p(s_i)} \tag{1}$$

Subsets of T with nonzero basic probabilities are called *focal elements*.

The probability distribution of space T, which is referred to as *the frame of discernment*, is constrained by the basic probability assignment. The lower probability and the upper probability of a set B subject to those constraints are called B's belief measures, denoted as $Bel(B)$, and B's plausibility measures, denoted as $Pls(B)$, respectively. These two quantities are obtained from the bpa as follows:

$$Bel(B) = \sum_{A \subset B} m(A) \tag{2}$$

$$Pls(B) = \sum_{A \cap B \neq \emptyset} m(A) \tag{3}$$

Hence, the belief interval $[Bel(B), Pls(B)]$ is the range of B's probability.

If m_1 and m_2 are two bpa's induced by two independent evidential sources, the combined bpa is calculated according to Dempster's rule of combination:

$$m_1 \oplus m_2(C) = \frac{\sum_{A_i \cap B_j = C} m_1(A_i) m_2(Bj)}{1 - \sum_{A_i \cap B_j = \emptyset} m_1(A_i) m_2(B_j)}$$

The basic combining steps that result in Dempster's rule are discussed in Section 4.5.

3   Previous Work

Zadeh was the first to generalize the Dempster-Shafer theory to fuzzy sets based on his work on the concept of information granularity and the theory of possibility [1, 8]. A possibility distribution, denoted by Π, is a fuzzy restriction which acts as an elastic constraint on the values of a variable [9, 10]. Zadeh first generalized the granule of a D-S compatibility relation to a conditional possibility distribution. Then he defined the *expected certainty*, denoted by $EC(B)$, and the *expected possibility*, denoted by $E\Pi(B)$, as a generalization of D-S belief and plausibility functions:

$$E\Pi(B) = \sum_i m(A_i) \sup_i (B \cap A_i)$$

$$EC(B) = \sum_i m(A_i) \inf_i (A_i \Rightarrow B) = 1 - E\Pi(B^c)$$

where A_i denotes fuzzy focal elements induced from conditional possibility distributions, $\sup(B \cap A_i)$ measures the degree that B intersects with A_i and $\inf(A_i \Rightarrow B)$ measures the degree to which A_i is included in B. It is easy to verify that the expected possibility and the expected certainty reduce to the D-S belief and plausibility measures when all A_i and B are crisp sets.

Following Zadeh's work, Ishizuka, Yager, and Ogawa have extended the D-S theory to fuzzy sets in slightly different ways [11, 2, 4]. They all extend D-S's belief function by defining a measure of inclusion $I(A \subset B)$, the degree to which set A is included in set B, and by using the following formula, similar to Zadeh's expected certainty EC(B).

$$Bel(B) = \sum_{A_i} I(A_i \subset B) m(A_i)$$

Their definitions of the measures of inclusion are listed below.

Ishizuka: $I(A \subset B) = \dfrac{\min_x[1, 1 + (\mu_B(x) - \mu_A(x))]}{\max_x \mu_A(x)}$

Yager: $I(A \subset B) = \min_x[\mu_{\overline{A}}(x) \vee \mu_B(x)]$

Ogawa: $I(A \subset B) = \dfrac{\sum_i \min[\mu_A(x_i), \mu_B(x_i)]}{\sum_i \mu_B(x_i)}$

Ishizuka and Yager arrive at different inclusion measures by using different implication operators in fuzzy set theory. Ogawa uses relative sigma counts to compute the degree of inclusion.

In order to combine two mass distributions with fuzzy focal elements, Ishizuka extended the Dempster's rule by taking into account the degree of intersection of two sets, J(A,B).

$$m_1 \oplus m_2(C) = \frac{\sum_{A_i \cap B_j = C} J(A_i, B_j) m_1(A_i) m_2(B_j)}{1 - \sum_{i,j}(1 - J(A_i, B_j)) m_1(A_i) m_2(B_j)}$$

$$\text{where} \quad J(A, B) = \frac{\max_x[\mu_{A \cap B}(x)]}{\min[\max_x \mu_A(x), \max_x \mu_B(x)]}$$

There are four problems with these extensions. (1) The belief functions sometimes are not sensative to significant change of focal elements because degree of inclusions are determined by certain 'critical' points due to the use of 'min' and 'max' operators. (2) The definitions of 'fuzzy inclusion operator' is not unique. Consequently, it is difficult to choose the most appropriate definition for a given application. (3) Although expected possibility and expected certainty (or, equivalently, expected necessity) degenerates to Dempster's lower and upper probabilities in the case of crisp sets, it is not clear that this is a 'necessary' extension. (4) The generalized formula for combining evidence is not well justified.

4 Our Approach

Instead of directly modifying the formulas in the D-S theory, we generalize the most primitive constructs of the theory and derive other extensions to the theory from these generalizations. Three primitive constructs that have been generalized are the compatibility relation, the objective function for calculating the belief function, and the probabilistic constraints imposed by focal elements. From these generalized basic components, we derive the belief function, the plausibility function, and the rule of combination for our generalized framework.

4.1 Generalizing the Compatibility Relation to a Possibility Distribution

The compatibility relation in the D-S theory can only record whether having s and t as answers to S and T respectively is completely possible (i.e., (s,t) is in the relation C) or completely impossible (i.e., (s,t) is not in the relation C). In general, however, the possibility that both s and t are answers to S and T is a matter of degree. To cope with this, we generalize Shafer's compatibility relation to a fuzzy relation that records joint possibility distribution of the spaces S and T.

Definition 1 *A generalized compatibility relation between the spaces S and T is a fuzzy relation* $C : 2^{S \times T} \rightarrow [0, 1]$ *that represents the joint possibility distribution of the two spaces, i.e.,* $C(s, t) = \Pi_{X,Y}(s, t)$, *where X and Y are variables that take values from the space S and the space T respectively.*

Shafer's compatibility relation is a special case of our fuzzy relation where possibility measures are either zeros or ones.

In fuzzy set theory, if the relationship of two variables X and Y are characterized by a fuzzy relation R and the values of variable X is A, the values of variable Y can be induced using the *composition Operation* defined as

$$\mu_{A \circ R}(y) = max_x\{min[\mu_A(x), \mu_R(x, y)]\}. \tag{4}$$

So, given a generalized compatibility relation $C : 2^{S \times T} \to [0, 1]$, the granule of an element s of S is defined to be the composition of the singleton s and C, i.e.,

$$G(s) = s \circ C = \Pi_{(Y|X=s)}. \tag{5}$$

Hence, we generalize granules to conditional possibility distributions just like Zadeh did; however, our approach is more general than Zadeh's approach because we go one step further to generalize compatibility relations to join possibility distributions. As we will see in Section 4.5, the generalized compatibility relation is important for justifying our generalization of Dempster's rule.

Given a probability distribution of the space S and a joint possibility distribution between space S and space T such that the granules of S's elements are normal fuzzy subsets,[1] a basic probability assignment (bpa) m to T is induced using equation 1. Adopting the terminology of the D-S theory, we call a fuzzy subset of T with nonzero basic probability a *fuzzy focal element*. A *fuzzy basic probability assignment* (bpa) is a bpa that has at least one fuzzy focal element.

4.2   An Optimization Formulation of Belief Functions

Pls(B) and Bel(B) are upper and lower probabilities of a set B under the probabilistic constraints imposed by a basic probability assignment. Therefore, Bel(B) can be viewed as the optimal solution of the following linear programming problem:

LP1: Minimize $\sum_{x_i \in B} \sum_j m(x_i : A_j)$ subject to the following constraints:

$$m(x_i : A_j) \geq 0, \qquad i = 1, ..., n; j = 1, ..., l. \tag{6}$$
$$m(x_i : A_j) = 0, \qquad \text{for all } x_i \notin A_j \tag{7}$$
$$\sum_i m(x_i : A_j) = m(A_j) \quad j = 1, ..., l. \tag{8}$$

Further discussion on formulating the D-S belief function as an optimization problem can be found in [12]. Since the distribution of each focals' masses do not interfere with each other, we partition these linear programming problems into subproblems, each one of which concerns the allocation of the mass of a focal element. The optimal solutions of these subproblems are denoted as $m_*(B : A_j)$ and $m^*(B : A_j)$. Adding the optimal

---

[1]A fuzzy subset A is normal if $sup_x \mu_A(x) = 1$. The assumption that all focal elements are normal is further discussed in Section 4.5.

solutions of subproblems, we get B's belief measure and plausibility measure, i.e.,

$$Bel(B) \quad = \quad \sum_{A_j \subseteq T} m_*(B : A_j) \tag{9}$$

$$Pls(B) \quad = \quad \sum_{A_j \subseteq T} m^*(B : A_j) \tag{10}$$

To compute the belief function of a fuzzy set B induced by a non-fuzzy bpa, we modify the objective functions to account for B's membership function:

$$\text{Minimize} \sum_{x_i} \sum_{A_j} m(x_i : A_j) \times \mu_B(x_i)$$

The optimal solutions of these modified minimization (maximization) problems can be obtained by assigning all the mass of a focal A to an element of A that has the lowest (highest) membership degree in B, i.e.,

$$m_*(B : A) \quad = \quad m(A) \times \inf_{x \in A} \mu_B(x) \tag{11}$$

$$m^*(B : A) \quad = \quad m(A) \times \sup_{x \in A} \mu_B(x) \tag{12}$$

4.3 Probabilistic Constraints of Fuzzy Focal Elements

To deal with fuzzy focal elements, we decompose them into nonfuzzy focal elements. An α-*level set* of A, a fuzzy subset of T, is a crisp set denoted by A_α which comprises all elements of T whose grade of membership in A is greater than or equal to α:

$$A_\alpha \quad = \quad \{x \mid \mu_A(x) \geq \alpha\}$$

A fuzzy set A may be decomposed into its level-sets through the *resolution identity* [13]

$$A \quad = \quad \sum_\alpha \alpha A_\alpha$$

where the summation denotes the set union operation and αA_α denotes a fuzzy set with a two-valued membership function defined by $\mu_{\alpha A_\alpha}(x) = \alpha$ for $x \in A_\alpha$ and $\mu_{\alpha A_\alpha}(x) = 0$ otherwise.

To decompose a fuzzy focal element, we distribute its basic probability among the focal's level-sets based on an observed relationship between the basic probabilities of crisp consonant focals and the possibility distribution of the frame of discernment. Dubois and Prade have shown that if a bpa is a set of nested focal elements, $A_1 \supset A_2 \ldots \supset A_n$, they can induce a possibility distribution, denoted as Poss(x), as follows:[2]

$$m(A_i) = \Pi_i - \Pi_{i-1} \tag{13}$$

where $\Pi_i = \inf_{x \in A_i} Poss(x)$, $\Pi_0 = 0$, and $\Pi_n = 1$. This result can be applied to decompose a fuzzy focal element whose basic probability value is one (i.e., m(A)= 1) because (1) the α-level sets of A form a set of nested focal elements $A_{\alpha_1} \supset A_{\alpha_2} \ldots \supset A_{\alpha_n}$

---

[2]We have paraphrased Dubois and Prade's results for the convenience of our discussion.

where $\alpha_1 < \alpha_2 \ldots < \alpha_n$, and (2) the membership function of a fuzzy focal element is a possibility distribution of the frame of discernment induced by a fuzzy compatibility relation. Since $inf_{x \in A_{\alpha_i}} Poss(x) = \alpha_i$, we replace the A_i and Π_i in equation 13 by level-sets A_{α_i} and its alpha value α_i. Thus, we get

$$m(A_{\alpha_i}) = \alpha_i - \alpha_{i-1} \tag{14}$$

In order to decompose fuzzy focal elements with arbitrary basic probability, we extend Equation 14 by multiplying the basic probability of the focal into the right-hand side of equation 14. Formally, the decomposition of a fuzzy focal element is defined as follows:

Definition 2 *The decomposition of a normal fuzzy focal element A is a collection of nonfuzzy subsets such that (1) they are A's α-level sets that form a resolution identity, and (2) their basic probabilities are the following.*

$$m(A_{\alpha_i}) = (\alpha_i - \alpha_{i-1}) \times m(A) \qquad i = 1, 2, \ldots, n \qquad \alpha_0 = 0, \ \alpha_n = 1 \tag{15}$$

When the focal element is a crisp set, its decomposition is the focal itself because the decomposition contains only one level set, which corresponds to the membership degree "one." The relationship between the decomposition of a fuzzy focal element and Shafer's consonant focals is discussed in Section 4.7.

The probabilistic constraint of a fuzzy focal is defined to be that of its decomposition, which is a set of nonfuzzy focals. Since we already know how to deal with nonfuzzy focals, decomposing a fuzzy focal into nonfuzzy ones allows us to calculate the belief functions that are constrained by the fuzzy focals.

Definition 3 *The probability mass that a fuzzy focal A contributes to the belief (and plausibility) of a fuzzy subset B is the total contribution of A's decomposition to B's belief (and plausibility), i.e.,*

$$m^*(B : A) \ = \ \sum_{\alpha} m^*(B : A_\alpha) \tag{16}$$

$$m_*(B : A) \ = \ \sum_{\alpha} m_*(B : A_\alpha) \tag{17}$$

4.4 A Generalized Belief Function

Based on formulating the belief function as an optimization problem, generalizing the objective function, and expressing the probabilistic constraints of fuzzy focal elements through their decompositions, we are able to derive the following formula for computing the belief function and the plausibility function.

$$Bel(B) \ = \ \sum_{A} m(A) \sum_{\alpha_i} [\alpha_i - \alpha_{i-1}] \times \inf_{x \in A_{\alpha_i}} \mu_B(x)$$

$$Pls(B) \ = \ \sum_{A} m(A) \sum_{\alpha_i} [\alpha_i - \alpha_{i-1}] \times \sup_{x \in A_{\alpha_i}} \mu_B(x)$$

It is also trivial to show that the dervied formula preserve the following important property of the D-S theory: *The belief of a (fuzzy) set is the difference of one and the plausibility of the set's complement.*

An Example

4.4.1 An Example

The following example illustrates how one applies the formula described in the previous section for computing the generalized belief function. Suppose a sensor is used to detect wind speed, which is represented as an integer between 1 and 50. Assuming a signal generated by the sensor is interpreted as **roughly 4 to 5** (denoted as fuzzy set A) with 0.7 basic probability and **about 6** (denoted as fuzzy set C) with 0.3 basic probability, i.e.,

$m(A) = 0.7$
$m(C) = 0.3$

where A and C are characterized below by lists in the form of $\mu_A(x_i)/x_i$:

$A = \{0.25/1, 0.5/2, 0.75/3, 1/4, 1/5, 0.75/6, 0.5/7, 0.25/8\}$
$C = \{0.5/5, 1/6, 0.8/7, 0.4/8\}$

Suppose we are interested in the degree of belief that the wind speed is **roughtly 3 to 5**, characterized by the fuzzy set B below:

$$B = \{0.5/2, 1/3, 1/4, 1/5, 0.9/6, 0.6/7, 0.3/8\} \tag{18}$$

The following discussion shows how we compute the belief measure and the plausibility measure of fuzzy set B in our generalized D-S framework.

The decomposition of fuzzy focal A consists of four nonfuzzy focals:

$A_{0.25} = \{1, 2, ..., 8\}$ with mass $0.25 \times m(A)$
$A_{0.5} = \{2, 3, ..., 7\}$ with mass $0.25 \times m(A)$
$A_{0.75} = \{3, 4, ..., 6\}$ with mass $0.25 \times m(A)$
$A_1 = \{4, 5\}$ with mass $0.25 \times m(A)$

and the decomposition of fuzzy focal C also consists of four nonfuzzy focals:
$C_{0.4} = \{5, 6, 7, 8\}$ with mass $0.4 \times m(C)$
$C_{0.5} = \{5, 6, 7\}$ with mass $0.1 \times m(C)$
$C_{0.8} = \{6, 7\}$ with mass $0.3 \times m(C)$
$C_1 = \{6\}$ with mass $0.2 \times m(C)$

Let us denote $\inf_{x \in A_{\alpha_i}} \mu_B(x)$ as $f_{B,A}(\alpha_i)$. So, we have

$m_*(B : A)$
$= m(A) \times [0.25 \times f_{B,A}(0.25) + 0.25 \times f_{B,A}(0.5) + 0.25 \times f_{B,A}(0.75) + 0.25 \times f_{B,A}(1)]$
$= m(A) \times [0.25 \times 0 + 0.25 \times 0.5 + 0.25 \times 0.9 + 0.25 \times 1]$
$= m(A) \times 0.6 = 0.7 \times 0.6 = 0.42$

$$m_*(B : C)$$
$$= m(C) \times [0.4 \times f_{B,C}(0.4) + 0.1 \times f_{B,C}(0.5) + 0.3 \times f_{B,C}(0.8) + 0.2 \times f_{B,C}(1)]$$
$$= m(C) \times [0.4 \times 0.3 + 0.1 \times 0.6 + 0.3 \times 0.6 + 0.2 \times 0.9]$$
$$= m(C) \times 0.54 = 0.3 \times 0.54 = 0.162$$

Thus, we have

$$Bel(B) = 0.42 + 0.162 = 0.582 \tag{19}$$

Similarly, we can calculate the plausibility of B:

$$Pls(B) = m(A) + 0.86 \times m(C) = 0.7 + 0.258 = 0.958 \tag{20}$$

Hence, the degree of belief in the hypothesis that the wind speed is **roughly 3 to 5** is [0.582, 0.958].

4.5 Generalizing Dempster's Rule of Combination

Dempster's rule combine the effect of two independent evidential sources, denoted as R and S, on the probability distribution of a hypothesis space, denoted as T. The rule can be viewed as a result of three steps: (1) constructing a combined compatibility relation between the product space $R \times S$ and T:

$$r\,C\,t \text{ and } s\,C\,t \implies [r,s]\,C\,t$$

where r, s, t, and [r, s] denote elements of R, S, T, and $R \times S$ respectively, (2) computing joint probability distributions of the two evidential sources based on the independence assumption: $P([r, s]) = P(r) \times P(s)$., and (3) normalizing the combined basic probability assignment to discard probability mass assigned to the empty set.

Two generalizations have to be made to Dempster's rule before it can be used to combine fuzzy bpa's in our generalized framework. (1) The first step above has to be extended to allow the combination of fuzzy compatibility relations. (2) The normalization step needs to consider subnormal fuzzy focal elements that result from combining fuzzy compatibility relations.

Combination of fuzzy compatibility relations A compatibility relation in our generalized D-S theory, as discussed in Section 4.1, is a joint possibility distribution. Thus, we have $C(r,t) = \Pi_{X,Z}(r,t)$ and $C(s,t) = \Pi_{Y,Z}(s,t)$ where X, Y, and Z are variables that take values from the spaces R, S, and T respectively. Let W be a variable that takes values from the space $R \times S$, the combined fuzzy compatibility relation can be expressed as $C([r,s],t) = \Pi_{W,Z}([r,s],t) = \Pi_{X,Y,Z}(r,s,t)$. By employing the assumption that the variables Y, Z and X, Z are *noninteractive*, a concept analogous to the independence of random variables, we obtain the joint possibility distribution from the two marginal possibility distributions:

$$\Pi_{X,Y,Z}(r,s,t) = \Pi_{Y,Z}(s,t) \wedge \Pi_{X,Z}(r,t).$$

Thus, the combined fuzzy compatibility relation can be obtained from the compatibility relations of two evidential sources:

$$C([r, s], t) = C(r, t) \wedge C(s, t).$$

For a fixed pair of r and s, applying the equation above to all possible elements in T gives us the following relationships between granules:

$$G([r, s]) = G(r) \cap G(s)$$

where $\cap$ denotes fuzzy intersection operator.

Normalizing Subnormal Fuzzy Focal Elements An important assumption of our work is that **all focal elements are normal**. We avoid subnormal fuzzy focal elements because they assign probability mass to the empty set. The probability mass assigned to the empty set by a subnormal fuzzy focal A is $[1 - max_x \mu_A(x)] \times m(A)$.

Although we have assumed that the focal elements of fuzzy bpa's are all normal, the intersections of focals, however, may be subnormal. Hence, the combination of fuzzy bpa's should deal with the normalization of subnormal fuzzy focal elements. To do this, we need to normalize the two components of a fuzzy focal element: the focal itself, which is a subnormal fuzzy set, and the probability mass assigned to the focal. It's straight forward to normalize the focal. Suppose A is a subnormal fuzzy set characterized by the membership function $\mu_A(x)$. A's normalized set, denoted as $\overline{A}$, is characterized by the membership function $\mu_{\overline{A}}(x) = \mu_A(x) / max_x \mu_A(x)$.

The criteria for normalizing the probability mass of a subnormal focal is that the probabilistic constraints imposed by the subnormal focal should be preserved after the normalization. Since we use the decomposition of a focal to represent its probabilistic constraint, this means that the probability mass assigned to a decomposed focal should not be changed by the normalization process. Since the α_i cut of the subnormal focal becomes the $k\alpha_i$ cut of the normalized focal, where k is the normalization factor $k = 1/ max_x \mu_A(x)$, the probability mass assigned to them should be the same, i.e.,

$$m(A_{\alpha_i}) = m(\overline{A}_{k \alpha_i}). \tag{21}$$

From this condition and the definition of fuzzy focal's decompositions, we can derive the following relationship between $m(\overline{A})$ and m(A): $m(\overline{A}) = m(A)/k$. Hence, mass of the normalized focal is reduced at the same rate its membership function has been scaled up. The remaining mass $(1 - 1/k) m(A)$ is the amount assigned to the empty set by the subnormal fuzzy focal and, hence, should be part of the normalization factor in the generalized Dempster's rule.

4.6   A Generalized Dempster's Rule

If m_1 and m_2 are two fuzzy bpa's induced by two independent evidential sources, the combined bpa is calculated according to the generalized Dempster's rule of combination:

$$m_1 \oplus m_2(C) = \frac{\sum_{\overline{A_i \cap B_j} = C} max_{x_i} \mu_{A \cap B}(x_i) m_1(A_i) m_2(B_j)}{1 - \sum_{i,j} (1 - max_{x_i} \mu_{A \cap B}(x_i)) m_1(A_i) m_2(B_j)} \tag{22}$$

Our extension generalizes the notion of *conflicting evidence* in the D-S theory to that of *partially conflicting evidence*. In original Dempster's rule, two pieces of evidence are either in conflict (i.e., the intersection of their focals is empty) or not in conflict at all (i.e., the intersection of their focals is not empty). In our generalized combining rule, two pieces of evidence are partially in conflict if the intersection of their focals is subnormal. The degree of conflict is determined by the peak (i.e., the maximum value) of the focal's membership function. The case of peak being zero corresponds to the case of total conflict in the D-S theory.

When both set A and set B are normal, Ishizuka's degree of intersection becomes $J(A, B) = \max_{x_i} \mu_{A \cap B}(x_i)$. His extension, formulated in equation 3, reduces to ours. However, unlike our approach, Ishizuka's extension is not justified using the possibility theory and the probability theory.

Although a fuzzy focal can be viewed as a set of consonant crisp focals in calculating belief functions, it differs from consonant focals in the evidence it represents. A fuzzy focal represents **one piece of evidence**, while a set of consonant focals represent **several pieces of evidence from one evidential source**, which is called the *inferential evidence* in [6].

4.7   Relationships to Consonant Support Functions

Several authors have discussed the similarity between possibility distribution and the plausibility function when the focal elements are nested, i.e., they can be arranged in order so that each is contained in the following one [7]. In this section, we first explain why the plausibility of consonant focals exhibit similar properties as possibility distribution, then we discuss their differences.

The plausibility function induced by a set of consonant focals is equivalent to that induced by a fuzzy set that is composed from the consonant focals. Suppose $A_1, A_2, ..., A_n$ are consonant focals such that $A_1 \subset A_2 \subset A_3 ... \subset A_n$. Then we can compose a fuzzy focal element A by treating A_k as a level set of A whose membership degree (i.e., α value) is $\sum_{i=1}^{k} m(A_i)$. It is straight forward to see that the decomposition of A is exactly the set of given consonant focals. Therefore, the plausibility function induced by the consonant focals is the same as that induced by the constructed fuzzy focal.

To show the relationship between consonant plausibility function and possibility distribution, we first prove that the highest basic probability that a fuzzy focal element can assign to an element is proportional to the degree that the element belongs to the fuzzy focal.

Theorem 1 *Let m be a bpa that assigns nonzero mass to a fuzzy subset A of the frame of discernment T, the maximum mass that can be allocated to an element t of T is proportional to the membership of t in A, i.e.,*

$$m^* (\{t\} : A) = m(A) \times \mu_A(t). \tag{23}$$

Proof: Let $\mu_A(t) = \alpha_k$. All the decomposed focals whose α values are smaller than α_k could contribute all of their masses to t. However, the decomposed focals whose α

values are higher than the membership degree of t can not assign their masses to t. Therefore, we have

$$
\begin{aligned}
m^* \left(\{t\} : A\right) &= m(A) \times \sum_{i=1}^{k}(\alpha_i - \alpha_{i-1}) \\
&= m(A) \times \alpha_k \\
&= m(A) \times \mu_A(t)
\end{aligned}
$$

It follows from the theorem that when a bpa consists of only one fuzzy focal element A, i.e., $m(A) = 1$, the plausibility of an element t becomes the membership degree of t in fuzzy set A, which characterizes a conditional possibility distribution, i.e., $Pls(\{t\}) = \mu_A(t)$. Since consonant focal elements can be used to construct a fuzzy focal element, the equation above explains why the plausibility of consonant focals exhibit similar properties as that of possibility measures.

Although consonant support function behaves like possibility distribution, it differs from possibility distributions in two major ways. (1) Consonant support functions are more restrictive in the kinds of evidence they can represent. More specifically, they are not appropriate for representing multiple fuzzy focal elements that are induced from a joint possibility distribution. (2) Combining consonant support function do not always yield another consonant support function. However, combining possibility distributions in our framework always result in another possibility distribution.

5 Conclusions

We have described a generalization of the Dempster-Shafer theory to fuzzy sets. Rather than generalizing the formula for computing belief function, we generalize the basic constructs of the D-S theory: the compatibility relations, the objective functions of the optimization problem for calculating belief functions, and the probabilistic constraints imposed by focal elements. As a result, we can compute the lower probability (i.e., the belief function) directly from these generalized constructs. Moreover, by employing the noninteractive assumption in possibility theory, we modified Dempster's rule to combine evidence that may be partially in conflict.

Our approach offers several advantages over previous work. First, the semantics of the D-S theory is maintained. Belief functions are lower probabilities in our extension. Second, we avoid the problem of 'choosing the right inclusion operators' faced by all previous approaches. Third, the belief function are determined by the shape of the whole focal elements, not just a critical point. Any change of focal elements directly affects its probabilistic constraints, which in turn affects the belief function. Finally, through our generalization, we have shown that the D-S theory could serve as a bridge that brings together probability theory and fuzzy set theory into a hybrid approach to reasoning under uncertainty and inexactness.

Acknowledgements

The author would like to thank Prof. Lotfi Zadeh for suggesting viewing consonant focals as a decomposition of a fuzzy focal element and for his comments on an earlier draft of the paper.

References

[1] L. A. Zadeh. Fuzzy sets and information granularity. In *Advances in Fuzzy Set Theory and Applications*, pages 3–18. 1979.

[2] R. Yager. Generalized probabilities of fuzzy events from fuzzy belief structures. *Information Sciences*, 28:45–62, 1982.

[3] M. Ishizuka. An extension of dempster and shafer's theory to fuzzy sets for constructing expert systems. *Seisan-Kenkyu*, 34(7):312–315, 1982.

[4] H. Ogawa and K. S. Fu. An inexact inference for damage assessment of existing structures. *International Journal of Man-Machine Studies*, 22:295–306, 1985.

[5] A. P. Dempster. Upper and lower probabilities induced by a multivalued mapping. *Annals of Mathematical Statistics*, 38:325–339, 1967.

[6] G. Shafer. *Mathematical Theory of Evidence*. Princeton University Press, Princeton, N.J., 1976.

[7] G. Shafer. Belief functions and possibility measures. Technical Report Working Paper No. 163, University of Kansas, School of Business, 1984.

[8] L. A. Zadeh. Possibility theory and soft data analysis. In L. Cobb and R. M. Thrall, editors, *Mathematical Frontiers of the Social and Policy Sciences*, pages 69–129. Westview Press, Boulder, Colorado, 1981.

[9] L. A. Zadeh. Fuzzy sets as a basis for a theory of possibility. *Fuzzy Sets and Systems*, 1:3–28, 1978.

[10] D. Dubois and H. Prade. *Possibility Theory*. Plenum Press, New York, N.Y., 1988.

[11] M. Ishizuka, K. S. Fu, and J. T. P. Yao. Inference procedures and uncertainty for the problem-reduction method. *Information Sciences*, 28:179–206, 1982.

[12] J. Yen. *Evidential Reasoning in Expert Systems*. PhD thesis, Department of Electrical Engineering and Computer Science, Computer Science Division, University of California, Berkeley, 1986.

[13] L. A. Zadeh. The concept of a linguistic variable and its application to approximate reasoning - i. *Information Sciences*, 8:199–249, 1975.

Uncertainty in Artificial Intelligence 4
R.D. Shachter, T.S. Levitt, L.N. Kanal, J.F. Lemmer (Editors)
© Elsevier Science Publishers B.V. (North-Holland), 1990

Parallel Belief Revision

Daniel Hunter
Northrop Research and Technology Center
One Research Park
Palos Verdes Peninsula, California 90274

Abstract

This paper describes a formal system of belief revision developed by Wolfgang Spohn and shows that this system has a parallel implementation that can be derived from an influence diagram in a manner similar to that in which Bayesian networks are derived. The proof rests upon completeness results for an axiomatization of the notion of conditional independence, with the Spohn system being used as a semantics for the relation of conditional independence.

1   Introduction

Belief revision concerns the problem of how to revise our beliefs in the light of new information. Although Bayesian probability theory gives a clear and well-founded method for revising *degrees* of belief, our beliefs are ordinarily not expressed in quantitative terms. Instead, beliefs tend to be *categorical*: one either believes, disbelieves, or suspends judgement, concerning some proposition. The problem of revising categorical beliefs is an active area of research within the fields of philosophy and artificial intelligence. Within the artificial intelligence community, the problem of categorical belief revision has been treated primarily in terms of various non-monotonic logics. Recent concern over anomalies in non-monotonic systems of logic [1] suggests that other approaches to belief revision should be considered. This paper examines a system of belief revision developed by the philosopher Wolfgang Spohn [2] and shows that it may be given an efficient parallel implementation by means of the technique of influence diagrams, which previously have been used almost exclusively in the context of probabilistic belief.

After a brief description of the Spohn system, we cite results that show that Spohn's system provides an adequate semantics for the notion of conditional independence and that influence diagrams are an appropriate representational tool for that notion of conditional independence. These results are then used to prove that Spohnian belief revision can be implemented via a parallel, distributed architecture analogous to Pearl's Bayesian Networks [3].

2 Spohnian Belief Revision

Let $\Theta = \{s_1, s_2, ..., s_n\}$ be a set of pairwise mutually exclusive and jointly exhaustive states of the world. In Spohn's theory, a state of belief is captured by an *ordinal conditional function* (OCF), which is a function from Θ into ordinals that assigns zero to at least one member of Θ. Although Spohn allows infinite ordinals, I will simplify matters by considering only those OCF's whose range consists entirely of natural numbers (0, 1, 2, ...). We call OCFs whose range is so restricted *natural conditional functions* or NCFs.

Intuitively, an OCF is a grading of states of the world in terms of their degree of *implausibility*. That is, the greater the value of the OCF for a given state, the more implausible that state is. Zero is a lower bound on degrees of implausibility, but there is no upper bound – no matter how implausible a state is, there could be an even more implausible one.

A *proposition* is a statement whose truth-value depends upon which member of Θ is the true state of the world. Propositions are true or false in states. We follow the convention of identifying a proposition with the set of states in which it is true. Formally, then, a proposition is simply a subset of Θ. An OCF κ can be extended to consistent (i.e. nonempty) propositions by defining for each nonempty subset A of Θ:

$$\kappa(\mathbf{A}) = \min\{\kappa(s_i)|s_i \in \mathbf{A}\}.$$

An OCF κ induces a *strength of belief* function β over proper subsets $\mathbf{A}$ of Θ as follows:

$$\beta(\mathbf{A}) =_{df.} \begin{cases} -\kappa(\mathbf{A}) & \text{if } \kappa(\mathbf{A}) > 0 \\ \kappa(\neg\mathbf{A}) & \text{otherwise} \end{cases}$$

It might seem from the above that the goal of analyzing deterministic belief has been forgotten and that the quite different notions of degrees of implausibility and strengths of belief have been introduced in its stead. However, deterministic belief is definable in this framework: A proposition $\mathbf{A}$ is *(deterministically) believed* if and only if $\kappa^{-1}(0) \subseteq \mathbf{A}$. In more intuitive terms, a proposition is believed if and only if it is true in all the most plausible worlds. If $\mathbf{A}$ is a proper subset of Θ this is equivalent to saying that $\mathbf{A}$ is believed if and only if $\beta(\mathbf{A}) > 0$. Note that belief is closed under logical implication on this definition of belief.

Now we can say how beliefs are revised when new information is obtained. Suppose that proposition $\mathbf{A}$ is learned with strength α. Let κ be the OCF before $\mathbf{A}$ is learned. Then we define κ', the OCF that results from learning $\mathbf{A}$, by its value for each state s as follows:

$$\kappa'(s) = \begin{cases} \kappa(s) - \kappa(\mathbf{A}) & \text{if } s \in \mathbf{A} \\ \kappa(s) - \kappa(\neg\mathbf{A}) + \alpha & \text{otherwise} \end{cases}$$

As shown in [2], Spohnian belief revision has several nice properties:

1. It automatically restores consistency to beliefs when information inconsistent with previous beliefs is received.

2. It is commutative: learning a and then learning b results in the same OCF as first learning b and then learning a, when a and b are independent.

			T0	T1	T2
1	PENGUIN	FLYS	2	2	1
2	PENGUIN	NOT-FLYS	1	1	0
3	TYPICAL-BIRD	FLYS	0	0	1
4	TYPICAL-BIRD	NOT-FLYS	1	1	2
5	NOT-BIRD	FLYS	0	1	2
6	NOT-BIRD	NOT-FLYS	0	1	2

Figure 1: Spohnian Belief Revision

3. It is easily reversible: if κ_2 results from κ_1 by learning proposition a with strength α, then κ_1 will result from κ_2 by learning proposition $\neg a$ with strength $\beta_1(\neg a)$, where β_1 is the strength of belief function corresponding to κ_1.

4. Notions of independence and conditional independence are definable and theorems analogous to those for probability theory are provable for these notions.

An example may aid understanding of Spohnian belief revision. Figure 1 shows three different OCFs for the six states corresponding to the rows of the table. The first OCF, for time T_0, gives one's beliefs about some unknown object. At T_1, one learns with strength 1 that the object is a bird and one's beliefs change accordingly. Note that the proposition BIRD is identified with the set of states $\{1,2,3,4\}$. Then at T_1, one believes that the object flys. At T_2 one learns with strength 1 that the object is a penguin and the OCF is again revised. In the OCF for time T_2, one believes that the object does not fly.

3   Influence Diagrams and Spohnian Conditional Independence

An *influence diagram* is a directed graph whose nodes are multi-valued variables. In Figure 2, for example, node C might be a variable whose values are possible diseases of a certain patient and nodes D and E might represent variables such as temperature and blood-pressure, whose values are influenced by the diseases. The values of a variable in an influence diagram are assumed to be mutually exclusive and exhaustive.

In the following, I will use "a", "b", "c", "d", and "e" to denote arbitrary values of A, B, C, D, and E, respectively; more generally, a small letter will be used to denote an arbitrary value of a variable denoted by the corresponding capital letter. A set of variables will be denoted by a capital letter from the end of the alphabet (U, V, W, X, Y, Z) and the corresponding lower-case letter will be used to denote a set of values of those variables.

An influence diagram is often given a causal interpretation in which a node is causally dependent upon all the nodes which have arrows pointing to it. But it can also be given an epistemic interpretation: it reveals certain conditional independencies

244

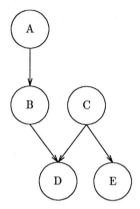

Figure 2: An Influence Diagram

between variables. To state this graphical criterion of conditional independence, we need the notion of d-separation, which is defined as follows:

Let X, Y, and Z be disjoint sets of variables. X and Y are *d-separated* by Z if and only if there is no path from a variable in X to a variable in Y such that: (1) no node along the path with an outgoing arrow is a member of Z; and (2) any node along the path with converging arrows is either a member of Z or a descendant of a member of Z.

The graphical criterion of conditional independence identifies conditional independence with d-separation: given an influence diagram D, we say that X and Y are conditionally independent given Z, written $I_D(X, Z, Y)$ if and only if Z d-separates X from Y.

Thus in Figure 2, D is separated from A and E by the set $\{B, C\}$, since any path from D to either A or E contains a node with outgoing arrows that is a member of $\{B, C\}$. However, B is *not* separated from C by $\{D\}$ since D is the only node on the path from B to C and the links meeting at D meet head-to-head.

In Spohn's system, a notion of conditional independence is definable in terms of OCFs. If **A** and **B** are consistent propositions (i.e. they have a non-empty intersection), we can define a *conditional* OCF $\kappa(\mathbf{A}|\mathbf{B})$ (the degree of disbelief in proposition **A** given proposition **B**) by:

$$\kappa(\mathbf{A}|\mathbf{B}) = \kappa(\mathbf{A}, \mathbf{B}) - \kappa(\mathbf{B}).$$

Note that this definition is analogous to the definition of conditional probabililty in probability theory, with subtraction replacing division. With this definition, we can define the conditional independence of **A** and **B** given **C**, relative to OCF κ (written $I_\kappa(\mathbf{A}, \mathbf{C}, \mathbf{B})$), by:

$$I_\kappa(\mathbf{A}, \mathbf{C}, \mathbf{B}) \text{ iff } \kappa(\mathbf{A}, \mathbf{B}|\mathbf{C}) = \kappa(\mathbf{A}|\mathbf{C}) + \kappa(\mathbf{B}|\mathbf{C}).$$

Again, note the similarity to the definition of conditional independence in probability theory, with addition in place of multiplication.

Spohn [2] proves that conditional independence relative to an OCF satisfies many of the properties of probabilistic conditional independence. From results in [4] and [5], we know that the graphical criterion of d-separation captures key formal properties of probabilistic conditional independence. It would not be too surprising, then, if Spohnian conditional independence also has a close connection to the d-separation criterion. Indeed, in [6] it is shown that it does.

To mesh the possible worlds framework used by the Spohn system with the representation in terms of multi-valued variables used by influence diagrams, we identify the set of worlds Ω with the cross-product space $\pi_{i=1}^{n} V_i$ of the variables $V_1, ..., V_n$. Value v_i of variable V_i is identified with the set of worlds having v_i in the ith position. Similarly, a set of values of variables is identified with the set of all worlds in which the variables in question have those particular values.

The definition of conditional independence relative to an OCF can be extended to sets of variables by defining for disjoint sets of variables X, Y, and Z:

$I_\kappa(X, Z, Y)$ iff for all values x of X, y of Y, and z of Z , $I_\kappa(x, z, y)$.

In [6], it is shown that d-separation captures the notion of conditional independence relative to an OCF and that the latter also captures crucial properties of our intuitive notion of conditional independence. The exact sense in which these three notions are equivalent is reflected in the soundness and completeness results described in the next section.

4 Soundness and Completeness Results

For the notion of conditional independence relative to an OCF to be useful, we would like to know that it satisfies certain intuitive properties of conditional independence. Moreover, for the results on Spohnian networks to be presented in the next section, we will need assurance that the graphical criterion of d-separation corresponds in an appropriate way with conditional independence relative to an OCF. Building on work by Geiger, Verma, and Pearl (see [4] and [5]), [6] established these results, a summary of which is given below.

What axioms should a relation of conditional independence, whether defined in terms of OCFs, probabilities, or some other way, satisfy? Let $I(X, Z, Y)$ mean that the set of variables X is independent of the set of variables Y given set of variables Z. Then the following axioms, listed in [4], seem to capture the intuitive notion of conditional independence:

$$(1a) \quad I(X, Z, Y) \Leftrightarrow I(Y, Z, X)$$
$$(1b) \quad I(X, Z, Y \cup W) \Rightarrow I(X, Z, Y)$$
$$(1c) \quad I(X, Z, Y \cup W) \Rightarrow I(X, Z \cup Y, W)$$
$$(1d) \quad I(X, Z \cup Y, W) \wedge I(X, Z, Y) \Rightarrow I(X, Z, Y \cup W)$$

We denote the set consisting of axioms (1a)-(1d) by "SG." A relation I that satisfies all the members of SG is a *semi-graphoid*. If the relation additionally satisfies the follow axiom, then it is a *graphoid*:

$$(1e) \quad I(X, Z \cup Y, W)\&I(X, Z \cup W, Y) \Rightarrow I(X, Z, Y \cup W),$$

where W is disjoint from X, Y, and Z.

[6] proves the following theorem:

Theorem 1 *The relation of conditional independence relative to an OCF is a graphoid.*

Let θ be a total ordering of the variables. A *causal list* (*relative to* θ) is a set of statements such that for each variable A there occurs in the list exactly one statement of the form

$$I(A, X, Y - X),$$

where Y is the set of ancestors of A and X is a subset of Y. The statement $I(A, X, Y - X)$ therefore says that given values for the X's, A is independent of all other predecessors in the ordering θ. A causal list can be used to produce an influence diagram by drawing arrows, for each statement $I(A, X, Y - X)$ in the list, from the variables in X to the variable A.

A causal list L entails independence statements other than those in L. For example, L will entail that given its parents, a variable A is independent, not just of all other ancestors, but of all non-descendant variables. We say that a causal list L entails an independence statement I, written $L \models I$, if and only if every OCF that satisfies every statement in L also satisfies I. We use $\Gamma \vdash \phi$ to denote that statement ϕ is derivable from the set of statements Γ in first-order logic.

So far we have seen three approaches to conditional independence: the definition in terms of OCFs, the axiomatic approach, and the graphical d-separation criterion. The following theorem, proved in [6], shows that these are equivalent for causal lists:

Theorem 2 *Let L be a causal list and D the corresponding influence diagram. Then the following statements are equivalent:*

$$(i) \quad L \models I(X, Z, Y)$$
$$(ii) \quad L \cup SG \vdash I(X, Z, Y)$$
$$(iii) \quad I_D(X, Z, Y).$$

5   Spohnian Networks

Given the equivalence, in the sense described above, between Spohnian conditional independence and d-separation in an appropriate influence diagram, a modified influence diagram can be used as a computational structure for belief querying and updating, much as Bayesian networks [3] are used for probabilistic belief.

For example, given the influence diagram of Figure 2, we can write the joint NCF κ over the variables A, B, C, D, and E as:

$$\kappa(a, b, c, d, e) = \kappa(a) + \kappa(c) + \kappa(b|a) + \kappa(d|b, c) + \kappa(e|c). \tag{1}$$

Equation (1) suggests a method for constructing an initial NCF: first, specify marginal NCFs for all parentless variables (in this case, A and C); second, for each remaining variable, specify a marginal NCF for that variable, conditional on each combination of values of the variables parents. By the conditional independencies implied by the influence diagram, such a specification will determine the joint NCF.

An unconditional NCF for each variable is determined as follows. Let Q be a variable with parents $P_1, ..., P_n$. Then $\kappa(q) = \min_{p_1,...,p_n} \{\kappa(q|p_1, ..., p_n) + \kappa(p_1, ..., p_n)\}$, where p_i is the value of variable P_i. Thus an initial marginal NCF for each variable can be computed in an obvious recursive manner.

To use an influence diagram as a computational structure for parallel distributed belief revision, we associate with each node in the diagram a marginal NCF constructed in the manner just described and for each node with parents, we also associate a matrix giving the NCF for the corresponding variable conditional on each combination of values of its parent variables. We now think of the nodes as individual processors that communicate only with their immediate neighbors. We call the resultant computational structure a *Spohnian network*.

The next three sections describe a parallel mechanism for propagating belief updates in a Spohnian network. In describing this mechanism, we avoid problems associated with loops in the network by assuming it to be *singly-connected*. A directed network is singly-connected if no more than one (undirected) path exits between any two nodes. A Spohnian network with loops can be transformed into a singly-connected network in a manner similar to that described in [3] for Bayesian networks.

6 Updating on a Single Piece of Uncertain Evidence

We take an update to occur when some information source external to the Spohnian network causes a change in the marginal NCF for some variable. If the NCF for variable R changes from κ to κ', it follows from the definition of belief revision for OCFs in Section 2 that $\kappa'(q)$, Q an arbitrary variable, is given by:

$$\kappa'(q) = \min\{\kappa(q|r) + \kappa'(r)\}.$$

We first focus on the case in which only a single variable is updated via an external source. Since we are assuming the network to be singly-connected, there can be at most one neighbor of a variable on the path between that variable and an updated variable. The next theorem shows that the update to a variable can be computed from information resident at the intervening neighbor variable.

Theorem 3 *Let NCF κ' result from NCF κ by updating on variable R. Let $Q \neq R$ be an arbitrary variable and let P be Q's neighbor on the path from Q to R. Then $\kappa'(q) = \min_p \{\kappa(q|p) + \kappa'(p)\}$.*

Proof. $\kappa'(q) = \min_r\{\kappa(q|r) + \kappa'(r)\} = \min_r\{\min_p\{\kappa(q|p,r) + \kappa(p|r)\} + \kappa'(r)\} =$ (by the fact that P d-separates Q from R) $\min_r\{\min_p\{\kappa(q|p) + \kappa(p|r)\} + \kappa'(r)\} = \min_p\{\kappa(q|p) + \min_r\{\kappa(p|r) + \kappa'(r)\}\} = \min_p\{\kappa(q|p) + \kappa'(p))\}$. □

The above theorem shows that an update can be propagated through a Spohnian network in parallel. For once a variable receives an update, the update can be propagated to all the variable's unvisited neighbors simultaneously, which in turn may propagate the update to their unvisited neighbors in parallel, and so on. Note that whether P is a child or a parent of Q, $\kappa(q|p)+\kappa'(p)$ may be computed from information stored at P and at Q.

An issue that may easily be overlooked here is whether or not updating preserves the relations of conditional independence. It is not the case that updating preserves all the conditional independencies implied by an influence diagram. For example, in Figure 2, variables B and C are independent given the null set, yet if D is updated, it may very well turn out that B and C are no longer independent given the null set. Although some conditional independencies may be destroyed by updating, the next theorem assures that after updating, the parents of a variable continue to "screen off" the effects of other non-descendant variables, thus allowing the decomposition of the joint NCF into marginal NCFs over the same subsets of variables as formed the domains of the prior NCFs.

Theorem 4 *Let C be a variable, X the set of parent variables of C, and Y the set of all remaining ancestors of C. If NCF κ' arises from κ by updating on variable D, then $\kappa'(c|x,y) = \kappa'(c|x)$.*

Proof. If D is connected to C via an ancestor of C, the result is trivial since if so, $\kappa'(c|x,y) = \kappa(c|x,y)$. We therefore assume that D either is identical with C or is a descendant of C. In either case, C d-separates D from $X \cup Y$ and we use this fact freely in what follows. "c^*" ranges over the values of the variable C. $\kappa'(c|x,y) = \kappa'(c,x,y) - \kappa'(x,y) = min_d\{\kappa(c,x,y|d) + \kappa'(d)\} - min_{c^*}\{\kappa(x,y|c^*) + \kappa'(c^*)\} = min_d\{\kappa(x,y) + \kappa(c,x) - \kappa(x) + \kappa(d|c) - \kappa(d) + \kappa'(d)\} - min_{c^*}\{\kappa(x,y) + \kappa(c^*,x) - \kappa(x) - \kappa(c^*) + \kappa'(c^*)\} = min_d\{\kappa(c,x) + \kappa(d|c) - \kappa(d) + \kappa'(d)\} - min_{c^*}\{\kappa(x|c^*) + \kappa'(c^*)\} = \kappa'(c,x) - \kappa'(x) = \kappa'(c|x)$. $\square$

7 Simultaneous Updating on Multiple Evidence Events

The previous section showed that a single piece of evidence may propagate through a Spohnian network in parallel. This section address the question of whether or not simultaneous multiple updates can propagate in parallel.

Unfortunately, if A and B are dependent variables, then updating first on A and then on B will not in general give the same result as updating in the reverse order. Thus simultaneous updating on dependent evidence events is problematic, since it is not clear what the answer should be.

One can approach the problem of simultaneous multiple updatings by first considering a special case in which the above problem does not arise. This is the case in which all the evidence events are learned with certainty. The strategy will be to prove that updating on several pieces of *certain* evidence can be done in parallel and then to argue that this case is not so special as it may appear.

To allow for learning with certainty, I extend the notion of an NCF to allow ∞ to be assigned to states. ∞ is a number such that adding or subtracting any finite number from it leaves it unchanged. To learn a proposition with certainty, then, is to assign ∞ to all states incompatible with that proposition, indicating that all those other states are "infinitely implausible."[1]

Another way of saying that a proposition is known with certainty is to say that its strength of belief is ∞. Hence $\kappa_{p,\infty}$ denotes the NCF that results from learning p with certainty. From the updating rule, we see that for any q compatible with p, $\kappa_{p,\infty}(q) = \kappa(q|p)$, while for any r incompatible with p, $\kappa_{p,\infty}(r) = \infty$.

The next thing to note is that if proposition p is learned with certainty, then it remains certain when any other *compatible* proposition is learned with any degree of strength.

Let C be an arbitrary node in a Spohnian network and suppose that the new evidence is learned with certainty. Let x^+ denote the values of the variables ancestral to C that are learned with certainty and let x^- denote the values of the descendant variables that are learned with certainty. Then the value of the new NCF, κ', for value c of C is given by:

$$\kappa'(c) = \kappa(c|x^+, x^-).$$

Since C d-separates X^+ from X^-, it is easy to show that

$$\kappa(c|x^+, x^-) = \alpha + \kappa(c) + \Delta_c^+ + \Delta_c^-,$$

where α is the constant $\kappa(x^+) + \kappa(x^-) - \kappa(x^+, x^-)$, Δ_c^+ is $\kappa(c|x^+) - \kappa(c)$, and Δ_c^- is $\kappa(c|x^-) - \kappa(c)$.

Since $\min_{c^*}\{\kappa'(c^*)\} = 0$, we must have $\alpha = -\min_{c^*}\{k(c^*) + \Delta_{c^*}^+ + \Delta_{c^*}^-\}$. Hence

$$\kappa'(c) = \kappa(c) + \Delta_c^+ + \Delta_c^- - \min_{c^*}\{k(c^*) + \Delta_{c^*}^+ + \Delta_{c^*}^-\}.$$

This result suggests the following algorithm for updating on multiple certain events. First, if $n_1, ..., n_s$ is any sequence of integers, positive or negative, define the *s-normalization* of $n_1, ..., n_s$ to be the sequence $n_1 - m, ..., n_s - m$, where m is $\min\{n_1, ..., n_s\}$. An s-normalized sequence of integers will be a possible NCF since all its members will be non-negative and it will have at least one zero member. The updating algorithm works by adding to each value c of variable C the terms Δ_c^+ and Δ_c^-, in any order, and then s-normalizing the resultant vector of integers.

It is also important to note that the updates originating from X^+ or from X^- do not have to be assimilated at C simultaneously, nor does the order in which the updates arrive make any difference in the final NCF. For example, let $x^+ = \{x_1, ..., x_k\}$. By writing Δ_c^+ as $\kappa(c) - \kappa(c|x_1, ...x_{k-1}) + [\kappa(c|x_1, ..., x_{k-1}) - \kappa(c|x_1, ..., x_k)]$, we see that if *changes* in NCF values are passed along, the result will be the same as assimilating the updates simultaneously. Moreover, since $\kappa(c|x_1, ..., x_k) = \kappa(c|x_{\pi(1)}, ..., x_{\pi(k)})$, π a permutation of 1,...,k, the order in which the updates arrive makes no difference in the final NCF. The same argument applies to the updates originating in X^-.

---

[1] Having an upper bound to degrees of implausibility or disbelief goes against the spirit of the Spohn system, which allows that any belief, no matter how strongly held, may be overturned by evidence. However, the existence of an upper bound is technically convenient, for the reasons given below, and can be thought of as an approximation to situations in which certain evidence events are believed to an extremely high degree.

8 Updating on Multiple Pieces of Uncertain Evidence

If simultaneous updates originate at variables $A_1, ..., A_n$, but these updates do not assign ∞ to specific values of these variables, there is a way of propagating these updates in parallel. Following the technique described in [3] for uncertain evidence in Bayesian networks, we add dummy nodes for binary variables $D_1, ..., D_n$ to the influence diagram with arrows pointing from A_i to D_i. We label the values of D_i by "d_i" and "$\bar{d}_i$." The Spohnian network corresponding to the augmented influence diagram will contain nodes with NCFs over the pairs $\{A_i, D_i\}$. The trick is to choose the NCFs so that $\kappa(a_i|d_i)$ equals the original updated value of a_i, for each a_i in A_i. Next, we set each value $\bar{d}_i$ to ∞. Then these updates on certain evidence are propagated as described in the previous section.

One must be aware, however, that this method will not in general produce a joint NCF in which the variables $A_1, ..., A_n$ have their original updates. This method seems to model a situation in which independent sources give updates for the A_i, one source for each variable, and the task is to combine the information from these sources. A different situation is one in which a single source stipulates that the A_i are to have certain new marginal NCFs and the task is to find some revised joint NCF that satisfies these marginals. The difference between these two tasks must be kept in mind in deciding whether or not the updating method described in this section is appropriate.

9 Discussion

I have described Wolfgang Spohn's system of belief revision and shown that there is an efficient parallel updating scheme for that system. A Common Lisp implementation of Spohnian networks has been written and runs on a Symbolics 3670 processor. The parallel updating algorithms have been tested in a C implementation running on a BBN Butterfly computer, a shared memory, parallel processor.

In my opinion, Spohnian belief revision offers an elegant and novel approach to many of the problems in the area of uncertain reasoning. The example of Figure 1 illustrates how Spohnian belief revision easily handles the problem of non-monotonic reasoning. One particularly promising area of application of Spohnian belief revision is to the Frame Problem in automatic planning – i.e., the problem of determining what changes and what stays the same when an action is performed. Spohnian belief revision also has application to causal and counterfactual reasoning (in fact, Spohn was led to his system through a consideration of how causation might be defined within the realm of deterministic belief). Space does not permit elaboration on these applications, which will be explored in future work. They are mentioned here merely to give the reader a sense of the rich potential of Spohnian belief revision.

References

[1] Hanks, S. and McDermott, D., "Nonmonotonic Logic and Temporal Projection," *Artificial Intelligence* (1987) 379.

[2] Spohn, W., "Ordinal Conditional Functions: A Dynamic Theory of Epistemic States," in: Harper, W. L. and Skyrms, B., (eds.), *Causation in Decision, Belief Change, and Statistics, II*, (D. Reidel, 1988).

[3] Pearl, J., *Probabilistic Reasoning in Intelligent Systems* (Morgan Kaufmann, San Mateo, 1988).

[4] Geiger, D. and Pearl, J., "On the Logic of Causal Models", this volume.

[5] Verma, T. and Pearl, J., "Causal Networks: Semantics and Expressiveness", this volume.

[6] Hunter, D. "Graphoids, Semi-graphoids, and Ordinal Conditional Functions," Technical Paper TP-8939, Northrop Research and Technology Center, 1989.

Uncertainty in Artificial Intelligence 4
R.D. Shachter, T.S. Levitt, L.N. Kanal, J.F. Lemmer (Editors)
© Elsevier Science Publishers B.V. (North-Holland), 1990

EVIDENTIAL REASONING COMPARED IN A NETWORK USAGE PREDICTION TESTBED: PRELIMINARY REPORT

Ronald P. Loui
Department of Computer Science
Washington University
St. Louis, MO 63130

This paper reports on empirical work aimed at comparing evidential reasoning techniques. While there is prima facie evidence for some conclusions, this is work in progress; the present focus is methodology, with the goal that subsequent results be meaningful.

The domain is a network of UNIX* cycle servers, and the task is to predict properties of the state of the network from partial descriptions of the state. Actual data from the network are taken and used for blindfold testing in a betting game that allows abstention.

The focal technique has been Kyburg's method for reasoning with data of varying relevance to a particular query, though the aim is to be able eventually to compare various uncertainty calculi.

The conclusions are not novel, but are instructive.

1. All of the calculi performed better than human subjects, so unbiased access to sample experience is apparently of value.

2. Performance depends on metric:

    (a) when trials are repeated, $net = gains - losses$ favors methods that place many bets, if the probability of placing a correct bet is sufficiently high; that is, it favors point-valued formalisms;

    (b) $yield = gains/(gains + losses)$ favors methods that bet only when sure to bet correctly; that is, it favors interval-valued formalisms.

3. Among the calculi, there were no clear winners or losers.

Methods are identified for eliminating the bias of the *net* as a performance criterion and for separating the calculi effectively: in both cases by posting odds for the betting game in the appropriate way.

1 TESTBED

States of a UNIX* cycle server network were described by asserting those sentences that hold in the state. For example,

(AND (weekend) (in-use 'castor) (logged-on 'marsh) (on 'cox 'antares))

described a state in which the machine "castor" was in use, the user "marsh" was logged on, and the user "cox" was logged onto the machine "antares", some time during the weekend.

All such descriptions were unified with deductive rules and forward chained, so that the above description was augmented by

> (NOT (weekday)),
> (logged-on 'cox),
> (in-use 'antares),

and of course, the tautology,

> (always-true).

The language allowed reference to such properties as machine load, number of users, kind of user, that is, whether a backup was in progress or there was a UNIX*-to-UNIX*-communication-protocal (uucp) user, number of ports, use of dial-in ports, and so forth. They could be combined with any logical connective, e.g.,

> (OR (logged-on 'marsh) (logged-on 'cox))

and with some quantifiers. All quantities were discretized, so that the property

> (very-very-many-network-users)

was used instead of $(> (\# \text{ network-users}) 20)$, for instance.

Given a state described partially, as above, what was at issue was the degree of belief in a sentence such as

> (logged-on 'jackson);

that is, the extent to which "marsh" and "cox" being so logged on a weekend provided evidence for "jackson" being logged on.

Several hundred snapshots of the network were taken at random times, i.e., states of the network were observed. Each snapshot was associated with a time, and was roughly the result of concatenating the results of the "rwho", the "ruptime", and the "date" commands under UNIX*.

Some of these data were provided to a program as sampling data. Typically, sixty snapshots were provided. If sampling was random, we would expect that one-seventh of these, or about nine, would be during the weekend; and of those hypothetical nine weekend snapshots, perhaps two were when "marsh" was logged on, and three when "cox" was logged on. Perhaps there was even one in which both were logged on, and so was "jackson". Sometimes the record of available data was limited to twenty snapshots instead of sixty.

For each query, such as the probability of (logged-on 'jackson) given (AND (logged-on 'marsh) ...), the snapshots were summarized as samples from populations of varying relevance:

> (s% ((AND (logged-on 'cox) (logged-on 'marsh)) (logged-on 'jackson)) (4 1))

> (s% ((weekend) (logged-on 'jackson)) (3 1))

> (s% ((AND (in-use 'castor) (logged-on 'marsh)) (logged-on 'jackson)) (2 2))

> (s% ((always-true) (logged-on 'jackson)) (20 4))

The first statement, for instance, reports that in the record of snapshots, there were four times when both "cox" and "marsh" were logged-on and "jackson" was also observed; in one of those four, "jackson" was logged-on too, in the other three, "jackson" was not logged-on.

In the general case, which includes twenty snapshots, "jackson" was logged-on four times. Note that in the record, there was no snapshot that captured all of (AND (weekend) (logged-on 'marsh) (on 'cox 'antares) (in-use 'castor)), nor even a snapshot in which (AND (weekend) (logged-on 'marsh) (logged-on 'cox)) held. So there are no samples from these classes.

2 BETTING

The following process was repeated an arbitrary number of times.

A test snapshot was selected from those that were not made available to the programs. Properties were chosen arbitrarily. They were determined to hold of the state of the network captured by the snapshot, or not, and an arbitrary number of them was announced. Typically three, eight, or sixteen properties were announced. Matching the discussion above, suppose the target property was (logged-on 'jackson) and four properties were announced: (weekend), (in-use 'castor), (logged-on 'marsh), and (on 'cox 'antares).

A lottery size, say 10, and payoff ratio, say .1, were chosen, arbitrarily, so that the following choice could be offered:

1. offer a pot of 10 for an ante of 1,

2. place an ante of 1 for a pot of 10, or

3. abstain.

For a rational agent who associates degrees of belief with willingness to bet, the choice was mandated by $Belief($ (logged-on 'jackson) given (AND (weekend) . . .)). If it was less than .1, option 1 was the rational choice. If it exceeded .1, then option 2 was the rational choice. If belief were an interval that included .1, say $Belief($ (logged-on 'jackson) given (AND (weekend) . . .)) $= [.05, .3]$, then, ostensibly, the rational choice was to abstain. Each program, or test subject, committed to one of these choices for each query.

The programs were forced to play the rational strategy for a single choice, without knowledge that the process was being repeated. That is, they had no knowledge that there would be more questions. The human test subjects were not prohibited from using the knowledge that the process was being repeated. So they could alter their betting strategies accordingly. They were, however, advised what would be the rational stragey for an unrepeated process. Any combination of choices was permitted, even though some combinations required a larger financial base. For example, the strategy that constantly offers pots requires more intial resource than the one that constantly abstains. There was no sense in which any agent went bankrupt from too much loss.

The actual snapshot was consulted to determine whether the target property held. Payoffs were awarded appropriately in the end, so there was no feedback during the questioning.

This process was repeated under various conditions for various kinds of queries. Relative success was usually stable after some 50 repetitions, though some of the runs reported here repeat the querying over 1000 times with fixed conditions.

3 UNCERTAINTY CALCULI

The original idea was to test Kyburg's method for determining probabilities from frequency information of varying relevance. It was to be compared against human performance. This paper reports those results.

This testbed, however, is natural for comparing one uncertainty calculus against another. This paper also reports intial considerations for such testing. *These data must be taken as preliminary, as the central conclusions of this paper are methodological at this stage of the research.*

The non-Kyburgian methods used here are based on approaches that have been discussed in the uncertainty literature, but are not necessarily applied appropriately. For instance, the Dempsterian rule of combination is applied to intervals, rather than beginning with belief functions constructed from sampling data, as Shafer suggests [8]. The method of similarity [7][9] is applied with an arbitrary similarity metric, with no attempt to optimize it for this domain. Subsequent research will apply these methods more appropriately. No prior probability information was used.

Kyburg. Kyburg's procedures [2][3] start with frequency data in the form of intervals, for example

(% ((weekend) (logged-on 'jackson)) (.2 .4)) .

So our sampling data must be converted into frequencies. This is done by approximating narrowest binomial confidence intervals at some level of confidence (usually .9). Some of these intervals can be combined on purely set-theoretic grounds. For example,

(% ((in-use 'castor) (logged-on 'jackson)) (.3 .5))

can be combined with the interval above to yield

(% ((XP (weekend) (in-use 'castor)) (X (logged-on 'jackson) (logged-on 'jackson)))
(g(.2, .3) g(.4, .5)));

where (XP (a) (b)) is

$\{< x,y > :$ (a) holds in x, (b) holds in y, and (logged-on 'jackson) holds in x just in case it holds in $y\}$;

where (X (a) (b)) is just a cross product: $\{< x,y > :$ (a) holds in x and (b) holds in $y\}$; and where $g(p, q) = pq/(1 - p - q + 2pq)$. These constructions are discussed in [5].

Of these intervals, Kyburg considers intervals that come from more specific sampling classes than intervals with which they disagree (intervals disagree if one does not nest in the other). The narrowest of such intervals is taken to be the probability.

Of the three intervals above, neither of the first two is considered because they disagree, and neither comes from a more specific class. The third disagrees with neither of the other two. So it would be considered if there were no other intervals.

Loui. Some reject Kyburg's rule for determining when intervals disagree. The intervals (.06 .63) and (.08 .73) disagree because neither is a sub-interval of the other. But neither would dispute the interval (.06 .73), and perhaps this could be taken as the probability. The author altered Kyburg's system to allow this [6]. This method for determining probabilities appears in this study, though under all conditions, since it demanded considerably more computation.

Naive Average. Another method takes the average of the maximum likelihood estimators for each sample, and this (point) value is taken to be the degree of belief. For n samples of sizes s_i with results r_i out of s_i, the belief would be

$(1/n)\Sigma_{all\ samples} r_i/s_i$.

With the four samples above, this would be $[(1/3) + (1/4) + (2/2) + (4/20)]/4$.

Maximal Average. Prior to averaging, estimators from sample classes are discarded if there is an estimator from a subclass. So a sample of snapshots in which (AND (in-use 'castor) (logged-on 'marsh)) held would make a sample in which just (in-use 'castor) held superfluous. Of the four samples above, only

(s% ((always-true) (logged-on 'jackson)) (20 4))

is discarded. It reports sampling from a superclass of (at least) one of the other classes reported, *e.g.*,

(AND (weekend) (logged-on 'jackson)),

which is really

(AND (weekend) (NOT weekday) (always-true (logged-on 'jackson))).

So the (point) value would be

$$(1/[\# \ of \ maximal \ classes])\Sigma_{samples \ from \ maximal \ classes} r_i/s_i$$

or $[(1/3) + (1/4) + (2/2)]/3$. Note that non-maximal sets are discarded irrespective of the size of the sample from its subset, and irrespective of whether they disagree about the estimate. These are considerations upon which Kyburg's system was designed.

Similarity. This method weighs each maximum likelihood estimator by the extent to which the sampled class matches the properties that are given. Also, samples contribute to the sum in direct proportion to their size. This is essentially the method used by Salzberg [7] to predict horse race winners and by Stanfill and Waltz [9] to project pronunciations of words from a small dictionary.

There are many possible weighting schemes. The weights used here were linear in the number of common properties. If $\#common(set, given)$ is the number of properties in common between *set* and *given*,*e.g.*,

#common((AND (always-true) (weekend) (in-use 'castor)),
        (AND (weekend) (on 'cox 'antares) (logged-on 'cox) (in-use 'antares) (logged-on 'marsh) (NOT (weekday)) (in-use 'castor) (always-true))) = 2,

then belief yielded by this method is

$$\Sigma_{all \ classes} \#common(class_i, given) r_i / \Sigma_{all \ classes} \#common(class_i, given) s_i$$

For the samples above, the (4 1) sample shares 3 properties with the given properties ((logged-on 'cox), (logged-on 'marsh), and (always-true)); the (3 1) sample shares 2 ((weekend) and (always-true)); the (2 2) sample shares 3 (logged-on 'marsh), (in-use 'castor), and (always-true)); and the (20 4) sample shares 1 ((always-true)). So the degree of belief in (logged-on 'jackson) is

$(3)(1) + (2)(1) + (3)(2) + (1)(4)$ divided by

$(3)(4) + (2)(3) + (3)(2) + (1)(20)$.

Naive Dempster. With the intervals above, simple mass functions can be constructed. The frequency statement

(% ((AND (logged-on 'marsh) (logged-on 'cox)) (logged-on 'jackson)) (.06 .63))

is converted to the mass function

$m_{(AND\ (logged-on\ 'marsh)\ (logged-on\ 'cox))}($ (logged-on 'jackson)) = .06

$m_{(AND\ (logged-on\ 'marsh)\ (logged-on\ 'cox))}($ (NOT (logged-on 'jackson))) = .37

$m_{(AND\ (logged-on\ 'marsh)\ (logged-on\ 'cox))}($ (OR (logged-on 'jackson) (NOT (logged-on 'jackson)))) = .57 .

This imputes a belief function, that is combined with the other belief functions constructed from the other intervals. An alternative way of constructing belief functions would start with the sample data directly, as Shafer suggests [8]. Note that the belief functions constructed from

(% ((logged-on 'cox) (logged-on 'jackson)) (.08 .73)) and from

(% ((AND (logged-on 'marsh) (logged-on 'cox)) (logged-on 'jackson)) (.06 .63))

would be combined by Dempsterian combination under this method, though they do not represent clearly distinct evidential sources.

This method tended to yield narrow intervals, reflected in the fact that it did not abstain much.

Maximal Dempster. Like maximal average, sources are discarded if they report on statistics about a class, and there is knowledge of statistics about some subclass. Of the above two frequency statements, (logged-on 'cox) is not as specific as (AND (logged-on 'marsh) (logged-on 'cox)). So a belief function is constructed only for the latter. It is then combined with other maximal sources of statistical information.

This method tended to yield the widest intervals of all the methods considered here; it abstained most often.

4 SOME PRELIMINARY DATA

A questionnaire with 40 choices was completed by some users of the network with varying knowledge of the patterns of its use. The questions were also answered using each of the techniques described. Human respondents did not have access to summarized sample information, but presumably had their own prior experience. It would be interesting to test the opposite situation, wherein agents respond only to the same syntactic information provided to the programs, with no additonal exposure to the domain.

Table 1 summarizes the results, sorted by *net*, which was *gains* less *losses*. An alternative performance criterion was *yield*, which was *gains/(gains + losses)*, or *gains/losses*. Figure 1 plots performance using both metrics.

Table 1. 40 questions sorted by *net*. *%max* is the per cent of the perfect score. *%rel* is the per cent of the highest achieved score. *#absts* reports the number of times the subject chose to abstain. *data* indicates the number of data points each program accessed, or else the familiarity of the subject with the usage patterns on the UNIX* network.

subject	data	net	%max	%rel	gains	losses	g/l	yield	#absts
naive dempster	60	172.5	68	100	213	41.5	5.1	.84	0
maximal average	60	160	63	93	207.5	47.5	4.4	.82	0
kyburg	60	136.5	54	79	168.5	32	5.3	.84	6
naive average	60	136.5	54	79	195.5	59	3.1	.76	0
maximal dempster	60	126.5	50	73	142	15.5	9.2	.90	13
loui	60	123	48	71	146	23	6.3	.86	12
similarity	60	92.5	36	53	173.5	81	2.1	.68	0
ai student	good	57	22	33	69	12	5.8	.85	24
systems student	good	44.5	16	25	149	105.5	1.4	.58	0
author	good	37.5	14	21	99	61.5	1.6	.62	17
vision student	fair	32	12	18	89.5	57.5	1.6	.62	22
vision faculty	fair	19.5	7	11	72	52.5	1.4	.58	16
systems student	good	11	4	6	58	47	1.2	.55	19
ai student	fair	−2	–	–	77	79	1.0	.50	16
psych student	poor	−7	–	–	117.5	124.5	0.9	.50	2

It was clear from the data that the uncertainty calculi, with access to unbiased sampling data, were outperforming the human subjects. In *net*, every system did better than every human subject. In *yield*, (which shares the same ordering as *gains/losses*), only one human subject did as well, though his score was quite high.

Note that human subjects performed poorly regardless of strategy: some tended to choose lotteries of which they were most certain and abstained frequently; others guessed recklessly. Even when subjects thought they knew the answer, they did not, so their *yields* suffered despite careful selection of bets to place. Note also that there was some correlation between subjects' familiarity with the system and with performance.

Subjects demonstrated the famous judgement biases [10]. For instance, the representativeness heuristic led most to overestimate the probability of (logged-on 'cheng) given there was a (backup-somewhere), since "cheng" was the user responsible for doing backups. But of course, backups ran much longer than "cheng's" logons.

It is not clear whether *net* or *yield* should be the performance criterion. Apparently, *net* favored agents who did not abstain much, while *yield* (or *gains* to *losses*) favored agents who were cautious about the choice of bets, so long as they did well on those bets that they did choose. *Had table 1 sorted by yield (or gains/losses), the ordering among the programs would have been largely reversed.*

Figures 2 and 3 show performance of the programs for different choices of payoff ratios (figure 2), and for different payoff ratios and different lottery values (figure 3). *Relative order among the programs is not robust for this small number of repetitions.*

Figure 4 shows the effect of limiting programs to 20 data points instead of 60. Sample sizes that may have been

gains/losses

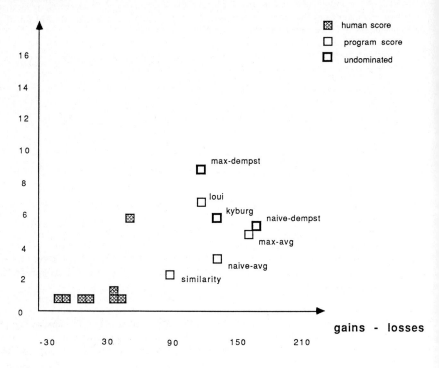

Fig. 1. 40 questions, various calculi.

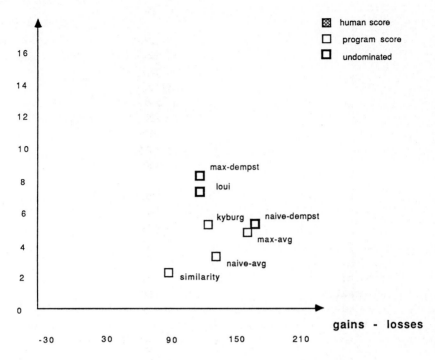

Fig. 2. Same 40 questions. Different fair betting ratios.

gains/losses

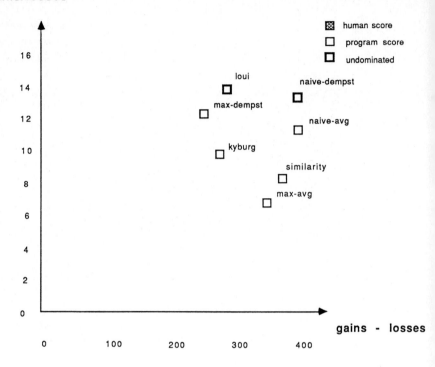

Fig. 3. Same 40 questions. Different fair betting ratios and lottery values.

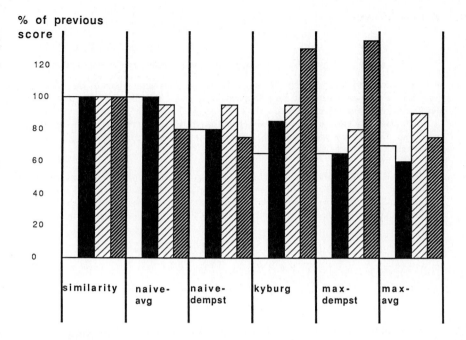

run 1, gains - losses
run 1, gains / losses
run 2, gains - losses
run 2, gains / losses

Fig. 4. Effect of using 20 data points instead of 60 from which to calculate probabilities. Note that for the wide-interval methods, the gains/losses score jumps because of more frequent abstaining.

(s% ((AND (logged-on 'marsh) (logged-on 'cox)) (logged-on 'jackson)) (4 1))

may have been reduced to

(s% ((AND (logged-on 'marsh) (logged-on 'cox)) (logged-on 'jackson)) (1 0))

or may have disappeared entirely. For methods that produce wide intervals, the *gains/losses* performance jumped because of more frequent abstaining. Diminished access to data had a detrimental effect on *net*, in general.

Elsewhere [4], I have suggested altering boldness, or width of intervals, as the size of stakes is altered. Table 2 gives prima facie evidence that this had a positive effect, though much more investigation needs to be done.

Table 2. Result of altering confidence levels. Kyburg(.7) applies Kyburg's methods to intervals constructed from samples at .7 confidence. Kyburg(.9) applies to intervals at .9 confidence. Kyburg(.7, .9) alters the confidence level between .7 and .9 depending on lottery size: the larger the lottery, the lower the confidence level appropriate for analysis of decision. 40 queries.

method	%rel	gains/losses
kyburg(.7, .9)	54	5.3
kyburg(.7)	50	4.0
kyburg(.9)	47	4.8

Again, wider intervals (from higher confidence level) results in more abstaining, a lower *net*, and a higher *yield*, all other things being equal.

We also investigated the effect of varying the number of properties announced to hold of each snapshot. It did not matter much. We had hypothesized that the maximal versions of the various calculi would fare better than the naive versions as the number of given properties increased. Intuitively, it seemed that the disparity in relevance between samples from classes such as

(AND (weekend) (in-use 'castor) (on 'cox 'antares) (logged-on 'marsh) (on 'lata 'lesath)
   ...)
and
(weekend)

would grow with increased number of properties. The more specific class should then bear more of the weight in determining the probability. Methods insensitive to such specificity would be confused. This was not observed in the data. Table 3 shows the result of 1650 queries.

Table 3. Different number of announced properties. The second column shows %rel for 8 properties as a percentage of %rel for 3 properties. The third column shows %rel for 16 properties as a percentage of %rel for 3 properties. Recall that %rel is the percentage of the method's *net* relative to the highest *net* among programs, for a particular run. With 16 given properties, assuming no forward chaining, there are potentially 2^{16} sampling classes. Of course, individuation among these classes is limited by the number of total data points, which was 60. 1650 queries total.

method	3 properties %rel%of3	8 properties %rel%of3	16 properties %rel%of3
kyburg	100	102	108
similarity	100	84	101
maximal average	100	101	100
naive dempster	100	98	100
naive average	100	89	99
maximal dempster	100	97	91

Only Kyburg's method fared consistently better with increased number of properties. In fact, the maximal version of Dempsterian combination fared successively more poorly, and the naive version seemed unaffected, with more numerous announced properties.

Although the relative performance of methods was fairly close for most runs, this should not lead us to complacency in our choice of uncertainty calculus, nor dissuade us from further investigation. The relative performance of these calculi can be made to differ markedly, when most of the choices are difficult. On a run of 40 queries, over half of the payoff ratios were such that all of the calculi agreed on the appropriate choice. It may have been obvious that the probability of (logged-on 'jackson) did not exceed .8, for instance. Table 4 shows the relative performance, in terms of *net*, on 750 queries when the payoff ratio was set by examining the belief of the programs.

Table 4. Relative *net* on difficult choices. In the first column, the payoff ratio equals the belief reported by the naive average method. In the second column, the payoff ratio equals the average of the beliefs of all the methods, where midpoints of intervals are used for interval-valued beliefs. 750 queries.

method	odds set by naive average %rel	odds set by average of beliefs %rel
naive dempster	100	100
maximal average	98	92
kyburg	77	85
naive average	–	68
similarity	−4	65
maximal average	33	5

Apparently, there could be large differences in relative performance for choices of this kind. Unfortunately, *yield* data was not kept for these queries. Future work will have to distinguish whether the methods with low *nets* fared as they did because of frequent abstaining (which was likely in the case of maximal average), or just poor guessing (which must be the case for similarity, since it does not abstain).

5 BIAS OF NET FOR REPEATED CHOICES

The major problem encountered above was defining the performance criterion. Both *net* and *yield* are sensible, and the partial order under $< net, yield >$ tuples is a natural compromise. It is natural to focus attention on the "pareto" frontier of undominated methods. In fact, one can study the convex hull that results by playing mixed strategies of method: this defines the frontier of $< net, yield >$ points that we know how to achieve.

But at the moment there is a problem with the *net* as a performance criterion. It is biased in favor of those who guess often, who abstain very little. This is okay, if guesses are good. It makes sense to reward repeated good guessing, and to penalize methods which lack courage.

How bad can a guess be, yet still be worth making? The calculations of figures 5 and 6 suggest that guesses are worth making if the probability of guessing right exceeds 1/2. Suppose an interval-valued belief straddles the payoff ratio; for example, [.4, .52] straddles .5. Nevertheless, when an interval straddles the payoff ratio in this way, the probability is greater than .5 by epsilon that the correct choice is to offer the pot (that is, to act as if the belief was entirely below .5). Even for small epsilon, it can be shown under certain assumptions that the expected gain is positive if the bet is taken. This is bad news for those methods that abstain.

Perhaps this invites too much courage in betting. Under repeated trials, this expected gain is manifest. Suppose p is the probability of guessing correctly, independently of whether the guess was to ante or to offer the pot. Also suppose the process is repeated, with l_i the lottery values, $i = 1, \ldots, k$. Then

$$(\Sigma_{1..k} l_i)(p - .5)$$

is the expected *net*. The expected *yield* is always p. Prior to analysis of individual choices, it can be determined that the optimal strategy is to bet twice, instead of once, or no times, if two lotteries are offered (so long as betting is done with a greater than one-half chance of betting correctly). Having made the commitment to place all bets offered, even interval methods can then be applied to determine which bet to place: whether to ante or offer the pot, having already ruled out abstaining. If interval methods do not legislate a choice, it is still optimal to choose one or the other out of indifference.

This is not how interval-valued bet-placing strategies were implemented. So point-valued methods are favored to perform well in *net* because they implement the optimal multi-stage solution by nature. Had the probability of guessing correctly been lower, perhaps the *net* would be biased against point-valued systems.

We are not interested in which method performs best on the multi-stage decision. We are interested in repeating the one-stage decision so that we obtain plausible long-run data about relative performance on one-stage bets. If we were interested in plausible data about relative performance on 40-stage bets, we would repeat play on the 40-stage game a few hundred times. Again, the optimal 4000-stage strategy might not be the same as the optimal 40-stage strategy, and methods that happen to implement the same strategy for both will be at an advantage. Nevertheless, it makes sense to reward methods that actually place good bets.

One remedy is to set odds very close to the degrees of belief yielded by each method, as described in table 4. In this way, it is not a trivial accomplishment to guess correctly more than one-half the time. In fact, when payoff ratios are taken to be the average of the various degrees of belief, the number of correct guesses (if guesses were forced and abstaining disallowed) should equal the number of incorrect guesses.

6 FUTURE WORK

This research began with an interest in showing that Kyburgian methods did what they were supposed to do: begin with raw, but limited sampling data of varying relevance, in a complex domain, and produce degrees of belief which are better in some sense than those that human experts would produce.

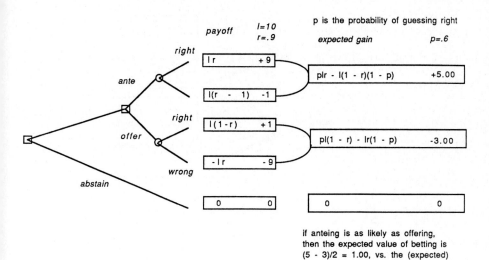

if anteing is as likely as offering,
then the expected value of betting is
(5 - 3)/2 = 1.00, vs. the (expected)
value of abstaining, 0.00.

Fig. 5. One Choice. The expected (gains - losses) = l(p - .5).
The expected (gains/(gains+losses)) = p.

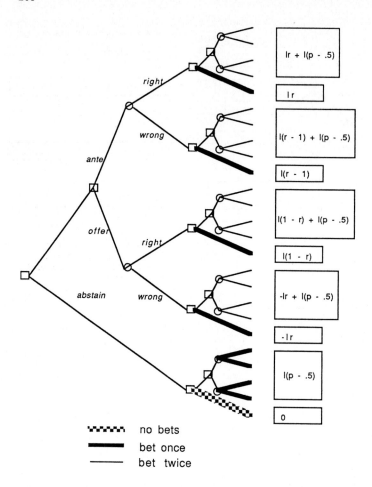

Fig. 6. Two choices. Expected (gains - losses) = 2l(p - .5).
Expected (gains/(gains+losses)) = p.

But the more interesting question is whether it was unbiased and indefatigable access to data that improved performance, so that any system would perform well; or, whether Kyburg's rules for processing the data were themselves responsible for success. Some preliminary study was made, with the following recommendations for future work.

In order to separate the methods effectively by relative performance, payoff ratios should be determined so that the probability of guessing correctly, p, is close to one-half. One way of doing this is taking the payoff ratio to be the average of the degrees of belief produced by the various methods. With p near one-half, the bias inherent in the use of *net* is tempered. Methods should still be partially ordered by $< net, yield >$ dominance. Undominated methods deserve attention, especially the methods that define the convex hull of performance. If the primary goal is comparison of techniques, techniques should be applied properly. This includes constructing belief functions from data, instead of interval, trying different similarity metrics, and altering confidence levels according to sizes of lotteries.

The prima facie conclusion is that the rules themselves are not responsible for the observed success: super-human performance was obtained with any of a number of methods. Nevertheless, subsequent research ought to be able to separate the better among them.

Acknowledgements. This work was supported at the University of Rochester by a basic grant from the U.S. Army Signals Warfare Center and at Stanford University by a Sloan Cognitive Science Postdoctoral Fellowship. It was originally prepared while at the Rockwell Science Center Palo Alto.

UNIX* is a trademark of AT&T.

The author thanks Jack Breese, Glenn Shafer, and an anonymous referee for comments, Michael McInerny, Bill Bolosky, Paul Cooper, Chris Brown, Cesar Quiroz, Dave Coombs, Joel Lachter, Leo Hartman, Eliz Hinkelman, and Josh Tenenberg for completing lengthy surveys, and the entire Rochester Computer Science Department for sacrificing so many cycles.

7 REFERENCES

[1] Dempster, A. "A Generalization of Bayesian Inference," *Journal of the Royal Statistical Society 2*, 1968.

[2] Kyburg, H. *Logical Foundations of Statistical Inference*, Reidel, 1974.

[3] Kyburg, H. "The Reference, Class," *Philosophy of Science 50*, 1982.

[4] Loui, R. "Interval-Based Decisions for Reasoning Systems," in *Uncertainty in AI*, L. Kanal and J. Lemmer, eds., Elsevier, 1986.

[5] Loui, R. "Computing Reference Classes," in *Uncertainty in AI v. II*, J. Lemmer and L. Kanal, eds., Elsevier, 1987.

[6] Loui, R. "Theory and Computation of Uncertain Inference and Decision," U. Rochester Dept. of Computer Science, Technical Report 228, 1987.

[7] Salzberg, S. "Good Hypotheses with Heuristics," in *AI in Statistics*, W. Gale, ed., Addison-Wesley, 1986.

[8] Shafer, G. *Mathematical Theory of Evidence*, Princeton, 1976.

[9] Stanfill, C. and D. Waltz. "Toward Memory-Based Reasoning," *Communications of the ACM 29*, 1986.

[10] Tversky, A. and D. Kahneman. "Judgement under Uncertainty: Heuristics and Biases," *Science 185*, 1974.

Uncertainty in Artificial Intelligence 4
R.D. Shachter, T.S. Levitt, L.N. Kanal, J.F. Lemmer (Editors)
© Elsevier Science Publishers B.V. (North-Holland), 1990

A Comparison of Decision Analysis and Expert Rules for Sequential Diagnosis

Jayant Kalagnanam & Max Henrion

Department of Engineering and Public Policy,
Carnegie Mellon University,
Pittsburgh, PA 15213.
Tel: 412-268-2670;

Abstract

There has long been debate about the relative merits of decision theoretic methods and heuristic rule-based approaches for reasoning under uncertainty. We report an experimental comparison of the performance of the two approaches to troubleshooting, specifically to test selection for fault diagnosis. We use as experimental testbed the problem of diagnosing motorcycle engines. The first approach employs heuristic test selection rules obtained from expert mechanics. We compare it with the optimal decision analytic algorithm for test selection which employs estimated component failure probabilities and test costs. The decision analytic algorithm was found to reduce the expected cost (i.e. time) to arrive at a diagnosis by an average of 14% relative to the expert rules. Sensitivity analysis shows the results are quite robust to inaccuracy in the probability and cost estimates. This difference suggests some interesting implications for knowledge acquisition.

1. Introduction

Although early work on automated diagnostic systems was much inspired by probabilistic inference and decision theory (Ledley & Lusted, 1959; Gorry & Barnett, 1968), many researchers later became disenchanted with this approach. Reasons cited include the difficulty of obtaining the required numerical probabilities and utilities, computational intractability, restrictive assumptions, and the apparent mismatch between the quantitative formalism of decision theory with human reasoning (Szolovits & Pauker, 1978). Thus, in the 1970s, this work was partly eclipsed by the development of AI approaches, which appeared more tractable and compatible with human thinking. More recently, however, there have been signs of renewed interest in the application of decision theoretic ideas in AI (Lemmer & Kanal, 1986; Horvitz, Breese & Henrion, in press). This has partly been due to increased misgivings about the assumptions and reliability of widely used heuristic methods for reasoning under certainty, and to the emergence of more tractable approaches based on probabilistic representations and decision analysis (e.g. Pearl, 1986; Henrion & Cooley, 1987).

Our focus here is on the application of decision analysis to troubleshooting, and particularly to sequential diagnosis, that is decisions about which diagnostic test to perform next and when to stop testing. We define the *test sequencing task* as the problem of finding the testing strategy that minimizes the total expected cost. This task is central in any kind of diagnosis, from medicine to mechanical and electronic devices.

If one has a causal model of the device that is entirely deterministic, logical analysis can identify possible explanations of the observed faults (e.g. Reggia et al, 1983; Genesereth, 1984; Milne, 1987). Intuitively it seems clear that test selection should involve some kind of balancing of the cost of the test against the chance it will provide useful information. This suggests that it is desirable to quantify the degree of belief in the logically possible explanations. Decision theory provides a way of quantifying the value of tests in the form of the *expected net value of information* (ENVI). This is a measure of the informativeness of the test, in terms of the expected value due to improved decision making, less the expected cost of performing the test.

Gorry & Barnett (1968) demonstrated the application of this approach to test sequencing in medical diagnosis. As they illustrate, the use of the ENVI can give one a voracious appetite for numbers. In addition to the expected costs of the tests and quantifications of their diagnosticity, one requires the prior probabilities of the alternative hypotheses (diseases), and the expected total cost to the patient for each combination of treatment and disease (both correct and incorrect diagnoses). Further, the ENVI for multiple tests are not additive, so the expected value of two tests is not the sum of their expected values. Typically, the ENVI for each testing strategy must be computed separately. With many possible tests, the number of strategies is vast. For this reason, Gorry & Barnett used a "myopic" approach that considers only one test at a time, rather than an entire strategy. This is suboptimal in general, but they found it to be a good heuristic.

In many ways troubleshooting of mechanical and electronic devices is much easier than medical diagnosis. The usual end point is the positive identification of the faulty component to be repaired or replaced, so the possibility of ultimate misdiagnosis can often be neglected. If all testing strategies result in the same end point, the costs of treatment (or mistreatment) are irrelevant. Only the costs of performing the tests are of concern when selecting tests. Typically these costs may be quantified relatively easily in terms of the time required, that is the costs of the diagnostician's time and/or the machine downtime. Further simplifying matters is the fact that there often exists a causal model of the device which is largely or entirely deterministic. Such a luxury is not usually available to the medical diagnostician. Moreover, for many machine components and subsystems, tests can determine with virtual certaintly whether they are faulty. These aspects of troubleshooting make test selection far more amenable to a decision analytic approach than in medicine. In some cases, the optimal test selection algorithm can be very simple, as we shall see.

Our purpose in this work is twofold: First, to demonstrate the practicality of decision analysis for test sequencing for troubleshooting; and second, to compare experimentally the performance of this decision theoretic approach with a more conventional expert system approach employing test selection rules obtained from expert diagnosticians. After presenting the decision analytic formulation we will describe its application to the example of diagnosing of motorcycle engines, to examine its performance in terms of the expected cost (or time) to complete the diagnosis. Finally, we will examine the robustness of the results, and discuss their practical implications.

2. Decision analytic approach

We start by presenting a decision analytic approach to sequential diagnosis for a device representable by a deterministic fault model. We will not develop the formulation beyond the generality required for the experimental example.

2.1. Single level test sequence task

Suppose the system to be diagnosed consists of a set of elementary components, i from 1 to n. We assume that each component is in one of two states, working or faulty, and that the system fails in some observable way if there is a fault in any element. Given the system failure, we assume that there is a fault in exactly one component. This is a reasonable assumption for most systems, where the chance of two elementary components failing simultaneously is negligible. We assume that, given the system has failed, the probability of a component i failing is p_i. Since the failures are mutually exclusive, the probabilities sum to unity.

We further assume that for each component there is a corresponding test which will tell us for certain whether it is working. The test might involve simple inspection, replacement of the component by an identical one known to work, probing with electronic test gear, or a variety of other operations. We assume that for each element i, the cost of testing is c_i, independent of the test sequence. We assume for simplicity that even if the fault is in the last element, which we can deduce if none others are faulty, we will test it anyway for positive identification.

The test sequence task is to find the strategy that minimizes the expected cost to identify the faulty component. It turns out that the optimal strategy is extremely simple: Select as the next element to test the one that has the smallest value of the ratio c_i/p_i, and continue testing until the faulty element is identified. We will call this the *C/P algorithm*.

It is not hard to prove this result. Let S_{jk} be the strategy of testing each element i in sequence for i from 1 to n, until we find the faulty component. We certainly will have to incur the cost C_1 of testing the first component e_1. If that is working, we will have to test the second element, and so on. The probability that the jth element having to be tested is the probability that none of its predecessors failed, which is also the probability that either the jth element or one of its successors has failed, i.e. $\sum_{i=j}^{n} p_i$. Let j and k be two successive elements in this sequence, so $k=j+1$. Then the expected cost of strategy S_{jk} is:

$$EC(S_{jk})=C_1+C_2\sum_{i=2}^{n}p_i+...+C_j\sum_{i=j}^{n}p_i+C_k\sum_{i=k}^{n}p_i+...+C_np_n \qquad (1)$$

Let S_{kj} be the same strategy, but with elements j and k exchanged. The expected cost of this strategy is:

$$EC(S_{kj}) = C_1 + C_2 \sum_{i=2}^{n} p_i + \dots + C_k [\sum_{i=k}^{n} p_i + p_j] + C_j [\sum_{i=j}^{n} p_i - p_k] + \dots C_n p_n$$

The difference in expected cost between these two strategies is then:

$$EC(S_{jk}) - EC(S_{kj}) = C_j p_k - C_k p_j$$

Assuming the probabilities are positive, we get:

$$EC(S_{jk}) > EC(S_{kj}) <=> C_j / p_j > C_k / p_k$$

In other words, strategy S_{kj} is cheaper than S_{jk} if and only if the *C/P* value for element *j* is greater than the *C/P* value for *k*. Thus any strategy with an element that has a higher C/P value than its successor can be improved upon by exchanging the successive elements. So for an optimal strategy, all elements must be in non-decreasing sequence of C/P value. This gives us our C/P algorithm.

This task is an example of what Simon & Kadane (1975) have called *satisficing search*. They show that a similar algorithm is optimal for the related search task, in which the events that each element contains a fault (or prize in their version) are independent rather than exclusive. They cite a number of similar results, and provide an algorithm for the generalized task with an arbitrary partial ordering constraint on the search sequence. See also Kadane & Simon (1977).

3. Experiment:

For the purposes of experimental comparison we chose the problem of diagnosing motorcycle engines. This choice was guided by two reasons. Firstly we had available an existing knowledge base for motorcycles. This allieviated the task of knowledge engineering. Secondly the motorcycle domain provided us with a problem that was small and simple enough to be manageable but still promising enough to make an interesting comparative study. The first goal was to explore the feasibility of implementing it in a real-world task domain, and obtaining the numerical probabilities and test costs required. The second goal was to evaluate its performance in terms of average cost to arrive at a diagnosis compared to the test sequence rules derived from human experts.

3.1. The rule-based approach:

Given the task domain, we identified 5 commonly occuring symptoms. Symptoms are understood as any deviations from expected behaviour. Symptoms can be directly observable or can be detected as a result of some measurement(s). Associated with each symptom is a set of elementary faults which might cause the given symptom. These elementary faults correspond to components that need to be repaired or replaced by the mechanic. The symptoms along with their corresponding symptoms are listed in table 3-1. Associated with each symptom is an *expert rule* that specifies the sequence of

Symptoms and Causes	
Symptoms	Corresponding Causes
poor-idling -due-to-carburettor	idle-speed-adjustment, clogged-speed-jet, air-leak-into-symptom, excess-fuel-from-accelerating-pump
starts-but-runs-irregularly	def-ignition-coil, def-ignition-module, improper-timing, dirty-carburettor, air-cleaner/carburettor-adjustments, engine-problems
charging-system-fails	stator-grounded, stator-defective, rotor-defective, def-regulator/rectifier
engine-turns-over-no-start-no-spark	air-gap-on-trigger-lobes, ignition-coil, circuit-between-battery-and-ignition-coil, ignition-module-defective
engine-turns-over-no-start-with-spark	spark-plugs, carburetion, advance-mechanism, improper-timing

Table 3-1: Symptoms and Causes

elements to be tested in that situation. These rules were obtained from extensive consultations with experienced mechanics and a standard reference manual (Harley Davidson). While eliciting these rules we asked the experts to keep in mind that the objective was to diagnose the fault as quickly as possible.

We interviewed three different mechanics. One of the mechanics refused to prescribe rules on the claim that all symptoms were quite straightfoward and with appropriate audio visual tests the faulty component could be exactly located. Unfortunately he was not able to characterize these tests beyond asserting that they are based on long years of experience. The other two experts did provide us with rules. Sometimes for a given symptom these rules differed markedly between experts. This difference did not affect our experimental study as we were only comparing the rules and C/p sequences for each given expert.

3.2. The decision analytic approach:
For purposes of comparison we applied the decision analytic approach to the same set of symptoms we developed for the rule-based approach. We preserved all the assumptions made in section 2 for both approaches. Firstly all variables (namely symptoms and components) are binary, either working or not working. Both approaches also assume that there is only a single elementary component at fault.

The failure probabilities and test costs were obtained by interviews from motorcycle mechanics of many years' experience. The failure probabilities were assessed in groups, conditional on their common symptom. Given a symptom, the approximate absolute probabilities for different components (which cause the symptom) were assessed. The numbers were subsequently normalized. The costs were estimated as the average time in minutes the expert would take to determine whether each component was working.

The cost estimates between experts differed by upto a factor of three. The ordering of costs for a given symptom was consistent between experts. The difference in the absolute cost estimates can be attributed to personal differences. On the other hand, the probability estimates across experts was starkly different. For a given symptom, even the relative ordering of failure rates of components did not match across experts. One likely cause for this is the fact that different experts saw different samples of motorcycles. The mechanics who worked at dealerships were more likely to service new bikes which they had recently sold. Mechanics working in garages were more likely to see older bikes. As mentioned earlier these differences are not critical for this study.

For each symptom, we applied the C/P algorithm to obtain a test sequence, which we will refer to as the *C/P sequence* to distinguish it from the expert rule. We also showed the C/P sequences to the expert to check real world feasibility.

3.3. Results
Using the estimated cost and failure probabilities, we computed the expected cost in minutes for identifying the failed element for each symptom for both the expert and C/p sequences. Table 3-2 demonstrates the method used for comparison for a selected symptom for a specific expert.

Selected Symptom: Poor - Idling due to Carburettor					
Components	Expert Rule	Cost (mins)	Prob	C/p	C/p sequence
idle-speed-adjustments	1	15	.263	57	2
clogged speed jet	2	30	.105	206	3
air leak into system	3	15	.526	29	1
excess fuel from pump	4	30	.105	206	4
Expected Cost	50				32

Table 3-2: Method for a selected symptom

For each given symptom, the expected cost of diagnosis for both the expert rule and C/p sequence is tabulated in Table 3-3. The C/p algorithm provides a reduction in expected cost of diagnosis for 3 to 4 out of 5 cases, reducing the diagnostic time by an average (across experts) by 14%.

3.4. Sensitivity Analysis
The failure probabilities and test costs are of course quite approximate, being subjective judgments by the expert. An important question for any approach based on expert judgment, be it decision analytic or heuristic, is how much the results depend on the

Expected Cost across different experts				
	Expert 1		Expert 2	
	Expert Rule	C/p sequence	Expert Rule	C/p sequence
poor-idling due to carburettor	8	8	50	32
starts-but-runs-irregularly	24	17	43	36
charging-system-fails	13.5	13.5	7	7
engine-turns-no-start-no-spark	17.5	16.6	55	53
engine-turns-no-start-spark	18.5	9	26.5	25.2

Table 3-3: Expected Cost for different experts

precise numbers used. Is it possible that the expert rules could in fact be optimal according to the C/P algorithm, if only we had obtained the expert's "actual" probabilities and costs? Let us examine how much bias or error would there have to be in the assessment process for this to happen.

For a given symptom, we associate with each component a probability distribution over the failure rate and the cost of testing. Since the failure rate itself is a probability it's range is [0,1]. Therefore we describe the failure rate as a logoddnormal distribution with the mean as the estimated value p and an error factor s. The range $[m/s, m.s]$ encloses 70% of the probability distribution. Similarly we associate a lognormal distribution for the cost with mean as the estimated value C and an error factor s. Now the *difference* between the expected cost for C/p sequence and the expert rule is itself a probability distribution with s as a parameter. We assume that s is the same for *all* the distributions. Figure 3-1 shows the cumulative density function of the *difference* (of the expected cost between the C/p sequence and expert rule) for a selected symptom with $s=2$. Figure 3-1 also graphs the boundaries for *difference* which encloses 70% of the distribution around the mean. From this graph we see that for $s \sim 2.5$, the lower boundary intersects the zero-line. In other words if the error factor is 2.5 then the expert rule and the C/p sequence have the same expected cost. Such an analysis for all symptoms, over all experts shows that the C/p sequence dominates the expert rule for error factors up to 2.5. This suggests that the results obtained are fairly robust to errors in cost and failure rate estimates.

3.5. Further consulations with experts

A major motivation for constructing formal models is the possibility that such models may improve on the intuitive inference of the expert. Hence when the formal models lead to results different from those suggested by experts, it becomes critical to explain these differences to the experts. If explanations (from within the formal framework) are acceptable and the results insightful then the formal models have served their purpose.

Keeping the above criterion in mind, we went back to the experts with the C/p sequences.

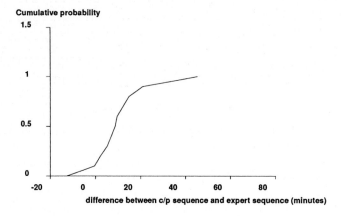

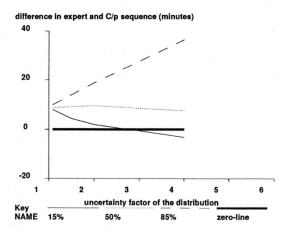

Figure 3-1: Sensitivity Analysis for "poor-idling"

Firstly, both experts found the C/p sequences to be feasible. Hence the C/p sequences did not violate any implicit realworld constraints. When it came to convincing the experts about the superiority of the C/p sequence the results were mixed. Expert 2 was a little surprised at the difference between his sequencing and the C/p sequencing. A careful explanation of the C/p algorithm convinced him of the dominance of the C/p sequence. He readily agreed that the C/p sequence was better at minimizing the expected cost. On the other hand expert 1 was not impressed by the C/p sequence. He felt that his sequences followed a causal pathway while checking for faults which he thought was more desirable. This bias for causal paths made him reject the C/p sequences.

4. Discussion

The results presented in section 3.3 suggest that the expected cost of diagnosis is significantly lower (at least for some cases) for the decision analytic approach. This result can be understood in light of the difference in test sequences obtained from human experts relative to those derived from the C/p algorithm. In order to explain and draw conclusions from this result we need to discuss three possible shortcomings of the experimental setup.

The cost and failure rate estimates are approximate. Therefore it is possible that the inaccuracies in these estimates might affect the test sequences derived from the C/p algorithm. However the sensitivity analysis in section 3.4 shows that the results are quite robust to inaccuracies in the cost and failure rate estimates.

The decision analytic approach sequences tests to optimize the expected cost of diagnosis. This approach is in fact too simple to model other constraints on test sequences which might arise from the shape and structure of the machine under consideration. As a result the C/p algorithm might in fact be ignoring implicit but vital constraints on the test sequences. On the other hand the expert rule might have implicitly accounted for such constraints and the difference in the two approaches might be attributed to this factor. In order to check for this possibility, we presented the experts in question with the C/p sequence for their comments. Specifically we were interested in the real world feasibility of the C/p sequences. We encouraged the experts to suggest reasons as to why the expert sequences might be preferable, so as to identify any implicit real world constraints that might be violated by the C/p sequence. The C/p sequences used are ones that were found acceptable to the experts. We interpret this to mean that the C/p sequences are indeed feasible ones.

The last question we need to worry about is whether the human experts (in the task domain) were actually attempting to minimize the expected time for diagnosis. There is a real possibility that the experts in fact had some other objective function. It is indeed more than plausible that experts have over time evolved these sequences to maximize economic return for each given symptom. The rules might maximize the time for diagnosis, subject to constraint that customer will not think it unreasonable.

5. Conclusions

The results of this study clearly indicate that the test sequences provide by the experts (in the task domain) are suboptimal. Unfortunately there is uncertainty regarding the objectives which motivate the expert test sequences. This restrains us from drawing firm conclusions about the efficacy of human intuition for this task domain. But it is important to remember that one of the experts accepted the validity of the C/p sequence and felt that the results are likely to be of practical interest. This suggests that normative theories of decision making are capable of obtaining results which go beyond current expert opinion.

This study also provides some valuable insights regarding knowledge acquistion for diagnostic expert systems. Diagnostic problem solving can be understood as follows:

- Given a symptom we have a set of components which can potentially explain the symptom. The physics and the structure of the problem provides a partial order on the set of test sequences allowable on the set of components. Since the partial order does not completely constrain the test sequence, we can optimize the expected cost of diagnosis over this set of feasible test sequences.

The knowledge required for this optimization could be acquired in two ways:

1. As an expert rule which picks one test sequence from this set of feasible test sequences. This corresponds to the rule-based approach of our study.

2. We can push level of knowledge acquistion a level deeper and explicitly represent the cost and failure rates. These are once again assessed from experts. This corresponds to the decision analytic approach of our study.

Our study suggests that it possible to explicitly represent the cost and failure rates and it provides better control on the objective of optimizing the expected cost of diagnosis.

Acknowledgements

This work was supported by the National Science Foundation, under grant IST 8603493. We are much indebted to David Keeler, Woody Hepner and Larry Dennis for lending us their expertise as motorcycle mechanics. We are grateful to Jeff Pepper and Gary Kahn of the Carnegie Group, Inc, for making available the expert system, and to Peter Spirtes and J. Kadane for valuable suggestions.

References

Cohen, J., Chesnick, E.I. & Haran, D. Evaluation of Compound Probabilities in Sequential Choice. In Kahneman, D., Slovic, P. & Tversky, A.,*Judgement under Uncertainty:Heuristics and Biases*. Cambridge: Cambridge University Press, 1982.

Genesereth, M.R. "The use of design descriptions in automated diagnosis", *Artificial Intelligence*, 24, pp411-436, 1984.

Gorry, G.A. & Barnett, G.O. "Experience with a Model of Sequential Diagnosis", *Computers and Biomedical Research*, Vol 1, pp490-507, 1968.

Harley-Davidson Inc., Service Manual, FX/FL Models, 1978 to 1984.

Henrion, M., Cooley, D.R., An Experimental Comparison of Knowledge Engineering for Expert Systems and for Decision Analysis. *In Proceedings of AAAI-87.* pg 471-476, Seattle, WA. 1987.

Henrion, M., "Uncertainty in Artificial Intelligence: Is probability epistemologically and heuristically adequate?", in *Expert Judgment and Expert Systems*, J. Mumpower,(Ed.), NATO ISI Series F, Volume 35, Springer-Verlag: Berlin, Heidelberg, 1987, pp.105-130.

Horvitz, E.J., Breese, J. & Henrion, M. "Decision theory in expert systems and AI", *J. of Approximate Reasoning*, (in press).

Kadane, J.B. & Simon, H.A. Optimal Strategies for a Class of Constrained Sequential Problems. *The Annals of Statistics*, 1977, Vol. 5, No. 2, 237-255.

Kahneman, D.,Slovic, P. & Tversky, A. *Judgement under Uncertainty: Heuristics and Biases*, Cambridge, Cambridge University Press, 1982. L.N. Kanal & J. Lemmer (eds.), *Uncertainty in Artificial Intelligence*, Machine Intelligence and Pattern Recognition, Volume 4, Elsevier: Amsterdam, 1986.

Ledley, R.S. & Lusted, L.B. "Reasoning foundations of medical diagnosis", *Science*, 130, pp9-21, 1959.

Milne, Robert. "Strategies for Diagnosis". *IEEE Transactions on Systems, Man & Cybernetics*, Vol. SMC-17, No. 3, May/June, 1987.

Pearl, J. Fusion, Propagation and Structuring in Belief Networks. *Artificial Intelligence*, Sept. 1986, 29(3), pp241-288.

Reggia, J.A., Nau, D.S. & Wang, P.Y. "Diagnostic expert systems based on a set covering model", *Int. J. Man-Machine Studies*, 19, pp437-460, 1983.

Simon, H.A. & Kadane, J.B. "Optimal Problem-Solving Search: All-or-None Solutions. *Artificial Intelligence*, 1975, 6, pp235-247.

Szolovits, P & Pauker, S.G. "Categorical and probabilistic reasoning in medical diagnosis", *Artificial Intelligence*, 11, pp115-144, 1978.

Uncertainty in Artificial Intelligence 4
R.D. Shachter, T.S. Levitt, L.N. Kanal, J.F. Lemmer (Editors)
© Elsevier Science Publishers B.V. (North-Holland), 1990

An Empirical Comparison of Three Inference Methods[1]

David Heckerman

Medical Computer Science Group
Knowledge Systems Laboratory
Departments of Computer Science and Medicine
Stanford, California 94305

In this paper, an empirical evaluation of three inference methods for uncertain reasoning is presented in the context of Pathfinder, a large expert system for the diagnosis of lymph-node pathology. The inference procedures evaluated are (1) Bayes' theorem, assuming evidence is conditionally independent given each hypothesis; (2) odds–likelihood updating, assuming evidence is conditionally independent given each hypothesis and given the negation of each hypothesis; and (3) a inference method related to the Dempster–Shafer theory of belief. Both expert-rating and decision-theoretic metrics are used to compare the diagnostic accuracy of the inference methods.

1   Introduction

Several years ago, before we had explored methods for reasoning with uncertainty, I and my colleagues began work on a large expert system, called Pathfinder, that assists community pathologists with the diagnosis of lymph-node pathology. Because the Dempster–Shafer theory of belief was popular in our research group at the time, we developed an inference method for our expert system inspired by this theory. The program performed fairly well in the opinion of the expert pathologist who provided the knowledge for the system.

In the months following the initial development of Pathfinder, several of us in the research group began exploring other methods for reasoning under uncertainty. We identified the Bayesian approach as a candidate for a new inference procedure. We realized that the measures of uncertainty we assessed from the expert could be interpreted as probabilities, and we implemented a new inference method—a special case of Bayes' theorem.

During this time, the expert was running cases through the program to test the system's diagnostic performance. One day, without telling him, we changed the inference procedure to the Bayesian approach. After running several cases with the new approach, the expert exclaimed, "What did you do to the program? This is fantastic!"

This experience was, and still is, in sharp contrast with the beliefs of many researchers in the artificial-intelligence community. At each of the first three workshops on uncertainty in artificial intelligence, one or more researchers argued that the particular inference method used does not affect performance significantly, at least in the context of large real-world systems. In this paper, I present a formal evaluation of the performance of several inference methods that

---

[1]This work was supported by the NSF under Grant IRI-8703710, and by the NLM under Grant RO1LM04529.

confirms our early experience with Pathfinder and refutes the claim made at the workshops. Specifically, I show that the Bayesian approach yields performance superior to that obtained with the other approaches in the domain of lymph-node pathology.

2   The Domain

Artificial-intelligence researchers working on uncertain reasoning often complain that the merits of one inference method versus those of another are evaluated on the basis of only theoretical considerations. Another complaint is that evaluations of performance are limited to small or artificial domains. This study is designed to address both of these complaints. The Pathfinder program reasons about virtually *all* diseases that occur in a human lymph node (25 benign diseases, 9 Hodgkin's lymphomas, 18 non-Hodgkin's lymphomas, and 10 metastatic diseases). In addition, the program includes an exhaustive list of clues or features that can be used to help determine a diagnosis. Over 100 morphologic features or patterns within a lymph node that can be easily recognized under a microscope are represented. The program also contains over 30 features reflecting clinical, laboratory, immunological, and molecular biological information that is useful in diagnosis.

Because this study focuses on only one domain, these results should not be extrapolated to other domains. Researchers interested in learning more about the relative merits of different inference methods should begin similar investigations in other domains.

3   The Inference Methods

The three inference methods evaluated are (1) a special case of Bayes' theorem, (2) an approach related to the parallel combination function in the certainty-factor (CF) model [1], and (3) a method inspired by the Dempster–Shafer theory of belief [2]. All three approaches take a set of observations and produce a belief distribution over disease hypotheses based on the same expert probability assessments. However, the second and third approaches deviate significantly from probabilistic reasoning.

All three approaches share the assumption that the hypotheses represented by the system are mutually exclusive and exhaustive. Furthermore, all three approaches assume that the diagnostic features are, in some sense, independent. The exact nature of independence varies from method to method and is discussed in detail in a later section. During the development of Pathfinder, the expert and I eliminated obvious dependencies among features by clustering highly dependent features. For example, a pattern called *necrosis* is seen in many lymph-node diseases. The size of necrosis (the percent area of lymph node showing this pattern) and the distribution of necrosis are two strongly interrelated features, and both are important for diagnosis. To remove the dependency, we created a single feature "necrosis size and distribution" that had the mutually exclusive and exhaustive values "nonextensive and focal," "nonextensive and multifocal," "extensive and focal," and "extensive and multifocal." We created these values by taking the cross-product of the values for individual features pertaining to necrosis size and necrosis distribution.

Before describing the inference methods, I shall introduce some definitions and notation. Each mutually exclusive and exhaustive disease hypothesis is denoted by the symbol d with a subscript—for example, d_j. Similarly, the symbol f_k refers to the kth feature in the knowledge base. Each feature is associated with a set of mutually exclusive and exhaustive *values*. The ith value of the kth feature is denoted by v_{ki}. A given feature and a value for that feature together constitute an *observation*. The term $f_k v_{ki}$ denotes an observation of the ith value for the kth feature. For the sake of brevity, a set of observations $f_1 v_{1i} \ldots f_n v_{ni}$ will be denoted by the symbol ξ. Finally, two assumptions of conditional independence associated with several of the inference procedures are introduced here for reference. The first assumption is that evidence is conditionally independent on disease hypotheses. Formally, the assumption is that, for any combination of observations $f_1 v_{1i} \ldots f_n v_{ni}$,

$$p(f_1 v_{1i} \ldots f_n v_{ni} | d_j) = p(f_1 v_{1i} | d_j) \ldots p(f_n v_{ni} | d_j) \tag{1}$$

The second assumption is that evidence is conditionally independent on the *negation* of the hypothesis. Specifically, for any combination of observations $f_1 v_{1i} \ldots f_n v_{ni}$,

$$p(f_1 v_{1i} \ldots f_n v_{ni} | \overline{d_j}) = p(f_1 v_{1i} | \overline{d_j}) \ldots p(f_n v_{ni} | \overline{d_j}) \tag{2}$$

Both Equations 1 and 2 apply to each disease hypothesis d_j.

3.1 Simple Bayes Method

The first inference method is Bayes' theorem under the assumption that features are conditionally independent on the disease hypotheses (Equation 1). In particular, if observations $\xi = f_1 v_{1i} \ldots f_n v_{ni}$ are made, the probability of the jth disease is given by

$$p(d_j | \xi) = \frac{p(d_j) p(f_1 v_{1i} | d_j) \ldots p(f_n v_{ni} | d_j)}{\sum_j p(d_j) p(f_1 v_{1i} | d_j) \ldots p(f_n v_{ni} | d_j)} \tag{3}$$

This inference procedure will be called the *simple Bayes method* to emphasize the conditional independence assumptions it embodies. Note that the only assessments required by this approach are the probabilities $p(f_k v_{ki} | d_j)$ for each combination of f_k, v_{ki}, and d_j, and the prior probabilities $p(d_j)$ for each disease. The other two inference methods require the same assessments.

3.2 Odds–Likelihood Method

The second inference method begins with a form of Bayes' theorem under the assumption that evidence is conditionally independent both on the hypotheses and on the negation of the hypotheses (Equations 1 and 2). Under these assumptions, Bayes' theorem for the jth disease given observations ξ can be written

$$\frac{p(d_j | \xi)}{p(\overline{d_j} | \xi)} = \frac{p(d_j)}{p(\overline{d_j})} \frac{p(f_1 v_{1i} | d_j)}{p(f_1 v_{1i} | \overline{d_j})} \cdots \frac{p(f_n v_{ni} | d_n)}{p(f_n v_{ni} | \overline{d_n})} \tag{4}$$

The ratio on the left-hand side and the first ratio on the right-hand side of Equation 4 are the *posterior* and *prior* odds of d_j, respectively. In general, the *odds* of an event is just a simple monotonic transformation of the probability of the event, given by

$$O = \frac{p}{1 - p}$$

The remaining terms of Equation 4 are called *likelihood ratios*. As can be seen from Equation 4, the likelihood ratio $p(f_k v_{ki} | d_j) / p(f_k v_{ki} | \overline{d_j})$ is a measure of the degree to which observing feature value $f_k v_{ki}$ updates or changes the degree of belief in disease hypothesis d_j.

In the version of this inference method evaluated in this paper, the likelihood ratios are not assessed directly. Instead, the numerator, $p(f_k v_{ki}|d_j)$ is assessed directly, and the denominator, $p(f_k v_{ki}|\overline{d_j})$, is computed using

$$p(f_k v_{ki}|\overline{d_j}) = \frac{p(f_k v_{ki}) - p(f_k v_{ki}|d_j)p(d_j)}{p(f_k v_{ki})}$$

where

$$p(f_k v_{ki}) = \sum_j p(f_k v_{ki}|d_j)p(d_j)$$

Thus, this inference method makes use of exactly the same assessments as does the simple Bayes approach. The likelihood ratios were not assessed directly because our expert found that they were much more difficult to assess than were conditional probabilities $p(f_k v_{ki}|d_j)$. It would be interesting to conduct a comparison similar to the one described in this paper using an expert who is willing to assess likelihood ratios directly.

Johnson [3] has demonstrated that the conditional-independence assumptions embodied in Equation 4 typically are not compatible with the updating of n mutually exclusive and exhaustive hypotheses, when n is greater than two. In particular, he has shown that consistently updating more than two mutually exclusive and exhaustive hypotheses under the conditional-independence assumptions used to derive Equation 4 is possible only when each hypothesis is updated by at most one observation.

In Pathfinder, this highly restrictive condition required for consistent updating is not met. Each disease hypothesis is updated by many observations in the knowledge base. As a result, Equation 4 produces an inconsistent probability distribution over diseases in which the posterior probabilities of disease do not sum to 1. To circumvent this problem, the disease probabilities are renormalized after Equation 4 is applied to the evidence. This completes the description of the second approach, which I call the *odds–likelihood method*.

The odds–likelihood approach is closely related to the parallel combination function used in the CF model. In fact, I showed that the multiplicative combination of likelihood ratios seen in Equation 4 maps exactly to the parallel combination function when a certainty factor is identified with a simple monotonic transformation of the likelihood ratio [4]. Moreover, in MYCIN—the expert system for which the CF model was designed—certainty factors of mutually exclusive and exhaustive sets of hypotheses are renormalized to sum to unity [5]. This form of renormalization does not correspond directly to the renormalization of probabilities in the second inference method, but it is similar in spirit.

3.3 Naive Dempster–Shafer Method

The third inference method has an interesting history. It was developed by researchers, including myself, who at the time knew little about methods for uncertain reasoning. As the method was primarily motivated by the Dempster–Shafer theory of belief, I call it the *naive Dempster–Shafer method*. The approach is fraught with difficulties, some of which will be addressed in Section 8. Perhaps the exposition will serve as a warning to the artificial-intelligence community regarding what can happen when a group of novice researchers attempts to cope with the conflicting uncertainty literature.

As members of a medical information-science group, we were familiar with the inference method used by INTERNIST-1, an expert system for the diagnosis of disease across all diseases in internal medicine [6]. The inference procedure used by INTERNIST-1 incorporates two measures of uncertainty, an *evoking strength* and a *frequency*. An evoking strength for disease d_j and observation $f_k v_{ki}$, denoted $ES(d_j, f_k v_{ki})$, represents the degree to which the observation "evokes" or "confirms" the disease [6]. In contrast, a frequency for disease d_j and observation $f_k v_{ki}$, denoted $FQ(d_j, f_k v_{ki})$, represents the "likelihood" of an observation given the disease [6].

Because we initially had planned to use the INTERNIST-1 inference procedure, our expert assessed both an evoking strength and a frequency (on a continuous scale from 0 to 1) for each disease–observation pair. Before we began programming the procedure, however, several members of our group argued that a more principled approach should be used to combine the measures of confirmation we had assessed. In particular, they argued that the Dempster–Shafer theory of belief should be used to combine evoking strengths.

After exploring of the Dempster–Shafer theory, we decided to construct a separate frame of discernment, $\theta_j = \{d_j, \overline{d_j}\}$, for each disease hypothesis d_j. In this framework, the evoking strength for a disease–observation pair is interpreted as a mass assignment to the singleton disease hypothesis:

$$m_{f_k v_{ki}}(\{d_j\}) = ES(d_j, f_k v_{ki}) \tag{5}$$

The remainder of the mass, $1 - ES(d_j, f_k v_{ki})$, is assigned to θ. Mass assignments of this form follow the approach taken by Barnett [7]. With this interpretation, Dempster's rule of combination can be used to determine the mass assigned to the singleton hypothesis $\{d_j\}$, given observations ξ. In particular, Barnett showed that

$$m_\xi(\{d_j\}) = 1 - \prod_k (1 - m_{f_k v_{ki}}(\{d_j\})) \tag{6}$$

In this framework of simple belief functions, the mass assigned to the singleton hypothesis $\{d_j\}$ is equal to the belief in d_j, denoted $Bel(\{d_j\})$. Thus, combining Equations 5 and 6, we can compute the belief in disease d_j given observations ξ, using

$$Bel_\xi(\{d_j\}) = 1 - \prod_k (1 - ES(d_j, f_k v_{ki})) \tag{7}$$

This inference method produces a number between 0 and 1 for each disease hypothesis.

At first, we ignored the frequencies provided by our expert. However, our expert kept insisting that his assessments of frequency were much more reliable than were his assessments of evoking strength. This led us to study the INTERNIST-1 inference method more carefully. It became clear to us and to our expert that the assessed evoking strengths were closely related to the posterior probability of disease given an observation. Also, it became apparent that the assessed frequencies corresponded to the probability of an observation given a disease. Thus, we discarded the directly assessed evoking strengths and replaced them with the calculated values

$$\begin{aligned} ES(d_j, f_k v_{ki}) &= p(d_j | f_k v_{ki}) \\ &= \frac{p(d_j) p(f_k v_{ki} | d_j)}{\sum_j p(d_j) p(f_k v_{ki} | d_j)} \end{aligned} \tag{8}$$

where each probability assessment $p(f_k v_{ki} | d_j)$ is given by the frequency $FQ(d_j, f_k v_{ki})$. Equation 8 follows from Bayes' theorem and the assumption that diseases are mutually exclusive.

Equations 7 and 8 together provide a method for computing the posterior degree of belief in each disease hypothesis from the prior probabilities of disease, d_j, and the probabilities of an observation given disease, $p(f_k v_{ki} | d_j)$. These are the same assessments that are required

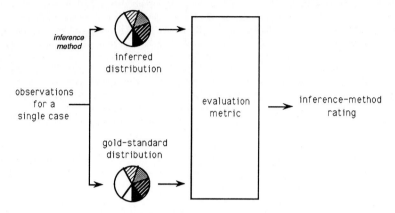

Figure 1: A schematic of the evaluation procedure.

The observed features for a given case are presented to an inference method. Based on the observations, the inference method produces an inferred distribution (represented by the shaded probability wheel at the top of the figure). In addition, a gold-standard distribution is determined from the same observations. An evaluation metric takes the two distributions and produces a scalar rating that reflects differences between them.

by the two approaches described previously. Note that the resulting belief distribution rarely sums to unity. The lack of normalization is not a problem conceptually, because the evaluation metrics used in the experimental comparison do not require probabilistic interpretations for the distributions. Nonetheless, the distributions produced by this inference method are renormalized to 1, so that, during the evaluation process, the expert is not able to recognize them immediately as being nonprobabilistic.

Like the odds–likelihood approach, the naive Dempster–Shafer method is related to parallel combination in the CF model. In fact, Equation 6 is exactly the parallel combination function for positive or confirming evidence if certainty factors are identified with singleton mass assignments.

4 The Evaluation Procedure

The procedure for evaluating an inference method is outlined in Figure 1. First, observations describing a biopsy of a patient's lymph nodes are presented to the inference method. Given these observations, the inference method produces an *inferred* probability distribution. The same observations also determine a *gold-standard* probability distribution, which represents the *true* distribution (see the following subsection). Then, an evaluation metric compares the inferred and gold-standard distributions and produces a scalar rating that reflects differences between the two distributions.

4.1   Gold-Standard Distributions

One of the most difficult tasks associated with this evaluation was the development a reasonable procedure for constructing gold-standard probability distributions. In a preliminary evaluation [8], we constructed the gold-standard distribution from the *true* disease. That is, we assigned a probability of 1.0 to the established diagnosis. In pathology, the disease that is manifesting in a lymph node is determined (1) by an expert pathologist examining tissue sections under a microscope; (2) by expensive immunology, molecular biology, or cell-kinetics tests; (3) through observations of the time course of a patient's illness; or (4) by a combination of these approaches.

There are two problems with this gold standard. First, the construction ignores the distinction between a good *decision* and a good *outcome*. For example, suppose the observations for a case suggest—say, through statistical data—that there is a 0.7 chance of Hodgkin's disease and a 0.3 chance of mononucleosis. Furthermore, suppose that mononucleosis is the true disease (not an unlikely event). In such a situation, an inference method that produces this distribution receives (unjustly) a lower rating than a distribution that produces a higher chance of mononucleosis. This difficulty is not serious, however. In general, we can diminish the differences between good decisions and good outcomes by considering a large number of cases.

A second, more serious problem with this construction stems from details of how microscopic observations are made by experts and nonexperts. In my experience, when experts examine such biopsies, they typically see many features at once and come to a diagnosis immediately. When asked to identify specific features that appear in the biopsy, these pathologists report mostly features that confirms their diagnosis. Moreover, it is difficult to train these experts to do otherwise, and essentially impossible to determine whether or not such training is successful. Thus, when experts are used to identify features, the three inference methods tend to perform well, and, in practice, it becomes impossible to identify significant differences from an experimental comparison. On the other hand, pathologists who do not specialize in the lymph-node domain misrecognize or fail to recognize some of features associated with diagnosis. It is unreasonable to compare the distributions produced by the inference methods, derived from one set of observations, with the true disease, derived from a different set of observations. In fact, in a separate study, I showed that errors in diagnosis resulting from the misrecognition and lack of recognition of features by a nonexpert were sufficient to obscure completely the differences between inference methods, when the true diagnosis was used as the gold standard [9].

As a consequence of these problems with the use of the true disease as the gold standard, we use the two procedures for constructing the gold-standard distributions shown in Figure 2. In one method (Figure 2a), a pathologist (other than our expert) reports features for a particular case. Then our expert is shown only these features, and is asked to assess a probability distribution over diseases. A difficulty with this procedure for constructing a gold standard is that people, including experts, often make mistakes when reasoning under uncertainty, in the sense that they violate highly desired principles of reasoning [10]. Indeed, the terms *descriptive* and *normative* often are used to distinguish how individuals actually reason from how they should reason. Thus, in a second approach (Figure 2b), the expert is shown both the features for the case and the distributions produced by each of the three inference methods. Of course, our expert is unlikely to appreciate his errors in reasoning, and to adjust his assessments accordingly, simply by observing the output of the inference methods. A decision analyst would argue, for example, that decision makers must iterate several times through the decision-analysis cycle—consisting of formulation, inference, and appraisal—before they can have any

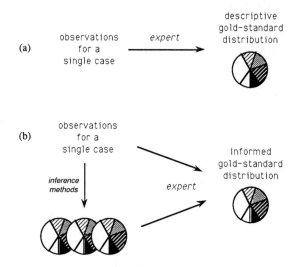

Figure 2: The construction of the gold-standard distributions.

Two gold-standards are used in the evaluation. (a) Given only the list of observations reported by another pathologist, the expert assesses the descriptive gold-standard probability distribution. (b) Given this same list of observations and the probability distributions generated by the three inference methods, the expert assesses the informed gold-standard probability distribution.

assurance that they are making good decisions. Such detailed iterations, however, are not possible in this experimental comparison because the principles of reasoning underlying each approach are not identical.[2] Developing a gold standard corresponding to a good decision under the principles associated with one of the inference methods would bias the results in favor of that inference method. We allow the expert to see the distributions generated by each approach, only so that gross errors in reasoning (such as lack of attention to rare diseases) will be reduced. I call the gold standards in Figures 2(a) and 2(b) the *descriptive* and *informed* gold standards, respectively.

4.2 A Decision-Theoretic Evaluation Metric

Two evaluation metrics are used to compare the inference methods. The one that we examine in this section is based on decision theory. Several researchers have suggested that decision-theoretic metrics be used to evaluate diagnostic computer systems [11,12,13]; some have actually employed such metrics in evaluations [14,15,16].

The fundamental notion underlying the decision-theoretic approach is that some errors in diagnosis are more serious than others are. For example, if a patient has a viral infection and is incorrectly diagnosed as having cat-scratch disease—a disease caused by an organism that is killed with antibiotics—the consequences are not severe. In fact, the only nonnegligible consequence is that the patient will take antibiotics unnecessarily for several weeks. If, however,

---

[2]In fact, the principles underlying the odds–likelihood and naive Dempster–Shafer approaches are unclear to me.

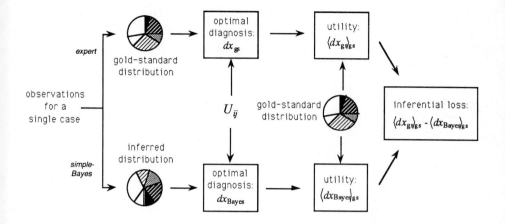

Figure 3: A decision-theoretic evaluation procedure for the simple Bayes method.

First, based on the features reported, the expert assesses a gold-standard distribution, and the simple Bayes method produces an inferred distribution. Then, we determine the optimal diagnosis dx_{gs} by identifying the disease that maximizes the expected utility of the patient. Similarly, we determine the optimal diagnosis associated with the inferred distribution, dx_{Bayes}. We then determine the expected utility of the two diagnoses with respect to the gold-standard distribution. Finally, the decrease in utility associated with the simple Bayes method, called the inferential loss, is computed.

a patient has Hodgkin's disease and is incorrectly diagnosed as having an insignificant benign disease such as a viral infection, the consequences are often lethal. If the diagnosis had been made correctly, the patient would have immediately undergone radio- and chemotherapy, with a 90-percent chance of a cure. If the patient is diagnosed incorrectly, however, and thus is not treated, it will progress. By the time major symptoms of the disease appear and the patient once again seeks help, the cure rate with appropriate treatment will have dropped to less than 20 percent.

A decision-theoretic approach to evaluation recognizes such variation in the consequences of misdiagnosis. The significance of each possible misdiagnosis is assessed separately. More specifically, for each combination of d_i and d_j, a decision maker is asked, "How desirable is the situation in which you have disease d_i and are diagnosed as having disease d_j?" The disease d_j is called the *diagnosis* and the preference assessed is called the *diagnostic utility*, denoted U_{ij}. Details of the utility-assessment procedure are discussed in Section 5.

Once the diagnostic utilities are assessed, it is a straightforward task to evaluate each of the inference methods relative to a gold standard. The procedure for evaluating the simple Bayes inference method is shown in Figure 3. First, observations for a case are presented to the expert, who then produces a gold-standard distribution (either descriptive or informed). In addition, the simple Bayes method produces an inferred distribution from the same observations.

Then, we determine the optimal diagnoses associated with the gold-standard and inferred distributions, denoted dx_{gs} and dx_{Bayes}, respectively, by applying the principle of maximum expected utility (MEU). In particular, the optimal diagnosis associated with a distribution is the diagnosis that maximizes the expected utility of the patient, given that distribution. Formally,

$$dx_{\text{gs}} = \text{argmax}_j \left[\sum_i p_{\text{gs}}(d_i) \, U_{ij} \right]$$

$$dx_{\text{Bayes}} = \text{argmax}_j \left[\sum_i p_{\text{Bayes}}(d_i) \, U_{ij} \right]$$

where $p_{\text{gs}}(d_i)$ and $p_{\text{Bayes}}(d_i)$ represent the probability of the the ith disease under the gold-standard and simple Bayes probability distributions.

Next, we compute a score for each of the two distributions. In a decision-theoretic framework, the natural choice for a score is the *expected utility* of a diagnosis. In computing expected utility, we use the gold-standard distribution, because this distribution presumably reflects the actual beliefs of the expert. Thus, we compute

$$< dx_{\text{gs}} >_{\text{gs}} = \sum_i p_{\text{gs}}(d_i) \, U_{i,dx_{\text{gs}}}$$

$$< dx_{\text{Bayes}} >_{\text{gs}} = \sum_i p_{\text{gs}}(d_i) \, U_{i,dx_{\text{Bayes}}}$$

Finally, we compute a decision-theoretic rating for the simple Bayes method that reflects the loss in utility associated with the use of that method. We call this quantity *inferential loss* (IL). Several functions of $< dx_{\text{gs}} >_{\text{gs}}$ and $< dx_{\text{Bayes}} >_{\text{gs}}$ are reasonable candidates for inferential loss. In this paper, we compute the loss as the simple difference between these two utilities. That is,

$$\text{IL} = < dx_{\text{gs}} >_{\text{gs}} - < dx_{\text{Bayes}} >_{\text{gs}}$$

By construction, inferential loss is always a nonnegative quantity. If both the gold-standard and simple Bayes distributions imply the same optimal diagnosis, then the inferential loss is zero, a perfect score.

We modify this procedure somewhat to evaluate the odds–likelihood and naive Dempster–Shafer inference methods. Specifically, we cannot interpret the degrees of belief produced by these methods as probabilities. Thus, we do not use the principle of maximum expected utility to compute the optimal diagnosis associated with a distribution produced by these methods. Instead, we determine the optimal diagnosis by identifying the disease with the highest degree of belief. This simple rule for decision making has been used in both Bayesian and nonBayesian systems [17,18]. Except for this modification, the computation of inferential loss for the odds–likelihood and naive Dempster–Shafer methods is the same as the computation for the simple Bayes method. To compare this simple decision rule with the principle of maximum expected utility, we compute the inferential losses associated with both rules, given distributions produced by the simple Bayes method. Thus, in total, four types of inferential loss are computed for each patient case: the inferential loss for the simple Bayes method using the MEU principle to determine an optimal diagnosis, and the inferential losses for the three inference methods using the simpler decision rule.

4.3 An Expert-Rating Evaluation Metric

In addition to the decision-theoretic approach, an expert-rating method is used to compare the inference methods. For each probability distribution, the expert is asked, "On a scale from zero to ten—zero being unacceptable and ten being perfect—how accurately does the distribution reflect your beliefs?" The ratings given by the expert are compared using standard statistical techniques. Note that gold standards do not need to be elicited explicitly in this approach. Other researchers have described approaches similar to this one for evaluating medical expert systems (see, for example [19]).

5 Utility Assessment

In this section, several important issues related to the assessment of diagnostic utilities are addressed, and details of the procedure for assessment are described.

An important consideration in the assessment of diagnostic utilities is that preferences will vary from one decision maker to another. For example, the diagnostic utilities of a decision maker (the patient) faced with the results of a lymph-node biopsy are likely to be influenced by the person's age, gender, and state of health. Consequently, the inferential losses computed in this evaluation are meaningful to an individual only to the degree that the diagnostic utilities used in the evaluation match the diagnostic utilities of that individual.

For this experimental comparison, the utilities of the expert on the Pathfinder project were used. The expert was chosen for two practical reasons. First, he was reasonably familiar with many of the ramifications of correct and incorrect diagnosis. Second, I had established a good working relationship with him during the construction of Pathfinder. The expert, because he is an expert, however, had biases that made his initial preferences deviate from those of a typical patient. For example, many sets of diseases of the lymph node currently have identical treatments and prognoses. Nonetheless, experts like to distinguish diseases within each of these sets, because doing so allows research in new treatments to progress. That is, experts often consider the value of their efforts to future patients. In addition, experts generally suffer professional embarrassment when their diagnoses are incorrect. Also, experts are concerned about the legal liability associated with misdiagnosis. In an effort to remove these biases, I asked the the expert to ignore specifically these attributes of utility. Further, I asked him to imagine that he himself had a particular disease, and to assess the diagnostic utilities accordingly.

Another important consideration in almost any medical decision problem is the wide range of severities associated with outcomes. As mentioned previously, one misdiagnosis might lead to inappropriate antibiotic therapy, whereas another might lead to almost certain death. How can preferences across such a wide range be measured in common terms? Early attempts to resolve this question were fraught with paradoxes. For example, in a linear willingness-to-pay approach, a decision maker might be asked, "How much would you have to be paid in order to accept a one in ten-thousand chance of death?" If the decision maker answered, say, $1000, then the approach would dictate that he would be willing to be killed for $10 million. This inference is absurd.

Recently, Howard has constructed an approach that avoids many of the paradoxes of earlier models [20]. Like several of its predecessors, the model deals with determining what an individual is willing to pay to avoid a given chance of death, and what he is willing to be paid to assume a given chance of death. Also, like many of its predecessors, Howard's model shows that, for small risks of death (typically, $p < 0.001$), the amount someone is willing to pay to avoid, or is willing to be paid to assume, such a risk is linear in p. That is, for small risks of death, an individual acts as would an expected-value decision maker with a finite value attached to his life. For significant risks of death, however, the model deviates strongly from linearity. For example, the model shows that there is a maximum probability of death, beyond which an individual will accept no amount of money to risk that chance of death. Most people find this result to be intuitive.[3]

In this paper, the details of the model will not be presented; for a discussion of the approach see [20]. Here, we need to assume only that willingness to buy or sell *small* risks of death is linear in the probability of death. Given this assumption, preferences for minor to major outcomes can be measured in a common unit, *the probability of immediate, painless death that a person is willing to accept to avoid a given outcome and to be once again healthy.* The desirability of major outcomes can be assessed directly in these terms. For example, a decision maker might be asked, "If you have Hodgkin's disease and have been incorrectly diagnosed as having a viral infection, what probability of immediate, painless death would you be willing to accept to avoid the illness and incorrect diagnosis, and to be once again healthy?" At the other end of the spectrum, the desirability of minor outcomes can be assessed by willingness-to-pay questions, and can be translated, via the linearity result, to the common unit of measurement. For example, a decision maker might be asked, "How much would you be willing to pay to avoid taking antibiotics for two weeks?" If he answered $100, and if his small-risk value of life were $20 million, then the answer could be translated to a utility of a 5 in 1,000,000 chance of death.

Thus, an important task in assessing the U_{ij} is the determination of the decision maker's small-risk value of life. Howard proposes a model by which this value can be computed from other assessments [20]. A simple version of the model requires a decision maker to trade off the amount of resources he consumes during his lifetime and the length of his lifetime, to characterize his ability to turn present cash into future income (summarized, for example, by an interest rate), and to establish his attitude toward risk. However, our expert did not find it difficult to assess the small-risk value of life directly.[4] When asked what dollar amount he would be willing to pay to avoid chances of death ranging from 1 in 20 to 1 in 1000, he was consistent with the linear model to within a factor of 2, with a median small-risk value of life equal to $20 million.

Note that, with this utility model, the inferential losses computed for the inference methods will have units "probability of death." In many cases, we shall see that the losses are small in these units (on the order of 0.001). Consequently, it is useful to define a *micromort*, a 1 in 1 million chance of death. In these units, for example, a decision maker with a small-risk value of life of $20 million should be willing to buy and sell risks of death at the rate of $20 per micromort. This unit of measurement is also useful because it helps to emphasize that the linear relationship between risk of death and willingness to pay holds for only small probabilities of death.

Another important consideration is the complexity of the utility-assessment procedure. There are 51 diseases represented in Pathfinder. The direct measurement of the U_{ij} therefore requires $51^2 = 2601$ assessments. Clearly, the measurement process would be tedious. Thus, several steps were taken to reduce the complexity of the task. First, the expert was asked to establish sets of disease hypotheses that have identical treatments and prognoses. An example of such a set is the collection of nine types of Hodgkin's diseases represented in Pathfinder. Patients with

---

[3] The result makes several assumptions, such as the decision maker is not suicidal and is not concerned about how his legacy will affect other people.

[4] Howard also has observed that the small-risk value of life can be assessed directly.

any of the nine types receive the same treatment and have the same prognosis.[5] The expert identified 26 such "equivalence classes," reducing the number of direct utility assessments required to $26^2 = 676$.

Next, the expert was asked to order the utilities U_{ii}— he was asked to order the desirability of having each disease and being diagnosed correctly. After he had completed this ranking, he was asked to assess each U_{ii} in the manner described previously. Note that the ordering of the U_{ii} was modified significantly during this process. About halfway through the procedure, the expert exclaimed, "The dollar is forcing me to think very carefully!" It would be interesting to determine whether most people respond in this way, as this observation tends to disconfirm one of the tenets of qualitative reasoning.

Finally, the off-diagonal utilities were assessed. For each disease, the expert was asked to quantify the desirability of having the disease and being diagnosed as having a different disease. First, he identified the most similar preexisting assessment. It was then a simple matter to identify the differences between the current assessment and the preexisting assessment, and to modify the utility appropriately. For example, given a patient with sinus hyperplasia, the only difference between him being diagnosed correctly and him being diagnosed with cat-scratch disease is that, in the latter case, the patient would take unnecessary antibiotics for several weeks. The expert said that he would be willing to pay \$100 to avoid taking the antibiotics unnecessarily, so this value (converted to micromorts) was subtracted from the utility of being correctly diagnosed with sinus hyperplasia.

6   Details of the Experiment

Whenever possible, the conditions of the experimental comparison were arranged to mimic the conditions under which Pathfinder would be used in clinical practice. For example, Pathfinder is expected to be used by community hospital pathologists to assist them in diagnosing challenging lymph-node cases. Currently, when a community hospital pathologist faces a difficult case, he refers the case to an expert, such as the expert on the Pathfinder project. Therefore, the cases selected for this experiment were chosen from a library of 3000 cases referred to our expert from community pathologists. Only cases diagnosed more than 4 months prior to the experiment were selected to decrease the chance that the memory of the expert would bias the results.

Twenty-six cases were selected at random from the expert's referral library such that no two diagnoses were the same. Repeat diagnoses were not allowed so that the inference methods would be evaluated over a larger portion of the lymph-node knowledge base. To account for the fact that some diseases are much more likely to occur than are others, we weighted the ratings derived from the metrics for each case by the relative likelihood of occurrence of the case. We computed the relative likelihoods by normalizing the prior probabilities (provided by the expert) of the true diagnosis of each case such that the latter summed to 1.

Although the cases were selected at random, a postexperiment analysis showed that the cases were more challenging than a set of average referral cases would be. The expert reported that 50 percent of the cases contained many more technical imperfections (such as tears and poor preservation) than is usual. He also thought that 70 percent of the cases were more difficult

---

[5] Prognosis for these nine types of Hodgkin's disease is determined by the clinical stage, not by the specific type of disease.

to diagnose than is the average case. The deviation from normal probably occurred because the case-selection process favored the inclusion of cases with rare diagnoses.

A pathology resident entered the observations for each case into a computer database after examining lymph-node biopsies through a microscope. The manner in which features were selected for identification deviated from the approach typically used in Pathfinder. Specifically, a pathologist usually enters only a few salient features and then receives recommendations from Pathfinder about what additional features are most useful for narrowing the diagnostic contenders. The pathologist then provides values for one or more of these recommended features, and the process cycles. To avoid confounding the performance of the inference methods with that of the feature-recommendation strategies, I asked the resident to enter all "salient features observed." At no time was the resident allowed to see the system's recommendations regarding what features should be evaluated.

Once features values had been identified for each case, they were presented to the three inference methods, producing three belief distributions. The expert was then given two evaluation sheets for each case. The first sheet included a list of the observations identified by the resident, as well as list of all the disease hypotheses represented in Pathfinder. The expert was asked to assign a probability distribution to the diseases based on the observations given. The descriptive gold standard was derived from this distribution. The second sheet was identical to the first, except that it included the distributions produced by the three inference methods. The distributions were displayed in columns in a random order for each case. The expert was asked to rate each belief distribution using the 0-to-10 scale described earlier, and again to assign a probability distribution to the diseases. He was allowed to refer to his first probability distribution during the second assignment. The informed gold standard was derived from this second distribution.

In two of the 26 cases, the simple Bayes and odds–likelihood methods produced inconsistent distributions in which all hypotheses were assigned a belief of 0. Later, we determined that the nonexpert had misidentified features in these cases. Consequently, these two cases were removed from the study.

7   Results

Average values for the four types of inferential loss described previously are shown in Table 1. "Simple Bayes MEU" refers to the procedure of selecting the disease that maximizes utility under the simple Bayes distribution. "Simple Bayes," "Odds–likelihood," and "Dempster–Shafer" refer to the procedures of selecting the most likely diseases under the simple Bayes, odds–likelihood, and Dempster–Shafer distributions, respectively. All losses are computed with respect to the informed gold-standard distribution.

The standard deviations of these losses are also given the table. Note that the standard deviations are quite large relative to the means. The reason for such large variances is easily appreciated. For each diagnostic approach, the diagnosis determined by the approach is identical to the diagnosis determined by the gold standard in many of the 24 cases. In particular, the simple Bayes MEU, simple Bayes, and odds–likelihood approaches select the gold-standard diagnosis in 17 of 24 cases. The naive Dempster–Shafer approach selects the gold-standard diagnosis in 12 of 24 cases. In these cases, the inferential loss associated with the inference methods is 0. In the remaining cases, the approaches select diagnoses that differ from the gold standard. These nonoptimal diagnoses are often associated with expected utilities that

Method	Inferential Loss (micromorts)	
	mean	sd
Simple Bayes MEU	811	4079
Simple Bayes	831	4078
Odds–likelihood	831	4078
Naive Dempster–Shafer	10,587	19,101

Table 1: Decision-theoretic inferential loss for the inference methods.

Method	Expert ratings (0 to 10)	
	mean	sd
Simple Bayes	8.52	1.17
Odds–likelihood	7.33	1.95
Naive Dempster–Shafer	0.03	0.17

Table 2: Expert ratings of the inference methods.

are significantly lower than is the expected utility associated with the gold-standard diagnosis. Thus, inferential losses fluctuate from 0 in many cases to large values in others.

Although the standard deviations are high, a Monte Carlo permutation test indicates that the performance of the naive Dempster–Shafer approach is significantly inferior to that of the other methods (achieved significance level = 0.004). No other significant difference exists among the other methods.

The expert ratings (0–to–10 scale) for each inference method are shown in Table 2. Because the ratings apply only to the belief distributions derived by each method, there is no distinction between the simple Bayes MEU and simple Bayes procedures. Using the expert-rating metric, we detect another significant difference. In particular, a Wilcoxon two-sample rank test shows that the simple Bayes inference procedure performs significantly better than does the odds–likelihood approach (achieved significance level = 0.07).

The inferential loss associated with descriptive gold standard relative to the informed gold standard was 84 micromorts, with a standard deviation of 1,273 micromorts. Thus, seeing the belief distributions generated by the inference methods, the expert did not change appreciably his opinion about the cases.

8 Discussion

Before we examine the results in detail, some general comments about the two evaluation metrics may be useful. An obvious advantage of the decision-theoretic approach over the expert-rating approach is that the results of the former are much more meaningful. For example, the difference between the simple Bayes and naive Dempster–Shafer ratings using the expert-rating metric is 8.5 on a scale from 0 to 10, and is deemed to be "significant" by a standard statistical test. The difference of approximately 10,000 micromorts between the two approaches as determined by the decision-theoretic metric, however, carries much more force; it implies that using the naive Dempster–Shafer approach instead of the simple Bayes approach is equivalent to assuming an additional one-in-100 risk of death!

A disadvantage of the decision-theoretic with respect to the expert-rating approach is that the results of the former have limited scope. Specifically, the differences among inference methods may be highly dependent on the assessments of diagnostic utility made by our expert. Furthermore, decision-theoretic comparisons of inference methods are likely to vary from one domain to another because there is room for wide variation in utility assessments among domains.

An advantage of the expert-rating metric over the decision-theoretic metric, as demonstrated in this experiment, is that the former can be much more sensitive to differences. For example, the decision-theoretic ratings of the simple Bayes and of the odds–likelihood methods are identical. In contrast, the expert-rating metric shows the two inference methods to be significantly different. High sensitivity is likely to be a property of the expert-rating approach across many domains. In a typical consulting session, an expert is hypersensitive to errors in diagnosis, whether or not such errors matter to a decision maker, because the integrity of the expert is on the line. It is likely that this hypersensitivity will carry over into expert ratings of diagnostic performance. Of course, the decision-theoretic metric can be modified to be more sensitive. Considerations of integrity or liability, for example, can be incorporated into the diagnostic utilities. Indeed, the fact that components of preference can be made explicit and are under the direct control of the expert is one advantage of the decision-theoretic approach.

Another advantage of the expert-rating metric is that it is less time consuming to implement. It took the expert approximately 20 hours, working with two people trained in decision-analytic techniques, to develop the utility model used in this evaluation. It took the expert less than 1 minute per case to rate the distributions produced by the three inference methods.

Overall, the two approaches are complementary. The expert-rating approach is useful for identifying differences in performance that may be important in *some* domain. The decision-theoretic metric reveals the degree of importance of such differences for a particular domain of interest. Note that information-theoretic metrics exist for measuring differences between probability distributions, such as relative entropy and the Brier score [21,22]. The advantages and disadvantages of the information-theoretic and expert-rating methods are similar with respect to the decision-theoretic approach, except that the information-theoretic methods require probabilistic interpretations for the distributions to be compared.

Given these considerations about the evaluation metrics, we can discuss differences in performance among the inference methods. In this experimental comparison, the method for selecting an optimal diagnosis with the highest decision-theoretic rank is simple Bayes MEU. The difference between the rank of this method and that of the gold standard is 811 micromorts. With the caveats described previously, this value can be seen to represent the maximum room for improvement in the knowledge base. Such improvements may include more careful assessments of probabilities in the knowledge base, and the representation of dependencies among features.

The difference in inferential loss between simple Bayes MEU and simple Bayes is only 20 micromorts and is not significant. This result suggests that, in the lymph-node domain, we gain little by using the more sophisticated decision rule. Three factors of this domain appear to be responsible for this observation. First, the resident pathologist recorded all salient features observed under the microscope for each case. Second, the lymph-node domain appears to be structured such that, when all salient features are entered, most of the probability mass will fall on one disease hypothesis or on a set of disease hypotheses within the same utility equivalence class. In 20 of the 24 cases, 95 percent of the probability mass falls on a set of diseases within the same equivalence class. Third, the structure of diagnostic utilities in the domain is such that a disease with small probability rarely will be chosen as the optimal diagnosis when the principle of maximum expected utility is used. In light of these factors, the relative value of decision rules should not be extrapolated to other domains without explicit justification.

Several interesting observations can be made about the relative performances of the simple Bayes and odds–likelihood inference methods. First, the expert-rating metric shows a significant difference between these methods, whereas the decision-theoretic metric shows no difference between them. This result is a clear example of the decreased sensitivity of the decision-theoretic approach to evaluation.

Second, the theoretical difference between the simple Bayes and odds–likelihood inference methods is that the former assumes evidence to be conditionally independent given the hypotheses, as shown in Equation 1, whereas the latter assumes evidence to be conditionally independent both given the hypotheses and given the negation of the hypotheses, as reflected in Equations 1 and 2. Thus, the decision-theoretic results suggest that the additional assumption of conditional independence given the negation of hypotheses is inconsequential in the lymph-node domain, but the expert-rating results suggest that the additional assumption may lead to significant degradation in performance in other domains.

Third, there is a regularity in the differences between the distributions produced by the two methods. Specifically, the simple Bayes distributions produced in this study are, with only one exception, more peaked. That is, the variance of these distributions are smaller than are those produced using the odds–likelihood approach. This difference can be traced to the additional assumption of conditional independence given the negation of hypotheses (Equation 2). To see this connection, we can consider a hypothetical example in which there are three mutually exclusive and exhaustive hypotheses—H_1, H_2, and H_3—that have equal prior probabilities. Suppose that there are many pieces of evidence relevant to these hypotheses such that each piece of evidence E_j has the same probability of occurrence for a given hypothesis. That is, $p(E_j|H_i) = p(E|H_i)$ for all E_j, and $i = 1, 2, 3$. Also suppose that the likelihoods have values such that

$$p(E|H_1) > p(E|H_2) > p(E|H_3)$$

$$\frac{p(E|H_1)}{p(E|\overline{H_1})} = \frac{2p(E|H_1)}{p(E|H_2) + p(E|H_3)} > 1$$

$$\frac{p(E|H_2)}{p(E|\overline{H_2})} = \frac{2p(E|H_2)}{p(E|H_1) + p(E|H_3)} > 1$$

$$\frac{p(E|H_3)}{p(E|\overline{H_3})} = \frac{2p(E|H_3)}{p(E|H_1) + p(E|H_2)} < 1$$

These constraints are satisfied easily (for example, $p(E|H_1) = 0.8$, $p(E|H_2) = 0.6$, and $p(E|H_3) = 0.2$). Under these conditions, evidence E is confirmatory for H_1, confirmatory to a lesser degree for H_2, and disconfirmatory for H_3. Using the simple Bayes inference procedure (Equation 3), we can show that, as the number of pieces of evidence grows, the posterior probability of H_1 tends to 1, whereas the posterior probabilities of both H_2 and H_3 tend to 0. However, using the odds–likelihood approach (Equation 4), where evidence is conditionally independent given the negation of hypotheses, we obtain a different result. In particular, we can show that, as the number of pieces of evidence grows, the posterior probabilities of both H_1 and H_2 tend to 1, whereas the posterior probability of H_3 tends to 0. In the odds–likelihood approach, these probabilities are renormalized, so the probabilities of H_1 and H_2 each approach 0.5. Thus, in this example, the odds–likelihood distribution is less peaked than is the simple Bayes distribution. In general, simple Bayes distributions will be more peaked, because this method tends to amplify differences in likelihoods, whereas the odds–likelihood method tends to wash out differences.

Unlike previous observations in this discussion, this one does not appear to be tied to the lymph-node domain. Provided a large body of evidence is reported such that the simple Bayes approach produces a sharp distribution, the odds–likelihood inference method should, in general, produce distributions that are less peaked. An important consequence of this phenomenon is that degradation in performance due to the incorrect assumption of conditional independence on the negation of hypotheses is likely to occur in other domains.

A final observation about the simple Bayes and odds–likelihood inference methods is that there is a regularity among the exceptional cases (5 of 24) in which distributions produced by odds–likelihood were preferred to the those produced by simple Bayes. Although obvious dependencies among features were captured by a clustering technique, subtle ones remained unrepresented in the lymph-node knowledge base. It seems that the failure to represent the more subtle dependencies led to decreased performance of the simple Bayes method relative to the odds–likelihood method. In particular, the incorrect assumption of conditional independence in the simple Bayes approach led to overcounting of evidential support. This overcounting, in turn, produced distributions that were overly peaked. In the odds–likelihood approach, evidence was also overcounted. However, it appears that such overcounting was partially compensated by the washout effect.

The performances of the odds–likelihood and naive Dempster–Shafer approaches are also interesting to compare. Both evaluation metrics revealed a significant difference between the two methods. There are two major theoretical differences between the inference procedures, one or both of which may be responsible for the differences in performance. First, from Equation 8, it is clear that each mass assignment in the inference method contains a component proportional to the prior probability of diseases. Thus, when the masses for many different observations are combined, the prior-probability components will be overcounted. Priors are not overcounted in the odds–likelihood approach. Second, due to the way mass is assigned in the naive Dempster–Shafer approach, disconfirmatory observations for disease hypotheses are not recognized. For example, if some observation completely rules out a disease hypothesis in the odds–likelihood method, the Dempster–Shafer mass for the disease–observation pair is 0. In the naive Dempster–Shafer inference method, a mass of 0 leaves the degree of belief of a hypothesis unchanged. Therefore, a hypothesis ruled out by an observation in the odds–likelihood approach is left with its degree of belief unchanged in the naive Dempster–Shafer approach. I suspect that this difference is more significant than is the overcounting of priors.

9 Future Work

The combination of the decision-theoretic and expert-rating approaches to performance evaluation provides useful insights about the inference process within the lymph-node domain. This same approach to evaluation can be used to probe many different components of Pathfinder. For example, we can use the decision-theoretic ratings to evaluate the cost-effectiveness of representing conditional dependencies among the features. Also, the Pathfinder research team has developed a set of procedures that recommends additional features for observation to the pathologist-user. The methods discussed in this paper should prove useful in evaluating the merits of these procedures. In addition, the Pathfinder group is currently exploring different techniques for constructing consensus knowledge bases that combine the beliefs of two or more experts. Again, the evaluation methods can be used to quantify the value of each approach. In yet another study, sensitivity to changes in the probabilities of the knowledge base could be examined. In general, we can use this approach to evaluate, in clear terms, a wide variety of issues related to the building of real-world expert systems.

Acknowledgments

I thank Eric Horvitz for his assistance with the assessment of the diagnostic utilities; Bharat Nathwani, the expert on the Pathfinder project, for his contributions to the construction and evaluation of the system; and Doyen Nguyen for her painstaking work to identify features under the microscope. Gregory Cooper, Lyn Dupre, Eric Horvitz, and Edward Shortliffe provided useful comments on earlier drafts of this manuscript.

References

[1] E.H. Shortliffe and B.G. Buchanan. A model of inexact reasoning in medicine. *Mathematical Biosciences*, 23:351–379, 1975.

[2] G. Shafer. *A Mathematical Theory of Evidence*. Princeton University Press, Princeton, NJ, 1976.

[3] R. Johnson. Independence and Bayesian updating methods. In L.N. Kanal and J.F. Lemmer, editors, *Uncertainty in Artificial Intelligence*, pages 197–202. North Holland, New York, 1986.

[4] D.E. Heckerman. Probabilistic interpretations for MYCIN's certainty factors. In L.N. Kanal and J.F. Lemmer, editors, *Uncertainty in Artificial Intelligence*, pages 167–196. North Holland, New York, 1986.

[5] E.H. Shortliffe. *MYCIN: A Rule-Based Computer Program for Advising Physicians Regarding Antimicrobial Therapy Selection*. PhD thesis, Stanford Artificial Intelligence Laboratory, Stanford, CA, October 1974.

[6] R.A. Miller, E.P. Pople, and J.D. Myers. INTERNIST-1: An experimental computer-based diagnostic consultant for general internal medicine. *New England Journal of Medicine*, 307:476–486, 1982.

[7] J. A. Barnett. Computational methods for a mathematical theory of evidence. In *Proceedings of the Seventh IJCAI*, pages 868–875. International Joint Conferences on Artificial Intelligence, 1981.

[8] D.E. Heckerman, E.J. Horvitz, and B.N. Nathwani. Pathfinder research directions. Technical Report KSL-89-64, Medical Computer Science Group, Section on Medical Informatics, Stanford University, Stanford, CA, October 1985.

[9] D.E. Heckerman, E.J. Horvitz, and B.N. Nathwani. Toward effective normative expert systems: The Pathfinder project. *Computers in Biomedical Research*, [submitted].

[10] A. Tversky and D. Kahneman. Judgement under uncertainty: Heuristics and biases. *Science*, 185:1124–1131, 1974.

[11] A.H. Murphy. A note on the utility of probabilistic predictions and the probability score in the cost–loss ratio decision situation. *J. Appl. Meteorol.*, 5:534–537, 1966.

[12] J. Pearl. An economic basis for certain methods of evaluating probabilistic forecasts. *Int. J. Man–Machine Studies*, 10:175–183, 1978.

[13] B. Wise. *An Experimental Comparison of Uncertain Inference Systems*. PhD thesis, The Robotics Institute and Department of Engineering and Public Policy, Carnegie–Mellon University, Pittsburgh, PA, June 1986.

[14] P. Smets, J. Willems, J. Talmon, V. DeMaertelaer, and F. Kornreich. Methodology for the comparison of various diagnostic procedures. *Biometrie–Praximetrie*, 15:89–122, 1975.

[15] B. Asselain, C. Derouesne, R. Salamon, M. Bernadet, and F. Gremy. The concept of utility in a medical decision aid: Example of an application. In *Proceedings of Medinfo*, pages 123–125. Medinfo, October 1977.

[16] J.D.F. Habbema and J. Hilden. The measurement of performance in probabilistic diagnosis IV: Utility considerations in therapeutics and prognostics. *Methods of Information in Medicine*, 20:80–96, 1981.

[17] F.T. de Dombal, D.J. Leaper, J.R. Staniland, A.P. McCann, and J.C. Horrocks. Computer-aided diagnosis of acute abdominal pain. *British Medical Journal*, 2:9–13, 1972.

[18] W.H. Cleckner. *Tactical Evidential Reasoning: An Application of the Dempster–Shafer Theory of Evidence*. PhD thesis, Naval Postgraduate School, Monterey, CA, September 1985.

[19] G.F. Cooper. *NESTOR: A Computer-based Medical Diagnostic Aid that Integrates Causal and Probabilistic Knowledge*. PhD thesis, Computer Science Department, Stanford University, Stanford, CA, November 1984. Rep. No. STAN-CS-84-48. Also numbered HPP-84-48.

[20] R.A. Howard. On making life and death decisions. In R.A. Howard and J.E. Matheson, editors, *Readings on the Principles and Applications of Decision Analysis*, volume II, pages 483–506. Strategic Decisions Group, Menlo Park, CA, 1980.

[21] M. Ben-Bassat. Myopic policies in sequential classification. *IEEE Transactions on Computers*, 27:170–178, 1978.

[22] D.J. Spiegelhalter. Probabilistic reasoning in predictive expert systems. In L.N. Kanal and J.F. Lemmer, editors, *Uncertainty in Artificial Intelligence*, pages 47–67. North Holland, New York, 1986.

Uncertainty in Artificial Intelligence 4
R.D. Shachter, T.S. Levitt, L.N. Kanal, J.F. Lemmer (Editors)
© Elsevier Science Publishers B.V. (North-Holland), 1990

MODELING UNCERTAIN AND VAGUE KNOWLEDGE IN POSSIBILITY AND EVIDENCE THEORIES

Didier DUBOIS - Henri PRADE

I.R.I.T. - L.S.I.
Université Paul Sabatier, 118 route de Narbonne
31062 TOULOUSE Cedex, FRANCE

This paper advocates the usefulness of new theories of uncertainty for the purpose of modeling some facets of uncertain knowledge, especially vagueness, in A.I.. It can be viewed as a partial reply to Cheeseman's (among others) defense of probability.

1. INTRODUCTION

In spite of the growing bulk of works dealing with deviant models of uncertainty in artificial intelligence, there is a strong reaction of classical probability tenants ([1]-[2] and [3] for instance), claiming that new uncertainty theories are "at best unnecessary, and at worst misleading" [1]. Interestingly enough, however, the trend to go beyond probabilistic models of subjective uncertainty is emerging even in the orthodox field of decision theory in order to account for systematic deviations of human behavior from the expected utility models (e.g. [4]). This paper tries to reconcile the points of view of probability theory and those of two presently popular alternative settings : possibility theory [5], [6] and the theory of evidence [7]. The focus is precisely on the representation of subjective uncertain knowledge. We try to explain why probability measures cannot account for all facets of uncertainty, especially partial ignorance, imprecision, vagueness, and how the other theories can do the job, without rejecting the laws of probability when they apply.

2. REPRESENTING UNCERTAINTY

Let $\mathcal{P}$ be a Boolean algebra of propositions, denoted by **a**, **b**,**c**... We assume that an uncertain piece of information can be represented by means of a logical proposition to which a number, conveying the level of uncertainty, is attached. The meaning of this number is partly a matter of context. Following Cheeseman [1], g(**a**) is here supposed to reflect an "entity's opinion about the truth of **a**, given the available evidence". Let g(**a**) denote the number attached to **a**. g is supposed to range over [0,1], and satisfies limit conditions g(**0**) = 0 and g(**1**) = 1, where **0** and **1** denote the contradiction and the tautology respectively.

2.1.   Some limitations of a probabilistic model of subjective uncertainty

If g is assumed to be a probability measure, then g(**a**) = 1 means that **a** is certainly true, while g(**a**) = 0 means that **a** is certainly false. This convention does not allow for the modeling of partial ignorance in a systematic way. Especially it may create some problems in the presence of imprecise evidence, when part of it neither supports nor denies **a**. First, to allocate an amount of probability P(**a**) to a proposition **a** compels you to allocate 1 - P(**a**) to the converse proposition 'not **a**' (¬**a**). It implies that P(**a**) = 1 means "**a** is true" and P(**a**) = 0 means "**a** is false". In case of total ignorance about **a**, you are bound to let P(**a**) = 1 - P(¬**a**) = .5. If you are equally ignorant about the truth of another proposition **b** then you must do it again : P(**b**) = 1 - P(¬**b**) = .5. Now assuming that **a** logically entails **b** (¬**a** ∨ **b** is the tautology **1**), you come up with the result that P(¬**a** ∧ **b**) = P(**b**) - P(**a**) = 0 ! (since P(¬**a** ∨ **b**) = 1 = 1 - P(**a**) + P(**b**) - P(¬**a** ∧ **b**)). This may seem paradoxical : how can your ignorance allow you to discard the possibility that ¬**a** ∧ **b** be true ! For instance **a** = "horse n° 4 will win the race" **b** = "horse with an even number wins the race", and this probabilistic modelling of ignorance leads you to the surprising statement "no horse with an even number other than 4 will win the race". Obviously, Bayesian tenants would not allocate probabilities that way ; they will consider that the information ¬**a** ∨ **b** = 1 constitutes a new context and that now the state of total ignorance is then represented by P(**a** ∧ **b**) = P(**a**) = 1/3 ; P(¬**a** ∧ **b**) = 1/3 ; P(¬**a** ∧ ¬**b**) = P(¬**b**) = 1/3 ; P(**a** ∧ ¬**b**) = 0. However we have now P(¬**a**) = 2 · P(**a**) and P(**b**) = 2 · P(¬**b**), which is not very satisfying if we consider that we only know that **a** entails **b**. What is pointed out is that probability theory offers no stable, consistent modelling of ignorance. Thus, the way a question is answered depends upon the existence of further information which may reveal more about the structure of the set of possible answers. This is psychologically troublesome.

Of course it can be argued that this is not the proper way of applying probability theory. First you should make sure about how many horses are in the race and then your ignorance leads you to uniformly distributing your probabilities among the horses following the principle of maximum entropy (Jaynes [8]). This is good for games of chance, when it is known that dice have only 6 facets. But in the expert system area, they usually play with objects without exactly knowing their number of facets. An important part of probabilistic modelling consists of making up a set of exhaustive, mutually exclusive alternatives *before* assessing probabilities. For instance, in the horse example, this set must account for the constraint "**a** implies **b**"; it leaves only three alternatives : **a**, ¬**a** ∧ **b**, ¬**b** to which probabilities must be assigned. The difficulty in artificial intelligence is that this job is generally impossible to do, at least to do once for all. Knowledge bases must allow for evolving representations of the universe, that is, the discovery of new unexpected events, without having to completely reconstruct a new knowledge base, upon such occurrences. At a given point in the construction of a knowledge base, the expert may not be aware of all existing alternatives. Of course you can always use a special dummy alternative such as "all other possibilities". But the uniformly distributed probability assignment derived from Laplace's insufficient reason principle is not very convincing in that case ! Moreover the expert may not always be able to precisely describe the alternatives he is aware of, so that these descriptions may overlap each other and the mutual exclusiveness property needed in probability theory, is lost. Despite this not very nice setting, one must still be able to perform uncertain reasoning in knowledge bases ! Quoting Cheeseman [1], "if the problem is undefined, probability theory cannot say something useful". But artificial intelligence tries to address partially undefined problems which human experts can cope with. This presence of imprecision forces us out of the strict probabilistic setting - this does not mean rejecting it, but enlarging it.

Even when an exhaustive set of mutually exclusive alternatives is available it is questionable to represent the state of total or partial ignorance by means of an uniformly distributed probability measure. The most recent justification for this latter approach seems to be the principle of maximum entropy [8]. However, in the mind of some entropy principle tenants, there seems to be a confusion between two problems : one of representing a state of knowledge and one of making a decision. The kind of information measured by Shannon's entropy is the amount of *uncertainty* (pervading a probability assignment) regarding which outcome is likely to occur next, or what is the best decision to be made on such ground. The word "information" refers here to the existence of reasons to choose one alternative *against* another. Especially you are equally uncertain about what will happen when flipping a coin whether you totally ignore the mechanical properties of this particular coin, or you have made 1,000,000 experiments with the coin, and it has led to an equal amount of heads and tails. You are in the same state of uncertainty but certainly not in the same state of knowledge : in the case of total ignorance, you have *no* evidence about the coin ; in the second situation, you are not far from having the *maximal* amount of evidence, although being uncertain due to randomness. In the first case the value of the probability is completely unknown, while in the second case it is quite precisely known. In artificial intelligence problems we want to have a model of our state of knowledge in which ignorance is carefully distinguished from randomness. This is important because when uncertainty is due to ignorance, there is some hope of improving the situation by getting more evidence (flip the coin, for instance). When uncertainty is due to experimentally observed randomness, it seems difficult to remove it by getting more information. Distinguishing between ignorance and randomness may be useful for the purpose of devising knowledge-based systems equipped with self-explanation capabilities. The maximal entropy principle was not invented to take care of this distinction, and looks irrelevant as far as the representation of knowledge is concerned. It may prove more useful for decision support-systems than for approximate reasoning systems.

2.2. Belief functions

In the situation of partial ignorance the probability P(**a**) of **a** is only imprecisely known, and can be expressed as an interval range [C(**a**), Pl(**a**)] whose lower bound can be viewed as a degree of certainty (or belief) of **a**, while the upper bound represents a grade of plausibility (or possibility) of **a**, i.e. the extent to which **a** cannot be denied. Total ignorance about **a** is observed when there is a total lack of certainty (C(**a**) = 0) and complete possibility (Pl(**a**) = 1) for **a**. A natural assumption is to admit that the evidence which supports **a** also denies 'not **a**' (¬**a**). This modeling assumption leads to the convention

$$C(\mathbf{a}) = 1 - Pl(\neg\mathbf{a}) \qquad (1)$$

which is in agreement with P(**a**) = 1 - P(¬**a**), where P(**a**) and P(¬**a**) are imprecisely known probabilities. This equality also means that the certainty of **a** is equivalent to the impossibility of ¬**a**. The framework of probability theory does not allow for modelling the difference between possibility and certainty, as expressed by (1). Functions C and Pl are usually called lower and upper probabilities, when considered as bounds on an unknown probability measure. See Walley & Fine [9] and Dubois & Prade [10] for surveys on lower and upper probabilities.

Using (1), the knowledge of the certainty function C over the Boolean algebra of propositions $\mathcal{P}$ is enough to reconstruct the plausibility function Pl. Especially the amount of uncertainty pervading **a** is summarized by the two numbers C(**a**) and C(¬**a**). They are such that C(**a**) + C(¬**a**) ≤ 1, due to (1). The above discussion leads to the following conventions, for interpreting the number C(**a**) attached to **a** :

i)   C(**a**) = 1 means that **a** is certainly true.

ii) C(¬**a**) = 1 ⇔ Pl(**a**) = 0 means that **a** is certainly false.

iii) C(**a**) = C(¬**a**) = 0 (i.e. Pl(**a**) = 1 = Pl(¬**a**)) means total ignorance about **a**. In other words **a** is neither supported nor denied by any piece of available evidence. This is a self-consistent, absolute reference point for expressing ignorance.

iv) $C(a) = C(\neg a) = 0.5$ (i.e. $Pl(a) = Pl(\neg a) = 0.5$) means maximal probabilistic uncertainty about **a**. In other words the available evidence can be shared in two equal parts : one which supports **a** and the other which denies it. This is the case of pure randomness in the occurence of **a** .

Note that total ignorance implies that we are equally uncertain about the truth of **a** and $\neg$**a**, as well as when $C(a) = C(\neg a) = .5$. In other words ignorance implies uncertainty about the truth of **a**, but the converse is not true. Namely, in the probabilistic case, we have a lot of information, but we are still completely uncertain because the evidence is contradictory. Total uncertainty is more generally observed whenever $C(a) = C(\neg a) \in [0,0.5]$. The amount of ignorance is assessed by $1 - 2\,C(a)$ in that case.

The mathematical properties of C depend upon the way the available evidence is modelled and related to the certainty function. In Shafer theory , a body of evidence $(\mathcal{F},m)$ is composed of a subset $\mathcal{F} \subseteq \mathcal{P}$ of n focal propositions, each being attached a relative weight of confidence $m(a_i)$ for all $a_i \in \mathcal{F}$. $m(a_i)$ is a positive number in the unit interval, and it holds

$$\Sigma_{i = 1,n}\, m(a_i) = 1 \qquad (2)$$
$$m(0) = 0 \qquad (3)$$

(3) expresses the fact that no confidence is committed to the contradictory proposition **0**. The weight $m(1)$ possibly granted to the tautology represents the amount of total ignorance since the tautology does not support nor deny any other proposition. The fact that a proposition **a** supports another proposition **b** is formally expressed by the logical entailment, i.e. $a \to b$ $(= \neg a \vee b) = 1$. Let $S(a)$ be the set of propositions supporting **a** other than the contradiction **0**. The function $C(a)$ is called a *belief function* in the sense of Shafer (and denoted 'Bel') if and only if there is a body of evidence $(\mathcal{F}, m)$ such that

$$\forall a, \quad Bel(a) = \Sigma_{a_i \in S(a)}\, m(a_i) \qquad (4)$$
$$\forall a, \quad Pl(a) = \Sigma_{a_i \in S(\neg a)^c - \{0\}}\, m(a_i) \qquad (5)$$

where 'c' denotes complementation. Clearly, when the focal elements are only atoms of the Boolean algebra $\mathcal{P}$ (i.e. $S(a_i) = \{a_i\}$, for all $i = 1,n$) then $\forall a$, $S(\neg a) = S(a)^c - \{0\}$, and $Pl(a) = Bel(a)$, $\forall a$. We recover a probability measure on $\mathcal{P}$. In the general case the quantity $Pl(a) - Bel(a)$ represents the amount of imprecision about the probability of **a**. Interpreting the Boolean algebra $\mathcal{P}$ as the set of subsets of a referential set Ω, the atoms of $\mathcal{P}$ can be viewed as the singletons of Ω and interpreted as possible worlds, one of which is the actual world. Then a focal element $\mathbf{a}_i$ whose model is the subset $M(\mathbf{a}_i) = A_i \subseteq \Omega$ corresponds to observing, as part of the available evidence, the actual world in A_i, $m(A_i)$ representing the relative confidence we put in this observation (e.g. the frequency of observing A_i, or the reliability of the source supplying the piece of information). When A_i is not a singleton, this piece of information is said to be imprecise, because the actual world can be anywhere within A_i. When A_i is a singleton, the piece of information is said to be precise. Clearly, Bel = Pl is a probability measure if and only if the available evidence is precise (but generally scattered between several disjoint focal elements viewed as singletons).

Note that although Bel($\mathbf{a}$) and Pl($\mathbf{a}$) are respectively lower and upper probabilities, the converse is not true, that is any interval-valued probability cannot be interpreted as a pair of belief and plausibility functions in the sense of (4) and (5) (see [9], [10]).

2.3. Possibility measures

When two propositions $\mathbf{a}$ and $\mathbf{b}$ are such that $\mathbf{a} \in S(\mathbf{b})$, we write $\mathbf{a} \vdash \mathbf{b}$, and $\vdash$ is called the entailment relation. Note that $\vdash$ is reflexive and transitive and equips the set $\mathscr{F}$ of focal elements with a partial ordering structure. When $\mathscr{F}$ is linearly ordered by $\vdash$, i.e., $\mathscr{F} = \{\mathbf{a}_1, ..., \mathbf{a}_n\}$ where $\mathbf{a}_i \vdash \mathbf{a}_{i+1}$, i = 1, n - 1, the belief and plausibility functions Bel and Pl satisfy the following properties [7]

$$\text{Bel}(\mathbf{a} \wedge \mathbf{b}) = \min\,(\text{Bel}(\mathbf{a}), \text{Bel}(\mathbf{b}))$$
$$\text{Pl}(\mathbf{a} \vee \mathbf{b}) = \max\,(\text{Pl}(\mathbf{a}), \text{Pl}(\mathbf{b})) \tag{6}$$

Formally, the plausibility function is a possibility measure in the sense of Zadeh [5]. The following equivalent properties then hold

$$\max\,(\text{Pl}(\mathbf{a}), \text{Pl}(\neg\mathbf{a})) = 1 \tag{7}$$
$$\min\,(\text{Bel}(\mathbf{a}), \text{Bel}(\neg\mathbf{a})) = 0 \tag{8}$$
$$\text{Bel}(\mathbf{a}) > 0 \Rightarrow \text{Pl}(\mathbf{a}) = 1 \tag{9}$$

In the following possibility measures are denoted Π for the sake of clarity. The dual measure through (1) is then denoted N and called a necessity measure [6]. Zadeh [5] introduces possibility measures from so-called possibility distributions, which are mappings from Ω to [0,1], denoted π. A possibility and the dual necessity measure are then obtained as

$$\forall\, A \subseteq \Omega, \left\{ \begin{array}{l} \Pi(A) = \sup\,\{\pi(\omega) \mid \omega \in A\} \\ N(A) = \inf\{1 - \pi(\omega) \mid \omega \in A^c\} \end{array} \right. \tag{10}$$

and we then have $\pi(\omega) = \Pi(\{\omega\})$, $\forall \omega$. Here π represents a state of incomplete information. The function π can be viewed as a generalized characteristic function, i.e. the membership function of a fuzzy set F [11]. Let F_α be the α-cut of F. i.e., the subset $\{\omega \mid \mu_F(\omega) \geq \alpha\}$ with $\pi = \mu_F$. It is easy to check that in the finite case the set of α-cuts $\{F_\alpha \mid \alpha \in (0,1]\}$ is the set $\mathcal{F}$ of focal elements of the possibility measure Π. Moreover, let $\pi_1 = 1 > \pi_2 ... > \pi_m$ be the set of distinct values of $\pi(\omega)$, let $\pi_{m+1} = 0$ by convention, and A_i be the π_i-cut of F, $i = 1,m$. Then the basic probability assignment m underlying Π is completely defined in terms of the possibility distribution π as [12, 6] :

$$\left\{ \begin{array}{l} m(A_i) = \pi_i - \pi_{i+1} \quad i = 1,m \\ m(A) = 0 \text{ otherwise} \end{array} \right. \tag{11}$$

Among the unjustified criticisms of possibility theory is the statement by Cheeseman [2] that it "contains rules such as $\Pi(\mathbf{a} \wedge \mathbf{b}) = \min(\Pi(\mathbf{a}), \Pi(\mathbf{b}))$". This is wrong. Only an inequality, $\Pi(\mathbf{a} \wedge \mathbf{b}) \leq \min(\Pi(\mathbf{a}), \Pi(\mathbf{b}))$ is valid, generally, just as in probability theory. The above equality holds in very special cases [6], namely when $\mathbf{a}$ and $\mathbf{b}$ pertain to variables which do not interact with each other. Possibility logic relies on (6) but certainly not on the equality mentioned by Cheeseman [2]. Possibility logic, just as probabilistic logic is not truth-functional. It can even be proved that in the presence of uncertainty, the two equalities $\Pi(\mathbf{a} \vee \mathbf{b}) = \max(\Pi(\mathbf{a}), \Pi(\mathbf{b}))$ and $\Pi(\mathbf{a} \wedge \mathbf{b}) = \min(\Pi(\mathbf{a}), \Pi(\mathbf{b}))$, $\forall \mathbf{a}, \forall \mathbf{b}$, are inconsistent. So it is wrong to claim, as Cheeseman [2] does, that possibility theory "assumes a state of maximal dependence between components".

The conventions adopted in this paper to quantify uncertainty can be visually illustrated by a rectangle triangle in a Cartesian coordinate system that is reminiscent of Rollinger [13]'s conventions (see Figure 1). Any point in the triangle has coordinates (Bel(a), Bel(¬a)). The x-axis quantifies support for

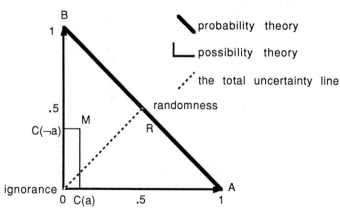

Figure 1

a, and the y-axis quantifies support for ¬**a**. Hence any point in the triangle AOB expresses a state of knowledge, viewed as a convex combination of total certainty for **a** (vertex A), for ¬**a** (vertex B), and total ignorance (vertex O). Probabilistic states of knowledge lie on the A-B segment, and possibilistic states of knowledge lie on the coordinate axes. Totally uncertain states are located on the segment bounded by O and R, R being the mid-point of the probabilistic segment.

3. A SHORT DISCUSSION OF COX'S AXIOMATIC FRAMEWORK FOR PROBABILITY

Traditionally, a degree of probability can be interpreted as

- either the ratio between the number of outcomes which realize an event over the number of possible outcomes. This is good for games of chance.
- or the frequency of occurrence of an event, after a sufficient (theoretically infinite) number of trials. This is the frequentist view.
- or a numerical translation of an entity's opinion about the truth of a proposition, given the available evidence as termed in [2]. This is the subjectivist view, which has been expressed in various settings : axiomatic [14], pragmatic (this is the Bayesian approach to betting behavior, and qualitative comparative probability (see [15]) ; we shall focus only on Cox's axiomatic view and ask whether such a view exist for belief and possibility functions ; see [16] for details. See [17] for other views of these functions.

Cox [14] tried to prove that probability measures were the only possible numerical model of "reasonable expectation". He started from the following requirements. Letting f(**b** | **a**) be a measure of the reasonable credibility of the proposition **b** when the proposition **a** is known to be true. Cox proposes two basic axioms :

C1. there is some operation * such that f(**c** ∧ **b** | **a**) = f(**c** | **b** ∧ **a**) * f(**b** | **a**)
C2. there is a function S such that f(¬**b** | **a**) = S(f(**b** | **a**))

The following additional technical requirements are used in [14] :

C3. * and S have both continuous second order derivatives

Then, f is proved to be isomorphic to a probability measure. The purely technical assumption (C3) is very strong and cannot be justified on common sense arguments. For instance * = minimum is a solution of C1 which does not violate the algebra of propositions, but certainly violates C3. In fact the unicity result does not require C3, which can be relaxed into a more intuitive continuity and monotonicity assumption. Cox's unicity result *only* holds under *strict* monotonicity assumption [18]. Cheeseman [2] proposes Cox's results as a formal proof that only probability measures are reasonable for the modeling of subjective uncertainty. His claim can be disputed. Although C1 sounds very sensible as a definition of conditional credibility function, C2 explicitly states that only one number is enough to describe both the uncertainties of **b** and ¬**b**. Clearly, this statement rules out the ability to distinguish between the notions of possibility and certainty. This distinction is the very purpose of belief functions, possibility measures, and any kind of upper and lower probability system. Hence the unicity result is not so surprizing, and Cox's setting, although being an interesting attempt at recovering probability measures from a purely non frequentist argument does not provide the ultimate answer to uncertainty modelling problems.

4. MODELING VAGUENESS

Cheeseman [2] has proposed a nice definition of vagueness which we shall adopt, namely : "vagueness is uncertainty about meaning and can be represented by a probability distribution over possible meanings". However, contrary to the author of this definition, we shall try to prove that this view is completely consistent with Zadeh's fuzzy set theory, as well as the set-theoretic view of belief functions.

4.1. Membership functions and intermediary grades of truth

The statement "Mary is young", can be represented by the logic formula $\mathbf{a} =$ young(x) where x stands for the actual value of Mary's age. The set of possible worlds is an age scale Ω. A rough model of "young" consists in letting $M(\mathbf{a}) = I_c$, an interval contained in Ω, for instance the interval [0,25] years. I_c is called the meaning of "young", the subscript c indicates the context where the information arises. Then "Mary is young" is true if $x \in I_c$ and false otherwise. Vagueness arises when there is uncertainty regarding which interval in Ω properly translates "young". Let m(A) be the probability that $I_c = A$. m(A) can be a subjective probability obtained by asking a single individual, or can be a frequency if it reflects a proportion of individuals thinking that A properly expresses "young".

Knowing the age $x = \omega$ of Mary, the grade of truth of the statement "Mary is young" is defined by the grade of membership $\mu_{young}(\omega)$ defined

$$\mu_{young}(\omega) = \Sigma_{A:\omega \in A} \, m(A) \qquad (12)$$

$\mu_{young}(\omega)$ estimates the extent to which the value ω is compatible with the meaning of "young", formally expressed under the form of a *random set* or equivalently [19] of a body of evidence in the sense of Shafer. This view is a translation of Cheeseman [2]'s definition of vagueness. It becomes exactly Zadeh's definition of a fuzzy set as soon as the family $\{A_i \mid m(A_i) > 0\}$ is a nested family so that the knowledge of the membership function μ_{young} is equivalent to that of the probabilities $m(A_i)$, because (11) is equivalent to (12) (see [12]). Of course this nested property is not always completely valid in practice, especially if the A_i's come from different individuals. However consonant (nested) approximations of dissonant bodies of evidence exist [20, 21], which are especially very good when $\cap_i A_i \neq \emptyset$, a usually satisfied consistency property which expresses that there exists at least an age in Ω, totally compatible with "young" for everybody in a given context. Hence a fuzzy set, with membership function $\mu : \Omega \rightarrow [0,1]$, can always be used as an approximation of a random set. However the word "random" may be inappropriate when the $m(A_i)$'s do not express frequencies. One might prefer the term "convex combination of sets" , which is more neutral but lengthy.

Cheeseman [2] claims that a membership function μ_{young} is nothing but a conditional probability P(young | x). This claims is debatable. Indeed the existence of a quantity such as P(young | x) may be understood as underlying the assumption that 'young' represents an event in the usual sense of probability. Hence 'young' is a given subset I_c of Ω. But then the value of P(young | x) is either 0 ($x \notin I_c$) or 1 ($x \in I_c$). This is because x and I_c belong to the same universe Ω. Admitting that P(young | x) $\in$ (0,1) leads to admit that 'young' is not a standard event but has a membership function ; Zadeh [11] has introduced the notion of the probability of a fuzzy event, defined, in the tradition of probability theory, as the expectation of the membership function μ_{young}.

$$P(young) = \int_\Omega \mu_{young}(\omega)dP(\omega) \qquad (13)$$

This definition assumes that the a priori knowledge on Mary's age x is given by a probability measure P. When calculating P(young | x), Mary's age is known ($x = \omega$) and P(young) = P(young | ω) = $\mu_{young}(\omega)$. But because in that case the available information ($x = \omega$) is deterministic, P(. | ω) is a Dirac measure ($P(A|\omega) = 1$ if $\omega \in A$, and 0 otherwise). and writing P(young | x) is just a matter of convention, one could write Bel(young | x), Π(young | x) etc... as well, since a Dirac measure is also a particular case of belief function, possibility measure, etc... !

If one admits as Hisdal [22] that concepts like 'young' have clear-cut meanings for single individuals, but become fuzzy when a group of individuals is considered, then P(young | ω) reflects the proportion of individuals that

probability, a natural approach would be to solve the following program (Ω is finite) :

$$\text{maximize}_p \ - \Sigma_{\omega_i \in \Omega} \ p(\omega_i) \log p(\omega_i)$$

under the constraint $P(I_c) \geq \alpha$ \qquad (20)

where $[\alpha,1]$ is a numerical translation of "probable" appearing in S. The interval I_c supposedly expresses the term "young". The solution to the above problem is simply

$$P(\{\omega\} \mid S) = \frac{\alpha}{\|I_c\|} \quad \text{if } \omega \in I_c$$

$$= \frac{1 - \alpha}{|\Omega| - \|I_c\|} \quad \text{if } \omega \notin I_c \qquad (21)$$

where $|.|$ denotes cardinality.

When $\alpha = 1$, we get a particular case of (19) where the a priori probability distribution is uniform. The above representation is good for *deciding* what is Mary's age, not for representing our state of knowledge, when the a priori probability distribution is not available. In that case, statement S translates into $C(I_c) = \alpha$ where $C(I_c)$ is a lower probability degree, here a degree of belief in the sense of Shafer. We need some least information principle, which, in the scope of simply representing knowledge, would maximize the imprecision contained in the belief function Bel = C. A simple evaluation of the imprecision of the statement "Mary is young", where "young" translates into the interval I_c, is the cardinality of I_c. When $\|I_c\| = 1$ then we know Mary's age precisely, when $I_c = \Omega$ we have no information. More generally if Mary's age in known under the form of a random set $(\mathcal{F},m)$, the imprecision is measured by the expected cardinality

$$|(\mathcal{F},m)| = \Sigma_{A \subseteq \Omega} m(A) \cdot |A|. \qquad (22)$$

Hence the problem of representing the meaning of a statement such as "Mary is probably young", where "probably" is viewed as specifying a lower bound on a probability value and "young" is viewed as a clearcut category approximated by a subset I_c, is that of solving the following program

$$\text{maximize}_m \ \Sigma_{A \subseteq \Omega} \ m(A) \cdot |A| \qquad (23)$$

under the constraint $\qquad \text{Bel}(I_c) \triangleq \Sigma_{A \subseteq I_c} m(A) = \alpha.$

This is the principle of minimum specificity (Dubois & Prade [22]). The solution of (23) is easily found :

$$m(I_c \mid S) = \alpha$$
$$m(\Omega \mid S) = 1 - \alpha. \qquad (24)$$

Note that this solution is a possibility measure whose distribution is $\pi(\omega|S) = 1$ if $\omega \in I_c$, $\pi(\omega|S) = 1 - \alpha$ otherwise (see Figure 2).

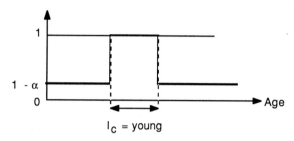

$$I_c = young$$

Figure 2 : Representation of "Mary is probably young"

Moreover it encompasses the solution given by the maximum entropy principle as a particular case, namely

$$\forall A \subseteq \Omega \qquad Bel(A|S) \leq P(A|S) \leq Pl(A|S) \qquad (25)$$

i.e. the probability measure obtained by (21) is in the set of probability measures implicitly defined by Bel and Pl, viewed as upper and lower probabilities.

This approach to the representation of uncertain knowledge can be extended to the case when "young" is expressed, not as an interval, but as a fuzzy interval (see Prade [24]). Note that the maximum entropy principle can also accommodate fuzziness in the statement of constraints changing $P(I_c)$ into $P(young)$ as defined by (13).

CONCLUSION

This paper has tried to show that as far as knowledge representation is concerned, there should not be any dispute regarding the well-foundedness of possibility and fuzzy set theory, belief functions, versus probability theory. The latter is older and is presently far more developed than the two former. So, they are easy to criticize from the stand-point of probability theory. However the development of new models of uncertainty for knowledge representation seems to be an important issue, because of limitations of probability theory in terms of descriptive power. The new models such as possibility and evidence theories are not built *against* probability theory, but in the same spirit ; indeed most of the new uncertainty measures can be viewed as upper and lower probability measures. Hence probability theory itself is a basic tool for the construction of new models of uncertain knowledge. The present situation of probability theory is similar to the situation of classical logic in the mid-seventies. Classical logic has been given up by some researchers, when modelling common sense knowledge, but the idea of a logic has been preserved, and new logics (default logics for instance) have arised. In the case of uncertainty models, it seems important to go beyond probability but consistently with probability theory itself. Of course the authors are aware of the bulk of work needed to bring possibility and evidence theories to the level of development of probability theory. In that sense many results reported in the literature about foundations and combination rules are certainly preliminary. But we strongly question dogmatic attitudes disputing alternative theories of uncertainty on behalf of rationality. Modelling uncertainty, and especially subjective uncertainty, cannot be but a compromise between the ideally optimal Bayesian theory and the limited precision and vagueness of the available, often subjective knowledge.

REFERENCES

[1] Cheeseman, P., In defense of probability, Proc. of 9th Inter. Joint Conf. on Artificial Intelligence, Los Angeles, 1985, pp. 1002-1009.
[2] Cheeseman, P., Probabilistic versus fuzzy reasoning, in : Kanal, L.N. and Lemmer, J.F., (eds.), Uncertainty in Artificial Intelligence (North-Holland, Amsterdam, 1986) pp. 85-102.
[3] Pearl, J., How to do with probabilities what people say you can't, Proc. of the 2nd Conf. on Artificial Intelligence Applications, Miami, Fl., Dec. 11-13, 1985, pp. 6-13.
[4] Munier B. (ed.), Risk, Decision and Rationality (D. Reidel, Dordrecht, 1988).
[5] Zadeh, L.A., Fuzzy sets as a basis for a theory of possibility, Fuzzy Sets and Systems 1 (1978) pp. 3-28.
[6] Dubois, D. and Prade, H., Possibility Theory : an Approach to Computerized Processing of Uncertainty (Plenum Press, New York, 1988).
[7] Shafer, G., A Mathematical Theory of Evidence (Princeton University Press, N.J., 1976).
[8] Jaynes, E.T., Where do we stand on maximum entropy ?, in : Levine, R.L. and Tribus, M. (eds.), The Maximum Entropy Formalism (MIT Press, 1979) pp. 15-118.
[9] Walley, P. and Fine, T., Towards a frequentist theory of upper and lower probability, The Annals of Statistics 10 (1982) pp. 741-761.

318

[10] Dubois, D. and Prade, H., Modelling uncertainty and inductive inference, Acta Psychologica 68 (1988) pp. 53-78.

[11] Zadeh, L.A., Probability measures of fuzzy events, J. Math. Anal. Appl. 23 (1968) pp. 421-427.

[12] Dubois, D. and Prade, H., On several representations of an uncertain body of evidence, in : Gupta, M.M. and Sanchez E. (eds.), Fuzzy Information and Decision Processes (North-Holland, Amsterdam, 1982) pp. 167-181.

[13] Rollinger, C.R., How to represent evidence - Aspects of uncertainty reasoning, Proc. of the 8th Inter. Joint Conf. on Artificial Intelligence, Karlsruhe, R.F.A., Aug. 8-12, 1983, pp. 358-361.

[14] Cox, R.T., Probability, frequency and reasonable expectation, American J. Phys. 14 (1946) 1-13.

[15] Fine, T., Theories of Probability (Academic Press, New York, 1973).

[16] Dubois, D. and Prade, H., Measure-free conditioning, probability, and non-monotonic reasoning, Proc. of the 11th Inter. Joint Conf. on Artificial Intelligence, Detroit, 1989, pp. 1110-1114.

[17] Dubois, D. and Prade, H., Representation and combination of uncertainty with belief functions and possibility measures, Computational Intelligence (Canada) 4(4) (1989) pp. 244-264.

[18] Dubois, D. and Prade, H., Conditioning in possibility and evidence theories - A logical viewpoint, To appear in Int. J. of Approximate Reasoning.

[19] Nguyen, H.T., On random sets and belief functions, J. Math. Anal. & Appl. 65 (1978) 531-542.

[20] Dubois, D. and Prade, H., A set-theoretic view of belief functions. Logical operations and approximations by fuzzy sets, Int. J. of General Systems 12 (1986) 193-226.

[21] Dubois, D. and Prade, H., Consonant approximations of belief functions. To appear in Int. J. of Approximate Reasoning, Special Issue on Belief Functions and Belief Maintenance.

[22] Hisdal, H., Reconciliation of the Yes-No versus grade of membership dualism, in : Gupta, M.M., Kandel, A., Bandler, W. and Kiszka, J.B. (eds.), Approximate Reasoning in Expert Systems (North-Holland, Amsterdam, 1985) pp. 33-46.

[23] Dubois, D. and Prade, H., The principle of minimum specificity as a basis for evidential reasoning, in : Bouchon, B. and Yager, R.R., Uncertainty in Knowledge-Based Systems (Springer Verlag, 1987) pp. 75-84.

[24] Prade, H., Reasoning with fuzzy default values, Proc. of the 15th IEEE Inter. Symp. on Multiple-Valued Logic, Kingston, Ontario, 1985, pp. 191-197.

Uncertainty in Artificial Intelligence 4
R.D. Shachter, T.S. Levitt, L.N. Kanal, J.F. Lemmer (Editors)
© Elsevier Science Publishers B.V. (North-Holland), 1990   319

PROBABILISTIC INFERENCE AND NON-MONOTONIC INFERENCE*

Henry E. KYBURG, Jr.

Computer Science and Philosophy
University of Rochester
Rochester, NY USA

1. INTRODUCTION

(1)   I have enough evidence to render the sentence S probable.
(1a)   So, relative to what I know, it is rational of me to believe S.
(2)   Now that I have more evidence, S may no longer be probable.
(2a)   So now, relative to what I know, it is not rational of me to believe S.

These seem a perfectly ordinary, common sense, pair of situations. Generally and
vaguely, I take them to embody what I shall call *probabilistic inference*. This form of inference is clearly non-monotonic. Relatively few people have taken this form of
inference, based on high probability, to serve as a foundation for non-monotonic logic or
for a logical or defeasible inference.

There are exceptions: Jane Nutter [16] thinks that sometimes probability has something to
do with non-monotonic reasoning. Judea Pearl [17] has recently been exploring the possibility.

There are any number of people whom one might call probability enthusiasts, who feel
that probability provides all the answers by itself, with no need of help from logic.
Cheeseman [1], Henrion [5] and others think it useful to look at a distribution of probabilities over a whole algebra of statements, to update that distribution in the light of new
evidence, and to use the latest updated distribution of probability over the algebra as a basis for planning and decision making. A slightly weaker form of this approach is captured
by Nilsson [15], where one assumes certain probabilities for certain statements, and infers
the probabilities, or constraints on the probabilities, of other statements.

None of this corresponds to what I call probabilistic inference. All of the inference that is
taking place, either in Bayesian updating, or in probabilistic logic, is strictly *deductive*.
Deductive inference, particularly that concerned with the distribution of classical probabilities or chances, is of great importance. But this is not to say that there is no important
role for what earlier logicians have called "ampliative" or "inductive" or "scientific" inference, in which the conclusion goes *beyond* the premises, asserts more than do the
premises. This depends on what David Israel [6] has called "real rules of inference". It is
characteristic of any such logic or inference procedure that it can go wrong: that statements
accepted at one point may be rejected at a later point.

---

*Research underlying the results reported here has been partially supported by the Signals Warfare Center
of the United States Army.

2. McCARTHY AND HAYES

As a matter of historical conjecture, I would suggest that it is the enormously influential article by John McCarthy and Pat Hayes [13] that slowed the exploration of probabilistic inference and focused attention on the problem of discovering a non-monotonic analog of classical logic. They offer powerful arguments against the use of probability as an approach to non-monotonicity. Since much of this argument (perhaps surprisingly) applies equally well to most formalizations of non-monotonic inference, it is worth rehearsing their objections.

They commence with first order predicate calculus, and add 3 operators: Consistent($\emptyset$), Normally($\emptyset$), Probably($\emptyset$). They consider a set σ of sentences, and add new sentences to it according to the rules:

1. Any consequence of σ may be added [to σ]

2. If $\emptyset$ is consistent with σ, consistent($\emptyset$) may be added

3. Normally($\emptyset$), Consistent($\emptyset$) $\Rightarrow$ Probably($\emptyset$)

4. $\emptyset \Rightarrow$ Probably($\emptyset$) is a possible deduction

5. If $\emptyset_1,...,\emptyset_n \Rightarrow \emptyset$ is a possible deduction, then

Probably($\emptyset_1$),..., Probably($\emptyset_n$) $\Rightarrow$ Probably($\emptyset$) is a possible deduction.

Two objections are offered against the use of probabilities:

"It is not clear how to attach probabilities to statements containing quantifiers in a way that corresponds to the amount of conviction people have." (p. 490)
"The information necessary to assign numerical probabilities is not ordinarily available.... Therefore ... epistemologically inadequate." (p.490)

A propos of these objections we only remark that Gaifman [4], Scott and Krauss [21], and others have provided schemes for assigning probabilities to quantified statements; and it is not obvious what information is necessary to assign numerical probabilities, so it's not obvious that we don't have it.

More telling is the example that McCarthy and Hayes offer:

P looks up Q's number;
So he knows it;
So he should believe that if he dials it, "he will come into conversation with Q."

In order to obtain this conclusion in terms of probability, we need to add to the rule:

6. Probably($\emptyset$) $\Rightarrow \emptyset$

We also need a rule for *deleting* statements from σ. But the details of these rules are not to the point. It is rather the intuitions that lie behind them (if not the axioms themselves) that have guided work in non-monotonic inference.

Rules (1) and (5) constitute the main stumbling blocks in the way of developing a system to embody these intuitions, even without (6). In particular, rule (1) requires that σ be strictly consistent; we shall argue later that this is neither necessary nor desirable.

From (1), (3), (4) and (5) and natural assumptions we get a lottery paradox [8]. (With (6) it becomes a contradiction.)

Assume: $\emptyset_i$: ticket i loses; $\emptyset$: all tickets lose; σ contains "~$\emptyset$"; Normally ($\emptyset_i$); Consistent ($\emptyset_i$);

By (3), Probably ($\emptyset_i$). By (1) {$\emptyset_i$ } $\Rightarrow$ $\emptyset$. Therefore by (5), Probably ($\emptyset$). But by (4), Probably (~$\emptyset$). If this isn't contradictory enough, add (6). Note that nothing self-referential is involved.

3. NON-MONOTONIC INFERENCE

In this section we will show that three well-known examples of efforts to codify non-monotonic inference stumble equally over the lottery paradox. Before doing so, it will be well to consider the question of what we want of this set σ of "believed" statements to do for us. Statements on that list should serve as *evidence* for other statements. They should be useful as premises in *planning* (the agent P is constructing a reasonable plan for talking to Q). They should define the limits (at a given point in the collection of evidence) of *reasonable* or *serious possibility*. It is the planning and designing function of σ that is of clearest importance in AI.

Don Perlis [18] has come up with the term "use-beliefs" to describe this set of sentences. Perlis has also argued [18] that standard systems of non-monotonic reasoning have difficulty in handling iterations of application. His zookeeper example -- one of the birds is sick and can't fly -- is just the lottery paradox made realistic. But Perlis still seems to want σ to be consistent.

Let us look at the system of Reiter [20]; it embodies the intuitions driving default logic particularly clearly.

The intuitive idea is to adopt a set of defaults D inducing an extension E of some underlying incomplete set of wffs W. The extension E need not be unique, but (1), (2) and (3) should be satisfied:

(1) $W \subset E$,
(2) E is deductively closed, and
(3) Suppose $(A:MB_1,...MB_n \,/\, C$) is a default, and each of B_i is consistent with E. Then C belongs to E.

The default rule is to be read as: if it's the case that A, and A, $B_1, ..\, B_n$ entail C, and the B_i are possible, then C may be in an extension of W. The lottery with n tickets: W = {sentences describing a fair lottery}; a perfectly natural default is :M ~$\emptyset_i \,/\emptyset_i$ - if you don't know that ticket i wins, i.e., if it is possible that it loses, it's reasonable to believe it loses.

This gives you n extensions E_i, each of which specifies one winner and n-1 losers. That seems implausible; it is clearly not useful for planning to have such a number of extensions. Note that it is deductive closure that prevents our having a single extension containing each $\emptyset_i$.

How does circumscription handle the lottery tickets? Roughly speaking: If x is a ticket, and x is not abnormal, then x loses the lottery. (Of course if you don't know how many tickets there are in the lottery, it might be the case that circumscription would lead you to conclude that there was only one, and that therefore you would win!) It is hard to know *exactly* what one can conclude, since [11] we "clearly" have to include domain dependent heuristics for deciding what circumscriptions to make and when to take them back. But waiving difficulties of quantification, it certainly seems right that in the case of just one ticket, we should be able to conclude that it does not win the lottery.

The question then is, "How often can we iterate this argument?" It would seem that the answer is roughly *n* /2: If we have considered less than half the tickets, the next ticket is still (statistically) likely to lose, relative to what we have taken ourselves to know.

The non-monotonic logic of McDermott and Doyle [14] construes the set of non-mono-tonic theorems as (roughly) the smallest fixed point under non-monotonic derivability. So it would seem that in lottery cases there would be no useful set of non-monotonic conclusions. And yet the lottery should not be dismissed as frivolous: consider the lottery as standing for any situation in which a certain outcome is taken to be "incredible", and consider an arbitrarily long sequence of such situations. We shall consider the specific non-frivolous case of *measurement* shortly.

4. THE CANONICAL EXAMPLES

Before considering the seriousness of the inability of standard non-monotonic inference systems to deal with the lottery, let us show that probabilities do work reasonably well on the standard examples of non-monotonic argument.

We assume that probabilities depend on our knowledge of frequencies or chances, and further than they depend on what we know about the object at issue.

Let E be evidence, K be the set of acceptable beliefs.

(1) Tweety.

> We know "almost all birds fly" in E.
> We know "all penguins are birds" in E.
> We know "no penguins fly" in E.

Suppose we add to E "Tweety is a bird". The probability that Tweety flies is high. High enough for us to accept "Tweety flies" in our body of knowledge (or use-beliefs) K.

Suppose we now add: "Tweety is a penguin" to E. The probability that Tweety flies, relative to E is now 0. We must *delete* "Tweety flies" And add "Tweety doesn't fly".

What we are doing here is using the *more specific reference class* as the basis for our probability. This principle is also given by McCarthy [12], Etherington [3] (as "inferential distance"), Poole [19] ("strictly more specific"), and others.

(2) Nixon Diamond:

Add "Nixon is a Quaker" to the standard E. It is then probable relative to E that Nixon is a pacifist; we add "Nixon is a pacifist" to K -- we plan on it.

Now add "Nixon is a Republican" to the standard E. Similarly: we add "Nixon is not a pacifist" to K.

Now add both. Knowledge about Republicans and knowledge about Quakers now conflict as a basis for asserting (or not) that Nixon is a pacifist. And we just don't know about the intersection. So it seems that we can't conclude anything. This conforms to the usual non-monotonic treatment. McCarthy [12] seems to give us a little more: we can conclude that Nixon is either an abnormal Quaker or an abnormal Republican. But the cash value of that is just that we don't know whether or not he is a pacifist.

Probabilities can do somewhat better, under some circumstances. See "Epistemological Relevance and Statistical Knowledge," in this volume [9].

(3) Cohabitation: [20]

$$\text{Spouse}(x,y)\&\text{hometown}(y)=z : M \text{ Hometown}(x) = z$$
$$\text{hometown}(x) = z$$
$$\text{Employer}(x,y)\&\text{Location}(y)=z : M \text{ hometown}(x) = z/\text{hometown}(x) = z$$

Consider John, whose spouse lives in Toronto and whose employer is located in Vancouver. We can derive an extension in which his hometown is Toronto, and one in which his hometown is in Vancouver.

Probability lets us conclude the disjunction: John's hometown is either Toronto or Vancouver. This may be false, of course, but that is the nature of probabilistic inference. The example suggests to Reiter: (1) ordering defaults (on what basis?) and (2) getting more information (a cop-out if we have to use what evidence we have; otherwise, it is available to probability).

Reiter [20] also suggests that default logic is useful for dealing with the frame problem. We use a default that says everything stays the same unless it is deducible that it has changed. Probability does even better here: When we add a new statement to E, it will not change most of the probabilities from which K is derived. So without a default: everything in K stays there unless its *probability* has changed.

This brings up the most serious charge against probable inference. Since what is probable depends on our whole body of evidence E, any addition to E requires the recomputation of all the probabilities on which K is based. But non-monotonic approaches require the same thing: "networks must be reconditioned after each update" (Touretzky [22]; Etherington [3]). How expensive that reconditioning is depends on how difficult it is to compute probabilities.

5. CONSISTENCY

How can K (the σ of McCarthy and Hayes) serve as a standard of serious possibility, as a basis for planning or designing, if it is inconsistent? Clearly, if it is deductively closed and inconsistent, it cannot. But if membership in K is determined by high probability, it *won't* be deductively closed. On the natural assumption that statements known to have the same truth value will have the same probability, it will contain (in principle) the logical consequences of statements that it contains. (Since if P entails Q, $P \equiv P\&Q$ will be logically true and thus part of the evidence E, and the probability of Q must be at least as great as that of $P\&Q$.)

Inconsistency is a good reason for avoiding deductive closure. But what is a good reason for having an inconsistent K? The lottery is frivolous. Is there a practical and natural counterpart?

The answer is yes, and it comes from the eminently respectable scientific domain of measurement. Suppose my job is measuring items produced by a certain machine. They are either OK or they aren't. It is clear that however sophisticated my measurements, it cannot be demanded that they be error free. Furthermore, there is no plausible way of bounding measurement error. What *can* be demanded is that of each measurement, the probability that it leads to a false assessment of OK be less than (say) .001. (Pick your own number if you don't like that one. But not 0.00.) For purposes of further manufacture, for purposes of design, for purposes of planning, it is obvious that I must believe, of each inspected piece, that it is OK.

It is also clear that I ought also to believe -- accept as a serious possibility, accept for planning or design -- that of a large number (10^6?) items, at least one will not be OK. Thus my beliefs -- my use-beliefs -- are flatly inconsistent. The deductive closure of K contains all the statements in the language. Yet I have no difficulty using this (unclosed!) set of statements K for planning, or as a standard of serious possibility. (Even though the *conjunction* of statements in K is impossible, K can serve as a standard of serious possibility in the sense that if a statement contradicts a *member* of K, it is not to be regarded as a serious possibility. That one of the pieces that has passed my inspection is not OK is not a *serious* possibility, though of course it is a *possibility*. And, at the same tiime, it is not a serious possibility that *all* the inspected pieces are OK.)

The probabilistic version of non-monotonic inference faces one irrefutable complaint. Real probability enthusiasts will say that the story I have just told, while reflecting the way in which people do talk, should be regarded simply as a rough approximation to the real truth which can only be represented by a probability distribution over all the states of the world (or all the sentences of the language). In particular, in planning to use one of the manufactured items for a certain purpose, what I must "really" be doing is evaluating the probability that it is OK, given that it has passed my inspection, multiplying that by the utility of using a piece that really is OK, and adding to that the negative expectation, similarly computed, of using a piece that is not OK. If the probability of a false acceptance were .25, and the number of pieces involved were 10, clearly the probabilistic analysis would be preferable. Why not when the probabilities are smaller and the numbers bigger?

To this one can reply by waving one's hands at the computations involved: acceptance into the body of beliefs K is not only realistic (as a representation of what humans do) but is the only computationally feasible way to go about these things. But that answer is not clearly correct. Here it seems to me that we will only be able to get good answers about which is the best way to represent practical knowledge or use-beliefs by constructing systems that embody each approach.

One thing that is controversial is whether or not there is any form of inference *other* than deductive inference. There is a tradition in philosophy that considers "inductive" or "ampliative" inference as a legitimate form of inference [7]. There is a new tradition, in artificial intelligence, according to which inference proceeds by rules that may not be truth-preserving in the sense that an addition to our knowledge base may require the rejection of a once acceptable conclusion. Such non-monotonic rules will (presumably) lead to truth for the most part.

David Israel [6] suggests that there is no other *logic* than classical deductive logic, but that "real" inference proceeds in non-deductive ways. This is just what inductive or ampliative inference, or more recently scientific inference, or non-monotonic inference, has been concerned with. Whether or not it is to be called a "logic" seems unimportant.

In artificial intelligence, this search is to be found in the search for representations of non-monotonic reasoning (such as circumscription), non-monotonic logics, default logics, logics of defeasible reasoning, and the like. We want to be able to *infer* that Tweety can fly. Since the kinds of inference under investigation do not preserve truth, we have to be able to back up: if we enlarge the premiss set, we *may* have to shrink the conclusion set. Non-monotonic inference is not generally taken to be probabilistic, but work on non-monotonic logic suggests that there is interest in inference rules -- that is, rules that lead from premises to the *acceptance* of a conclusion -- that need not be truth preserving. Many people want to be able to detach conclusions from their premises. Not all approaches to non-monotonic logic allow full detachment; de Kleer's ATMS [2], for example, requires that tags reflecting the assumptions used in an inference be carried along with the conclusions.

6. CONCLUSIONS

We have not provided an algorithm for performing probabilistic inference, though some efforts have been made along these lines [10]. We have not argued that pure probabilism is unworkable in principle. We have argued that many of the usual arguments against probabilistic inference are equally applicable to other forms of non-monotonic reasoning. We have argued that, in fact, once the single hurdle of "inconsistency" is overcome, probabilistic inference offers advantages (in some contexts) or at least no disadvantages (in most contexts) compared to other forms of non-monotonic reasoning. We have argued that the ability to live comfortably with certain sorts of inconsistency is an important feature of probabilistic inference, and that it allows us to take as a basis for planning exactly those individual probable conclusions that are collectively impossible to credit.

All this is not to say that the various forms of non-monotonic reasoning that have been explored are not useful for special purposes. It does suggest both that specific instances of non-monotonic argument can be justified by reference to probabilities, and that any sort of inference that was incompatible with probabilistic inference would have some strikes against it.

REFERENCES

[1]   Cheeseman, Peter (1985): "In Defense of Probability," *IJCAI 85,* Morgan Kaufmann, Los Altos, 1002-1009.
[2]   de Kleer, J. (1986): "Formalizing Non-Monotonic Reasoning Systems," *Artificial Intelligence* **31**, 41-86.
[3]   Etherington, D. W. (1987): "Formalizing Non-Monotonic Reasoning Systems," *Artificial Intelligence* **31**, 41-86.

[4]   Gaifman, Haim (1964): "Concerning Measures on First Order Calculi," *Israeli Journal of Mathematics* **2**, 1-18.

[5]   Henrion, Max, and Cooley, Daniel (1987): "An Experimental Comparison of Knowledge Engineering for Expert Systems and for Decision Analysis," *AAAI 87*, Morgan Kaufman, Los Altos, 471-476.

[6]   Israel, David (1980): "What's Wrong with Non-Monotonic Logic?" *IJCAI 80*, Stanford, 99-101.

[7]   Kneale, W. and Kneale, M., (1962): *The Development of Logic*, Oxford University Press.

[8]   Kyburg, Henry E., Jr. (1961): *Probability and the Logic of Rational Belief,* Wesleyan University Press, Middletown.

[9]   Kyburg, Henry E., Jr., "Epistemological Relevance and Statistical Knowledge," this volume.

[10] Loui, Ronald P. (1986): "Computing Reference Classes," *Proceedings of the 1986 Workshop on Uncertainty in Artificial Intelligence*, 183-188.

[11] McCarthy, John (1980): "Circumscription -- A Form of Non-Monotonic Reasoning," *Artificial Intelligence* **13**, 27-39.

[12] McCarthy, John (1986): "Applications of Circumscription to Formalizing Common-Sense Knowledge," *Artificial Intelligence* **28**, 89-116.

[13] McCarthy, John, and Hayes, Pat (1969): "Some Philosphical Problems from the Standpoint of Artificial Inteligence," *Machine Intelligence* **4**, 463-502, reprinted in Weber and Nilsson (eds) *Readings in Artificial Intelligence*, Tioga Publishing, Palo Alto, 1981.

[14] McDermott, D., and Doyle, J. (1980): "Non-Monotonic Logic I," *Artificial Intelligence* **13**, 41-72.

[15] Nilsson, Nils (1986): "Probabilistic Logic," *Artificial Intelligence* **28**, 71-87.

[16] Nutter, Jane Terry (1987): "Uncertainty and Probability," *IJCAI 87*, Morgan Kaufman, Los Altos, 373-379.

[17] Pearl, Judea (1988): *Probabilistic Reasoning in Intelligent Systems*, Morgan Kaufman, Los Altos.

[18] Perlis, Donald (1986): "On the Consistency of Commonsense Reasoning," *Computational Intelligence* **2**, 189-190.

[19] Poole, David L. (1985): "On the Comparison of Theories: Preferring the Most Specific Explanation," *IJCAI 85*, 144-147.

[20] Reiter, R. (1980): "A Logic for Default Reasoning," *Artificial Intelligence* **13**, 81-132.

[21] Scott, Dana, and Krauss, Peter (1966): "Assigning Probabilities to Logical Formulas," in Hintikka and Suppes (eds) *Aspects of Inductive Logic*, North Holland, Amsterdam, 219-264.

[22] Touretzky, D. S.(1986): *The Mathematics of Inheritance Systems,* Morgan Kaufman, Los Altos, 1986.

Uncertainty in Artificial Intelligence 4
R.D. Shachter, T.S. Levitt, L.N. Kanal, J.F. Lemmer (Editors)
© Elsevier Science Publishers B.V. (North-Holland), 1990

Multiple decision trees

Suk Wah Kwok† and Chris Carter‡

Basser Department of Computer Science
University of Sydney
Australia

This paper describes experiments, on two domains, to investigate the effect of averaging over predictions of multiple decision trees, instead of using a single tree. Other authors have pointed out theoretical and commonsense reasons for preferring the multiple tree approach. Ideally, we would like to consider predictions from all trees, weighted by their probability. However, there is a vast number of different trees, and it is difficult to estimate the probability of each tree. We sidestep the estimation problem by using a modified version of the ID3 algorithm to build good trees, and average over only these trees. Our results are encouraging. For each domain, we managed to produce a small number of good trees. We find that it is best to average across sets of trees with different structure; this usually gives better performance than any of the constituent trees, including the ID3 tree.

Keywords: machine learning, transduction, empirical evaluation

1. Introduction

A common goal in machine learning is to make predictions based on previous data. In this paper we consider classification tasks – where predictions are restricted to assigning data points to one of a small number of mutually exclusive and exhaustive classes.

Many classification systems use the data to select one model – from a given class of models – and then use this model to make predictions. Using Self and Cheeseman's terminology (Self and Cheeseman, 1987) we call this method *abduction*. Many authors have pointed out that this method is not optimal (Howard, 1970; Self and Cheeseman, 1987). Self and Cheeseman give an example involving a military commander who is unsure of the location of his enemy. Abduction corresponds to chosing the most likely location, and then proceeding as if it were a fact.

Ideally, we would like to use predictions from all possible models, weighted by the probability of each model. We call this method *transduction* (Self and Cheeseman, 1987) Using the military example, we should consider all possible locations of the enemy, not just the most likely. The difference between these methods is greatest when there is a

---

† Currently a knowledge engineer at the Computer Power Group in Sydney.

‡ Currently at the Australian Graduate School of Management, University of New South Wales, Sydney.
e-mail chrisc@agsm.unsw.oz

small amount of data available. In this case, there is little basis for preferring any one model over the others, so abduction may give misleading results.

When using transduction, however, it may be computationally infeasible to consider all possible models, and it may be difficult to estimate the probability of each model. The practical result is that we are restricted to models and probabilities that facilitate the calculations.

This paper describes a hybrid approach proposed by Buntine (Buntine, 1989). We use *decision trees*, a class of models that has performed well in classification problems (Quinlan, Compton, Horn and Lazarus, 1987), and average over a small number of models each with a high probability. We hope to get some of the benefits of transduction, whilst retaining the complex models possible with abduction. Our results are encouraging; we find improved performance with a very small number of models on a variety of domains. We show that, for the small number of models we used, it is important that the models be as different as possible. Since we had trouble constructing many different models, this is a key area for future work.

2. Overview of ID3

The ID3 algorithm, and related algorithms, have been used with considerable success in classification tasks (Quinlan et. al., 1987; Breiman, Friedman, Olshen and Stone 1984; Michie, 1987). It is normally used to select a single model from data; this model is then used to predict the class of future data.

The data is described by a fixed set of *attributes*. The attributes are chosen to be predictive of the class. For example, if we were considering first year computer science students, and the class we wish to predict is whether the student passed or failed first year computer science, the following attributes might be appropriate.

High school result with numeric values.
High school maths result with numeric values.
Previous programming experience with values {yes and no}.
Temperment with values {patient and impatient}.

ID3 uses a *training set* of classified data to construct a decision tree. Figure 1 shows a decision tree for the student example. Each internal node of the tree contains a test on the value of an attribute, and each leaf of the tree is assigned a class.

```
high school result < 62.5%: fail (2)
high school result > 62.5%:
|       temperment = patient: pass (3)
|       temperment = impatient:
|       |       high school maths result < 82.5%: fail (2)
|       |       high school maths result > 82.5%: pass (1)
```

Figure 1. A decision tree

To construct this tree, ID3 uses a top-down approach, first chosing the test for the root of the tree, and then working downwards. Tests are chosen using a heuristic called the maximum *information-gain* (Quinlan, 1986), which tries to build a simple tree that fits the training set. The algorithm terminates when the tree correctly classifies the training set.

Once a tree has been built, it can be *pruned* by collapsing subtrees into leaves. This has been shown to generally improve performance (Quinlan, 1987a). After pruning some leaves may have training set objects of different classes. The proportion in each class can be used as an estimate of the probability of each class. We call this a *class probability tree* (Breiman, et. al., 1984; Carter and Catlett, 1987; Quinlan, 1987b).

3. Background theory

The motivation for our work comes from a Bayesian analysis of decision tree methods by Buntine (Buntine, 1989). This analysis shows that it is difficult to calculate the posterior probability of decision tree models. The difficulty lies in calculating the prior probability of the trees. Thus a strict application of the transduction approach does not seem possible. Buntine proposes a hybrid approach, which we adopt, where a few trees of high posterior probability are used to get some of the averaging effect of transduction.

Bayesian analysis

Buntine considers the case when there are two classes, (positive and negative) and a finite number of possible data points (that is, all attributes take discrete values). Let C be the number of different data points, and ϕ_i be the probability of type i data point having positive class, for $i = 1$ to C. We call the vector $\Phi = (\phi_1, \phi_2, ..., \phi_C)$ a classification rule.

The Bayesian approach is to work with the distribution, $p(\Phi)$, and analyse how this distribution is updated by the training set, $\mathbf{x}$. Thus, we wish to calculate

$$p(\Phi \mid \mathbf{x})$$

using Bayes' Theorem

$$p(\Phi \mid \mathbf{x}) = \frac{p(\mathbf{x} \mid \Phi)p(\Phi)}{p(\mathbf{x})}$$

where $p(\mathbf{x})$ is a normalising constant. Buntine shows that, if there are n_i type i data points in the training set, r_i of which have positive class, then

$$p(\mathbf{x} \mid \Phi) \propto \Pi_{i=1,...,C} \phi_i^{r_i} \phi_i^{n_i - r_i}$$

so the updating formula for classification rules is straightforward.

However, Buntine points out difficulties in the choice of the prior $p(\Phi)$. He argues that the success of ID3 with small training sets (a fraction of the number of data point types) means that strong correlations between data must be justified a priori. He also points out that the prior must incorporate Occam's Razor because of the observation that simple trees are superior, and because simple trees are easier to understand, so they are a more effective representation of domain knowledge.

A simplified approach

These difficulties lead us to follow Buntine's suggestion and abandon (at least for the time being) calculating the posterior probability of each classification rule. Instead, we generate several rules of high posterior probability and average across them.

We're interested in two main areas: the distribution of classification rules, $p(\Phi \mid \mathbf{x})$, and the effect of combining a small number of classification rules with high posterior probability.

The shape of the distribution of classification rules, $p(\Phi \mid \mathbf{x})$, is of particular interest. If it is fairly flat (so there are many rules of equal posterior probability) then the abduction approach of choosing one rule may give poor results. However, if it has a sharp peak, (a few rules dominate) then the abduction approach is probably adequate.

Regarding the combination of classification rules, we wish to know whether the performance of the combination is better than the performance of single rules. We would also like to know how the number of rules affects the performance of the combination.

4. Experiments

To investigate the areas mentioned above, we performed a number of experiments using decision trees built by a interactive version of ID3 (Kwok, 1987). We chose ID3, and decision trees, because of their successful track record in classification tasks. This track record suggests that the ID3 decision trees have reasonably high posterior probability, though possibly not optimal.

These experiments address the following questions:

- Is the ID3 tree special? That is, can we build other simple trees with competitive performance, and if so, how many?
- Does averaging across a group of good trees improve accuracy?
- What happens when we increase the number of trees?

Building multiple trees

Because we weight the trees equally when calculating the average, we require a systematic method of building many trees of comparable accuracy to the original ID3 tree. Recall from Section 3 that ID3 generates a single tree in a top-down manner, at each node choosing the test with the highest information gain. We adopt an interactive version of the ID3 algorithm that allows the user to select the test. We still calculate the information gain for each test, and we present the user with a ranked list of tests for guidance, with the highest information gain test as the default.

We find that, if we use a test with an information gain that is close to the maximum, the resulting tree does not perform significantly worse. In fact, some trees perform better.

In our experiments, we only try to override the default test at the top tree levels. This is because the choice of test at the top tree levels affects all the tests that appear below it; by doing this we hope to obtain trees that are substantially different from each other.

Combining multiple trees

We use each tree independently to classify data points and then average the results. There are several ways of doing this. First, individual trees can return a categorical result (decision trees) or probability estimates (class probability trees). In both cases, we can take the estimates and average them. This average can be changed to a categorical result, or left as a probability estimate.

To interpret the average categorically, we choose the class with the highest estimate. We call this the *voting* method. A result from Buntine (Buntine, 1989) shows that the voting method minimizes the expected error, given that we must return a categorical result. To evaluate performance, we calculate the percentage error over a test set of data.

We call leaving the average as a probability estimate the *class probability* method. We evaluate the performance of this method by calculating the Half-Brier score (one-half the mean square error) (Brier, 1950) over a test set of data.

5. Results

We performed experiments using two domains, Weather and Student, selected from a set of ten candidate domains (Kwok, 1987). We selected these particular domains because ID3 gives moderate performance on them, and there are several good attributes to choose at the root of the tree. Reasonable performance is important because, first, if performance is too poor ID3 is not an appropriate method anyway, and, second, if the performance is too good it is difficult to detect any improvement.

Weather data

The weather data (Allen, Bolam and Ciesielski 1986) contains daily meteorlogical observations described by 35 attributes including humidity, pressure pattern, wind direction, cloud amount and temperature. The task is to decide whether it will rain on the following day. There are 5516 observations: 3000 in the training set, and 2516 in the test set.

Student data

The student data (Kwok, 1987) contains information on first year Computer Science students at the University of Sydney in 1983. Students are described by attributes such as High School mark, High School maths units and mark, faculty, sex, and answers to two questionaires on their background in computing, opinions on the computer science course and expectation of their results. The task is to determine the performance of a student in the computer science course. There are two classes: pass or fail. The data contains 446 observations: 250 in the training set, and 196 in the test set.

Performance of individual trees

For each domain, a number of trees were built using the interactive method described in Section 4. We also pruned each tree. Table 1 gives the accuracy and size (measured by the number of nodes) of individual trees before and after pruning. Tree 0 is the ID3 tree (built uninterrupted). In both domains our tree-building method (Section 4) found a group of trees with competitive performance to the ID3 tree (8 for the weather data, 7 for the student data). The ID3 tree is not the best tree in any of the domains, though it is a good tree. (2 better trees for the weather data, 4 for the student data).

In the student domain we obtain a larger group of good trees than in the weather domain. (in the case of pruned trees, 4 have better performance than the pruned ID3 tree, with trees 2, 3 and 5 significantly better.) This may be expained by the fact that in the student domain there are 6 or 7 attributes that yield good information gain at the top few levels of the ID3 tree, whereas, in the weather domain, there are only 2 or 3 good attributes.

TABLE 1. Performance of individual trees

	Weather				Student			
	unpruned		pruned		unpruned		pruned	
tree	% error	size	% error	size	% error	size	% error	size
0	31.48	915	29.61	523	27.04	160	24.49	23
1	32.71	909	30.29	507	22.96	162	24.49	31
2	30.37	887	28.97	479	25.00	159	21.94	18
3	32.51	913	30.09	523	26.02	149	21.94	39
4	32.43	917	30.52	501	25.00	162	23.47	34
5	30.05	887	28.50	509	29.08	164	20.41	27
6	33.74	889	31.20	539	27.55	154	24.49	23
7	32.23	927	29.77	515				
Average	31.94	906	29.87	512	26.09	159	23.03	28

Different combinations of trees

We used the weather data to experiment with different combinations of unpruned and pruned trees. The weather data has a limited number of good attributes at the root of the tree, so some of the 8 trees we built are fairly similar – either having common roots or common second tree level nodes. This allows us to compare the performance of combinations of similar trees to combinations of different trees.

We expect that combining similar trees will not result in much improvement in accuracy. An intuitive explanation for this is that the group of similar trees give a "biased vote" for a particular class.

We tried different combinations of three trees; the individual result from each tree is interpreted as a probability estimate, and combined using the voting method to return a categorical result (as described in Section 4).

TABLE 2. Different combinations of three pruned trees

3 fairly different trees			3 trees with common second level node			3 trees with common root		
	% error			% error			% error	
comb	unpruned	pruned	comb	unpruned	pruned	comb	unpruned	pruned
0 1 2	28.42	27.98	0 1 4	31.20	29.01	0 2 4	31.00	29.25
0 1 3	29.33	28.06	0 1 5	29.01	28.38	0 2 5	30.48	28.50
0 2 3	29.17	28.06	0 1 6	32.04	29.69	0 4 5	31.48	29.49
0 2 6	28.50	27.90	0 2 4	31.00	29.25	1 3 6	32.00	29.77
0 2 7	28.50	27.86	0 2 5	30.48	28.50	1 3 7	32.23	29.57
0 6 7	28.93	27.42	0 3 4	30.68	28.74	3 6 7	31.52	29.25
Average	28.81	27.88		30.74	28.93		31.45	29.31

Table 2 confirms our prediction that combinations of different trees have better performance than combinations of similar trees (common roots or common second tree level nodes). This is the case for both unpruned and pruned trees.

The effect of using more trees

To investigate whether increasing the number of trees improves accuracy, we progressively increase the number of pruned and unpruned trees. For unpruned trees, since individual trees return a categorical result, odd numbers of trees were used to avoid ties. For each number of trees, the average percentage error over many different combinations is given in Table 3. The combinations were chosen so that the constituent trees are as different as possible. So some possible combinations were ignored because the constituent trees were too similar.

TABLE 3. Percentage error for increasing number of trees

	Weather				Student			
	unpruned		pruned		unpruned		pruned	
# trees	%error	# comb.	%error	# comb.	%error	# comb.	%error	# comb.
1	31.94	8	29.87	8	26.09	7	23.03	7
2			30.23	27			21.04	21
3	28.62	23	27.52	23	23.92	35	19.49	35
4			27.33	9			19.48	35
5	28.33	9	27.2	9	24.05	21	19.00	21
6			26.96	5			18.80	7
7	28.66	6	27.25	6	24.49	1	19.90	1
8			27.19	1				

For the limited numbers considered, increasing the number of trees initially improves performance. After only a few trees, however, the error rate reaches an optimal point; after that, additional trees slightly degrade performance. The overall improvement in performance is significant. In the case of unpruned trees, using multiple trees gives an improvement of 3.6% for weather and 2.2% for student. As a comparison, Table 1 (averages row) shows that the well-established technique of pruning gives an improvement of 2.1% for weather and 3% for student. For pruned trees, using multiple trees gives a further average improvement of 2.9% for weather and 4.2% for student over single trees.

Class probability method

So far we have used the voting method to return a categorical result. We now investigate the effect of returning the average class probability estimate. We used the Half-Brier score as our measure of error. To give some feel for the Half-Brier score, if all probability estimates are 0 or 1, the Half-Brier score corresponds to the error rate. Figure 2 shows a similar pattern to Table 3 (using the voting method). The Half-Brier score (a measure of error) decreases as the number of trees increase. The decrease is initially large and gradually slows down as more trees are added.

6. Conclusion

The purpose of our experiments was to see whether a limited form of transduction could improve the accuracy of classification methods using decision trees. Our limited form of transduction is to only use good trees, since we do not know how to accurately calculate the posterior probability of trees.

For each domain, our tree-building method produced a small number of trees of competitive size and performance to the ID3 tree. We found that it is best to average

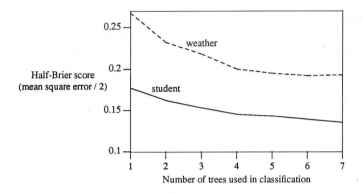

Figure 2. Error (Half-Brier score) against number of pruned trees

across sets of different trees; this usually gives better peformance than any of the constituent trees, including the ID3 tree. Unfortunately, our tree-building method did not produce sufficient numbers of different trees to allow a thorough investigation of the effect of increasing the number of trees.

We would like to find a tree-building algorithm that produces more good trees. If we cannot build sufficient good trees, we would like to investigate the effect of weighting the individual trees, however approximate are the weights.

Acknowledgement

We would like to thank Wray Buntine for his many useful suggestions on this work.

References

Allen, G., Bolam, W. and Ciesielski, V. (1986). Evaluation of an Expert System to forecast rain in Melbourne, *First Australian Artificial Intelligence Conference,* Melbourne, Nov 1986.

Breiman, L., Friedman, J.H., Olshen, R.A. and Stone, C.J. (1984). *Classification and Regression Trees,* Wadsworth, Belmont, Calif.

Brier, (1950). Verification of Forecasts Expressed in Terms of Probability, *Monthly Weather Review,* 1950, 78, 1-3.

Buntine, W. (1989). Decision tree induction systems: a bayesian analysis, pp 109-127, *Uncertainty in Artificial Intelligence 3,* Kanal, L.N., Levitt, T.S., and Lemmer, J.F. (eds) North-Holland, Amsterdam, 1989.

Carter, C.K., and Catlett, J. (1987). Assessing credit card applications using machine learning, *IEEE Expert, Fall 1987,* Special edition on AI applications in Financial Systems.

Howard, R.A. (1970). Decision Analysis: Perspectives on Inference, Decision, and Experimentation, *Proc. of the IEEE.,* Vol. 58, No. 5, May 1970.

Kwok, S.W. (1987). Induction and manipulation of decision trees, Unpublished Honours Thesis, Basser Dept. of Computer Science, University of Sydney.

Michie, D. (1987). Current Developments in Expert Systems, *Applications of Expert Systems*, Quinlan, J. R. (ed), Addison Wesley.

Quinlan, J.R. (1986). Induction of decision trees, *Machine Learning 1*, 1, 1986.

Quinlan, J. R., Compton, P. J., Horn, K. A., Lazarus, L. (1987). Inductive Knowledge Acquisition: A case study, *Applications of Expert Systems*, Quinlan, J. R. (ed), Addison Wesley.

Quinlan, J.R. (1987a). Simplifying Decision Trees, in *Int. J. Man-Machine Studies*.

Quinlan, J.R. (1987b). Decision trees as probabilistic classifiers, *Proc. Fourth Int'l Workshop on Machine Learning*, Morgan Kaufmann, Los Altos, Calif., June 1987.

Self, M., Cheeseman, P., (1987). Bayesian Prediction for Artificial Intelligence, *Proc. Uncertainty in Artificial Intelligence*, Seattle, July 1987.

Section III

KNOWLEDGE ACQUISITION AND EXPLANATION

Uncertainty in Artificial Intelligence 4
R.D. Shachter, T.S. Levitt, L.N. Kanal, J.F. Lemmer (Editors)
© Elsevier Science Publishers B.V. (North-Holland), 1990

KNET: Integrating Hypermedia and Normative Bayesian Modeling

R. Martin Chavez and Gregory F. Cooper
Medical Computer Science Group
Stanford University
Stanford, California 94305

December 11, 1989

Abstract

KNET is a general-purpose shell for constructing expert systems based on belief networks and decision networks. Such networks serve as graphical representations for decision models, in which the knowledge engineer must define clearly the alternatives, states, preferences, and relationships that constitute a decision basis. KNET contains a knowledge-engineering core written in Object Pascal and an interface that tightly integrates HyperCard, a hypertext authoring tool for the Apple Macintosh computer, into a novel expert-system architecture. Hypertext and hypermedia have become increasingly important in the storage, management, and retrieval of information. In broad terms, hypermedia deliver heterogeneous bits of information in dynamic, extensively cross-referenced packages. The resulting KNET system features a coherent probabilistic scheme for managing uncertainty, an object-oriented graphics editor for drawing and manipulating decision networks, and HyperCard's potential for quickly constructing flexible and friendly user interfaces. We envision KNET as a useful prototyping tool for our ongoing research on a variety of Bayesian reasoning problems, including tractable representation, inference, and explanation.

1. Motivation

1.1 User Interfaces

Rowley *et al.* observe that "advances in computer science are often consolidated as programming systems that raise the abstraction level and the vocabulary for expressing solutions to new problems. We have seen little permanent consolidation of this form in AI" [15]. The authors note that some artificial intelligence (AI) systems place too many restrictions on the admissible paradigms; almost all insulate the AI kernel from the surrounding programming environment; few support the inclusion of facilities that were not coded within the original framework. Our experience has illustrated shortcomings in many of the available knowledge-engineering products, including EMYCIN [2], KEE [12], S-1 [17], and Personal Consultant Plus. Consultations with knowledge bases developed in EMYCIN and Personal Consultant Plus must conform to a rigidly specified, linear sequence of questions and answers. The certainty factor model of EMYCIN, Personal Consultant Plus, and S-1 implicitly assumes that rules must form tree-structured chains of inference. KEE provides no facilities for the management of uncertainty.

KNET combines normative probabilistic modeling techniques with a front end that offers the flexibility and expressive power of hypertext. Perhaps more important, KNET cleanly separates the design of a tailored, domain-specific user interface from all other aspects of the system. In addition, KNET strictly adheres to the Macintosh human-interface guidelines. Buttons, icons, scrolling text fields, color illustrations, menus, and mouse-sensitive screen objects streamline the construction and validation of new knowledge bases. HyperCard, an authoring tool for hypermedia, facilitates the design of intuitive user interfaces. A custom-designed interprocess communications channel transfers information from the object-oriented KNET core (written in Object Pascal) to HyperCard and back.

The entire KNET environment runs on low-cost, general-purpose hardware. Using HyperTalk [6], HyperCard's object-oriented authoring language, knowledge engineers and even relatively naive users can incorporate sound, synthesized speech, videodisc images, and animation into their knowledge-intensive applications. Our experience has indicated that we can prototype, debug, and refine radically different hypertext presentations of the knowledge captured by a Bayesian model in a single session. Workers in the field have observed that powerful and understandable user interfaces can absorb much of a project's design and implementation cycle. We believe that KNET has altered the software-engineering balance: With HyperCard as the front end, development of an appropriate user interface takes much less of the development cycle than heretofore possible.

1.2 Belief networks and decision networks

Henrion [8] characterizes belief networks and decision networks (also known as influence diagrams) as tools for constructing coherent probabilistic representations of uncertain expert opinion. For more than a decade now, decision analysts have used decision networks to construct formal descriptions of decision problems and to capture knowledge in a representation that people with varying degrees of technical proficiency can understand. Belief networks are specialized decision networks that lack value and decision nodes. Belief networks are particularly useful for diagnostic applications. Pearl [14] has proposed an elegant distributed algorithm for belief maintenance and updating in such networks.

Decision networks represent the alternatives, states, preferences, and relationships that constitute a decision model [11]. We define decision networks as directed acyclic graphs with nodes that represent propositions or quantities of interest and arcs that summarize the interactions between those nodes. Decision networks provide a direct mapping between the expert's knowledge and the internal computational formalism. Their intuitive pictorial structure facilitates knowledge acquisition and communication [9].

Rectangular decision nodes represent actions under direct control of the decision maker. Arcs that enter a decision node represent the information available at the time of action. Circular chance nodes represent uncertain states of the world. Diamond-shaped value nodes summarize the preferences of the decision maker. The decision maker will select a course of action that maximizes his expected value.

After drawing a decision network, the knowledge engineer must quantitate the influences of parent nodes on their children. Chance nodes without predecessors require prior-probability distributions. Chance nodes with predecessors require probability distributions conditioned on their parents. Next, the engineer must encode the decision maker's attitudes toward risk according to the axioms of utility theory. Value nodes require the specification of a function

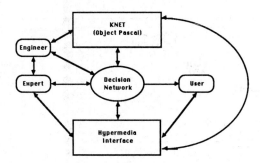

Figure 1: THE KNET ARCHITECTURE INTEGRATES OBJECT PASCAL AND HYPERCARD.

over all parent decision and chance nodes. An inference algorithm for belief networks will calculate posterior odds, based on all the available evidence, for each chance node of interest. An inference algorithm for decision networks will isolate the sequence of decisions with the highest expected value.

Shachter has designed DAVID, a decision network processing system that runs on the Macintosh and provides operations for expected-value decision making and sensitivity analysis. He observes that "the criticisms of probabilistic models of uncertainty are overcome by an intelligent graphical interface that explicitly incorporates conditional independence" [16]. Shachter's encouraging results show that students have been able quickly to build and solve decision models with DAVID. Henrion [8] has demonstrated the feasibility of constructing decision networks of moderate size (with about 30 nodes) for diagnosing and treating disorders of apple-tree roots. MUNIN [13], an expert system based on belief networks for electromyography diagnosis, pursues a similar knowledge-engineering approach. Experience suggests, therefore, that belief networks and decision networks can serve as effective representations for communication between people and machines. The elicitation of those normative network models, moreover, entails the application of tests that can remove imprecise language, force clear explication of an expert's model, and clarify the interrelationships of causal influences.

As always, the development of practical skills, algorithms, and software lags behind the theoretical discovery of a new modeling paradigm. Shachter [16] proposes, but does not define, an architecture that integrates decision networks and traditional expert systems. KNET is a step toward that goal: The system provides sophisticated graphical tools, powerful Hyper-Card templates for defining user interfaces, a Bayesian decision-making kernel, and an open architecture that encompasses Object Pascal, HyperTalk, and in the near future, Common-Lisp. Figure 1 summarizes the KNET architecture and illustrates the interactions among the knowledge engineer, the expert, the user, the HyperCard interface, and the Pascal inferencing algorithm. The target user never needs to observe the details of uncertainty management in KNET, inasmuch as the hypermedia interface hides the irrelevant details.

KNET differs substantially from DAVID, the closest previous research, in three respects:

1. The final output of DAVID consists of tables that indicate preferred decisions and expected value for every possible instantiation of the observed chance variables. As such, DAVID's paradigm does not optimally represent large diagnostic problems that have dozens or

342

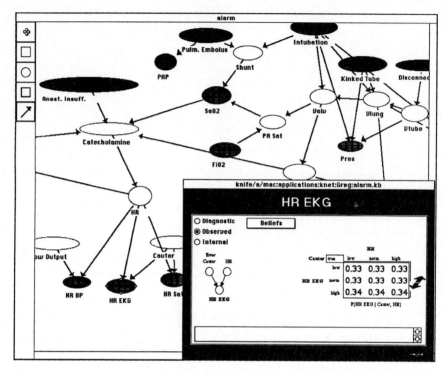

Figure 2: A SMALL PORTION OF THE ALARM BELIEF NETWORK, AS DISPLAYED BY KNET. ALARM
ENCODES KNOWLEDGE ABOUT THE VENTILATION STATUS OF A PATIENT IN THE ICU.

even hundreds of observations. For example, if the value of 20 binary symptom variables
were known for a given patient, then DAVID would produce a table of size 2^{20} relating all
combinations of the 20 symptom variables to a particular disease of interest. Only one
of the 2^{20} entries, however, actually corresponds to the current patient's condition.

2. DAVID provides a single interface for the knowledge engineer and end user. KNET, on the
other hand, envisions a multiplicity of target audiences that require different interfaces.

3. KNET specifies an open architecture for probabilistic expert systems. A distributed server
that runs on fast hardware could, for instance, perform updating of the decision model.
A networked implementation will allow the Macintosh to offer maximum responsiveness,
whereas superior number-crunching hardware will execute the inferencing algorithm.

Wellman and Heckerman [19] have described modularity and modifiability as essential
characteristics of a sophisticated representation. Without either of those attributes, knowledge
bases rapidly lose their transparency, portability, and relevance. The analysis of Heckerman

and Horvitz [7] shows that the certainty-factor model of EMYCIN entails strong conditional-independence assumptions that rarely obtain in practice. Decision networks, on the other hand, accommodate a weaker form of semantic modularity (in which propositions can be added or deleted from the decision model without requiring reassessment of every influence) appropriate for plausible reasoning. KNET provides the myriad tools that can help bring theoretically motivated decision networks into the practical world of applied knowledge engineering.

2. Knowledge engineering in the Bayesian framework

In its present form, KNET uses Pearl's distributed updating algorithm [14] to maintain belief assignments in a belief network. The system accomodates decision nodes by using a technique [5] that transforms any belief-network algorithm into a decision-network algorithm.

Design of a belief network follows the canonical principles of decision analysis [11]. First, the knowledge engineer must extract the relevant state variables and their admissible values. In certain domains, such as clinical epidemiology, where few terms possess a unique denotation, the engineer must elicit detailed descriptions that pass a clarity test. In other words, a clairvoyant with access to all the relevant information could unambiguously assign a value to each state variable without requiring further clarification.

Second, the knowledge engineer and expert must group the state variables into a directed acyclic graph by drawing arcs that represent influences. Arcs may, but do not necessarily, denote cause-and-effect relationships. The absence of an arc implies specific probabilistic statements of conditional independence. Pearl [14] and Wellman [18] describe the implications of graph connectivity in detail.

Anyone who has used standard Macintosh graphics software can create a decision network in KNET. After invoking a HyperCard stack entitled "Belief Networks," the engineer presses a button labeled "New Knowledge Base." Two empty windows immediately appear: One displays a palette of graphical shapes, and the other contains a scrollable list of variable names. The engineer clicks the mouse on the palette to select ellipses for chance nodes, squares for decision nodes, diamonds for value nodes, and arrows for influence arcs. Using mouse gestures that the Macintosh design group has standardized, the knowledge engineer creates a color picture of the network (Figure 2). KNET supports all the sophisticated screen operations that Macintosh users have come to expect, including dragging, coloring, shading, naming, and resizing of nodes. KNET's pop-up window scroller allows the engineer immediately to situate herself within a potentially enormous knowledge base and to extract a view of any slice of the domain.

After drawing a network and rearranging its nodes for maximum esthetic appeal, the engineer can double-click on a node and thereby open that node for further definition and inspection. A HyperCard corresponding to the node appears on the screen (Figure 3). At present, KNET provides only one template for the knowledge engineer's view of a node; we plan to offer several, inasmuch as the design of a new format with different text fields, buttons, labels, and illustrations takes only minutes, and presupposes no deep knowledge of HyperTalk.

The inferencing core for belief networks requires only that the HyperCard interface specify mutually exclusive and collectively exhaustive values for each node, a prior belief assignment for each value of orphan nodes (those that have no incoming arcs), and a conditional probability distribution over the values of each parent node. We have extended HyperCard to share hypertext fields with Pascal objects. The communication mechanism, although complex

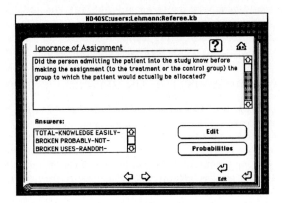

Figure 3: A HYPERCARD VIEW OF A CHANCE NODE, IGNORANCE OF ASSIGNMENT, FROM THE REFEREE BELIEF NETWORK. DIFFERENT KNOWLEDGE BASES MIGHT PRESENT DOMAIN-SPECIFIC HYPERTEXT RENDITIONS OF THEIR CONCEPTS.

at the implementation level, presents a powerful interface that the HyperTalk script designer can invoke with just one line of code. In effect, the HyperCard interface can create arbitrarily sophisticated and graphically appealing views of the decision network's hidden structure. More important, the KNET programmer can tailor those views to the requirements of diverse knowledge engineers who are operating in radically different domains.

An example illustrates the key ideas. A prototypical HyperCard view (Figure 3) into a chance node of the belief network contains a scrolling text field labeled "QUESTION," a field labeled "LEGALVALUES," a "NAME" field at the top, a button labeled "PROBABILITIES," and a return arrow at the bottom. The return arrow contains a simple HyperTalk script with the command "activate KNET"; when the user clicks on that button, HyperCard returns control to the KNET knowledge-engineering core, and the belief network becomes the foremost window on the screen. The "PROBABILITIES" button has a script that transfers control to another HyperCard (not shown), one that gathers numbers for the conditional probability distribution incident upon that node. The probability-gathering card has at its disposal all the computational, text-manipulation, and painting capabilities of HyperTalk. The card need only insert the new distribution into an invisible hypertext field; the interface shares that field transparently with Object Pascal.

HyperCard provides a number of useful templates. One of those prototype cards contains HyperTalk scripts that produce attractive histograms and pie charts corresponding to arbitrary numerical data. With 5 minutes of effort, the first author was able to paste the chart-drawing card into his KB stack, to create a new button on the probability-gathering card, and to write a five-line script that switches instantaneously between graphical and numeric views of the conditional probability distribution. Such a facility might demand an entire week of a professional programmer's time; a requirement for user-specified dimensions, labels, and background illustrations could quickly turn into a tedious, lengthy task for the system's programmer. With

KNET and HyperCard working together, however, the KNET designer needn't anticipate every possible feature required by every conceivable target audience. KNET provides the templates and hooks; HyperCard users, be they domain experts, knowledge engineers, or application programmers, can do the rest.

3. Using the Bayesian model

A fully specified belief network enumerates the possible values or discretized ranges for each state variable, the relevant conditional probability distributions at each local event group, and prior probabilities for the root nodes. A single line of HyperTalk code, "command consult," tells KNET to instantiate the belief network, to calculate evidential and diagnostic support for each node, to compute the current belief assignment, and to build a new consultation object. We have extended the EMYCIN metaphor of a decision session as a consultation with the expert's knowledge base; in KNET, however, the consultation can use the power of hypertext to maximize the flow of information between knowledge base and the user. We have enhanced HyperTalk with simple commands that extract the belief assignment for a given node and feed new observations into the belief network. The KNET architecture hides the irrelevant details of belief updating and propagation. From the user's point of view, observations automatically propagate through the network and make themselves apparent through graphical interactions with the HyperCard interface.

The KNET designer's imagination alone limits the applicability of HyperCard's Bayesian modeling functions. The current consultation format (Figure 4), which the first author designed and built in a few hours, allows the user to explore the belief network by pointing and clicking on the obvious icons. Transition from one card to the next happens instantaneously; on-screen buttons provide helpful information, illustrate the user's context within the model, and effect transitions among different levels of the model. One button provides easy access to a dictionary of terms; others break complicated queries into more easily managed parts. Labeled scales translate mouse gestures into belief updates. Clearly marked buttons, when activated, reveal a node's current belief assignment in either numerical or graphical form. By pointing and double-clicking, the user can switch between arbitrary color views of the belief network and hypertext presentations of the equivalent information; users may even choose to have both displays available simultaneously. In short, the current version of KNET provides a consultation format that fully exploits a decade of progress in the design of human interfaces. More significant, KNET offers this generality and flexibility within a normative Bayesian framework.

4. Applications

REFEREE [3] is an expert system that incorporates into a belief network a biostatistician's expert knowledge about the methodology of randomized clinical trials (RCTs). An original EMYCIN prototype revealed ambiguity in the goals of the project and in the precise definition of state variables (also known as "parameters" in EMYCIN). Perhaps more significant, the EMYCIN implementation assigned conflicting interpretations to certainty factors, which simultaneously served as measures of belief and as continuous measures of quality. In addition, EMYCIN's facilities for observing the interrelationships among rules and for guiding the user through a

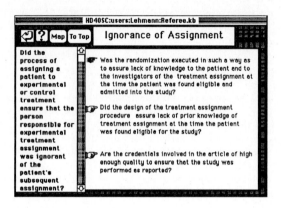

Figure 4: A SCREEN VIEW FROM A CONSULTATION WITH REFEREE SHOWS THE RELATION-
SHIP BETWEEN THE BELIEF NETWORK AND THE HYPERCARD INTERFACE. BY CLICKING
ON THE POINTING-HAND ICONS, THE USER CAN FOCUS THE SYSTEM'S ATTENTION FROM
IGNORANCE OF ASSIGNMENT TO MORE SPECIFIC QUESTIONS ABOUT THE RANDOMIZATION OF
THE CLINICAL STUDY.

consultation with the expert's knowledge base simply did not measure up to the task at hand.
Without advanced tools for clarifying questions and for providing the necessary contextual
clues, experts and knowledge engineers became confused about the underlying structure and
purpose of the system.

Three months of experimentation with KEE revealed a dearth of facilities for plausible
reasoning. The dynamic creation of active images in KEE proved to be too slow and cumbersome
for general use. Personal Consultant Plus, M-1, and S-1 suffer from related deficiencies; all
employ the certainty-factor model.

In parallel with the design and implementation of KNET on the Macintosh, we drew the
REFEREE belief network and wrote scripts to transfer the old knowledge-base frames (from
a prototype implementation on the TI Explorer) into HyperCard. To date, we have found
that we can act on the REFEREE team's suggestions, regardless of their complexity, and can
demonstrate an enhanced version of the HyperCard interface within hours or a few days. We
have constructed a belief network that represents the REFEREE expert's subjective knowledge
about the interpretation of randomized, controlled studies that measure the effect of a treatment intervention on mortality. We are now validating and adjusting the expert's numerical
assessments.

The KNET implementation of REFEREE places the ease and power of HyperCard at our disposal. In a few hours, we can experiment with various presentation formats that optimize
clarity and completeness. We can encode user models as HyperCard templates and thereby
tailor the presentation to a specific agent's requirements. We can provide dictionaries, illustrations, suggestive examples, and extensive help facilities, all within the HyperCard framework.
By carefully structuring and refining the information we present in the interface according to

a Bayesian clarity test, we increase our expert's enthusiasm and our own confidence in the correctness and relevance of the model.

5. Future work

KNET has begun to serve as our research group's standard vehicle for investigating the design of large knowledge-intensive systems with coherent schemes for managing uncertainty. We have planned and initiated the following activities:

- The general Bayesian inferencing problem is NP-hard [4]. We are investigating randomized algorithms that may yield significant time reductions for networks with particular topologies. Inasmuch as KNET hides the details of belief propagation, we can develop and test new algorithms without altering existing knowledge bases.

- Belief networks can encode meta-knowledge about how to manage and focus a user's interaction with a Bayesian model. KNET offers a general facility for designing and verifying belief networks; we can then neatly package and reference those networks through extensions to HyperTalk. In the coming months, we will apply KNET to ongoing work on belief networks for control reasoning.

- Our expert has suggested the use of color as an explanation facility; nodes might be shaded or colored according to their influence on the goal node. Inasmuch as HyperCard can control the presentation of a decision network by setting red, green, blue tuples in hypertext fields, the basic facilities already exist. In consultation with our expert, we shall experiment with various color-coded semantics for explanation.

- KNET presently uses a primitive custom database to store large quantities of information, including numerical data, network topology, color coding, shading, and discretization. We are presently incorporating a relational-database management system (DBMS) into the KNET architecture [1]. We shall access the DBMS from both Object Pascal and HyperCard. The DBMS will store risk-preference curves, probability distributions, pictorial data, incremental revisions of the knowledge base, and consultation histories.

- As a test of KNET's flexibility and general utility, we shall convert the PATHFINDER knowledge base [10] to KNET format. PATHFINDER presently assumes conditional independence of evidence given diseases; the KNET implementation will allow us to relax that assumption. We shall measure the time required for the transition to KNET and the construction of an appropriate HyperCard consultation interface.

- We shall offer KNET as a programming environment for our department's course in expert systems. The students who use the system will provide important feedback.

Only further experience will unequivocally establish the efficacy of Bayesian methods in the design of large-scale expert systems. Now, at last, KNET offers all the software tools we need to design, debug, and validate Bayesian models suitable for use by a large and diverse target audience.

Acknowledgments

Harold Lehmann made essential contributions to the development of KNET. Diana Forsythe, David Heckerman, Eric Horvitz, and Bruce Buchanan provided important feedback. Lyn Dupre edited the manuscript. Bill Brown and Dan Feldman devoted their time and insight as domain experts.

This work was supported by the National Library of Medicine under Grant LM-04136, the National Institutes of Health under a Medical Scientist Training Program Grant GM07365, and the National Science Foundation under Grant ISt83-12148. Computing facilities were provided by the SUMEX-AIM resource under NIH Grant RR-00785.

References

[1] T. Barsalou. An object-based architecture for biomedical expert database systems. In R.A. Greenes, editor, *Proceedings of the Twelfth Symposium on Computer Applications in Medical Care*, pages 572–578, Washington, DC, November 1988. IEEE Computer Society Press.

[2] B. G. Buchanan and E. H. Shortliffe. *Rule-Based Expert Systems: The MYCIN Experiments of the Stanford Heuristic Programming Project*. Addison-Wesley, Reading, MA, 1984.

[3] R.M. Chavez and H.P. Lehmann. REFEREE: A belief network that helps evaluate the credibility of a randomized clinical trial. In *Proceedings of the 1988 AIM Workshop*, pages 15–16, Stanford, CA, 1988. American Association for Artificial Intelligence.

[4] G. F. Cooper. Probabilistic inference using belief networks is NP-hard. Technical Report KSL-87-27, Medical Computer Science Group, Knowledge Systems Laboratory, Stanford University, Stanford, CA, May 1987.

[5] G. F. Cooper. A method for using belief networks as influence diagrams. In *Proceedings of the Fourth Workshop on Uncertainty in Artificial Intelligence*, University of Minnesota, Minneapolis, MN, August 1988. American Association for Artificial Intelligence.

[6] D. Goodman. *The Complete HyperCard Handbook*. Bantam Books, New York, NY, 1987.

[7] D. E. Heckerman and E. J. Horvitz. DAVID: Influence diagram processing system for the Macintosh. In *Uncertainty in Artificial Intelligence 2*, pages 23–34. North-Holland, Amsterdam, 1988.

[8] M. Henrion. Some practical issues in constructing belief networks. In *Uncertainty in Artificial Intelligence 3*, pages 161–174. North-Holland, Amsterdam, 1989.

[9] E. J. Horvitz, J. S. Breese, and M. Henrion. Decision theory in expert systems and artificial intelligence. *International Journal of Approximate Reasoning*, 2:247–302, 1988.

[10] E.J. Horvitz, D. E. Heckerman, B. N. Nathwani, and L. M. Fagan. Diagnostic strategies in the hypothesis-directed PATHFINDER system. In *First Conference on Artificial Intelligence Applications*, pages 630–636. IEEE Computer Society, 1984.

[11] R. A. Howard and J. E. Matheson. Influence diagrams. In *Readings on the Principles and Applications of Decision Analysis*, volume II, pages 719–762. Strategic Decisions Group, Menlo Park, CA, 1981.

[12] Inc. Intellicorp. *Intellicorp KEE Software Development System User's Manual*. 1986.

[13] S. L. Lauritzen and D. J. Spiegelhalter. Local computations with probabilities on graphical structures and their application to expert systems. *Journal of the Royal Statistical Society*, 50(2), 1988.

[14] J. Pearl. Fusion, propagation, and structuring in belief networks. *Artificial Intelligence*, 29:241–288, 1986.

[15] S. Rowley. JOSHUA: Uniform access to heterogeneous knowledge structures, or, Why Joshing is better than Conniving or Planning. In *Proceedings of the Sixth National Conference on Artificial Intelligence*, pages 48–52, Seattle, WA, July 1987. American Association for Artificial Intelligence.

[16] R. D. Shachter. DAVID: Influence diagram processing system for the Macintosh. In *Uncertainty in Artificial Intelligence 2*, pages 191–196. North-Holland, Amsterdam, 1988.

[17] Inc. Teknowledge. *S.1 Reference Manual*. 1984.

[18] M. P. Wellman. Qualitative probabilistic networks for planning under uncertainty. In *Uncertainty in Artificial Intelligence 2*, pages 197–208. North-Holland, Amsterdam, 1988.

[19] M. P. Wellman and D. E. Heckerman. The role of calculi in uncertain reasoning. In *Proceedings of the Third Workshop on Uncertainty in Artificial Intelligence*, pages 321–331, Seattle, WA, July 1987. American Association for Artificial Intelligence.

Uncertainty in Artificial Intelligence 4
R.D. Shachter, T.S. Levitt, L.N. Kanal, J.F. Lemmer (Editors)
© Elsevier Science Publishers B.V. (North-Holland), 1990   351

GENERATING EXPLANATIONS OF DECISION MODELS
BASED ON AN AUGMENTED REPRESENTATION OF UNCERTAINTY

Holly B. Jimison
Medical Computer Science
Stanford University
Stanford, California

Many real world models can be characterized as weak, meaning
that there is significant uncertainty in both the data input and
inferences. This lack of determinism makes it especially
difficult for users of computer decision aids to understand and
have confidence in the models. This paper presents a
representation for uncertainty and utilities that serves as a
framework for graphical summary and computer-generated
explanation of decision models. The application described that
tests the methodology is a computer decision aid designed to
enhance the clinician-patient consultation process for patients
with angina (chest pain due to lack of blood flow to the heart
muscle). The angina model is represented as a Bayesian
decision network. Additionally, the probabilities and utilities
are treated as random variables with probability distributions
on their range of possible values. The initial distributions
represent information on all patients with anginal symptoms,
and the approach allows for rapid tailoring to more patient-
specific distributions. This framework provides a metric for
judging the importance of each variable in the model
dynamically.

1. Introduction

It is often difficult to give an intuitive summary and explanation of a
complicated decision problem. Yet, if a computer decision-support
system is to be successful, it is important that it provide the user with
insight into the decision model and a justification for the resulting
recommendations. Many decisions must be made in a timely manner
with incomplete and sometimes unreliable information. Computer
decision aids can provide valuable assistance for these types of
problems, however, it is important that a system provide an intuitive
overview and explanation for the resulting recommendation.

With therapy decisions for chronic diseases, there is generally significant uncertainty in the prediction of health outcomes and the decisions are often sensitive to a patient's preference on the quality of life associated with the health outcomes. We chose to look at the therapy of angina (chest pain due to lack of blood flow to the heart muscle) as a representative chronic disease decision problem. For simplicity, we limited the decision alternatives to treatment with coronary artery bypass surgery or medical management using drug therapy. This choice for patients involves the tradeoff between the increased chance of relief of pain associated with the bypass surgery and the mortality also associated with the surgical procedure. As with many chronic diseases, a patient's preferences for the quality of life of the various health states is a very important component of a complete decision model. These factors are often difficult for clinicians to incorporate in their decisions on what to recommend for individual patients.

In designing a computer aid for angina patients and clinicians, we chose to emphasize the presentation of information. The purpose of the system is to enhance a user's understanding of an underlying complex and quantitative model and to improve the quality of communication between the clinician and patient. For this reason we refer to the system as the *Angina Communication Tool.*

2.   Motivation for Using a Decision Network Model

Given the importance of uncertainty and patient utilities in the angina decision model, a decision theory formulation for a model seemed most appropriate. The advantages to this approach are that patient utilities, incorporating preferences and risk attitudes, are explicitly modeled and that the probabilistic representation of uncertainty is axiomatic and provides the range of quantification necessary to represent the small but important differences in likelihood of death in surgery as well as the less critical likelihoods of drug side effects. While it is important to represent the probabilities and utilities with care in this type of model, quantitative models of complex problems have been notoriously difficult for clinicians and patients to understand. An understanding of a model and its recommendations is required for a user to have confidence in and to act in accordance with the recommendation.

To improve user understanding of a complex probabilistic model, we chose to use the graphical representation of a Bayesian decision network (also known as an influence diagram[1,2]), and to augment the uncertainty representation by treating sensitive probabilities and utilities as random variables. Traditionally, decision theory models are represented as decision trees, as shown in Figure 1. This example is taken from Stephen Pauker's 1976 *Annals of Internal Medicine* article[3]. It shows that the decision being modeled is whether or not to have bypass surgery for a patient with angina. The chance outcomes that are modeled are surgical death, death from myocardial infarction (heart attack), and subsequent anginal pain. The possible outcomes are listed on the right side of the figure at the end of each branch of the tree. In the article Pauker provides probabilities and utilities on outcomes for various types of patients.

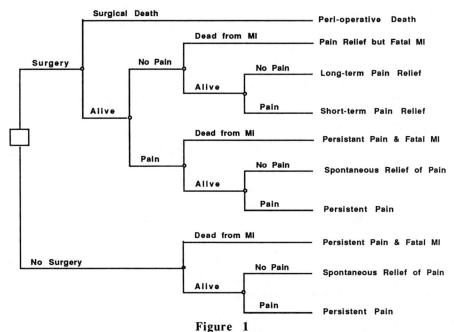

Figure 1
Decision Tree for Coronary Artery Bypass Surgery
Adapted from Pauker, S.G. Coronary Artery Surgery: The Use of Decision Analysis, Annals of Internal Medicine, 85:8-18, 1976.

The equivalent decision network version of the Pauker decision tree model is shown in Figure 2. The square node represents the decision between bypass surgery or continued medical management of angina with drugs. Inputs to the utility model are are seen more clearly in this representation as being the number of years alive and the number of those years that are without pain. It can also be seen that the choice of surgery or medical management influences the likelihood of the health outcomes of subsequent pain, fatal myocardial infarction, and operative death. These variables in turn influence the number of years alive and years without pain. A probabilistic network, such as this, is an acyclic graph where the arrows between nodes represent probabilistic dependence. For example, in the Pauker model in Figure 2 the probability of a fatal myocardial infarction depends on whether the patient had bypass surgery or was treated with medications.

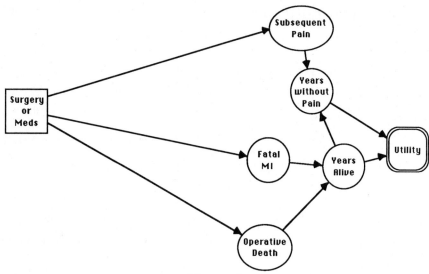

Figure 2
Decision network representation of Pauker's decision tree.

The graphical representation of a decision network is useful in providing the user with clear view of the model variables and the relationship between them. The visual complexity of a decision tree grows exponentially with additional variables as the tree fans out, while adding a variable to a network diagram involves adding a single node and a limited number or arcs. Also, inputs to the utility function are clearly defined by the variables with direct arcs into the utility node.

3.   Augmenting the Uncertainty Representation

To provide additional explanatory capabilities and efficient patient modeling, we added additional nodes for sensitive probabilities and utilities in the model.   In the Pauker example described above, the article showed the explicitly modeled variables, but also implicitly referred to additional variables that defined how to assign probabilities for the various health outcomes and how to assign utilities for years alive and years without pain based on patient characteristics, such as coronary anatomy or previous pain.   This additional representation is shown in a modified decision network in Figure 3.   The implicit variables that were mentioned in Pauker's article but not included in his model are now explicitly represented in this augmented network model.   These new variables that describe the individual patient are highlighted in this figure.

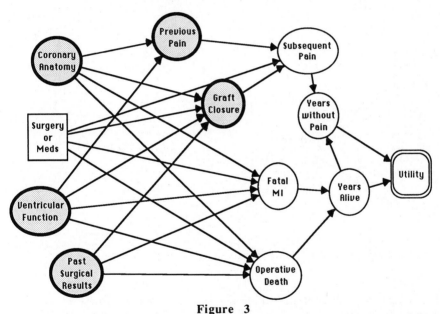

Figure 3
Expansion of the decision network to include patient variables
that were used to determine patient probabilities and utilities.

The augmented network of Figure 3 provides a general structure for all patients with angina.   The nodes with no input arcs have prior probability distributions for their possible values.   This generic model can be tailored for a specific patient when the data for a patient's coronary anatomy, ventricular function, and past surgical results replace the prior distributions for these variables. These specific values then modify the probabilities for subsequent pain, fatal myocardial infarction and operative death. While this representation offers the obvious advantage of automating the selection of these probabilities, it also offers explanatory power through the ability to compare the patient-specific model with the generic model.

The decision network for the Angina Communication Tool is based on several classic angina decision tree models from the literature, notably articles by Weinstein, Pauker, and Pliskin[3,4,5,6]. These are all articles that show a decision tree model for individual patients, but also provide a series of hypothetical patients or data on how to assign probabilities and utilities for individual patients. The synthesis of these models is shown in decision network graphical form in Figure 4.

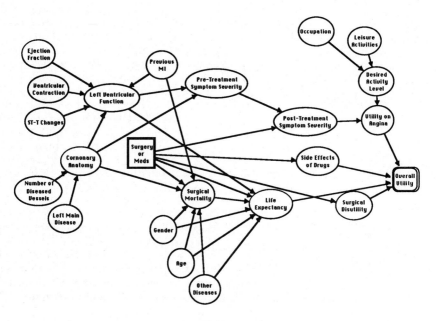

Figure 4
Decision network for the Angina Communication Tool

In this model there are several input variables that are used to describe the patient, such as the values of test results and patient history. These are variables that have no incoming arcs. The ejection fraction, ventricular contraction, and ST-T changes are the results of and exercise test and thallium scan. The values for the variables describing number of disease coronary vessels and whether or not the left main coronary artery is diseased are determined from an angiography test. Information from the patient's chart regarding previous myocardial infarctions, other diseases, age, and gender are also used as input to tailor the model to the patient. Finally, a patient's occupation and leisure activities are used to predict whether a patient is active or sedentary, and this information in turn predicts a patient's utility for angina. The distribution data for the utility component of the model comes from Pliskin's 1980 article entitled "Utility Functions for Life Years and Health Status" in *Operations Research*[5].

Ideally, the data for distributions for this type of model would come from large patient databases. For this prototype system we used data from the literature[3,4,5,6] and restricted ourselves to only modeling the surgical and medication alternatives available at that time. However, the representation and methodology for generating model explanation are general and the probability distributions for variables in the model can come from a variety of sources. The distributions can be derived "objectively" from a database or from articles in the literature, or they can be generated "subjectively" through interviewing the clinical user or experts in the field.

4. Defining a Generic Model

As the angina decision model is tailored to a patient, the overall graphical structure, consisting of the variables and their dependencies, remains the same. It is the probability distributions on the values for the variables in model that are refined and become more patient-specific. The model containing the original population distributions for variables is defined as the *generic* model for angina. The general structure, consisting of alternative tests and treatments, chance events, and possible outcomes is applicable to all patients with angina. The prior distributions for the probabilities and utilities of the model represent the population of all patients encountered in this domain. The "typical" patient is described using the mean of each distribution and the "typical" recommendation is defined by the treatment with the highest mean expected utility. These distributions are refined and narrowed using information from patient assessment questions. The assessment questions serve as predictors that assign patients to more homogeneous subgroups with more specific distributions.

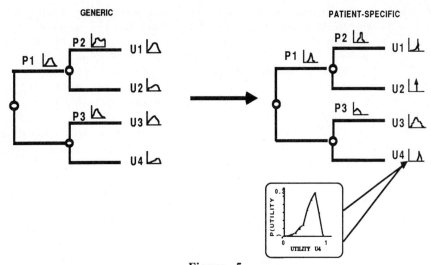

Figure 5

Population distributions on probabilities and utilities become more narrow and patient-specific as patient data is entered into the model.

Figure 5 shows how this refinement would occur for a small section of a model in decision tree form. The tree on the left is part of the generic model, where the wide distributions are the prior probability distributions reflecting information from the whole patient population. With data from the patient assessment questions these distributions become more patient-specific, as is shown in the tree on the right. The new distributions come from data on more homogeneous subgroups that match the patient in question. Figure 6a shows how the prior distribution for the probability of surgical death becomes more specified after learning the patient's age, sex, and other diagnosed diseases. For the random variable of the utility of the quality of life with angina pain, Figure 6b shows that the wide prior distribution of utility values is narrowed after the patient's occupation and leisure activities are used to classify the patient as either sedentary or active. In this example the patient has been classified as sedentary, and the distribution shows that, on average, sedentary patients do not devalue living with occasional angina pain as much as the group of more active patients.

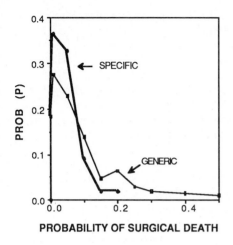

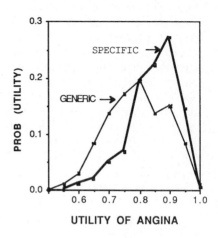

Figure 6a
Generic and specific distributions for the probability of surgical death.

Figure 6b
Generic and specific distributions for the utility of angina.

5. Efficient Generation of Patient-Specific Models

There are several advantages associated with representing prior distributions on variables in a decision model, and with including sensitive probabilities and utilities and variables (as opposed to point parameters) in the model. Measurements of sensitivity and expected value-of-information may be made as the model is tailored to the patient. The utility variables have been selected to allow the system to predict a patient's utilities based on population data. This means that the utility assessment questions can be designed to be more clear and easy for a patient to answer. This is in contrast to traditional assessment techniques where the patient must understand probability, the possible medical outcomes, and the notion of choosing between hypothetical lotteries and/or hypothetical time trade-off questions. Currently, data for constructing the distributions on probability variables exists for some of the relevant subgroups of patients, but with a few exceptions[7,8] the population data necessary for utility models does not exist for clinical applications. Ideally, the data would be carefully collected from patients familiar with the medical outcome of interest and also educated with regard to the assessment techniques. While we have chosen to make use of the limited amount of data in the literature, it is also possible to obtain subjective distributions from an expert during system development. Experts can either give subjective frequency distributions or simply provide parameters for assumed parametric distributions. The goal of the approach is to trade off the added complexity of system design for user interface and decision quality benefits derived during real time use. The distribution means are used to decide among treatment and test alternatives at any point in the consultation, but it will be shown that the variances of the distributions are important in directing the interaction with the patient and in placing appropriate emphasis on the most important variables in the model.

In real-time use the assessment questions are ranked by expected value of information. The assessment questions also have a cost associated with them, and in the Angina Communication Tool the cost of the assessment questions are assigned based on the estimated time and difficulty associated with the question. Questions on age, sex, and test results already noted in the chart are basically free of cost, while a set of hypothetical standard gamble questions used to obtain a point utility would be much more costly. Functional questions such as number of blocks walked per day would fall somewhere in between. This metric, comparing expected value of information of a question versus its cost, serves to dynamically order the assessment questions and provides a suggested stopping rule that notes when the cost of asking a question exceeds its expected value of information. This approach optimizes the efficiency of patient-specific modeling. The major part of the model building is done during system development in the creation and encoding of a generic model. The real time use in the clinician-patient consultation simply involves tailoring the generic model to the patient at hand. The ordering of the assessment questions then optimizes this tailoring by focusing on the most important variables for that patient and minimizing the time and complexity of assessment by letting the user know when the decision is sufficiently robust and dominant.

6.   Computer-Generated Explanation

A major focus and design goal for the Angina Communication Tool was to provide the clinician and patient with an intuitive understanding of the factors most critical to deciding among treatment alternatives for the patient and to provide feedback on the progress of the assessment procedure. One of the graphics displays is a histogram representation of the distributions on expected utilities for each of the relevant alternatives. The example shown in Figure 7 represents the expected utilities for bypass surgery and medical management. The histograms on the left show that for most of the population of patients with angina (using the literature results), surgery is the preferred alternative, however, there is significant overlap in the standard deviations on these distributions. For the patient-specific model in this example medical management is the preferred alternative and there is now minimal overlap in the distributions, signifying that the decision is robust.

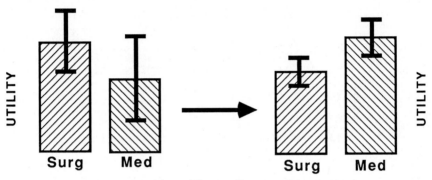

Figure 7
Dynamic Display of Overall Model Uncertainty

The importance of this display is that it gets updated with each new piece of information about the patient. The expected utilities and the associated error bars can be computed using Monte Carlo simulation. On each iteration a point is randomly chosen from each cumulative distribution, thereby selecting representative samples from the probability distributions for each variable. Sampling from each distribution essentially provides one instantiation of the overall model, as if it were the description of a particular patient. The expected utility for each alternative is calculated for this instantiation and these points contribute to the histogram distribution on expected utilities for repeated instantiations. The overlap of the expected utility distributions for the alternatives gives the user of the system a feel for how dominant the decision is, given what is known about the patient. This is a characterization of overall model sensitivity, and this information is displayed for the user as a dynamically changing histogram of mean expected utilities for the relevant alternatives as shown in Figure 5. The error bars on the graph represent +/- one standard deviations of expected utility. The feedback showing changes in mean expected utilities as well as the overlap between alternatives provides the user with a sense of how the assessment is progressing and how robust the decision would be at that point in time.

The graphical of the decision network can also be augmented using information from the distributions of the generic and specific models. Variables that that remain sensitive with respect to the treatment decision and those that are more than a standard deviation from the mean of the prior distribution are highlighted in the display. One can use node size, line width, or a pattern fill to highlight these nodes in a model. An example of a display is shown in Figure 8.

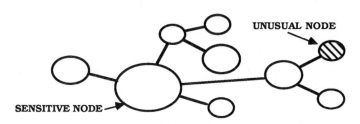

Figure 8
**Nodes emphasized according to sensitivity
and deviation from normal.**

These two forms of graphical model overviews serve to aid the clinician and patient in focusing on what is currently most important for the patient's decision, while also giving a sense of how the model refinement is progressing. The purpose of these system features is to enhance the information transfer between the clinician and patient, both in understanding and efficiency.

The comp··ter-generated text explanation for the patient-specific model makes use of the same information that is used to modify the graphics. There is a pre-compiled explanation for the overall generic aspects of the model and the text explanation for the patient model emphasizes differences between the variable distributions in each. Using the same metric of expected value of information and sensitivity as described previously, the variables can be ranked according to importance and selected for explanation.

Figure 9a shows an unusual patient value compared to the prior distribution. If this variable were age, for example, the explanation would mention the patient's extreme advanced age and also mention the factors dependent upon age (e.g. surgical risk). In Figure 9b we note that the mean of the patient-specific distribution is not very different from the prior generic distribution. However, this change critically affects the choice between treatments 1 and 2. Thus, this variable is selected for explanation of the patient-specific model. An

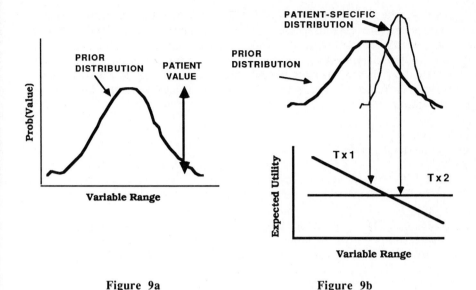

Figure 9a
Unusual Patient Variable

Figure 9b
Sensitive Patient Variable

example of this is comes from the distribution data for the utility of angina pain, as shown previously. In both cases the patient-specific distribution is referenced to the prior generic distribution to measure its importance for explanation. As with the graphical display, the methodology serves to focus the attention and communication on aspects of the decision model that are most relevant for the patient.

7. Conclusion

A decision model for the treatment of angina has been describe. The representation in the form of a Bayesian decision network has been augmented by representing the sensitive probabilities and utilities as random variables with distributions on their sets of possible values. The prior distributions define a generic model, which is made patient-specific through an assessment process that dynamically creates an optimal ordering for questions according to a metric based on each question's expected value of information. The approach allows for the rapid tailoring of the model while providing a metric for judging the importance of each variable in the model. The graphical interface uses this information to display interactively a concise representation of the overall model and its associated uncertainty. Text explanation and summary of the patient-specific model is referenced to an assumed

364

understanding of what is normally done for the typical patient, as defined by the generic model. The explanation emphasizes components of the patient's model that are sensitive and/or deviate from what is typically observed. These techniques serve to keep the explanation of the decision model concise, allowing the clinician and patient to focus on the issues that are most important for that individual patient.

Acknowledgements

Harold C. Sox, Jr. and Charles Dennis have made essential contributions to the clinical aspects of this project, while Misha Pavel has provided invaluable advice in the areas of measurement theory and user interface. This work was supported in part by a traineeship from the National Library of Medicine, with computing facilities provided by the SUMEX-AIM resource under the NIH Grant RR-00785.

References

[1] Howard, R.A. and Matheson, J.E., (eds.), Readings on the Principles and Applications of Decision Analysis (Strategic Decisions Group, Menlo Park, Ca., 1981).

[2] Shachter, R.D., Evaluating Influence Diagrams, Operations Research, 34 (1986) 871-882.

[3] Pauker, S.G., Coronary Artery Surgery: The Use of Decision Analysis, Annals of Internal Medicine, 85 (1976) 8-18.

[4] Weinstein M.C., Pliskin, J.S, Stason, W.B., Risk-Benefit and Cost-Benefit Analysis of Coronary Artery Bypass Surgery, in Bunker, J.P., Barnes, B.A., Mosteller, F., (eds.), Costs Risks and Benefits of Surgery (New York, Oxford University Press, 1977) pp. 342-371.

[5] Pliskin, J.S., Shepard D.S., Weinstein, M.C., Utility Functions for Life Years and Health Status, Operations Research 28 (1980) 206-224.

[6] Pliskin, J.S., Stason, W.B., Weinstein, M.C., et al, Coronary Artery Bypass Graft Surgery, Medical Decision Making, 1(1) (1981)

[7] Wennberg, J., Dartmouth Study on TURP Patients, Personal communication (1986)

[8] Eraker, S., University of Michigan Study on Utilities for Cardiac Patients, Unpublished data.

[9] Cox, R., American Journal of Physics 14(1) (1946) 1-13.

[10] Critchfield, G. C., and Willard, K. E., Probabilistic Analysis of Decision Trees Using Monte Carlo Simulation , Medical Decision Making 6(2) (1986) 85-92.

[11] de Finetti, B., Theory of Probability (Wiley, New York, 1970)

[12] Good, I.J., Subjective Probability as the Measure of a Non-measurable Set, Logic, Methodology, and Philosophy of Science: Proceedings of the 1960 International Congress, Stanford University Press (1962) 319-329.

[13] Spetzler, C. S., and Stael von Holstein, C. S., Probability Encoding in Decision Analysis, Management Science 22 (1975) 340-358.

[14] Clarke, John R., A Comparison of Decision Analysis and Second Opinions for Surgical Decisions, Arch Surg 120 (1985) 844-847.

[15] Bunker, JP, Barnes, BA, and Mosteller F (eds), Cost, Risks and Benefits of Surgery (New York, Oxford University Press, 1977)

[16] Weinstein MC, Fineberg, HV (eds), Clinical Decision Analysis, (Philadelphia, WB Saunders Co., 1980)

[17] Rutkow, IM, Gittelshon, AM, Zuidema, GD, Surgical Decision Making: The Reproducibility of Clinical Judgment, Arch Surg 117 (1982) 337-340.

[18] Eiseman B (ed), Prognosis of Surgical Disease, Philadelphia, (WB Saunders Co., 1980)

[19] Pauker S.G., Kassierer J.P., Clinical Decision Analysis by Personal Computer, Arch Intern Med 141 (1981) 1831-1837.

[20] Sox, H.C., Jr., Probability Theory in the Use of Diagnostic Tests, Annals of Internal Medicine 104 (1986) 60-66.

[21] Cooper, G.F., NESTOR: A Computer-Based Medical Diagnostic Aid that Integrates Causal and Probabilistic Knowledge (Technical Report HPP-84-48, Medical Computer Science, Stanford, CA. 1984)

[22] Pearl, J., Fusion, Propagation, and Structuring in Belief Networks, Artificial Intelligence 29 (1986) 241-288.

[23] Thomas, J.C., and Schneider, M.L. (eds), Human Factors in Computer Systems, (Ablex Publishing Co., Norwood, New Jersey 1984)

[24] Weiner, D.A., and Frishman W.H., Therapy of Angina Pectoris (Marcel Dekker, Inc., New York, 1986)

Section IV

APPLICATIONS

Uncertainty in Artificial Intelligence 4
R.D. Shachter, T.S. Levitt, L.N. Kanal, J.F. Lemmer (Editors)
© Elsevier Science Publishers B.V. (North-Holland), 1990   369

INDUCTION AND UNCERTAINTY MANAGEMENT
TECHNIQUES APPLIED TO VETERINARY
MEDICAL DIAGNOSIS

M. CECILE and M. MCLEISH†

Department of Computing and Information Science
University of Guelph
Guelph, Ontario, Canada   N1G 2W1

P. PASCOE

Ontario Veterinary College
Guelph, Ontario, Canada   N1G 2W1

W. TAYLOR

NASA AMES, Moffett Field,
CA 94035

ABSTRACT
      This paper discusses a project undertaken between the Departments of Computing
Science, Statistics, and the College of Veterinary Medicine to design a medical diagnostic
system. On-line medical data has been collected in the hospital database system for
several years. A number of induction methods are being used to extract knowledge from
the data in an attempt to improve upon simple diagnostic charts used by the clinicians.
They also enhance the results of classical statistical methods - finding many more
significant variables. The second part of the paper describes an essentially Bayesian
method of evidence combination using fuzzy events at an initial step. Results are
presented and comparisons are made with other methods.

1.0 INTRODUCTION
      This paper discusses the progress to date on a large project undertaken primarily at
the University of Guelph, which is the home to one of Canada's major (and few) Veterinary Colleges. The larger goal of the project is to build a general diagnostic shell for

---

† This research has been supported by NSERC operating grant #A4515.

veterinary medicine. Work has begun on a prototype involving the diagnosis of surgical versus medical colic in horses. This is a significant problem in veterinary medicine having led to many studies, use of diagnostic charts etc. to aid owners and veterinarians in recognizing serious cases[6,7,24]. Horses suspected of requiring surgery must be shipped at a significant cost to the veterinary hospital, where further tests are conducted and a final decision is made. We are endeavoring to provide a computerized diagnostic tool for use in the hospital as well as on a remote access basis for practicing veterinarians.

The animal hospital at Guelph has a computer system call VMIMS (Veterinary Medical Information Management System). This system was originally programmed in Sharp APL and handles usual admission and billing procedures. However, the system also stores a considerable amount of medical information on each patient, including bacteriology, clinical pathology, parasitology, radiology and other patient information such as age, sex, breed, presenting complaint, treatment procedures, diagnosis and outcome. In clinical pathology, much of the data is electronically generated by the lab equipment. The database currently holds about 48,000 records with 30,000 unique cases, requiring 500 megabytes of disk storage. The current project is being designed to make use of the vast amounts of on-line data to aid the diagnostic process. Other database issues concerning the implementation of our system are discussed by M. McLeish, M. Cecile, and A. Lopez in [12]. A diagram of the proposed system is given in [13].

Medical expert systems have been under development for human medicine for many years, especially as seen in major projects like MYCIN (Stanford) [3]. These recent systems have been largely based on the assumption that to have expert capability, they must somehow mimic the behavior of experts. Earlier work, using mathematical formalisms (decision analysis, pattern matching, etc.) were largely discarded and attention to the study of the actual problem-solving behavior of experienced clinicians. In a recent paper [21] by Drs. Patil, Szolovits and Schwartz, it is suggested that the time has come to link the old with the new: "now that much of the A.I. community has turned to casual, pathophysiologic reasoning, it has become apparent that some of the earlier, discarded strategies may have important value in enhancing the performance of new programs ...." The authors recognize the difficulty of this approach when they state that "an extensive research effort is required before all these techniques can be incorporated into a single program."

This project is truly an attempt to allow rules and other types of information extracted from data to enchance or complement an "expert opinion" driven system. The paper discusses our current progress with induction processes and uncertainty management methods.

Classical statistical methods of discriminant analysis and logistic regression were run on data sets involving about 45 input parameters. The results of these analyses are summarized in section 2.1. Problems with the predictive power and variable selection of these methods are discussed. Reasons are provided for looking at other methodologies to help deal with these problems.

Section 2.2 discusses the use of Bayesian classification and how the results of this method can extend the information discovered in section 2.1. It also outlines how Bayesian classification may be used predictively for the type of problem at hand. Section 2.3 briefly describes some other induction methods which have been applied to the data.

Section 3 outlines a method of evidence combination which is based on a form of Bayesian updating but uses infinite valued logic as a basis for the representation of events. Some initial results of its use are tabulated. Finally section 4 highlights work which is planned and currently in progress.

2.1 CLASSICAL STATISTICAL METHODS

The data used for these studies represented 253 horses presented at the teaching hospital at Guelph. The horses were all subjected to the same clinical tests and the same pathology data were collected. This data set was used for all the studies discussed in this paper. Outcome information of the following type was available: whether surgery was performed, whether or not a surgical lesion was actually found and the final state of the animal (i.e. lived, died, or euthanized). The objective of the study was to assess which variables obtained during examination of the horses with abdominal pain were significant in differentiating between horses that required surgery versus non-surgical treatment.

The types of parameters which were studied included rectal temperature, heart rate, respiratory rate, temperature of extremities, colour of mucous membranes, capillary refill times, presence and severity of abdominal pain, abdominal distension, peristalsis, and the results of naso-gastric intubation and rectal examination. Clinico-pathological parameters evaluated included hematocrit (HCT) and the total plasma concentration of abdominal fluid. These variables were sometimes continuous and when descriptive (pain levels, etc.) were translated into discrete integer variables. Missing data was handled by elimination of cases. There are 20 parameters in each of the two data sets (*clin* and *clin-path*).

A multiple stepwise discriminant analysis in a recursive partition model was used to determine a decision protocol. The decision protocol was validated by a jackknife classification and also by evaluation with referral population in which the prevalence of surgical patients was 61% [c.f. 6, 7]. The significant parameters were found to be abdominal pain, distension and to a lesser extent, the color of abdominal fluid. The use of the decision tree yielded a significant number of false positives and virtually eliminated false negatives in one study. Unnecessary surgery is even more undesirable in animals than humans due to costs (usually borne by the owner) and the debilitating effects of surgery on a productive animal. Other difficulties with these results concerned the fact that the clinical pathology data appeared entirely non-predictive - a result contrary to the medical belief that, at least in serious cases, certain of these measured parameters do change significantly. Discriminant analysis can miss effects when variables are not linearly behaved. Missing data was another serious problem. Other methods described in section 3 helped overcome some of these problems.

Logistic Regression [11] was also run on the same data set. Here, a regression model of the form

$$Y_i = \log_e[\frac{P_i}{1-P_i}] = \beta_0 + \beta_1 X_1 + \cdots \beta_k X_k$$

is used where the β_i's are slope parameters relating each of the X_i independent variables to the Y_i's (log odd's ratio). P_i is the probability of a response and can be estimated by the back transformation: $P = \dfrac{e^Y}{(1-e^Y)}$. When a new case is to be diagnosed, the probability of requiring surgery may be calculated. The data was run for all three possibilities: surgical lesion found (SL), surgery performed (S) and outcome (O). The outcome, O, can take on the values of lived, died or euthanized. Pulse, distension and a variable representing the presence of firm feces in the large intestine (A2) were the significant predictors. However, testing against whether the doctors decided to do surgery, pain and A2 were the most significant. (These results were obtained from the clinical data only.) Outcome found several other variables to be significant; the probability of death is increased by pain, cold extremities, a high packed cell volume and low NGG reading (Naso-gastric tube emissions). Again, problems were caused by the presence of missing data. Some modifications of these results were found when missing data were estimated using stepwise regression methods. The reasons for the missing data were complicated and various - sometimes records ended because euthanasia was chosen as a solution for cost reasons. Thus, estimating missing data was not a very reliable technique.

2.2 Bayesian Classification

This methodology uses Baye's Theorem to discover an optimal set of classes for a given set of examples. These classes can be used to make predictions or give insight into patterns that occur in a particular domain. Unlike many clustering techniques, there is no need to specify a "similarity" or "distance" measure or the number of classes in advance. The approach here finds the most probable classification given the data. It allows for both category-valued information and real-valued information. For further details on the theory, the reader is referred to [4,5,22].

A program called Autoclass I (see also [5]) was run on the combined clinical and pathological data sets. All 51 variables were included; that is, all outcome possibilities, as described in section 2, were included as variables and lesion type (four possibilities) was also added. A total of 13 classes were found and in most cases the probabilities of a horse belonging to a class were 1.00. The type of information available consisted of relative influence values for every attribute to the over-all classification. For each class and each attribute, influence values are produced indicating the relative influence of each attribute to that class. This information is available in tabular and graphical form.

The classes provide related groups of cases which are useful for case studies (OVC is also a teaching institution). The information may be used predictively. For example, the class with the highest normalized weight, class 0, was found to have surgical lesion as a very high influence factor. The variables of abdominal distension, pulse, abdomen (containing A2 mentioned earlier) and pain, found significant by earlier methods, were also influential factors for this class. Some other variables not flagged by earlier methods were found to be influential as well (total protein levels and abdominocentesis, in particular). The horses in class 0 were found to not have surgical lesions. It is thus possible to see from the features of horses in this class, which attributes and what type of attribute values are significant for this to be the case. New cases can be categorized into classes according to their attribute values and if found to be in class 0, this would indicate a very small chance of surgery being required. Class 1, however, is predominantly a class where surgeries are required.

Actually, there is a wealth of information to be gleaned from the results and much of this interpretive work is ongoing at this time. One may infer that certain variables are not very predictive. For example, a variable distinguishing young from old animals has low influence value in all major classes, but is slightly more significant in a couple of the smallest classes. Studying these small classes, however, can be particularly fascinating because they flag situations which are more unusual. That is, methods which simply find variables which are *usually* the most predictive, cannot perform well on cases which do not conform to the normal pattern. For example, class 11 has four cases all of which required surgery. A number of pathology variables were the most influential, with pain, abdomen, and distension being only moderately important. Surgical type was a very influential variable and indeed three of the cases actually had a strangulated hernia involving the small intestine and one a strangulation problem of the small intestine called intussuception. (The number of possible precise diagnoses was approximately 12x4x3x11.) This class was also interesting because two of its cases were young (less than nine months). The percentage of young cases in the whole population was less than 8%.

Other classes pinpoint cases difficult to diagnose. Class 12 contains three cases which were all operated on, but only one out of three was actually found to have a surgical lesion. Two cases had a simple large colon obturation and the third a large colon volvulus or torsion (requiring surgery). That is, two unnecessary surgeries were performed. A close study of the influential variables and their parameter values for this class of cases - with very close but importantly different diagnoses - provides extremely valuable information.

A significant question arises as to whether or not outcome information should be included initially in the program run. If the data were highly predictive, it should not matter. However, it was not clear from the onset how true this was. The data was run twice again: once with all outcome information removed and once with the doctor's decision information deleted. When all outcome information was removed, one notes that some interesting prognosis information still remains. Class 1 indicated cases virtually all of which lived and whose condition, whether or not surgery was required, was generally good. The question often arises whether or not to operate even given that the animal has a lesion if the general prognosis is bad. This class would indicate that surgery should be performed in such cases. Class 2 (42 cases) was extremely well discriminated with 91% having a surgical lesion. Of the remaining classes (again there were 13 in total), 3/4 were also reasonably well discriminated on the basis of lesion. Others flagged items such as young animals or cases that had very poor over-all prognosis.

New data has been obtained and code written to take new cases and determine a probability distribution, for this case over the classes, from which a probability of outcome may be calculated. It is interesting to note that the use of Bayesian classification for medical diagnosis in this fashion is in a sense a mathematical model of the mental process the clinicians themselves use. That is, they try to think of similar cases and what happened to those cases in making predictions. The technique for making predictions outlined above provides a sophisticated automation of this process. It is impossible within the scope of this paper to document all the information obtained from using Bayesian inductive inference. A sample case will be provided in Section 3.5 which will show the usefulness of combining information from the results of Bayesian inductive inference with the other methodologies.

2.3 Other Induction Techniques

Several other methods have been tried on the data sets. The probabilistic learning system [c.f. 19, 20] also classifies data. Classes are optimally discriminated according to an inductive criterion which is essentially information-theoretic. To accommodate dynamic and uncertain learning, PLS1 represents concepts both as prototypes and as hyperrectangles. To accommodate uncertainty and noise, the inductive criterion incorporates both probability and its error. To facilitate dynamic learning, classes of probability are clustered, updated and refined. The references describe the methodology in detail. We give here some of the results of the application to the veterinary data.

Two classes of data were given to the program (1: no surgery, 2:surgery) and 14 clinical pathology variables were processed according to the PLS1 algorithm. The results can be interpreted as rules and also flag the most prominent variables. (The data sets were reduced due to the presence of missing data. Dr. Rendell is currently revising the PLS1 algorithm to allow it to run with a minimum loss of data when missing values are present.) The current version of PLS1 required that the data be scaled between 0 and 255. The variable X1 represents total cell numbers, X8 is mesothelial cells and X13 is inflammation. These were found to be the most significant variables for the prediction of no surgery. For the purpose of predicting surgery, again X1 and X13 were significant, as well as X9, a measure of degenerate cells. Uncertain rules can also be obtained from the results. Further work is being done to revise the learning algorithm to be able to handle missing data without losing entire cases (i.e. all parameter values when only one is absent). The statistical methods lose all case information and it would be a considerable advantage to employ a method less sensitive to this problem.

Quinlan's algorithm [18] for rule extraction has been run on the clinical data. Continuous data has been converted to discrete values. The important variables are mucous membranes, peristalsis, rectal temperature, packed cell volume, pulse, abdominal condition, and nasogastric reflux. A number of variables appeared significant using this technique which were deemed unimportant using discriminant analysis. A decision tree was generated but some implementational difficulties, due to the number of variables used and missing data, led to a tree which was not very complete or reliable. These problems are currently being addressed to develop a more robust version of the algorithm.

Further details and output on the methods just discussed can be found in [13]. The method in the following section uses all variables provided, rather than reducing the variable set and basing the diagnoses on only a few parameters.

3.1 OVERVIEW

This section describes a method of evidence combination performs Bayesian updating using evidence that may be best modelled using an infinite valued logic such as that which fuzzy set theory provides. The methodology described in this section provides a unified approach for intelligent reasoning in domains that include probabilistic uncertainty as well as interpretive or "fuzzy" uncertainty.

A formulation central to several components of the methodology is that of the "weight of evidence" and is therefore introduced in section 3.2. The description (and justification) of the use of an infinite valued logic is presented in section 3.3. Section 3.4 explains how "important" symptom sets are discovered and section 3.5 relates the performance of this method in the domain of equine colic diagnoses.

3.2 The Weight of Evidence

A.M. Turing originally developed a formulation for what he called the "weight of evidence provided by the evidence E towards the hypothesis H" or W(H:E). Good [8,9] has subsequently investigated many of the properties and uses of Turing's formulation which is expressed as:

$$W(H:E) = \log\left[\frac{p(E/H)}{p(E/\bar{H})}\right] \quad Or \quad W(H:E) = \log\left[\frac{O(H/E)}{O(H)}\right]$$

where O(H) represents the odds of H, $\frac{p(H)}{p(\bar{H})}$. Weight of evidence plays the following part in Bayesian inference:

$$Prior\ log\ odds + \sum_i weight\ of\ evidence_i = posterior\ log\ odds$$

A weight of evidence which is highly negative implies that there is significant reason to believe in $\bar{H}$ while a positive W(H:E) supports H. This formulation has been most notably used in a decision support system called GLADYS developed by Spiegelhalter [23].

In any formulation for evidence combination using higher order joint probabilities there exists the problem of evidence that may appear in many different ways. For example, a patient has the following important symptom groups: (High pain), (High pain, high temp.), (High pain, high temp, high pulse). Which of these symptom groups should be used? Using more than one would obviously be counting the evidence a number of times. The rule we have chosen to resolve this situation is to choose the symptom group based on a combination of the group's size, weight, and error. In this way we may balance these factors depending upon their importance in the domain. For example, if higher order dependency is not evident in a domain then the size of a group is of little importance.

3.3 Events as Strong α - Level Subsets

Infinite valued logic (IVL) is based on the belief that logical propositions are not necessarily just true or false but may fall anywhere in [0,1]. Fuzzy set theory is one common IVL which provides a means of representing the truth of a subjective or interpretive statement. For example, what a physician considers to be a "normal" temperature may be unsure or "fuzzy" for certain values. For these values the physician may say that the temperature is "sort of normal" or "sort of normal but also sort of high". This is different from the likelihood interpretation where the probability of a normal temperature in certain ranges is between 0 and 1. Implicitly, probability theory (in both the belief and frequency interpretations) assume that an event either happens or does not (is true or false). On the practical side, we have found that the concept and estimation of membership functions is intuitively easy for physicians.

Let F be a **fuzzy subset** of a universe, U. F is a set of pairs $\{x, \mu_F(x), x \in U\}$ where $\mu_F(x)$ takes a value in [0,1]. This value is called the grade of membership of x in F and is a measure of the level of truth of the statement "x is a member of the set F".

A strong α - **level subset**, A_α, of F is a fuzzy set whose elements must have a grade of membership of >= α. Formally defined,

$$A_\alpha = \{\mu_{A_\alpha}(x) \mid \mu_{A_\alpha}(x) >= \alpha\}$$

For example, if we have the fuzzy set F = {x1/0.2, x2/0.7, x3/0.0, x4/0.4} then the strong α - level set $A_{\alpha=0.2}$ = {x1/0.2 x2/0.7, x4/0.4}.

Because we wish to perform probabilistic inference we need to have a means of calculating the probability of fuzzy events. Two methods have been suggested for this: the first from Zadeh [26] and the second from Yager [25]. Zadeh's formulation is as follows:

$$P(A) = \int_{R^N} U_A(x)dp = E[U_A(x)]$$

U_A is the membership function of the fuzzy set A, and $U_A \in [0,1]$. Yager argues that "... it appears unnatural for the probability of a fuzzy subset to be a number.". We would further argue that Zadeh's formulation does not truly provide a probability of a fuzzy event but something quite different: the expected truth value of a fuzzy event. Yager proposes that the probability of a fuzzy event be a fuzzy subset (fuzzy probability):

$$P(A) = \bigcup_{\alpha=0}^{1} \alpha \left[\frac{1}{P(A_\alpha)} \right]$$

where α specifies the α - level subset of A and since $P(A_\alpha) \in [0,1]$, P(A) is a fuzzy subset of [0,1]. This fuzzy subset then provides a probability of A for every α - level subset of A. Thus, depending on the required (or desired) degree of satisfaction, a probability of the fuzzy event A is available. In our case the desired level of truth is that which maximizes the the bias of this event to the hypothesis. For example, if we wish to set a degree of satisfaction for the proposition "x is tall" and we are primarily interested in whether x is a basketball player then we wish to choose an α level which allows us to best differentiate BB players from non-BB players. We define this optimal α - level to be:

$$\underset{\alpha}{Max} \; |W(H:E_\alpha)| \quad \alpha \in [0,1]$$

$W(H:E_\alpha)$ is the weight of evidence of the strong α - level subset E_α provided towards the hypothesis H. The α -level which maximizes the bias of a fuzzy event to a hypothesis (or null hypothesis) is the optimal α - level for minimizing systematic noise in the event.

3.4 Discovery of Important Attribute Sets

The identification of important sets of symptoms or characteristics is done commonly by human medical experts and other professionals. For example, the combination of (abdominal pain, vomiting, fever) may indicate appendicitis with a certain probability or level of confidence. Our motivation for trying to discover important symptom groups is twofold: to identify which groups are important in a predictive sense and to quantify how important a group is. Also a factor in the decision of using symptom groups instead of individual variables is the belief that there exists many high order dependencies in this and other real-life domains. For example, a high pulse rate, a high respiratory rate, and high temperature are obviously dependent in many ways that are violations of the Bayesian independence assumption if taken as single symptoms. In using higher order joint distributions for several groups of symptoms we can account for higher order dependencies in the domain and hopefully not violate the assumptions of the Bayesian model.

An symptom set may be of any size between 1 and N where N is number of possible symptoms. To find all such symptom sets requires an exhaustive search of high combinatorial complexity. This may be reduced somewhat by not examining groups that contain a subset of symptoms which are very rare. For example, if freq(High pain, low pulse) is very low then we need not look at any groups containing these two symptoms. Our present implementation examines sets up to size three. The weight of evidence of each symptom group is measured from the data and a test of significance decides whether this group has a weight significantly different from 0.

Of significant interest is the clinician's endorsement of the important symptom sets that this method found. Those sets which showed as being important using the weight of evidence are symptom groups that the clinician would also deem as being significant.

3.5 Implementation and Results

Implementation was on a Sequent parallel processor with 4 Intel 80386's. The method was coded in C and Pascal and made much use of a programming interface to the ORACLE RDBMS. This provided a powerful blend of procedural and non-procedural languages in a parallel programming environment.

Data was obtained for a training set of 253 equine colic cases each composed of 20 clinical variables. Also included for each case are several pertinent diagnostic codes: clinician's decision, presence of a surgical lesion, and lesion type. The prototype system provides a prediction for the presence of surgical lesions. Veterinary experts commonly have problems in differentiating between surgical and non-surgical lesions. Of primary concern to the clinicians is the negative predictive value: that is, how often a surgical lesion is properly diagnosed. If a surgical lesion is present and is incorrectly diagnosed then the lesion is usually fatal for the horse. Presented below is a summary of our results using 89 cases from the training set.

Comparison of Predictive Power (89 Cases)		
Method	Negative Predictive Value	Positive Predictive Value
Clinician†	87.6%	100%
Weight of Evidence	96.7%	86.6%

† Figures obtained from these 89 cases. Previous studies have shown these values to be 73% and 93% respectively over a large sample.

From these results we can see that the method of evidence combination achieved an accuracy for negative prediction which exceeded the clinician's. Incorrect diagnoses are being reviewed by the clinician to see if some explanation can be found. There seems to be no correlation between clinician's errors and the computer technique's. This perhaps indicates that the clinician is adept at cases which are difficult for our techniques (and vice versa).

The following example shows our results for a case which had a surgical lesion but was not operated on by the clinicians. The horse displayed the following symptoms:

> 6 months old	High rect temp	V high pulse	high resp rate
Cool xtrem	Reduced per pulse	Nm muc memb	Cap refill < 3s
Depressed	Hypomotile	Mod abdom dist	Sl naso reflux
No reflux	Elev Reflux PH	Nm rectal Xam	Dist lg intestine
Norm pcv	Norm tot prot	serosang centesis	H abd Tot Protein

and the method determined that the following evidence was important:

Evidence in Favor of Surgical Lesion:	
Symptom Group	W(H:E)
> 6 months,Hypomotile,Mod abdom dist	1.053
Sl nasogastric,Distended L.I.,Normal Tot. Protein	0.861
V high pulse,Reduced per pulse, C refill < 3s	0.861
Cool temp Xtrem,No reflux,Normal PCV	0.661
High rect temp, depressed	0.372
Serosang abdominocentesis	0.312
Evidence Against Lesion:	
High resp rate,norm mucous mem,normal rectal Xam	-0.547

Final Results:

Prior Log Odds	=====	0.530
+ W(H:E)	=====	3.573
= Post. Log Odds	=====	4.103

==> p(surg lesion) = 0.804

For this case, this method strongly supports the surgical lesion hypothesis. It is interesting to compare these results to that of the classical regression model. Using this model the probability of a lesion, p, is predicted by: $p = \dfrac{e^Y}{(1-e^Y)}$, where

$$Y = 7.86 - 1.73(A2) - 1.54(ln\,(pulse)) - 0.498(Distension)$$

In this case A2 was 1 because the horse had a distended large intestine, the pulse was 114, and the distension was 3 (moderate). Substituting into the formula we get:

$$Y = 7.86 - 1.73 - 1.54(ln\,(114)) - 0.498(3)$$

and when we solve for p we find that p = 0.5818

Thus the classical regression analysis produces a p value rather than .5, but which is not strongly convulsive. We speculate that this may be due to the fact that so few variables are considered by this method.

It is interesting to combine these findings with the results of Bayesian classification. This case belongs to autoclass 4 (determined with outcome information excluded). In this class, 80.1% of the 22 cases had a lesion, close to the value predicted but the weight of evidence formula. However, in this class only 19% of the cases lived and only 15% of the animals which had a lesion and were operated on actually lived. Pathology variables were particularly important for determining that class and abdominal distension was only moderately significant (although the doctors and logistic regression rely on this variable). The Autoclass information suggests a poor outcome prognosis in any case and indeed this was a situation in which the clinicians decided on euthanasia. Regression and weight of evidence techniques alone would not have suggested this decision.

4.0 CONCLUSIONS AND FURTHER WORK

This paper has attempted to provide an idea of the methods being used to extract information from data in the development of an information system for medical diagnoses. Several techniques have been presented and some initial comparisons made.

Some tests of performance were accomplished by keeping aside portions of the test data. A new data set is currently being gathered with 168 cases which will be used to both test the methodologies and then refine the present diagnostic results. This new data set has been difficult to retrieve as not all the data used in the original set was on-line. We are taking care to ensure the information taken from hard copy records is entirely consistent with the first training set.

We are also looking at a more standard Bayesian model and trying to understand the dependencies and other conditioning in the data. The methodologies used here also help shed some light on this. The works by J. Pearl [16] and Spiegelhalter [10] are being considered for this approach.

In terms of developing an actual system using the methodologies of part 3, a prototype has already been implemented which considers symptom groups up to a size of three. A more advanced algorithm which tests independence between groups and provides an error estimate is currently being implemented in a blackboard architecture.

Terminals exist in the hospital in the work areas used by the clinicians and we are now proceeding to make the results available on incoming cases. Any final system would provide the doctors with selected information from several methodologies. This is to help especially with the diagnosis of difficult cases - as the real question is not just to be statistically accurate a certain percentage of the time, but to have diagnostic aids for the harder cases.

Acknowledgements

The authors wish to thank the Ontario Veterinary College computing group, Dr. Tanya Stirtzinger (OVC) and Ken Howie for their help, especially with data collection. The Statistical consulting group at the University of Waterloo (C. Young) helped with some analyses. The encouragement of Dr. D.K. Chiu is also gratefully acknowledged.

References

1. Adlassnig, K.P., *Fuzzy Set Theory in Medical Diagnosis*, IEEE Transactions on Systems, Man and Cybernetics, vol. 16, 1986, pp. 260-265.

2. Berge, C., *Graphs and Hypergraphs*, North Holland Press, 1973.

3. Buchanan, B. and Shortcliffe, E., *Rule-Based Expert Systems: The MYCIN Experiments of the Stanford Heuristic Programming Project* , Addison-Wesley, 1986.

4. Cheeseman, P.C., *Learning Expert Systems for Data*, Proc. Workshop of Knowledge-Based Systems, Denver, December 1984, pp. 115-122.

5. Cheeseman, P.C., Kelly, J., Self, M. and Stutz, J., *Automatic Bayesian Induction of Classes*, AMES Report, 1987.

6. Ducharme, N., Pascoe, P.J., Ducharme, G. and Lumsden, T., *A Computer-Derived Protocol to Aid in Deciding Medical or Surgical Treatment of Horses with Abdominal Pain*

7. Ducharme, N., Ducharme G., Pascoe, P.J. and Horney, F.D., *Positive Predictive Value of Clinical Explanation in Selecting Medical or Surgical Treatment of Horses with Abdominal Pain*, Proc. Equine Colic Res., 1986, pp. 200-230.

8. Good, I. J., *Probability and the Weighting of Evidence*, New York: Hafner, 1950.

9. Good, I. J., *Weight of Evidence, Corroboration, Explanatory Power, Information, and the Utility of Experiments*, JRSS B,22, 1960, p. 319-331.

10. Lauritzen, S.L., Spiegelhalter, D.J., *Local Computations with Probabilities on Graphical Structures and Their Application to Expert Systems*, accepted for JRSS, Series B.

11. Matthews, D. and Farewell, V., Using and Understanding Medical Statistics , Karger Press, 1985.

12. McLeish, M., Cecile, M. and Lopez-Suarez, A., *Database Issues for a Veterinary Medical Expert System*, The Fourth International Workshop on Statistical and Scientific Database Management, 1988, June 88, pp. 33-48 and Springer-Verlag Lecture Notes in Computer Science, #339, 1989, pp.177-192.

13. McLeish, M., *Exploring Knowledge Acquisition Tools for a Veterinary Medical Expert System*, The First International Conference on Industrial and Engineering Applications of Artificial Intelligence and Expert Systems, June 1988,p778-788.

14. McLeish, M., *Comparing Knowledge Acquisition and Classical Statistical in the Development of a Veterinary Medical Expert System*, The Interface in Statistics and Computing, Virginia, Apr 1988, pp.346-352.

15. Minsky, M. and Selfridge, O. G., *Learning in Random Nets*, Information Theory (ed. Colin Cherry; London Butterworths), p. 335-347.

16. Pearl, J., *Distributed Revision of Composite Beliefs*, Artificial Intelligence, Oct. 1987, p.173-215.

17. Popper, K.R., *The Logic of Scientific Discovery*, London: Hutchinson, 1959.

18. Quinlan, U.R., *Learning Efficient Classification Procedures and Their Applications to Chess End Games*, in Machine Learning: An Artificial Intelligence Approach , edited by R. Michalski, Tioga, 1983, pp. 463-482.

19. Rendell, L.A., *A New Basis for State-space Learning Systems and a Successful Implementation*, in Artificial Intelligence , vol. 4, 1983, pp. 369-392.

20. Rendell, L.A., *A General Framework for Induction and a Study of Selective Induction*, in Machine Learning, vol. 2, 1986, pp. 177-226.

21. Schwartz, W., Patil, R. and Szolovits, P., *Sounding Board, Artificial Intelligence in Medicine*, New England Journal of Medicine, vol. 16, no. 11, 1987, pp. 685-688.

22. Self, M. and Cheeseman, P., *Bayesian Prediction for Artificial Intelligence* , Proceedings of the Third AAAI Workshop on Uncertainty Management, 1987, pp. 61-69.

23. Spiegelhalter, D.J. and Knill-Jones, R.B., *Statistical and Knowledge-based Approaches to Clinical Decision Support Systems*, JRSS, B, 147, p35-77

24. White, N.A., Moore, J.N., Cowgil, L.M. and Brown, N., *Epizootiology and Risk Factors in Equine Colic at University Hospitals*, Proc. Equine Colic Res., vol. 2, 1986.

25. Yager, R. R., *A Note on Probabilities of Fuzzy Events*, Information Sciences 18, 1979, p.113-129.

26. Zadeh, L. A., *Probability Measures of Fuzzy Events*, J. Math. Anal. Appl. 23, 1968,p. 421-427.

Uncertainty in Artificial Intelligence 4
R.D. Shachter, T.S. Levitt, L.N. Kanal, J.F. Lemmer (Editors)
© Elsevier Science Publishers B.V. (North-Holland), 1990   383

Predicting the Likely Behaviors of Continuous Nonlinear Systems in Equilibrium

Alexander Yeh*

MIT Laboratory for Computer Science
545 Technology Sq., NE43-413
Cambridge, MA 02139
USA

This paper introduces a method for predicting the likely behaviors of continuous nonlinear systems in equilibrium in which the input values can vary. The method uses a parameterized equation model and a lower bound on the input joint density to bound the likelihood that some behavior will occur, such as a state variable being inside a given numeric range. Using a bound on the density instead of the density itself is desirable because often the input density's parameters and shape are not exactly known. The new method is called SAB after its basic operations: *split* the input value space into smaller regions, *and* then *bound* those regions' possible behaviors and the probability of being in them. SAB finds rough bounds at first, and then refines them as more time is given. In contrast to other researchers' methods, SAB can (1) find all the possible system behaviors, and indicate how likely they are, (2) does not approximate the distribution of possible outcomes without some measure of the error magnitude, (3) does not use discretized variable values, which limit the events one can find probability bounds for, (4) can handle density bounds, and (5) can handle such criteria as two state variables both being inside a numeric range.

1   Introduction

This paper introduces a method called SAB to predict the likely behaviors of a continuous nonlinear system in equilibrium in which the input values can vary. SAB uses a parameterized equation model and a lower bound on the input joint density to bound the likelihood that one or more state variables stay inside or outside of a given set of numeric ranges (the likelihood of meeting some criteria).

The reason for using one or more bounds on the probability density, and not the density itself, is that density parameters (means, etc.) and density shape are often not exactly known: One may only have confidence intervals or estimated ranges for some parameters. In fact, the actual parameters may vary (periodically) over time, such as the mean blood pressures in the chest which rise and fall due to pressure changes caused by the breathing cycle. Even if one has point estimates for all the parameters, they may be unusable due to slight inconsistencies. For example, the correlation estimates may

---

*This research was supported in part by the National Heart, Lung, and Blood Institute through grant R01-HL33041.

be slightly inconsistent, especially if some correlations are estimated using intuition or heuristics, as opposed to applying statistics over a large data-base. By relaxing correlation estimates to be ranges of values around the original estimates, one can examine densities with that type of correlation structure. For example, if some correlation coefficient estimate of 0.8 was found to be inconsistent with the other density parameters, one could still do preliminary analysis with a density where that correlation coefficient is high (near 0.8) by allowing that coefficient to be anywhere in the range of 0.7 to 0.9 (assuming some value within this range is consistent with all the other density parameters).

An alternative to using bounds on the probability density is to use a sample of possible probability densities. However, sampling is not as complete an examination as bounding. Some class of important behaviors may lie between all the samples and not be observed.

Other prediction-making methods have one or more of the following problems: not finding the likelihood of behaviors or only finding the likelihood of the variable values falling in certain ranges; producing approximate results without estimating the error and being unable to improve on an initial result's accuracy when given more computation time; not being able to handle density bounds, or handling them too slowly; needing all the set(s) of input values that satisfy the criteria to be explicitly mentioned.

Compared to the these other techniques, SAB produces analytic bounds, improves its answers as more samples or iterations are allowed, and deals with distributions of continuous variable values.

The next section of this paper gives a more detailed description of some other methods. Section 3 gives a simple example of using SAB. It is followed by three sections which give in order an overview of SAB, a demonstration of how it runs in the simple example, and SAB's details. The paper ends with a discussion section and an appendix on some bounds derivations.

2   Other Techniques

Other prediction-making methods fit into one of four categories. The first category of methods finds all the possible system behaviors (sometimes including impossible ones), but does not tell the likelihood of the behaviors. Such methods include systems either performing qualitative reasoning [1, 2], or providing numeric bounds [3].

Category two methods estimate the distributions of possible outcomes without giving some measure of each estimate's error and will not improve the accuracy of those estimates when given more computation time. One of these methods is using moments [4]. This method uses truncated Taylor series expansions of the model equations to find various moments (mean, variance, etc.) of the distributions of interest.

A third category is evidential reasoners [5, 6], which include most of the current work done on uncertainty in AI. These reasoners can only handle a variable value in terms of the possibility of it belonging to one or more regions in a preset discretization of the possible variable values. For example, blood pressure (bp) may be only thought of in terms of being low, normal, or high. This limitation is a problem because what is considered normal, desirable, etc. can change with each use of a model. For example, when trying to lower a patient's bp, an acceptable pressure depends on the patient's former normal blood pressure and the patient's ability to withstand therapy side-effects.

Monte Carlo techniques [4, 7, 8], which fall into two general classes, constitute the fourth category. The first class simulates a system by generating samples according to some probability distribution. Most methods in this class cannot handle density bounds. The acceptance/rejection method can handle density bounds, but it is too slow due to the large number of potential samples it rejects.

The second class of Monte Carlo techniques integrates the density or density bound involved. These integration techniques include hit-or-miss and sample-mean Monte Carlo. Unfortunately, determining the interval(s) to be integrated over (the region(s) satisfying the criteria) is very hard. As an illustration of this, consider the PVR example to be given in Section 3. The interval of all possible input values is the region defined by $PAP \in [10, 80]$, $LAP \in [2, 45]$, and $CO \in [1, 30]$. To find a bound on $\Pr(PVR > 1.62)$, one needs to integrate over the density bound in all the regions of possible input values where the criterion of $1.62 < PVR = (PAP - LAP)/CO$ is satisfied. Two of these regions are

$$PAP \in [19, 80], LAP \in [2, 15], CO \in [1, 2]$$
and
$$PAP \in [19, 80], LAP \in [2, 11], CO \in [2, 4].$$

Finding all such regions in the interval of all possible input values is difficult. Also, as with all Monte Carlo techniques, every answer is inexact and has a standard deviation associated with it.

3   Simple Example Using PVR

A simple example of using SAB involves finding a patient's pulmonary vascular resistance (PVR) given the constraint

$$PVR = (PAP - LAP)/CO \tag{1}$$

and information on the patient's pulmonary arterial pressure (PAP), left atrial pressure (LAP) and cardiac output (CO). PVR is of interest because a high value indicates that the heart's right ventricle has to work very hard to keep the blood moving through the lungs [9, p. 234]. One threshold condition is $PVR \leq 1.62 mmHg/(l/min)$. Critically ill surgical patients with values above this are less likely to survive [10, p.54-59].[1] PAP, LAP, and CO have patient and time dependent values, and are not easy to measure accurately. Table 1 gives some statistics for the patient of interest, a heart attack victim. The question is, given information on PAP, LAP, and CO for the patient involved, is PVR at all likely to be above the threshold? If so, one ought to monitor PVR.

The numbers are close enough so that the answer is not obvious from looking at Table 1: For example, substituting the mean values into Equation 1 results in $PVR < 1.62$, but increasing PAP's value in the substitution by 3.38 (one standard deviation) while maintaining LAP and CO's values would result in $PVR > 1.62$. However, the latter is not that likely to happen because LAP tends to increase when PAP does (high positive correlation).

---

[1] Assume that patients have a body surface area of $1.74m^2$, the average for humans.

NAME	MEAN	STD DEV	Correlation Coef. PAP	LAP	CO
PAP	23.94	3.38	1.0	.861	.096
LAP	15.29	3.08	.861	1.0	-0.044
CO	6.49	1.20	.096	-0.044	1.0

Table 1: PVR Example

Gaussian   Uniform Max   Vary Mean

Figure 1: 3 Lower Density Bounds

So, one has to look at the joint density of PAP, LAP, and CO. Like most statistics, the ones in Table 1 are subject to sampling error, and in addition, the density shape is not exactly known. To get around this difficulty, one can hypothesize plausible bounds on the joint density and let SAB bound the probabilities of satisfying the criteria given each density bound. Ideally, the set of density bounds used will cover all the possible variations.

In this example, three lower density bounds are considered. They show the types of bounds that SAB can handle. One dimensional views of these are in Figure 1, where the areas under the density bounds are marked by vertical lines. As will be described later, the right-most bound covers all Gaussian densities where CO's mean is somewhere within a bounded interval and all the other parameters are as given in Table 1. The details on getting the results are given later on.

The first "bound" is a regular joint Gaussian density with the parameters listed in Table 1 and is shown in the left diagram of Figure 1. A 1000-sample Monte Carlo simulation with this bound (a normal probability density) indicates that $PVR > 1.62$ about 20% of the time. SAB analytically bounds this to be between 4% and 57%. This is consistent with the Monte Carlo simulation and with patient data, where 4 of 17 (23.5%) data points had $PVR > 1.62$.[2]

The second density bound is a

1. joint Gaussian density with the parameters listed in Table 1

2. in which the maximum value is limited to that of a jointly uniform density with the same means and standard deviations.

In other words, the density bound looks like a Gaussian far from the variables' means, but has the low flat top of a uniform density near the means. It is shown in the middle diagram of Figure 1. Integrating the bound indicates that it includes $\sim 70\%$ of the probability mass. Using this bound SAB analytically bounds $\Pr(PVR > 1.62)$ to be between 4% and 79%. This is again consistent with the patient data.

The third density bound is the lower bound of a Gaussian density where CO's mean is allowed to be anywhere between 6.20 to 6.78.[3] This constraint might have been

---

[2] Here, the data could have been used by itself to answer the question of whether $PVR > 1.62$ is at all likely. SAB is meant to be used when such data is not available.

[3] The variances, covariances, and other means could also be allowed to vary.

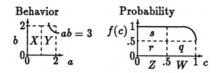

Figure 2: Examples of Splitting

determined by using information in some confidence interval for CO's mean. The right diagram of Figure 1 shows this bound: CO's mean can lie anywhere between the two $*$'s. The lower density bound is the intersection of the areas under all the densities possible due to allowable variations in CO's mean. Because Gaussian densities are unimodal, the lower density bound is the intersection of the areas under the two Gaussian density curves[4] shown. Integrating the bound indicates that it includes $\sim 65\%$ of the probability mass. Using this bound SAB analytically bounds $\Pr(PVR > 1.62)$ to be between 1% and 76%. This is also consistent with the patient data.

In all three input bound cases, $\Pr(PVR > 1.62) > 1\%$, so PVR should be monitored. Note that the results for each of the input bounds can be tightened. See the end of Section 5 for details.

4   SAB: Overview

SAB tightens the probability bound of achieving or failing some criteria by repeatedly selecting a region of possible input values, *splitting* that region into smaller regions α_i's, and then *bounding* both the possible behaviors within the α_i's and the probability of being in the α_i's (using the input probability density bound). SAB marks the α_i's whose possibilities always satisfy or fail the criteria.

Figure 2 shows two examples of splitting. In the one marked *Behavior*, the criterion is $ab < 3$, and the original region is $a, b \in [0, 2]$. In this region $ab \in [0, 4]$, so it sometimes passes and sometimes fails the criterion. Split the region along $a = 1$ into the two sub-regions X and Y. In X, $a \in [0, 1]$, so $ab \in [0, 2]$, and the criterion is always satisfied. Mark X. $a \in [1, 2] \to ab \in [0, 4]$ in Y, so Y is not marked. In the example marked *Probability*, α, the original region, is $c \in [0, 1]$, and $f(c)$ is a lower bound on probability density at c. SAB finds a lower bound on $\Pr(\alpha)$, the probability of being in α, of 0.5 (sum areas q and r) by multiplying 1, α's length, by 0.5, the lowest value of $f(c)$ in α.[5] Split the region at $c = 0.5$ into the two sub-regions Z and W. By a method similar to the one above, SAB finds a lower bound on $\Pr(Z)$ of 0.5 (sum areas r and s), and a lower bound on $\Pr(W)$ of 0.25 (area q). Sum the lower bounds of $\Pr(Z)$ and $\Pr(W)$ to get a new lower bound of 0.75 on $\Pr(\alpha)$.

As hinted by these two examples, *as long as* the bounding method used tends to reduce the range of possibilities as a region of input value space gets smaller, this continued splitting will mark more and more of the value space. And *as long as* the bounding method tends to reduce the gap between a density bound's upper and lower

---

[4]They are the ones with the extreme CO mean values.

[5]Better methods of bounding probabilities are described later.

bound[6] in a region as the region gets smaller, the bound on the probability of being in a marked region will improve.

To find a lower bound on Pr(satisfy criteria) sum the lower probability bounds of all the regions marked as satisfying the criteria. Similarly, one can find a lower bound on Pr(fail criteria). One minus the latter is an upper bound on Pr(satisfy criteria).

5 PVR Example Revisited

This section re-examines the introduction's PVR example when using the Gaussian density as a "bound" (first density bound). To bound $\Pr(PVR > 1.62)$, SAB looked at the space of inputs (given to SAB as one region):

$$PAP \in [1.0, 88.0], LAP \in [1.0, 88.0], CO \in [1.0, 100].$$

A lower bound on PVR, written $lb(PVR)$, is

$$\max(0, [lb(PAP) - ub(LAP)]/ub(CO)) = 0,$$

and an upper bound $(ub(PVR))$ is

$$[ub(PAP) - lb(LAP)]/lb(CO) = 87.0.$$

PVR can be either greater or less than 1.62, so SAB split the space in two along the CO dimension:

subspace1 : $PAP \in [1.0, 88.0], LAP \in [1.0, 88.0], CO \in [1.0, 50.5]$
subspace2 : $PAP \in [1.0, 88.0], LAP \in [1.0, 88.0], CO \in [50.5, 100.0]$

SAB then checked and split as appropriate. Regions like

$$PAP \in [20.75, 25.47], LAP \in [15.95, 17.32], CO \in [6.41, 7.19], (PVR \in [0.756, 1.484])$$

where PVR is either always $>$, or ≤ 1.62, were marked. SAB found lower bounds on the probabilities of being in these marked regions (the one above has a probability ≥ 0.002).

As SAB recursively splits and checks regions, it tightens the probability bound for satisfying the criteria. When the bound is tight enough, or SAB runs out of time or another resource, it can be stopped. In this example, when SAB was stopped, it gave a lower bound of 0.438 on the probability of being in a passing region (one where $PVR \leq 1.62$), and 0.042 for a failing region ($PVR > 1.62$). If a tighter bound was desired, one could have restarted SAB with the then current set of regions. Since this input joint density bound includes all of the probability mass, SAB can, barring round-off error in the floating point math, get the bound to be arbitrarily tight if given enough computing time. In general, if an input joint density bound includes $n \times 100\%$ of the probability mass, SAB can, barring round-off error, get the bound to have a gap of $1.0 - n$ between the upper and lower figure. So if a density bound includes 70% of the probability mass, the tightest bound SAB could give on the chances of passing some criteria would have a gap of 0.3 between the lower and upper figures (such as a lower bound of 0.6 and an upper bound of 0.9).

---

[6]Yes, we are bounding a bound here.

6 SAB: Details

6.1 Main Loop

Perform the following cycle until told to stop:

1. Select the region α with the highest *rank* (see below). SAB can start with either one universal region (as in the example), or any number of predefined regions.

2. What type of region is it?

   (a) *Marked* for being known to always satisfy or fail the given criteria. An example is when a region's PVR range is 0.0 to 1.2 and the criterion is $PVR \leq 1.62$. Here, split the region into two, and using the given density bound, estimate and bound the greatest lower probability bound of being in each of the two sub-regions. Mark them for the same reason as the original region.

   (b) *Unsure.* The region can still either pass or fail the given criteria. An example is when a region's PVR range is 0.0 to 2.0 and the criterion is $PVR \leq 1.62$.

      i. If the possibilities of the region (PVR's range in the PVR example) have not been bounded yet, bound them (in the PVR example, use the given formulas for an upper and lower bound on PVR). *If* the region should be marked, do so and bound the probability of being in it.

      ii. If the possibilities have been bounded, split the region in two. Bound both sub-regions' possibilities, and estimate the greatest lower probability bound of being in each sub-region. *If* a sub-region should be marked, do so and bound that sub-region's probability.

The probability estimations made are just used to suggest the next best step for SAB by helping to rank the sub-regions. They are *not* used as part of any probability bound.

The only overlap allowed between regions is shared borders. No overlap is permitted if the probability density bound has impulse(s).[7]

6.2 Ranking Regions & Estimating Region Probabilities

A region's *rank* estimates how much splitting it will increase the known lower bound on the probability of either satisfying or failing the criteria. An "unsure" (unmarked) region's rank is the estimated greatest lower probability bound (using the given density bound) of being in that region. Estimate as follows:

1. Observe how many input and parameter sample points (out of a thousand picked using a "density" which resembles the given joint density bound) fall within the region. If > 10 samples (1%) fall inside, the fraction falling inside is the estimate.

---

[7]An impulse occurs when part of the bound becomes infinitely high and leads to a non-zero probability of the variables taking on a particular set of values. An example of such a set for the variables PAP and LAP is $(PAP = 45) \wedge (LAP = 30)$.

2. If ≤ 10 samples fall inside, estimate with a formula that quickly, but approximately integrates the density bound in the region. The PVR example uses formula $C_n : 3\text{-}3$ in [11, page 230].

These two parts compensate for each other's weaknesses:

1. The first part is bad for low probabilities because any region α will have large gaps between the sample points within it. So many sub-regions of α will have no sample points even though they may have high values for the lower probability density bound.

2. The second part is bad for high probabilities because the regions involved are either large or probably contain a complicatedly shaped part of the density bound.[8] The integration formulas only work well when a region's section of the density bound is easily approximated by a simple polynomial.

A marked region's rank is the gap between the estimated greatest lower probability bound of being in the region and the known lower bound on that probability. This works better than the gap between the upper and lower bounds on the greatest lower probability bound because SAB often finds very loose upper bounds, while the estimates are usually accurate.

6.3   Bounding Region Probabilities

The basic way SAB finds a lower bound on the probability of being in a region is to multiply the region's volume[9] by its minimum probability density lower bound value (found by the bounding mechanism described below). I derived the PVR example's first density bound expression (a Gaussian density) by taking the density parameters (Table 1) and substituting them into the general form for a Gaussian density. After some simplification, I got (numbers rounded-off):

$$0.01033 \exp(-0.01323(13.70P^2 - 26.09PL - 10.36PC + 16.42L^2 + 10.77LC + 28.08C^2))$$

where $P = (PAP - 23.94)$, $L = (LAP - 15.29)$, and $C = (CO - 6.487)$.

To help tighten this bound, SAB tries to use any monotonicity and/or convexity present in the region's part of the density bound in the following manner (derivations in Appendix A):

Let $f(x_1, \ldots, x_n)$ be the probability density and within a region α let x_i range between l_i and h_i. The probability of being in α is

$$F = \int_{l_n}^{h_n} \cdots \int_{l_1}^{h_1} f(x_1, \ldots, x_n) dx_1 \ldots dx_n.$$

If $\partial f/\partial x_1$ is always > 0 in α, then

$$F \geq [\prod_{i=1}^{n}(h_i - l_i)][(\min_* f(l_1, x_2, \ldots, x_n)) + (\min \frac{\partial f}{\partial x_1}(x_1, \ldots, x_n))(\frac{h_1 - l_1}{2})],$$

---

[8]Most of the common probability densities only have complicated shapes where the density values are high. I am assuming that this complication will be reflected in the corresponding part of the bound.

[9]For a region α, let its variables x_i ($i = 1 \ldots n$) range between l_i and h_i. Then α's volume is $\prod_{i=1}^{n}(h_i - l_i)$. SAB only deals with n-dimensional rectangular regions.

Figure 3: 1-D Convex Density and Lower Bound

where the minimization of f is over the x_2 through x_n values within α (min$_*$ means that x_1 is NOT part of the minimization) and the minimization of $\partial f/\partial x_1$ is over the x_1 through x_n values within α. This bound is tighter than the basic lower bound:

$$[\prod_{i=1}^{n}(h_i - l_i)][\min f(x_1,\ldots,x_n)].$$

Similar expressions can be derived for the other variables and for when $\partial f/\partial x_i < 0$. If $\partial^2 f/\partial x_1^2$ is always ≤ 0 in α (convex down), then

$$F \geq [\prod_{i=1}^{n}(h_i - l_i)][(\min_* f(l_1, x_2,\ldots,x_n)) + (\min_* f(h_1, x_2,\ldots,x_n))]/2,$$

where the minimizations of f are over the x_2 through x_n values within α. This bound is also tighter than the basic one. See Figure 3 for the one dimensional case: the ∩ curve is the density, the area under the diagonal line is F's new lower bound, and the area under the horizontal line is the original bound. Similar expressions can be derived for the other variables.

Several methods exist to integrate a region's probability density bound, including Monte Carlo [7] and quadrature (numeric integration) methods [11]. These cannot truly bound the integration error because they only take numeric samples at particular points.

6.4 Splitting Regions

SAB may split a selected region α in either step 2a or step 2(b)ii. In either, SAB picks a variable in α to split along and then bisects α. Select the variable as follows: in step 2(b)ii, find the one with the largest difference between its upper and lower bound within the region, normalized by its standard deviation. In step 2a, find the one with the largest apparent variation in the density's slope with respect to it.

6.5 Finding Numeric Bounds

Many of SAB's parts need to bound expressions. For algebraic expressions (the type in the models to be used), perfect bounding algorithms have not been built. The type of algorithm used here will find bounds that indicate the truly unachievable,[10] but may not be the tightest possible. Example: saying that $x < 7$, when in fact, $x < 3$. I have implemented an augmented version of bounds propagation [3]. It does the following interval arithmetic [12]:

- Bound an operation's result using bounds on the operation's operands. For example: $ub(a + b) \leq ub(a) + ub(b)$.

---

[10]In practice, the accuracy of this may be limited by round-off error.

- Bound an operand using bounds on an operation's result and the operation's other operands. For example: $ub(a) \leq ub(a+b) - lb(b)$.

The "bounder" examines expressions and updates bounds with these operations. It *iterates* over the expressions until every one that might produce a change has been examined at least once and all the recent bound changes are below a certain threshold.

7 Discussion

This paper introduces a method called SAB which uses a lower bound on the input joint density to analytically bound the likelihood of some possible behavior.

SAB entails much computation. When possible, first estimate the probability with some approximation method like moments [4] and then use SAB to insure that the probability is within certain bounds. Also, once regions are made in response to one set of criteria, they can be reused when examining other sets. This will cut down much of the computation for the remaining sets.

Future work on SAB itself includes testing how large a problem it can handle and expanding it to more quickly bound a variable's mean, variance, median, 90% confidence interval, etc. I will also explore splitting a region at the selected variable's median value (or some approximation) within the region. This can handle infinite intervals (bisection cannot), which permits an initial region where each variable is within the all-inclusive range of $[-\infty, \infty]$.

Another question about SAB is how important is its inability to handle upper density bounds. Some preliminary answers to this question and the question of SAB's speed can be found in [13], which is based on work done after the original version of this paper was written.

On matters other than algorithms, work needs to be done on finding the types of density bounds that are the most common, easiest to specify, and most useful. Candidates for easy-to-specify bounds are common densities with bounded parameters. An example is a Gaussian density with a mean between 0 and 1. One can generate such bounds by using information from parameter confidence intervals.

Despite uncertainty in input density shapes and parameter values, bounds on input densities have not really been utilized to bound the chances of events. This work describes a bounding method which has the features of being able to handle events beyond the ones in a pre-enumerated list, producing analytic probability bounds, and giving better answers as more iterations or samples are allowed.

A   Some Region Probability Bounds Derivations

This appendix shows derivations for some of the expressions that bound the probability of being in a region α. Let $f(x_1, \ldots, x_n)$ be the probability density, and within α let x_i range between l_i and h_i. Then the probability of being in α is

$$F = \int_{l_n}^{h_n} \cdots \int_{l_1}^{h_1} f(x_1, \ldots, x_n) dx_1 \ldots dx_n.$$

A.1 Basic Bound

This subsection derives the following lower bound on F:

$$[\prod_{i=1}^{n}(h_i - l_i)][\min f(x_1, \ldots, x_n)],$$

which is the 'volume' of the region multiplied by the lowest density value within it. The minimization of f is over the x_1 through x_n values within α.

$$F \geq \int_{l_n}^{h_n} \cdots \int_{l_1}^{h_1} [\min f(x_1, \ldots, x_n)] dx_1 \ldots dx_n$$

$$[\min f(x_1, \ldots, x_n)] \int_{l_n}^{h_n} dx_n \cdots \int_{l_1}^{h_1} dx_1$$

$$[\min f(x_1, \ldots, x_n)] \prod_{i=1}^{n}(h_i - l_i)$$

A.2 Bound Using Monotonicity

This subsection shows that if $\partial f / \partial x_1$ is always > 0 in α, then

$$F \geq [\prod_{i=1}^{n}(h_i - l_i)][(\min_{*} f(l_1, x_2, \ldots, x_n)) + (\min \frac{\partial f}{\partial x_1}(x_1, \ldots, x_n))(\frac{h_1 - l_1}{2})],$$

where the minimization of f is over the x_2 through x_n values within α (min$_*$ means that x_1 is NOT part of the minimization), and the minimization of $\partial f / \partial x_1$ is over the x_1 through x_n values within α.

$$F = \int_{l_n}^{h_n} \cdots \int_{l_1}^{h_1} f(x_1, \ldots, x_n) dx_1 \ldots dx_n$$

$$= \int_{l_n}^{h_n} \cdots \int_{l_1}^{h_1} [f(l_1, x_2, \ldots, x_n) + \int_{l_1}^{x_1} \frac{df}{dx_1}(x_1, \ldots, x_n) dx_1] dx_1 \ldots dx_n$$

$$= \int_{l_n}^{h_n} \cdots \int_{l_1}^{h_1} [f(l_1, x_2, \ldots, x_n) + \int_{l_1}^{x_1} [\sum \frac{\partial f}{\partial x_i}(x_1, \ldots, x_n) \frac{dx_i}{dx_1}] dx_1] dx_1 \ldots dx_n$$

Since the x_i's are integrated independently of one another, dx_i/dx_1 is 0 for $i \neq 1$ and 1 for $i = 1$. So, the sum collapses down to the $\partial f / \partial x_1$ term:

$$F = \int_{l_n}^{h_n} \cdots \int_{l_1}^{h_1} [f(l_1, x_2, \ldots, x_n) + \int_{l_1}^{x_1} \frac{\partial f}{\partial x_1}(x_1, \ldots, x_n) dx_1] dx_1 \ldots dx_n$$

$$\geq \int_{l_n}^{h_n} \cdots \int_{l_1}^{h_1} [(\min_{*} f(l_1, x_2, \ldots, x_n)) + \int_{l_1}^{x_1} (\min \frac{\partial f}{\partial x_1}(x_1, \ldots, x_n)) dx_1] dx_1 \ldots dx_n$$

$$\geq [\int_{l_1}^{h_1} [(\min_{*} f(l_1, x_2, \ldots, x_n)) + (\min \frac{\partial f}{\partial x_1}(x_1, \ldots, x_n)) \int_{l_1}^{x_1} dx_1] dx_1] \times$$

$$[\int_{l_n}^{h_n} dx_n \cdots \int_{l_2}^{h_2} dx_2]$$

$$\geq [\int_{l_1}^{h_1} [(\min_{*} f(l_1, x_2, \ldots, x_n)) + (\min \frac{\partial f}{\partial x_1}(x_1, \ldots, x_n))(x_1 - l_1)] dx_1] \prod_{i=2}^{n}(h_i - l_i)$$

$$\geq [[(\min_{*} f(l_1, x_2, \ldots, x_n)) - l_1(\min \frac{\partial f}{\partial x_1}(x_1, \ldots, x_n))] \int_{l_1}^{h_1} dx_1$$

$$+ (\min_* \frac{\partial f}{\partial x_1}(x_1,\ldots,x_n)) \int_{l_1}^{h_1} x_1 dx_1)] \prod_{i=2}^{n}(h_i - l_i)$$

$$\geq \quad [(\min_* f(l_1, x_2,\ldots,x_n))(h_1 - l_1)$$

$$+ (\min_* \frac{\partial f}{\partial x_1}(x_1,\ldots,x_n))[-l_1(h_1 - l_1) + (\frac{h_1^2 - l_1^2}{2})]] \prod_{i=2}^{n}(h_i - l_i)$$

$$\geq \quad [(\min_* f(l_1, x_2,\ldots,x_n))(h_1 - l_1) + (\min_* \frac{\partial f}{\partial x_1}(x_1,\ldots,x_n))\frac{(h_1 - l_1)^2}{2}] \prod_{i=2}^{n}(h_i - l_i)$$

$$\geq \quad [(\min_* f(l_1, x_2,\ldots,x_n)) + (\min \frac{\partial f}{\partial x_1}(x_1,\ldots,x_n))\frac{(h_1 - l_1)}{2}] \prod_{i=1}^{n}(h_i - l_i)$$

A.3 Bound Using Convexity

This subsection shows that if $\partial^2 f/\partial x_1^2$ is always ≤ 0 in α (convex down), then

$$F \geq [\prod_{i=1}^{n}(h_i - l_i)][(\min_* f(l_1, x_2,\ldots,x_n)) + (\min_* f(h_1, x_2,\ldots,x_n))]/2,$$

where the minimization of f is over the x_2 through x_n values within α (min$_*$ means that x_1 is NOT part of the minimization). Within α, f is convex down with respect to x_1, so $f(x_1,\ldots,x_n)$ is $\geq$ than the linear combination of

$$q(x_1)f(l_1, x_2,\ldots,x_n) + (1 - q(x_1))f(h_1, x_2,\ldots,x_n),$$

where $q(x_1) = (x_1 - l_1)/(h_1 - l_1)$. So,

$$F \geq \int_{l_n}^{h_n} \cdots \int_{l_1}^{h_1} [q(x_1)f(l_1, x_2,\ldots,x_n) + (1 - q(x_1))f(h_1, x_2,\ldots,x_n)]dx_1 \ldots dx_n$$

$$\geq \int_{l_n}^{h_n} \cdots \int_{l_1}^{h_1} [q(x_1)(\min_* f(l_1, x_2,\ldots,x_n))$$

$$+ (1 - q(x_1))(\min_* f(h_1, x_2,\ldots,x_n))]dx_1 \ldots dx_n$$

$$\geq \quad [(\min_* f(l_1, x_2,\ldots,x_n)) \int_{l_1}^{h_1} q(x_1)dx_1$$

$$+ (\min_* f(h_1, x_2,\ldots,x_n)) \int_{l_1}^{h_1}(1 - q(x_1))dx_1] \int_{l_n}^{h_n} dx_n \cdots \int_{l_2}^{h_2} dx_2$$

$$\geq \quad [(\min_* f(l_1, x_2,\ldots,x_n))[\frac{x_1^2/2 - l_1 x_1}{h_1 - l_1}]_{l_1}^{h_1}$$

$$+ (\min_* f(h_1, x_2,\ldots,x_n))[x_1 - \frac{x_1^2/2 - l_1 x_1}{h_1 - l_1}]_{l_1}^{h_1}] \prod_{i=2}^{n}(h_i - l_i)$$

$$\geq \quad [(\min_* f(l_1, x_2,\ldots,x_n))(\frac{h_1 - l_1}{2}) + (\min_* f(h_1, x_2,\ldots,x_n))(\frac{h_1 - l_1}{2})] \prod_{i=2}^{n}(h_i - l_i)$$

$$\geq \quad [(\min_* f(l_1, x_2,\ldots,x_n)) + (\min_* f(h_1, x_2,\ldots,x_n))][\prod_{i=1}^{n}(h_i - l_i)]/2$$

Acknowledgments

The idea for SAB arose after a thought-provoking discussion with Mike Wellman, who also, along with Peter Szolovits, William Long, Alvin Drake and Peter Kempthorne have reviewed parts of this paper.

References

[1] Daniel G. Bobrow, editor. *Qualitative Reasoning about Physical Systems.* MIT Press, 1985. Reprinted from *Artificial Intelligence,* vol. 24, 1984.

[2] Brian C. Williams. MINIMA: A symbolic approach to qualitative algebraic reasoning. In *Proceedings of the National Conference on Artificial Intelligence,* pages 264–269. American Association for Artificial Intelligence, August 1988.

[3] Elisha P. Sacks. Hierarchical reasoning about inequalities. In *Proceedings of the National Conference on Artificial Intelligence,* pages 649–654. American Association for Artificial Intelligence, 1987.

[4] G. Hahn and S. Shapiro. *Statistical Models in Engineering.* John Wiley & Sons, Inc., 1967.

[5] Eric J. Horvitz, David E. Heckerman, and Curtis P. Langlotz. A framework for comparing alternative formalisms for plausible reasoning. In *Proceedings of the National Conference on Artificial Intelligence,* pages 210–214. American Association for Artificial Intelligence, 1986.

[6] Peter Szolovits and Stephen G. Pauker. Categorical and probabilistic reasoning in medical diagnosis. *Artificial Intelligence,* 11:115–144, 1978.

[7] J. M. Hammersley and D. C. Handscomb. *Monte Carlo Methods.* Barnes and Noble, Inc., 1965.

[8] Mark Johnson. *Multivariate Statistical Simulation.* John Wiley and Sons, New York, 1987.

[9] Dean T. Mason. *Congestive Heart Failure, Mechanisms, Evaluation, and Treatment.* Dun-Donnelley, New York, 1976.

[10] William C. Shoemaker. Physiology, monitoring and therapy of critically ill general surgical patients. In William C. Shoemaker and Edward Abraham, editors, *Diagnostic Methods in Critical Care,* chapter 4, pages 47–86. Marcel Dekker, Inc., New York, 1987.

[11] A. H. Stroud. *Approximate Calculation of Multiple Integrals.* Prentice-Hall, Inc., 1971.

[12] H. Ratschek and J. Rokne. *Computer Methods for the Range of Functions.* Halsted Press: a division of John Wiley and Sons, New York, 1984.

[13] Alexander Yeh. Finding the likely behaviors of static continuous nonlinear systems. *Annals of Mathematics and Artificial Intelligence.,* 1990. Revised version of the preliminary paper in the 2nd Intl. Workshop on AI and Statistics. Accepted for a corresponding special issue of the journal.

Uncertainty in Artificial Intelligence 4
R.D. Shachter, T.S. Levitt, L.N. Kanal, J.F. Lemmer (Editors)
© Elsevier Science Publishers B.V. (North-Holland), 1990

The structure of Bayes networks for visual recognition

John Mark Agosta

Robotics Laboratory
Stanford University
Stanford, CA 94305
johnmark@coyote.stanford.edu

I. The problem

This paper[1] is part of a study whose goal is to show the efficiency of using Bayes networks to carry out model based vision calculations. [Binford et al. 1987] Recognition proceeds by drawing up a network model from the object's geometric and functional description that predicts the appearance of an object. Then this network is used to find the object within a photographic image. Many existing and proposed techniques for vision recognition resemble the uncertainty calculations of a Bayes net. In contrast, though, they lack a derivation from first principles, and tend to rely on arbitrary parameters that we hope to avoid by a network model.

The connectedness of the network depends on what independence considerations can be identified in the vision problem. Greater independence leads to easier calculations, at the expense of the net's expressiveness. Once this trade-off is made and the structure of the network is determined, it should be possible to tailor a solution technique for it.

This paper explores the use of a network with multiply connected paths, drawing on both techniques of belief networks [Pearl 86] and influence diagrams. We then demonstrate how one formulation of a multiply connected network can be solved.

II. Nature of the vision problem

The objects within a visual image offer a rich variety of evidence. The image reveals objects by their surface edges, textures, color, reflectance, and shadows. Save for extreme cases, only a part of this evidence is necessary to recognize an object. The vision problem is no simpler because of the surfeit of evidence: Each kind of evidence presents a new problem. The researcher may approach the preponderance of clues by concentrating only on a limited variety, such as those which are easiest to calculate, or lead to the most efficient algorithm. Bayes methods encourage the use of a wider variety of evidence since they traditionally have been developed to integrate diverse and subtle sources of evidence.

The problem of image recognition has close kin. By considering other varieties of evidence, an object could be identified by those not available in a visual image, such as tactile feel or motion when it is disturbed. Similarly there are vision problems for which recognition is not necessary, such as visual obstacle avoidance. Recognition is one aspect of understanding the scene; the scene

---

[1] This paper grew out of extensive discussions with Tom Binford, Dave Chelberg, Tod Levitt and Wallace Mann. I owe a special debt of gratitude to Tom for introducing me to both the problem and a productive way to approach it. As usual, all errors are the sole responsibility of the author.

398

also may be analyzed to infer the location of the viewer relative to the object and to make other functional statements. Conceivably the process of recognition might proceed to a higher level recognition of some situation or "Gestalt." These concerns are outside the scope of this paper.

Model based vision consists of two activities; first, modelling the objects to be looked for – the predictive phase, then identifying objects by analyzing a raster image – the inferential phase. Vision models are built from a top down decomposition of an object's geometry into geometric primitives that further decompose into primitive observable features. The model of the object is decomposed into sub-assemblies that are in turn decomposed to obtain relations among volume filling primitives, in our case "generalized cylinders" and their intervening joints. Volumes have surfaces that appear as patches in the image. The patches are projected onto the image visual plane as regions bounded by edges and junctions, the lowest level features in the hierarchy.

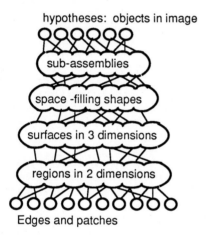

hypotheses: objects in image
sub-assemblies
space -filling shapes
surfaces in 3 dimensions
regions in 2 dimensions
Edges and patches

Vision recognition based on a model proceeds by grouping image features at a lower levels to identify features at higher levels.The bottom up grouping process is driven by the decomposition model of objects expected to be within the image.

III. Issues in formulation

Grouping is a primary process of recognition, and occurs at each level of the decomposition hierarchy. A predictive arc from a feature to a lower level feature implies both the appearance of a lower level feature and its location relative to the feature. If a predictive arc did not entail some position information, then the network could not perform grouping of features. Consider the contrary case: A network constructed out of complete but non-localized evidence of the number and kind of low level features that compose an object. This is still only weak evidence for the appearance of the object. Unfortunately grouping adds dependencies that complicate the network structure. Here I discuss the formulation of these dependencies.

A. *Tree structured hierarchies.*

The formulation of a decomposition model implies a probability network where top level constructs predict the appearance of lower level ones. When the observable parts at a stage can be decomposed independently, the network becomes tree structured. The tree is rooted (at the "top", an unfortunately confusing use of terms) in a hypothesis about the appearance of an object. It grows "down" to leaf nodes that represent image primitives. The process of recognition begins when evidence from an image instantiates primitives. Then by inference from lower level nodes to higher levels, the calculation results in the probability of the object hypothesis given the evidence.

For example, a generalized cylinder consists of a face, an axis and a sweeping function for the face along the path of the axis. The face of the generalized cylinder appears independently of the axis. The lower level observables of both face and axis remain independent. In contrast, the sweeping rule and the limbs that it predicts depend on both the face and axis.

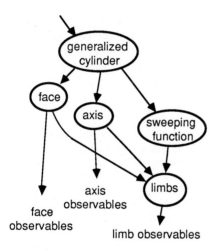

B. *Ambiguity*

Optical illusions that can appear to be different objects are an example of ambiguity functioning in the human vision system. The novelty of such images indicates their rarity. This is evidence that the eye, in the process of bottom up grouping rarely resorts to backtracking. Ambiguity can be formulated as the existence of a higher level construct that clarifies an ambiguity more than one level below. It is expressed by influences that skip over levels. They express kinds of arguments that stand in contrast to the grouping-at-each-level kind of reasoning we apply. Hopefully, the intermediate constructs in the hierarchy are rich enough so that they are not necessary.

C. *Exclusion*

Multiple parents in the network may be used to express exclusion, so that recognizing one object implies the other does not exist.

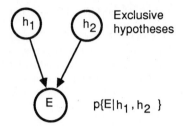

Exclusive
hypotheses

$p\{E|h_1,h_2\}$

The evidentiary node for their exclusion is a sibling of both objects. Instantiating E offers evidence for one hypothesis but not both. The distribution function of the evidence given the object hypotheses, $p(E \mid h_1,h_2)$, resembles an exclusive-or function. We can demonstrate the strong dependence between object nodes that this evidence generates by flipping the direction of the arc between a hypothesis and the evidence. By Bayes rule this generates an arc between hypotheses. Thus the truth of one hypothesis upon observing the evidence depends strongly on the truth of the other. This characteristic multiple parent structure allows formulation by Bayes networks of conflicting hypotheses sets as presented by Levitt [Levitt 1985]. It is useful for the purposes of formulation to have evidentiary nodes that excludes hypotheses for different objects from evidence the same location.

D. Co-incidence

Just as multiple parents can express exclusion, they can be used to infer two models at the same location. Enforcing co-incident locations for different models could be a useful modeling tool. Imagine an object that could be posed as two separate models depending on the level of detail. For instance the "Michelin Man" could be modeled as both a human figure and as a stack of tires. As evidence for him, the perceptor would expect to find both a man and a stack of tires in the same location.

More common objects may also be composed as a set of co-incident models. For example a prismatic solid may be interpreted differently as generalized cylinders, depending on the choice of major axis. We may infer more than one of these generalized cylinders occupying the same location from which we infer the one object that predicted the set.

Composition of the same object as several co-incident models is not to be confused with the decomposition hierarchy. Decomposition is essentially a conditional independence argument, that the separate features into which an object is decomposed can be recognized, given the object appears in the view. Composition as several co-incident models, like exclusion formulations, depends on one lower level feature being predicted by multiple higher level features. Such multiple parent structures describe relations among their ancestors. In co-incident models, furthermore, the multiple higher level features are resolved into the one ancestor that admits of co-incident interpretations. This generates a network with multiple paths.

E. Global location and the use of proximity information.

In general, evidence for exclusion and co-incidence is of the kind from which the proximity of two higher level constructs may be inferred. For instance, when an observable feature in the image is due to the joint between two other features, then the proximity of these two may be inferred.

Further, all parts of the hierarchy are influenced by object position, orientation and articulation. All variables are a function of these global variables. They form a set of variables with universal influences, as shown here:

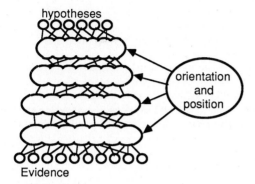

This generates a set of arcs that violate tree type hierarchies. These dependencies allow information about feature orientation and position to be made available to all superior nodes, once an inference about it can be made from a lower level.

Again a question arises about the trade-off between making this influence explicit, or entailing "softer" proximity information within the network structure. Since the geometric modeling and resulting dependencies that complete orientation information require is demanding, it is worth considering whether less specific proximity information could be substituted effectively. Arguably a person can recognize an image with distorted orientations among components, much as the subject of a cubist painting can be recognized.

Thus, if as I have argued, the network cannot be formulated with independence required by a tree structured decomposition, it is likely that local relationships – exclusion, co-incidence, proximity and orientation – can be exploited that do not require "completely global" influences.

IV. Single verses multiply connected networks

When more than one feature predict one lower level observable, the recognition network will have nodes with multiple paths. Fortunately the hierarchical method creates networks with influences only between adjacent levels. This section presents a solution to a simple case of multiple connections between levels that suggests their may be efficient solution techniques that apply to hierarchical networks.

A. The Concept of a solution

Both influence diagram and belief network solution methods result in the same solution to a Bayes network. Solving the network by influence diagram techniques derived from Bayes rule transforms the network so that a subset of the nodes, the set of hypotheses is conditioned upon the rest. The initial distribution over the set of hypotheses, known as the prior, is part of the network specification. In the process of solution, evidentiary nodes are transformed so that they are not conditioned by other nodes. Solving the network also imputes a distribution over the evidence, known as the *pre-posteriors* or *marginals*. The *pre-posteriors* – the distribution imputed by prior beliefs before observations are made – has significance for the solution only as it relates to collection of information – only indirect significance for the solution. As evidence nodes are instantiated, their distributions are replaced by degenerate distributions (e.g. observed values), and repeated application of "Jeffrey's rule" changes the hypotheses to distributions posterior to the evidence. These posteriors are the results, by which choices can be made.

When solving by belief network operations, marginal distributions, or "beliefs" are maintained at all times for all nodes. Initially these are, for the hypotheses, the priors, and for the evidence, the pre-posteriors. As nodes are instantiated, message passing schemes update all node marginals to their distributions given the evidence observed.

The subset of singly connected Bayes networks to which Pearl's solution technique applies has the particular and useful property of being modular in space and proportional in time to the network diameter. There are several extensions for more complicated nets, by conditioning over cut sets [Pearl, 1985] and by star decomposition [Pearl 1986]. At the other extreme of complexity, Shachter [1986] shows that any directed acyclic probability graph has a solution in finite number of steps.

B. Networks with multiple hypotheses

When the various objects that may appear can each be decomposed into a different tree then these trees can be linked to a common set of leaf nodes. The result is no longer a tree, although it does not contain multiple directed paths. One may conjecture that when the leaves are instantiated and are no longer probabilistic, the trees effectively separate into a forest, and the solution is equivalent to evaluating each tree independently. Then Pearl's algorithm could be applied to each tree. This conjecture is wrong. As Pearl recognizes, [Pearl 1985] nodes with multiple parents cannot be the separating nodes in a cut-set. The parents of each leaf are not conditionally independent given the leaf node. This is apparent by application of Bayes rule through influence diagram transformations to condition the parent nodes upon the leaf node. Reversing a parent-to-leaf arc generates an arc between parents. This dependence is mediated in Pearl's algorithm by message passing at the leaf nodes.

In terms of message passing, incoming πs are reflected at leaves and affect the upward propagating λs even when the leaf value is certain, as shown by the propagation formula at an instantiated leaf node for λs:

(1) $$\lambda_i = \alpha \, \Sigma_j \, \pi_j \, p\{E_k / P_i P_j\},$$

[Pearl 86, from equation 21] where P_i is the parent receiving the lambda message, P_j is the parent sending the π message and k indicates the state at which the evidence is instantiated.

For separation such that multiple parents remain independent after evidence arrives, the evidence must be distributed thus:

(2) $$p\{E \mid P_1, P_2\} \propto p\{E \mid P_1\}p\{E \mid P_2\} .$$

This is equivalent to evaluating each tree separately in trees where the leaves contain probabilities $p\{E \mid P_i\}$. Equivalently, this assumption makes the outgoing λs in (1) equal to the certainty value of the leaf node.

In exchange for the complexity that common leaf nodes add, we gain the ability to express exclusion and co-incidence among hypotheses of the different trees. This is the significance of (1): the $p\{E \mid P_1, P_2\}$ express the effect of one hypothesis on another.

C. Solving a simple multiply connected network.

Its a reasonable conjecture that some multiply connected networks lend themselves to time-efficient solution techniques. We offer one example where a multiply connected network can be solved by an extension of Pearl's technique. For this simple case consider a pair of common-leaved trees only one level deep, with two hypotheses and two evidentiary nodes, shown this diagram:

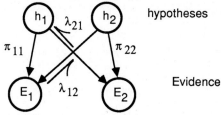

This network has a closed form solution in terms of Pearl's messages. From the top-down propagation rule for root nodes [Pearl 1986, p. 260] the hypothesis sends down a π_{HE} message vector that is the term by term product of its prior with the λ message it receives:

(3) $$\pi_{HE} = \alpha\,\pi_i\,\lambda_i.$$

For each hypothesis node, write this as the product of a vector (all λs and πs now represent vectors) and a diagonal matrix $\underline{h}$ of the prior

(4) $$\pi_{22} = \alpha\,\underline{h}_2\,\lambda_{12}$$
(5) $$\pi_{11} = \alpha\,\underline{h}_1\,\lambda_{21}$$

where α normalizes π, and $\underline{h}$ is the matrix with the terms of h on its diagonal.

From (1) reflection equations at the leaves are, in vector notation:

(6) $$\lambda_{21} = \alpha\,P_2\pi_{22}$$
(7) $$\lambda_{12} = \alpha\,P_1\pi_{11}$$

where, as before, the likelihood, $P_i = p(E_{i_k} | h_1, h_2)$, is instantiated as indicated by k. So for each leaf node, the λ propagating up is the matrix product of the likelihood with the π it receives. Substituting together (4)(5)(6)(7) obtains

(8) $$\pi_{11} = \alpha\,\underline{h}_1 P_2\,\underline{h}_2\,P_1\pi_{11}.$$

This expresses the cycle of messages passed in one direction. For the other cycle containing π_{21}, the P matrix transpose appears in the corresponding leaf reflection equations.

Viewed as a recursion equation, if this has a solution, messages converge to steady values. Dividing through by the normalization constant puts this in the form of an eigenvector problem for the matrix $A = \underline{h}_1 P_2\,\underline{h}_2\,P_1$ with eigenvalue $1/\alpha$. Its eigenvector is the solution to the recursion relation. From this eigenvector, the beliefs of all nodes can be calculated. For example, let the evidence at both leaves have the same P matrices, and both $\underline{h}$ functions represent a uniform prior. Then

$$P = \begin{bmatrix} .52 & .18 \\ .08 & .22 \end{bmatrix} \quad Bel(h_1) = \begin{bmatrix} .811 \\ .190 \end{bmatrix}$$

$$\alpha = .562 \quad Bel(h_2) = \begin{bmatrix} .345 \\ .655 \end{bmatrix}$$

$$\pi = \begin{bmatrix} .811 \\ .190 \end{bmatrix}$$

Further simplifications occur for a rigid hierarchy. Notice that in a singly connected network we need only propagate upward to all nodes since determining the resulting marginal beliefs of evidentiary nodes is uninteresting as far as hypotheses distribution updates are concerned. Generally, with multiple connections above, we can ignore downward propagation in singly connected extents below. This follows from the lambda updating formula. As its shows, λs in a single parent node depend only on the λs arriving from below, and not on the node's marginal belief, nor on πs descending the tree. This is not symmetric with propagation downward; the πs interact with the λs on their way down. Thus, in a true tree, the hypothesis posterior can be updated solely by lambda propagation upward. This is equivalent to so-called "naive Bayes" updating schemes.

If we think of a network equivalent to the rigid hierarchy, but instead with all nodes at a level coalesced into one node, then the same argument about λ propagation applies: To update the hypotheses we need only propagate up between levels.

V. Further directions.

Empirical tests will determine whether the directions described in this paper improve the ability of vision based modeling systems. There are also a host of formulation and solution questions to pursue.

What is the relation of the attachment graph – the graph of geometric relations – and the graph that predicts observable features –the "recognition network" discussed here? They are related, but they are not the same thing. We have given arguments that the recognition network may have structural regularities that simplify its solution. The design of a general purpose vision machine also requires that the recognition network can be constructed in the process of recognition. The structure we have proposed has implications for the automatic generation of these networks, which we have yet to explore.

As we consider scenes with a wider variety of objects and the vision machine gains flexibility by having more models from which to chose, the recognition network becomes bushier. With even a small number of models it may not make sense to solve the whole network. There is a need for partial evaluation methods for large networks. One hopes also that the value and decision node structure of influence diagrams suggest techniques to control inference and to guide automatic generation of hypotheses over sets of evidence.

References.

[Binford 71]
Binford, Thomas O., "Visual Perception by Computer," **IEEE Conf. on Systems and Control,** Miami, (December 1971).
[Binford et al. 87]

Binford, Thomas O., Tod S. Levitt and Wallace B. Mann, "Bayesian Inference in Model-Based Machine Vision," in L.N. Kanal , Tod S. Levitt and John F. Lemmer, **Uncertainty in Artificial Intelligence 3,** (Elsevier Science Publishers, Amsterdam, 1989).

[Levitt 85]

Levitt, Tod S. "Probabilistic Conflict Resolution in Hierarchical Hypothesis Spaces," in L.N. Kanal and John F. Lemmer, **Uncertainty in Artificial Intelligence ,** (Elsevier Science Publishers, Amsterdam, 1986).

[Pearl 85]

Pearl, Judea,"A constraint propagation approach to probabilistic reasoning,"in L.N. Kanal and John F. Lemmer, **Uncertainty in Artificial Intelligence ,** (Elsevier Science Publishers, Amsterdam, 1986).

[Pearl 86]

Pearl, Judea, "Fusion, Propagation, and Structuring in Belief Networks" **Artificial Intelligence, 29** (1986) 241-288.

[Shachter 86]

Shachter, Ross, "Evaluating Influence Diagrams," **Operations Research, 34** (November - December 1986) 871-882.

Uncertainty in Artificial Intelligence 4
R.D. Shachter, T.S. Levitt, L.N. Kanal, J.F. Lemmer (Editors)
© Elsevier Science Publishers B.V. (North-Holland), 1990

Utility-Based Control for Computer Vision

Tod S. Levitt*, Thomas O. Binford**, and Gil J. Ettinger*

*Advanced Decision Systems, Mountain View, California
**Stanford University, Stanford, California

1 Introduction

Several key issues arise in implementing computer vision recognition of world objects in terms of Bayesian networks. Computational efficiency is a driving force. Perceptual networks are very deep, typically fifteen levels of structure. Images are wide, e.g., an unspecified number of edges may appear anywhere in an image 512 x 512 pixels or larger. For efficiency, we dynamically instantiate hypotheses of observed objects. The network is not fixed, but is created incrementally at runtime. Generation of hypotheses of world objects and indexing of models for recognition are important, but they are not considered here [4, 11]. This work is aimed at near-term implementation with parallel computation in a radar surveillance system, ADRIES [5, 15], and a system for industrial part recognition, SUCCESSOR [2].

For many applications, vision must be faster to be practical and so efficiently controlling the machine vision process is critical. Perceptual operators may scan megapixels and may require minutes of computation time. It is necessary to avoid unnecessary sensor actions and computation. Parallel computation is available at several levels of processor capability. The potential for parallel, distributed computation for high-level vision means distributing non-homogeneous computations. This paper addresses the problem of task control in machine vision systems based on Bayesian probability models.

We separate control and inference to extend the previous work [3] to maximize utility instead of probability. Maximizing utility allows adopting perceptual strategies for efficient information gathering with sensors and analysis of sensor data. Results of controlling machine vision via utility to recognize military situations are presented in this paper. Future work extends this to industrial part recognition for SUCCESSOR.

2 Bayesian Network for Evidential Accrual

The relationship between models, hypotheses, and decisions is pictured in Figure 1. Models represent physical objects in the world, such as military units, formations, industrial parts, components of parts, and attributes such as color, reflectivity, etc.

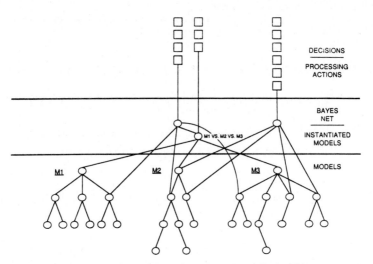

Figure 1: Model-Hypothesis-Decision relationships.

As such, we view our models as causal; i.e., a physical object is viewed as "causing" its component sub-parts.

Object models are physical models; their geometry is represented by part/whole graphs and by interlocking taxonomic graphs. Figure 2 shows two part-of slices of the (taxonomic) is-a hierarchy for a model of a military brigade of the evil empire of Mordor. The part-of hierarchy corresponds to (physical) military sub-units. The is-a hierarchy is obtained by taking the common set of unit type and formation constraints for military units that can be confused based on uncertain observations. For example, if we are too far away to distinguish steam engines from catapults, we might still recognize them as vehicles, and be uncertain as to whether we are observing a Catapult Battalion or a Steam Engine Team. For military units, the models of military organization predict the existence and location of other sub-units, given the observation of another.

In optical part recognition for manufacturing, we represent objects as part-of hierarchies based on generalized cylinder volume primitives. Object models are recursively broken up into joints composed of parts; those parts may in turn be broken into sub-joints and sub-parts, or they may be primitive. Joints are relationships between parts, incorporating observable effects of joining parts. Such a hierarchy forms a directed acyclic graph (DAG), where nodes are parts or relations and arcs indicate part-of relationships. Generalized cylinders (GCs) are defined by a cross section swept along a space curve, the axis, under a sweeping transformation [13]. Compound object models are DAGS of primitives represented in a simple modelling language. Models also include material modeling of optical properties, i.e., reflectives, specularities, and color [6, 7]. Figure 3a shows an elbow without threads. Figure 3b shows the line drawing of the elbow without hidden line suppression to show its subparts.

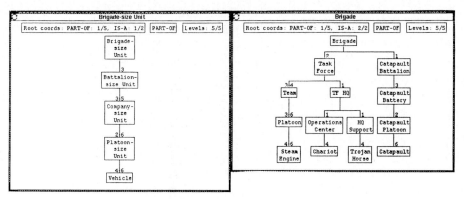

Figure 2: Brigade model.

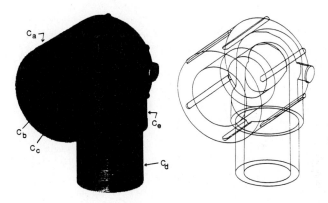

Figure 3: a. Elbow without threads. b. Line drawing of elbow without threads.

At each node of the Bayes net, there is a probability distribution over the set of mutually exclusive and exhaustive possible interpretations of the visual evidence accrued to that level in the hierarchy. A node is a set of hypotheses, e.g., catapult-battalion vs. task-force vs. non-military-unit, or t-joint versus elbow-joint versus non-joint. Although they do not have to be simultaneously instantiated, the possible links between nodes are hard-wired, a priori, by the models of objects and relationships, and the criteria for node instantiation that determine which pieces of evidence can generate conflicting hypotheses. Each alternative hypothesis at a node contributes some probability to the truth of an alternative hypothesis at a parent node (e.g., the part supports the existence of the whole) and also contributes to the truth of supporting children. When new evidence appears at a node, it is assimilated and appropriate versions of that evidence are propagated along all other links entering or exiting the node. We use the propagation algorithms of Pearl [3, 12].

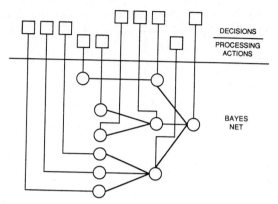

Figure 4: Separable influence diagram.

As we dynamically create the Bayes net at runtime, node instantiation is guided by the a priori models of objects, the evidence of their components, and their relationships. System control alternates between examination of the instantiated Bayes nodes, comparing against the models, and choosing what actions to take to grow the net, which is equivalent to seeing more structure in the world. Thus, inference proceeds by choosing actions from the model space that create new nodes and arcs in the Bayes net. All possible chains of inference that the system can perform are specified a priori in the model-base. This feature clearly distinguishes inference from control. Control chooses actions and allocates them over available processors, and returns results to the inference. Inference uses the existing Bayes net, the current results of actions (i.e., the collected evidence) generates Bayes nodes and arcs, propagates probabilities over the net, and accumulates the selectable actions for examination by control. In this approach, it is impossible for the system to reason circularly, as all instantiated chains of inference must be supported by evidence in a manner consistent with the model-base.

The prioritization and selection of actions can be viewed as a decision-making procedure. By representing the selection of actions at a single Bayes-node as a single decision, we create an influence diagram [14] with the property that severing any decision node from the diagram leaves the Bayes-net intact. Figure 4 illustrates this design. This allows us to construct control algorithms over the influence diagram where evidence accrual in the Bayes-net, and decisions of actions to execute, appear as modular operations.

3   Computing Values for Inference Actions

Our approach to selecting actions by utility theory is to compute the estimated value and cost of each currently executable action, then the value/cost of all actions as

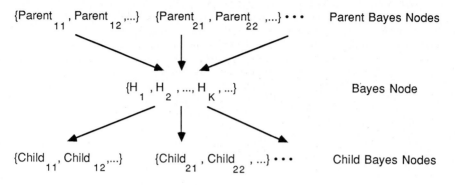

Figure 5: Bayes net structure.

inputs to a resource allocation algorithm that assigns actions to processors for execution. In our current implementation, we define cost of an action as the average processing time for the action. If the action is an algorithm that can be performed on different processors with radically different computation times, we can model this as two different actions.

We define the Bayes node structure to be a set, $\{H_K\}$, of mutually exclusive and exhaustive hypotheses, a set of pointers to its $\{Parents\}$, each of which is a predecessor Bayes nodes, and a set of pointers, $\{Children\}$, to its successor Bayes nodes (see Figure 5).

For each H_K, there is a corresponding model node (which we also call H_K) that has a set, $\{Actions\}$, of procedures that gather evidence in support of the presence of absence of H_K in an image.

The computation of value is performed hierarchically over the Bayes net, where the hierarchy is the hierarchy inherent in the model space. That is, we view computing the value of an action, A, at the child-hypothesis, H_K, as the increment in evidential value achieved at the parent hypothesis, P. We define the value V of an action at a child node H_K of a Parent node to be:

$$V \text{ (Child, Action)} = V (H_k, A)$$
$$= \sum_{\text{Parents}} \mid p(\text{Parent} \mid H_k, A) - p(\text{Parent} \mid H_k) \mid \cdot V(\text{Parent})$$

Where $p(Parent|H_K)$ is the conditional probability of the presence of the Parent in an image, given that the Child, H_K, is observed in the image. Similarly, $p(Parent|H_K, A)$ is the probability that Parent is present given the Child, H_K, and that action A has already been executed and the evidence accrued in support or denial of Parent.

Thus, we can begin at the top level of the model hierarchy and assign values to recognizing, for example, the various military units or industrial parts. We then recursively compute the value at each child, or sub-part, down the model hierarchy. In the instantiated Bayes net, this computation is proportional to the number of instantiated levels in the hierarchy. For example, in trying to confirm or deny the presence of a task force, we can assign a task-based value (not a probability) of .8 to H_1 = task force, .1 to H_2 = catapult battalion and .1 to H_3 = other. These are the objects in the goal Bayes node. The actions include "search for sister sub-unit", "get closer observation of vehicle types", and "adjust match of formation based on adaptation to underlying terrain".

If we have a set of child hypotheses, H_K, at Bayes node N, then the value of taking action A at node N is defined as

$$V\ (N,A\ ) = \sum_k V\ (H_k,A\ )$$

In general, the increase in belief in the parent depends on the results of computations performed in the action, which can, in turn, depend on many other results of processing at other nodes corresponding to sub- and super-hypotheses. To compute it, we begin by applying Bayes rule,

$$p\ (\text{Parent} \mid \text{Child, Action}) = \frac{p\ (\text{Child, Action} \mid \text{Parent})\ p\ (\text{Parent})}{p\ (\text{Child, Action})}$$

and note that $p(Parent)$ is known at runtime. When a Bayes node is already instantiated, then $p(Child, Action)$ can be interpreted as the accuracy with which the results of the action can be measured, given the state of the child. For example, if the child is a boundary of a generalized cylinder of the parent and the action is a curvature measurement, then the joint probability can determine how accurately the curvature can be measured, given the pixels observed on the boundary.

The term $p(Child, Action \mid Parent)$ is defined as

$$\int_{\text{outcomes of action}} p\ (\text{Child, Outcome} \mid \text{Parent})$$

where $p(Child, Outcome \mid Parent)$ is computed and stored a priori. For example, if the child is a pair of generalized cylinders, the action is an angular measurement between them, and the parent is a joint with known angular measure; then the above formula specifies the probability we would observe a given outcome (angle) given the true (model) angle. See [1, 3] for examples of such a computation.

There is an implicit assumption in this approach that all executable actions are represented in the model space a priori, and that values are calculated to account for continuous ranges of values for individual pieces of evidence. For example, executing a procedure to infer the curvature of a part may depend upon hypothesizing and testing against possible curvatures. We use the expected value of a quasi-invariant measure given its observation as in [1].

Now if a higher level Bayes node, e.g., a generalized cylinder, is not yet instantiated, but we wish to compute the value of actions at an instantiated lower level node, e.g., an observed edge of a generalized cylinder, then the probability, $p(generalized\ cylinder)$, must be estimated a priori for the recursive computation of value at the

```
Until ((time exceeded or (termination condition achieved))
    Instantiate new Bayes nodes
    For each instantiated Bayes node
        Get list of possible actions from node
        Instantiate new decision nodes
        Evaluate value/cost of each action
    End for
    Until (all processors allocated or all actions selected)
        Allocate highest value/cost task to a processor
    End Until
    Until ((a node's probability ratio exceeds threshold)
        or (all k actions return values))
            propagate evidential returns over Bayes net
    End Until
End Until
```

Figure 6: Control algorithm.

observed edge node. We take these priors to be the task-based likelihood that given objects are present in a scenario. For example, in an assembly line application, based on the current manufacturing task, we have an a priori notion of what parts to expect on the line.

4   Control of the Dynamic Influence Diagram

An influence diagram is dynamically created to represent both the state of the Bayes net and the possible processing options, i.e., decisions, available to the computer vision system at a single point in time. This is done as follows.

At a given time, we have a Bayes net where non-leaf nodes represent sets of hypotheses, each of which is the instantiation of a model. Referencing the model, there is a set of actions that can be used to gather evidence relating to the presence of an instance of this model in imagery. The union over an instantiated Bayes node of all such executable actions are grouped to form a decision node pointed into by the Bayes node. This is done for each Bayes node, yielding the structure pictured in Figure 4.

Control in the influence diagram is effected by the top-level loop of: form new Bayes nodes, form new decision nodes, accrue probabilities, compute value/cost for each executable action in decision nodes, choose actions to execute, and execute them. A version of this algorithm in terms of the Bayes-net is given in Figure 6.

Execution of actions can occur on multiple machines in a distributed environment. Results are summarized and returned asynchronously to the Bayes net. We have structured the model space, and therefore the Bayes net, such that the assumptions of Pearl's algorithm [12] are fulfilled. This allows asynchronous updating and propagation of probabilities, throughout the net. Because no decision nodes are between Bayes nodes, Pearl's algorithm applies over the subsets of the influence diagram that are connected Bayes-nets. Note that this structuring of the influence diagram, see Figure 4, was necessary to permit a control structure in which probability accrual and decision making are separable operations.

In our current system, we are using a greedy, best-first algorithm for actions prioritized by value/time, as indicated in Figure 6. Obviously any resource allocation algorithm could be substituted at this point in the top-level control loop. Previously, [9], we used an approach of maximizing utility. However, this required "time-chunking" the control process in order to provide a fixed set of times in which to optimize task to processor assignments. Given the uncertainty in these processes, studies such as [10] of such algorithms are unlikely to do better than more traditional job-queue types of assignment algorithms.

5 Examples

The following examples present the use of utility-based control to drive the recognition of military units from aerial imagery in the ADRIES system. The aerial imagery used is assumed to be relatively low resolution so that individual vehicles are difficult to identify due to their small size and a high false alarm rate. As a result, additional contextual forms of evidence, such as terrain, are used to recognize the military forces. The acquired evidence is matched against known military force models in order to determine its degree of support. The force models resident in the system are shown in Figure 2. The recognition system normally commences processing by generating hypotheses for the coarse models and proceeds by refining them and using them to generate higher-level hypotheses. The Bayes net is then used to group conflicting hypothesis configurations and to propagate beliefs throughout the hypothesis space.

In both of the following examples we run the system on the same scenario, but with different utility parameters. Actual processing results on simulated input data are given. In this scenario the system is attempting to confirm the presence of a Brigade in the boxed region in the upper portion of the map shown in Figure 7a. The system is initialized by locating possible vehicle detections in the available imagery. These detections are then clustered into Company-size Unit hypotheses based on coarse parameters in the model database such as inter-vehicle distance, number of vehicles in a unit, and maximum extent of a unit. By initializing the Bayes net with Company-size Units and not individual vehicles we achieve a large reduction in combinatorics. The initial cluster units are shown in Figure 7b.

After initialization, the system progresses by performing any of the following actions on the appropriate Bayes nodes:

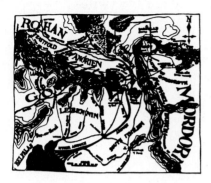 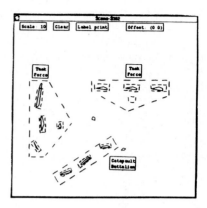

Figure 7: a. Area of interest. b. Initial hypotheses (solid lines) and actual ground truth (dashed lines).

- Refine a Bayes net hierarchy by using the more detailed force type model description (Refine-type).

- Search for matches among lower-level force hypotheses in order to generate higher-level force hypotheses (Search).

- Refine a Bayes net hierarchy by using a more detailed formation description (Refine-formation).

- Attach terrain evidence to a Bayes node by examining the support the underlying terrain provides for the given force (Terrain-support).

- Attach classification evidence to a Bayes leaf node indicating the support for the given force type obtained from high resolution sensors–an accurate process that is normally expensive to perform (Classification-support).

As results of actions are incorporated into the Bayes net, new actions are generated and queued for execution. The currently best queued action, based on the utility/cost ratio, is then selected for execution. New actions are thus generated as the state of the Bayes net changes. The net's state is reflected by the location, identity, and belief of the system's hypotheses. Processing continues until no new actions can provide additional information towards satisfying the goal or until the allotted time expires.

The actions performed by the system for the first test run (Test 1) are shown in Figure 8. Several snapshots of the system were taken to capture the state of the system after the main net restructuring actions (Figures 9 through 12). Snapshot 0, Figure 9, shows the state of the Bayes net right after initialization of the net. At this stage,

```
                *[SNAPSHOT 0]*
(REFINE-TYPE of (<B2226> <B2223> <B2220> <B2229>))
        [Refine Company-size Units to Teams, Task Force
        Headquarters, and Catapult Batteries]
                *[SNAPSHOT 1]*
(CLASSIFICATION-SUPPORT for hypotheses in <B2344>)
(TERRAIN-SUPPORT for hypotheses in <B2344>)
(CLASSIFICATION-SUPPORT for hypotheses in <B2299>)
(CLASSIFICATION-SUPPORT for hypotheses in <B2380>)
(TERRAIN-SUPPORT for hypotheses in <B2299>)
(TERRAIN-SUPPORT for hypotheses in <B2380>)
(CLASSIFICATION-SUPPORT for hypotheses in <B2321>)
(TERRAIN-SUPPORT for hypotheses in <B2321>)
(SEARCH for matches of hypotheses in (<B2344> <B2321> <B2380> <B2299>))
        [Match Teams, Task Force Headquarters, and Catapult
        Batteries into Task Forces and Catapult Battalions]
                *[SNAPSHOT 2]*
(SEARCH for matches of hypotheses in (<B2739>))
        [Match Task Forces and Catapult Battalions into Brigades]
(REFINE-FORMATION of <B2739>)
        [Include additional formation features in matches]
(TERRAIN-SUPPORT for hypotheses in <B2739>)
(TERRAIN-SUPPORT for hypotheses in <B3230>)
                *[SNAPSHOT 3]*
```

Figure 8: Action sequence for Test 1.

several Company-size Unit hypotheses have been generated. The attached probabilities are the ones obtained from the detection likelihoods and clustering matches.
Subsequent actions performed by the system refined the hypotheses, generated larger
ones, and accrued evidence for them. Final results, shown in Snapshot 3 (Figure 12),
indicate that the best hypothesis is an accurate explanation of the scene, given the
ground truth.

As a second test, some of the utility cost parameters were adjusted so that the
system will select a different inference path–i.e., a different sequence of inference
actions. The action sequence for this test run (Test 2) is shown in Figure 13.

The main difference between these two tests is that in the second test the Search
action is performed before the Refine-type action. One of the most time-consuming
tasks, matching companies into battalions, was performed on the typed companies in
Test 1 (matching Teams, Task Force Headquarters, and Catapult Batteries into Task
Forces and Catapult Battalions) while being performed on the generic companies in
Test 2 (matching Company-size Units into Battalion-size Units and then refining the
battalions into Task Forces and Catapult Battalions). Since matching is an inherently

417

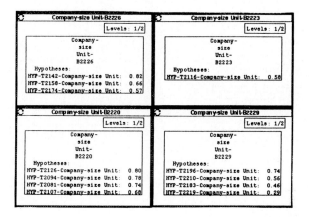

Figure 9: Test 1 – Snapshot 0: State of Bayes net upon initialization.

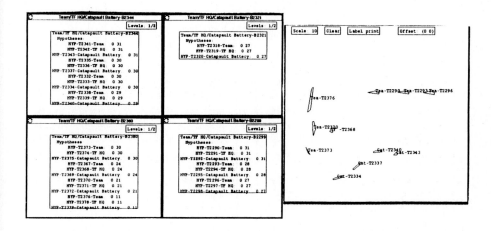

Figure 10: Test 1 – Snapshot 1: Highest Bayes net nodes and locations of representative component hypotheses.

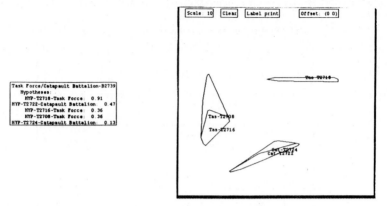

Figure 11: Test 1 – Snapshot 2: Highest Bayes net node and locations of highest belief component hypotheses.

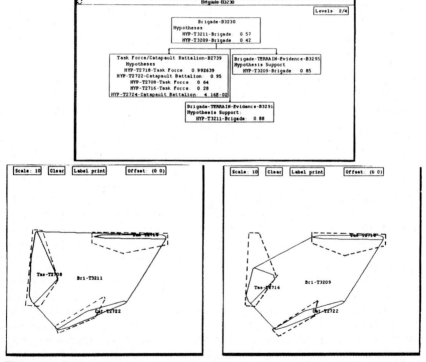

Figure 12: Test 1 – Snapshot 3: Final Bayes net and locations of final hypotheses (solid lines) shown compared against ground truth (dashed lines). Hypothesis #T3211 is selected as best hypothesis.

```
(SEARCH for matches of hypotheses in (<B606> <B597> <B603> <B600>))
            [Match Company-size Units into Battalion-size Units]
(TERRAIN-SUPPORT for hypotheses in <B597>)
(TERRAIN-SUPPORT for hypotheses in <B606>)
(TERRAIN-SUPPORT for hypotheses in <B603>)
(TERRAIN-SUPPORT for hypotheses in <B600>)
(REFINE-TYPE of (<B745>))
            [Refine Battalion-size Units to Task Forces and Catapult
            Battalions]
(SEARCH for matches of hypotheses in (<B898>))
            [Match Task Forces and Catapult Battalions into Brigades]
(CLASSIFICATION-SUPPORT for hypotheses in <B901>)
(TERRAIN-SUPPORT for hypotheses in <B901>)
(REFINE-FORMATION of <B898>)
            [Include additional formation features in matches]
(CLASSIFICATION-SUPPORT for hypotheses in <B901>)
(TERRAIN-SUPPORT for hypotheses in <B901>)
(TERRAIN-SUPPORT for hypotheses in <B898>)
(TERRAIN-SUPPORT for hypotheses in <B6427>)
```

Figure 13: Action sequence for Test 2.

exponential process while force type refinement is linear, Test 1 has less favorable combinatorics. The tradeoff being that Test 1 is performing more accurate matching (highest belief hypotheses expected to be more accurate) so we would expect more accurate results in Test 1. The final results of Test 2 are shown in Figure 14. The best final hypothesis (#T6374) is shown to have still identified the correct brigade unit, but a little less accurately than in Test 1. The other identified hypothesis (#T6382) had additional discrepancies in that it assigned the wrong refined force type names to the battalion units, but the system correctly assigned it much lower belief. The reason the results of the two tests are not exactly the same is that the system selects the best hypotheses to continue exploring at each step. By taking different action sequences, the ordering of hypotheses may not be exactly the same, but since the system is always maintaining *multiple* conflicting hypotheses, many of them will be similar across the different runs.

Overall, these and other tests performed on the system show that its performance is robust in that even though many different inference paths are possible in order to satisfy a given goal, the final results vary smoothly across the different operating conditions. As expected a main tradeoff is accuracy vs efficiency, but the utility-based control mechanism coupled with the dynamic nature of the inference process provide a means for controlling that tradeoff and making this approach adaptable to diverse situations.

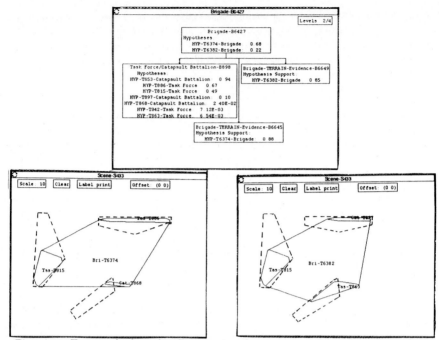

Figure 14: Test 2 – final results: Bayes net and comparison of final hypotheses (solid lines) against ground truth (dashed lines). Hypothesis #T6374 is selected as best hypothesis.

6 Conclusions

We have developed a methodology for vision system control based on utility theory applied to model-based Bayesian inference. We have implemented this methodology in ADRIES, a radar surveillance system, and are implementing it in SUCCESSOR, a system for computer vision of industrial parts in optical imagery. Many technical innovations were developed including:

- Representation of control and inference in a cognitively tractable model promoting clean and efficient system designs.

- Separation of decision making from evidence accrual.

- Dynamic instantiation of Bayes nets and influence diagrams.

- Hierarchical value computation achieved by assigning values only at the top model-level.

- Handling real world problems.

The approach to dynamic influence diagram instantiation used in this work requires theoretical substantiation. In particular, the coherence of the algorithm for incremental Bayes net updating and decision making needs to be justified with respect to existing theories of influence diagram updating [14]. We have taken an empirical approach in the near term, with a long term approach toward proving the underlying principles as expressed in [9]. The key continuing issue is the theoretical justification of this approach.

Another critical issue is the methodology for allocation of tasks to processors. We have used a greedy, best-first algorithm, based on value/cost of processing tasks. However, many other criteria including task priority, load balancing, communication overhead, processor specificity, etc. might be considered in optimization [10]. For example, [8] suggests a control approach that accounts for control parameters not represented in the ADRIES or SUCCESSOR systems.

The value/cost computation involves the control parameters in current use in ADRIES. However, a full decision theoretic control representation can also account for the cost of mis-interpretation of world objects, as well as the cost of communication between distributed processors. We have not incorporated the cost of mis-interpretation because of a lack of specificity of the tasks that provide values for the top level models.

Presumably the tasks for which a machine vision system is providing input determines the priority of the recognition of particular world objects, and the penalty for mis-recognition. Along with the problem of determining top-level values, this points to a need for detailed task analysis. The relationship between task analysis for automation and problem structuring and value assignment as understood in decision analytic applications, [16], is one that deserves considerable study.

7 Acknowledgments

This work was supported by the Advanced Digital Radar Imagery Exploitation Systems (ADRIES) project sponsored by the Defense Advanced Research Projects Agency (DARPA) and the U.S. Army Engineer Topographic Laboratories (USAETL) under U.S. Government Contract No. DACA76-86-C-0010, and by the Knowledge-Based Vision Techniques project sponsored by USAETL and DARPA under U.S. Government Contract No. DACA76-85-C-0005. This work benefited greatly from many insightful discussions with Larry Winter and Charlie Turner of SAIC, Tucson, AZ. They are also co-developers of the ADRIES system. Thanks are due to Angela Dorendorf for document support.

References

[1] T.O. Binford. Generic surface interpretation: observability model. In *Proceedings of the International Symposium of Robotics Research*, 1987.

[2]   T.O. Binford. Image understanding: intelligent systems. In *Proceedings of the DARPA Image Understanding Workshop*, 1988.

[3]   T.O. Binford, Levitt T.S., and W.B. Mann. Bayesian inference in model-based machine vision. In L.N. Kanal, T.S. Levitt, and J.F. Lemmer, editors, *Uncertainty in Artificial Intelligence III*, North Holland, 1988.

[4]   G.J. Ettinger. Large hierarchical object recognition using libraries of parameterized model sub-parts. In *Proceedings of the Computer Vision and Pattern Recognition Conference*, Ann Arbor, Michigan, June 1988.

[5]   J.E. Franklin, C.L. Carmody, K. Keller, T.S. Levitt, and B.L. Buteau. Expert system technology for the military. In *Proceedings of the IEEE*, 1988.

[6]   G. Healey and T.O. Binford. A color metric for computer vision. In *Proceedings of the DARPA Image Understanding Workshop*, 1988.

[7]   G. Healey and T.O. Binford. The role and use of color in a general vision system. In *Proceedings of the International Conference on Artificial Intelligence*, August 1987.

[8]   E.J. Horvitz. Reasoning under varying and uncertain resource constraints. In *Proc. AAAI*, Minneapolis, Minnesota, August 1988.

[9]   T.S. Levitt, J.M. Agosta, and T.O. Binford. Model-based influence diagrams for machine vision. In *Proceedings of the 5th Uncertainty in Artificial Intelligence Workshop*, Windsor, Ontario, August 1989.

[10] V.M. Lo. Heuristic algorithms for task assignment in distributed systems. *IEEE Trans. on Computers*, Vol. 37(No. 11), November 1988.

[11] R.K. Nevatia and T.O. Binford. Structured descriptions of complex objects. In *Third International Conference on Artificial Intelligence*, Stanford, California, 1973.

[12] J. Pearl. Fusion, propagation, and structuring in bayesian networks. *Artificial Intelligence*, 1986.

[13] J. Ponce and G. Healey. Using generic geometric and physical models for representing solids. In *Proceedings of the DARPA Image Understanding Workshop*, 1988.

[14] R.D. Shachter. Evaluating influence diagrams. *Operations Research*, Vol. 34(No. 6):871-882, December 1986.

[15] Levitt T.S. Bayesian inference for radar imagery based surveillance. In *Uncertainty in Artificial Intelligence II*, North Holland, 1988.

[16] D. VonWinterfeldt and W. Edwards. *Decision Analysis and Behavioral Research*. Cambridge University Press, Cambridge, MA, 1986.